lonely planet

Discover
USA's
Best National Parks

Contents

Throughout this book, we use these icons to highlight special recommendations:

The Best...
Lists for everything from bars to wildlife – to make sure you don't miss out

Don't Miss
A must-see – don't go home until you've been there

Detour
Special places a little off the beaten track

If you like...
Lesser-known alternatives to world-famous attractions

These icons help you quickly identify reviews in the text and on the map:

Sights

Eating

Drinking

Sleeping

Information

D1113678

Contents

Plan Your Trip

On the Road

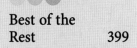

p195

p65 Glacier

Acadia p29

Olympic &
Mt Rainier

p243 Yellowstone &
Grand Teton

Yosemite

p307

p357

p217 Rocky Mountain

p141

p173

p93

Zion &
Bryce Canyon

Great Smoky
Mountains
& Shenandoah

Joshua Tree
& Death
Valley

Grand
Canyon

Everglades p49

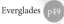

USA's Best National Parks

The moment you roll up to a national park entry kiosk, you feel it. You're entering someplace special. Maybe it's the mountain air or the smell of the trees. Most likely, it's because you're about to see something *big*. Something indescribable. A canyon so deep you can see two billion years of geological history in its walls. Trees so massive you could fit buildings inside them. Rock formations so strange they can only be called 'hoodoos.'

America's national parks hold some of earth's most spectacular scenery. A collection of superlatives, they encompass the highest and lowest points in North America. One park is home to the greatest concentration of geothermic features on the planet. Another encompasses the world's densest collection of natural stone arches. In yet another, the continent's highest waterfall plummets over a cliff amid the greatest expanses of exposed granite on earth.

Indeed, the national parks are our greatest treasure. They protect 85,000 miles of the country's most beautiful rivers and streams, and over 43,000 miles of our wildest shoreline. They are home to 27,000 historic structures and nearly 70,000 archeological sites. They also protect 400 endangered species – plants and animals that might very well be gone if not for the parks.

We can thank some early visionaries for their existence. The John Muirs, Theodore Roosevelts, Stephen Mathers and Horace Albrights. The conservationists and naturalists who fought to protect these swaths of land for the enjoyment of *all*. But the preservation of the parks today are the efforts of so many more. Since the creation of the first national park, over 2.4 million people have together logged more than 97 million work hours, without pay, to make these places better.

No wonder our skin tingles upon entry to a national park. Behind those entry kiosks lie landscapes that are vastly beautiful, histories that are inspirational, an idea that was, as novelist Wallace Stegner famously put it, America's best.

> " Behind those entry kiosks lie landscapes that are vastly beautiful "

Old homestead, Grand Teton (p286)

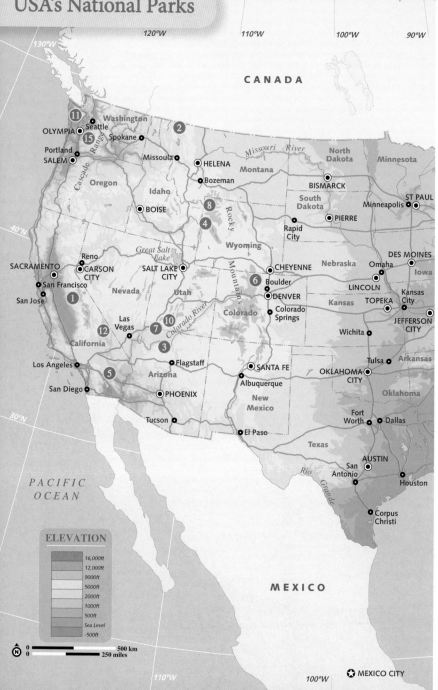

USA's National Parks

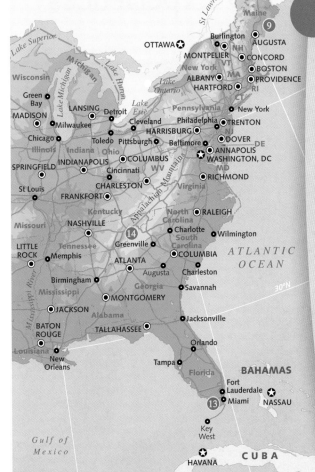

15
Top Experiences

1. Yosemite Valley, Yosemite
2. Going-to-the-Sun Road, Glacier
3. Sunset, Grand Canyon
4. Wildlife Watching on Snake River, Grand Teton
5. Rock Climbing, Joshua Tree
6. Longs Peak, Rocky Mountain
7. The Narrows, Zion
8. Wildlife Watching, Yellowstone
9. Sunrise, Cadillac Mountain, Acadia
10. Bryce Amphitheater, Bryce Canyon
11. Hoh Rainforest, Olympic
12. Mesquite Flat Sand Dunes, Death Valley
13. Paddling, Everglades
14. Cades Cove Historic Buildings, Great Smoky Mountains
15. Wildflower Season, Mt Rainier

15 USA's Best National Parks' Top Experiences

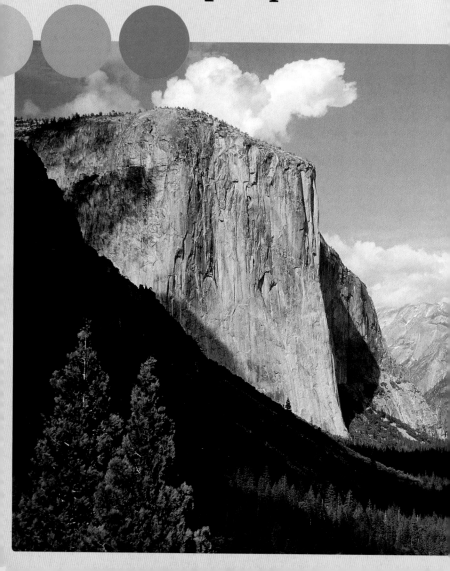

Yosemite Valley, Yosemite

In Yosemite Valley (p314), the national park system's crown jewel, massive granite rock formations tower thousands of feet over the Merced River. Wild creeks plummet from the cliff tops, creating a spectacle of waterfalls unlike anywhere on earth. And presiding over it all stand the iconic and mighty sentinels of rock, including El Capitan, Half Dome, the Royal Arches, the Three Brothers and Cathedral Rocks. No matter what people tell you about the summer crowds, the sights of Yosemite Valley are so astonishing that almost nothing can detract from the experience.

1

Going-to-the-Sun Road, Glacier

Going-to-the-Sun Rd (p69) offers steely-nerved motorists the drive of their life. Chiseled out of the mountainside and punctuated by some of the sheerest and most vertiginous drop-offs in the US, this 50-mile, vista-laden strip of asphalt offers drivers access to some of the most astounding sights in the Rockies.

Sunset, Grand Canyon

When Bob Dylan wrote of God and Woody Guthrie, he said 'I may be right or wrong/You'll find them both/In the Grand Canyon/At sundown.' Of all the places to watch the sunset in the world, few can measure up to the Grand Canyon. Lipan Point (p104) is one of the finest spots to do it. Or, if you're feeling leisurely, simply grab a drink and a porch swing on the patio of El Tovar lodge (p116), where you can watch the sunset in style. Toroweap Overlook (p137)

Wildlife Watching on Snake River, Grand Teton

Spilling down from Jackson Lake beneath the mighty Teton Range, the wild and scenic Snake River offers some of the most dramatic mountain scenery in the country. Not only are its waters the perfect place to gawk at the Tetons themselves (including the 13,775ft Grand Teton), but they're prime for wildlife watching. Numerous outfitters (see p303) offer float trips ranging from gentle to giant water. No matter which you choose, prepare to be awed. View from Oxbow Bend (p291)

The Best...
Hiking

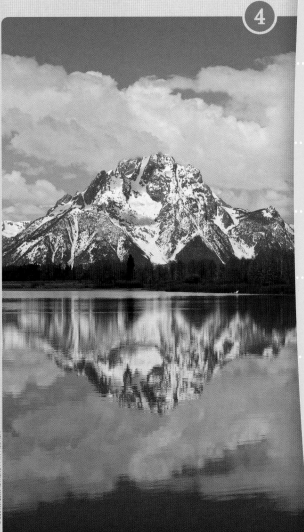

VERNAL & NEVADA FALLS, YOSEMITE
Yosemite's most stunning waterfalls plummet over granite cliffs. (p332)

ICEBERG LAKE, GLACIER
Icebergs float in azure waters beneath a massive glacial cirque. (p79)

GRANDVIEW TRAIL, GRAND CANYON
Grueling trail with epic canyon views. (p109)

LONGS PEAK, ROCKY MOUNTAIN
Views are endless from atop this 14,259ft peak. (p223)

THE NARROWS, ZION
Narrow slot canyon with a river for a trail. (p370)

Rock Climbing, Joshua Tree

Whether you're a rock-climbing novice or a bouldering goddess, you'll find heaven above earth when you take to Joshua Tree's granite (p180). With more than 8000 established climbing routes, this is truly one of the world's rock meccas. There are classes for beginners, and the 400-plus climbing formations offer endless fun for seasoned enthusiasts. Amid the giant boulders and sweaty climbers, the bizarre Joshua trees themselves lend the scenery an otherworldly character.

TYLER ROEMER / LONELY PLANET IMAGES ©

The Best...
Wildlife Watching

LAMAR VALLEY, YELLOWSTONE
Bison, moose, wolves and elk roam the 'American Serengeti.' (p253)

OXBOW BEND, GRAND TETON
Moose, elk, bald eagles, trumpeter swans, blue herons and more can be seen at this special place in Grand Teton. (p291)

ANHINGA TRAIL, EVERGLADES
Crowded as it is, this trail offers wildlife up close, including anhingas, alligators and turtles. (p57)

MANY GLACIER, GLACIER
This remote, mountainous sector of Glacier has the park's best wildlife viewing. (p77)

ENCHANTED VALLEY, OLYMPIC
Moose and black bears are common sights along this spectacular Olympic hike. (p203)

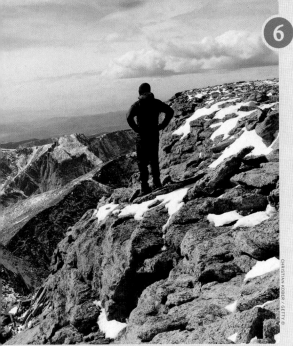

CHRISTIAN KOBER / GETTY ©

Longs Peak, Rocky Mountain

6

Whether you hike to the top of its 14,259ft summit or just ogle its glaciated slopes from below, Longs Peak (p223) is truly a feast for the eyes. Given it's the highest peak in the park, it should be. Those who attempt the ascent via the Keyhole Route must first brave the hair-raising Ledges, before conquering the Trough and inching across the Narrows, which finally give way to the (whew!) Homestretch. The views from the top are mind-boggling.

The Narrows, Zion

Check your claustrophobia at the door and prepare to get wet on this hike up the Virgin River into a 2000ft-deep slot canyon (p370). As you make your way upriver, the cliffs press inward, towering higher and higher until, finally, you reach Wall Street, where the width of the canyon narrows to under 30ft.

Wildlife Watching, Yellowstone

No matter how many nature shows you've seen, nothing can prepare you for the first time you spot a moose in the wild. And in Yellowstone (p263), if you don't see a moose – or a bison or a herd of elk or a bear – you probably have your eyes closed. On par with the Galápagos, the Serengeti and Brazil's Pantanal, Yellowstone is one of the world's premier wildlife-watching destinations. Big mammals are everywhere. The knowledge that grizzlies, wolves and mountain lions are among them simply adds to the rush.

Sunrise, Cadillac Mountain, Acadia

Catching the country's 'first sunrise' from the top of Cadillac Mountain (p33) is, hands down, one of the finest ways to kick off a day. At 1530ft, Cadillac Mountain is the highest point on Maine's Mount Desert Island, and the views over the Atlantic are sublime. The island is one of the easternmost points in the USA, and, while it's technically not the *first* place that catches the morning sun, we prefer to do what everyone else up top does at sunrise: ignore the technicalities and bliss out.

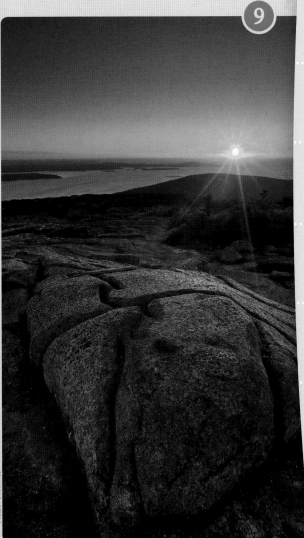

The Best...

Views

CAPE ROYAL POINT, GRAND CANYON
The earth seems to disappear beneath your feet. (p130)

OBSERVATION POINT, ZION
The hike is a doozy, but the views make the 2150ft climb worth every grunt. (p372)

BRYCE POINT, BRYCE CANYON
Mysterious hoodoos tower up from the Silent City below. (p386)

GOING-TO-THE-SUN ROAD, GLACIER
Every turn in this road offers breathtaking Rocky Mountain views. (p69)

CADILLAC MOUNTAIN, ACADIA
Head here to watch the first sunrise over America. (p33)

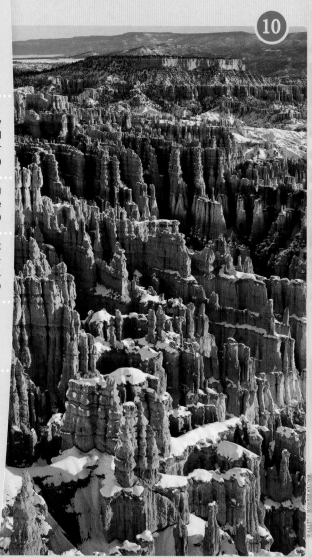

Bryce Amphitheater, Bryce Canyon

Proof that nature has a wild imagination, hoodoos are one of the strangest formations on the planet. From the rim of southern Utah's Bryce Amphitheater (p386) you can look down upon thousands of these bizarre, ancient rock spires as they tower out of the so-called Silent City, a conglomeration of hoodoos so vast that you'd be forgiven for thinking you'd landed on another planet. Sunrise over the amphitheater is one of life's treats.

The Best...
Winter Wonderlands

YOSEMITE VALLEY
Frozen waterfalls, snowy cliffs, and a silent, magical white valley await winter visitors. (p314)

ROCKY MOUNTAIN
You'll practically have the park to yourself. (p220)

YELLOWSTONE
Without the crowds, wild-life watching is even better. (p246)

GRAND TETON
Miles of cross-country ski trails snake beneath massive peaks. (p286)

EVERGLADES
A subtropical paradise for those who want to be warm in winter. (p52)

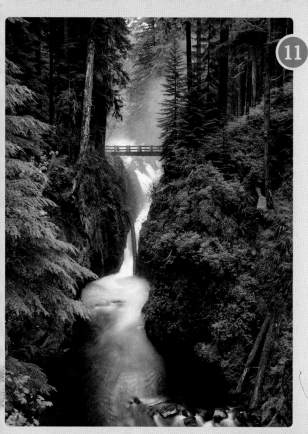

Hoh Rainforest, Olympic

11

Embrace the rain! It's what makes this temperate rainforest (p201), in all its Tolkienesque beauty, one of the greenest places in North America. With an average rainfall of up to 170in (that's 14ft), it is also one of the wettest. This tremendous amount of water creates a forest covered in mosses, lichens and ferns, with a canopy so dense the forest floor seems trapped in the perpetual lowlight of dusk. Pack your rain jacket and watch for the Roosevelt elk.

Mesquite Flat Sand Dunes, Death Valley

12

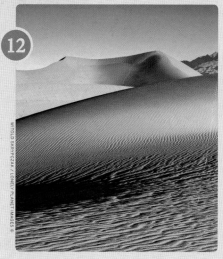

Wind and sand make for magical bedmates in Death Valley, where dune fields rise from the desert floor and kindle the imagination with their shadowy, wind-hewn ripples. And just as you'd expect from the scene, it's hot! Located between the ominously named Stovepipe Wells and Furnace Creek, Mesquite Flat Sand Dunes (p187) are the easiest series of dunes to reach. With crescent, linear and star-shaped sand dunes, Mesquite Flat provides the complete experience.

Paddling, Everglades

The country's third-largest national park (p49) is a paddler's paradise, with kayak and canoe 'trails' meandering through mangrove swamps and freshwater marshes that teem with wildlife. Crocodiles, alligators, turtles, cormorants, herons, egrets and fish are just some of the wildlife boaters come across while paddling around this subtropical park. Thanks to the National Park Service's handy (and free) kayak and canoe trail maps, navigating the waters is fairly straightforward.

Cades Cove Historic Buildings, Great Smoky Mountains

Pick up a self-guided tour booklet and poke your way around the historic buildings of Cades Cove (p146). Beneath the backdrop of Thunderhead Mountain, pioneer churches, a gristmill, graying old homes and plank-board barns take you back to the 19th century, when settlers carved out their home in this idyllic valley.

Tipton Place (p147)

Wildflower Season, Mt Rainier

Mt Rainier (p208) gets over 650in of snow annually. It's covered in glaciers, and the high meadows are blanketed in white for nearly nine months of the year. Once the snow finally melts and the meadows are exposed, wildflowers, somehow knowing they have only a short time to do their thing, explode into bloom. Avalanche lilies, beargrass, bog orchids, wood nymphs and dozens of other flowers turn the slopes of the Cascade's highest mountain into a rainbow of color. July and August are peak season.

The Best...
Adventures

RAFTING THE COLORADO RIVER, GRAND CANYON
Hands down, the best way to see the Grand Canyon. (p110)

CANYONEERING, ZION
Rappelling into Zion's slot canyons is hair-raising fun. (p374)

ROCK CLIMBING, YOSEMITE
The world's holy grail of rock climbing is accessible to all. (p337)

PADDLING, EVERGLADES
Paddle the 99-mile Wilderness Waterway between Everglades City and Flamingo. (p58)

MOUNTAINEERING, MOUNT RAINIER
Some 10,000 people attempt this 14,411ft summit every year. Try it and find out why. (p211)

The Parks Month by Month

 ## January

Strap on your snowshoes or cross-country skis and enjoy the white winter magic in Yellowstone, Glacier and Grand Teton. Joshua Tree is lovely, and the subtropical Everglades are sublime.

🏃 Snowshoeing

Leave the crowds behind and take to the trails of the national parks with snowshoes on your feet. Seeing the high-elevation and northern parks when they're blanketed in snow is a magical experience. Rangers at some of the parks even host guided snowshoe hikes.

March

The biting cold of winter fades from the desert parks, and wildflowers begin to bloom at lower elevations. Snow activities are still good at high elevations.

Frozen Dead Guy Days

Join the living in Nederland, CO (near Rocky Mountains National Park) and celebrate a dead guy – a Norwegian named Grandpa Bredo Morstoel – who is cryogenically frozen in a local lab, patiently awaiting reanimation. The festival (go to 'events' at www.nederlandchamber. org) spans three days in early March and includes music and coffin races.

April

Wildflowers are in full swing at lower elevations, and waterfalls begin pumping at full force with the beginning of the snowmelt. Weather in the desert parks is beautiful.

Yosemite Falls (p317), Yosemite
PHOTOGRAPHER: EMILY RIDDELL / LONELY PLANET IMAGES ©

⊙ Spring Wildflowers

Wildflowers put on dazzling springtime displays at the lower-elevation parks, especially at Death Valley, Shenandoah, Great Smoky Mountains, Zion and sometimes Joshua Tree. Check the National Park Service websites for wildflower walks, talks and celebrations.

⊙ Yosemite Waterfalls

Most people who visit Yosemite in July and August have no idea – until they get there – that the Valley's famous falls (p317) are but a trickle of their springtime selves. April, May and June are the best months to see the falls in full force.

✿ National Park Week

For an entire week every April, admission to the national parks is free. Early in the year, the US president announces when National Park Week will fall that year. Many of the parks also host free activities.

May

Temperatures in Zion, Bryce, Grand Canyon, Yosemite Valley, Death Valley and Joshua Tree are delightful. The summer crowds have yet to materialize, waterfalls are at their peak, and river and stream levels are high.

✿ Strawberry Music Festival

Twice a year (Memorial Day and Labor Day weekend), lovers of country and folk music make a beeline to this wildly popular music festival (www.strawberrymusic.com) held in a meadow at Camp Mather, 10 miles west of Yosemite's Big Oak Flat Entrance.

✿ Joshua Tree Music Festival

Over a long weekend in May, numerous bands rock Joshua Tree Lake Campground during a family-friendly indie music fest (www.joshuatreemusicfestival.com). It's followed by a soulful roots celebration in mid-October.

June

It's still possible to beat the crowds of summer in early June. By late June, the parks are jammed but the weather is stellar in many of them. Upper-elevation roads are still closed in the Sierras and Rocky Mountains.

✿ Utah Shakespeare Festival

Near Zion National Park, Cedar City kicks off its three-month-long Shakespeare Festival (www.bard.org) in late June, bringing famed actors to the stage for dozens of top-notch performances. Activities include classes, literary seminars, magic shows and more.

July

High elevation sectors of the Rockies, Sierras and Cascades begin opening. It's prime hiking time in the high-country, where wildflowers are at their peak. Desert parks, including Grand Canyon, are sweltering.

☺ Cody Stampede

In Yellowstone's gateway communities, rodeo is the major cultural event of the year. Cowboys take to the saddle throughout June, July and August in various communities. The largest rodeos are the Cody Stampede (www.codystampederodeo.com) and the Wild West Yellowstone Rodeo (www.yellowstonerodeo.com).

✿ North American Indian Days

In the second week of July, head to the Blackfeet Indian Reservation, immediately east of Glacier National Park, for traditional drumming, dancing and the annual crowning of the year's Miss Blackfeet. The four day festival (www.browningmontana.com/naid.html) is a wonderful display of Blackfeet traditions.

campsite is reserved. First-come-first-served campgrounds are your best bet. Head to the high-country, where the weather is superb.

Christmas in August

Join the Christmas caroling in one of the parks' oddest celebrations, Yellowstone's Christmas in August (celebrated on the 25th). The event dates back to the turn of the last century, when a freak August snowstorm stranded a group of visitors in the Upper Geyser Basin.

September

The crowds begin to thin out, and by the end of the month things are pretty quiet. If you don't mind brisk evenings, this can be a beautiful time to visit the parks. High-country sectors close by the end of the month.

Mountain Life Festival

Participate in hearth cooking demonstrations and help make historic farm staples like hominy, apple butter, apple cider and soap. The event is celebrated every year in mid-September at the Mountain Farm Museum in Great Smoky National Park.

October

From Yosemite to the Great Smoky Mountains, fall color is nothing short of fabulous in many of the parks. Grand Canyon, Zion, Joshua Tree and Death Valley are especially beautiful. Crowds are nonexistent and the temperatures are dropping quickly. High-elevation sectors are closed.

Pioneer Days

On the third weekend in October, the town of Twentynine

Summer Wildflowers

There's nothing like hiking through high-country meadows that are blanketed in wildflowers. In high-elevation parks such as Glacier, Rocky Mountain, Yellowstone, Grant Teton and parts of Yosemite, wildflowers bloom intensely during the short growing season between snows.

Grand Teton Music Festival

Over 40 classical music concerts are held throughout the Jackson Hole region near Grand Teton National Park. Everything from children's concerts to full orchestras are on the menu. Concerts take place almost nightly throughout July and into August. See www.gtmf.org for calendars and to purchase tickets.

August

Hello crowds! It's the height of summer, it's blazing hot, and every hotel and

Palms, near Joshua Tree National Park, celebrates Pioneer Days (www.visit29.org) with an Old West-themed carnival featuring a parade, arm-wrestling and a giant chili dinner.

November

Winter is creeping in quickly. The best parks to visit are those in southern Utah, Arizona and the California deserts, where the weather is cool but still beautiful.

 ### Death Valley '49ers

In early or mid-November, Furnace Creek hosts this historical encampment (www.deathvalley49ers.org), featuring cowboy poetry, campfire sing-alongs, a gold-panning contest and a western art show. Show up to this Death Valley festival

early to watch the pioneer wagons come thunderin' in.

December

Winter is well under way in most of the parks. High-elevation roads and park sectors are closed, and visitor center and business hours are reduced. Think snowshoeing and cross-country skiing.

National Audubon Society Christmas Bird Count

Every year around Christmastime, thousands of people take to the wilds to look for and record birds for the Audubon Society's annual survey. Many of the parks organize a count and rely on volunteers to help. Check the National Park Service websites for information.

Far left: Cross-country skier, Yellowstone (p270) **Left:** Orchestra at Grand Teton Music Festival

PHOTOGRAPHERS: (FAR LEFT) LEE FOSTER / LONELY PLANET IMAGES ©; (LEFT) BRADLEY BONER

Get Inspired

Books

Our National Parks (1901) The words of John Muir inspired a nation to embrace national parks.

Ranger Confidential: Living, Working & Dying in the National Parks (2010) Former park ranger Andrea Lankford tells you what it takes to fill the shoes of our favorite park employee.

Lost in My Own Backyard (2004) Chuckle your way around Yellowstone with Tim Cahill.

A Sand County Almanac (1949) Aldo Leopold's nature classic embodies the conservation ethic that lies at the heart of our national parks.

Films

American Experience: Ansel Adams (2004) Inspire your snapshots with this PBS documentary.

Vacation (1983) Perfect comedy kick-starter for any family vacation.

Thelma & Louise (1991) The classic American road-trip flick is a joy to watch, despite the terrible circumstances.

Into the Wild (2007) Follow Chris McCandless as he kisses his possessions goodbye and hitchhikes to Alaska.

Music

Classic Old-Time Fiddle (2007) Perfect fiddle compilation for trips to Great Smoky Mountains and Shenandoah.

Joshua Tree (1987) Crank up this U2 classic, whether you're heading to Joshua Tree or not.

Beautiful Maladies (1998) Nothing spells 'road trip' like a good Tom Waits tune.

This Land is Your Land: The Asch Recordings, Vol. 1 (1997) Woodie Guthrie sings everything from 'This Land is Your Land' to 'The Car Song'.

Websites

Lonely Planet (www.lonelyplanet.com) Lodging information, Thorn Tree, Trip Planner and more.

RoadsideAmerica.com (www.roadsideamerica.com) Don't miss all those weird roadside attractions!

The National Parks (www.pbs.org/nationalparks) Online portal of Ken Burn's national park PBS classic.

Short on time?

This list will give you an instant insight into the national parks.

Read Ansel Adam's *In the National Parks* (2010) is the next best thing to being there.

Watch Ken Burns' 12-hour PBS miniseries, *The National Parks, America's Best Idea* (2009) is a must.

Listen Dig into the blues, folk and country roots of America with Harry Smith's *Anthology of American Folk Music* (1952).

Log on National Park Service websites (www.nps.gov) are jammed with information on everything from hiking to stargazing.

Top: Half Dome (p316), Yosemite; Left: Black bear (p432)

Need to Know

Entry Fees
$0 (Great Smoky) to $25 (Yellowstone); valid for seven consecutive days.

America the Beautiful Annual Pass
Valid for all national parks for 12 months from purchase. Buy through National Park Service (📞 888-275-8747, ext 1; www.nps.gov).

ATMs
Most parks have at least one ATM; widely available in gateway towns.

Credit Cards
Major credit cards widely accepted; Forest Service, BLM and other campgrounds accept cash and/or checks only.

Cell Phones
Coverage inside parks is spotty at best.

Wi-Fi
Some park lodges have wireless. Outside the parks, most cafes and hotels offer free wireless. Chain hotels charge.

Tipping
Tip restaurant servers 15–20%; porters $2 per bag; hotel maids $2 to $5 per night.

When to Go

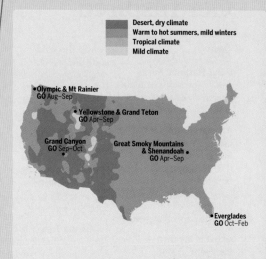

Desert, dry climate
Warm to hot summers, mild winters
Tropical climate
Mild climate

●Olympic & Mt Rainier
GO Aug–Sep

● Yellowstone & Grand Teton
GO Apr–Sep

Grand Canyon
GO Sep–Oct

Great Smoky Mountains & Shenandoah ●
GO Apr–Sep

● Everglades
GO Oct–Feb

High Season
(Jun–early Sep)
○ High-country sectors in the Rockies, Sierras and Cascades are guaranteed to be open.
○ July and August are crowded; reservations are a must.

Shoulder
(May–mid-Jun & mid-Sep–Oct)
○ Waterfalls in Yosemite and Great Smoky Mountains are at their peak in spring.
○ High elevation roads are still closed in spring.

Low Season
(mid-Sep–May)
○ Cross-country skiing and snowshoeing are excellent in the Rockies and Sierras.
○ High season for the subtropical Everglades.

Advance Planning
○ **Twelve months before** Reserve campsites and historic lodge accommodations.
○ **Six months before** Reserve hotel rooms in satellite towns if visiting in summer. Book flights.
○ **Three months before** Start training if planning to backpack. If you haven't reserved sleeping arrangements, do so.
○ **One month before** Secure rental car. Take your own car in for a safety inspection and tune up if planning a long drive.

Your Daily Budget

Budget less than $50

○ Campsites: $10–25

○ Plenty of self-catering options in gateway towns; pricier at stores inside parks

○ Park entry: $0–25

○ Park shuttles and visitor sites free with admission

○ Gas costs depend on distances and vehicle

Midrange $50-250

○ Budget hotels: $50–99

○ B&Bs, midrange hotels, most park lodges: $100–200

○ Two can eat well at local cafes for $25

Top end more than $250

○ Better B&Bs and four-star hotels: over $200

○ High-end restaurants in gateway towns: $50 per person

Exchange Rates		
Australia	A$1	$1.01
Canada	C$1	$1
Euro zone	€1	$1.41
China	Y10	$1.54
Japan	¥100	$1.22
Mexico	MXN10	$0.86
New Zealand	NZ$1	$0.79
UK	£1	$1.62

For current exchange rates see www.xe.com.

What to Bring

○ **Rain jacket** Thin shell that's easy to pack; afternoon thundershowers common in summer.

○ **Layers** Layered clothing keeps you warmest and is best for adjustability.

○ **Binoculars** A must for wildlife watching.

○ **Insect repellent** Critical for high-country in summer, when mosquitoes and black flies are out. Also use for ticks in woodsy, low-elevation areas.

○ **Camp chair** Always relax in style.

○ **Sun protection** Hat, sunglasses and sun block.

○ **First aid kit** Buy one or make your own.

○ **Flashlight** Critical for campers.

Arriving at a National Park

○ **Information** Pick up a park newspaper at the entry kiosk and hang onto it; they're packed with useful information.

○ **Camping** If you're going for a first-come-first-served site, head straight to the campground. Try to arrive no later than mid-morning Friday.

○ **Parking** People not spending the night inside a park will find parking difficult. Arrive early, park and take free shuttles whenever possible.

○ **Visitor Centers** Best places to start exploring the parks. Purchase books and maps, ask rangers questions, check weather reports and trail and road conditions.

Getting Around

○ **Car** Most convenient way to travel between the parks. A few park roads are gravel. Traffic inside some parks can be horrendous.

○ **Park Shuttles** Many parks have excellent shuttle systems with stops at major visitor sites and trailheads.

○ **Bicycles** Some parks have rentals. Good for getting around developed areas. Elsewhere, roads can be steep and shoulders narrow.

Accommodations

○ **Campsites** Reservation and first-come-first-served sites both available in all parks. Flush toilets are common, hot showers are not. Full hookups for RVs usually found outside parks.

○ **Park Lodges** Wonderful experience. Usually lack TV; some have wi-fi.

○ **B&Bs** Available in gateway towns outside parks; often excellent and usually include wi-fi.

○ **Hotels** Occasionally inside parks; most in gateway towns. Nearly all have wi-fi.

Acadia National Park

Acadia is an unspoiled wilderness of surf-pounded beaches and quiet lakes, with pink granite painting the backdrop. Indeed, the park's dramatic coastal mountains loom as the highest along the North Atlantic seaboard.

At just 73 sq miles, Acadia National Park packs an amazing variety into a relatively small space. You can opt to take a leisurely shoreline stroll or stretch your quads along a mountain ridge, dip a paddle into New England's only fjord or hop on a cruise to an offshore island.

With soulful views in every direction, it's little wonder that Acadia was once a favorite summer retreat for affluent Americans like John D Rockefeller Jr, who donated much of the land that forms the park. Today, one of the highlights of Acadia is hiking and cycling along the handsome carriage roads that Rockefeller once rode his horse and buggy on.

Otter Cliffs (p33)
EDDIE BRADY / LONELY PLANET IMAGES ©

Acadia Itineraries

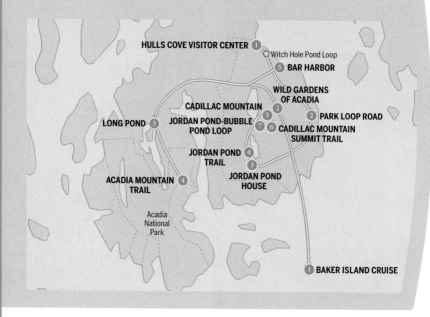

HULLS COVE VISITOR CENTER ①
○ Witch Hole Pond Loop
⑤ BAR HARBOR

WILD GARDENS
OF ACADIA

CADILLAC MOUNTAIN
②
② PARK LOOP ROAD
LONG POND ③ JORDAN POND-BUBBLE ⑤
POND LOOP ⑦ ⑥ CADILLAC MOUNTAIN
SUMMIT TRAIL

JORDAN POND ①
TRAIL
③
ACADIA MOUNTAIN ④ JORDAN POND
TRAIL HOUSE

Acadia
National
Park

① BAKER ISLAND CRUISE

Two Days

① **Hulls Cove Visitor Center** (p43) Start your explorations at this helpful place, where you'll find the perfect introduction to Acadia, including a nifty 3D diorama of the entire park and the latest scoop on what's happening.

② **Park Loop Rd** (p33) Now it's time to hit the road and see the real deal on this 27-mile loop of beaches, dramatic sea cliffs and quiet woodlands. Take your time, get out and stroll – there's a full morning of fun to be had here.

③ **Jordan Pond House** (p42) Lunch on fresh Maine seafood at this classic teahouse restaurant with an irresistible view of Jordan Pond.

④ **Jordan Pond Trail** (p37) Work off that popover and jam dessert with a relaxing afternoon walk around the park's favorite pond.

⑤ **Cadillac Mountain** (p33) Start day two by catching the sunrise atop Acadia's highest peak, the first place in the USA to catch the sun's rays.

⑥ **Cadillac Mountain Summit Trail** (p36) You brought your camera, didn't you? With its panorama of ocean, mountain and island views in every direction, this short hike could fill a picture book.

⑦ **Jordan Pond-Bubble Pond Loop** (p39) The hard-packed, pea-gravel carriage roads that John D Rockefeller Jr built for his horse and buggy rides are ideal for cycling, and this one's the prettiest of them all.

➡ THIS LEG: 36 MILES

Four Days

1 Baker Island Cruise (p40) Acadia National Park doesn't stop at the shoreline. On day three, join a ranger-led cruise to Baker Island – one of the more remote niches of the park – and count the seals and seabirds along the way. Take a hike around the island and climb to the top of the historic Baker Island lighthouse for a towering view.

2 Wild Gardens of Acadia (p33) Sample a microcosm of the many habitats that make up this diverse national park by walking the trails of these fragrant gardens and visiting the adjacent Sieur de Monts Nature Center.

3 Long Pond (p41) On day four, rent a canoe and paddle the deep blue waters of Long Pond, exploring secluded coves on the way. Be sure to bring a picnic lunch – there are lots of scenic spots along the shore begging for a leisurely stop.

4 Acadia Mountain Trail (p38) You've seen the view from Cadillac Mountain on the east side of the park – now it's time to take in the vista from the west. Your reward at the top will be a stunning view of the Cranberry Islands and Mount Desert Island's 5-mile-long fjord.

5 Bar Harbor (p43) End your stay with a night on the town. Mount Desert Island's largest town, Bar Harbor, sits right on the doorstep of the national park. It not only has entertainment and eateries that will sate any appetite, but it also boasts an inviting shoreline trail of its own.

THIS LEG: 45 MILES

Acadia Highlights

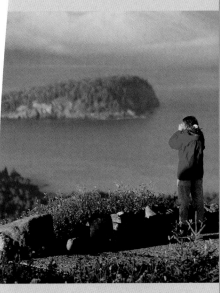

1 Best View: Cadillac Mountain (p33) An unbeatable panorama of islands, lakes and forests from the summit.

2 Best Drive: Park Loop Rd (p33) Explore Acadia's top sights along this 27-mile drive.

3 Best Afternoon Break: Jordan Pond House (p42) Relax like a Rockefeller and take your tea on the lakeside lawn.

4 Best Hike: Acadia Mountain Trail (p38) On the quieter west side of the park, overlooking the only fjord on the USA's east coast.

5 Best Family Outing: Witch Hole Pond Loop (p39) Cycle past beaver ponds on this gentle carriage road path.

View from Cadillac Mountain (p33)
JOHN ELK III / LONELY PLANET IMAGES ©

Discover Acadia

ACADIA NATIONAL PARK

The park includes about two-thirds of Mount Desert Island as well as part of the Schoodic Peninsula, Isle au Haut and Baker Island. From shoreline to summit, woodland to lake, the park's diversity is a large part of its appeal.

Jordan Pond House (p42)

History

Indigenous Wabanaki settlers were living on Mount Desert Island when the first Europeans arrived. French explorer Samuel Champlain landed on the island in 1604 but made no attempt at settlement. In 1688, King Louis XIV granted Mount Desert Island to Antoine de la Cadillac, who stayed just briefly before moving on to establish the city of Detroit; today, Mount Desert's highest mountain and Detroit's top car both bear Cadillac's name.

The first permanent European settlement was established in 1761 but the area remained a quiet backwater until the 1840s when artists from the Hudson River School, attracted by the natural beauty of Mount Desert, came to paint landscapes. Their works inspired others and tourists soon began arriving in droves.

By the 1890s Mount Desert Island had become a magnet for Rockefellers, Vanderbilts and other rich urbanites who built lavish summer mansions, dubbed 'cottages,' along the shoreline. Led by Harvard University president Charles Eliot, these wealthy summer residents formed a land trust in 1901 to preserve large tracts of the island. In 1919 Congress designated the land as a national park, the first to be established east of the Mississippi River.

When to Go

The park is open year-round. The busiest time is summer; in July and August the park is absolutely packed. June and September are great months to visit – ranger-led programs are still taking place but it's not nearly as crowded. In late September and early October the foliage blazes in reds, yellows and russets, making hiking and cycling an absolute delight. For those hardy souls that show up during the winter months, the carriage roads double as scenic cross-country ski runs.

When You Arrive

The gateway to Acadia National Park is Hulls Cove Visitor Center, where you can get oriented with all the park has to offer before setting off.

Orientation

Most of the park is on Mount Desert Island – which, like Maine, is shaped like a lobster claw – with the long, narrow Somes Sound separating the east and west sides. The east side of the park, adjacent to Bar Harbor, is crowned by the park's highest peak, Cadillac Mountain, and is home to the park's main sights.

 Sights

Scenic landscapes of green forests, blue ponds and pink granite mountains abound in this region. Watch for white-tailed deer, industrious beavers, soaring raptors and colorful wildflowers.

HULLS COVE VISITOR
CENTER   Visitor Center
(📞 207-288-3338; www.nps.gov/acad; ME 3; ⊙ 8am-4:30pm mid-Apr–Jun & Oct, 8am-6pm Jul & Aug, 8am-5pm Sep) Conveniently perched near the start of Park Loop Rd, this friendly visitor center should be your first stop. Inside you'll find maps, the latest on wildlife spotting and a short introductory film to the park. Have kids? Ask about the Junior Ranger program.

PARK LOOP ROAD   Scenic Drive
The 27-mile Park Loop Rd, the main sightseeing jaunt, circumnavigates the eastern portion of the park, covering many of Acadia's highlights. There are plenty of stops along the way where you can get out and explore. One caveat: parking is tight at top spots. Your best bet during the busy summer months

is to either drive the route early in the morning or take advantage of the park's free Island Explorer bus system. On the Ocean Drive section, be sure to stop at **Thunder Hole** to watch surf crashing into a cleft in the granite; when there's a strong incoming tide, it roars thunderously. From Thunder Hole look south to see rock climbers scaling the vertical pink granite of **Otter Cliffs**.

JORDAN POND   Pond
Midway along the Park Loop Rd, picturesque Jordan Pond sates both body and soul. Shoreline trails, afternoon tea overlooking the pond and dining with a view make this a prime stop on any itinerary.

CADILLAC MOUNTAIN   Mountain
The majestic centerpiece of Acadia National Park is Cadillac Mountain (1530ft), the highest coastal peak in the eastern US. By car it's reached via a 3.5-mile spur road off Park Loop Rd. Four trails also lead to the summit from four directions should you prefer hiking boots to rubber tires. The summit's breathtaking 360-degree view of ocean, islands and mountains is a winner any time of the day, but it's truly magical at dawn when hardy souls flock to the top to watch the sun rise over Frenchman Bay. The mountaintop is susceptible to high winds, so if you're coming up for sunrise bring an extra layer of clothing.

🚩 WILD GARDENS OF
ACADIA   Gardens
(📞 207-288-3003; Sieur de Monts exit off Park Loop Rd; admission free; ⊙ dawn-dusk) This 1-acre botanical garden showcases 12 of Acadia's biospheres in miniature, from bog to coniferous woods to meadow, all nicely identified with labels. At the head of the garden is the one-room **Sieur de Monts Nature Center**, with stuffed creatures like bald eagles, beaver and coyote.

🚩 ABBE MUSEUM AT SIEUR
DE MONTS   Museum
(www.abbemuseum.org; Sieur de Monts exit off Park Loop Rd; adult/child $3/1; ⊙ 10am-5pm late May–mid-Oct) Today this is a branch of

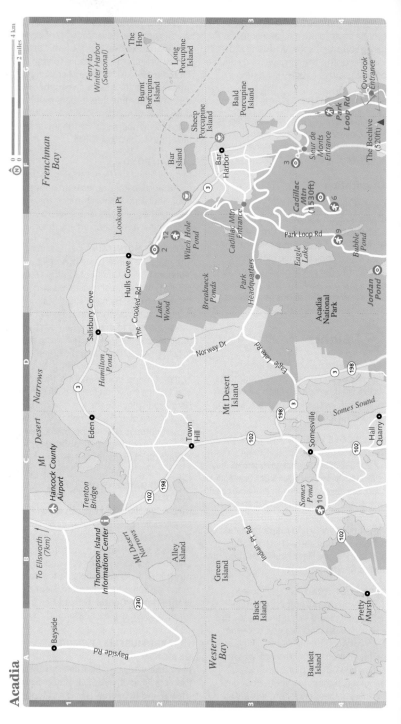

DISCOVER ACADIA

Acadia

34

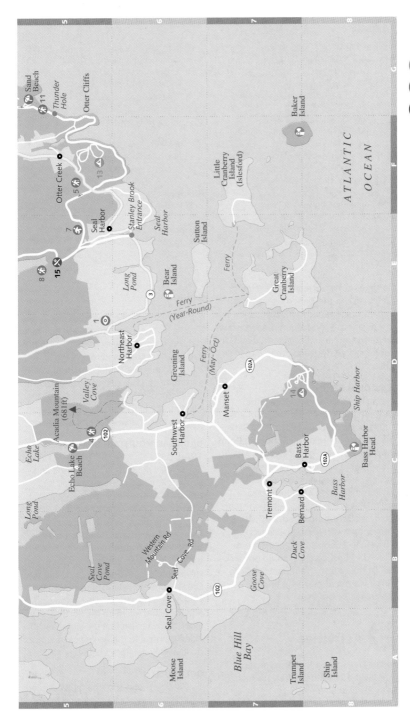

Acadia

the larger Abbe Museum in Bar Harbor, but this inside-the-park museum is the original, first opened in 1928. It centers on indigenous life on Mount Desert Island before the arrival of Europeans, displaying stone tools, pottery and other Wabanaki artifacts.

SCHOODIC PENINSULA   Peninsula
Jutting into the Atlantic Ocean, the southern tip of this peninsula contains a quiet portion of Acadia National Park. The 7.2-mile shore drive, **Schoodic Point Loop Rd**, offers splendid views of Mount Desert Island and Cadillac Mountain. This one-way loop road is excellent for cycling since it has a smooth surface and relatively gentle hills. Along the loop you'll find **Schoodic Head**, a 400ft-high promontory with fine ocean views.

To get to Schoodic Peninsula by car, follow US 1 east and turn south onto ME 186. Or take a ferry from Bar Harbor to Winter Harbor and pick up the free Island Explorer bus from there.

 **Activities**

Acadia National Park offers a plethora of activities for both leisurely hikers and adrenaline junkies.

Hiking

Some 140 miles of hiking trails crisscross Acadia National Park, from easy half-mile nature walks and level rambles to mountain treks up steep and rocky terrain. You can pick up a free leaflet with brief trail summaries or buy detailed trail guides at the visitor center. In addition to dedicated hiking trails, hikers are also welcome on the extensive network of carriage roads.

CADILLAC MOUNTAIN SUMMIT TRAIL   Hiking
Some folks drive up to the summit and somehow miss this view-studded loop trail that crowns Cadillac Mountain. With ocean and mountain vistas galore, this may be the most rewarding 15-minute hike you'll ever make. It begins on a paved footpath at the southern end of the parking lot. As you walk, sweeping views unfold from Southwest Harbor and Great Cranberry Island in the south to Bar Harbor and Frenchman Bay in the east and mainland Maine to the north. Plaques along the way describe the views and provide insights into the geological origins of Acadia National Park's highest peak.

OCEAN PATH   Hiking
This 4-mile round-trip trail runs between Sand Beach and Otter Cliffs and takes

in the most dramatic coastal scenery in the park, including Acadia's most popular sight – the roaring chasm of Thunder Hole. Start the Ocean Path at the parking lot for Sand Beach, where you can enjoy a swim before heading off. The trail runs south along the coast paralleling Park Loop Rd and makes an easy two-hour walk, best done in the morning before traffic picks up. Along the way short spur trails lead down to ledges and a rocky shoreline with tidepools. You'll also find curious canyon-like formations cut into the pink granite cliffs by eons of pounding winter waves. While the entire route is worthwhile, the most interesting scenery is packed into the first mile, so if time is short you could cut your walk in half by taking it as far as Thunder Hole before returning. You'll miss Otter Point, the park's steepest ocean cliffs, but you can catch it later as a stop on the Park Loop Rd drive.

JORDAN POND TRAIL   Hiking

A stroll around Jordan Pond and its surrounding forests and flower meadows is one of Acadia's most popular and family-friendly activities. It's a delightfully peaceful walk with gently lapping waters along the shoreline and open vistas across the pond. On clear days, the glassy waters of this 176-acre pond reflect the image of Penobscot Mountain like a mirror. Since the path skirts the pond, it can get a bit muddy after rain, but wet conditions are more common in spring than in summer or fall. Start the 3.2-mile trail at the Jordan Pond parking area on Park Loop Rd, 200yd north of the Jordan Pond House.

If you want to sample a 15-minute taste of this trail, the Jordan Pond Nature Trail edges the scenic south side of the pond in front of the Jordan Pond House.

CADILLAC MOUNTAIN SOUTH RIDGE TRAIL   Hiking

At 7.4 miles round-trip, the South Ridge Trail to the summit of Cadillac Mountain is the longest hike in the national park. The trail has a moderate ascent and true to its name follows a ridge, rewarding hikers with unobstructed views along the way.

The hike starts in the woods on the north side of ME 3, 100ft south of the Blackwoods Campground entrance. A mile past the trailhead, a short loop trail, marked Eagles Crag, spurs off to the right offering a view of the village of

Jordan Pond (p33)

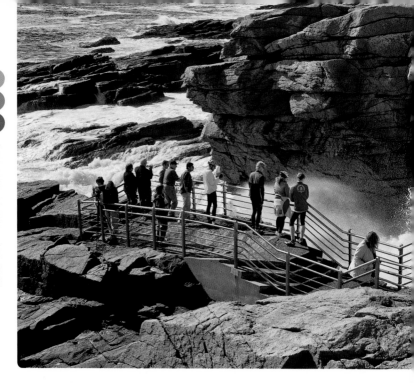

Otter Creek before rejoining the South Ridge Trail a few minutes later. As you continue, the trail climbs gradually past ledges where you can stop and enjoy more eye-popping coastal vistas to the south and east. After 2.3 miles the trail crosses Canon Brook Trail before making the climb for the final haul to the summit, where the grandest panorama of all unfolds. The hike takes about four hours round-trip but you could have someone meet you at the summit and make it a one-way event.

ACADIA MOUNTAIN TRAIL   Hiking

Of all the trails on the west side of Acadia National Park, this climb up the park's namesake mountain stands out for the sheer variety of stunning water views. It's also one of the more strenuous, thanks to the numerous rocks you'll need to scramble up. Parking for the hike is on ME 102, three miles south of Somesville. The trail begins up stone stairs on the opposite side of the road. After 0.1 mile the trail forks; bear left. The trail then crosses

a babbling brook and a gravel fireroad before reaching the first of the granite boulders you'll be maneuvering over.

About 30 minutes into the hike you'll break out of the forest for your first views, with scenic Echo Lake and Beech Mountain appearing to the west. That's just a taste of what's to come – keep climbing and the deep-blue arm of Somes Sound, the only fjord in the eastern US, comes into view. About an hour into the hike you'll reach the summit, where a breathtaking panorama of the entire fjord, the picturesque villages of Northeast and Southwest Harbors, and the low-lying southern islands unfolds.

From the summit the trail continues east along the ridge, providing more watery vistas in all directions. Blue blazes mark the way but keep an eye open where the descent begins so you don't go astray. As you descend the mountain you'll have to scurry down some rocky ledges before you reach the final leg of this 2.5-mile hike, a gentle path through the woods along the Man O' War fireroad. Follow the

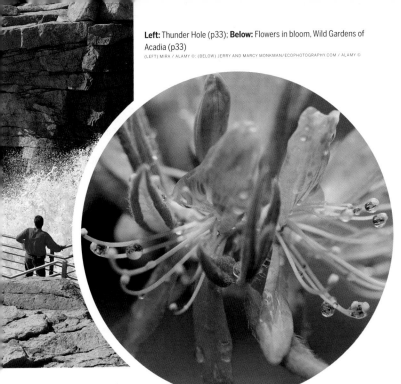

Left: Thunder Hole (p33); **Below:** Flowers in bloom, Wild Gardens of Acadia (p33)

(LEFT) MIRA / ALAMY ©; (BELOW) JERRY AND MARCY MONKMAN/ECOPHOTOGRAPHY.COM / ALAMY ©

fireroad all the way back to ME 102 – the trail parking lot will be visible 100yd to the south. Give yourself three hours to do the hike, enjoy the views and pick a few blueberries along the way.

Cycling

The park's 45 miles of carriage roads are ideal for cycling.

JORDAN POND-BUBBLE POND LOOP
Cycling

The 8.3-mile Jordan Pond-Bubble Pond Loop of the carriage road system packs forest, mountain and pond views into one of the prettiest cycling paths in the park. Starting at the northeast side of the loop, Cadillac Mountain offers a superb scene, shooting straight up from the carriage road with Bubble Pond in the foreground. The route continues over arching stone bridges and past the classic gate lodge at Jordan Pond, where you can stop and enjoy afternoon tea before continuing on

to the final leg. The route is considered moderate and takes about 2½ hours.

WITCH HOLE POND LOOP
Cycling

This 3.3-mile carriage road loop makes a fun, easy outing for families and those looking for a short pedal close to the park's main entrance and Bar Harbor. You'll encounter some gentle hills but the route is largely flat, skirting bogs and small ponds with log-stacked beaver lodges. This is one of the park's most popular routes but unlike other carriage road sections, horses are prohibited, so it's all cyclists and hikers on this one.

ACADIA BIKE
Bicycle Rental

(📞 207-288-9605; www.acadiabike.com; 48 Cottage St, Bar Harbor; rental per day $22; ⏰ 8am-8pm) You can rent quality mountain bikes, replaced new at the start of each season, from this reliable outfitter.

DISCOVER ACADIA ACTIVITIES

39

Rock Climbing

With all that granite, Acadia National Park is a mecca for rock climbers. A favorite spot is Otter Cliffs, where pink rocks rise vertically out of the sea.

ACADIA MOUNTAIN GUIDES   Rock Climbing
(207-288-8186; www.acadiamountainguides.com; 228 Main St, Bar Harbor; half-day outing $60-140; May-Oct) Rates vary depending on the number in your party and include a guide, instruction and equipment.

Ranger Programs

Scores of ranger-led programs are offered from mid-May to early October. These include short nature walks, longer hikes, peregrine falcon watches, tidepool exploration and children's programs. Get the latest schedule online or at the visitor center.

Boat Cruises

In summer, park rangers, working in conjunction with commercial boat operators, offer interpretive tours of Frenchman Bay and some of the offshore islands.

BAR HARBOR WHALE WATCH   Boat Cruise
(207-288-2386; www.barharborwhales.com; 1 West St, Bar Harbor; adult/child $45/22; Jun-Oct;) Cruise along Acadia's rugged shoreline on a ranger-led tour to **Baker Island**, a 130-acre island that's part of Acadia National Park but reachable only by boat. The company also offers whale-watching and puffin trips.

Acadia's Carriage Roads

Acadia National Park's 45 miles of handcrafted carriage roads stand out as one of the park's most distinctive features. They're also a major draw for visitors.

The carriage roads were built by national parks philanthropist John D Rockefeller Jr. Rockefeller was an accomplished equestrian with a love of auto-free wilderness who wanted a way to get into the heart of Mount Desert Island solely by horse and buggy.

Considered the nation's finest example of broken-stone road building, Acadia's iconic carriage roads were constructed over a 27-year period beginning in 1913. Rockefeller had a keen eye for landscape architecture and aligned the roads to blend carefully with Acadia's landscape and to take advantage of its incredible views.

The hand-hewn stonework, made of locally quarried granite, also includes 17 handsome stone bridges and two gate lodges that once served as entry points to the carriage road system. The gate lodges – one of which is opposite Jordan Pond House and the other in Northeast Harbor – are styled to resemble rustic European hunting lodges and use hues and materials that meld harmoniously with their surroundings.

The roads themselves are a generous 16ft in width and include unique features like roughly-cut granite coping stones, dubbed 'Rockefeller's teeth,' that serve as guardrails.

Today, as in Rockefeller's day, cars are forbidden from the carriage roads, leaving them a unspoiled haven for hikers, cyclists and horseback riders...and, of course, horse and buggy rides!

DOWNEAST WINDJAMMER CRUISES Boat Cruise

(☎207-288-4585; www.downeastwind jammer.com; 27 Main St, Bar Harbor; adult/child $38/28; ☉May–mid-Oct; ⛵) For a cruise of Frenchman Bay in style, hop aboard the four-mast schooner *Margaret Todd,* which sets sail three times a day. Cruises are led by rangers and concentrate on the bay's history and wildlife.

Canoeing & Kayaking

Long Pond, the largest of Acadia's many lakes, is the top paddling destination in the park. Aptly named, the pond is long – 7.5 miles – cut with coves to explore and rich with mountain views.

NATIONAL PARK CANOE & KAYAK RENTAL Canoe & Kayak Rental

(☎207-244-5854; www.nationalparkcanoe rental.com; Ponds End, ME 102; 3hr rental $27-35; ☉8am-5pm May-Oct) At the north end of Long Pond, this outfitter rents canoes, solo kayaks and tandem kayaks in three-hour blocks. It frequently books out, so call ahead for reservations.

Carriage Rides

 CARRIAGES OF ACADIA Tour

(☎877-276-3622; www.carriagesofacadia.com; adult/child 1hr tour $18/9, 2hr tour $24.50/10; ☉May-Oct; ⛵) Operating out of Wildwood Stables on the Park Loop Rd, this local outfit leads a variety of leisurely, family-friendly horse-drawn carriage tours with narration recalling the romance of Rockefeller's horse and buggy days. Choose between tours that feature the carriage road bridges and Jordan Pond Gate Lodge, and others that center around mountain vistas and scenic views. Private carriage charters are also available.

Swimming

BEACHES Swimming

The park offers two choices for cooling off on a hot summer day. Brave the icy

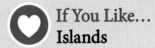

If You Like... Islands

If you like exploring Baker Island, you might also like the lightly populated **Cranberry Isles** (www.cranberryisles.com), which are connected to Mount Desert Island by passenger boat.

1 LITTLE CRANBERRY ISLAND
This 400-acre island, home to the village of Islesford, is about 20 minutes offshore from Mount Desert Island's Southwest Harbor. Sights include a few galleries and a general store, where the 80-odd year-rounders and 400-odd summer folk gather around like it's their own kitchen.

2 GREAT CRANBERRY ISLAND
The biggest of the Cranberry Isles has a small historical museum (admission free) and a mile-long trail that leads through woods to a quiet beach.

3 SUTTON ISLAND
Largely a summer colony, Sutton is so lightly developed that it doesn't even have a road, just footpaths, and its only 'sight' is a cemetery...now, how quiet is that?

(55°F/12.7°C even in midsummer!) ocean waters of **Sand Beach** or take a dip in the calm waters of **Echo Lake**, which provides a more temperate swim.

🛏 Sleeping

The park has two campgrounds, both wooded and with running water, showers and barbecue pits, but no hookups for RVs. Both national park campgrounds are within a 10-minute walk of the ocean. If these are full, several commercial campgrounds can be found on the outskirts of Acadia National Park; for details, go to www.acadiainfo.com. No other lodging is available in the park, but there are scores of inns and hotels in Bar Harbor, just a mile beyond the park.

STEVEN EMERY / GETTY ©

Don't Miss Jordan Pond Viewpoint

For a picture-perfect view of Jordan Pond, take the steps to the observation deck atop the Jordan Pond Gift Shop. From this vantage you can gaze across the sloping lawn to the south side of the pond. Clear across the waters, the voluptuous rounded double hills known as the Bubbles form the backdrop, rising sublimely above the north side of the pond. It's one of the loveliest views in the entire park.

BLACKWOODS CAMPGROUND Campground $
(☎877-444-6777; www.recreation.gov; ME 3; campsites $20; ☉year-round) This 279-site campground, 5 miles south of Bar Harbor, accepts advance reservations.

SEAWALL CAMPGROUND Campground $
(☎877-444-6777; www.recreation.gov; ME 102A; campsites $14-20; ☉late May-Sep) This 210-site campground, 4 miles south of Southwest Harbor, is first-come, first-served, but accepts some advance reservations.

 **Eating & Drinking**

The park has only one restaurant, but it's a good one! Do expect a crowd.

JORDAN POND HOUSE American $$
(☎207-276-3316; www.thejordanpond house.com; afternoon tea $9, mains $10-22; ☉11:30am-9pm mid-May–Oct) For a memorable midday break, sit on the lawn overlooking the pond and order afternoon tea served with warm popovers and homemade strawberry jam. Lunch, served until 5:30pm, features lobster rolls, salads and tender Atlantic scallops, all accompanied by a popover with jam. Dinner fancies it up with the likes of bouillabaisse and prime rib.

Shopping

JORDAN POND GIFT SHOP Souvenirs
(www.acadiashops.com; Park Loop Rd) In the same complex as Jordan Pond House,

this shop carries quality crafts and souvenir items including Acadia National Park logo clothing and coffee mugs, Maine maple syrup and blueberry jam, and bags of Jordan Pond House's famous popover mix.

HULLS COVE GIFT SHOP Maps, Books (Hulls Cove Visitor Center, ME 3) This national park concessionaire sells maps and field guides, plus crafts and some fun kids games.

ℹ Information

Entrance Fees & Passes

An admission fee is charged from May 1 to October 31. The fee, which is valid for seven consecutive days, is $20 per vehicle between mid-June and early October, and $10 from May to mid-June and early October to October 31. Pedestrians, cyclists and motorcyclists pay $5 for a seven-day pass.

Opening Dates

The park is open year-round, though Park Loop Rd and most facilities are closed because of snow in winter.

Tourist Information

Hulls Cove Visitor Center (☏207-288-3338; www.nps.gov/acad; ME 3; ⊙8am-4:30pm mid-Apr–Jun & Oct, 8am-6pm Jul & Aug, 8am-5pm Sep)

Park Policies & Regulations

Parking, camping and fires are permitted only in designated areas. If you must stray from trails, hike on durable surfaces, like granite rock, when possible. To prevent the spread of the Asian longhorned beetle and other pests, it's prohibited to bring in firewood from neighboring states.

Maps

The best map of the park is the *Acadia National Park Hiking & Biking Trail Map* ($5), sold at Hulls Cove Visitor Center.

Websites

You can find tons of information on the Acadia National Park (www.nps.gov/acad) website.

ℹ Getting There & Around

Air

US Airways Express (www.usairways.com) connects Bar Harbor and Boston with daily flights year-round. Hancock County Airport (BHB), also called Bar Harbor Airport, is in nearby Trenton, off ME 3, just north of the Trenton Bridge.

Bus

Island Explorer (☏207-667-5796; www.exploreacadia.com; rides free; ⊙late Jun-early Oct) runs eight shuttle bus routes throughout Acadia National Park as well as to adjacent Bar Harbor, linking sightseeing spots, trailheads, campgrounds and accommodations. Taking these propane-powered buses is not only an ecofriendly way to travel but it eliminates queuing up for a parking space at busy sights, like Thunder Hole, which is commonplace in summer.

Car & Motorcycle

Acadia National Park is 275 miles from Boston, and 160 miles from Portland, Maine, via I-95 to ME 1 and then to ME 3, which runs into the park. While getting to Acadia should pose few problems with traffic, keep in mind that with millions of visitors arriving each year, the roads within the park can get frustratingly crowded during the high season. Fortunately, Acadia's free summertime bus shuttle service lets visitors minimize the need to drive on park roads.

For car rental, Hertz (www.hertz.com) and Enterprise Rent-a-Car (www.enterprise.com) have booths at the airport.

AROUND ACADIA
Bar Harbor

Set at the northeastern edge of Acadia National Park, this alluring coastal town once rivaled Newport, Rhode Island, as a trendy summer destination for wealthy Americans. Today many of the old mansions have been turned into inviting inns and the town has become a magnet for outdoor enthusiasts. Its busy downtown is packed with outfitters, souvenir shops and cafes catering to park visitors.

◉ Sights & Activities

ABBE MUSEUM   *Museum*
(☎207-288-3519; www.abbemuseum.com; 26 Mount Desert St; adult/child $6/2; ⊙10am-5pm) The main Abbe Museum, in the center of Bar Harbor's downtown, has fascinating presentations on the Native American tribes that hail from this region. The thousands of artifacts range from pottery dating back more than a millennium to contemporary woodcarvings and baskets.

SHORE PATH   *Walking*
For a picturesque view of the harbor, take a stroll along Bar Harbor's Shore Path. This half-mile walkway, first laid down in 1880, begins near Agamont Park and continues past birch-tree-lined Grant Park, with views of the Porcupine Islands offshore and the historic mansions set back from the path.

👉 Tours

Numerous outfits offer adventures out on the water. Keep in mind that it is often

Horse-drawn carriage crossing (p41)

20°F (11°C) cooler on the water than on land, so bring a jacket.

COASTAL KAYAKING TOURS   *Kayaking*
(☎207-288-9605; www.acadiafun.com; 48 Cottage St; 2½/4hr tours $38/48; ⊙8am-8pm) Guided kayaking tours typically go to the islands in Frenchman Bay or the west side of Mount Desert Island, depending on which way the wind's blowing. This outfit offers personalized tours, taking out a maximum of six kayaks at a time.

ACADIAN NATURE CRUISES   *Cruise*
(☎207-288-2386; www.acadiannaturecruises. com; 1 West St; adult/child $27/16; ⊙mid-May– Oct) See bald eagles, seals and coastal sights on these narrated two-hour nature cruises.

🛏 Sleeping

Since there are no places to stay in the national park other than two camp-grounds, most park visitors spend their nights at one of the many guesthouses and small hotels in Bar Harbor. Book early if you're arriving in summer; getting a

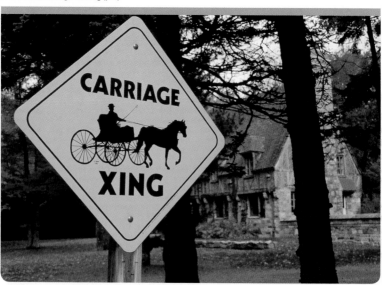

room without a reservation is not a challenge the rest of the year. More accommodation options can be found at www.barharborinfo.com.

HOLLAND INN B&B $$
(☎207-288-4804; www.hollandinn.com; 35 Holland Ave; r incl breakfast $95-175; ❋ ☎) Nine cheery rooms with frill-free decor, a hearty breakfast and innkeepers who make you feel at home are in store at this B&B just a short stroll from the town center and waterfront.

ANNE'S WHITE COLUMNS INN B&B $$
(☎207-288-5357; www.anneswhitecolumns. com; 57 Mount Desert St; r incl breakfast $75-165; ❋) Once a Christian Scientist church, this B&B's name refers to its dramatic columned entrance. Rooms have a quirky Victorian charm, with plenty of florals and bric-a-brac. Get here in time for the afternoon wine and cheese reception.

AYSGARTH STATION INN B&B $$
(☎207-288-9655; www.aysgarth.com; 20 Roberts Ave; r incl breakfast $115-155; ❋) On a quiet side street near the town center, this 1895 B&B has six cozy rooms with homey touches. Request the Tan Hill room, which is on the 3rd floor, for a view of Cadillac Mountain.

ACADIA PARK INN Motel $$
(☎207-288-5823; www.acadiaparkinn.com; ME 3; r incl breakfast $109-169; ❋ ☎) This good-value motel has comfy renovated rooms in a woodsy setting 2 miles north of the park's main entrance.

BASS COTTAGE Inn $$$
(☎207-288-1234; www.basscottage.com; 14 The Field; r incl breakfast $190-370; ❋ ☎) Have a 'Great Gatsby' moment at this Gilded Age mansion just steps from the heart of town.

AURORA INN Motel $$
(☎207-288-3771; www.aurorainn.com; 51 Holland Ave; r $89-169; ❋ ☎) This retro motor lodge has 10 simple rooms and a convenient in-town location.

 Eating & Drinking

CAFE THIS WAY American $$
(☎207-288-4483; www.cafethisway.com; 14½ Mount Desert St; breakfast $6-9, dinner $15-24; ⏱7-11:30am Mon-Sat, 8am-1pm Sun, 5:30-9pm nightly; ☞) *The* place in Bar Harbor for breakfast – the feather-light blueberry pancakes topped with real maple syrup melt in your mouth. Vegans will love the scrambled tofu chock-full of veggies, while old-schoolers should order the eggs Benedict with smoked salmon.

MCKAYS American $$
(☎207-288-2002; www.mckayspublichouse. com; 231 Main St; mains $10-20; ⏱4:30-9:30pm Tue-Sun) This buy-local-and-organic-when-possible pub-style eatery dishes up Maine crab cakes, farm-raised chicken and good ol' beer-battered fish and chips.

TRENTON BRIDGE LOBSTER POUND Seafood $$
(☎207-667-2977; ME 3, Ellsworth; lobsters $10-15; ⏱10:30am-8pm Mon-Sat; ♿) Sit at a picnic table and crack open a boiled lobster at this traditional lobster pound. It borders the causeway connecting Mount Desert Island to mainland Maine.

FINBACK ALEHOUSE Pub $$
(☎207-288-0233; www.finbackalehouseme. com; 30 Cottage St; mains $10-20; ⏱11am-1am) Creative Maine-centric fare featuring locally caught seafood and juicy grass-fed sirloin burgers. Great selection of local beers and live music on weekends.

2 CATS Cafe $$
(☎207-288-2808; www.2catsbarharbor.com; 130 Cottage St; mains $8-17; ⏱7am-1pm; ☞) The perfect place for scones and tea on drizzly days. Awesome lobster omelettes, and good veggie options too!

HAVANA Cuban $$$
(☎207-288-2822; www.havanamaine.com; 318 Main St; mains $19-29; ⏱5-10pm) Maine goes Latin at this elegant dinner restaurant presenting seafood with a Cuban twist. Award-winning wine list.

ⓘ Information

Bar Harbor Chamber of Commerce (☏207-288-5103; www.barharborinfo.com; 1201 Bar Harbor Rd/ME 3, Trenton; ⏰8am-6pm late May–mid-Oct, 8am-5pm Mon-Fri mid-Oct–late May) Has a convenient welcome center on Thompson Island just before reaching Mount Desert Island, and a branch on the corner of Cottage and Main streets in Bar Harbor.

Northeast Harbor

Called 'Northeast' by locals, this fishing village is a popular getaway for the preppy East Coast yachtie set. The tiny Main St is dotted with art galleries and cafes, and the hillsides are lined with Gilded Age mansions hidden behind the trees.

◉ Sights

🖋ASTICOU AZALEA GARDEN
Gardens

(www.gardenpreserve.org; ME 3; suggested donation $5; ⏰dawn-dusk May-Oct) Designed in

1900, this lovely 200-acre garden is laced with paths, little shelters and ornamental Japanese-style bridges. It's so zen-like you might think you're in Kyoto. Azaleas and rhododendrons bloom profusely from mid-May to mid-June. Wander up to the garden's century-old **Thuya Lodge** (⏰10am-4:30pm late Jun-early Sep) to see the reflecting pool and well-tended English gardens. The terraces zigzag through the woods and down to the water.

Southwest Harbor & Bass Harbor

More laid-back and less affluent than Northeast Harbor, 'Southwest' is also quite tranquil. But looks can be deceiving: it's also a major boat-building center and a commercial fishing harbor.

From the Upper Town Dock – a quarter-mile along Clark Point Rd from the flashing light in the center of town – boats venture out into Frenchman Bay to the Cranberry Isles.

A few miles south of Southwest Harbor lies the somnolent fishing village of Bass Harbor, home to the **Bass Harbor Head Light**. Built in 1858, the 26ft lighthouse still has a Fresnel lens from 1902.

Isle au Haut

Half of Isle au Haut, a rocky island 6 miles long, is under the auspices of Acadia National Park. Remote from the rest of the park, the island lies about 20 miles southwest of Mount Desert Island. To get here requires a 60-mile drive from Mount Desert Island to the village of Stonington, at the southern end of ME 15, and then a ride on a mail-boat. On the plus side, since Isle au Haut is much harder to get to, this rugged island avoids the crowds that flock to the rest of the national park.

Kayaker, Bar Harbor (p43)

Detour:
Ellsworth

Just north of Mount Desert Island, the small town of Ellsworth is a slice of old-time Americana, with a pretty Main St lined with shops, galleries and restaurants. A highlight is the **Woodlawn Museum** (www.woodlawnmuseum.com; ME 172; adult/child $10/3; ⊙10am-5pm Tue-Sat & 1-4pm Sun Jun-Sep, 1-4pm Tue-Sun May & Oct), located 0.25 miles south of US 1. This former home of three generations of the wealthy Black family dates from the early 19th century and has marvelously preserved furnishings, decorations and family artifacts dating from 1820 to 1920. Formal gardens and a picturesque lawn surround the mansion, with a pleasant trail circling the woods.

Afterwards, treat yourself to a meal at Ellsworth's top eatery, **Cleonice** (☎207-664-7554; www.cleonice.com; 112 Main St; meals $10-35; ⊙11:30am-9pm), where they take their own homegrown ingredients and prepare them with Mediterranean flair in dishes like lamb burgers with feta, and halibut ceviche. The landmark building, with black-and-white tiled floors and tables hidden in carved wooden alcoves, has a charming old-world vibe.

 **Activities**

Bicycles can be rented on the island for $25 a day.

ISLE AU HAUT BOAT
SERVICES
Boat Trips
(☎207-367-5193; www.isleauhaut.com; round-trip adult/child $37/19) Operates daily, year-round mail-boat trips between Stonington and Isle au Haut. In summer, five boats a day make the 45-minute crossing from Monday through Saturday. Service is lighter at other times. Bicycles, kayaks and canoes (no cars) can be carried to the island for a fee.

 Sleeping & Eating

Duck Harbor
Campground
Campground $$
(☎207-288-3338; www.nps.gov/acad; campsites $25; ⊙mid-May–mid-Oct)Serious hikers can tramp the island's miles of trails and camp for the night at this campground, which has five lean-to shelters maintained by the National Park Service.

Inn at Isle au Haut
Inn $$$
(☎207-669-2751; www.innatisleauhaut.com; r incl breakfast, lunch & dinner $300-375; ⊙Jun-Sep) For a less rustic experience, the Inn offers four cheerfully decorated rooms with antique furniture and quilted bedspreads; three rooms have ocean views. Meals are included in the rate and are generally excellent.

Everglades National Park

More than Miami, the Everglades make South Florida truly unique. Called the 'River of Grass' by Native Americans, this is not just a wetland, or a swamp, or a lake, or a river, or a prairie, or a grassland – it is all of the above, twisted together into a series of soft horizons, long vistas, sunsets that stretch across your entire field of vision and the creeping grin of a large population of dinosaur-era reptiles.

When you watch anhinga flex their wings before breaking into corkscrew dives, or the slow, Jurassic flap of a great blue heron gliding over its domain, or the sun kissing miles of unbroken sawgrass as it sets behind humps of skeletal cypress domes, you'll start to have an idea of what we're speaking of. In a nation where natural beauty is measured by its capacity for drama, the Everglades subtly, contentedly, flows on.

Aerial view of Everglades welands
JIM WARK / LONELY PLANET IMAGES ©

Everglades Itineraries

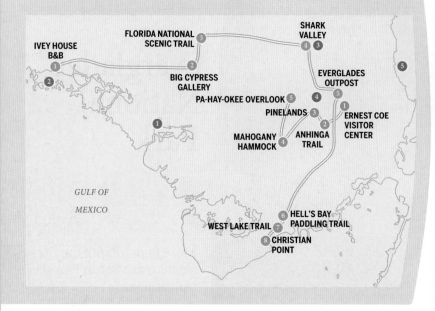

IVEY HOUSE B&B

FLORIDA NATIONAL SCENIC TRAIL

SHARK VALLEY

BIG CYPRESS GALLERY

EVERGLADES OUTPOST

PA-HAY-OKEE OVERLOOK

PINELANDS

ERNEST COE VISITOR CENTER

MAHOGANY HAMMOCK

ANHINGA TRAIL

GULF OF MEXICO

HELL'S BAY PADDLING TRAIL

WEST LAKE TRAIL

CHRISTIAN POINT

One Day

1 **Ernest Coe Visitor Center** (p57)
Introduce yourself to the United States' largest subtropical wilderness the easy way: at the park's excellent Ernest Coe Visitor Center, only 34 miles from Miami. Interactive exhibits, a film about the park and brochures aplenty will orient you and help you decide what you most want to see.

2 **Anhinga Trail** (p57) Spot alligators soaking up the sun and watch for the trail's namesake birds as they spear their prey with their razor-sharp bills. The short, easy hike is a great way to experience the Everglades without exerting too much effort.

3 **Pinelands** (p58) Wander through a section of the Everglades' pine forests on the Pinelands trail, not far from the Ernest Coe Visitor Center. The unique ecosystem is home to numerous plants that grow only in the Everglades.

4 **Mahogany Hammock** (p58) Explore an 'island' of hardwood forest – including gumbo-limbo trees, bromeliads and massive mahogany trees – on the short walk along this lovely boardwalk.

5 **Pa-hay-okee Overlook** (p58) Close the day watching the sun set from this stunning viewpoint over the River of Grass.

THIS LEG: 30 MILES

Three Days

1 Ivey House B&B (p60) If you'd rather skip sleeping under the stars, head to Everglades City and bed down at this modern B&B. The owners offer outstanding paddling trips to boot.

2 Big Cypress Gallery (p61) To get an aesthetic appreciation of the beauty of the Everglades, head to this gallery for some of the best photography of the surrounding swamps, forests, beaches and sea.

3 Florida National Scenic Trail (p58) On day three, slather on the bug juice and sun block and explore Big Cypress National Preserve along this rugged 31-mile trail.

4 Shark Valley (p57) Make sure to stop at Shark Valley, where you can head down some quick walking paths. Don't forget to either rent a bicycle or book a ticket on the Shark Valley Tram Tour, which winds its way past 'Glades wildlife to a watchtower where you can look over the low horizon.

5 Everglades Outpost (p62) Stop in and support the animal rescue operations underway at the Everglades Outpost, where you can take a peak at gibbons, tigers, wolves, cobras and other animals the center has rescued.

6 Hell's Bay Paddling Trail (p59) With plenty of time on your hands, you can spend days canoeing or kayaking into this tangled and beautiful morass of red creeks and slow blackwater. Those with camping gear and the proper boat can spend the night at one of the many backcountry campsites along the way.

7 West Lake Trail (p58) If you'd rather stay on dry land, hike this trail through the largest protected mangrove forest in the Northern Hemisphere.

8 Christian Point (p58) At the end of the day, wander along this mellow trail and take in the dramatic views of Florida Bay.

⊙ **THIS LEG: 175 MILES**

Everglades Highlights

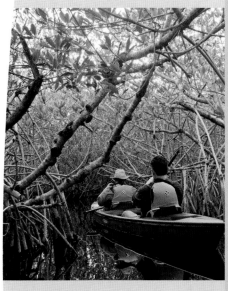

1 Best Paddle Trip: Wilderness Waterway (p59) This 99-mile path between Everglades City and Flamingo is the longest canoe trail in the area.

2 Best Boating: 10,000 Islands (p56) The Gulf Coast Visitor Center is the jumping-off point for exploring these waterways.

3 Best cycling: Shark Valley (p57) The flat, 15-mile trail through this forested area of the park makes for superb pedaling.

4 Best Alligator Spotting: Royal Palm Visitor Center (p57) With trails, exhibits and nighttime ranger walks, how can you go wrong?

5 Best snorkeling: Biscayne National Park (p61) This vast marine reserve near the Everglades is home to the world's third-largest reef.

Kayaking through mangroves (p59)
JAMES CALDWELL / ALAMY ©

51

Discover Everglades

EVERGLADES NATIONAL PARK

Forget what you've heard about airboats and swamp buggies – the Everglades should be approached with the same silence and gentle persuasion it shows its animal inhabitants; instead, explore by canoe, bike, kayak or foot. To understand the way that a nutrient-rich patch of water produces a mosquito that feeds a frog, who becomes lunch for a gator, who snaps up a fish that nearly got speared by a diving anhinga, you need to be still. When you are, you realize that the Everglades, so often dismissed as a swamp, possess a quiet, expansive beauty unlike anywhere else in the United States.

History

It's tempting to think of the Everglades as a swamp, but 'prairie' may be a more apt description. The Glades (Colonial cartographer Gerard de Brahm named the region 'River Glades,' which became Everglades on later English maps) are grasslands that are flooded for most of the year. Run-off water from central Florida flows down the peninsula via streams and rivers, over and through the Glades, and into Florida Bay. Small wonder the Calusa Indians called the area Pa-hay-okee (grassy water). Conservationist Marjory Stoneman Douglas called the Everglades the River of Grass.

Starting in 1905, Floridians cut hundreds of canals to separate the Glades from the state's natural flow of water. The idea was to 'reclaim' the land and turn it into farmland. Unfortunately, this effort has upset the water cycle and replenishment of the Florida aquifer (the state's freshwater supply).

In 2011, the water level in Okeechobee was almost 2.7 inches below normal levels. The number of wading birds nesting has declined by 90% to 95% since the 1930s. Currently, there are 67 threatened and endangered plant and animal species in the park. At this stage, scientists estimate that the wetlands have been reduced by 50% to 75% of their original size.

Alligator

The Comprehensive Everglades Restoration Project (CERP; www.evergladesplan.org) is designed to address the 'root' issue of water, but political battles have significantly slowed the implementation of CERP. The cost of the project has bloomed from around $7.8 billion to $15 billion, and rather than sharing a 50/50 split with the federal government, at the time of research, Florida has footed 79% of the CERP bill. In the meantime, Florida's funding has fallen from $200 million during the Jeb Bush years to $17 million under Rick Scott.

When to Go

Dry season, December through March, brings optimum wildlife viewing along watercourses. However, some kayak routes will be difficult during that time. The weather heats up April through June, but there's a good mix of water and wildlife. July through November means heat, bugs and (except October and November) chances of hurricanes.

When You Arrive

Upon entry, be sure to pick up park brochures, which detail hiking trails, paddling routes, campgrounds, business hours and other useful information from the Ernest Coe, Shark Valley or Gulf Coast Information centers.

Orientation

There are three main entrances and three main areas of the park: one along the southeast edge near Homestead and Florida City (Ernest Coe section); another at the central–north side on the Tamiami Trail (Shark Valley section); and a third at the northwest shore (Gulf Coast section), past Everglades City.

 Sights

Shark Valley Section

The northern and western portion of the park hugs the Tamiami Trail/US 41. Here you'll find flooded forests and swampy bottomlands.

SHARK VALLEY — Park
(☏ 305-221-8776; www.nps.gov/ever/planyourvisit/svdirections; car/bicycle $10/5; ◷ 8:30am-6pm) Shark Valley sounds like it should be the headquarters for the villain in a James Bond movie, but it is in fact a slice of National Park Service grounds heavy with informative signs and knowledgeable rangers. Shark Valley is located in the cypress, hardwood and riverine section of the Everglades, a more traditionally jungly section of the park than the grassy fields and forest domes surrounding the Ernest Coe Visitor Center. A 15-mile paved trail takes you past small creeks, tropical forest and 'borrow pits' – manmade holes that are now basking spots for gators, turtles and birdlife. The pancake-flat trail is perfect for bicycles, which can be rented at the entrance for $7.50 per hour. Bring water with you.

TRAM TOUR — Tram
(☏ 305-221-8455; www.sharkvalleytramtours.com; adult/child under 12yr/senior $18.25/11.50/17.25; ◷ departures 9:30am, 11am, 1pm, 3pm May-Dec, 9am-4pm every hour on the hour Jan-Apr) If you don't feel like exerting yourself, the most popular and painless way to immerse yourself in the Everglades is via the two-hour tram trip that runs along Shark Valley's entire 15-mile trail. If you only have time for one Everglades activity, this should be it, as guides are informative and witty, and you'll likely see gators sunning themselves on the road. Halfway along the trail is the 50ft-high **Shark Valley Observation Tower**, an ugly concrete tower that offers dramatically beautiful views of the park.

BIG CYPRESS GALLERY — Gallery
(☏ 941-695-2428; www.clydebutcher.com; Tamiami Trail; ◷ 10am-5pm Wed-Mon) The highlight of many Everglades trips, this gallery showcases the work of Clyde Butcher, an American photographer who follows in the great tradition of Ansel Adams. His large-format black-and-white

Everglades

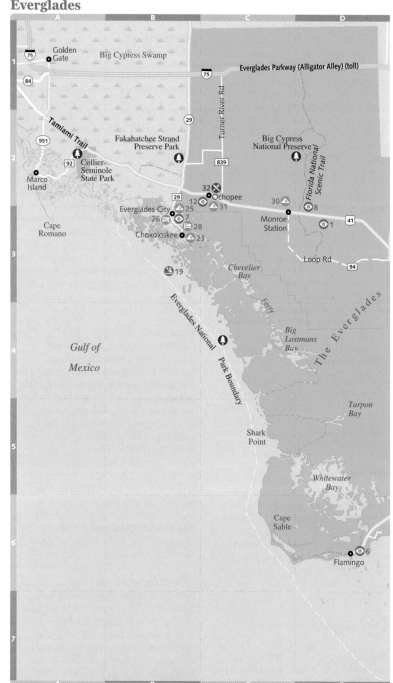

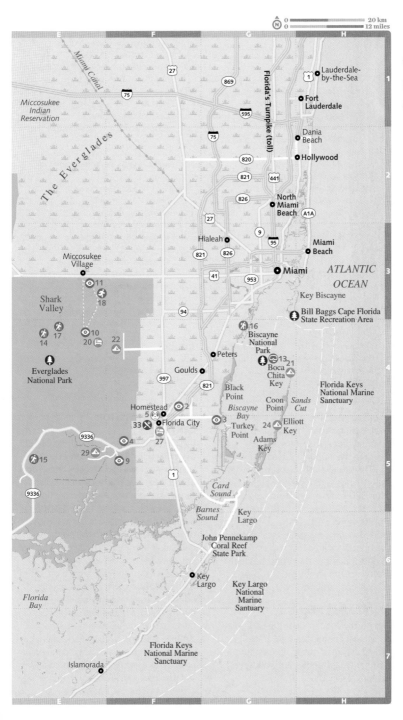

0   20 km
0   12 miles

Lauderdale-
by-the-Sea

Fort
Lauderdale

Dania
Beach

Hollywood

North
Miami
Beach

Miami
Beach

Miami

ATLANTIC
OCEAN

Key Biscayne

Bill Baggs Cape Florida
State Recreation Area

Miami Canal

Miccosukee
Indian
Reservation

The Everglades

Miccosukee
Village

Shark
Valley

Everglades
National Park

Biscayne
National
Park

Boca
Chita
Key

Florida Keys
National Marine
Sanctuary

Peters

Goulds

Homestead

Florida City

Black
Point

Biscayne
Bay

Turkey
Point

Adams
Key

Coon
Point

Sands
Cut

Elliott
Key

Card
Sound

Barnes
Sound

Key
Largo

John Pennekamp
Coral Reef
State Park

Key
Largo

Key Largo
National
Marine
Santuary

Florida
Bay

Florida Keys
National Marine
Sanctuary

Islamorada

55

Everglades

images elevate the swamps to a higher level. Butcher has found a quiet spirituality in the brackish waters and you might too, with the help of his eyes. Every Labor Day (first weekend in September), the gallery holds a gala event, which includes a fun $20 swamp walk onto his 30-acre property; the party attracts swamp-stompers from across the state. At the time of writing, the gallery was setting up two homes located in the cypress woods as guesthouses – the properties look pretty nice, can sleep four to six people and will cost around $200 per night.

Gulf Coast Section

The northwest corner of the park rubs up against Everglades City, an old Florida fishing village of raised houses, turquoise water and scattershot emerald-green mangrove islands.

GULF COAST VISITOR CENTER Visitor Center
(☎ 239-695-3311; Hwy 29, Everglades City, 815 Oyster Bar Ln; ⏱ 9am-4:30pm May-Oct, from 8am Nov-Apr; tours from $25, boat rentals from $13 per hr) This is the northwestern-most ranger station for Everglades National Park, providing access to the **10,000 Islands** area. Boat tours depart from the downstairs marina into the mangrove flats and green islands – if you're lucky you may see dolphins springing up beside your craft. This tangled off-shore archipelago was a major smuggling point for drugs into the mainland USA during the late 1970s and early '80s; bales of marijuana were nicknamed 'square grouper' by local fishermen. It's great fun to go kayaking and canoeing around here; boats can be rented from the marina, but make sure to take a map

with you (they're available for free in the Visitor Center).

Ernest Coe Section

The southern and eastern portions of the park can be accessed from Homestead, an hour south of Miami. This part of the park consists of grassy prairies, small creeks and small wooded copses.

ERNEST COE VISITOR CENTER
Visitor Center

(✆305-242-7700; www.nps.gov/ever; 40001 State Rd 9336; ⏰8am-5pm) You'll enter Everglades National Park at this friendly visitor center. Have a look at the excellent exhibits, including a diorama of 'typical' Floridians.

ROYAL PALM VISITOR CENTER
Visitor Center

(✆305-242-7700; State Rd 9336; ⏰8am-4:15pm) Four miles past Ernest Coe Visitor Center, Royal Palm offers the easiest access to the Glades in these parts. Two trails, the **Anhinga** and **Gumbo Limbo** (the latter named for the gumbo-limbo tree, also known as the 'tourist tree' because its bark peels like a sunburned Brit), take all of an hour to walk and put you face to face with a panoply of Everglades wildlife. Gators sun on the shoreline, anhinga spear their prey and wading birds stalk haughtily through the reeds. Come at night for a ranger walk on the boardwalk and shine a flashlight into the water to see one of the coolest sights of your life: the glittering eyes of dozens of alligators prowling the waterways.

FLAMINGO VISITOR CENTER
Visitor Center

(✆239-695-2945; State Rd 9336; ⏰8am-4:15pm) The most isolated portion of the park is a squat **marina** (✆239-696-3101, 239-695-2591), where you can rent boats or go on a backcountry boat tour, but facilities were shut down for renovations during our visit. In the past, boat tours have run for around $20/10 for adult/child, while canoes (one hour/half-day/full day $8/22/32) and sea kayaks (half-/full day $35/45) were available

---

Skunk Ape Research Headquarters

Ah, Florida. You can't make this stuff up. To whit: the **Skunk Ape Research Center** (✆239-695-2275; www.skunkape.info; 40904 Tamiami Trail E; ⏰7am-7pm, 'zoo' closes around 4pm), topped by a giant panther statue, dedicated to tracking down Southeastern USA's version of Bigfoot, the eponymous Skunk Ape (a large gorilla-man who supposedly stinks to high heaven).

We didn't end up seeing a Skunk Ape here, but you can see a corny gift shop and, in the back, a reptile and bird zoo run by a true Florida eccentric, the sort of guy who wraps albino pythons around his neck for fun. Donate a few bucks at the entrance when you arrive.

---

for rental. You're largely left to explore the channels and islands of Florida Bay on your own. Be careful in coastal areas here during rough weather, as storm surges can turn an attractive spread of beach into a watery stretch of danger fairly quickly.

 **Activities**

Be it by boat, bicycle or your own feet, there are plenty of ways to explore the wet wild of the Everglades.

Hiking
SHARK VALLEY

At the park entrance, the easy **Bobcat Boardwalk** makes a loop through a thick copse of tropical hardwoods before emptying you out right back into the Shark Valley parking lot. A little ways along is the **Otter Cave Trail**, which heads over a limestone shelf that has been Swiss-cheesed into a porous sponge by

rainwater. Animals now live in the eroded holes (although it's not likely you'll spot any); Native Americans used to live on top of the shelf.

FLORIDA NATIONAL SCENIC TRAIL
Hiking

(www.nps.gov/bicy/planyourvisit/florida-trail. htm) Some 31 miles of this national scenic trail lie within Big Cypress National Preserve. From the southern terminus, which can be accessed via Loop Rd, the trail runs 8.3 miles north to US 41. The way is flat, but it's hard going: you'll almost certainly be wading through water, and you'll have to pick your way through a series of solution holes (small sinkholes) and thick hardwood hammocks. There is often no shelter from the sun, and the bugs are... *plentiful*. There are primitive campsites (free) with water wells along the trail; pick up a map at the visitor center. **Monument Lake** (May-Dec 14 free, Dec 15-Apr $16) has water and toilets.

ERNEST COE TO FLAMINGO POINT

State Rd 9336 cuts through the soft heart of the park; all of the following walks leading off from this road are half-a-mile long. **Mahogany Hammock** leads into an 'island' of hardwood forest floating on the waterlogged prairie, while the **Pinelands** takes you through a copse of rare spindly swamp pine and palmetto forest. Further on, **Pa-hay-okee Overlook** is a raised platform that peeks over one of the prettiest bends in the River of Grass. The **West Lake Trail** runs through the largest protected mangrove forest in the Northern Hemisphere. Further down, you can take a good two-hour, 1.8-mile hike to **Christian Point**, which ends with a dramatic view of the windswept shores of Florida Bay.

Kayaking & Canoeing
GULF COAST

The **10,000 Islands** consist of tiny islands (but not really 10,000) and a mangrove swamp that hugs the southwestern-most

border of Florida. The
Wilderness Waterway, a 99-
mile path between Everglades City
and Flamingo, is the longest canoe trail in
the area, but there are shorter trails near
Flamingo.

Adhere to National Oceanic &
Atmospheric Administration (NOAA)
tide and nautical charts. Going against
the tides is the fastest way to have a
miserable trip. The Gulf Coast Visitor
Center sells nautical charts and gives out
free tidal charts; it also rents canoes and
kayaks for extended periods.

ERNEST COE TO FLAMINGO POINT

There are plenty of push-off points in the
southeast of the park, with names that
sound like they were read off Frodo's map
to Mordor, including **Hell's Bay**, the **Night-
mare**, **Snake Bight** and **Graveyard Creek**.

NORTH AMERICAN CANOE
TOURS   Canoeing
(NACT; ☏ 941-695-3299/4666; www.everglades
adventures.com; Ivey House B&B, 107 Camellia

St; ☉ Nov–mid-Apr) Rents out camping
equipment and canoes for full/half-days
($35/$25) and touring kayaks ($45 to
$65).

Sleeping

If you don't feel like camping in the park,
there are good hotels in Everglades City
(near the Gulf Coast section of the park)
and Homestead (near the Homestead
section of the park).

Everglades City

EVERGLADES CITY MOTEL   Motel $$
(☏ 239-695-4244, 877-567-0679; www.ever
gladescitymotel.com; 310 Collier Ave; r from $80;
❄ 🛜 👪) With large renovated rooms that
have flat-screen TVs, air-conditioning and
a fantastically friendly staff that will hook
you up with whatever tours your heart
desires, this is an exceptionally good value

59

lodge for those looking to spend some time near the 10,000 Islands.

IVEY HOUSE B&B
B&B $$

(☎239-695-3299, 877-567-0679; www.ivey house.com; 107 Camellia St; lodge $74-120, inn $99-209; ❄🛜🛗) This family-run tropical inn serves good breakfasts in its small Ghost Orchid Grill. Plus, it operates some of the best nature trips around.

Inside the Park

NATIONAL PARK SERVICE CAMPSITES
Campground $

(NPS; ☎800-365-2267; www.nps.gov/ever/ planyourvisit/camping; sites May-Oct free, Nov-Apr $16) There are campgrounds run by the NPS located throughout the park. Most sites are primitive and do not have hookups. NPS visitor centers can provide a map of campsites, as does the park website. **Long Pine Key** (☎305-242-7873; May-Oct free, Nov-Apr $16) is a good bet for car campers, while the **Flamingo Campground**(☎877-444-6777; May-Oct free, Nov-Apr $30) has electrical hookups.

Homestead

EVERGLADES INTERNATIONAL HOSTEL
Hostel $

(☎305-248-1122, 800-372-3874; www.ever gladeshostel.com; 20 SW 2nd Ave, Florida City; camping $18, dm $28, d $61-75; P❄🛜🛝) Located in a cluttered, comfy 1930s boarding house, this friendly hostel has good-value dorms, private rooms and 'semi-privates' (you have an enclosed room within the dorms and share a bathroom with dorm residents). But what they've done with their back yard...wow! It's a serious garden of earthly delights. There's a tree house, a natural rock-cut pool with a waterfall, a Bedouin pavilion that doubles as a dancehall, a gazebo, an open-air tented 'bed room' and an oven built to resemble a tail-molting tadpole. It all needs to be seen to be believed, and best of all, you can sleep anywhere in the backyard for $18.

Eating

Old Florida fare, rich produce, fresh seafood and Southern cuisine are the name of the game.

JOANNIE'S BLUE CRAB CAFÉ
American $

(www.joaniesbluecrabcafe.com; Tamiami Trail; mains $9-17; ⊗9am-5pm) This quintessential shack, east of Ochopee, with open rafters, shellacked picnic tables and alligator kitsch, serves delicious food of the 'fried everything' variety on paper plates. There's live music most days.

ROBERT IS HERE
Market $

(www.robertishere.com; 19200 SW 344th St, Homestead; ⊗8am-7pm Nov-Aug) More than a farmer's stand, Robert's is an institution. This is

Boca Chita Key, Biscayne National Park

Detour:
Big Cypress National Preserve

The 1139-sq-mile Big Cypress Preserve (named for the size of the park, not its trees) is the result of a compromise between environmentalists, cattle ranchers and oil-and-gas explorers. The rains that flood the preserve's prairies and wetlands slowly filter down through the Glades. About 45% of the cypress swamp (actually a group of mangrove islands, hardwood hammocks, slash pine, prairies and marshes) is protected. Great bald cypress trees are nearly gone, thanks to pre-preserve lumbering, but dwarf pond cypress trees are plentiful.

The Oasis Visitor Center (☏ 239-695-4758, 941-695-1201; 33000 Tamiami Trail E; ☷ 8am-4:30pm Mon-Fri), about 20 miles west of Shark Valley, has great exhibits for the kids and an outdoor, water-filled ditch popular with alligators.

Old Florida at its kitschy best, in love with the Glades and the agriculture that surrounds it. There's a petting zoo for the kids, live music at night, plenty of homemade preserves and sauces, and while everyone goes crazy for the milkshakes – as they should – do not leave without having the fresh orange juice. It's the best in the world. What's up with the funny name? Well, back in the day the namesake of the pavilion was selling his dad's cucumbers on this very spot, but no traffic was slowing down for the produce. So a sign was constructed that announced, in big red letters, that Robert was, in fact, here. He has been ever since, too.

ℹ Information

Everglades National Park (☏ 305-242-7700; www.nps.gov/ever; car/bicycle & pedestrian $10/5 for 7 days) is open 365 days a year.

ℹ Getting There & Away

Miami International Airport (MIA; ☏ 305-876-7000; www.miami-airport.com) is 42 miles (about one hour by car) northeast of the Ernest Coe entrance station (near Homestead). In Miami, 8th St SW becomes US-41/Tamiami Trail. Shark Valley is also about an hour west of Miami. There are no buses into the park.

AROUND THE EVERGLADES
Biscayne National Park

Just to the east of the Everglades is Biscayne National Park, or the 5% of it that isn't underwater. A portion of the world's third-largest reef sits here off the coast of Florida, along with mangrove forests and the northernmost Florida Keys. Fortunately, this unique 300-sq-mile park is easy to explore independently with a canoe, via a glass-bottom-boat tour or a snorkeling or diving trip.

Sights & Activities

Boating and **fishing** are popular and often go hand in hand, but to do either you'll need to get some paperwork in order. Boaters will want to get tide charts from the park (or from www.nps.gov/bisc/planyourvisit/tide-predictions.htm). Make sure you comply with local slow-speed zones, designed to protect the endangered manatee.

The slow zones currently extend 1000ft out from the mainland, from Black Point south to Turkey Point, and include the marinas at Black Point and Homestead Bayfront Parks. Another slow zone extends from Sands Cut to Coon

If You Like...
Roadside Attractions

After getting battered into rubble by Hurricane Andrew in 1992, Homestead was haphazardly rebuilt around fast-food stops, car dealerships and gas stations. Yet, Homestead, for all her sprawl, houses two great attractions of the Florida roadside.

1 CORAL CASTLE
(www.coralcastle.com; 28655 S Dixie Hwy; adult/child 7-18yr $12/7; ⏰8am-6pm, to 8pm Sat & Sun) The Coral Castle is one Latvian immigrant's monument to unrequited love. The rough-hewn rock compound includes a throne room, a sun dial and a stone stockade (his intended's 'timeout area'). Audio stations explain the site in a replicated Latvian accent, so it feels like you're getting a narrated tour by Borat.

2 EVERGLADES OUTPOST
(www.evergladesoutpost.org; 35601 SW 192nd Ave; recommended donation $20; ⏰10am-4pm Sat & Sun, by appointment Mon-Fri) If the Coral Castle is amusing, the Everglades Outpost is moving. Volunteers house, feed and care for wild animals that have been seized from illegal traders, abused, neglected or donated by people who could not care for them. Residents include gibbons, a lemur, wolves, cobras, alligators and a pair of tigers. During the week, call ahead to visit.

Point; maps of all of the above can be obtained from rangers, and are needed for navigation purposes in any case.

For information on boat tours and rental, contact **Biscayne Underwater** (www.biscayneunderwater.com), which can help arrange logistics.

BISCAYNE NATIONAL PARK   Park
The **Dante Fascell Visitor Center** (📞305-230-7275; www.nps.gov/bisc; 9700 SW 328th St; ⏰8:30am-5pm) at the park itself offers canoe rentals, transportation to the off-shore keys, snorkeling and scuba-diving trips, and glass-bottom-boat viewing of the exceptional reefs. All tours require a minimum of six people, so call to make reservations. Three-hour glass-bottom-boat trips ($45) depart at 10am and are very popular; if you're lucky you may spot some dolphins or manatees. Canoe rentals cost $12 per hour and kayaks $16; they're rented from 9am to 3pm. Three-hour snorkeling trips ($45) depart at 1:15pm daily; you'll have about 1½ hours in the water. Scuba trips depart at 8:30am Friday to Sunday ($99). You can also arrange a private charter boat tour around the park for $300.

MARITIME HERITAGE TRAIL   Trail
One of the only trails of its kind in the USA, the Maritime Heritage Trail was still technically under development at the time of research, but already taking 'hikers'. If you've ever wanted to explore a sunken ship, this may well be the best opportunity in the country. Six are located within the park grounds; the trail experience involves taking visitors out, by boat, to the site of the wrecks where they can swim and explore among derelict vessels and clouds of fish – there are even waterproof information site cards placed among the ships. Five of the vessels are suited for scuba divers, but one, the *Mandalay,* a lovely two-masted schooner that sank in 1966, can be accessed by snorkelers.

 Sleeping

Primitive camping on Elliott and Boca Chita Keys costs $15 per tent, per night; you pay on a trust system with exact change on the harbor (rangers cruise the keys to check your receipt). There is potable water on the island, but it always pays to be prepared. It costs $20 to moor your boat overnight at Elliott or Boca Chita harbors, but that fee covers the use of one campsite for up to six people and two tents.

Wilderness Camping

Three types of backcountry campsites are available: beach sites, on coastal shell beaches and in the 10,000 Islands; ground sites (mounds of dirt built up above the mangroves), and 'chickees', wooden platforms built above the water line where you can pitch a free-standing (no spikes) tent. Chickees, which have toilets, are the most civilized – there's a serenity found in sleeping on what feels like a raft levitating above the water.

Warning: if you're paddling around and see an island that looks pleasant for camping but isn't a designated campsite, beware – you may end up submerged when the tides change.

From November to April, camping permits cost $10, plus $2 per person per night; from May to Oct sites are free, but you must still self-register at Flamingo and Gulf Coast Visitor Centers or call ☎239-695-2945.

Some backcountry tips:

• Store food in a hand-sized, raccoon-proof container (available at gear stores).

• Bury your waste at least 10in below ground, but keep in mind that some ground sites have hard turf.

• Use a backcountry stove to cook. Ground fires are only permitted at beach sites, and you can only burn dead or drowned wood.

❶ Information

Dante Fascell Visitor Center (☎305-230-7275; www.nps.gov/bisc; 9700 SW 328th St; ⏰8:30am-5pm) Located at Convoy Point, the grounds around the center are popular for picnics. Also showcases local artwork.

❶ Getting There & Away

To get here, you'll have to drive about 9 miles east of Homestead (the way is pretty well signposted) on SW 328th St (North Canal Dr) into a long series of green-and-gold flat fields and marsh.

Glacier National Park

Glacier is one of the country's wildest parks. Rising like giant Gothic cathedrals above western Montana's wind-swept prairies, its jagged, snow-blanketed ridges and glacier-sculpted horns tower dramatically over aquamarine lakes and meadows blanketed in wildflowers. Beneath its lofty peaks, grizzly bears, bighorn sheep, wolves, mountain goats and myriad other animals forage and hunt for food in the fleeting but glorious Rocky Mountain summer.

At the same time, visitors descend on the park to hike its 700-plus miles of trails, float its alpine lakes, stare at glaciers, drive the famous Going-to-the-Sun Rd, and sleep in the park's historic handcrafted lodges. Fortunately, for those who want to escape the crowds, most visitors stick to the areas around Going-to-the-Sun Rd, leaving sectors such as the spectacular Two Medicine Valley open for solitary exploration.

St Mary Lake (p69)
CRAIG LIEB / LONELY PLANET IMAGES ©

Glacier Itineraries

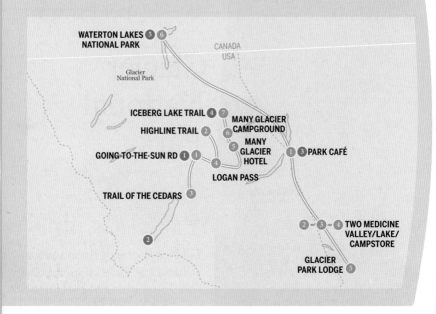

Two Days

1 Going-to-the-Sun Rd (p69) Make this famous and hair-raising scenic road your introduction to Glacier National Park. You'll be glued to the window of your car for every one of its 53 scenic miles.

2 Highline Trail (p76) Set out early and you can stop midway up Going-to-the-Sun Rd to hike this epic trail past Glacier's famous Garden Wall. The glacial carved wall is an iconic sight and getting up close is the best way to see it.

3 Trail of the Cedars (p72) Wander along this paved path that departs Going-to-the-Sun Rd for a quick glimpse of Glacier's alpine scenery. Views have never been so easy!

4 Logan Pass (p72) Park the car, check out the visitor center and take in the vistas from the highest point accessible by road in the park. Several trails fork out from the pass if you get the itch to roam.

5 Many Glacier Hotel (p84) Ensconce yourself in this historic lodge, which sits smack in the middle of some of the park's most glorious scenery. The hotel was constructed by the Great Northern Railroad in 1915 and is the centerpiece of the spectacular Many Glacier Valley.

6 Many Glacier Campground (p83) Campers, nab a site at Many Glacier Campground for easy access to some of the best trails in the park.

7 Iceberg Lake Trail (p79) On day two, hike this justifiably popular trail to an alpine lake set inside a vast glacial cirque and filled with floating icebergs.

· ·

THIS LEG: 130 MILES

Four Days

1 **Park Café** (p88) Begin day three with a giant breakfast at this Glacier classic, where the portions are nearly as vast as the views. Oh, and be a glutton. Order the huckleberry pie for dessert. Who cares if it's not even 10am!

2 **Two Medicine Valley** (p73) Stomach filled, head to Two Medicine Valley and explore what many consider the heart and soul of the park. Surprisingly, there are far fewer people in this region of Glacier.

3 **Two Medicine Lake** (p73) Rent a canoe or kayak, pack a lunch and paddle across the azure waters of this glacial lake while gazing at the massive Rising Wolf Mountain above.

4 **Two Medicine Campstore** (p85) Pop into this historic general store for a Glacier souvenir (grizzly T-shirt anyone?) and reflect on the history: Franklin D Roosevelt gave one of his famous fireside chats here.

5 **Glacier Park Lodge** (p88) Spend the night at this historic park lodge with a sublime setting in East Glacier. Reading a book in the grand main lobby while the other guests are sleeping is an experience you won't forget.

6 **Waterton Lakes National Park** (p89) On day four, get up early and drive to Waterton Lakes National Park to hike the Carthew-Alderson Trail. Some consider it the best hike in the Rockies.

➡ THIS LEG: 150 MILES

Glacier Highlights

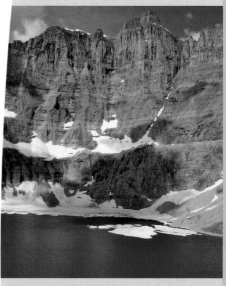

1 **Best Drive: Going-to-the-Sun Rd** (p74) You'll never look at asphalt the same way again.

2 **Best Hotel: Village Inn** (p82) On the shore of Glacier's largest lake, this rustic hotel takes the concept of 'lake views' to a new height.

3 **Best Pie: Park Café** (p88) No visit to Glacier is complete without a slice of Park Café's delicious homemade pie.

4 **Best Hike: Iceberg Lake Trail** (p79) Icebergs, wildflowers, a massive glacial cirque – this is what Glacier is all about.

5 **Best Detour: Waterton Lakes National Park** (p89) The trails alone are reason enough to head to Canada to visit Glacier's neighboring park.

Iceberg Lake (p79)
DANITA DELIMONT / ALAMY ©

Discover Glacier

GLACIER NATIONAL PARK

Few of the world's great natural wonders can rival the US national park system, and few national parks are as magnificent and pristine as Glacier. Created in 1910 during the first flowering of the American conservationist movement, Glacier ranks among other national park classics such as Yellowstone and Yosemite. Perennial highlights include its quartet of historic 'parkitecture'

lodges, the spectacular Going-to-the-Sun Rd, and a rare fully intact pre-Columbian ecosystem. This is the only place in the lower 48 states where grizzly bears still roam in abundance and smart park management has kept the place accessible yet, at the same time, authentically wild. Among a slew of other outdoor attractions, the park is particularly noted for its hiking, wildlife-spotting, and fishing and boating lakes.

Although Glacier is popular, few people stray far from the Going-to-the-Sun Rd and almost all visit between June and September. Choose your moment and splendid isolation is yours.

History

The ancestors of Montana's present-day Native Americans have inhabited the Glacier region for over 10,000 years. At the time of the first European contact, the region's eastern prairies were controlled by the Blackfeet, while the valleys in the west were the hunting grounds of the Salish and Kootenay.

In the 1800s, a white wanderer named James Willard Shultz spent many years living among the Blackfeet and became one of the first European American men to lay eyes on much of Glacier's interior. In the 1880s he introduced the area to Dr George Bird Grinnell, a leading conservationist who lobbied Congress vociferously for a decade until, in 1910, President Taft signed the bill that created Glacier National Park.

Visitors began coming regularly to the park around 1912, when the Great Northern Railroad instigated an intense building program to promote the newly inaugurated line. Railway employees built grand hotels and a network of tent camps and mountain

Alpine wildflowers

chalets. With the advent of automobile travel, construction of Going-to-the-Sun Rd began in 1921 and was finally opened in 1932. The historic road crossed the Continental Divide at the 6646ft Logan Pass and opened the park to millions. That same year, Glacier joined with Waterton Lakes in the world's first International Peace Park, a lasting symbol of peace and friendship between the USA and Canada.

WWII forced the closure of almost all hotel services in the park, and many of Glacier's rustic chalets fell into disrepair. Fortunately, nine of the original 13 'parkitecture' structures survived and form the basis of the park's accommodations today.

When to Go

Peak season in Glacier – for tourists as well as wildflowers – is July and August. Because this is a high-altitude park, many facilities don't even open until July. Hardy travelers trickle in to the lower elevations as early as May, when the snows begin to melt. September means fewer crowds, quieter campgrounds and a reliable weather window before the first snows

When You Arrive

Staff at the entrance stations hand out free detailed Glacier-Waterton maps, a quarterly newspaper and the *Glacier Explorer,* a schedule of events and activities, including ranger-led day trips.

Orientation

Cocooned in northwest Montana and abutting the border with the Canadian provinces of Alberta and British Columbia, Glacier is bisected by the Continental Divide and contained within the 'Crown of the Continent' natural ecosystem. The 1562-sq-mile park's natural delineators are the North Fork Flathead River (west), Marias Pass on US 2 (south), US 89 and the Blackfeet Indian Reservation (east), and the Canadian border (north).

The park's main areas, clockwise roughly northeast to northwest, are Goat Haunt, at the base of Upper Waterton

Lake; Many Glacier, a popular hiking valley; St Mary, best known for its photogenic namesake lake; Two Medicine, a rugged but secluded valley replete with wildlife; Logan Pass, at the apex of the Going-to-the-Sun Rd; the Lake McDonald Valley, home to Apgar Village; and the North Fork Valley, the most remote and least visited corner of the park.

 ## Sights

Going-to-the-Sun Road

If it were possible to mathematically measure 'magnificence', the Going-to-the-Sun Rd would surely hit the top end of the scale. Chiseled out of raw mountainside and punctuated by some of the sheerest and most vertiginous drop-offs in the United States, this vista-laden artery of asphalt that bisects the park west to east is an engineering marvel without equal. In the circumstances, it is hardly surprising that it's considered by many motorists to be the best drive in the country. The best way to experience it, of course, is to drive it (see p75).

ST MARY LAKE   Lake
Located on the park's dryer eastern side, where the mountains melt imperceptibly into the Great Plains, St Mary Lake lies in a deep, glacier-carved valley famous for its astounding views and ferocious winds. Overlooked by the tall, chiseled peaks of the Rockies and scarred by the landscape-altering effects of the 2006 Red Eagle Fire, the valley is spectacularly traversed by the Going-to-the-Sun Rd and punctuated by numerous trailheads and viewpoints.

SUNRIFT GORGE   Canyon
Just off the Going-to-the-Sun Rd and adjacent to a shuttle stop lies this narrow canyon carved over millennia by the gushing glacial melt-waters of Baring Creek. Look out for picturesque **Baring Bridge**, a classic example of rustic Going-to-the-Sun Rd architecture, and follow a short, tree-covered trail down to misty **Baring Falls**.

Glacier

DISCOVER GLACIER

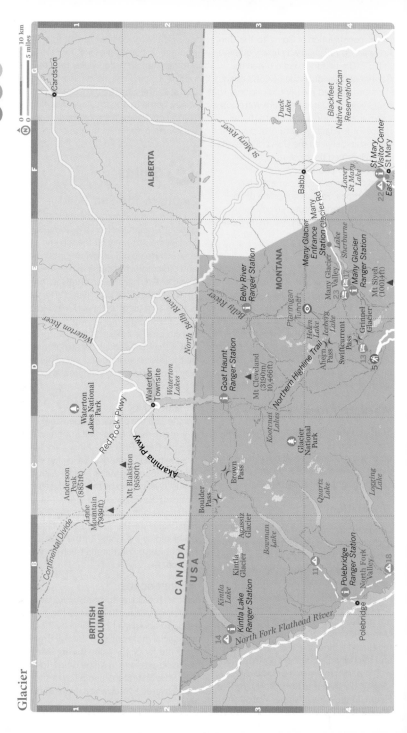

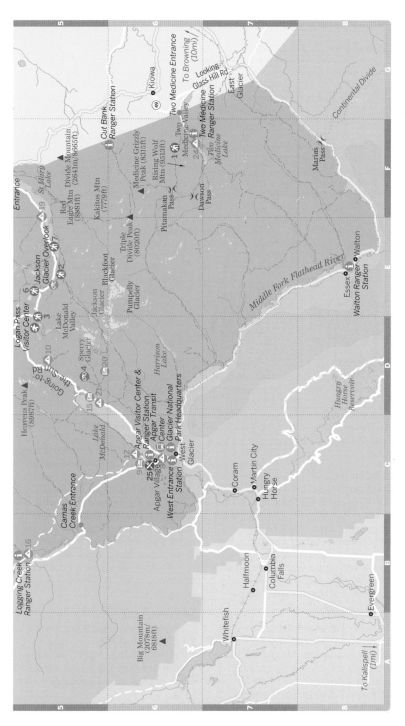

Glacier

LOGAN PASS   Landmark

Perched above the tree line, atop the wind-lashed Continental Divide, and blocked by snow for most of the year, 6646ft Logan Pass is the park's highest navigable point by road. Two trails, Hidden Lake Overlook and Highline, lead out from here.

GARDEN WALL   Landmark

The sharp steep-sided arête that parallels the Going-to-the-Sun Rd as it ascends to Logan Pass from the west was carved by powerful glaciers millions of years ago. Its western slopes, bisected by the emblematic Highline Trail, are covered by a quintessential Glacier Park feature: steep velvety meadows embellished by an abundance of summer wildflowers.

WEEPING WALL   Waterfall

A couple of thousand feet below the Garden Wall, the glistening Weeping Wall creates a seasonal waterfall that was formed when Going-to-the-Sun Rd construction workers drilled their way across a network of mountain springs. The water has subsequently been diverted over the lip of a 30ft man-made cliff, and frequently gives unwary cars and motorbikes a good soaking.

LAKE MCDONALD VALLEY   Lake, Forest

Greener and wetter than the St Mary Valley, the Lake McDonald Valley harbors the park's largest lake and some of its densest and oldest temperate rainforest. Crisscrossed by a number of popular trails, including the wheelchair-accessible 0.8 miles **Trail of the Cedars**, the area is popular with drive-in campers, who frequent the Sprague Creek and Avalanche Creek campgrounds, and winter cross-country skiers, who use McDonald Creek and the Going-to-the-Sun Rd as seasonal skiing trails.

APGAR VILLAGE   Landmark

In contrast to the sizeable townsites in Banff, Jasper and Waterton National Parks, Apgar Village is minuscule, supporting little more than a couple of lodges, a gift shop and a restaurant, all of which sit quietly on the western shores of Lake McDonald.

South of Going-to-the-Sun Road

With no hotels, no restaurants and only one dead-end road, the **Two Medicine Valley** is a favorite haunt for ambitious hikers intent on reaching one of a trio of high-altitude passes that guard the gusty Continental Divide. The more intrepid forge further west, beyond Cut Bank Pass, where faintly marked trails descend into the barely visited Nyack Creek Wilderness, a rough mélange of fordable rivers and primitive campsites that surround the isolated hulk of Mt Stimson, the park's second-highest peak at 10,142ft.

Hikers can grab a picnic at the historic **Two Medicine Campstore**, once the dining hall for the now defunct Two Medicine Chalets and the venue for one of President FD Roosevelt's famous 'fireside chats.' Towering authoritatively over sublime **Two Medicine Lake** is the distinctive hulk of **Rising Wolf Mountain**, named for Canadian-turned-Peigan Indian, Hugh Monroe, who was the first white person to explore the region in the mid-19th century.

A few miles to the northwest, 8020ft **Triple Divide Peak** marks the hydrologic apex of the North American continent. Empty a bucket of water on its summit and it will run into three separate oceans: the Pacific, the Atlantic and the Arctic.

North of Going-to-the-Sun Road

You can penetrate the park's rugged north from both the east and the west sides. The northeast is accessible through the popular Many Glacier nexus and is crowned by an historic lodge. The northwest is more remote and requires a good car, self-sufficiency and an adventurous spirit.

North Fork Valley, Glacier's most isolated nook, is a riot of grassy meadows and regenerated forest that protects the park's only pack of wolves and hides some of its best backcountry trails and campgrounds.

Glacier's Glaciers

Unless you've been living on the moon for the last decade, you'll know all about melting glaciers and the global preoccupation with climate change. Glacier National Park currently lists 25 glaciers, significantly less than other American national parks such as the North Cascades (with 300) and Mt Rainier (with 26 on one mountain). But, thanks to a Glacier Research Monitoring program carried out by the US Geological Survey, the Montana park's icy monoliths have been more studied than any of their counterparts.

Current figures procured by hi-tech sensing equipment and repeat photography suggest that, if current trends continue, the park could be glacier-free by 2030. These tentative estimates are based on studies undertaken on the Sperry, Agassiz, Jackson and Grinnell glaciers, all of which have lost approximately 35% of their volume since the mid 1960s. However, whatever scenario ultimately transpires, the park – contrary to popular opinion – will not have to change its name. The 'glacier' label refers as much to the dramatic ice-sculpted scenery as it does to its fast-melting rivers of ice, and these remarkable geographical features ought to be dropping jaws for a good few millennia to come.

 **Activities**

Driving Tours

Blessed with one of America's most spectacular roads, Glacier promises steely nerved motorists the drive of their life. Those less enthusiastic about crawling in second gear up gravity-defying chicanes can find solace in the park's less demanding back routes.

GOING-TO-THE-SUN ROAD Scenic Drive
One of the greatest and most spectacular drives in the US, Going-to-the-Sun Rd starts inauspiciously at the park's western entrance and tracks east alongside translucent **Lake McDonald**. Encased in dense rainforest and characterized by the famous Lake McDonald Lodge, the valley here is lush and verdant, though a quick glance through the trees will highlight the graphic evidence of the destruction wreaked by the 2003 Robert fire on the opposite side of the water.

After tracking alongside McDonald Creek for approximately 10 miles, the road begins its long, slow ascent to Logan Pass with a sharp turn to the southeast at the famous **Loop**, a hiking trailhead and the start of an increasingly precipitous climb toward the summit. Views here vary from amazing to even more amazing as the road cuts precariously into the **Garden Wall**, a 8999ft granite arête that delineates the west and east regions of the park along the Continental Divide. Look out for **Bird Woman Falls** at 27 miles, stunning even from a distance, and the more in-your-face (literally, if you've got the roof down) **Weeping Wall** at 29 miles, as the gaping chasm to your right grows ever deeper.

Nearly everybody stops at the 6646ft **Logan Pass**, at 32 miles, to browse the visitor center or stretch their legs amid alpine meadows on the popular Hidden Lake Overlook Trail. Be forewarned: the Logan Pass parking lot can resemble a shopping-mall parking lot in July and

August, particularly between 11am and 3pm.

Descending to the east the scenery almost grows in grandeur. At 36 miles, you can pull over to spy one of only 25 remaining park glaciers at the **Jackson Glacier Overlook**, while a few clicks further on, you can sample narrow **Sunrift Gorge** near the shores of St Mary Lake. With an elevation of 9642ft, majestic **Going-to-the-Sun Mountain** – for which the road is named – is omnipresent to the north. **Wild Goose Island** is a tiny stub of land with a handful of lopsided trees that perches precariously in the middle of St Mary Lake, providing a perfect photo op for incurable camera-clickers. If you're in need of gifts or a bite to eat, **Rising Sun** has a store and a no-nonsense restaurant.

The St Mary Visitor Center, at 53 miles, on the lake's east end, is journey's end. The plains on this side of the park stretch east from St Mary to Minneapolis.

No vehicles over 21ft are allowed from east of Sun Point to Avalanche Creek. The entire one-way drive is 53 miles and takes about three hours with stops.

Hiking

You don't have to be an aspiring Everest climber to enjoy the well-tramped trails and scenic byways of Glacier National Park. Indeed, two of the park's most popular hikes are wheelchair accessible, while countless more can be easily tackled by parents with children, vacationing couch potatoes or nervous novices.

GOING-TO-THE-SUN ROAD

AVALANCHE LAKE TRAIL   Hiking
A handy stop on the new shuttle route, the Avalanche Lake Trail provides quick and easy access to one of Glacier National Park's most gorgeous alpine lakes – and you don't have to bust a gut to get there. As a result, the trail is invariably

heaving in peak season with everyone from flip-flop-wearing families to stick-wielding seniors making boldly for the tree line. But don't be deceived; while the walk itself might be relatively easy, it is highly recommended you come prepared with bottled water, layered clothing and the appropriate footwear.

The 4-mile round-trip trail starts on Going-to-the-Sun Rd and follows the paved Trail of the Cedars to a signposted three-way junction. Bear right here. Allow about 2½ hours for the hike.

HIDDEN LAKE OVERLOOK TRAIL   Hiking

For many Glacier visitors, this relatively straightforward hike is the one occasion in which they step out of their cars and take a sniff of the sweet-scented alpine air for which the area is famous. Starting at the busy Logan Pass Visitor Center, the hike ascends gradually along a raised boardwalk (with steps) through expansive alpine meadows replete with monkey-flower and pink laurel.

Just before you reach the **overlook** itself, you cross the Continental Divide – probably without realizing it – before your first stunning glimpse of deep-blue Hidden Lake (and a realization of what all the fuss is about).

Hearty souls continue on to Hidden Lake via a 1.5-mile trail from the overlook, steeply descending 765ft. Sans this detour, it's an easy-to-moderate, 3.2-mile hike. Allow about two hours.

SUN POINT TO VIRGINIA FALLS   Hiking

Handily served by the free park shuttle, the myriad of trailheads along the eastern side of the Going-to-the-Sun Rd offer plenty of short interlinking hikes, a number of which can be pooled together to make up a decent morning or after-noon ramble.

If you take the busy **St Mary Falls Trail**, you'll climb undemanding switchbacks through the trees to the valley's most picturesque falls, set amid colorful foliage on St Mary River. Beyond here, a trail branches along Virginia Creek, past a narrow gorge, to mist-shrouded (and quieter) **Virginia Falls** at the foot of a

hanging valley. It's approximately 7 miles round-trip to Virginia Falls and back. The easy hike takes about four hours.

HIGHLINE TRAIL   Hiking

A Glacier classic, the Highline Trail cuts like an elongated scar across the famous Garden Wall, a sharp, glacier-carved ridge that forms part of the Continental Divide, and the summer slopes which are cov-ered with an abundance of alpine plants and wildflowers. The stupendous views here are some of the best in the park and, with little elevation gain throughout its 7.6-mile course, the treats come with minimal sweat.

Allow about 7½ hours for the one-way hike. From here you have three options: you can retrace your steps back to Logan Pass; head for Swiftcurrent Pass and the Many Glacier Valley; or descend 4 miles to the Loop, where you can pick up a shuttle bus to all points on the Going-to-the-Sun Rd.

MT BROWN LOOKOUT   Hiking

This demanding hike is a means to an end; a steep 5.4-mile grunt up through thick forest to a historic 1929 lookout (7425ft) last manned in 1971 (and refur-bished in 1999) on the southwest ridge of 8565ft Mt Brown, located about 1500ft below the summit. The views from here are outstanding but no mountaineering skills are required – just a strong pair of lungs.

The hike starts on the Going-to-the-Sun Rd opposite the Lake McDonald Lodge on the heavily used Sperry Chalet trail.

PIEGAN PASS   Hiking

A popular hike among Glacier stalwarts, this trail starts on the Going-to-the-Sun Rd at a handy shuttle stop on Siyeh Bend just east of Logan Pass and deposits you in Glacier's mystic heart, Many Glacier, with transport connections back to St Mary. It also bisects colorful Preston Park, one of the region's prettiest and most jubilant alpine meadows. The trail starts at the Siyeh Bend shuttle stop.

MARK NEWMAN / LONELY PLANET IMAGES ©

Don't Miss **Many Glacier**

Dubbed the 'heart and soul' of Glacier by park purists, Many Glacier is a magical mélange of lush meadows and shimmering lakes, where the pièce de résistance is the strategically positioned **Many Glacier Hotel**, constructed by the Great Northern Railroad in 1915. Known traditionally for its 'rivers of ice' – though there aren't *quite* so many of them these days – the valley nurtures some of the park's most accessible glaciers, including the rapidly shrinking Grinnell Glacier, first spotted by conservationist and naturalist George Bird Grinnell in 1885, and the Salamander Glacier that sits tucked beneath the saw-toothed Ptarmigan Ridge, so-named for its distinctive amphibian-like shape. Other 'unmissables' include **Iceberg Lake**, where turquoise waters are fed from a surrounding snowfield, and the **Ptarmigan Tunnel**, a 183ft corridor through the rock, blasted out of the mountain in the 1930s.

Many Glacier is probably the best place in the park to spot wildlife. Avalanche chutes around the lakes attract bears, and mountain goats are easy to pick out on the steep scree slopes above Swiftcurrent Lake. It's also home to some of its greatest trails, including the spectacular Iceberg Lake Trail.

Many Glacier is accessed by road from the park's eastern side. To get to there by public transportation, take the free shuttle to the St Mary Visitor Center then board one of the Glacier Park Inc's shuttles to Many Glacier.

NORTH OF THE GOING-TO-THE-SUN ROAD

SWIFTCURRENT LAKE NATURE TRAIL — Hiking

From civilization to bear-infested wilderness in less than 60 seconds; natural juxtapositions don't get much more dramatic than this. Anchoring the trail system that connects Many Glacier's three navigable lakes – Swiftcurrent, Josephine and Grinnell – this easy flat nature trail offers a potent taste of the valley's rugged essence. Take note: despite heavy usage and its proximity to the hotel, the trail often posts bear warnings. It takes about

Lake McDonald (p74)

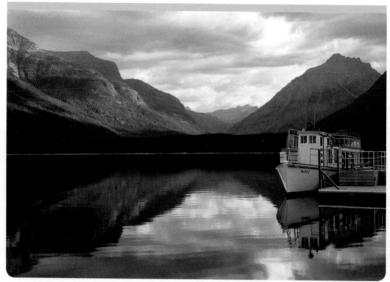

an hour to walk the 2.5 miles of trail. Start and finish at Many Glacier Lodge.

SWIFTCURRENT PASS TRAIL Hiking
After meandering through the Many Glacier Valley, this 7.6-mile trail climbs up to the Continental Divide and passes waterfall vistas, Redrock Lake and Bullhead Lake en route. The switchbacks on the ascent are numerous and the path, which cuts sharply into the mountainside, becomes ever more vertiginous as you climb. The Continental Divide at **Swiftcurrent Pass** is marked by an unruly pile of rocks surrounded by dwarf trees. For a far better view, take the spur trail up a further set of switchbacks to the **Swiftcurrent Lookout** for one of the park's most tower-topping views. Returning to the pass, either retrace your steps, or head 0.9 miles down to the Granite Park Chalet to link up with other trails. The trail departs from the west side of the Swiftcurrent Motor Inn parking lot and can be linked up with the Loop or Highline Trails for longer hikes.

Backpacking

Backcountry hiking is what Glacier is all about and hitting the high trails will quickly introduce intrepid travelers to a side of the park that few other visitors see. Two of the most popular hikes are the two-day **Gunsight Pass Trail** and the **Northern Highline-Waterton Valley Trail**. You can also split the 18.8-mile **Dawson-Pitamakin Loop Trail** into a two-day hike. Another option is to join the Swiftcurrent Pass Trail with the Highline Trail, overnighting in the Granite Park Chalet or campground. Visitor centers provide information on backpacking and trails and reservations.

Canoeing & Kayaking

McDonald, Bowman, Swiftcurrent, Two Medicine and St Mary Lakes have launching ramps available for boats. Sailors might find St Mary Lake's winds to their liking.

GLACIER PARK BOAT COMPANY
Boat Hire

(www.glacierparkboats.com) Rents out small boats (kayaks, canoes and rowboats) in the summer at Apgar, Lake McDonald, Two Medicine and Many Glacier for US$15 per hour. Rowing boats cost US$18 per hour.

Fishing

The fishing season in streams and rivers is late May to late November, though lakes are open for fishing year-round. While anglers explore easily accessible waters like Lake McDonald and St Mary Lake, it is some of the hike-in destinations that can prove the most tranquil getaways; try Hidden Lake, Oldman Lake or Red Eagle Lake. A Montana state fishing license is not required within Glacier National Park. Anglers are generally limited to possession of five fish daily, with caps varying by species. Read the park's Fishing Regulations pamphlet.

Horseback Riding

Back in the 'old' days, before the Going-to-the-Sun Rd was built, getting around by horse between the various tourist chalets was the primary means of transport and horses still run a regular supply line up to the Sperry Chalet, a route that can be incorporated into an excellent day ride with **Swan Mountain Outfitters** (www.swanmountainoutfitters.com; ⊗early May-early Sep), the park's *only* horseback-riding guides. The company offers a variety of other trips. All trips are led by experienced wranglers who'll furnish you with plenty of entertaining tales.

Ranger Programs

Throughout the summer there are a whole host of free evening ranger talks, slide shows and guided walks available in Glacier National Park's hotels, campgrounds and visitor centers. Topics vary from culture and history to ecology

Iceberg Lake Trail

Famed for the bobbing bergs that float like miniature ice cubes in its still waters all summer long, Iceberg Lake has long been a classic Glacier National Park pilgrimage. The popularity of the hike is understandable. Enclosed in a deep glacial cirque and surrounded on three sides by stunning 3000ft vertical walls, the lake is one of the most impressive sights anywhere in the Rockies. The 1200ft ascent to get there is gentle, and the approach is mostly at or above the tree line, affording awesome views. Wildflowers fans will go ga-ga in the meadows near the lake.

Start at the trailhead by the Swiftcurrent Motor Inn. The hike kicks off with a steep ascent, packing most of its elevation gain into the first few kilometers. But once you emerge onto the scrubby slopes above Many Glacier the gradient is barely perceptible. After 2 miles the path enters a small section of mature forest and arrives at Ptarmigan Creek, crossed by a footbridge, just upstream from **Ptarmigan Falls**. Here you climb gently through pine to the Ptarmigan Tunnel Trail junction, which heads right.

Continuing toward Iceberg Lake, you'll fall upon the first of several beautiful meadows under **Ptarmigan Wall**. Descend for a short distance to cross Iceberg Creek via a footbridge, and then climb up past **Little Iceberg Lake** before dropping down to the shores of your hallowed destination, the icy-blue cirque lake.

Allow about 5½ hours for the 9 mile, round-trip hike.

and 'Native American Speaks'. You'll find a printed schedule posted at all park visitor centers, or listed in the *Activity Schedule* newspaper. Alternatively, you can scan the official park website at www.nps.gov/glac.

Golf

Two golf courses lie just outside the park limits. **Glacier Park Lodge Golf Course** (www.glacierparkinc.com), in East Glacier, the oldest course in Montana, is the most picturesque. **Glacier View Golf Club** (www.glacierviewgolf.com), in West Glacier, is another scenic gem that overlooks the Middle Fork of the Flathead River. Green fees are US$20/29 for 9/18 holes. Club rental starts at US$14.

Cross-Country Skiing & Snowshoeing

Self-sufficient cross-country skiers can choose from a number of popular marked but ungroomed trails in the park, the bulk of them emanating from Apgar Village and Lake McDonald. A well-used favorite is to ski along an unplowed section of the Going-to-the-Sun Rd from the Lake

McDonald Lodge to Avalanche Creek. The road is always plowed as far as the lodge, allowing easy access by car. Another regularly tackled trail is the 11.5-mile **McGee Meadow Loop** heading up the unplowed Camas Rd and back down the Inside Fork Rd to Apgar Village. Far more difficult is the steep 5.2-mile ascent to the **Apgar Lookout**.

Although all hotels and restaurants stay closed and the park registers only a handful of visitors, Glacier's mountains and valleys remain gloriously open all winter to those intrepid enough to breach them. For ultimate safety organize a guided backcountry ski tour with **Glacier Park Ski Tours** (☎ 406-892-2173; www. glacierparkskitours.com), which operates out of Whitefish.

 Tours

Horseback rides (p79)

🌿 **RED JAMMER BUSES**   Bus
Run by **Glacier Park Inc** (www.glacier parkinc.com), Glacier's stylish red 'jammer' buses (a legacy of when drivers had to 'jam' hard on the gears) are synonymous

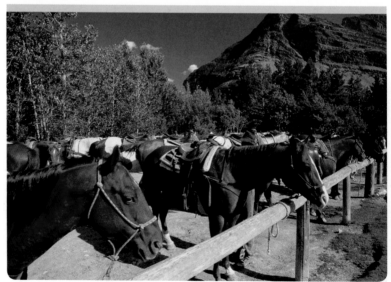

Boat & Hike Combos

Six historic boats – some dating back to the 1920s – ply five of Glacier's attractive mountain lakes and some of them have the added bonus of combining the watery ride with a short guided hike led by interpretive, often witty guides. One of the best excursions leaves from the Many Glacier Hotel twice daily (July to September) and chugs slowly across shallow Swiftcurrent Lake to a landing point on the opposite (southern) side. From here, groups disembark and stroll a quarter of a mile to the shores of Josephine Lake, where another boat whisks you ever closer to the continental divide. Upon landing, your guide will lead you a further 1.5 miles overland to Grinnell Lake for wondrous glacial views. This is prime grizzly bear country and the safety-in-numbers puts many nervous hikers at greater ease.

A similar boat-hike combo can be undertaken on Two Medicine Lake, marrying a 45-minute cruise with a 2-mile walk to double-flumed Twin Falls. On St Mary Lake boats departing from Rising Sun incorporate a 1.5 hour cruise with a longer 3-mile hike to St Mary Falls.

All boat trips are run by the **Glacier Park Boat Company** (www.glacierparkboats. com) and can be booked in person at boat docks in Many Glacier, Lake McDonald Lodge, Two Medicine and Rising Sun (St Mary Lake). The cost is a generic adult/child US$25/12.

with the park and a nostalgic reminder of the pioneering days of early motorized transportation. Introduced on the Going-to-the-Sun Rd between 1936 and 1939, the buses have been serving the park for over 70 years. As much a part of the scenery as the glaciers themselves, it is difficult to imagine the park without them.

Jammer tours range from the **Western Alpine Tour** (adult/child US$50/25), a 3½-hour trip between Lake McDonald Lodge and Logan Pass, to the **Big Sky Circle Tour** (adult/child US$80/40), an 8½-hour journey that circles the park via US 2. The **International Peace Park Tour** departs Many Glacier (adult/child US$55/27.50) and St Mary Lodge (adult/child US$65/32.50) daily, rumbling through the east side of the park before heading to Waterton Lakes National Park in Canada in time for an optional high tea at the Prince of Wales Hotel.

SUN TOURS   Bus
(☎406-226-9220; www.glaciersuntours.com)
Blackfeet tribal members lead these interpretive tours (adult/child US$40/20)

of the Going-to-the-Sun Rd. Air-conditioned buses leave from various points in East Glacier, St Mary and Browning; tours last approximately four hours.

 Sleeping

In the early 1910s James Hill's Great Northern Railroad built a series of grand hotels to lure rich tourists to Glacier National Park. Two of these so-called parkitecture structures, Many Glacier Lodge and Lake McDonald Lodge, still stand within the park boundaries, conjuring up nostalgic memories of times gone by.

In keeping with the park's back-to-nature ethos, the lodges have been kept religiously 'rustic', ie they are bereft of distracting modern appliances such as TVs, room phones and wi-fi. All are also nonsmoking and offer at least one wheelchair-accessible room.

Glacier National Park (☎reservations 800-365-2267; www.recreation.gov) operates 13 campgrounds. Sites at Fish Creek and

81

St Mary Campgrounds can be reserved up to six months in advance, and at Apgar up to a year in advance. All other sites are first-come, first-served.

Glacier park lodges are operated by **Glacier Park Inc** (☎406-892-2525; www.glacierparkinc.com) and can be booked online or over the phone.

Going-to-the-Sun Road

Camping

All of the Going-to-the-Sun Rd campgrounds act as bus stops on the free summer shuttle route, making link-ups with trailheads and visitor centers refreshingly easy.

Two campgrounds – St Mary and Apgar – are open in the winter. St Mary takes advance reservations. Phone ahead on ☎406-888-7800.

AVALANCHE CREEK CAMPGROUND   Campground $
(campsites US$20; ☺mid-Jun–early Sep) This lush campground abutting the park's old-growth cedar forest gets more rainfall than most. Some sites are overshadowed by old stands of hemlock, cedar and Douglas fir, but you're close to Lake McDonald and right in the path of a couple of popular trailheads.

RISING SUN CAMPGROUND   Campground $
(campsites US$20; ☺early Jun–early Sep) Situated on Glacier's more unprotected eastern side, 5 miles west of the St Mary entrance station, sites here vary, with lush and diverse vegetation providing some shade. A host of facilities, including the Rising Sun Motor Inn, a store, a restaurant and a boat launch, are nearby.

SPRAGUE CREEK CAMPGROUND   Campground $
(campsites US$20; ☺mid-May–mid-Sep) Quiet, tent-only campground on Lake McDonald.

ST MARY CAMPGROUND   Campground $
(☎406-888-7800; campsites US$23; ☺late May-late Sep, Dec-late Mar) Cottonwood and

aspen trees predominate in the most shaded sites at this campground, on the eastern end of Going-to-the-Sun Rd.

APGAR CAMPGROUND   Campground $
(campsites US$15-20; ☺early May-Oct, Dec-late Mar) Large wooded campground near Apgar Village.

TWO MEDICINE CAMPGROUND   Campground $
(Two Medicine; campsites US$15; ☺late Jun-late Oct) Good sites near Two Medicine Lake and some nice wooded spots. Southwest of Two Medicine entrance.

Lodging

VILLAGE INN   Motel $$
(☎406-888-5632; www.villageinnatapgar.com; s/d US$130/185; ☺late May-late Sep) Occupying a serene setting at the southern end of Lake McDonald in Apgar Village, this well-placed accommodation option is far posher than its motel billing implies. The rooms are the usual rustic, gadget-free zones, but lean out on your sunrise-facing balcony and you are, quite literally, within cherry stone-spitting distance of the park's largest and most tranquil lake.

▉LAKE MCDONALD LODGE   Hotel, Cabins $$
(☎406-888-5431; www.lakemcdonaldlodge.com; r cabin/motel/lodge US$122/134/153; ☺late May–mid-Sep; ☎) Built on the site of an earlier lodge commissioned by park pioneer George Snyder in the 1890s, the present building was constructed in 1913 in classic US parkitecture style. Fronting luminous Lake McDonald, the establishment originally welcomed its guests by boat, meaning that present-day visitors must enter the lodge through the back door. Once inside, a huge fireplace ignites a cozy ambience and colorfully painted paper lamps add an attractive Native American touch. Small, old-fashioned lodge rooms (sans TV and air-con) are complemented by cottages and a 1950s motel. The location, next to boat docks and hiking trails, is perfect.

🖉 RISING SUN MOTOR INN   Motel $$

(☎406-732-5523; www.risingsunmotorinn.com; r motel/cabin US$118/122; ⏱mid-Jun–early Sep) One of two classic 1940s-era motor inns in the park, Rising Sun lies on the upper north shore of St Mary Lake, in a small complex that includes a store, campground, restaurant and boat launch. Rustic motel and cabin rooms with wooden floors offer everything an exhausted hiker could hope for, although tele-addicts and obsessive Blackberry users might find the dearth of technical gadgets a shock to the system.

APGAR VILLAGE LODGE   Motel, Cabins $$

(☎406-888-5484; r US$95-135, cabins US$125-200; ⏱May–mid-Oct) The only privately owned accommodations within the park; this lodge (one of two in Apgar Village) offers well-maintained motel-style rooms and cabins. The cabins are spacious and most come with kitchenettes, while the smaller rooms are more rustic.

North of Going-to-the-Sun Road

All campgrounds in this area, including those not mentioned here, are first-come, first-served, except Fish Creek.

Camping

MANY GLACIER CAMPGROUND   Campground $

(Many Glacier; campsites US$15; ⏱mid-Jun–late Oct) Its access to phenomenal trails makes this campground, next to Swiftcurrent Motor Inn, one of the park's most popular with the hiking set. It's also strolling distance from a restaurant, hot showers, a laundry, camp store and the sublime Many Glacier Hotel with its relaxing lobby.

BOWMAN LAKE CAMPGROUND   Campground $

(North Fork; campsites US$12; ⏱mid-May–mid-Nov) Rarely full, this campground, 6 miles up Inside North Fork Rd from Polebridge, offers spacious sites in forested grounds. There is a visitor's information tent here with reference books and local hiking information.

FISH CREEK CAMPGROUND   Campground $

(☎406-888-7800; campsites US$23; ⏱early Jun-Sep) Cocooned inside a dense cedar-hemlock forest, 3.5 miles northwest of the main park entrance, this campground offers sites that are tucked among the trees.

KINTLA LAKE CAMPGROUND   Campground $

(Inside North Fork Rd; campsites US$15; ⏱late May–mid-Nov) You'll find little to disturb you at this primitive campground.

Skier, Logan Pass (p72)
HOLGER LEUE / LONELY PLANET IMAGES ©

LOGGING CREEK CAMPGROUND
Campground $

(Inside North Fork Rd; campsites US$10; ⏱early Jul-late Sep) Remote, primitive campground about 20 miles north of West Glacier.

QUARTZ CREEK CAMPGROUND
Campground $

(Inside North Fork Rd; campsites US$10; ⏱early Jul-late Nov) The campground here, on Inside North Fork Rd, is similar to the one at Logging Creek, though its thicker vegetation lends a more private air.

Lodging

MANY GLACIER HOTEL
Historic Hotel $$

(☎406-732-4411; www.manyglacierhotel.com; Many Glacier Valley; r US$145-180; ⏱mid-Jun–early Sep) Enjoying the most wondrous setting in the park, this fine old parkitecture-style lodge sits pretty on the northern shore of aquamarine Swiftcurrent Lake, within binocular-viewing distance of shimmering glaciers and foraging bears. Built in the style of a huge Swiss chalet by the Great Northern Railroad in 1915, the hotel sprawls over five floors with an imposing open-plan lobby, complete with a huge fireplace and a resident pianist tinkling on the ivories. Large bar windows frame a postcard-perfect view, while upstairs rustic rooms offer comfortable beds, but no TVs or phones.

SWIFTCURRENT MOTOR INN
Motel $$

(☎406-732-5531; www.swiftcurrentmotorinn.com; Many Glacier Valley; cabin shared/private bath US$70/90, motel US$134; ⏱mid-Jun–early Sep) A relic from the early days of the motor car, the Swiftcurrent, conveniently located next to numerous Many Glacier trailheads, offers cabins and motel-style rooms all bereft of modern luxuries such as TV and air-con.

Eating

Going-to-the-Sun Road

RUSSELLS FIRESIDE DINING ROOM
International $$$

(Lake McDonald Lodge; lunch & dinner US$12-30; ⏱late May–mid-Sep) Lake views and stuffed animal heads characterize the interior

Lake McDonald Lodge (p82)

of this handsome restaurant at the Lake McDonald Lodge, where you can enjoy hash browns for breakfast, substantial sandwiches for lunch, and crab cakes and Caesar salad for dinner.

TWO DOG FLATS
GRILL   American, Tex-Mex $$
(Rising Sun Motor Inn; mains US$15-20; ⊙mid-Jun–early Sep) With zilch competition, and a clientele made up primarily of tired, famished hikers, the Two Dog doesn't have to try too hard, embellishing its standard Montana fare with a faintly discernable Tex-Mex twist.

EDDIE'S CAFE   American $$
(Apgar Village; mains US$12-22; ⊙late May–mid-Sep; 🚼) The menu here includes meatloaf, fish and chips, and buffalo burgers. Order smoothies, muffins and bucket-sized cups of coffee from a walk-up window, too.

JAMMER JOE'S
GRILL & PIZZERIA   Pizzeria, American $
(Lake McDonald Lodge; meals US$7-10; ⊙late May–mid-Sep; 🚼) Serves decent pizza that tastes great after a hike.

South of Going-to-the-Sun Road
TWO MEDICINE
CAMPSTORE   Self-Catering $
(☎406-892-2525; ⊙7am-9pm) While Two Medicine Valley has no standard restaurants, you can purchase coffee, ice cream and enough ingredients to make up a decent picnic at this historic building-cum-grocery store.

North of Going-to-the-Sun Road
PTARMIGAN DINING
ROOM   International $$$
(Many Glacier Hotel; mains US$15-30; ⊙mid-Jun–early Sep) Stay safe at the top of the food chain inside this refined Many Glacier Hotel restaurant where you can enjoy steak, seafood, and pasta as bears munch on berries in the bushes outside.

ITALIAN GARDEN
RISTORANTE   Pizzeria, Italian $
(Swiftcurrent Motor Inn; breakfast US$6-13; ⊙mid-Jun–early Sep) Take the Italian moniker with a pinch of salt. *Molto bene* this isn't, though the pizzas and soup/sandwich combos taste good after a day on the trail.

🛈 Information

Entrance Fees & Passes
Glacier National Park (www.nps.gov/glac) is open year-round. Entry per car, or RV, costs US$25. People arriving on foot, bicycle or motorcycle pay US$12 per person. Both tickets are valid for seven days. Entrance fees are reduced in winter.

Opening Dates
The park is open 24 hours a day, 365 days a year, although many amenities and a couple of park roads close in winter.

Tourist Information
The park has three informative visitor centers and three fully staffed ranger stations scattered within its midst. All are overseen by knowledgeable and helpful rangers during peak season. Visitor centers usually offer other amenities such as restrooms, drinking water, bookstores, maps and interpretive displays. Call in at any of the following:

Apgar Visitor Center (☎406-888-7939; ⊙early May-late Oct, Sat & Sun only in winter) A small information center in the village, close to all amenities.

Logan Pass Visitor Center (⊙usually early Jun–mid-Oct) Opens when the Going-to-the-Sun Rd is fully functional. Books, toilets, water and interpretive displays, but no food.

Many Glacier Ranger Station (☎406-732-7740; ⊙late May–mid-Sep) Call here for local hiking information and details of recent bear activity.

Polebridge Ranger Station (☎406-888-7842; ⊙late May–mid-Sep) A small historic station with North Fork information.

St Mary Visitor Center (☎406-732-7750; ⊙early May–mid-Oct) Holds interesting geological exhibits and an auditorium featuring slide shows, ranger talks and Native American Speaks.

Two Medicine Ranger Station (☏406-226-4484; ☺late May–mid-Sep) A good source for Two Medicine area hikes.

Park Policies & Regulations

Pets are prohibited from all park trails and backcountry campgrounds. Elsewhere, they must be leashed at all times.

Park regulations allow visitors to collect up to a pint of berries per person per day, but think twice before going on a picking binge. Bears and other creatures depend on this food for sustenance.

The speed limit is 45mph on all park roads, dropping to 25mph at the upper part of the Going-to-the-Sun Rd and 10mph in campgrounds.

Dangers & Annoyances

Glacier is prime grizzly bear country and, although you're more likely to get into a car accident than be maimed by a bear, attacks have happened. Drive-in campers should store their edibles in a hard-sided vehicle or in a bear-proof food locker. Stoves, coolers, containers and utensils (even if clean) and scented toiletries should never be left out unattended. Garbage should be disposed of in the bear-proof bins available in all frontcountry campgrounds.

ⓘ Getting Around

Air

There are three airports within reasonable driving distance of Glacier:

Glacier Park International Airport (FCA; ☏406-257-5994; www.iflyglacier.com) Near Kalispell, MT, approximately 30 miles from West Entrance.

Missoula International Airport (MSO; ☏406-728-4381; www.flymissoula.com) In Missoula, MT, approximately 150 miles south of the West Entrance.

Great Falls International Airport (GTF; ☏406-727-3404; www.gtfairport.com) In Great Falls, MT, approximately 140 miles southeast of East Glacier.

Bicycle

Getting around by bike is feasible on the Going-to-the-Sun Rd at certain times of day – although the ride is tough. With all trails out of bounds, cyclists are confined to plying the park's scant road network. A 2.5-mile path runs between Apgar Village and West Glacier.

Bus

All of the park's major trailheads (bar those in the remote North Fork area) are well served by public transportation. Smaller 12-seater shuttles on the western side of the park ferry passengers from the Apgar Transit Center (via Apgar Village) up to Logan Pass. Here you must change to a larger 24-seater shuttle to continue on down to the St Mary Visitor Center. Shuttle services run every 15 to 30 minutes between 7am and 8:30pm, from July 1 to Labor Day. The buses are wheelchair accessible and run on biodiesel. Clear route maps are provided at every shuttle stop or can be viewed on the park website at www.nps.gov/glac.

On the park's eastern side, the **East Side Shuttle** runs a less comprehensive paying service between East Glacier and Waterton (Canada), calling at Two Medicine, Cut Throat Creek, St Mary, Many Glacier and Chief Mountain. Journeys cost US$10 per trip segment and are rarely full; contact **Glacier Park Inc** (www.glacierparkinc.com) for more details. Shuttle buses generally run from July 1 to Labor Day.

Car & Motorcycle

The only paved road to completely bisect the park is the 53-mile Going-to-the-Sun Rd. The unpaved Inside North Fork Rd links Apgar with Polebridge. To connect with any other roads, vehicles must briefly leave the park and re-enter via another entrance.

Cars can be rented from **Kruger Helicop-Tours** (☏406-387-4565; www.krugerhelicopters.com), one mile west of West Glacier on US 2. Other outlets can be found at Glacier Park International Airport and in the nearby town of Whitefish.

Train

Largely responsible for opening up the region in the 1890s, the train has been a popular method of transport to Glacier since the park's inception in 1910. Amtrak's *Empire Builder* continues to ply the Great Northern Railroad's historic east–west route from Chicago to Seattle once daily (in either direction) stopping in both East Glacier (6:45pm westbound, 9:54am eastbound) and West Glacier (8:23pm westbound, 8:16am eastbound). The

SHANNON NACE / LONELY PLANET IMAGES ©

same train also connects with Whitefish and (by request only) Essex.

AROUND GLACIER NATIONAL PARK

St Mary

Sitting on the Blackfeet Indian Reservation just outside the park's east entrance, St Mary makes a handy base for exploring Glacier's dryer eastern side. Though less salubrious than its western counterpart, West Glacier, the views of the mountains are better here and it's a shorter walk (0.6 miles) to the first free shuttle stop on the Going-to-the-Sun Rd (outside the St Mary visitor and transit center). A cluster of handy services not found inside the park crowd around the junction of Hwy 89 and the Going-to-the-Sun Rd including campgrounds, a motel, a supermarket, a gas station and the region's swankiest modern hotel. The East Side shuttle provides easy access to East Glacier, Two Medicine, Many Glacier and Waterton.

 Sleeping & Eating

ST MARY LODGE & RESORT Resort $$
(☏406-732-4431; www.glacierparkinc.com; cnr Hwy 89 & Going-to-the-Sun Rd; r US$139-179, cabins US$279; ☉mid-May–early Oct; ❄ 🛜)
Myriad facilities include a gift shop, coffee bar, the Snowgoose Grill and a grand stash of rooms, from motel-style to luxury teepees to plush rooms in the main Great Bear Lodge. Most rooms have TVs, coffee machines and other gadgets. Located just outside the park boundary.

JOHNSON'S OF ST MARY Campground, Cabins $
(☏406-732-4207; www.johnsonsofstmary. com; off US 89; tent/RV sites US$25/35, cabins US$149; 🚻) Set on a knoll overlooking the village, RV sites here get gorgeous views of St Mary Lake with the crenellated peaks of the Continental Divide glimmering in the background. Tents sites are shaded peacefully by some alder trees. Also available are cabins, a cottage and Johnson's World Famous Historic Restaurant onsite.

PARK CAFÉ Breakfast, American $
(www.parkcafe.us; US 89; breakfast $7-12;
7am-10pm) Almost as celebrated as the
historic Going-to-the-Sun Rd, the Park
Café is lauded, less for its astounding
views, and more for its astoundingly delicious huckleberry pie. Playing a strong
supporting role are the fortifying breakfasts best enjoyed at the diner counter
while discussing the merits of bear spray
over playing dead.

Information

St Mary lies less than 0.6 miles from the park's
eastern entrance where the Going-to-the-Sun Rd
meets US 89. Most facilities can be found at the
convenience store, gift shop and gas station that
adjoin the Park Café.

Getting There & Around

The free Going-to-the-Sun Rd shuttles terminate
at the St Mary Visitor Center, a five-minute stroll
from St Mary's diminutive core. They run every 30
minutes July to September. The three-times-daily
East Side shuttle links St Mary with Waterton,
Many Glacier, Cut Throat Creek, Two Medicine and
East Glacier.

East Glacier Park

A summer-only stop on Amtrak's *Empire
Builder* route, East Glacier Park grew up
around the train depot (which splits the
small slightly scruffy settlement in half)
and the adjacent Glacier Park Lodge.
While its eating and sleeping options
offer more variety than West Glacier, its
location away from the Going-to-the-Sun
Rd make quick forays into the park less
convenient.

Sleeping & Eating

**GLACIER PARK
LODGE** Historic Hotel $$
(☎406-226-5600; www.bigtreehotel.com; r
$140-180, ste $359; ⊙mid-May–late Sep; 🛜🏊)
Set in attractive flower-filled grounds
and overlooking Montana's oldest golf
course, this historic 1914 lodge was built
in the classic national park tradition with
a splendid open-plan lobby supported
by lofty 900-year-old Douglas fir timbers
(imported from Washington State).

BROWNIE'S Hostel $
(☎406-226-4426; www.brownieshostel.com;
1020 Hwy 49; dm US$20, r US$55) Above
Brownie's Grocery & Deli, this
casual HI hostel is packed with
travelers staying in eight-per-
son single-sex dorms or pri-
vate doubles. It has a com-
mon room and kitchen, and
lockout is roughly 10am
to 4pm. Sheets, blankets
and pillows are provided
free of charge.

**FIREBRAND PASS
CAMPGROUND**
Campground $
(☎406-226-5573) This
small campground, 3
miles west of East Glacier
Park and off US 2, has 26

Sunrise, St Mary Lake (p69)
JOHN ELK III / LONELY PLANET IMAGES ©

Detour:
Waterton Lakes National Park

This little known Canadian national park is nearly identical to Glacier geographically, but, with a compact townsite within its boundaries, lenient trail regulations, a golf course, and a stash of modern hotels, the park is definitely different. Despite the development, Waterton's diminutive size has ensured that its trail network remains both multifarious and accessible. Indeed, the park is unrivaled in North America for offering almost instant access to rugged stretches of high-alpine terrain located well above the tree-line. It also equals Glacier for flora and fauna – the park is a sanctuary for numerous iconic animals – grizzlies, elk, deer and cougar – along with 800-odd wildflower species.

Waterton Lakes National Park lies in Alberta's southwestern corner, 81 miles from Lethbridge. The one road entrance into the park is in its northeast corner along Hwy 5. Most visitors coming from Glacier and the USA reach the junction with Hwy 5 via Hwy 6 (Chief Mountain International Hwy) from the southeast.

If you only have time for one hike in this park, make it the 11-mile Carthew-Alderson Trail, which many consider the best in the Rockies.

Campgrounds, lodgings and restaurants are plentiful. For information, stop into the **Waterton Visitor Centre** (403-859-5133; www.parkscanada.gc.ca/waterton; 8am-7pm, early May–early Oct), across the road from the Prince of Wales Hotel.

Glacier Park Inc (www.glacierparkinc.com; departures 3pm) runs East Side shuttles (round-trip only) from the Prince of Wales Hotel in Waterton to Chief Mountain (US$10), Many Glacier (US$20), St Mary (US$30) and Glacier Park Lodge (US$50) in Glacier.

sites for both tent and full RV hookup. The grassy, shady grounds have an air of seclusion.

Information

East Glacier Park lies just outside the park's southeastern corner at the junction of Hwy 49 and US 2. Facilities include a post office, ATMs, internet at Brownie's and a couple of gas stations.

Getting There & Around

The three-times-daily East Side shuttle links East Glacier with Two Medicine (US$10), Cut Throat Creek (US$20), St Mary (US$30), Many Glacier (US$40) and Waterton (US$50). The **Amtrak** (www.amtrak.com) *Empire Builder* stops at the train depot once a day traveling in either direction.

West Glacier

Lying not half a mile from the park's busiest entrance gate and equipped with an Amtrak train station, West Glacier is the park's most pleasant gateway town with its attractive cluster of serviceable facilities befitting Glacier's rustic parkitecture image. Known as Belton until 1949, the settlement was the site of the park's oldest hotel, the Belton Chalet, built in 1910 and still hosting guests.

Sleeping & Eating

 BELTON CHALET Historic Hotel $$
(406-888-5000; www.beltonchalet.com; r US$155-170) Built and opened the same year as the national park (1910), this affectionate Swiss chalet overlooking

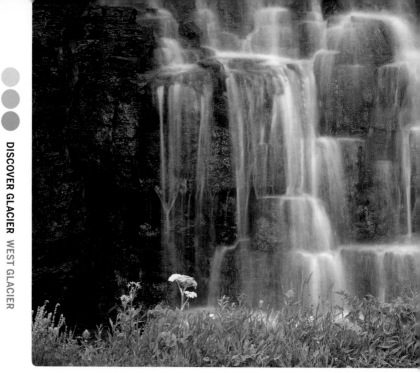

the railroad tracks in West Glacier was Glacier's first tourist hotel and has a plusher feel than many of the park's other vintage lodges. The onsite **Belton Chalet Grill Dining Room & Taproom** (www.beltonchalet.com; mains US$25-34; ⊙3-10pm) is well worth a visit for its food and beer selection.

VISTA MOTEL
Motel $

(📞406-888-5311; www.glaciervistamotel.com; US 2; r US$95-125; 🛜 🏊) A cheap and relatively cheerful motel, the no-nonsense Vista does at least have a vista, along with comfortable beds, powerful showers and a spatially challenged swimming pool. Located a half mile hike along US 2 from the West Glacier train depot.

🌿 GLACIER GUIDES LODGE
B&B $$

(📞406-387-5555; www.glacierguides.com; Highline Blvd; r US$171; ❄ 🛜) Newly refurbished to meet environmental LEED standard, this wooden B&B-style lodge run by a local guide company is a good option for people who want rustic authenticity without forsaking wi-fi and the TV. It's just off US 2 opposite the Amtrak station.

GLACIER CAMPGROUND
Campground $

(📞406-387-5689) This campground, 1 mile west of West Glacier and off US 2, sits on 16 hectares (40 acres) of lovely wooded grounds. It also offers basic wooden cabins.

WEST GLACIER RESTAURANT & BAR
American $$

(200 Going-to-the-Sun Rd; mains US$11-17; ⊙7am-10pm May-Sep) Perched invitingly on the cusp of the park, this ultra-friendly restaurant is a sure bet for filling, calorie-packed Montana cooking. The breakfast classic is a stack of buttery pancakes while dinner veers toward spaghetti and meatballs.

🛈 Information

Most basic facilities can be found here including a gas station, a grocery-gift store, a post office and an ATM.

Left: Waterfall near Logan Pass (p72); **Below:** Mountain goat

Glacier National Park Headquarters (☏406-888-7800; www.nps.gov/glac; West Glacier, MT 59936; ⊗8am-4:30pm Mon-Fri) Inhabits a small complex just south of the west entrance station. This location is the focus for visitor information from November to April.

Glacier Natural History Association (www.glacierassociation.org; US 2; ⊗8am-4:30pm Mon-Fri) This nonprofit association, in West Glacier's train depot, is an excellent resource for books, maps and information.

ℹ Getting There & Around

A 2.5-mile paved cycle path links West Glacier with Apgar Village and the transit center inside the park, from where you can catch free Going-to-the-Sun Rd shuttles. Amtrak's *Empire Builder* stops at the train depot once a day traveling in either direction.

Grand Canyon National Park

Talk to anyone who's been here about their visit and they get the same faraway look in their eyes. It happens the moment they start describing their first walk out to the rim and that unforgettable initial glimpse over the edge. A mile deep, 18 miles wide and 227 river-miles long, the Grand Canyon is a chasm in the earth that defies description.

While the views from the rim are the Grand Canyon's iconic experiences, the park is also home to a wealth of history, both human and geologic in scope. The hiking here is different than in any other park – it's like climbing a mountain in reverse. And the rafting? Let's just say it's well worth the year-long wait that's usually required to land yourself a coveted spot in a raft on the Colorado.

Mather Point (p103)

Grand Canyon Itineraries

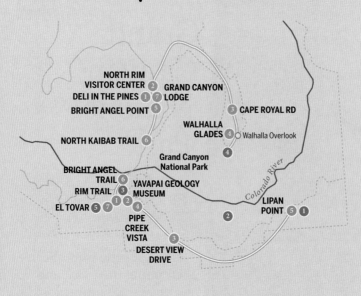

Two Days

1 Rim Trail (p105) Explore the edge of the Grand Canyon's South Rim by walking part or all of the 12-mile Rim Trail, one of the few flat trails in the park.

2 Yavapai Geology Museum & Observation Station (p100) Orient yourself with the canyon's geologic formations with a giant relief map and take in the incredible canyon views from the viewing platform.

3 Desert View Drive (p103) In the late afternoon, take a spin down the Grand Canyon's quintessential roadway, a 25-mile meander past some of the park's most epic viewpoints.

4 Pipe Creek Vista (p103) Mather Point is one of the most popular viewpoints along Desert View Drive, but hike just 1.3 miles from the parking area out to Pipe Creek Vista and you'll leave the crowds behind.

5 Lipan Point (p104) Time your drive out Desert View Drive so that you catch the sunset at Lipan Point, one of the last stops on the route and possibly the best place to watch the setting sun light up the canyon walls.

6 Bright Angel Trail (p107) On day two, still on the South Rim, set out early and hike below the canyon rim on the Bright Angel Trail.

7 El Tovar (p116) Close the evening at El Tovar lodge, where you can lull yourself into a blissful stupor on a porch swing or take in the views over a delicious dinner.

➡ THIS LEG: 50 MILES

Four Days

1 Deli in the Pines (p139) On day three, wake up, pack the car, and make the 215-mile drive to the Grand Canyon's North Rim. Once you're there, shake out your driving cramps and eat lunch in this modest but delightful deli beside the Grand Canyon Lodge.

2 North Rim Visitor Center (p139) Pop into the only visitor center on the North Rim, ask questions, get weather reports and orient yourself with the park.

3 Cape Royal Rd (p130) Once you're rested and fed, jump back in the car and take the short drive out to Cape Royal, where you can marvel at the views of the Colorado River below. It's the only place on the North Rim where you can actually see the river.

4 Walhalla Glades (p130) While driving Cape Royal Rd, stop at Walhalla Overlook and explore the ruins of an ancient Puebloans' summer home.

5 Bright Angel Point (p132) Close the evening watching the sunset from this iconic viewpoint lyiing at the end of a short, paved trail along a breathtaking precipice over the canyon.

6 North Kaibab Trail (p134) On day four, wake up with the sun and hike into the canyon on North Kaibab Trail. Those who would rather skip the walking part can hire a mule and head down by hoof. Setting out early is a must.

7 Grand Canyon Lodge (p136) After grunting and groaning your way back up to the canyon rim, grab an ice-cold beer from the lodge's bar. Then plonk yourself into an Adirondack chair and enjoy the Grand Canyon sunset in comfort and style.

. . . .

THIS LEG: 240 MILES

Grand Canyon Highlights

1 Best sunset: Lipan Point (p104) You've hardly lived until you see the sunset from Lipan Point.

2 Best thrill: Grandview Trail (p109) Check your vertigo at the door before hiking this frightening trail.

3 Best South Rim viewpoint: Hopi Point (p103) Three massive rapids on the mighty Colorado are visible from this epic viewpoint.

4 Best North Rim viewpoint: Cape Royal Point (p130) The earth just falls away, and there are no guardrails impede the view.

5 Best meal: El Tovar Dining Room (p118) Without a doubt, one of the best restaurant views in the world.

Lipan Point (p104)
JOHN ELK III / LONELY PLANET IMAGES ©

Discover Grand Canyon

SOUTH RIM

Step up to a South Rim overlook, and as the maw dramatically opens out before you, with a breeze carrying a soaring California condor along with high-desert hints of piñon and sage, you can expect to feel very small.

Taking in the grandeur from the rim is as far as most visitors go. But ranging below the rim brings the sheer immensity and splendor of the gorge into perspective; even hiking down a short way reveals fossils embedded in sandstone, and rock art left by ancient Native Americans. Hiking up exposes the canyon's scale in a new, sweat-sheened light.

Desert wildflowers bloom out of rock in the springtime, autumn leaves light up the landscape in the fall, and the canyon's spires and temples are breathtaking when frosted with snow. All the while, light and shadow creep across the canyon, constantly recreating the landscape before you.

History

The Grand Canyon's rich history dates back more than 10,000 years, when Paleo-Indian hunters first passed through it in search of Pleistocene megafauna such as mammoths and giant sloth. As Native American groups settled and migrated in response to the cycles of climate change, they left their mark on the canyon in the form of extensive trail systems, rock art and artifacts hinting at their cultures.

Eventually, the fate of modern Native Americans in the Grand Canyon would be determined not by the rhythms of nature but by inexorable European encroachment and, ultimately, the United States government. As the park was incrementally protected as a game reserve and national monument, it eventually became, in 1919, the country's 17th national park. As its primary administrator, the National Park Service now collaborates with the US Forest Service and neighboring reservations to maintain a sustainable balance between Native American land rights, resource management and future preservation of the park's ecology.

Mather Point (p103)

When to Go

Unlike the North Rim, the South Rim is open all year. Summer is hot and extremely busy. Spring is much cooler, has fewer people and occasionally gets a dusting of snow. Fall is a particularly pleasant time to visit, both in terms of weather and the relative lack of crowds. Winter is crowd-free but cold; snow-capped temples and buttes in the canyon can be beautiful.

When You Arrive

Upon entry, you'll receive a map and a copy of *The Guide*, a National Park Service (NPS) newspaper with current park news, and information on ranger programs, hikes, accommodations and park services.

Make your first stop at Canyon View Information Plaza to get your bearings, walk out to Mather Point and then carry on with your day.

Orientation

The park's South Rim comprises four distinct sections: Grand Canyon Village, Hermit Rd, Desert View Dr and the below-the-rim backcountry.

You'll find most services in and around Grand Canyon Village, where lodges, restaurants, two of the three developed campgrounds, the backcountry office, visitor center, clinic, bank, grocery store, shuttles and other services almost comprise a full-fledged town.

Hermit Rd follows the rim from the village 8 miles west to Hermits Rest, offering seven viewpoints along the way.

Desert View Dr spans 25 miles from Grand Canyon Village through Desert View to the East Entrance, passing several excellent viewpoints, picnic areas and the Tusayan Ruins and Museum.

Tourist services, including restaurants and hotels, are available just outside the park in Tusayan, 2 miles south of Grand Canyon Village; and in Williams, 59 miles south of the village.

 Sights

While you'll obviously want to marvel at the main attraction, the South Rim is also the site of notable buildings and museums that offer some fascinating and enriching historical perspective on your canyon experience. Many of the historic buildings on the South Rim were designed by visionary architect Mary Colter, painstakingly researched and designed to complement the landscape and reflect the local culture.

Consider purchasing the self-guided *Walking Tour of Grand Canyon Village Historical District* brochure ($1) at park bookstores.

VERKAMP'S VISITOR CENTER   Historic Building
(Grand Canyon Village; ⊙8am-7pm) In 1898 John G Verkamp sold souvenirs from a tent outside Bright Angel Lodge to persevering travelers who arrived at the canyon after long, arduous stagecoach rides. He was a little before his time, however, as there weren't enough customers to make a living, and he closed down his operation after only a few weeks. The arrival of the railroad in 1901 opened up the canyon to more and more tourists, and in 1905 Verkamp returned to build the modified Mission-style Verkamp's Curios at its present location beside Hopi House. After running the shop for more than 100 years, Verkamp's ancestors closed down the business, and the NPS revamped the building as a visitor center in 2008.

BRIGHT ANGEL LODGE   Historic Building
(Grand Canyon Village) By the 1930s, tourism to the park had boomed, and Fred Harvey decided to build a more affordable alternative to El Tovar. Designed by Mary Colter, the log-and-stone Bright Angel Lodge was completed in 1935. Just off the lobby is the History Room, a small museum devoted to Fred Harvey, the English immigrant who, in conjunction with the Atchison, Topeka and Santa Fe Railway, transformed the Grand Canyon into a popular tourist destination. Don't miss

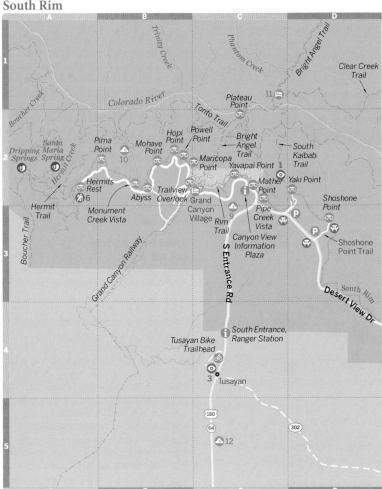

the fireplace, built of Kaibab limestone and layered with stones that represent the canyon strata from river to rim.

The first stagecoach to the South Rim left Flagstaff on May 19, 1892. Eventually, stages made the 11-hour ride to the park thrice weekly, and three stations along the way allowed visitors to stretch their legs, dust off and prepare for the next leg of the journey. Red Horse (originally called Moqui Station) was built 16 miles south of the village in the 1890s; in 1902 Ralph Cameron, who controlled Bright Angel

Trail, moved the building to its present site (on the Bright Angel Lodge grounds) and converted it into the Cameron Hotel. It served as a post office from 1907 to 1935. When Mary Colter designed Bright Angel Lodge in the early '30s, she insisted the station be preserved and incorporated into the lodge.

GRAND CANYON
TRAIN DEPOT   Historic Building
(Grand Canyon Village) Designed by Francis Wilson for the Atchison, Topeka & Santa

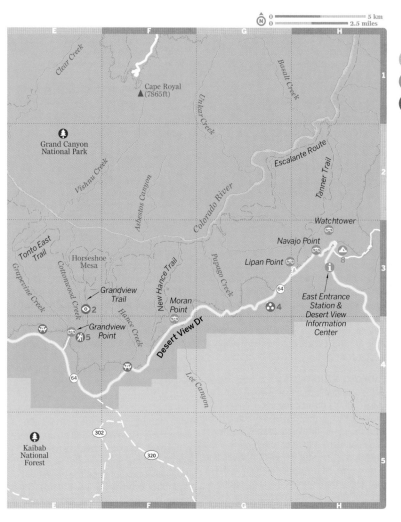

Map labels:

5 km
2.5 miles

Clear Creek
Cape Royal
▲ (7865ft)
Unkar Creek
Busali Creek
Grand Canyon National Park
Vishnu Creek
Escalante Route
Tanner Trail
Colorado River
Asbestos Canyon
Watchtower
Navajo Point
Tonto East Trail
Horseshoe Mesa
Lipan Point
New Hance Trail
Papago Creek
Cottonwood Creek
Grapevine Creek
Grandview Trail
Moran Point
64
East Entrance Station & Desert View Information Center
Grandview Point
Hance Creek
Desert View Dr
4
64
Led Canyon
Kaibab National Forest
302
320

Fe Railway, this train depot was completed in 1909, eight years after the first train arrived in the village from Williams. It's one of three remaining log depots in the country and one of only 14 log depots ever constructed in the US. The logs are squared on three sides to create a flat-walled interior. The 1st floor was used for passenger services, and the 2nd floor was a two-bedroom apartment for the ticket agent. Today, a Grand Canyon Railway train pulls into the station from Williams daily.

HOPI HOUSE Historic Building

(Grand Canyon Village; ⊙8am-8pm) Another beautiful stone building designed by Mary Colter for Fred Harvey, Hopi House was built largely by Hopi Indians and was finished a few weeks before the completion of El Tovar in 1905. It was modeled after the pueblos at Old Oraibi, a Hopi settlement on the Third Mesa in eastern Arizona that vies with Acoma, New Mexico, for the title of longest continually inhabited village in the US. The interior does resemble an ancient pueblo, featuring adobe walls

South Rim

and concrete floors made to look like dirt, corner fireplaces and a timbered ceiling. Exterior ladders and interior staircases connect each story. In the park's early days, Hopi Indians lived here, sold crafts and entertained travelers with nightly dances. Today, it's a wonderful place to shop for quality Native American jewelry, basketwork, pottery and other crafts.

LOOKOUT STUDIO   Historic Building

(Grand Canyon Village; ☼8am-sunset) Like Mary Colter's other canyon buildings, Lookout Studio (c 1914) was modeled after the stone dwellings of the Southwest Pueblo Indians. Made of rough-cut Kaibab limestone – the stone that comprises one of the layers of the upper canyon walls – with a roof that mirrors the lines of the rim, the studio blends into its natural surroundings. The interior features an arched stone fireplace, stone walls and a timber-framed ceiling. Inside, you'll find a small souvenir shop and a tiny back porch that offers spectacular canyon views. There's also a stone stairway snaking below Lookout Studio leading to another terrace, which may be closed in bad weather.

KOLB STUDIO   Historic Building

(Grand Canyon Village; ☼8am-7pm) Photographer brothers Ellsworth and Emery Kolb first came to the Grand Canyon from Pennsylvania in 1901 and 1902, respectively. The pioneering brothers built their photography studio in 1904 and made their living photographing parties traveling the Bright Angel Trail. In 1911, after having boats custom-made for the expedition, they filmed their own trip down the Green and Colorado Rivers, and canyon visitors flocked to their small auditorium to see the film, in which both brothers repeatedly tumble into the water. Emery continued to show the film to audiences twice daily until his death at 95 in 1976.

Today, their studio, perched on the edge of the canyon, holds a small but well-stocked bookstore and an art gallery with changing exhibits. You can still see clips of the original Kolb river film, though not projected on the big screen (nor introduced by the late Emery). Their home, built on two stories and beneath the bookstore, is maintained by the Grand Canyon Association and occasionally opened to the public for tours.

YAVAPAI GEOLOGY MUSEUM &
OBSERVATION STATION   Museum

(Grand Canyon Village; ☼8am-7pm) Panoramic views of the canyon unfold behind the plate-glass windows of this observation station on Yavapai Point, one of the South Rim's best viewpoints. Plaques beneath the large windows identify and explain the formation of the landmarks upon which you're gazing. With a topographic relief model of the canyon itself and a model illustrating and explaining the canyon's sedimentary layers, this is an excellent place to bone up on Grand Canyon geology before hiking down. If the exhibits here spark your curiosity, consider attending a ranger talk about canyon geology (check *The Guide* for locations and times).

 **Activities**

From the rim to the Colorado River, the Grand Canyon is an adventure waiting to happen, whether you navigate the scenic drives or float the raging rapids below.

Driving Tours

Two scenic drives follow the contour of the rim on either side of the village: Hermit Rd to the west and Desert View Dr to the east. The rim dips in and out of view as the road passes through the piñon-juniper and ponderosa stands of Kaibab National Forest. Pullouts along the way offer spectacular views and interpretive signs that explain the canyon's features and geology.

The road to Yaki Point and the South Kaibab Trailhead is closed year-round to all traffic except bicycles and the green Kaibab Trail Route shuttle. From March 1 to November 30, Hermit Rd is closed to all traffic except bicycles and the red Hermits Rest Route shuttle. Both scenic drives may close due to snow or ice buildup from November through March; call ☏928-638-7888 for current road and weather conditions.

HERMIT ROAD Scenic Drive

This popular road offers several exceptional views. It begins at the west end of Grand Canyon Village and ends at Mary Colter's distinctive Hermits Rest, built as a rest stop for early park tourists. Hermit Rd is closed to private vehicles from March through November, but the Hermits Rest shuttle route will take you to all the sites detailed here.

Trailview Overlook offers a great view of Bright Angel Trail, the lush vegetation at Indian Garden and Grand Canyon Village on the rim to the east. If you arrive early in the morning, you may see the tiny specks of a faraway mule train descending into the canyon.

In 1890 prospector Daniel Lorain Hogan discovered what he believed to be copper 1100ft below **Maricopa Point**. He filed a mining claim for the area, including 4 acres on the rim, and set about making his fortune. After more than 40 years of minimal success, Hogan realized that the real money at the canyon was in tourism, so in 1936 he built tourist cabins,

Buckey O'Neill Cabin

On the grounds of Bright Angel Lodge, the **Buckey O'Neill Cabin** (☏888-297-2757; www.grandcanyonlodges.com) is the longest continually standing building on the rim. It was built in the 1890s by a man named William Owen O'Neill. Nicknamed 'Buckey' because he 'bucked the odds' in a card game, O'Neill moved to Arizona in 1879 and worked as an author, journalist, miner, politician and judge. Drawn to a copper deposit near Anita, about 14 miles south of today's Grand Canyon Village, he lived in this cabin and worked on the side as a tour guide.

As was the case with so many other prospectors, Buckey found mining to be an unprofitable venture, so he eventually sold his land to the railways and went on to become mayor of Prescott, Arizona. He was one of Teddy Roosevelt's Rough Riders in the Spanish American War and died the day before the assault on San Juan Hill. Today, the cabin is a guesthouse and the lucky few who make reservations well in advance can stay in his cabin.

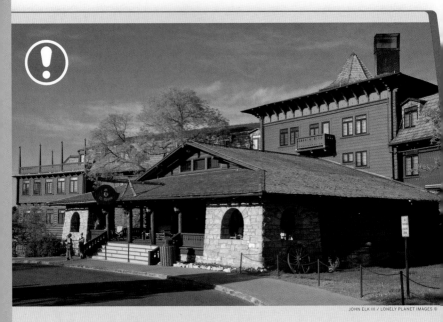

Don't Miss **El Tovar**

With its unusual spires and dark-wood beams rising behind the Rim Trail, elegant El Tovar (Map p98) remains a grande dame of national-park lodges. El Tovar was built in 1905 for the Atchison, Topeka & Santa Fe Railway and designed by architect Charles Whittlesey as a blend between a Swiss chalet and the more rustic style that would come to define national-park lodges in the 1920s. Spacious rooms (many with sleigh beds and rim overlooks), a dining room with panoramic views, and wide, inviting porches with rocking chairs offered visitors a comfortable and elegant place to relax after a long journey to the park.

Today the public spaces look much as they did when the lodge opened, though many of the rooms are smaller, and it remains the most luxurious lodge on the South Rim. Moose and elk trophy heads, reproduction Remington bronzes and Craftsman-style furniture lend the interior a classic Western feel. A gift shop and restaurant adjoin the lobby, and the helpful concierge can book bus tours and answer questions. The lodge sits about 100 yards from the rim, and though it's thronged with tourists by day, the scene mellows in the evening. The back porch, a sweet spot to relax with a drink, looks out over a small lawn, one of the park's few grassy areas and a great place for small children to play. If the back porch is full, take your drink to the side porch – it's closer to the Rim Trail but has a delightful bench swing that's the perfect perch after a long hike.

a trading post and a saloon on the rim. In 1947 he sold the property to Madelaine Jacobs, who would end up making the fortune Hogan never did – in uranium, not copper.

Perched at **Powell Point**, the Powell Memorial was erected in 1915 in honor of John Wesley Powell, the intrepid one-armed Civil War veteran, ethnologist and geologist who led the first white-water run through the canyon on the Colorado in 1869. The park was officially dedicated at this spot in 1920.

One of the park's best viewpoints, **Hopi Point** juts out further than any other overlook along Hermit Rd and offers huge, spectacular views of plateau upon plateau and the Colorado River a mile below. Notable canyon features here include the Isis and Osiris Temples. Until completion of Hermit Rd in 1912, Hopi Point was the westernmost spot on guided tours. Nowadays, it's a popular place to watch the sunset and is often crowded on summer evenings.

If you're doing the Grand Canyon speed-demon tour and only have time for a couple of stops, make them count at Mohave and Hopi Points. **Mohave Point** serves up a delicious array of cliff views in all directions. It's also a particularly good place to see the Colorado, as three rapids – Salt Creek, Granite and Hermit – are visible below, downstream.

Aptly named, the **Abyss** is a beautiful example of how steep some canyon drop-offs can be. If you're at all acrophobic, consider stopping at a different viewpoint, as sheer cliffs drop 2600ft to the Redwall limestone below. If heights don't bother you, walk about a quarter mile westward along the Rim Trail and (carefully) check out the dizzying drop.

The overwhelming maw of the Grand Canyon can truly be appreciated from **Pima Point**, where you can see for miles to the west, north and east. **Hermits Rest** (like Hermit Rd and Hermit Rapid) is one of the 13 canyon features named after one of the park's most famous residents, Louis Boucher (aka 'The Hermit'). Boucher was a Canadian immigrant who worked as a prospector and tourist guide and lived alone at Dripping Springs in Boucher Canyon, below Hermits Rest, from 1889 to 1912.

DESERT VIEW DRIVE   Scenic Drive
(Map p98) The 25-mile Desert View Dr is the red-carpet welcome to the Grand Canyon (sans paparazzi and hype), starting at the East Entrance and including historic architecture, a Native American ruin and inspiring vistas.

Six well-marked viewpoints (plus several unmarked ones), an ancient Puebloan site with accompanying small museum and Mary Colter's Watchtower give you a dash of culture with your canyon views. A leisurely drive, with plenty of time for every stop, takes about four hours.

As it sits beside the Canyon View Information Plaza parking lot (300 yards away), **Mather Point** can be the most crowded of all the viewpoints. However, its roomy overlooks extend to two promontories that jut out over the canyon, providing views of the Bright Angel and South Kaibab Trails ribboning down into the canyon. Or you can walk 1.3 miles east along the Rim Trail to **Pipe Creek Vista** to escape the crowds.

Closed year-round to private vehicles, **Yaki Point** lies just north of Desert View Dr and is accessed by the green Kaibab Trail Route shuttles. East of the trail, you'll get an excellent look at Zoroaster Temple and Wotan's Throne beyond.

If you don't see many cars as you drive by the unsignposted **Shoshone Point Trailhead**, make time for the wonderful 1-mile walk to this peaceful picnic spot and viewpoint.

They didn't call the next overlook **Grandview Point** for nothing. Peter Berry (another prospector-turned-entrepreneur) and his partners built the Grandview Toll Trail in 1893 to access copper claims more than 2000ft below on Horseshoe Mesa. In 1897 he built the Grand View Hotel here on the rim, and when he wasn't hauling copper, he led tourists into the canyon on foot and by mule. Today thousands make a steep descent into the canyon via Berry's Grandview Trail, while others enjoy impressive canyon views from the spot where his hotel once thrived.

The oft-visited **Moran Point** is named after Thomas Moran, the landscape painter who spent just about every winter at the canyon from 1899 to 1920 and whose romantically dramatic work was instrumental in securing the canyon's national-park status. From here you can see down the river in both directions, and peer down onto the reddish-orange Hakatai shale of Red Canyon below.

The tiny **Tusayan Ruins & Museum** (admission free; ⏲9am-5pm) houses only a few displays of pottery and jewelry, but the 4000-year-old split-twig figures of animals on exhibit are worth a stop at this beautiful little stone building. From here you can take a short self-guided walk through the remains of an ancient Pueblo village that was excavated in 1930. Tree-ring analyses date the structure to 1185, and archaeologists estimate that about 30 people lived here.

One of the most spectacular viewpoints on the South Rim, **Lipan Point** gives a panoramic eyeful of the canyon and makes a magnificent spot to watch the sunset. From here, you'll get an unobstructed view of Unkar Rapid just to the west. To the northeast, the sheer cliffs called the Palisades of the Desert define the southeastern wall of the Grand Canyon, beyond which the Echo and Vermilion Cliffs lie in the distance.

The Escalante and Cardenas Buttes are the immediate features you'll see from **Navajo Point** (7498ft), beyond which

you'll get good views of several miles' worth of the Colorado River. You can also look back at Desert View to the east and the **Watchtower**, the top floor of which, at 7522ft, edges out Navajo Point as the highest spot on the rim itself. Designed by Mary Colter and built in 1932, the 70ft circular stone Watchtower was inspired by ancient Pueblo watchtowers. You'll enter through the gift shop, above which a small terrace offers beautiful views. Stairs lead up to the 4th floor, where binoculars and big windows offer expansive views in every direction.

Hiking

Hiking along the South Rim is among park visitors' favorite pastimes, with options for all levels and persuasions. The popular river-bound corridor trails (Bright Angel and South Kaibab) span the 7 to 10 miles to the canyon floor, following paths etched thousands of years ago by drainage routes. Several turnaround spots make these trails ideal for day hikes

Left: Picnicking beside the Colorado River; **Below:** Prickly pear cactus

(LEFT) ANDREW PEACOCK / LONELY PLANET IMAGES ©; (BELOW) JOHN ELK III / LONELY PLANET IMAGES ©

of varying lengths. Both can get packed during summer with foot and mule traffic. For more solitude, opt for a less trodden trail like Hermit or Grandview.

Most of the trails start with a super-steep series of switchbacks that descend quickly to the dramatic ledge of Coconino sandstone about 2 miles beneath the rim. Hike another 3 miles and you'll hit the sun-baked Tonto Platform, which after another couple of miles opens up to inner gorge vistas. From the platform it's a fast and furious pitch to the canyon floor and Colorado River. Most day hikers will want to stay above the Tonto Platform, particularly in summer.

Day hiking requires no permit, just preparation and safety. In the following descriptions, we specify whether the listed distances are one way or round-trip. (Hiking time depends largely on each hiker's ability.)

The first two hikes listed here are excellent for families, as neither involve significant elevation change.

RIM TRAIL   Hiking

(Map p98) The 12-mile Rim Trail can be walked in its entirety in a day, with stops at scenic viewpoints, or explored in short segments by hopping on and off the shuttles.

It makes a lovely stroll at sunrise, sunset or under a starry sky, times when the crowds really thin out.

Stretching from Hermits Rest on the rim's western edge through Grand Canyon Village to Pipe Creek Vista and with an elevation change of a mere 200ft, the Rim Trail connects a series of scenic points and is hands down the easiest long walk in the park. By no means a nature trail, it's paved from Powell Point (2 miles west of Kolb Studio) to the South Kaibab Trailhead (4.6 miles east of Kolb Studio), which makes it accessible to wheelchairs and more easily navigable for those with mobility issues.

Still, flexibility is a big draw, with the shuttles making it simple to jump on for a segment and hike for as long as you like. Every viewpoint from Hermits Rest to Yaki Point is accessed by one of three shuttle routes, which means you can walk to a vista and shuttle back, or shuttle to a point, walk to the next and shuttle from there. A helpful map inside *The Guide* shows the shuttle stops and hiking distances along each segment of the trail.

The trail passes many of the park's historical sights, including **El Tovar**, **Hopi House**, **Kolb Studio**, **Lookout Studio** and **Verkamp's Visitor Center**. The 3 miles or so that wind through the village are usually packed with people, but the further west you venture, the more you'll break free from the crowds.

One very pretty stretch is the mile east of **Pima Point**, where the trail is set far back from the road, offering stunning views and relative solitude. Winding through piñon-juniper woodlands, it passes several viewpoints; see the Hermit Rd drive (p101) for details. **Mohave** and **Hopi Points** offer great views of the Colorado River, with three visible rapids (Salt Creek, Granite and Hermit) below and downstream.

SHOSHONE POINT Hiking
(Map p98) The gentle and cool amble out to Shoshone Point, accessible only by foot or bike, can be a welcome pocket of peace during the summer heat and crowds. This little-known 2-mile round-trip hike is also ideal for children. Chances are you won't see another person, which means you can have the spectacular views all to yourself. It can be done in about an hour.

The trail starts from a dirt pullout along Desert View Dr, 1.2 miles east of Yaki Point or 6.3 miles west of Grandview Point. There's no official trailhead or signpost, so look for the dirt road barred by a closed and locked gate. The park service deliberately downplays this trail, which they make available from May to October for weddings and other private events. If the parking lot is full of cars, refrain from hiking out, out of respect for any private events taking place. When it hasn't been reserved for a special gathering, and during winter months, hikers are welcome on the trail. Because the trail is sandy, it isn't wheelchair-friendly.

Lookout Studio (p100)

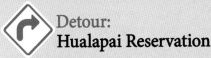

Detour:
Hualapai Reservation

The Hualapai Reservation borders many miles of the Colorado River northeast of the town of Kingman. In 1988, the Hualapai Nation opened **Grand Canyon West** (☎ 928-769-2636, 888-868-9378; www.grandcanyonwest.com) and the much-hyped **Skywalk** (per person $43-87; ⏰ 7am-7pm Apr-Sep, 8am-5pm Oct-Mar), offering a less-chaotic alternative to the South Rim.

The Skywalk itself is a horseshoe-shaped glass bridge cantilevered 4000ft above the canyon floor. Jutting out almost 70ft over the canyon, it allows visitors to see the canyon in one of the eeriest ways imaginable: through a glass walkway under your feet. Although the views here are less dramatic than those on the South Rim, the Skywalk is a completely novel – and exhilarating – experience.

Kingman lies 175 miles southwest of Grand Canyon Village via Hwy 180 and Hwy 40. The drive takes about three hours.

This is a great spot for a family gathering, as you'll find picnic tables, BBQ grills and portable toilets. Nearby Shoshone Point juts out into the canyon, offering magnificent views of the North Rim's full sweep. Unlike the other scenic points, there are no safety railings here. You can walk to the tip of the slender plateau and its Easter Island moai-like formation, where it feels almost possible to reach out and touch **Zoroaster Temple**.

BRIGHT ANGEL TRAIL   Hiking
(Map p98) The most popular of the corridor trails, the Bright Angel is wide, well graded and easy to follow. Although it's steep, it's equally attractive to first-time canyon hikers and seasoned pros, as well as mule trains, making it a heavily trafficked route. But the din doesn't lessen the sheer beauty. The steep and scenic 7.8-mile descent to the Colorado is punctuated with four logical turnaround spots, including two well-appointed resthouses (one at 1.5 miles down, another at 3 miles down) for opportunities to seek shade and hydration. Even if you're wary of crowds, you won't regret taking a jaunt of some length on the Bright Angel.

There is both shade and seasonal water on the Bright Angel (unlike the South Kaibab). Still, the summer heat can be crippling; day hikers should either turn around at one of the two resthouses or hit the trail at dawn to safely make the longer hikes to Indian Garden (4.6 miles down) and Plateau Point (6.1 miles down). Hiking to the Colorado for the day is not an option during the summer.

The trailhead of the oft-crowded Bright Angel Trail is smack in Grand Canyon Village, just west of Kolb Studio and Bright Angel Lodge. There's ample nearby parking, or you can take the shuttle bus to the Hermits Rest transfer stop and walk from there. The piñon-fringed trail quickly drops into some serious switchbacks as it follows a natural break in the cliffs of Kaibab limestone, the Toroweap formation and Coconino sandstone. The trail soon passes through two tunnels – look for the Indian pictographs on the walls of the first. After passing through the second, **Mile-and-a-Half Resthouse**, 1131ft and nearly an hour's hike from the top, comes into view. It has restrooms, an emergency phone and drinking water from May to September. Turning around here makes for a 2½-hour round-trip.

Continuing downward through different-colored rock layers, more switchbacks eventually deposit you 2112ft down at **Three-Mile Resthouse**, which has seasonal water and an emergency phone but no restrooms. Down below, you'll see the iridescent green tufts of Indian Garden tucked into a canyon fold, as well as the broad expanse of Tonto Platform, a nice visual reward before beginning the ascent back to the rim. First-time Grand Canyon hikers should strongly consider making Three-Mile Resthouse their turnaround point. Those with strong legs and a tolerance for heat can push on to the shady oasis of Indian Garden or, for a real challenge, Plateau Point and its gorgeous views of the inner gorge. Indian Garden can take five to seven hours round-trip and Plateau Point can take 10 hours round-trip.

SOUTH KAIBAB TRAIL   Hiking
(Map p98) One of the park's prettiest trails, the moderate-to-difficult South Kaibab combines stunning scenery and adventurous hiking with every step. The only corridor trail to follow a ridgeline instead of a drainage route, the red-dirt path traverses the spine of a crest, allowing for unobstructed 360-degree views. Blasted out of the rock by rangers in the mid-1920s, the South Kaibab is steep, rough and wholly exposed. The dearth of shade and water, combined with the

sheer grade, make ascending the South Kaibab particularly dangerous in summer, and rangers discourage all but the shortest of day hikes. The trail sees a fair number of rescues, with up to a half-dozen on a hot June day. Even if you're just hiking a few miles, plan on bringing a gallon of water.

Summer day hikers should turn around at **Cedar Ridge** (1.5 miles from the trailhead), perhaps the park's finest short day hike. Up to a two-hour round-trip with a 1140ft change in elevation, Cedar Ridge is a dazzling spot, particularly at sunrise, when the deep ruddy umbers and reds of each canyon fold seem to glow from within. This hike can also be done with a ranger; see p113. During the rest of the year, the continued trek to Skeleton Point, 1.5 miles beyond Cedar Ridge and 2040ft below the rim, makes for a fine three to five hour day hike – though the climb back up is a beast in any season.

The trailhead is 4.5 miles east of Grand Canyon Village along Yaki Point Rd, just shy of the point itself. To keep crowds in check during the high season, you're only permitted to park at the trailhead between December and February; all

Rafting (p110) on the Colorado River

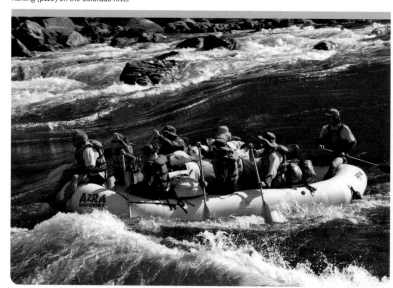

History of the Bright Angel

In one form or another, the Bright Angel Trail has been in continuous use for thousands of years. It was originally forged by the Havasupai tribe to access present-day Indian Garden, where they grew crops and farmed until the early 20th century. In the early 1890s prospectors Ralph Cameron and Pete Berry – who built the Grand View Hotel – improved the trail, eventually extending it to the river. Seeing a golden opportunity, Cameron imposed a $1 toll on anyone using the trail in 1903, a widely criticized decision. In response, the Atchison, Topeka and Santa Fe Railway and others constructed alternative toll-free trails, such as the Hermit, to draw the burgeoning mule tourism trade. In 1928 the park service took the reins of the Bright Angel and lifted the toll, thus ending mule traffic on the Hermit.

other times require a ride aboard either the Kaibab Trail Route shuttle or the far more direct Hikers' Express shuttle. Water and toilets are available at the trailhead.

GRANDVIEW TRAIL Hiking
(Map p98) One of the steepest trails in the park – dropping 1200ft in the first three-quarters of a mile – Grandview is also one of the finest and most popular day hikes. The payoff following the stunning (and grueling) descent is an up-close look at one of the inner canyon's sagebrush-tufted mesas and a wonderful sense of solitude. The trail spirals down to a sprawling horseshoe-shaped mesa, where Hopi people once collected minerals.

In 1892 miner Pete Berry improved the former Native American route and constructed the current trail to access his Last Chance Mine at Horseshoe Mesa. For the next 15 years mules carted high-grade copper from there to the rim.

The **Grandview Trailhead**, right beside where the hotel once stood, is at Grandview Point, 12 miles east of the village on Desert View Dr, with year-round parking. While rangers don't recommend the trek to Horseshoe Mesa in summer (there's no water on the very exposed trail, and the climb out is a doozy), it's not overly long and certainly doable for strong hikers strapped with a hydration system and hiking early or late. For a shorter but

still rewarding option, you can hike to **Coconino Saddle** and turn around there. Though it's only a 1.5-mile round-trip, it packs a quick and precipitous punch as you plunge 1600ft over less than a mile. With the exception of a few short level sections, the Grandview is a rugged, narrow and rocky trail and probably not the best choice for those skittish of heights or occasional loose footing. The steep drop-offs can be a bit scary, but although the trail is no longer maintained, Berry's metal-reinforced switchbacks have held up quite nicely.

HERMIT TRAIL Hiking
(Map p98) This wilderness trail descends into lovely Hermit Canyon by way of a cool spring. It's a rocky trip down, with some knee-wrenching switchbacks and long traverses that wend through the Supai cliffs. But if you set out early in the morning and take it slow, the Hermit offers a wonderfully serene day hike and glimpses into hidden corners. Offering several good turnaround spots and a clear shot to the Colorado River, the trail is equally appealing to both day hikers and backcountry adventurers. The hike can take up to four hours.

In 1912 the Atchison, Topeka and Santa Fe Railway developed the trail (originally called El Tovar) for tourists to avoid tolls on the then privately controlled Bright Angel Trail. Mule trains ferried travelers to cushy Hermit Camp, which boasted a fancy stone cabin outfitted with a stove, glass windows, beds, and wood floors adorned with Navajo rugs. Supplies arrived via tram from Pima Point.

The trail was eventually renamed in honor of Louis 'The Hermit' Boucher (see Hermits Rest, p103). When the NPS gained control of Bright Angel in 1928, luring away the mule tourism business, the Hermit was abandoned. Though officially untended since then, the trail is in remarkably good condition.

The best destinations for day hikers are to **Santa Maria Spring** (5 miles round-trip, 1760ft elevation change) or to **Dripping Springs** via a spur trail (around 7 miles round-trip, 1440ft elevation change). For a shorter but still worthwhile hike, turn around at the Waldron Trail junction in Waldron Basin, a round-trip of just under 3 miles with 1240ft of elevation change. The upper section of the Hermit is well shaded in the morning, making it a cool option in summer.

The **Hermit Trailhead** is at the end of its namesake road, 8 miles west of Grand Canyon Village and about 500ft from Hermits Rest. Although the road is only accessible via shuttle bus during the summer peak season, overnight backpackers are permitted to park at the lot near the trailhead throughout the year, while day hikers may park here in the winter.

Backpacking

Without venturing below the rim, it's impossible to truly appreciate the grandeur and depth – both literal and figurative – of the Grand Canyon, one of the world's deepest chasms. Hiking down through ancient layers of rock is a singularly surreal journey through geologic time, and the difference in ecology between rim and river is truly unique. Outdoor enthusiasts should plan to spend at least a night or two in the inner gorge to explore side canyons and tributaries of the rich wilderness along the Colorado.

Overnight hikes into the canyon require a backcountry permit, applications for which are taken up to four months in advance. If you didn't secure a backcountry permit beforehand, try your luck at the **Backcountry Information Center** (Grand Canyon Village; ☏/fax 928-638-7875; ⏰8am-noon & 1-5pm), located near Maswik Lodge.

The Bright Angel Trail is a superb option for both first-time and veteran canyon hikers alike. This well-marked trail (p107) can be extended into a three-day, 18.6 mile round-trip backpacking adventure.

Another option is hiking South Kaibab to Bright Angel, a difficult 16.1-mile one-way trek that takes two days.

The two-day Hermit Trail to Hermit Creek Camp is a steep but rewarding out-and-back trek that descends to the river and Vishnu schist, the oldest exposed rock of the canyon's layers. It's a 15.6-mile round-trip hike beginning at Hermits Rest Trailhead. The same trailhead is the starting point for the Hermit Trail to Bright Angel hike, a 27-mile trek that takes three to four days. This is a stunning journey but may require some route finding, making it off limits for first-time canyon hikers.

River Rafting

Rafting the national park stretch of the Colorado is a virtual all-access pass to the Grand Canyon, in all its wildness, peace and ancient glory. The canyon section of the river, which runs 277 miles from Lees Ferry to Lake Mead, has more than 160 sets of rapids. The biggest single drop (from the top to the base of the rapids) is 37ft, and nearly 20 rapids drop 15ft or more. Along the length of the river, the side canyons and tributaries feeding into the Colorado provide a wealth of hidden places to explore.

The river is run year-round, though access to some sections is limited under certain conditions. Most commercial trips operate between April and October, with June, July and August being the peak months. Due to their popularity, rafting trips often sell out a year in advance. However, a small percentage of

JOHN ELK III / LONELY PLANET IMAGES ©

Don't Miss Dripping Springs Trail

What better reason to tackle a hike than to answer the question 'What would the Hermit do?' The trailhead at which you will address this inquiry is at Hermits Rest. From here, you will begin an excellent day hike to Dripping Springs, a must see destination for South Rim hikers curious to see why Louis Boucher (p101) made this secluded spot his home.

From the trailhead, follow the Hermit Trail for 2 miles. At the junction with the Dripping Springs Trail, turn left and head west along the narrow path as it climbs and meanders along the slope's contours. In a mile you'll hit the Boucher Trail; turn left here to continue following the Dripping Springs Trail as it wends up toward the water source, which sprouts from an overhang not far beneath the rim. Droplets shower down from the sandstone ceiling, misting a myriad of maidenhair ferns, and here you will find your answers.

This moderate-to-difficult hike is 7 miles round-trip and takes up to five hours and has an elevation change of 1440ft.

cancellations do occur, so it's sometimes possible to get in on a trip at the last minute.

The easiest way to book river trips is to contact the Flagstaff-based booking agency **Rivers & Oceans** (☺928-526-4575, 800-473-4576; www.rivers-oceans.com); it works with all of the area's companies running trips on the Colorado and doesn't charge a booking fee. The company can

point you to the few operators that offer daytrips.

Arizona Raft Adventures Rafting
(☏928-786-7238, 800-786-7238; www.azraft.com; 6-day Upper Canyon hybrid trips/paddle trips $1940/2040, 10-day Full Canyon motor trips $2830) This multigenerational family-run outfit offers paddle, oar, hybrid (with opportunities for both paddling and floating) and motor trips.

Mule rides, Bright Angel Trail

JOHN ELK III / LONELY PLANET IMAGES ©

Arizona River Runners   Rafting
(☎602-867-4866, 800-477-7238; www.raft arizona.com; 6-day Upper Canyon oar trips $1795, 12-day Full Canyon motor trips $2695) Has been at the game since 1970, offering oar-powered and motorized trips.

Colorado River & Trail Expeditions   Rafting
(☎801-261-1789, 800-253-7328; www.crateinc. com; 5-day Upper Canyon oar, paddle or hybrid trips $1857, 9-day motor trips $2752) Offering a range of motorized and oar-powered trips, this outfit also includes transportation to or from Las Vegas.

Grand Canyon Whitewater   Rafting
(☎928-645-8866, 800-343-3121; www.grand canyonwhitewater.com; 6-day Upper Canyon oar trips $1600, 8-day Full Canyon motor trips $2355) With a new name, this formerly family-owned business is run by a new team of old hands who have been running the Colorado since the '70s. Offers both oar and motorized trips.

Hatch River Expeditions   Rafting
(☎800-856-8966; www.hatchriverexpeditions. com; 4-day Upper Canyon motor trips $1199, 7-day Full Canyon oar trips $2310) Hatch has been

around since 1929 – though of course the motorized rafts are a more recent introduction – and is a reliable company for those seeking a faster trip down the river.

OARS   Rafting
(☎209-736-4677, 800-346-6277; www.oars. com; 6-day Upper Canyon oar trips $2608, 15-day Full Canyon dory trips $5010) One of the best outfitters out there, OARS offers oar, paddle and dory trips and gives you the option of carbon-offsetting your trip.

Western River Expeditions   Rafting
(☎801-942-6669, 866-904-1160; www.western river.com; 7-day Upper & Middle Canyon motor trips $2695) Taking out at Whitmore Wash, these river trips can last for six or seven days. There are also half- to two-day paddle or inflatable kayak trips starting and ending in Moab, Utah.

Wilderness River Adventures   Rafting
(☎928-645-3296, 800-992-8022; www. riveradventures.com; 6-day Full Canyon motor trips $2135, 12-day Full Canyon oar trips $3520) Wilderness River Adventures also offers hybrid trips that offer rafters the chance to paddle or float as on an oar-powered trip. Day trips are offered as well.

Cycling

Cyclists have limited options inside the park, as bicycles are only allowed on paved roads and the Greenway Trail. The multi-use Greenway Trail, open to cyclists as well as pedestrians and wheelchairs, stretches about 13 miles from Hermits Rest all the way to the South Kaibab Trailhead.

Hermit Rd offers a scenic ride west to Hermits Rest, about 16 miles round-trip from the village. Shuttles ply this road every 10 to 15 minutes between March and November (the rest of the year, traffic is minimal). They are not permitted to pass cyclists, so for the first 4 miles you'll have to pull over each time one drives by. However, starting from the Abyss, a completed section of the Greenway Trail diverges from the road and continues separately all the way to Hermits Rest.

Alternatively, you could ride out to the East Entrance along Desert View Dr (p103), a 50-mile round-trip from the village. The route is largely shuttle-free but sees a lot of car traffic in summer. Just off Desert View Dr, the 1-mile dirt road to Shoshone Point (p106) is an easy, nearly level ride that ends at this secluded panoramic vista, one of the few places to escape South Rim crowds.

BRIGHT ANGEL BICYCLES   Bicycle Rental
(Map p98; ☎928-814-8704; www.bikegrand canyon.com; full-day adult/child $35/25; ⏱8am-6pm May-Sep, 10am-4:30pm Mar-Apr & Oct-Nov, weather permitting) Located in the P4 parking lot of the Grand Canyon Visitors Center, Bright Angel Bicycles rents 'cruiser' bikes for rides around the South Rim. Rates include helmet and bicycle-lock rental; child trailers also available. You can even arrange for shuttle pickups and/or drop-offs.

Mule Rides

Mosey into the canyon the way tourists traveled a century ago, on the back of a sure-footed mule. Half-day and overnight mule trips into the canyon depart every day of the year from the corral west of Bright Angel Lodge.

Due to erosion concerns, the NPS has limited inner-canyon mule rides to those traveling all the way to Phantom Ranch. Rather than going below the rim, three-hour day trips ($119) now take riders along the rim, through the ponderosa, piñon and juniper forest to the Abyss overlook. Riders dismount to enjoy the view and a snack before heading back to the village.

Overnight trips (one/two people $482/850) and two-night trips (one/two people $701/1170) still follow the Bright Angel Trail to the river, traveling east on the River Trail and crossing the river on the Kaibab Suspension Bridge. Riders spend the night at Phantom Ranch. It's a 5½-hour, 10-mile trip to Phantom Ranch, but the return trip up the 8-mile South Kaibab Trail is an hour shorter. Overnight trips include dorm accommodations and all meals at Phantom.

Don't plan a mule trip assuming it's the easiest way to travel below the rim. It's a bumpy ride on a hard saddle, and unless you're used to riding a horse regularly you will be saddle-sore afterwards. Mule trips are popular and fill up quickly; to book a trip more than 24 hours and up to 13 months in advance, call **Xanterra** (☎888-297-2757, 303-297-2757; www.grandcanyon lodges.com/mule-rides-716.html). If you arrive at the park and want to join a mule trip the following day, ask about availability at the transportation desk at Bright Angel Lodge (your chances are much better during the off season).

Ranger Programs

Free ranger programs are one of the park's greatest treasures. Lasting 30 minutes to four hours, the talks and walks cover subjects ranging from fossils to condors to Native American history. Programs are held throughout the park and often involve a short walk. *The Guide* provides a complete listing of current ranger programs, including a short description and the location, time and duration of each program. A kiosk at Canyon View

Information Plaza also clearly explains current programs.

The **Cedar Ridge Hike** is one regular offering. It involves a strenuous 3-mile hike (two to four hours round-trip) 1140ft below the rim on the South Kaibab Trail. While you can take this trail by yourself, the ranger will explain canyon geology and history as you hike. It departs from the South Kaibab Trailhead at 8am. Take the green Kaibab Trail Route shuttle from Canyon View Information Plaza to access the trailhead.

On the one-hour **Geology** and **Fossil Walks**, both offered daily, you can brush up on your knowledge of brachiopods and learn about the canyon's rich history. The Fossil Walk is an easy half-mile one-way walk to exposed fossil beds along the rim, a particularly nice activity if you plan on hiking into the canyon from Hermits Rest. If you attend the ranger talk, you'll be able to recognize fossils that lie about 10 minutes down the trail.

Each evening program at McKee Amphitheater examines a significant aspect of the canyon's natural or cultural history. Subjects change nightly; check the kiosk at the Canyon View Information Plaza.

Cross-Country Skiing

From November to March, depending on snowfall, the surrounding national forest offers several trails for cross-country skiing and snowshoeing. Trails around Grandview Point may be groomed. Contact the **Tusayan Ranger Station** (☏ 928-638-2443) for current information. You can rent skis from several outdoor shops in Flagstaff, where you'll also find plenty of cross-country and downhill trails.

Flyovers

At press time, over 300 flyovers of the Grand Canyon were still departing daily from Tusayan and Las Vegas. However, the NPS and the Federal Aviation Administration were also inviting public comments on a draft environmental impact report in June 2011, which may have implications for the number or existence of scenic flyovers at Grand Canyon National Park. Flights have already been restricted in number, altitude and routes to reduce noise pollution affecting the experience of

Kolb Studio (p100)

DAVID TOMLINSON / LONELY PLANET IMAGES ©

other visitors and wildlife. If you choose to take a flight and you're concerned about flight noise, ask whether the company uses quiet technology (QT) helicopters, which provide a quieter experience. Flight operators include the following:

Grand Canyon Airlines (866-235-9422, 928-638-2359; www.grandcanyonairlines.com)

Grand Canyon Helicopters (928-638-2764, 702-835-8477; www.gtgrandcanyonhelicoptersaz.com)

Maverick Helicopters (888-261-4414; www.maverickhelicopter.com)

Papillon Grand Canyon Helicopters (888-635-7272, 702-736-7243; www.papillon.com)

Scenic Airlines (866-235-9422; www.scenic.com)

Tours

Narrated bus tours offer a good introduction to the canyon, as drivers stop at the best viewpoints, point out the various buttes, mesas and plateaus, and offer historical anecdotes. Bus tours depart daily from Maswik, Yavapai and Bright Angel Lodges, last two to four hours and cost anywhere from $14.50 to $57.

The best places to book bus tours are at the **Transportation Desks** (928-638-2631, ext 6015; 8am-5pm) in the lobbies of Bright Angel, Yavapai and Maswik Lodges. You can also book same- or next-day mule trips, and staff can answer questions about horseback rides, scenic flights and smooth-water float trips.

Sleeping

At the South Rim, you can sleep under the stars in one of the park's three campgrounds or choose a cabin or comfortable lodge room. Mather and Trailer Village campgrounds take reservations and are open year-round, while Desert View is open May through September and does not accept reservations. There's a seven-day limit at all three campgrounds.

Xanterra (888-297-2757; www.grandcanyonlodges.com) operates all park lodges, as well as Trailer Village. You can make reservations up to 13 months in advance; visit the website for more information and photos. For same-day reservations or to reach any lodge, call the **South Rim switchboard** (928-638-2631).

In summer or during the holidays, you may find that there are no rooms left at the village inns; instead, consider a chain hotel or motel in Tusayan or, for better options, Williams.

Camping

The **National Park Service** (877-444-6777; www.recreation.gov) operates Mather and Desert View Campgrounds. Reservations for Mather are accepted up to six months in advance until the day before your arrival. From mid-November through February, sites at Mather Campground are first-come, first-served.

DESERT VIEW CAMPGROUND Campground $
(Map p98; 928-638-7893; campsites $12; May–mid-Oct) Set back from the road in a quiet piñon-juniper forest near the East Entrance, this first-come, first-served campground is a peaceful alternative to the more crowded and busy Mather Campground. The lovely sites are spread out enough to ensure some privacy. You'll find toilets and drinking water but no showers or hookups.

MATHER CAMPGROUND Campground $
(Map p98; 928-638-7851; campsites/group sites $18/50; year-round) Though Mather has over 300 campsites, it's actually a pleasant and relatively quiet place to camp. Piñon and juniper trees offer plenty of shade, sites are well dispersed and the flat ground offers a comfy platform for your tent. If you're longing for pristine wilderness, look elsewhere, but if you just want a guaranteed site with ample facilities, this is your best bet. You'll find pay showers, laundry facilities, drinking water, toilets and grills, but no hookups.

Detour:
Sedona

Nestled amid alien-looking red sandstone formations at the south end of Oak Creek Canyon, Sedona attracts spiritual seekers, artists, healers, and day-trippers from Phoenix trying to escape the oppressive heat. Many New Agers believe that this area is the center of vortexes (not 'vortices' in Sedona) that radiate the earth's power, and Sedona's combination of scenic beauty and mysticism draws throngs of tourists year-round. You'll find all sorts of alternative medicines and practices, from psychic channeling, past-life regression, crystal healing, shamanism and drumming workshops to more traditional massages, yoga, tai chi and acupressure. The surrounding canyons offer excellent hiking and mountain biking, and the town itself bustles with art galleries and expensive gourmet restaurants.

There are plenty of lodging options in town, including the wonderful **Briar Patch Inn** (☎ 928-282-2342, 888-809-3030; www.briarpatchinn.com; 3190 N Hwy Alt 89; cottages $219-395; 🛜 👪), which has 19 log cottages nestled into nine wooded acres along Oak Creek.

Rancho Sedona RV Park (☎ 928-282-7255, 888-641-4261; www.ranchosedona.com; 135 Bear Wallow Ln; RV sites $31-63) includes a laundry, showers and 30 RV sites, most with full hookups. There are also several **USFS campgrounds** (☎ 928-282-4119, 877-444-6777; www.recreation.gov) along Hwy Alt 89.

Sedona lies 108 miles (130 minutes by car) south of Grand Canyon Village, via Hwy 180 and Hwy Alt 89.

Lodging

EL TOVAR
Lodge $$$

(Map p98; ☎ 888-297-2757; www.grandcanyonlodges.com; d $178-273, ste $335-426; ❄ 🛜)
Its exposed beams, dark-wood interiors, bronzes and stately presence continue to define El Tovar as a quintessential 1905 national-park lodge. It appeals to those visitors seeking more than a roadside motel, and even day-trippers are lured in by the wide, inviting porches that wreathe the rambling wood structure, offering pleasant spots for people-watching and canyon sunsets. The original guestrooms were remodeled to accommodate private baths, thus many of the standard double rooms are incredibly small – ask for the slightly more expensive deluxe room. Those in a mood to splurge can stay in one of three rim-view suites, all with sitting rooms and private porches looking out onto full canyon views. These are the only rooms in the park with a full rim view, and they're often booked more than a year in advance.

BRIGHT ANGEL LODGE
Lodge $$

(Map p98; www.grandcanyonlodges.com; Grand Canyon Village; d without/with private bath $81/92, cabin $113-178; ⊙year-round; ❄ @ 🛜)
Built in 1935, this log-and-stone lodge on the ledge offers travelers more historic charm and nicer rooms than you'll find at most other accommodations on the South Rim. You will find two restaurants, a snack bar and a small, nondescript bar with a TV. In 2001 all rooms at Bright Angel were refurbished in keeping with architect Mary Colter's original design. The least expensive rooms in the park are the doubles with shared (immaculate) bath, which offer a double bed, a desk and a sink. The bathroom is down the hall, there are no TVs, and the pleasant rooms are nothing extraordinary, but this is a great price for a perch right on the rim (no views, however). Powell suites feature two bedrooms and a tub but no

shower or TV; each holds up to seven people.

Cabins at Bright Angel, many decorated in rustic Western style, offer more character.

PHANTOM RANCH Cabins $

(Map p98; ☎888-297-2757; dm $43; ❄) Sitting at the bottom of the canyon floor, Phantom can only be reached by foot, mule or floating river conveyance. Built along the north bank of the Colorado River, stone cottages offer cozy private cabins sleeping up to 10 on bunks, as well as dormitory-style bunks in single-sex cabins outfitted for 10 people. Bunk prices include bedding, soap, shampoo and towels; meals are extra and must be reserved. If you'd rather skip the expensive meals, you may bring your own food and stove. After dinner each night, the dining room converts into a canteen that serves beer, wine and hot drinks – it's a good venue to meet fellow riverside ramblers.

MASWIK LODGE Lodge $$

(Map p98; d South/North $92/173, cabins $92; ❄@🛜) Located a quarter-mile from the rim near the Backcountry Information Center, the Maswik Lodge comprises 16 two-story wood-and-stone buildings set in the woods. Rooms at Maswik North feature private patios, high ceilings and forest views, while rooms at the less expensive Maswik South are smaller and don't offer much of a view.

YAVAPAI LODGE Lodge $$

(Map p98; d West/East $114/163; ⏾Apr-Oct; ❄🛜) Sure, it's your basic motel, but it lies more than a mile from the traffic and chaos of the central village. The lodgings are stretched out amid a peaceful piñon and juniper forest,

yet you can pull your car right up to your door.

KACHINA & THUNDERBIRD LODGES Lodge $$

(Map p98; d streetside/rimside $173/184; ❄) Beside the Rim Trail between El Tovar and Bright Angel, these institutional-looking lodges offer standard motel-style rooms with two queen beds, full bath and TV. It's worth spending up a little for the rimside rooms, some with partial canyon views. Neither lodge has a lobby or front desk – guests at Kachina check in at El Tovar, while those at Thunderbird check in at Bright Angel.

Eating & Drinking

Grand Canyon Village has all the eating options you need, whether it's picking up picnic parts at Canyon Village Marketplace, enjoying an après-hike ice-cream cone at Bright Angel Fountain or sitting down for a celebratory dinner at El Tovar.

O'Neill Butte, South Kaibab Trail (p108)
JOHN ELK III / LONELY PLANET IMAGES ©

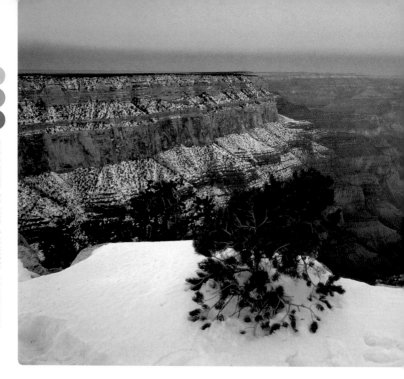

Hours listed here are for the summer and may vary in slower seasons.

All South Rim bars close at 11pm, and drinks are prohibited along the rim itself.

EL TOVAR
DINING ROOM International $$$

(Map p98; ☎928-638-2631, ext 6432; El Tovar; mains $18-31; ☺6:30-11am, 11:30am-2pm & 5-10pm) If at all possible, treat yourself to at least one meal at historic El Tovar. The memorable surroundings feature dark wood, tables set with china and white linen, and huge picture windows with views of the rim and canyon beyond. The service is excellent, the menu creative, the portions big and the food very good – much better than you might expect at a place that knows it's the only gig in town.

Inside the bar at El Tovar is a dark and cozy lounge, with big, cushioned chairs and stained glass. But if you prefer a sunnier outlook, the patio just outside the bar is a great spot to sit with a glass of sustainable sauvignon blanc and watch people strolling along the rim.

ARIZONA ROOM American $$

(Map p98; Bright Angel Lodge; mains $8-28; ☺11:30am-3pm Mar-Oct & 4:30-10pm Mar-Dec) A wonderful balance between casual and upscale, this busy restaurant is one of the best options for dinner on the South Rim. Antler chandeliers hang from the ceiling, and picture windows overlook a small lawn, the rim walk and the canyon beyond. Waits are long unless you get there when the doors open.

BRIGHT ANGEL
RESTAURANT American $$

(Map p98; Bright Angel Lodge; mains $10-26; ☺6:30am-10pm; ⁂) With exposed wood beams and an adobe-style interior, this busy family-style restaurant is not without its simple charm. Menu offerings include burgers, fajitas, salads, pasta and other down-home sorts of dishes.

Families with small children gravitate here, so it can get loud.

PHANTOM RANCH CANTEEN
American $$$

(Map p98; Phantom Ranch; mains $27-42; ☾5am & 6:30am breakfast, 5pm & 6:30pm dinner) On the canyon floor, Phantom Ranch offers family-style meals on a set menu: hearty stew, steaks and vegetarian chili, as well as hearty breakfasts and sack lunches for the trail. Seating hours change seasonally. You must make meal reservations before your descent, ideally when you reserve your accommodations. The canteen is open to the public for cold lemonade and packaged snacks between 8am and 4pm, and for beer, wine and hot drinks from 8pm to 10pm.

CANYON VIEW DELI
Cafeteria $

(Map p98; ☎928-631-2262; Market Plaza; mains $4-7; ☾7am-8pm) This counter in the village grocery store is the best place to find a freshly made sandwich for a picnic, as well as premade salads and hot dishes like pizza and fried chicken. Morning offerings include breakfast burritos, doughnuts and coffee.

MASWIK CAFETERIA
Cafeteria $

(Map p98; Maswik Lodge; mains $4-10; ☾6am-10pm) The term 'cafeteria' should tip you off to the fare, setup and seating. Though fairly predictable, the food encompasses a nice variety and isn't too greasy. The various food stations serve burgers, sandwiches, fried chicken, Mexican food and even Vietnamese *pho*.

The adjoining Maswik Pizza Pub shows sporting events on TV and serves a decent selection of draft beer and wine.

CANYON VILLAGE MARKETPLACE
Market $

(Map p98; ☎928-631-2262; Market Plaza; ☾8am-8pm) The biggest source for supplies on either rim, this market offers everything you'd expect from your local grocery store, including a fair selection of organic items and over-the-counter medications. You may prefer to stock up on groceries in Williams, Flagstaff or Sedona, as prices and selection are better outside the park.

 Information

Entrance Fees & Passes

The $25-per-vehicle park entrance fee permits unlimited visits to both rims within seven days of purchase. Those entering by bicycle, motorcycle or on foot pay $12. Interagency and senior passes are valid.

Opening Dates

The South Rim, including campgrounds, lodging and restaurants, is open 24 hours a day, 365 days a year. Entrance kiosks are unstaffed at night.

Tourist Information

Canyon View Information Plaza (Map p98; ☎928-638-7644; ☺8am-5pm) Three hundred yards behind Mather Point, Canyon View Information Plaza encompasses this visitor center and the Books & More Store. Outside the visitor center, bulletin boards and kiosks display information on ranger programs, the weather, tours and hikes. Rangers offer daily talks on a variety of subjects.

Desert View Information Center (Map p98; ☎928-638-7893; ☺9am-5pm) Housed in a small stone building near the East Entrance, this staffed information center also offers books and maps.

Verkamp's Visitor Center (Grand Canyon Village; ☺8am-7pm) Next to Hopi House, Verkamp features a display about the building's history.

Park Policies & Regulations

○ Bicycles are allowed only on roads open to other vehicles, and on the Greenway Trail on the South Rim.

○ This is extremely dry country, and the slightest spark may cause a devastating wildfire. Open fires are prohibited in the park except at established campgrounds on the rim.

○ Dogs are permitted on developed South Rim trails and in the campgrounds but must be leashed at all times. Pets are not allowed in park lodges or below the rim, except for certified service dogs.

○ Weapons of any kind, including guns and bows, are prohibited on park grounds.

○ It's illegal to feed wildlife in the park, including jump-in-your-lap squirrels and forward ravens. This is not only for your safety (squirrels can carry bubonic plague!), but also for the well-being of the animals.

Maps

The Grand Canyon National Park Service website (www.nps.gov/grca) has numerous good maps to peruse (or print) before you head out. The park newspaper also contains a good, non-topographical map for basic park orientation.

Dangers & Annoyances

For the casual visitor to the park, health and safety usually requires little effort apart from keeping sufficiently hydrated and not goofing around on the rim.

As the South Rim is more than 7000ft above sea level and the North Rim 8801ft at its highest point, altitude sickness is fairly common.

If you're hiking below the rim, beware of flash floods. Even if the sky overhead is clear, distant rainstorms can send walls of water, debris and mud roaring through side canyons without warning.

Finally, there are the ledges. Just about every year people fall to their death at the Grand Canyon. Stay on the trails, refrain from stepping over guardrails, and absolutely do not allow children to run along the rim. There isn't as much railing as you may expect.

ⓘ Getting There & Around

Air

Phoenix's **Sky Harbor International Airport** (PHX; ☎602-273-3300 www.skyharbor.com) is 230 miles (about four hours) south of Grand Canyon Village. The next closest major international airport is Las Vegas' **McCarran International Airport** (LAS; ☎702-261-4636; www.mccarran. com), 275 miles west of Grand Canyon Village.

Car

The South Rim has two vehicle entrances: the South Entrance and the East Entrance. The South Entrance is reached by Hwy 180 from Tusayan (two miles south), Valle (22 miles south) and Flagstaff (80 miles south). From Williams (30 miles west of Flagstaff on I-40), Hwy 64 heads north to Valle, where it connects with Hwy 180 to the park.

For the East Entrance, take Hwy 89 from Flagstaff to Cameron, where Hwy 64 heads west to the park entrance. It is 25 miles from the East Entrance to Grand Canyon Village.

Once parked outside your hotel or in a public lot, your car can remain there as long as you're on the South Rim. All services and points of interest are accessible via the free shuttles, a hassle-free alternative to traffic and parking.

Shuttle

Free shuttle buses ply three routes along the South Rim. In the pre-dawn hours, shuttles run every half-hour or so and typically begin running about an hour before sunrise; check *The Guide* for current sunrise and sunset information. From early morning until after sunset, buses run every 15 minutes. *The Guide* features exact seasonal operating hours relevant to your visit, along with a map of shuttle stops. Maps are also posted at all shuttle stops and inside the shuttles themselves.

 Sights

NATIONAL GEOGRAPHIC VISITOR CENTER   Visitor Center
(Map p98; ☏928-638-2468; www.explorethe canyon.com; 450 Hwy 64; adult/child $13/10; ⏱8:30am-8:30pm Mar-Oct, 10:30am-6:30pm Nov-Feb) Hourly, on the half-hour, the IMAX theater here screens a terrific 34-minute film called *Grand Canyon – The Hidden Secrets*. With exhilarating river-running scenes and virtual-reality drops off canyon rims, the film plunges you into the history and geology of the canyon through the eyes of ancient Native Americans, John Wesley Powell and a soaring eagle.

 Sleeping

Some of these motels offer a touch more character than you'd find at most other American roadside motels, but don't expect anything particularly memorable.

AROUND THE SOUTH RIM

Tusayan

The friendly little town of Tusayan, situated 1 mile south of the park's South Entrance along Hwy 64, is basically a half-mile strip of hotels and restaurants catering to Grand Canyon visitors. It makes a good base if accommodations inside the park are booked up, and it does offer conveniences like a general store, gas station, souvenir shop and espresso bar with internet access. The Tusayan Ranger Station sits just outside the park's South Entrance.

Horseback riders at sunset
HOLGER LEUE / LONELY PLANET IMAGES ©

GRAND HOTEL
Hotel $$$

(☎ 928-638-3333, 888-634-7263; www.grand canyongrandhotel.com; 149 Hwy 64; d $190-220; ❄ 🛜 ≋) Public spaces at this Western themed hotel include a big fireplace, high ceilings, woven rugs, stone floors and faux pine beams. Relatively large, comfortable rooms are filled with pleasing Mission-style furniture, and the ones in back face the woods.

BEST WESTERN GRAND CANYON SQUIRE INN
Hotel $$$

(☎ 928-638-2681, 800-622-6966; www. grandcanyonsquire.com; 100 Hwy 64; d $260; ❄ @ 🛜 ≋ 👬) This is the only resort-style accommodation in Tusayan. Amenities include a restaurant, popular sports bar, bowling alley, pool tables, fitness center, coin laundry and outdoor pool (open seasonally).

TEN-X CAMPGROUND
Camping $

(Map p98; ☎ 928-638-7851; sites per vehicle $10; ☽ May-Sep) Woodsy and peaceful, this first-come, first-served USFS campground lies 2 miles south of Tusayan on Hwy 64. It has 70 sites and can fill up early in the summer. You'll find large sites, picnic tables, fire rings and BBQ grills, water and toilets, but no showers. There are pull-through sites for RVs but they don't have hookups.

Eating

Considering the number of tourists that pass through Tusayan annually, the village manages to retain a sort of old-fashioned, roadside-hub pace. There's an OK variety of eateries to choose from, but as yet no one has established a notable culinary presence.

SOPHIE'S MEXICAN KITCHEN
Mexican $$

(☎ 928-638-1105; 110 Hwy 64; mains $10-16; ☽ 11am-9pm; 👬) Festooned with colorful *papel picado* (cut-paper banners), this cheery restaurant in Tuayan's Grand Canyon Village Shops offers Mexican food like street-style tacos, fajitas and a few vegetarian options like chile rellenos.

RP'S STAGE STOP
Cafe $

(☎ 928-638-3115; 400 Hwy 64; mains $3-7; ☽ 7am-8pm; 🛜) The only place in Tusayan to grab an espresso drink and pick up a sandwich for your picnic lunch.

Grand Canyon Railway train

STEPHEN SAKS / LONELY PLANET IMAGES ©

WE COOK PIZZA & PASTA   Pizzeria $$

(☑ 928-638-2278; 504 Hwy 64; mains $10-20; ⏰ 11am-10pm; 👤) This cavernous, busy pizza joint is the kind of place where you order, take a number, and then unceremoniously chow down on mediocre pizza.

CORONADO ROOM   American $$$

(☑ 928-638-2681; 100 Hwy 64; mains $13-30; ⏰ 5-10pm; 👤) In a town where the pickings are very slim, the house restaurant at the Best Western Grand Canyon Squire Inn serves the classiest cuisine around.

ℹ Information

Park passes are available at the National Geographic Visitor Center when a ranger is on duty.

ℹ Getting Around

You can walk to most places along the highway through Tusayan.

Williams

A pretty slow spot by day, Williams comes to life in the evening when the Grand Canyon Railway train returns with passengers from the South Rim...and then closes down on the early side. Route 66 passes through the main historic district as a one-way street headed east; one-way Railroad Ave parallels the tracks and heads west.

Lining these two thoroughfares is downtown Williams.

◎ Sights & Activities

There are plenty of opportunities for **hiking** and **biking** in nearby Kaibab, Coconino and Prescott National Forests. Ask at the visitor center or at the ranger station for maps and information.

GRAND CANYON RAILWAY   Rail Tour

(☑ 800-843-8724; www.thetrain.com) Following a 9:30am **Wild West show** by the tracks, the historic Grand Canyon Railway train departs for its two-hour ride to the South Rim. If you're only visiting the rim for the day, this is a fun and hassle-free way to travel. You can leave the car behind and enjoy the park by foot, shuttle or tour bus.

BEARIZONA   Zoo

(☑ 928-635-2289; www.bearizona.com; 1500 E Route 66; adult/child/under 4yr $16/8/free; ⏰ 8am-5pm Mar-Nov) Established in 2010, the awesomely named Bearizona is a drive-through 'wildlife park' inhabited by indigenous North American fauna. Visitors drive themselves along a road that winds through various fenced enclosures over 160 acres, where they can see roaming gray wolves, bison, bighorn sheep and black bears up close. There's also a walk-through section that features bobcats, javelinas, skunks and heart-meltingly adorable baby bears.

Sleeping

Camping

Three pleasant USFS campgrounds near Williams offer year-round camping without hookups. Contact the visitor center or the Williams Ranger Station for information.

CATARACT LAKE CAMPGROUND   Campground $

(tent & RV sites $14; ⏰ May-Sep) To get to this pleasant, woodsy USFS campground, take exit 161 off I-40 and head north for 2 miles. Note that the campground is not only right next to pretty Cataract Lake but also the BN-Santa Fe Railway tracks – trains run regularly all night long.

WHITE HORSE LAKE CAMPGROUND   Campground $

(tent & RV sites $18) Nineteen miles southeast of town, this campground offers a hiking trail and fishing; from town, drive 8 miles on 4th St and turn left on FR 110.

RAILSIDE RV RANCH   RV Campground $

(☑ 928-635-4077, 888-635-4077; www.railsidervranch.com; 877 Rodeo Rd; RV sites $36-38; 📶 👤) The closest campground to downtown Williams, with 96 RV hookups. There's no shade, but the campground has coin showers, a pet wash, free wi-fi and a playground.

Lodging

RED GARTER BED & BAKERY
B&B $$

(☎928-635-1484, 800-328-1484; www.redgarter.com; 137 W Railroad Ave; d $120-145; ❄️📶) Up until the 1940s, gambling and girls were the draw at this 1897 bordello-turned-B&B across from the tracks. Nowadays, the place trades on its historic charm and reputation for hauntings. Of the four restored rooms, the suite was once reserved for the house's 'best gals,' who would lean out the window to flag down customers. Set back from the road, the other three rooms are smaller and quieter.

GRAND CANYON HOTEL
Boutique Hotel $

(☎928-635-1419; www.thegrandcanyonhotel.com; 145 W Route 66; dm $28, d with shared bath $60, d $70-125; ❄️@📶) This charming spot is just what this town needed – a European-style hotel in a historic 1889 building right on Route 66. There's air-con in interior rooms and the place is run by very friendly proprietors.

FIRELIGHT B&B
B&B $$

(☎928-635-0200, 888-838-8218; www.firelightbedandbreakfast.com; 175 W Meade Ave, Williams; r $160-175, ste $250; ❄️📶) Four well-appointed and tastefully decorated rooms in this Tudor-style house all have their own fireplaces. A gourmet breakfast is served every morning by your hosts Debi (the interior designer) and Eric. This romantic spot is adults only.

LODGE ON ROUTE 66
Motel $$

(☎928-635-4534, 877-563-4366; www.thelodgeonroute66.com; 200 E Route 66; r $85-100, ste $135-185; ❄️📶) The Lodge is a beautifully designed blend of Route 66 motel with low-key Southwestern style (ie no Kokopelli motif). Sturdy dark-wood furniture and wrought-iron accents give an elegant feel. Standard rooms are on the cramped side, but roomier suites feature kitchenettes.

GRAND LIVING BED & BREAKFAST
B&B $$

(☎928-635-4171, 800-210-5908; www.grandlivingbnb.com; 701 Quarter Horse Rd; r & ste $140-290; ❄️📶) Spacious rooms are named after flowers in this bigger B&B, grandly designed with antique oak and cherry furniture, king- or queen-sized beds, TVs and fireplaces. Gourmet breakfasts are served in the airy dining room.

CANYON MOTEL & RV PARK
Motel $

(☎928-635-9371, 800-482-3955; www.thecanyonmotel.com; 1900 E Rodeo Rd; RV sites $35-38, cottages $74-78, train cars $78-160; ❄️📶♨️🐾) Stone cottages and rooms in two railroad cabooses and a former Grand Canyon Railway coach car offer a quirky alternative to a standard motel. Kids love the cozy train cars, which sport bunk beds and private decks. Cottages feature wood floors and kitchenettes. There's a heated indoor pool and a playground on the premises.

CANYON COUNTRY INN
Motel $

(☎928-635-2349, 877-405-3280; www.thecanyoncountryinn.com; 422 W Route 66; r $66-$98; ❄️📶) Rooms at this family-run inn are a step up from typical motel rooms and give you more of a B&B feel at a reasonable rate. An 'extended' continental breakfast includes yogurt, fresh fruit, bagels and muffins.

HIGHLANDER MOTEL
Motel $

☎928-635-2541, 877-635-2541; 533 W Route 66; d $49-59; ❄️📶) Good, clean budget choice with cutesy Old West decor, microwave, fridge, cable TV and spacious bathrooms.

 Eating & Drinking

AMERICAN FLYER COFFEE COMPANY
Cafe $

☎928-635-0777; www.americanflyercoffeeco.com; 326 W Route 66; mains $2-6; ⏰7am-2pm Sun-Thu, 7am-6pm Fri & Sat; 📶) This extremely friendly cafe/bike-repair shop offers wi-fi access, freshly baked pastries and healthy items like salads and wraps along with its excellent house-roasted coffee.

RICHARD I'ANSON / LONELY PLANET IMAGES ©

Board games, mellow music and cushy couches create a welcoming space.

DARA THAI CAFÉ — Thai $

(☎928-635-2201; 145 W Route 66, Suite C; mains $8-12; ⏱11am-2pm & 5-9pm Mon-Sat) A breath of fresh lemongrass on the Williams culinary scene, Dara Thai offers a lighter alternative to meat-heavy menus elsewhere in town. Lots of choice for vegetarians, and all dishes are prepared to your specified spiciness. Despite its address, the front door is found along S 2nd St.

RED RAVEN RESTAURANT — American $$

(☎928-635-4980; www.redravenrestaurant. com; 135 W Route 66; mains $10-22; ⏱11am-2pm & 5-9pm Tue-Sun) White tablecloths and candlelight set the mood at the family-run Red Raven, delivering the most upscale dining experience you'll find in Williams. Simple but creative dishes (such as medallions of pork loin with pineapple and cranberry salsa) are complemented by a straightforward wine list.

ROD'S STEAK HOUSE — Steakhouse $$

(☎928-635-2671; www.rods-steakhouse.com; 301 E Route 66; mains $13-26; ⏱11am-9:30pm Mon-Sat) Locals say service here can be inconsistent. But the cow-shaped sign and menus spell things out – if you want steak and potatoes, this has been the place to come since 1946 (though there are a few non-cow items on the menu). Diners with limited mobility should note that restrooms are down a flight of stairs.

CRUISERS CAFÉ 66 — American $$

(☎928-635-2445; www.cruisers66.com; 233 W Route 66; mains $10-20; ⏱3-10pm) Housed in an old Route 66 gas station and decorated with vintage gas pumps and old-fashioned Coke ads, this cafe is a fun place for kids. Expect BBQ fare, such as burgers, spicy wings, pulled-pork sandwiches and mesquite-grilled ribs (cooked on the outdoor patio). In summer you can sit outside and enjoy live music.

ℹ Information

Visitor center (☎928-635-4061, 800-863-0546; www.williamschamber.com; 200 W Railroad Ave; ⏱8am-5pm) Inside the historic former train depot; offers a small bookstore with titles on the canyon, Kaibab National Forest and other areas of interest.

125

Williams Ranger Station (📞928-635-5600; 742 S Clover Rd; ⏰8am-4pm Mon-Fri) You'll find USFS rangers at both the visitor center and here.

ℹ Getting There & Around

Amtrak (📞800-872-7245; www.amtrak.com; 233 N Grand Canyon Blvd) Trains stop at Grand Canyon Railway Depot.

Arizona Shuttle (📞928-225-2290, 800-563-1980; www.arizonashuttle.com) Offers three shuttles a day to the canyon (per person $22) and to Flagstaff (per person $19).

NORTH RIM

A single stone and timber lodge, with floor-to-ceiling windows, perches directly on the canyon rim, and miles of trails wind through meadows thick with wildflowers, willowy aspen and towering ponderosa pines. At the end of every day, the lodge's small rimside sun porch fills with dusty, weary hikers, doffing baseball caps, Camelbaks and backpacks. They grab a beer from the saloon and mingle on the porch, settling into the Adirondack chairs, comparing notes and sharing experiences. After the sun sets, when most of the children have gone to sleep and darkness has subdued the canyon's ferocity, folks bundle in their fleeces and sit quietly, studying the stars, breathing in the canyon's emptiness, listening to the silence. This is the kinder, gentler Grand Canyon, and once you've been here you'll never want to see the canyon from anywhere else.

When to Go

Between mid-October and mid-May, all visitors services on the North Rim, including lodging and campgrounds, are closed. During this time, Hwy 67 to the North Rim is often closed due to snow. Summertime on the North Rim is noticeably cooler than surrounding canyon lands. September, when the sun is especially gentle, can be a lovely time to visit.

When You Arrive

Upon entry, you'll receive a map and a copy of *The Guide*, the National Park Service (NPS) newspaper with information on ranger programs, hikes and park services. Do not lose your entrance receipt, as you'll need it if you intend on leaving and re-entering the park.

A park pass of $25 per car, good for seven days on both rims, can be purchased at the gate. If you arrive after-hours, a posted note will direct you – remember to pay the fee when you depart. From here, it is 14 miles to Grand Canyon Lodge.

Orientation

The North Rim Entrance sits 30 miles south of Jacob Lake on Hwy 67. The road dead-ends at Grand Canyon Lodge. At the lodge entrance you'll find the **North Rim Visitor**

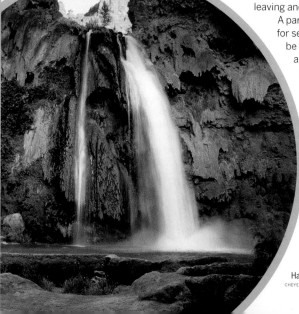

Havasu Falls, Supai
CHEYENNE ROUSE / LONELY PLANET IMAGES ©

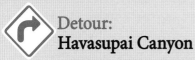

Detour:
Havasupai Canyon

One of the Grand Canyon's true treasures is Havasu Canyon, a hidden valley with four stunning, spring-fed waterfalls and inviting azure swimming holes in the heart of the 185,000-acre Havasupai Reservation. Parts of the canyon floor, as well as the rock underneath the waterfalls and pools, are made up of limestone deposited by flowing water. These limestone deposits are known as travertine, and they give the famous blue-green water its otherworldly hue. Because the falls lie 10 miles below the rim, most trips are combined with a stay at either **Havasu Lodge** (☎928-448-2111, 928-448-2101; PO Box 159, Supai, AZ 86435; r $145; ❄) or at the **Havasu Campground** (☎928-448-2121, 928-448-2141; Havasupai Tourist Enterprise, PO Box 160, Supai, AZ 86435; per night per person $17).

Supai is the only village within the Grand Canyon, situated 8 miles below the rim, and is the most remote village in the lower 48 states. Getting there is half the adventure. The village lies at the end of an 8-mile trail from Hualapai Hilltop, a parking area located 69 miles northeast of Peach Springs. (Online mapping sites may give you directions from Grand Canyon Village, but the road is 4WD only.)

Center (☎928-638-7864; ⏱9am-6pm, closed mid-Oct–mid-May) as well as a cafeteria, saloon, cafe and other amenities.

 Sights

Every drive and hike on the North Rim includes a canyon overlook, and one of the best is from the sun porch of Grand Canyon Lodge. From here, steps lead to two rocky overlooks (they don't have a name, but you can't miss them), and Bright Angel Point is an easy amble along a precipitous rocky outcrop. You can drive paved roads to Point Imperial and Cape Royal, or a dirt road to Point Sublime. Widforss Point, Cape Final and the North Kaibab down to Coconino Overlook make excellent day-hike destinations, and just outside the park boundary, the Kaibab National Forest offers trails and dirt roads through aspen and meadows to remote overlooks.

POINT IMPERIAL   Viewpoint
(Map p128) At 8803ft, Point Imperial is an easy drive away and the highest overlook on either of the rims. Expansive views of the canyon's eastern half and the desert

beyond include Nankoweap Creek, the Vermilion Cliffs, the Painted Desert and the Little Colorado River. An interpretive sign identifies the sights and geologic formations. There are no stops along the road to Point Imperial. From the Grand Canyon Lodge, the point is a 20 minute, 11-mile one-way drive.

 **Activities**

Whether you're on hoof, wheel, foot or ski, there are plenty of ways to explore the vast beauty of the Grand Canyon's north side.

Driving Tours

Driving on the North Rim involves miles of slow roads through dense stands of evergreens and aspen to the region's most spectacular overlooks. To reach Cape Royal and Point Imperial Rds, head 3 miles north from Grand Canyon Lodge to the signed right turn. From here, it is 5 miles to the Y-turn for Point Imperial and Cape Royal Rds. The road to Point Sublime offers amazing views, but requires at least four hours round-trip navigating

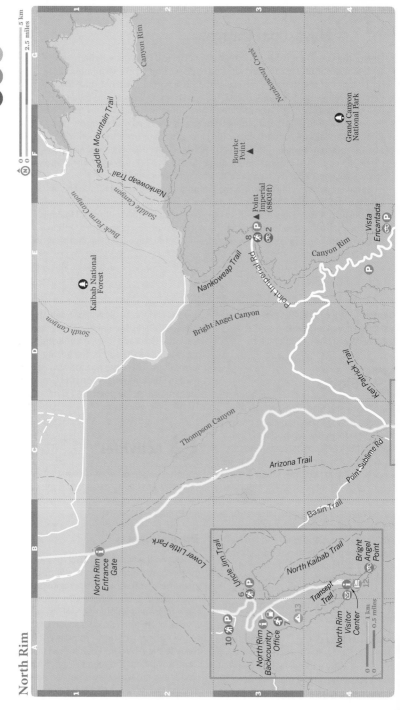

DISCOVER GRAND CANYON NORTH RIM

North Rim

5 km
2.5 miles

Canyon Rim

Nankoweap Creek

Saddle Mountain Trail

Nankoweap Trail

Buck Farm Canyon

Saddle Canyon

Kaibab National Forest

South Canyon

Bourke Point

Point Imperial (8503ft)

Grand Canyon National Park

8

2

Point Imperial Rd

Nankoweap Trail

Bright Angel Canyon

Vista Encantada

Canyon Rim

P

Ken Patrick Trail

Thompson Canyon

Arizona Trail

Point Sublime Rd

Basin Trail

North Rim Entrance Gate

Uncle Jim Trail

Lower Little Park

10 P

6 P

Bright Angel Point

North Kaibab Trail

Transept Trail

North Rim Visitor Center

North Rim Backcountry Office

13

12

1 km
0.5 miles

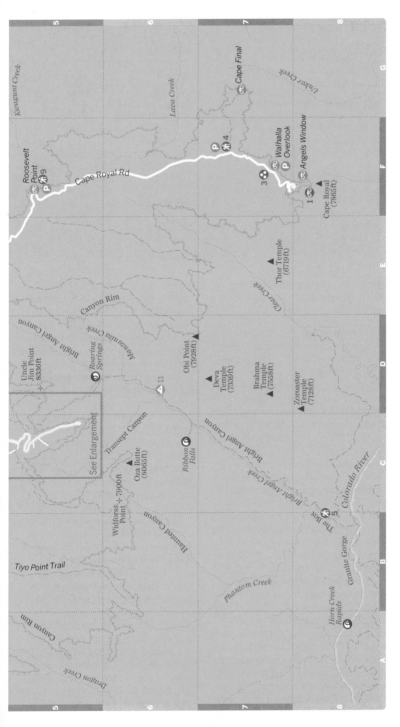

Kwagunt Creek

Cape Final

Lava Creek

Unkar Creek

Roosevelt Point

Cape Royal Rd

Walhalla Overlook

Angels Window

Cape Royal (7865ft)

Thor Temple (6719ft)

Clear Creek

Canyon Rim

Bright Angel Canyon

Manzanita Creek

Uncle Jim Point +8336ft

Roaring Springs

Obi Point (7928ft)

Deva Temple (7339ft)

Brahma Temple (7558ft)

Zoroaster Temple (7128ft)

Widforss +7900ft Point

Oza Butte (8065ft)

Transept Canyon

Ribbon Falls

Bright Angel Canyon

Bright Angel Creek

Colorado River

See Enlargement

Tiyo Point Trail

Haunted Canyon

Phantom Creek

The Box

Granite Gorge

Canyon Rim

Dragon Creek

Horn Creek Rapids

129

North Rim

a treacherous dirt road. You can hike to Point Imperial but no trails connect the viewpoints.

CAPE ROYAL ROAD   Scenic Drive
(Map p128) Descending gradually from 8200ft at Grand Canyon Lodge to 7685ft at Cape Royal, this 23-mile paved road is a must and is the only spot on the North Rim where you can see the Colorado River; once at Cape Royal parking lot, it's an easy 15-minute walk to the Cape Royal overlook. The one-way drive takes about 45 minutes.

From the Y-turn for Point Imperial and Cape Royal Rds, it's 2.5 miles to **Greenland Lake**. Look for the small parking lot on the right. A two-minute walk leads to a meadow and alpine pond and, a few minutes further, an old, empty salt cabin. This is the only stop on the drive without rim views, and it makes an excellent spot for a picnic.

Cape Royal Rd continues 2 miles to **Vista Encantada**. Views from this overlook extend from Nankoweap Creek within the canyon to the Vermilion Cliffs and Painted Desert in the distance. You'll find a few picnic tables, but because the tables are right next to the road and parking lot it's not a particularly nice spot to eat. After taking in the view, continue 1.6 miles to **Roosevelt Point**. From here,

you can see the confluence of the Little Colorado and Colorado Rivers, the Navajo Reservation, the Painted Desert and the Hopi Reservation. The easy 0.2-mile round-trip rimside **Roosevelt Point Trail** loops through burnt-out forest to a small bench at the canyon edge.

The next stop is **Walhalla Overlook**, 6.5 miles past Roosevelt Point. Just below the rim lies Unkar Delta, a plateau composed of sand and rocks deposited by Unkar Creek. This was the winter home of ancestral Puebloans from AD 850 to 1200. On the north side of the parking lot, a path crosses the street and leads to **Walhalla Glades**, the ancient Puebloans' summer home. A short self-guided walk leads past six small ruins.

The road ends 1.5 miles past Walhalla Overlook at the Cape Royal parking lot. From here, a 0.3-mile paved path, lined with piñon, cliffrose and interpretive signs, leads to **Angels Window**, a natural arch, and **Cape Royal Point**, arguably the best view from this side of the canyon. The path splits at the view of Angels Window, a few minutes from the trailhead. To the left, a short path leads to a precipice overlook that juts into the canyon and drops dramatically on three sides – here, you are literally standing atop Angels Window. To the right, the path continues to the rocky outcrop of Cape

Royal Point. The Colorado River can be seen directly below the point.

While the path is plenty wide for strollers and wheelchairs, they can't access Angels Window and the point itself is rocky. Several pleasantly shaded picnic tables sit at the far end of the parking lot. The **Wedding Site** features great canyon views – an ideal spot for a sunrise picnic.

This road may be closed in the late fall and early spring, and during heavy wind.

Hiking

Do not underestimate the effect of altitude. If you can, spend a few days acclimatizing with scenic drives, short walks and lazy days before conquering longer trails. The only maintained rim-to-river trail from the North Rim is the North Kaibab, a steep and difficult 14-mile haul to the river; day hikers will find multiple turnaround spots. Under no circumstances should anyone attempt to hike to the Colorado River and back in one day – as a ranger told us, the Grand Canyon wants to kill you.

WIDFORSS TRAIL   Hiking

(Map p128) The moderate, 10-mile (round-trip) Widforss Trail meanders through stands of spruce, white fir, ponderosa pine and aspen to **Widforss Point**. Tall trees offer shade, fallen limbs provide pleasant spots to relax, and you likely won't see more than a few people along the trail.

After an initial 15-minute climb, the canyon comes into view. For the next 2 miles, the trail offers wide views of the canyon to one side and meadows and woods to the other. About halfway into the hike, the trail jags away from the rim and dips into gullies of lupines and ferns; the canyon doesn't come into view again until the end. From Widforss Point (elevation 7900ft), take the small path to the left of the picnic table to a flat rock, where you can sit and enjoy your sandwich, the classic view and the silence. Though the total elevation change is only 440ft, rolling terrain makes this six-hour hike a moderate challenge. The trail starts at Widforss Trailhead.

Terrace, Grand Canyon Lodge (p136)

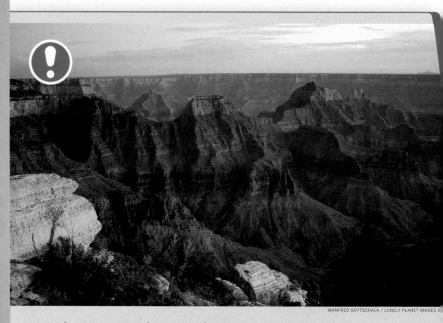

MANFRED GOTTSCHALK / LONELY PLANET IMAGES ©

Don't Miss **Bright Angel Point**

More a walk than a hike, this quarter-mile paved trail wraps up, down and out along a narrow finger of an overlook that dangles between Transept Canyon and Roaring Springs Canyon.

This is one of the few trails on the North Rim where you feel like you're walking along a precipice, with the canyon dropping off from either side of the trail. Anyone with a fear of heights should think twice before strapping on their walking shoes. There are few guardrails, and the edges are crumbling rock and sand – hold onto your children's hands and do not veer from the established trail. While it is officially paved and easy, the few steep inclines, rocky spots and narrow path make this half-hour walk dangerous for strollers and prohibitive to wheelchairs. A few benches and boulders offer pleasant spots to rest along the way.

The overlook itself gives unfettered views of the mesas, buttes, spires and temples of Bright Angel Canyon, as well as a straight shot of the South Rim, 10 miles across the canyon as the crow flies, and the distant San Francisco Peaks towering over Flagstaff.

The trail begins on the left side of the Grand Canyon Lodge sun porch, or you can start at a second trailhead in the log shelter in the parking area by the visitor center.

CAPE FINAL   Hiking
(Map p128) Hike this trail for the destination, not the hike. It's so dry, with nothing but brown ponderosa and brittle needles for most of the hike, that it feels like you're walking through a box of kindling, and what you see at the trailhead is what you'll see for just about the entire hike. But it's almost completely flat, quite easy, and you're rewarded with an amazing canyon overlook. The entire 4-mile round-trip hike takes about 2 hours and departs from the Cape Final Trail parking area off Cape Royal Rd.

After the initial, moderate 10-minute incline, the trail levels off. In about a half hour, a short side trail veers left to a beautiful view – take a few minutes to rehydrate, and return to the main trail. There is one more view before the trail narrows, turns rocky and heads a couple of minutes downhill. The ponderosa give way to piñon, sagebrush and cliffrose, and a flat, rocky triangle roughly 25ft by 25ft extends into the canyon with incredible views. Hike five more minutes through cactus and scramble up some boulders to **Cape Final**. Here, a small, rocky overlook sits at the edge of the canyon, offering a 270-degree view of lower Marble Canyon, Eastern Grand Canyon and one of the canyon's most famous formations, Vishnu Temple. The ease of this hike makes it great for children, but it's a frighteningly dangerous overlook and there are no guardrails.

TRANSEPT TRAIL   Hiking

(Map p128) Conveniently connecting Grand Canyon Lodge to the campground, this rocky dirt path with moderate inclines follows the rim and meanders through the aspen and ponderosa pine.

From the bottom of the steps off the Grand Canyon Lodge sun porch, follow the trail along the rim to the right. This is particularly nice in the evening, as you can relax in the woods and watch the sun set across a side canyon. In about 15 minutes, you'll come to a log bench with a quiet, lovely view of the canyon. With plenty of room to run, this is a nice spot for a picnic with children. From here, the trail veers from the edge and the path becomes relatively level, more a walk through the woods than a hike. The trail passes a small **ancient Puebloan site** and several viewpoints before reaching the rim-view tent sites of the campground, and the general store beyond. From the campground, the trail begins behind the general store. The 1.5-mile trail starts at the Grand Canyon Lodge and finishes at North Rim Campground and takes about 45 minutes each way.

POINT IMPERIAL   Hiking

(Map p128) This forested, two-hour round-trip walk leads to a rock that juts over the canyon, offering spectacular views.

From the Point Imperial parking lot, this trail heads northeast along the rim, veers through areas burned by the 2000 fire, and ends at the park's northern border, where it connects with the backcountry Nankoweap Trail and US Forest Service (USFS) roads. Though this quiet trail rolls gently along the rim, the high elevation (8800ft) can make it seem more difficult.

KEN PATRICK TRAIL   Hiking

(Map p128) Offering rim and forest views, this challenging trail ascends and descends numerous ravines as it winds through an old, deep forest, crosses Cape Royal Rd after 7 miles and continues for another 3 miles to Point Imperial.

The trail starts with a gentle climb into the woods, winding through gambel oak, ponderosa pine, white fir and aspen woodland. Views are intermittent, offering quick glimpses of Roaring Springs Canyon. The trail sees a lot of mule traffic, and it shows – particularly on the first mile, where the soft dirt path, worn into sandy grooves by hooves and softened by mule urine, can be smelly and hard on the feet. After a mile the mules head off on the Uncle Jim Trail, while the Ken Patrick veers to the left. Beyond this junction the trail grows increasingly serene, at times faint but still discernible, and involves several difficult uphill stretches.

For excellent views and a shorter, easier, mule-free walk, start at Point Imperial and hike 3 miles to Cape Royal Rd, and turn around. This stretch is the steepest but also the prettiest and the quietest. The trail alternates between shady conifer forests and panoramic views of Nankoweap Canyon, the Little Colorado River gorge, Marble Platform and the Painted Desert, and the San Francisco Peaks far to the south. Allow four hours for this round-trip journey.

UNCLE JIM TRAIL   Hiking

This spur trail leads to a canyon overlook and was named after a hunting advocate and forest-service warden who shot hundreds of mountain lions on the North Rim to 'protect' resident deer. It's a moderate, 5-mile, three-hour loop, sharing the Ken Patrick Trailhead. The two trails are the same for the first mile, then Uncle Jim heads right. After a bit of down and up, the trail soon reaches the 2-mile loop out to the point – it makes little difference if you go left or right. Near the tie-up area for mules at **Uncle Jim Point**, you'll have a terrific view of the North Kaibab switchbacks, Roaring Springs, the Walhalla Plateau and the South Rim. Tree trunks carved into chairs and stools offer a perfect resting spot before your return. Note that this trail is also used by mules.

Backpacking

Backpacking down into the canyon from the North Rim can be challenging but extremely rewarding. All overnight hiking requires a backcountry permit, available at the **North Rim Backcountry Office** (Map p128; ☎928-638-7875; ⏲8am-noon & 1-5pm, closed mid-Oct–mid-May).

The two most popular trails are the **North Kaibab Trail** and the **Clear Creek Trail**. The heavily used North Kaibab Trail leads 7.4 miles down to the backcountry **Cottonwood Campground** and then another 4 miles to the Colorado River. The clearly marked trailhead lies about 2 miles north of Grand Canyon Lodge.

The Clear Creek Trail, which begins 0.3 miles north of Phantom Ranch, leads 8.4 miles, past Phantom Overlook, to a lovely little cottonwood-fringed backcountry campground alongside tiny Clear Creek. The trail, built in 1935, was originally created as a mule trail so visitors to Phantom Ranch could access a side canyon and do some trout fishing in the stocked creek. The views into the gorge and across the canyon are magnificent. Even the first few miles provide gorgeous views, so just hiking a couple miles and turning around makes a lovely day hike

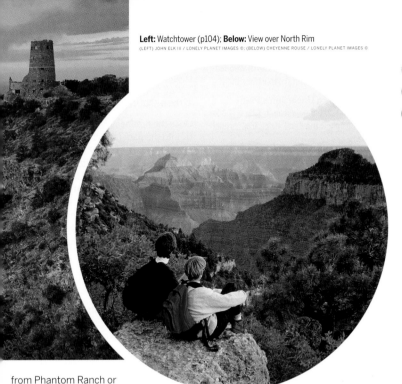
Left: Watchtower (p104); **Below:** View over North Rim
(LEFT) JOHN ELK III / LONELY PLANET IMAGES ©; (BELOW) CHEYENNE ROUSE / LONELY PLANET IMAGES ©

from Phantom Ranch or Bright Angel Campground. Be warned, however, that because it lies on the south-facing slope, the entire trail bears the brunt of the sun from sunrise to sunset. It is unspeakably hot during the summer, and there's no shade or water anywhere. Bring plenty of water to drink and get an early start.

Cycling

Because bikes are allowed on blacktop roads only, options for biking on the North Rim are limited to Hwy 67 into the park, Point Imperial Rd, and Cape Royal Rd. The two exceptions are the 17-mile dirt road to Point Sublime and the utilitarian Bridle Trail that follows the highway from the lodge to the North Kaibab Trail parking area. **North Rim Outfitter Station** (⏰7am-7pm, closed mid-Oct–mid-May), in the gas station next to the campground, rents surrey, mountain and tandem bikes as well as jogging strollers. Prices vary.

In the surrounding Kaibab National Forest just outside the park entrance, bikes are allowed on a seemingly endless network of forest roads and all trails, including the spectacular 18-mile **Rainbow Rim Trail** connecting five remote overlooks.

Mule Rides

Family-run **Canyon Trail Rides** (☎435-679-8665; www.canyonrides.com; ⏰mid-May–mid-Oct) take reservations anytime for the upcoming year. Unlike mule trips on the South Rim, however, you can usually book a trip upon your arrival at the park. Just duck inside the Grand Canyon Lodge to the **Mule Desk** (☎928-638-9875; ⏰7am-5pm). Mule rides from the North Rim don't go into the canyon as far as the Colorado River, but the half-day trip gives a taste of life below the rim, doesn't follow precipitous canyon ledges, and is

135

suitable even for folks a bit shy around horses and scared of heights.

One Hour Rim of the Grand Canyon (7yr age limit, 220lb weight limit; $40) Wooded ride to an overlook. Several departures daily.

Half-Day Trip to Uncle Jim's Point (10yr age limit, 220lb weight limit; $75; ⏱7:30am & 12:30pm) Follow the Ken Patrick Trail through the woods.

Half-Day Canyon Mule Trip to Supai Tunnel (10yr age limit, 200lb weight limit; $75; ⏱7:30am & 12:30pm) Descend 1450ft into the canyon along the North Kaibab Trail.

Ranger Programs

Ranger programs are small, informal gatherings that reflect the summer-camp mood of the North Rim. Several after-noon and evening talks are held around the fireplace on the sun porch of Grand Canyon Lodge – a highlight of any visit. When skies are clear, guests gather to gaze through telescopes while a ranger describes the night sky. Other programs are conducted at the campground am-phitheater, inside Grand Canyon Lodge, or at the Walhalla Overlook parking lot. *The Guide* publishes a seasonal schedule, and daily events are posted at the visitor center and at the campground.

Cross-Country Skiing

Once the first heavy snowfall closes Hwy 67 into the park (as early as late October or as late as January), you can cross-country ski the 44 miles to the rim and camp at the campground (no water, pit toilets). Camping is permitted elsewhere with a backcountry permit, available from rangers year-round. You can ski any of the rim trails, though none are groomed. The closest ski rental is in Flagstaff.

Sleeping

The closest lodging outside the park is Kaibab Lodge, 18 miles from the rim, or Jacob Lake Inn, 44 miles from the rim. Beyond that, you'll have to drive 78 miles north to Kanab, Utah, 85 miles northeast to Marble Canyon or 125 miles northeast to Page, Arizona. Contact the back-country office or Pipe Spring National Monument for permits to camp at remote North Rim overlooks or at backcountry sites below the rim; you can camp for free without a permit anywhere in the bucolic North Kaibab National Forest, just outside the park gate.

GRAND CANYON LODGE Historic Hotel $$ (Map p128; ☏928-638-2611 same-day reservation, 877-386-4383 reservations up to 12 months in advance, 480-337-1320 reservations from outside the USA; www.foreverlodging.com; r for 2 $116, cabin for 2 $121-187, $10 for each additional guest over 15yr; ⏱mid-May–mid-Oct; 🛜👪) Made of wood, Kaibab

Toroweap Overlook

WITOLD SKRYPCZAK / LONELY PLANET IMAGES ©

Detour:
Toroweap

One of the park's most impressive overlooks, Toroweap (also known as Tuweep) offers a landscape and views unlike anywhere else on the North Rim. Its 4552ft elevation, lower than either rim, supports piñon, junipers, cacti and small flowering desert plants, and sheer cliffs drop directly into the canyon and the Colorado River below. But Toroweap is not for everyone. It sits 150 miles from the North Rim Entrance Gate, requires at least two hours on a rough desert dirt road, there are no facilities and it's almost unbearably hot and dry during the summer. Toroweap is, in fact, a Paiute term meaning 'dry or barren valley.' For those who venture out here, however, Toroweap promises a Grand Canyon experience like nothing else. You literally have to crawl on your belly to see the river below, and there are no guardrails. Lava Falls, perhaps the roughest water in the canyon, is visible 1.5 miles downstream, and Vulcans Throne, basalt remnants of a cinder cone eruption 74,000 years ago, rises from the Esplanade Platform. Across the canyon is the Hualapai Reservation and 25 miles east sits the mouth of Havasu Canyon, home to the Havasupai.

The most reliable way to get here is to drive 7 miles west of Fredonia on Hwy 389 and look for a dirt road and the sign 'Toroweap.' Take this road 55 miles south to the **Tuweep Ranger Station**, which is staffed year-round.

The road to Toroweap, notorious for flattening tires, keeps garages in Kanab in business, and a tow can cost upwards from $1000! Drive under 25mph to minimize your chances, have at least one spare tire, and bring plenty of water. There is none at Toroweap, and shade is scarce. The ranger is not always available, and cell service is spotty at best.

limestone and glass, with a 50ft-high sunroom, a spacious rimside dining room and panoramic canyon views, this is the canyon as it was meant to be. The original lodge, designed by Gilbert Stanley Underwood and built in 1928 by the Union Pacific Railroad in anticipation of a direct train link to the North Rim, burned down in 1932. It was rebuilt in 1937, but the train and masses of tourists never did come. The lodge, listed on the National Register of Historic Places, remains today much as it was then. Two small stone sun porches, each with Adirondack chairs and one with a massive fireplace, sit directly on the canyon edge. It just doesn't get any better than sitting here with a cold beer after a long, dusty hike, watching the sun set over the canyon.

There are no rooms in the lodge itself, but a series of cabins, ranging from rustic and cramped to bright and spacious, occupy outlying grounds. The 'Western' cabins offer the best views. Make reservations up to a year in advance.

NORTH RIM
CAMPGROUND Campground $
(Map p128; ☎877-444-6777, 928-638-7814; www.recreation.gov; sites $18-25; 🐾) Set back from the road beneath ponderosa, 1.5 miles north of Grand Canyon Lodge, North Rim Campground offers pleasant sites on level ground blanketed in pine needles. The proximity of some sites to the edge makes them unsuitable for children and, while they are beautiful, they are particularly windy. Site number 10, backed by woods, and site number eight, nestled in a little aspen grove, are the nicest of the standard sites.

Eating & Drinking

Part of the North Rim's charm lies in the striking contrast between the intimacy of its facilities and the wildness of the canyon. With only one restaurant, one cafeteria and one saloon, you'll find yourself bumping into the same folks, sharing stories over a glass of wine. Visitors can contact the following establishments through the **North Rim Switchboard** (☎ 928-638-2612, 928-638-2611).

GRAND CANYON LODGE DINING ROOM
American $$

(Map p128; mains $12-24; ⏰ 6:30-10am, 11:30am-2:30pm, 4:45-9:45pm, closed mid-Oct–mid-May) Some people get downright belligerent if they can't get a window seat, but the canyon-view windows are so huge, it really doesn't matter where you sit. While the solid menu includes buffalo steak and several vegetarian options, don't expect culinary memories. Make reservations in advance of your arrival to guarantee a spot for dinner (reservations are not accepted for breakfast or lunch).

GRAND CANYON COOKOUT EXPERIENCE
American $$

(Map p128; adult $30-35, 6-15yr $12-22, under 6yr free; ⏰ 6-7:45pm Jun-Sep) Chow down on BBQ, skillet cornbread and southwestern baked beans, served buffet style, while husband and wife Woodie and Cleda Jane entertain with Western songs and cheesy jokes. It sounds corny, but it's a lot of fun, very old-school national park and great for kids. A little train is supposed to shuttle folks from the lodge to the chuck wagon tent next to the campground, but most of the time it doesn't work so they have to use a van, or you can just walk the mile up the Bridle Trail. Buy tickets in advance, usually available same-day.

ROUGHRIDER SALOON & COFFEE SHOP
Bar $

(Map p128; snacks $2-5; ⏰ 5:30-10:30am & 11:30am-11pm, closed mid-Oct–mid-May) If you're up to catch the sunrise or enjoy an early-morning hike, stop at this small saloon on the boardwalk beside the lodge for an espresso, a freshly made cinnamon roll and a banana. Starting at 11:30am the saloon serves beer, wine and mixed drinks, as well as hot dogs and Anasazi chili.

Grand Canyon Lodge Dining Room

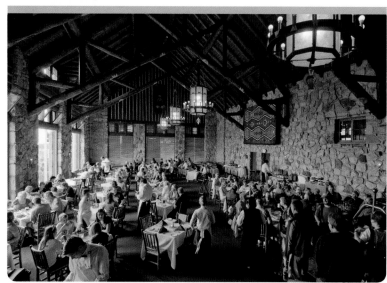

DELI IN THE PINES Cafeteria $

(Map p128; mains $4-8; ⏱7am-9pm, closed mid-Oct–mid-May) This small cafeteria beside the lodge serves surprisingly good food. The limited menu includes sandwiches, pizza and chili. There are a few indoor tables, but you're better off taking your plate outside to enjoy the high mountain air.

NORTH RIM GENERAL STORE Market $

(Map p128; ⏱7am-8pm, closed mid-Oct–mid-May; 📶) Adjacent to the campground and just over a mile from the lodge, the general store primarily services the needs of campers. You'll find canned soup, instant oatmeal, pasta, beer, wine and frozen hamburgers and steak, as well as picnic supplies like bread, cheese, peanut butter and, if you're lucky, a few fresh fruits and vegetables. There's also camping gear, including tents and first-aid basics, and it's the only place to find children's Tylenol.

ⓘ Information

Entrance Fees & Passes

A park pass of $25 per car, good for seven days on both rims, can be purchased at the gate. Those entering on foot, by bicycle or by motorcycle pay $12 per person.

Opening Dates

All services on the North Rim are closed from mid-October through mid-May, but rangers are always on hand. Day-trippers are welcome year-round (no charge). You can stay at the campground (with water and a bathroom but no services) until the first heavy snowfall closes the road from Jacob Lake; after that you'll need a backcountry permit (available directly from winter rangers after the backcountry office closes). Public showers and laundry facilities are next to the campground.

Tourist Information

North Rim Visitor Center (📞928-638-7864; ⏱8am-6pm, closed mid-Oct–mid-May) At the entrance to Grand Canyon Lodge.

Park Policies & Regulations

For park rules and regulations, see p120.

Maps

For information on maps, see p120.

Dangers & Annoyances

Hikes and overlooks on the North Rim range from 8000ft to almost 9000ft in elevation, and it can take a couple days to acclimate. Simply drinking lots of water can often prevent headaches, nausea, shortness of breath and exhaustion, all symptoms of elevation sickness. There is an ice-maker (free) and a cold-water faucet for drinking water behind the visitor center. If you need ice to fill your cooler, the North Rim General Store sells bagged ice.

ⓘ Getting There & Around

There is no public transportation to the North Rim, and once there, the only way to get around is by car, bicycle, motorcycle or foot. Both the 1.2-mile Transept Trail and a 1-mile leg of the Bridle Trail link the lodge and campground, and the Bridle Trail continues a mile or so to the North Kaibab Trailhead.

Car & Motorcycle

Chevron Service Station (⏱8am-5pm, 24hr pay at the pump, closed mid-Oct–mid-May) Next to the campground, has gas and sells oil, but does not have a garage or towing services. The closest full-service garage and 24-hour towing is located in Kanab, 78 miles north of Grand Canyon Lodge.

Shuttles

Hikers' Shuttle (⏱5:45am & 7:10am, seasonal variations) Complimentary shuttle takes folk from the Grand Canyon Lodge 2 miles to the North Kaibab Trailhead twice daily. You must sign up for it at the front desk; if no one signs up the night before, it will not run. Note that there is no service from North Kaibab Trailhead back to the lodge.

Trans-Canyon Shuttle (📞928-638-2820; one-way/round-trip $80/150) Departs from the Grand Canyon Lodge at 7am daily to arrive at the South Rim at 11:30am. Cash only. Reserve at least two weeks in advance.

Great Smoky Mountains & Shenandoah National Parks

Escape to the misty, magical Blue Ridge Mountains.

Running down the spine of the ancient Appalachians, both Great Smoky Mountains and Shenandoah National Parks offer visitors a chance to experience deep, mossy, mysterious old-growth forests. Great Smoky Mountains, America's most visited national park, is beloved for its many waterfalls, scalable peaks, and highly photogenic preserved mountain villages, complete with old clapboard churches, settlers cabins, one-room schoolhouses and working grist mills. Shenandoah's single road, the winding Skyline Drive, is one of America's most glorious scenic byways, with stirring views over the patchwork valleys and silvery rivers of the Shenandoah Valley. The drive is dotted with lodges, snack bars and scenic overlooks, so you can stop as much as you like. Both parks have grand hiking, splendidly rustic campgrounds and the chance to get up-close-and-personal (but not *too* close, please) with the wildlife of Appalachia – bobcats and otters and bears, oh my!

Great Smoky Mountains & Shenandoah Itineraries

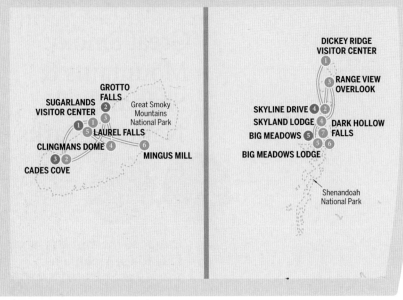

Two Days in Great Smoky

1 Sugarlands Visitor Center (p145) One of Great Smoky's two major visitor centers, bustling Sugarlands has a small museum of animal dioramas, a nice bookstore and a squadron of friendly rangers at the ready with maps and info. Sign on for a ranger-led walk in the morning, or watch the free 20-minute video, buy a hiking map and set off on your own.

2 Cades Cove (p146) Next, explore crumbling family cemeteries and humble farmers' cottages on the 11-mile driving loop surrounding this historic 19th-century mountain settlement.

3 Grotto Falls (p153) Later in the afternooon, pass beneath a transparent wall of water on this one-of-a-kind 2.6-mile hike, which actually takes you behind a waterfall. Don't forget your camera – this is one of the park's classic photo spots.

4 Clingmans Dome (p145) The next morning, drive your car to the top of the park's highest peak, where an observation tower offers jaw-dropping 360° views of the mist-shrouded mountains.

5 Laurel Falls (p154) Later, hit the 2.6 mile (round-trip) path to this double-decker waterfall, one of Great Smoky's most accessible - and lovely - hikes. If it's warm out, whip off your shoes and wade around in the icy pool beneath the falls.

6 Mingus Mill (p148) Near the Cherokee entrance, this working grist mill straddles a burbling river, its enormous millstone grinding wheat and corn just like it has since 1886. Stop for a late-afternoon picnic here, or stroll the short wooded nature trail.

➡ **THIS LEG: 63 MILES**

Two Days in Shenandoah

1 **Dickey Ridge Visitor Center** (p162) Start your trip at the more northern of the park's two visitor centers for maps, ranger info and neat displays on the park's flora and fauna.

2 **Skyline Drive** (p162) The serpentine 105-mile-long Skyline Drive is the park's only road and its main attraction. Pull over at any one of its 75-plus scenic overlooks to gaze into the silvery-green Shenandoah Valley. No matter what you do, don't miss a sunset from one of the western-facing overlooks.

3 **Range View Overlook** (p170) All the park overlooks are glorious, but Range View is particularly awe-inspiring, with a clear vista over a 14-mile stretch of peaks ranging from Stony Man's craggy face to the Blue Ridge, Massanutten and beyond.

4 **Skyland** (p164) On your second day in the park, make a pit stop at this 1890s lodge, on Shenandoah's highest peak. Order a Coke at the sweetly old-fashioned snack bar and cool your heels at the outdoor patio.

5 **Big Meadows** (p168) A striking grassy expanse at the park's heart, this is the place to stop for a picnic and bust out the binoculars for some deer and bird watching.

6 **Dark Hollow Falls** (p165) If you've only got time for one hike, make it this moderately challenging 1.4-mile round-trip, where a 70ft waterfall flows over craggy, ancient volcanic turf. If you've got a little longer, keep hiking further to see more small falls and rock pools.

7 **Big Meadows Lodge** (p169) Don't miss the lodge's wonderfully old-fashioned wood-beamed Great Room, with a stone fireplace, cozy couches and million-dollar views. Then retire to one of the park's motel rooms or cabins for a tranquil night's sleep.

THIS LEG: 30 MILES

Great Smoky Mountains & Shenandoah Highlights

1 **Best Hike: Alum Cave Bluffs** (p153) All you could want in a hike, including a natural arch, a field of wild blueberries and a rock shelter.

2 **Best Waterfall: Grotto Falls** (p153) How many waterfalls can you actually walk behind?

3 **Best Historic Area: Cades Cove** (p146) See real 19th-century Appalachian homesteads.

4 **Best Scenic Drive: Skyline Drive** (p162) 105 miles of eye-popping vistas and stomach-dropping turns.

5 **Best Lodge: Big Meadows** (p169) Cozy rooms and an inviting wood-paneled Great Room filled with board games.

Grotto Falls (p153), Great Smoky Mountains
RICHARD I'ANSON / LONELY PLANET IMAGES ©

Discover Great Smoky Mountains & Shenandoah

GREAT SMOKY MOUNTAINS NATIONAL PARK

The Cherokee called this territory Shaco-nage (shah-*cone*-ah-jey), meaning, roughly, 'land of the blue smoke,' for the heather-colored mist that hangs over these ancient peaks. The Southern Appalachians is the world's oldest mountain range, with landscapes ranging from deep, dim spruce forest to sunny meadows carpeted with daisies and Queen Anne's lace to silvery rivers and rushing waterfalls. The land is home to such an astonishing variety of animals and plants that it has been designated an International Biosphere Reserve and a World Heritage Site.

Great Smoky is a magic place for hikers, bikers, wildlife-watchers, history buffs and lovers of scenic drives. In fact, the 815-sq-mile park is the country's most popular, attracting nearly 10 million visitors a year. While the main arteries and attractions can get crowded, studies have shown that 95% of visitors never venture further than 100yd from their cars, so it's easy to leave the teeming masses behind – you'll be glad you did.

History

For millennia, these misty mountains were the primary domain of the Cherokee people. The Native Americans were later supplanted by Scotch-Irish, French and German settlers, a conglomeration that one early settler characterized as 'a heady brew.' In Cades Cove and Cataloochee the historic log homes, churches, mills and schoolhouses of these mountain people still stand with doors wide open.

The park was founded in 1934, and much of its infrastructure was built by Civilian Conservation Corps workers during the Great Depression. Unlike most other national parks, Great Smoky charges no admission fee, nor will it ever; this proviso was written into the park's original charter as a stipulation for a $5-million Rockefeller family grant.

Autumn in Great Smoky Mountains
CHARLES COOK / LONELY PLANET IMAGES ©

When to Go

The park is open year-round, but summer and fall are the most popular seasons. Some facilities are closed late fall through early spring, and roads may be closed in winter due to inclement weather.

When You Arrive

Great Smoky Mountains National Park is open every day, year-round. However, Newfound Gap Rd often closes during winter storms, and several others, including Clingmans Dome Rd, close during the winter months. As there are no fee stations, you will have to stop by a visitor center to pick up a park map.

Orientation

Great Smoky Mountains National Park straddles the North Carolina and Tennessee border, which runs diagonally through the heart of the park, shadowed by the Appalachian Trail (AT). The park encompasses some 521,000 acres and more than 800 square miles. As the crow flies, it is roughly 65 miles wide and 25 miles long.

The north–south Newfound Gap Rd/ Hwy 441 spans the park from one end to the other, connecting the gateway towns of Gatlinburg, Tennessee on the north–central border and Cherokee, North Carolina on the south–central border.

Great Smoky's most-used entrances lie just outside the gateway towns of Gatlinburg and Cherokee, at opposite ends of Newfound Gap Rd/Hwy 441.

Also heavily used is the Hwy 73 entrance near Townsend, Tennessee, which offers a straight shot to Cades Cove.

 Sights

Great Smoky sights fall into two rough categories: nature and history. In the nature camp are the park's peaks, waterfalls and nature-watching areas, while the history camp includes preserved 19th century historic settlements like Cades Cove and Mingus Mill.

While the park is massive, most of the most popular sights are just off the park's main artery, Newfound Gap Rd. The Cades Cove area, the one exception, is less than an hour from Gatlinburg.

Gatlinburg Entrance

The Gatlinburg entrance is the park's most trafficked, so plan accordingly, especially in high season.

SUGARLANDS VISITOR
CENTER   Visitor Center
(⊙ 9am-7pm in summer, off-season hours vary) If you're entering the park from the Tennessee side, your first stop should be this excellent visitor center which features exhibits on the park's flora and fauna (check out the wild boar diorama), a large bookstore, a free 20-minute film and an info desk staffed with helpful rangers. During the summer, visitors are welcomed with frequent ranger presentations. Ranger-led walks to nearby Cataract Falls leave from the patio area several times daily in summer – check in at the center for times.

MT LECONTE   Mountain
Mt LeConte (6593ft) is the park's third-highest peak, and one of its most familiar sights, visible from practically every viewpoint. The only way to get to the top is on foot. It is accessible by six trails, which range from 5–10 miles in length. At the summit, LeConte Lodge is the park's only non-camping lodging, but you better book ahead – it's often full up to a year in advance.

CLINGMANS
DOME   Mountain, Viewpoint
'On top of Old Smoky' is Clingmans Dome (elevation 6643ft), the park's highest peak. At the summit a steep, half-mile paved trail leads to an observation tower offering a 360-degree view of the Smokies and beyond. It can be cold and foggy up here, even when the sun is shining in Sugarlands, so bring a jacket.

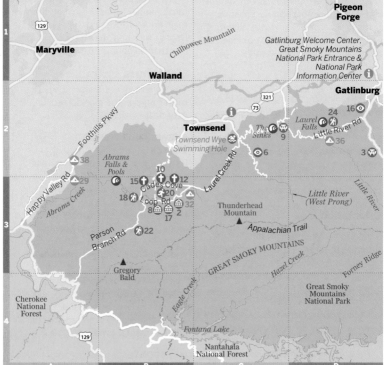

Cades Cove Area

A cove, in Appalachian parlance, means a valley, but Cades Cove is far more than that. Many consider this special place to be a national treasure, thanks to its poignant cultural legacy, telling pioneer architecture and plentiful wildlife. Settled by English, Scotch-Irish and Welsh pioneers in the 1820s, the cove was a thriving village of churches, gristmills and homesteads. Today, thanks to the excellent preservation efforts of the NPS, you can still get a vivid sense of life in 19th century Cades Cove by visiting more than a dozen preserved buildings.

An 11-mile loop road encircles the cove, with parking areas at the base of the various sights. Be warned, though – Cades Cove is the park's most popular area, and the road is the site of horrid

summer traffic jams. So plan ahead. The loop is open to traffic from dawn to dusk except on summer Wednesdays and Saturdays, when bikers and hikers rule the road. Pick up the self-guided auto tour booklet ($1) from any visitor center or the entrance to Cades Cove itself. Cades Cove is located about 45 minutes' drive west of the Sugarlands Visitor Center. The following represent a few of the cove's top sights.

CABLE MILL HISTORIC
AREA & VISITOR CENTER   Gristmill

In order to get bread on the table, early residents of Cades Cove first had to mill their grains and corn. Above all other staples, corn was the most important. Every meal included foods made from cornmeal, including cornbread, mush, hoecakes and spoon bread. Built in the

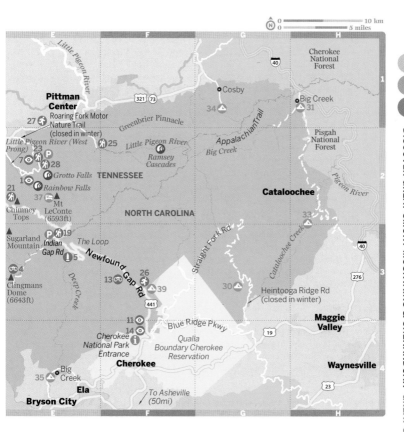

early 1870s by John Cable, Cable Mill was once one of four or five water-powered gristmills to serve Cades Cove's peak population of 700 residents. Powered by Mill Creek, whose waters were routed into the mill via a 235ft flume, Cable Mill features a classic overshot waterwheel. The other historic buildings surrounding the mill were brought from other locations in the park to create a living history museum. There's a blacksmith shop, a barn, a smokehouse, a sorghum mill and a homestead, as well as a visitor center and shop – stop by to pick up a bag of corn ground on-site.

CHURCHES   Churches

Three rural churches remain standing in Cades Cove: the 1887 Primitive Baptist Church, the 1902 Methodist Church with a small but picturesque white steeple,

and the Missionary Baptist Church (which was built by former Primitive Baptist Church members who were kicked out for advocating missionary work). In the Primitive Baptist Church cemetery, look out for the grave of Russell Gregory, 'murdered by North Carolina rebels' during the Civil War for being a Union sympathizer.

TIPTON PLACE   Historic Home

The picturesque Tipton homestead was built by Mexican War veteran 'Colonel Hamp' Tipton in the early 1870s. The grounds include a spacious two-floor cabin, blacksmith and carpentry shops and a cantilever barn.

JOHN OLIVER PLACE   Historic Home

Built in the early 1820s, this rustic log cabin is the oldest in Cades Cove. Check

Great Smoky Mountains

out the stone chimney, made with mud mortar. The home was built by one of the cove's earliest settlers and remained in the family until the park was founded more than 100 years later.

Cherokee Entrance

Near the gateway town of Cherokee, the primary southern portal into Great Smoky, is an area known as Oconaluftee, once home to the Cherokee. In the language of the Cherokee, the word means simply 'by the river.' This fertile land has been inhabited for 8000 years, but it wasn't until the 1880s that non-native settlers put down permanent roots here. Today the area is known for its visitor center, the Mountain Farm Museum and Mingus Mill.

OCONALUFTEE VISITOR CENTER
Visitor Center

(⊘ 8am-7pm in summer, shorter hours in off-season) Housed in a handsome brand-new building, this busy visitor center 2 miles north of Cherokee has a bookstore and wonderful exhibit on mountain life in the 19th and early 20th centuries. Don't miss the recorded oral histories, which give you a sense of what a mountain-dweller's accent was like 100 years ago. The Oconaluftee River Trail, one of only two in the park that allows leashed pets, leaves from the visitor center and follows the river for 1.5 miles to the boundary of the Cherokee reservation.

MINGUS MILL
Gristmill

In 1886 the Mingus family built this lovely mill on their eponymous creek. Today, to the delight of visitors, the turbine-powered mill still grinds wheat and corn much as it always has. The cornmeal pouring into the bag is still warm from the friction caused by the mammoth mill stones and, when it's in operation, the entire building vibrates and hums. A pleasant path enters the woods to follow the 100yd-long board-walled canal, which delivers water to the mill from Mingus Creek. For a good time that doesn't cost a nickel, toss a couple of leaves into the water for an unhurried leaf race.

MOUNTAIN FARM MUSEUM
Historic Homestead

Adjacent to the Oconaluftee Visitor Center, the excellent Mountain Farm Museum and its collection of historic buildings evoke life on a typical farmstead from the late 19th century. Together these structures paint a poignant picture of the mountain people who once eked out their sustenance from this rugged and isolated wilderness. The buildings include a meat house, where a mountain farm's most valuable commodity was butchered, dried and smoked. Other structures are dedicated to chickens, apples, corn, water and blacksmithing. The well-tended garden and old-strain cornfields are beautiful to behold any time of year.

Cataloochee Valley
The Cherokee named these lands Gadalutsi, which means 'standing up in a row' or 'wave upon wave.' This less-visited former frontier outpost in the park's isolated eastern edge remains a delightful secret waiting to be discovered. Accessed via a narrow, winding 11-mile road, Cataloochee offers lush old-growth forests, restored farms and homesteads and opportunities for thrilling wildlife sightings of elk, wild turkeys and black bears. Settlers in Cataloochee were drawn by the bountiful reserves of game and fish and fertile bottomlands. Today community buildings such as Palmer Chapel, Beech Grove School and Little Cataloochee Church stand open for visitors to explore. Facilities include Cataloochee Campground, ranger and information stations, restrooms and a frontcountry horse camp. Pick up the Cataloochee Auto Tour brochure ($1) from any visitor center or at the valley's entrance.

Greenbrier
This wild day-use area 6 miles east of Gatlinburg off Hwy 321 was once one of the most populous communities in the Smokies. Today it's a terrific place to fish, swim or picnic along the gorgeous Middle Prong of the **Little Pigeon River**, or you can hike to some of the most beautiful wildflower spots in the park. The road into Greenbrier cove follows the river and offers many places to pull off and enjoy the scenery. At Mile 3.2 it forks; the left fork leads to the trailhead for Old Settlers Trail and Ramsey Cascades, while the right fork passes two picnic areas and dead-ends at a turnaround after 4 miles. At the turnaround, an easy, 1-mile path leads to old homesteads, a cemetery and plenty of wildflowers during the spring and early summer.

 # Activities

Scenic drives and hiking are by far the park's most popular activities. But if you're here for more than a day or two, there are plenty of other things to try, from horseback riding to river rafting.

Driving Tours

Many visitors to Great Smoky never leave their cars, and while we don't recommend that, it's understandable – this park has some of the loveliest scenic drives around. Most of the drives have *Auto Tour* brochures ($1) available at the visitor centers.

NEWFOUND GAP ROAD
Scenic Drive

The park's main artery, Newfound Gap Rd/Hwy 441 begins just outside of Gatlinburg and heads the 30 winding miles to Cherokee, NC. Along the way are many turnouts, picnic areas, nature trails, quiet walkways and overlooks – everything that you came for.

Between Mile 5.6 and Mile 7.1, you'll have several opportunities to pull over and admire one of the park's best-known geologic features. The Cherokee thought these twin stony outcroppings high on the ridge resembled a pair of antlers, while white settlers characterized them as a pair of stone chimneys. The challenging

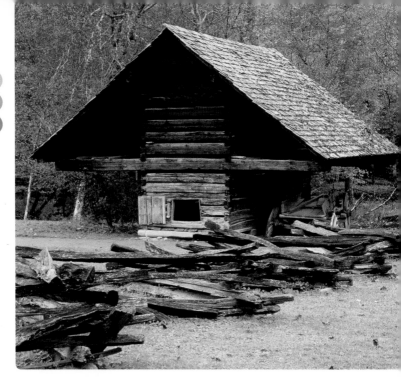

DISCOVER GREAT SMOKY MOUNTAINS & SHENANDOAH   GREAT SMOKY MOUNTAINS NATIONAL PARK

Chimney Tops Trail leads to the top and offers some truly spectacular views.

At Mile 7.3 there is a famous patch of road known as The Loop. Here the highway passes through a tunnel and crosses over itself, a necessity required by the steep slope.

The trailhead and parking area for one of the park's most popular hikes, Alum Cave Bluffs is at Mile 8.8. Over the next 1.5 miles, this stretch of road offers several turnouts for access to the roaring West Prong of the Little Pigeon River.

At Mile 12.2 you'll know you've entered the upper elevations of the Smokies as you come to the spruce fir forest that dominates the high mountain slopes. The weather is considerably more prickly up here; on average it's 10°F to 15°F degrees cooler than in the lowlands, annual rainfall regularly exceeds 80in and the wind can be fierce.

At Newfound Gap (Mile 12.5), travelers pass from Tennessee into North Carolina and the Appalachian Trail crosses the road. In the olden days, the road passing over the crest of the Smokies did so at Indian Gap, 1.5 miles west of the current site. When this easier passage was discovered in 1850, it was immediately and permanently dubbed 'Newfound Gap.' Straddling the state line is a monument marking the spot where Franklin D Roosevelt formally dedicated the park in 1940. From here you get your first privileged view into North Carolina.

The turnoff for Clingmans Dome Rd is at Mile 13.4. Shortly thereafter, at Mile 13.9, is a large parking area for the Oconaluftee Valley Overlook, where you will be treated to impressive views into the Oconaluftee River Valley.

At Mile 28.7, Mingus Mill still grinds corn into meal just as it has done for more than a century. The mill is in operation from early spring through fall, though visitors are welcome anytime.

At Mile 29.2, the Oconaluftee Visitor Center and Mountain Farm Museum signal the end of the driving tour.

Left: Corn crib, Cable Mill Historic Area (p146), Great Smoky Mountains;
Below: Screech owl

(LEFT) RICHARD CUMMINS / LONELY PLANET IMAGES ©; (BELOW) MARK NEWMAN / LONELY PLANET IMAGES ©

CADES COVE
LOOP   Scenic Drive

Some two million people visit Cades Cove each year, most of them via this 11-mile one-way loop road encircling the valley. Cades Cove has the widest variety of historic buildings of any area in the park, including churches, a gristmill, log houses and cantilever barns.

The cove's wide-open expanses offer some of the best opportunities for wildlife viewing. Bear sightings are fairly common – if one lumbers within sight of the road, traffic comes to a standstill as normally sensible people leap from their cars fumbling with their cameras. You may also hear the peculiar gobbling of wild turkeys or see a multitude of deer, their bobwhite tails sticking straight up in the air as they leap wire fences to cross the road.

You'll pass several historic buildings with parking areas before coming to the midway point of the loop, home to Cades Cove's biggest attraction, the Cable Mill.

Traffic congestion continues to be a major issue in Cades Cove, but on Wednesday and Saturday mornings until 10am cars are banned to make way for cycle and foot traffic.

ROARING FORKS MOTOR
NATURE TRAIL   Scenic Drive

The Roaring Fork area is well loved for its surging streams and waterfalls, glimpses of old-growth forest and its excellent selection of preserved cabins and gristmills.

The six-mile loop road begins and ends a short distance from downtown Gatlinburg. From Hwy 441, turn onto Airport Rd at the eighth traffic light. Airport becomes Cherokee Orchard Rd, and the Roaring Fork Motor Nature Trail begins 3 miles later.

The first stop on Cherokee Orchard Rd is the Noah 'Bud' Ogle Nature Trail, providing an enjoyable jaunt into a mountain farmstead with a streamside tub mill (an improvised contraption built

151

to crush or grind the family corn) and an ingenious wooden-flume plumbing apparatus.

Immediately following the Rainbow Falls Trail you can either turn around and head back to Gatlinburg or continue on Roaring Fork Rd, a narrow, twisting one-way road. The road follows Roaring Fork, one of the park's most tempestuous and beautiful streams. It passes through an impressive stand of old-growth eastern hemlocks, some of which reach heights of more than 100ft and have trunks stretching as much as 5ft across.

From the Trillium Gap Trail the delicate Grotto Falls can be reached via an easy, short hike through a virgin hemlock forest.

Of considerable historical interest is the hardscrabble cabin at the Home of Ephraim Bales, and also the more comfortable 'saddlebag' house at the Alfred Reagan Place (painted with 'all three colors that Sears and Roebuck had'). Reagan was a jack-of-all-trades who served his community as a carpenter, blacksmith and storekeeper.

A wet-weather waterfall called Place of a Thousand Drips provides a wonderful conclusion to your explorations.

LITTLE RIVER ROAD Scenic Drive

Formerly an old railroad roadbed serving the timber industry, Little River Rd shadows the snaking Little River to connect Sugarlands Valley with Townsend and Cades Cove. The meandering 18-mile route can take as long as 1½ hours to drive.

A short 3.7 miles from Sugarlands is the trailhead for the paved Laurel Falls Trail, one of the most popular hikes in the park.

Ten miles from Sugarlands you'll see a bridge leading to Metcalf Bottoms Picnic Area, a large and pretty day-use area on the Little River. Bear sightings are common here. A 1-mile path leads to the delightful Little Greenbrier School, a charming, 19th century split-log schoolhouse that also served as a church. Original classroom accoutrements, including desks, benches and a painted blackboard, still line the room.

Another mile and a half down Little River Rd brings you to The Sinks, an ominous stretch of white water that once swallowed a derailed logging train whole, according to folklore.

The next major landmark is the Townsend Wye, where the West Prong joins Little River and Hwy 73 peels off for Townsend. At this favorite swimming spot you'll find a placid stretch of river with grassy banks. From this point, as you drive into Cades Cove, the road's name changes to Laurel Creek Rd.

Less than a mile past the junction is the opportunity to turn left onto Tremont Rd, an uncrowded, 3.2-mile route into an interesting and scenic area of the

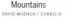

Laurel Falls (p154), Great Smoky Mountains
DAVID MUENCH / CORBIS ©

park that once was home to one of the largest and last logging camps in the Smokies.

The Great Smoky Mountains Institute at Tremont, a research facility with a small visitor center and bookstore, is also worth a visit. Two trails provide pleasant river walks with impressive cascades: the West Prong Trail, on the right just before the institute, and the Middle Prong Trail, at the end of the road.

Hiking

Whether you have an irrepressible urge to climb a mountain or just want to get some fresh air, hiking in Great Smoky Mountains National Park is the single best way to experience the sublime beauty of this singular place. Even if you're only here for a short visit, be sure to include at least one hike in your itinerary. Trails range from flat, easy and short paths to longer, more strenuous endeavors. Many are excellent for families, some are wheelchair accessible, and the majority of trailheads begin from major sights. No matter what your physical ability or endurance level, there's a hike out there for you.

ALUM CAVE BLUFFS   Hiking

The well-loved, 4.5-mile round-trip Alum Cave Bluffs hike provides a representative sampling of the park's diverse pleasures. Some rate this satisfying hike, which passes through old-growth forest and follows a series of streams as it winds its way up the southern slope of Mt LeConte, to be the finest the park has to offer. However, the pleasures of the hike must be earned; it's a steady uphill slog all the way from the parking area to the bluffs.

Highlights include Arch Rock, where handcrafted stone steps ascend steeply through the portal of an impressive stone arch that looks like something Frodo was compelled to climb. Beyond this interesting formation, the trail crosses the Styx Branch and begins a steep ascent. The forest gives way to open sky at the next point of interest, a large heath bald where mountain laural and blueberry bushes grow in a dense mass. After some huffing and puffing, you'll be repaid

The Best...
Waterfall Hikes

for your efforts at a scenic vista called Inspiration Point. From here, it's a short climb to Alum Cave Bluffs. As it turns out, the name is a misnomer. Waiting for you is not a cave, but rather a rock overhang. Moreover, the rocks contain not alum, but rather sulfur and rare minerals, some not known to occur elsewhere. Alum Cave Bluffs are the end of this hike, but if you're game for more delightful punishment, you can continue on to the summit of Mt LeConte, 2.7 miles up the trail. Access the trailhead from Newfound Gap Rd.

GROTTO FALLS   Hiking

This moderate 2.6-mile round-trip hike passes through mature forests supporting old-growth hemlocks to another of Great Smoky's gorgeous waterfalls. The trailhead is on Roaring Fork Motor Nature Trail, 1.7 miles from the start of the one-way road. The parking area may fill up in summer, so get there early in the day. You will be hiking along Trillium Gap Trail, one of the main arteries leading to the summit of Mt LeConte (6.6 miles from the parking area). The well-maintained trail makes a moderate ascent all the way to the falls. There are a number of easy creek crossings along the way. You might encounter large black-and-white pileated woodpeckers or hear their insistent drumming on the trunks of dead trees. During the spring you might see liverworts or silverbells in bloom or, on warm days, salamanders doing push-ups at the edge of a stream. Grotto Falls is a favorite subject of photographers. Here, Roaring Fork spills 20ft from an overhanging ledge as the trail passes behind a transparent wall of water – very cool.

LAUREL FALLS   Hiking

With its close proximity to Gatlinburg and Elkmont Campground, this easy 2.6-mile round-trip waterfall hike has become so wildly popular that the park service has paved the entire length of the trail to head off the erosion caused by countless pairs of clomping boots. The paved passage is wheelchair accessible (with considerable assistance).

The trail to Laurel Falls climbs gently through a forest of oak and pine. At the top, Laurel Branch bursts from a grove of mountain laurel and falls nearly 50ft to collect in a pool that is ideal for soaking your weary gams. From here, the water spills another 40ft to a second pool below. Plan on spending about 1.5 hours on this hike.

ABRAMS FALLS   Hiking

The 5-mile day-hike to Abrams Falls and back is the most popular walk in Cades Cove, and for good reason. After following the boisterous Abrams Creek and its many tributaries, you will arrive at an enormously appealing waterfall that spills into one of the park's largest natural pools. However, the beauty of this place is certainly no secret, and unless it is a gray and rainy day, you can expect to share the experience with scores of others. You'll find the turnoff for the trailhead 5 miles from the beginning of Cades Cove Loop Rd, just prior to the Cable Mill area. Be careful around the mossy rocks at the bottom of the falls – they're highly slippery, and there have been numerous accidents in recent years.

CHIMNEY TOPS   Hiking

This hike is one of the most popular in the park, due to its short length (4 miles round-trip) and easy access from Newfound Gap Rd. The view from the twin peaks of Chimney Tops is nothing short of spectacular. However, before you set out, you should know that this grueling climb could cause a priest to mutter expletives within earshot of children.

After several stream crossings, a rhododendron thicket and a climb through a mixed forest punctuated with

Cades Cove (p146), Great Smoky Mountains

giant yellow buckeye trees, you'll begin the arduous uphill trek to the top. After a half mile of extremely steep trail, the path eases up and ascends more moderately along Sugarland Mountain. Be careful of rocky outcrops, which can be slippery, and look out for high winds or lightning. From here you can attempt to climb straight up to the first 'chimney' (a peak of bare, metamorphic rock), or take the alternate route to the right to gain access to the saddle between the peaks. You will enjoy an exceedingly fine panoramic view. To the northeast stand the imposing peaks of Mt LeConte (6593ft), Great Smoky's third-highest mountain; to its right is the narrow ridgeline called the Boulevard. Northeast is Mt Mingus (5802ft). Some hikers try to make it to the second hump, but to do so is extremely dangerous.

RAINBOW FALLS   Hiking
Seeing Rainbow Falls takes a bit of dedication (and lungpower) – one must climb 1700ft in a scant 2.8 miles. But oh, is it worth it. A long uphill slog is finally rewarded by the sight of misty Rainbow Falls, one of the prettiest and most delicate waterfalls in the park. Rivulets of crystalline water spill over an 80ft bluff and then flow through a mossy boulder field in a succession of gentle cascades. The entire trail is about 5.4 miles and takes about four hours (round-trip) to hike. The trailhead is off Roaring Fork Motor Nature Trail.

Backpacking

More than 800 miles of well-marked backcountry trails crisscross these mountains, including 70 miles of the 2,181-mile Appalachian Trail. Popular hikes include the 11.4-mile Gregory Bald at Cade's Cove, the 13.4-mile Trillium Gap trail to the summit of Mt LeConte, and the 31.2-mile stretch of the Appalachian Trail East (you must make reservations to sleep in the AT's hiking shelters). Backcountry camping is free, but you must obtain a permit at one of the ranger stations or visitor centers.

Cycling

Bicycles are welcome on most park roads, with the exception of the Roaring Fork Motor Nature Trail. However, it is important that you choose your road wisely. Due to steep terrain, narrow byways and heavy car traffic, many park roads are not well suited for safe or enjoyable riding. Great Smoky has no mountain biking trails. Bicycles are allowed only on the Gatlinburg Trail, the Oconaluftee River Trail and the Lower Deep Creek Trail. They are prohibited on all other park trails.

By far the best place for a carefree cycling tour is Cades Cove, particularly when the road is closed to cars (Wednesday and Sunday before 10am from mid-May to late September). In summer and fall, rent cycles from **Cades Cove Campground Store** (☏ 865-448-9034; www.explorecadescove.com; adult/child per hr $6/4).

Horseback Riding

A staggering – or should we say galloping – 550 miles of the park's hiking trails are open to horses and their humans. Assuming you're not towing your own horse, sign on for a trail ride at one of the park's three stables, all open between mid-March and mid-November. Trail rides are about $25 per person.

Cades Cove Riding Stables (☏ 865-448-9009; www.cadescovestables.com)

Smokemont Riding Stables (☏ 828-497-2373; www.smokemontridingstable.com)

Smoky Mountain Riding Stables (☏ 865-436-5634; www.sugarlandridingstables.com)

 ## Sleeping

Great Smoky Mountains National Park provides varied camping options, but only one place where you can get a room, and you have to hike to the top of a mountain to enjoy this privilege. Gatlinburg has

Detour:
Asheville

About an hour and a half drive from the North Carolina park gateway town of Cherokee, Asheville is one of North Carolina's – and America's – hippest small cities. Long a vacation destination for moneyed East Coasters (F Scott Fitzgerald was a fan), the city now has a huge artist population and a highly visible contingent of hard-core hippies. The art-deco buildings of downtown remain much the same as they were in 1930, though the area is now hopping with decidedly modern boutiques, restaurants, vintage stores and record shops.

Asheville's number one attraction by far is **Biltmore Estate** (www.biltmore.com; adult/child under 17 $59/29.50; ☺9am-4:30pm). With 43 bathrooms, 65 fireplaces and a private bowling alley, the Gilded Age estate is a veritable American Versailles. The country's largest private home and Asheville's number-one tourist attraction, it was built in 1895 for shipping and railroad heir George Washington Vanderbilt II, who modeled it after the grand chateaux he'd seen on his various European jaunts. Viewing the estate and its 250 acres of gorgeously manicured grounds and gardens takes several hours.

The town's food scene is one of its major draws. Don't miss chowing down on New Southern specialties like sweet potato pancakes with artisan jam or pork chops with mango salsa at **Tupelo Honey** (☎828-255-4863; www.tupelohoney.com; 12 College St; mains $9-22; ☺9am-10pm), or tasting the renowned small-batch chocolates at the **French Broad Chocolate Lounge** (www.frenchbroadchocolates.com; 10 S Lexington; snacks $2-6; ☺11am-11pm, to midnight Fri & Sat).

by far the most sleeping options of any gateway town.

Camping

The National Park Service maintains developed campgrounds at 10 locations in the park. Each campground has restrooms with cold running water and flush toilets, but there are no showers or electrical or water hookups in the park. Each individual campsite has a fire grate and picnic table.

Campsites at Cades Cove, Cataloochee, Cosby, Elkmont, and Smokemont may accept **reservations** (☎800-365-2267; www.recreation.gov), but only between May 15 and October 31. Sites may be reserved up to six months in advance. All other campgrounds are first-come, first-served. There are a number of options for group camping for groups of eight or more – check out the park website for more info. Backcountry

camping is allowed by permit only – pick one up at any one of the visitor centers.

CADES COVE Campground $
(campsite $17-20; ☺year-round) This campground is always full on summer weekends and during the autumn leaf-peeping season, but there's plenty of room the rest of the year. The 159 sites are shady but situated a mite too close together. In late afternoon the place takes on a downtown feel as everyone hops on bicycles or socializes. In the evenings the Cades Cove amphitheater provides entertainment in the form of ranger programs. A tiny camp store serves the itinerant camper community.

The campground is 6 miles southwest of the Townsend Wye via Laurel Creek Rd.

ELKMONT Campground $
(Little River Rd; campsite $17-23; ☺Mar-Nov) The largest campground in the park and the closest to Gatlinburg, Elkmont features wooded sites along the Little River.

During peak season the 220 sites often fill to capacity by noon. Even though it's larger than Cades Cove Campground, this is a much quieter place. Sections A and B tend to be the most crowded. Nearby hiking trails include the Elkmont Nature Trail, Little River Trail and Jakes Creek Trail. The maximum RV length is 32ft.

SMOKEMONT   Campground $
(campsite $17-20; ⏱year-round) Near Cherokee, this large and attractive 140-site campground along the wooded banks of the Oconaluftee River is open year-round. Sections B and C feature sunny creekside spots; section F is for RVs (up to 35ft long) only. The campsite is off Newfound Gap Rd.

BALSAM MOUNTAIN   Campground $
(campsite $14; ⏱May-Oct) This small highlands campground is considered by many to be the park's loveliest, thanks to its privileged placement within an 'island' forest of red spruce and Fraser firs. Though the 46 campsites are somewhat small, the upside to this is that it discourages behemoth RVs from roosting (though RVs up to 30ft are allowed). The campground

is 8 miles from the Blue Ridge Parkway via Heintooga Ridge Rd.

DEEP CREEK   Campground $
(campsite $17; ⏱Apr-Oct) Near Bryson City, this medium-sized family campground with 92 sites offers a good variety of choices and splendid opportunities for hiking and bird-watching. Section C features creekside tent-only sites; section D, a loop road through the woods, affords more privacy. The waters of Deep Creek give much joy to inner-tubers and anglers. Near the entrance to the campground is the village of Big Creek, with a snack bar and tube rentals. To get there from the depot in Bryson City, turn right onto Depot St, then left on Ramseur Rd, then immediately right on Deep Creek Rd.

CATALOOCHEE   Campground $
(campsite $20; ⏱Mar-Oct) This remote campground in a forest of hemlock and white pine has spacious campsites arranged off a loop road; six of the 27 sites lie along the excellent fishing waters of Cataloochee Creek. The campground fills up on summer evenings. Take exit 20 off I-40, go west on Hwy 276 to Cove Creek Rd and follow it to Cataloochee Rd.

Sunrise, Great Smoky Mountains

COSBY
Campground **$**

(campsite $14; ⏰Mar-Oct) This large, beautifully forested campground is a good alternative to the heavily used Elkmont and Cades Cove sites; it's rarely if ever crowded. Several loops are lined with 165 spacious campsites that afford a remarkable degree of privacy. The campground lies off Hwy 32 near the Tennessee town of Cosby.

ABRAMS CREEK
Campground **$**

(campsite $14; ⏰Mar-Oct) This small, remote campground on the western edge of the park takes a bit of effort to get to, but you'll be well compensated for your journey. Half of the 16 sites face pretty Abrams Creek; the others are arranged along the edge of the woods. Abrams Creek is a popular fishing spot. The campground lies 7 miles north of Hwy 129 via Happy Valley Rd.

BIG CREEK
Campground **$**

(campsite $14; ⏰Mar-Oct) The smallest of Great Smoky's campgrounds is a walk-in affair used mostly by hikers. RVs are not welcome here. Five of the 12 sites sit beside the cacophonous Big Creek. You must haul your gear from the car a distance of 100ft to 300ft. To get here, take Tennessee exit 451 off I-40, then proceed upstream beside the Pigeon River to the ranger station.

LOOK ROCK
Campground **$**

(campsite $14; ⏰May-Oct) Due to its out-of-the-way location, this campsite always has sites available. The 68 sites are fairly small, but chances are you won't have neighbors. The campground's on Foothills Pkwy W, which begins at the intersection of Hwy 321, just north of Townsend.

Lodging

LECONTE LODGE
Lodge **$$**

(☎865-429-5704, www.lecontelodge.com; summit of Mt Le Conte; adult/child incl breakfast & dinner $116/85; ⏰Mar-Nov) At the summit of the crown jewel mountain of the Great Smokies, the park's only lodge is not your average hotel. Accessible only by hiking (six trails lead to the top, ranging from 5 to 10 miles), with no electricity and all food and supplies packed in by llamas (yep, you heard us), LeConte is a once-in-a-lifetime experience. The lodge can accommodate 50 guests per night, housed in rustic cabins or group sleeping lodges. The cabins have upper and lower double bunk beds and sleep two couples or a family of four to five. The lodges accommodate 10 to 13 people each. Kerosene lamps provide illumination, but definitely pack a flashlight.

Hearty all-you-can-eat family-style breakfasts and dinners are served in the lodge dining room; lunch is included for guests staying more than one night. The lodge fills up FAST – book your reservations

Little Pigeon River (p149), Great Smoky Mountains

Hiking the Appalachian Trail

The storied Appalachian Trail is an irresistible draw for many hikers. For some it's the only reason they come to Great Smoky. Seventy of the AT's 2174 miles pass through the park, and many through-hikers consider these to be the highlight of the entire trail. For the most part, the trail follows the crest of the Great Smoky Mountains, shadowing the shared border between North Carolina and Tennessee.

An excellent time to make the trip is in September or October, when traffic on the trails has dissipated somewhat and autumn leaves are at their finest. In October, however, snow should be expected.

Hikers on the AT sleep in backcountry shelters spaced 3 to 8 miles apart; reservations are required. During the summer, you'll likely need to make the necessary consecutive reservations well in advance.

Check out the **Appalachian Trail Conservancy's website** (www.appalachiantrail.org) for more information.

months, if not a full year, in advance. The lodge begins taking reservations on October 1 for the following year's season. Reservation cancellations are not uncommon, so if you have no reservation and would like to find space on short notice, try your luck by calling the office; the lodge just might be able to accommodate you.

 Eating

Nuts and berries notwithstanding, there's nothing to eat in Great Smoky Mountains National Park, save for guests-only fare at LeConte Lodge, vending machines at Sugarlands Visitor Center and the meager offerings sold at the Cades Cove Campground store. Luckily, there are lots of restaurant options in the surrounding towns. See p161 for listings.

ℹ Information

The National Parks Services' **Great Smoky Mountains National Park website** (www.nps.gov/grsm) has comprehensive and extremely valuable information about campgrounds, hiking trails, activities, visitor center hours and much more.

Entrance Fees & Passes

Entrance to Great Smoky Mountains National Park is free. The park is open year-round.

Park Policies & Regulations

Campers must store all food in bear-proof containers or on storage poles. Backcountry campfires are forbidden. If you plan to fish, you need either a North Carolina or Tennessee fishing license, which are sold at sporting goods stores and gas stations outside the park.

Maps

A variety of useful maps, hiking guides and driving tours are available for sale at all the visitor centers.

Dangers & Annoyances

Black bears are active throughout the park, and can be dangerous. Campers should keep all food in their cars or tied to cables, and hikers should never approach or feed bears. If a bear approaches you, back away slowly. If the bear continues to approach, shout or wave your arms to intimidate it. As a last resort, throw rocks or other objects, or try to deter the bear with a large stick. Never try to run.

Getting There & Around

The closest major airport is Knoxville's McGhee Tyson Airport, 45 miles from the Gatlinburg entrance. For information on the airport and on public shuttles from Gatlinburg, see p161.

AROUND GREAT SMOKY
Gatlinburg

Wildly kitschy Gatlinburg hunkers at the entrance of the Great Smoky Mountains National Park, waiting to stun hikers with the scent of fudge and cotton candy. Tourists flock here to ride the ski lifts, shop for Confederate-flag undershorts, get married at the many wedding chapels, and play hillbilly-themed mini-golf. Love it or hate it, the entire village is a gin-u-wine American roadside attraction.

Souvenir shopping, mini-golf, comedy shows, arcades, and carnival-style museums and attractions are the order of the day in Gatlinburg. There are several wildly popular Ripley's attractions, including a Believe it or Not! museum of oddities, and a huge and high-quality aquarium. Both make fun family trips on rainy days.

🛏 Sleeping

Gatlinburg has thousands upon thousands of hotel rooms, most in the budget to midrange price category. Prices rise in summer, on weekends, and during October leaf-peeping season. Look for a comprehensive list of accommodations at www.gatlinburg.com.

BUCKHORN INN   B&B $$
(☎865-436-4668, www.buckhorninn.com; 2140 Tudor Mountain Rd; r incl breakfast $115-175; P ❄ 🛜) A few minutes' drive and several light years away from the kitsch and crowds of downtown Gatlinburg, the tranquil Buckhorn has nine elegant rooms and seven private cottages on a well-manicured haven of a private property, complete with wandering swans. If the unbroken views of Mt LeConte don't relax you enough, have a wander through the fieldstone meditation labyrinth.

Mountain Farm Museum (p149), Great Smoky Mountains

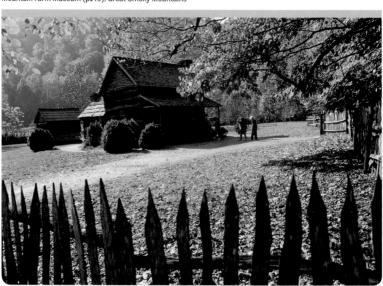

GATLINBURG INN   Hotel **$**

(☎865-436-5133, www.gatlinburginn.com; 755 Parkway; r $58-110; P✲🛜🏊) Looking like the home of an eccentric country music star c 1963, this downtown classic has all the wood paneling, gold rugs, rococo light fixtures and Jesus paintings you can handle. Check out the bear in the lobby.

ROCKY WATERS MOTOR INN   Motel **$**

(☎865-436-7861, www.rockywatersmotorinn.com; 333 Parkway; r from $59; P✲🛜) This pleasantly retro motel has clean, comfy rooms perched above the river. It's walking distance from downtown, but at a serene remove from the noise and lights.

 Eating

Gatlinburg dining is mostly high-volume and middlebrow. Pancake restaurants, steakhouses and ye olde country kitchen-style buffets are all big. But if you're emerging from a day of hiking in the park, you'll be happy enough to tuck into a massive plate of greasy ribs. Expect waits at the more popular restaurants during busy season.

PANCAKE PANTRY   Breakfast **$**

(www.pancakepantry.com; 628 Parkway; mains $8-11; ⏱7am-4pm Jun-Oct, to 3pm Nov-May) Gatlinburg has a thing for pancakes, and this is the place that started it all. The Pantry's secret is simple: real butter, honest-to-goodness fresh whipped cream and everything made from scratch. We recommend the Swedish pancakes, with lashings of lingonberry jam. At lunch there's gourmet sandwiches with funny names like The Polish Aristocrat, which can be ordered ahead for picnics by the waterfalls of Great Smoky.

THE PEDDLER   Steakhouse **$$$**

(☎865-436-5794; www.peddlergatlinburg.com; 820 River Rd; mains $19-30; ⏱5pm-varies) In a large rustic lodge with exposed timbers and native stone fireplaces, this always slammed spot is loved for its dripping hunks of prime rib, grilled mountain trout and American-sized salad bar. Kids meals

are priced by the child's age in dollars, making this a popular family spot.

SMOKY MOUNTAIN BREWERY   American **$$**

(www.coppercellar.com; 1004 Parkway; mains $9-20; ⏱11:30am-1am) American pub grub like quesadillas, chicken fingers, pizzas, burgers and pasta dishes are A-OK, but it's the microbrewed beer, multiple TV sets and raucous ski-lodge atmosphere that really packs in the crowds.

ℹ️ Information

The visitor's bureau runs an info-packed **website** (www.gatlinburg.com). There are several Welcome Centers downtown, all stocked with brochures and maps.

ℹ️ Getting There & Away

The vast majority of visitors arrive in Gatlinburg by car. The nearest airport is Knoxville's **McGhee Tyson Airport** (www.tys.org), 55 miles away, and there's no regular intercity bus service.

The **Gatlinburg Trolley** serves downtown, and the trolley's tan line ($2) goes into the park between July and October, with stops at Sugarlands Visitor Center, Laurel Falls and Elkmont Campground.

Cherokee

On the other end of Newfound Gap Rd from Gatlinburg, the North Carolina town of Cherokee is the park's other major base town. The area has a rich but sad Native American history – many of the Smokies' original Cherokee inhabitants were forced off their lands during the 1830s and marched to Oklahoma on the Trail of Tears. Descendants of those who escaped are known as the Eastern Band of the Cherokee, about 12,000 of whom now occupy the 56,000-acre Qualla Boundary territory at the edge of the park. Cherokee, a rather unlovely town, anchors the Qualla Boundary with motels, ersatz Native American souvenir shops, fast-food joints and **Harrah's Cherokee Casino** (www.harrahs.com). The best sight is the modern **Museum of the Cherokee Indian** (www.cherokeemuseum.org; cnr Hwy 441 & Drama Rd; adult/child $10/6; ⏱9am-5pm), with an informative exhibit on the Trail of Tears and eerily realistic dioramas.

SHENANDOAH NATIONAL PARK

Some say that *Shenandoah* means 'daughter of the stars'; others translate it as 'river of high mountains.' Whatever interpretation, the park deserves a beautiful appellation such as these. A lush and verdant stretch of the Blue Ridge Mountains, the park is home to more glorious viewpoints than your camera can handle, with the green-and-silver Shenandoah River Valley to the west and the gently rolling hills of Piedmont Virginia to the east.

The park's only road, the spectacular 105-mile Skyline Drive, twists and climbs from 600ft to more than 4000ft. Numerous trails sprout from this main artery, providing visitors with many opportunities to dip into the great outdoors.

History

First proposed as a park in 1926, this area of the Blue Ridge Mountains was set aside to provide a peaceful refuge for nearby urban populations. It took 10 years for the people who had lived here to relocate, and in 1936 President Roosevelt dedicated the park, naming it Shenandoah. It was considered a novel experiment to take an over-logged and overgrazed area and allow it to return to its natural state. The experiment worked. Former cropland and pasture have become wild forest once again, complete with a healthy population of black bears, deer, bobcats, turkeys and 200 species of birds.

When to Go

The park is open year-round, but fall leaf-peeping season is by far the more popular time to visit. Some facilities and visitor centers are only open from April through November.

When You Arrive

Most visitors enter the park by car, but pedestrians and cyclists are also admitted for a fee. Fees for individuals (including bicycles) are $8 and vehicles are $15. Both fees are good for seven days.

Orientation

The famous and spectacularly scenic Skyline Drive is the only road through the park. Twisting like a loose ribbon, it weaves along the top of the Blue Ridge Mountains for 105 miles, ending at the North Entrance of the Blue Ridge Parkway. Concrete mileposts (referenced in this chapter as MP) on either side of the road indicate location and serve as reference points.

Vehicles access the park from four entrances. The Front Royal (North) Entrance (Map p163) is accessible via I-66 east to US 340 south. To access the Thornton Gap (North–Central) Entrance (Map p163) from the east, take the Gainesville (US 29) exit off I-66 and head south to Warrenton, then take US 211 west to the park; from the west, take US 211 east from Luray. Enter the Swift Run Gap (South–Central) Entrance (Map p166) from the east by staying on US 29 to Stanardsville, then taking US 33 west; from the west, follow US 33 east from Elkton. The Rockfish Gap (South) Entrance can be reached from the east by staying on US 29 to Charlottesville and taking I-64 west; if you're coming from the west, take US 250 east from Waynesboro. There are also several pedestrian and cyclist entrances.

Sights

All the sights in the park are along **Skyline Drive**, which has more than 75 viewpoints for drivers to pull off and admire the valleys below.

DICKEY RIDGE VISITOR CENTER
Visitor Center

(MP 4.6; Map p163) Dickey Ridge is one of the park's two main information centers and contains a little bit of everything you'll need to get you started on your trip along Skyline Drive, including a slide show, exhibits, rest rooms and water.

Shenandoah (North)

0 — 10 km
0 — 5 miles

Strasburg

Front Royal

Front Royal (North)
Entrance Station

Shenandoah
National Park

4

6

Skyline Dr

George
Washington
National Forest

522

630

Mt Marshall
(3368ft)

The Peak
(3000ft)

9

Washington

15

7

5

Pignut
Mountain
(2530ft)

Shenandoah
National Park

Three
Sisters

Pass
Mountain
(3052ft)

Thornton Gap
(North–Central)
Entrance

211

Marys
Rock

Hazel
Mountain

Luray

8

Pinnacles

Stony Man
Mountain
(4011ft)

Skyline Dr

10

Pinnacle
Peak
(3401ft)

Old Rag
(3268ft)

340

Stanley

2

Hawksbill
(4050ft)

12

600

340

14

Big Meadows

1   11   3

670

649

Tanners Ridge

Hazeltop
(3812ft)

Shenandoah (North)

HARRY F BYRD VISITOR CENTER
Visitor Center

(MP 51; Map p163) The park's second visitor center also has plenty of maps, info and backcountry camping permits.

SKYLAND
Lodge, Activities

(MP 41.7; Map p163) Naturalist George Freeman Pollock envisioned a lofty summer resort where wealthy city folks (who had come to spend the hot months in the clear air of the high mountains) would be toted around in sightseeing wagons and fed elaborate meals as they observed nature. He got it. Skyland Lodge opened in 1890; over the years it grew to incorporate about 15 historic buildings and nature sites. Today it marks the highest point on Skyline Drive and one of the park's primary tourist facilities. Visitors can tour those same 15 sites Pollock created, as well as enjoy horseback rides, ranger activities and evening programs at the lodge.

HAWKSBILL MOUNTAIN
Mountain

(MP 45.6) The highest peak in the park (4050ft) is also a well-known nesting area for peregrine falcons. Stand on the rustic stone observation platform at the end of the trail for long-lasting impressions of the park's wondrous beauty.

 Activities

While hiking is the main draw, bird-watching, cycling and ranger-led activities are also popular.

Hiking

TRACES
Hiking

One of the easiest and prettiest day hikes in the park, this 1.7-mile round-trip is a good bet for small children. The 'traces' you'll pass include an old mountain settlement as the trail winds through a cool, mature oak forest. Start from the Mathews Arm Campground, where the trail quickly winds past pieces of former foundations and roads. Enveloped in a canopy of red oaks, the trail soon rises above the campground amphitheater. Near the end of the trail, a solitary oak stands like a beacon, and there are points ahead where you can take in mountain vistas.

HAWKSBILL SUMMIT
Hiking

This tremendous climb to the park's highest peak offers an unforgettable picture of the mountain landscape. There are two options for this climb – either a 2.8-mile loop or 1.7-mile up-and-back. (This description follows the latter.)

Start at the Hawksbill Gap parking area (MP 45.6) and look for the Lower Hawksbill Trail, which leads into the woods. The steep ascent is lined with mountain ash and red spruce– beware of small, frequent rockslides along the jumbled path. When you encounter a cement post, you'll know you're close to the summit. Go right until you see a three-sided building, the Byrds Nest Shelter 2 (no water or camping here). A little further up is the observation platform, which offers breathtaking vistas in every

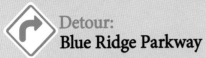

Detour:
Blue Ridge Parkway

Commissioned by president Franklin D Roosevelt as a Depression-era public-works project, the glorious Blue Ridge Pkwy traverses the southern Appalachians connecting Shenandoah National Park at Mile 0 to the Great Smoky Mountains National Park at Mile 469. The National Park Service **campgrounds and visitor centers** (☏877-444-6777; www.blueridgeparkway.org; tent sites $16) are open May to October. Parkway entrance is free; be aware that restrooms and gas stations are few and far between.

Parkway highlights and campgrounds include the following:

- **Peaks of Otter** (Mile 86) Three scenic mountain peaks with camping and a lodge.

- **Rocky Knob & Mabry Mill** (Miles 169, 176.2) Rental cabins and a historic gristmill.

- **Cumberland Knob** (Mile 217.5) NPS visitor center, easy walk to the knob.

- **Doughton Park** (Mile 241.1) Gas, food, trails and camping.

- **Moses H Cone Memorial Park** (Mile 294.1) A lovely old estate with pleasant walks and a craft shop.

- **Julian Price Memorial Park** (Mile 296.9) Camping.

- **Grandfather Mountain** (Mile 305.1) Hugely popular for its mile-high pedestrian 'swinging bridge.'

- **Linville Falls** (Mile 316.4) Short hiking trails to the falls and campsites.

- **Linville Caverns** (Mile 317) Limestone cave with neat formations and underground streams; tours $7.

- **Crabtree Meadows** (Mile 339.5) Camping.

- **Mt Mitchell State Park** (Mile 355.5) Highest peak east of the Mississippi (6684ft); hiking and camping.

- **Folk Art Center** (Mile 382) Local crafts for sale.

- **Mount Pisgah** (Mile 408.8) Hiking and camping.

possible direction of Browns Mountain, Stony Man and even the town of Luray twinkling in the distance. After taking a peek at the cool compass embedded in the cement post, retrace your steps to the parking lot.

DARK HOLLOW FALLS   Hiking

This small waterfall is only 0.7 miles away from the Skyline Drive parking area, but the rocky terrain makes for a tough hike in certain sections, and the return trip is all uphill. It's not unusual for hikers to suffer accidents here, so take extra caution when stepping over slippery rocks and

make use of those handrails – they're there for a darn good reason!

Start at the Dark Hollow Falls parking area (MP 50.7). Upon entering the forest, you'll encounter a small stream. Less than a mile ahead you'll see the 70ft Dark Hollow Falls pouring over a craggy ancient lava flow. Descend about 0.1 mile to the base of the falls and imagine what was racing through the mind of one of the forefathers, Thomas Jefferson, when he was a frequent visitor to this area.

You can either hike further down to see more small waterfalls and cascades created by Hogcamp Branch (which will

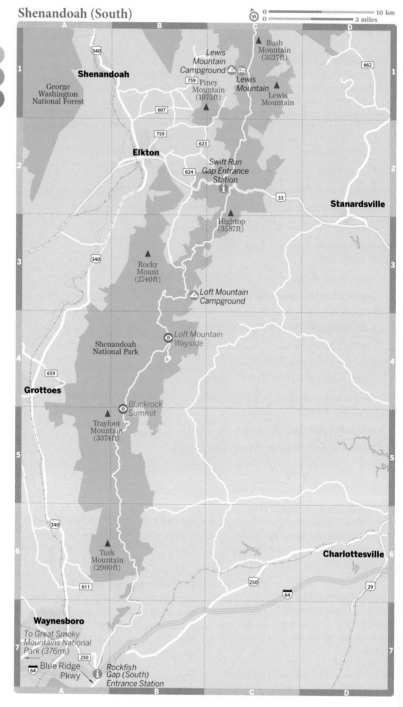

eventually put you out at the Rose River Fire Rd) or take a deep breath and begin that arduous ascent back to the trailhead.

FOX HOLLOW Hiking
This 1.2 mile loop is a nice, kid-friendly trail that offers a good introduction to how the forests of the Shenandoah area have repopulated themselves and covered what used to be abundant farmland. It's also home to a colorful assortment of birds like the hairy woodpecker, Carolina chickadee and American goldfinch.

Start at the Dickey Ridge Visitor Center and cross the street. You'll soon run into the Dickey Ridge Trail. Turn left and proceed about 0.2 miles until you meet up with the Fox Hollow Trail. Continue walking alongside a stone wall that used to mark the Fox family property. After turning right, you'll soon descend to a hollow with a small, crumbly cemetery. This is the Fox Family Cemetery, named for the family who worked a farmstead on this land. Be on the lookout for pickerel frogs, which flourish in the spring. The end of the trail turns sharply upward and pops out into a clearing. You'll see a sign for the Snead Farm Loop Trail – if you want to extend your hike, this loop is a mild, 1.4-mile trek through apple orchards past an old barn.

Backpacking

Shenandoah has several overnight hikes for dedicated trail-walkers with their own gear. Backcountry camping is free, but you must have a permit – pick one up at any visitor center or ranger station. Popular trails include the 13.5-mile Mt Marshall loop and the 9.3-mile Riprap Trail loop. Riprap Trail parking is at MP 90, while the Mt Marshall trailhead is at MP 12.5.

Cycling

Cycling is only permitted on Skyline Drive. Cycling or mountain biking on backcountry trails and fire roads is not allowed. Normal cycling rules apply – use correct lighting at night, travel single file and keep to the right. Even though many cyclists told us they were discouraged from riding Skyline Drive's narrow, sometimes blind-curve route, it remains a popular and challenging route for two-wheelers.

Bird & Wildlife Watching

More than 200 bird species have been spotted in the park, not to mention more than 40 species of mammals, 50 species of reptiles and amphibians, and 20 species of fish. Rockfish Gap is a particularly good place to see hawks in flight. Big Meadows is the best spot to view an interesting assortment of wildlife, from wild turkeys to white-tailed deer to loping bears lolling about in the fields.

Horseback Riding

Riding is allowed on designated trails. **Skyland Stables** (☏540-999-2210; www.visitshenandoah.com; rides per hour $40; ☉May-Oct) offers guided rides along neighboring trails; children saddle up on ponies (15/30 minutes $6/12).

 Sleeping

The park has two lodges, four campgrounds, a number of rental cabins and free backcountry camping.

Camping

The following campgrounds all allow RVs except for Lewis Mountain. Big Meadows, Loft Mountain and Mathews Arm accept advance **reservations** (☏877-444-6777; www.recreation.gov).

BIG MEADOWS CAMPGROUND Campground $
(Map p163; MP 51.3; campsite $20; ☉Mar-Nov) Find the perfect spot among 217 sites and you might just snap a quick photo of a resident bear lumbering past your campfire. This campground tends to be crowded, especially during fall, but it's smack in the middle of Skyline Drive and a convenient base for all exploration.

STEPHEN SAKS / LONELY PLANET IMAGES ©

Don't Miss Big Meadows

There's no doubt you've reached Big Meadows when the trees disappear and the land becomes an open meadow. A sprawling expanse of silvery grassland favored by grazing deer and other critters, this is one of the park's most unique biozones, so pack a picnic, bring your binoculars, and get ready for some nature-watching. The spacious Harry F Byrd Visitor Center houses an exhibit on the landscape and history of Shenandoah, as well as a plethora of books, maps and even mountain music. Grab a bite to eat at the wayside coffee shop before gassing up, or head just down the road to check out the views from the Great Room at the Big Meadows Lodge, which has the park's coziest dining area and soul-wrenching views down into the Shenandoah Valley. There's a snack bar, a gift shop, and a tall stack of well-worn board games in the lodge's Great Room.

The Big Meadows area stretches between MP 51.3 and MP 51.9. The lodge restaurant is open for breakfast, lunch and dinner.

MATHEWS ARM CAMPGROUND   Campground $

(Map p163; MP 22.1; campsite $15; ⊙May–Oct) This campground doesn't have a store (there's one 2 miles south at Elkwallow), but does boast plenty of rushing water – Overall Run Falls, the highest waterfall in the park, is accessible from here.

LEWIS MOUNTAIN CAMPGROUND   Campground $

(Map p166; MP 57.5; campsite $15; ⊙Apr–Oct) The smallest campground (only 31 sites)

is also the most intimate when it comes to getting close to Mother Nature. The tent-less should check out the onsite cabins.

LOFT MOUNTAIN CAMPGROUND   Campground $

(Map p166; MP 79.5; campsite $15; ⊙mid-May–Oct) This 'lofty' campground features some serious altitude on top of Big Flat Mountain. It's also the largest, so expect crowds.

Lodging

Skyland and Big Meadows are the park's main sleeping and activity centers, with onsite restaurants, taprooms, gift shops and playgrounds. They're also the starting points for a few trails. To the prices quoted below, add about $10 to $20 for fall high season.

SKYLAND LODGE Lodge, Cabins $$
(Map p163; MP 41.7; 📞800-999-4714; www.visitshenandoah.com; r $129-166, ste $159-219, cabins/family cabins $109/256; ⊙Mar-Nov; 🐾) Located at the highest point on the drive, Skyland Lodge is also one of the park highlights. Most of the rooms are motel-type units only a quick hike from the main lodge, but there are a few rustic cabins, and many of the accommodations offer magnificent views of the Shenandoah Valley.

BIG MEADOWS LODGE Lodge, Cabins $$
(Map p163; MP 51.3; 📞800-999-4714; www.visitshenandoah.com; r $109-166, cabins/ste $109/164; ⊙mid-May–Nov; 🐾) The old-fashioned Great Room inside the lodge is the perfect place to end a strenuous day, nestled beside the cozy stone fireplace playing board games or rocking in the line of chairs that overlook the valley. Rustic cabins are the way to go for their earthy silence – end cabins get you your own fireplace. Don't be surprised to see deer or a bear stroll by your steps. Some rooms have TVs, but none have phones.

LEWIS MOUNTAIN Cabins $$
(Map p166; MP 57.5; 📞800-999-4714; www.visitshenandoah.com; cabins $109; ⊙early Apr–early-Nov; 🐾) Think of these rustic one-room cabins as 'camping with walls and a bed,'

plus a few modern conveniences thrown in, like heat and private bathrooms. Though there's electricity and running water, there's no fridge or stoves, so guests must bring coolers and all their own cooking implements.

Eating

Elkwallow, Big Meadows and Loft Mountain have wayside snack bars. Skyland and Big Meadows have snack bars in addition to the following sit-down dining rooms.

POLLOCK DINING ROOM American $$
(Map p163; MP 41.7; www.visitshenandoah.com; mains $13-24; ⊙Mar-Nov) Skyland's dining room serves squares a day. Lunch is sandwiches and burgers, while dinner aims a little fancier – stick to classics like 'Rapidan Camp Trout' and 'Roosevelt Chicken.'

SPOTTSWOOD DINING ROOM American $$
(Map p163; MP 51.3; www.visitshenandoah.com; mains $13-23; ⊙May-Nov) Big Meadows'

Appalachian Trail (p159), Shenandoah
ANDRE JENNY / ALAMY ©

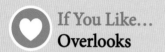

If You Like…
Overlooks

There are over 75 scenic overlooks in Shenandoah, so you could easily pull over every mile or two if you wish. Following are a few of our favorites:

1 GOONEY RUN OVERLOOK
(Map p163; Mile 6.8) Overlooking the white-water rapids that share its name, Gooney Run was a key marching point for General Stonewall Jackson during the Civil War. From this vantage point you can see the snaky outline of the South Fork of the Shenandoah River and the undulating peaks of the Massanutten Range.

2 RANGE VIEW OVERLOOK
(Map p163; Mile 17.1) Like an encyclopedic illustration of mountains and ranges, this impressive vista takes in a 14-mile stretch of peaks ranging from Stony Man's craggy face to the Blue Ridge and Massanutten, reaching even as far as the Alleghenies on exceptionally clear days.

3 PINNACLES & PINNACLE PEAK OVERLOOK
(Map p163; Mile 36.7) From the second parking lot, there's a very quick hike (20 minutes) along the AT down to a sweeping overlook of Hogback Mountain and Mt Marshall.

4 CRESCENT ROCK OVERLOOK
(Map p163; Mile 44.4) The commanding peaks of the Massanutten Range, Hawksbill Mountain and Naked Top stretch across the Shenandoah Valley like a panoramic photograph.

dining room serves essentially the same menu as Skyland's, with an old-fashioned rustic lodge ambiance.

ⓘ Information
The National Parks Service website (www.nps.gov/shen) for Shenandoah is full of hiking and outdoors information, while the Visit Shenandoah site (www.visitshenandoah.com) covers information about the park's privately run concessions like lodges, restaurants and horseback riding.

Entrance Fees & Passes
Fees for individuals (including bicycles) are $8, vehicles are $15. Both are good for seven days. Annual passes are $30.

Opening Dates
Shenandoah is open year-round. Parts of Skyline Drive may be closed during bad weather in winter, and at night during the November–January deer-hunting season.

Park Policies & Regulations
Campers must store all food in bear-proof containers or on storage poles. Backcountry campfires are forbidden. You may not bring firewood into the park because of the risk of invasive insects – firewood is sold at the campgrounds. If you plan to fish, you need a permit – these are available at the Big Meadows' wayside, or at sporting goods stores outside the park.

Maps
Basic maps are distributed at the park entrance; more detailed hiking maps are available for purchase at the visitor centers and the lodge gift shops.

Dangers & Annoyances
Bears can be a problem in the park. Never approach or try to feed a bear, and keep all food securely locked away in your car or bear-proof container. If you're planning to hike the Old Rag Trail, check out the safety video on the Parks Service website (www.nps.gov/shen) – the hike is the park's most hazardous.

ⓘ Getting There & Around
There are four main park entrances. The Front Royal (North) Entrance is accessible via I-66 east to US 340 south. To access the Thornton Gap (North–Central) Entrance from the east, take the Gainesville (US 29) exit off I-66 and head south to Warrenton, then take US 211 west to the park; from the west, take US 211 east from Luray. Enter the Swift Run Gap (South–Central) Entrance from the east by staying on US 29 to Stanardsville, then taking US 33 west; from the west, follow US 33 east from Elkton. The Rockfish Gap (South)

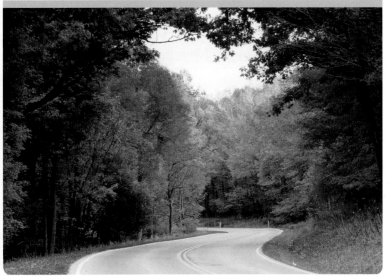

WITOLD SKRYPCZAK / LONELY PLANET IMAGES ©

Entrance can be reached from the east by staying on US 29 to Charlottesville and taking I-64 west; if you're coming from the west, take US 250 east from Waynesboro.

The nearest airport is in Swift Run Gap, Virginia, about 27 miles away. The nearest major airport is in Washington, DC, 56 miles away.

There is no public transportation in the park.

AROUND SHENANDOAH

Front Royal

At the park's northernmost tip, this medium-sized town is cute enough, with a handful of B&Bs, grocery stores for resupplying, and a number of area vineyards open for wine-sipping tours. Other than that, there's not much to detain the visitor.

Sleeping & Eating

KILLAHEVLIN BED & BREAKFAST
B&B $$

( 540-636-7335, www.vairish.com; 1401 N Royal Ave; r $155-215, ste $255-465; P ❄ 🛜) Front Royal's most elegant B&B is Irish down to the shamrocks in the wallpaper. Sleep under crisp linens in the handsome, antiques-filled rooms, then wake to breakfast on homemade scones. Later, a Harp on tap in the tiny pub is just the ticket after a long Shenandoah hike.

SPELUNKERS
Fast Food $

(www.spelunkerscustard.com; 116 S St; mains $3-5; ⏰11am-10pm) 'Cavern burgers' and superlative homemade custard are all-American good eats at this beloved local fast-food spot.

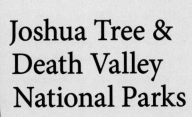

Joshua Tree & Death Valley National Parks

Good things come to those who wait. When Congress passed the California Desert Protection Act in 1994, it finally elevated two national monuments in California – Joshua Tree and Death Valley – to higher status. In the process, it added more than 2000 sq miles to the latter and confirmed what millions of people knew about both: that these unique desert regions merit the National Park Service's highest title – national park.

From the massive boulders and bizarre plants of Joshua Tree, to the singing sand dunes and shady oases of Death Valley, there is certainly no shortage of things to see. Despite being deserts, these unique national parks are full of wildlife, including bighorn sheep, tiny pupfish and, in Death Valley, one of the grandest displays of wildflowers anywhere in the United States. What took Congress so long?

RICHARD CUMMINS / LONELY PLANET IMAGES ©

Joshua Tree & Death Valley Itineraries

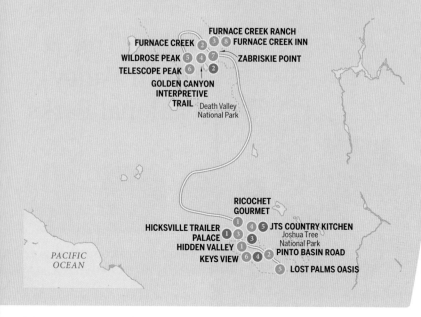

FURNACE CREEK RANCH
FURNACE CREEK ❷ ❸ ❻ FURNACE CREEK INN
WILDROSE PEAK ❺ ❹ ❼ ZABRISKIE POINT
TELESCOPE PEAK ❻ ❷
GOLDEN CANYON
INTERPRETIVE
TRAIL   Death Valley
National Park

PACIFIC
OCEAN

RICOCHET
GOURMET
❶
HICKSVILLE TRAILER ❶ ❹ ❺ JTS COUNTRY KITCHEN
PALACE ❸ Joshua Tree
HIDDEN VALLEY ❶ ❸ National Park
KEYS VIEW ❻ ❹ ❷ PINTO BASIN ROAD
❺ LOST PALMS OASIS

Two Days in Joshua Tree

❶ **Hidden Valley** (p181) Ever been curious about monzogranite? Get to know one of Joshua Tree's finest natural features – rock – by hiking this short trail and playing around on the boulders. No need to be a rock climber to have fun on this stuff!

❷ **Pinto Basin Road** (p177) Unroll the windows, hit the gas and explore this 30-mile scenic drive from the high Mojave Desert to the low Colorado Desert.

❸ **Hicksville Trailer Palace** (p182) Lay your head down at one of California's quirkiest places to stay, an oasis of vintage trailers, custom decorated in the finest of retro-chic style.

❹ **JT's Country Kitchen** (p183) On day two slurp down some Cambodian noodles somewhere you'd least expect them – in an American roadside breakfast joint.

❺ **Lost Palms Oasis** (p179) Hike out to Joshua Tree's largest fan-palm oasis, where you can experience the subtle beauty of the park's unique desert oases.

❻ **Keys View** (p177) Close the evening atop this stunning lookout point, which has 360-degree views of the Coachella Valley and Southern California's highest mountains. If you squint, you can even see the Salton Sea, which is 235ft below sea level.

⮕ THIS LEG: 160 MILES

174

Two Days in Death Valley

1 **Ricochet Gourmet** (p183) Get up early and treat yourself to a hearty and wholesome breakfast, and then pack the car for the drive to Death Valley National Park.

2 **Furnace Creek** (p187) Drive 275 miles north to the official headquarters of Death Valley National Park, where you can explore the park's beloved Borax Museum and, if you time it right, meet all 24 of Furnace Creek's permanent residents.

3 **Furnace Creek Ranch** (p191) Check in at this family-friendly ranch and take a dip in the spring-fed swimming pool.

4 **Golden Canyon Interpretive Trail** (p190) Take a leisurely stroll through Golden Canyon and gaze at the surreal, multihued cliffs of Red Cathedral.

5 **Wildrose Peak** (p190) On day two, wake up early and hike to the summit of Wildrose Peak for a view of the park from 9064ft above sea level.

6 **Telescope Peak** (p190) If you're a fit hiker with a thirst for extremes, skip Wildrose Peak and tackle the park's highest peak, 11,049ft Telescope Peak. Despite its location in Death Valley, it's covered in ice and snow in winter.

7 **Zabriskie Point** (p187) In the afternoon, set out by car for Zabriskie Point, where you can take in stellar views of the park. While you're gazing, ponder the fact that the great French philosopher Michel Foucault dropped acid up here in 1975.

8 **Furnace Creek Inn** (p191) Close the day with a sunset cocktail on the patio of Death Valley's exquisite Furnace Creek Inn.

· ·

➡ **THIS LEG: 415 MILES**

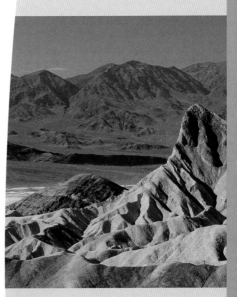

Joshua Tree & Death Valley Highlights

1 **Best Place to Sleep: Hicksville Trailer Palace** (p182) Who knew a trailer could be so stylish?

2 **Best View: Zabriskie Point** (p187) One of California's most famous viewpoints.

3 **Best Oasis: 49 Palms Oasis** (p178) You won't drink the water, but the sight of this oasis is stunning.

4 **Best Bike Ride: Geology Tour Road** (p178) Pedal into the geological past on a mountain-bike ride down this scenic dirt road.

5 **Best Lunch: JT's Country Kitchen** (p183) Cambodian noodles have never tasted so good.

View from Zabriskie Point (p187), Death Valley
WITOLD SKRYPCZAK / LONELY PLANET IMAGES ©

Discover Joshua Tree & Death Valley

JOSHUA TREE NATIONAL PARK

Taking a page from a Dr Seuss book, the whimsical Joshua trees (actually tree-sized yuccas) welcome visitors to this 794,000-acre (321,000-hectare) park at the convergence of the Colorado and Mojave Deserts. Rock climbers know 'JT' as the best place to climb in California, but kids and the young-at-heart also welcome the chance to scramble up, down and around the giant boulders. Hikers seek out hidden, shady fan-palm oases fed by natural springs and small streams, while mountain bikers are hypnotized by the desert vistas seen from dirt 4WD roads. The park is especially lovely in springtime when the Joshua trees send up a huge single cream-colored flower, and the octopus-like tentacles of the ocotillo cactus shoot out crimson flowers.

History

Visitors to Joshua Tree are often surprised to learn that this arid desert has supported humans for at least 5000 years. The first people known to inhabit the area were the Pintos, hunter-gatherers who sought large mammals in the Pinto Basin region. Much later, the Serrano, the Chemehuevi and the Cahuilla cultures all lived, gathered food and hunted in different regions of the park. All three cultures relied on the desert's oases, particularly the Mara Oasis (now called Twentynine Palms). During the California gold rush, miners began scouring the region for gold, but few struck it big. The only fruitful mine was the Lost Horse Mine, which was eventually purchased by a wealthy Montanan named JD Ryan, who hauled in the 10-stamp mill that can still be seen there today.

By the early 1900s, the region's indigenous people were almost gone, forced from their villages by settlers or killed by smallpox. The Lost Horse Mine was abandoned in 1931. Five years later, Joshua Tree became a national monument. It finally gained national-park status with the passage of the California Desert Protection Act in 1994.

Joshua trees
RUTH EASTHAM & MAX PAOLI / LONELY PLANET IMAGES ©

When to Go

The best time to visit Joshua Tree is arguably in spring, when temperatures are still tolerable and the wildflowers are in bloom. However, spring is also peak tourist season, and the park is at its busiest. Fall temperatures are also comfortable. Summer is sweltering and visitation is low. During winter, days are cool and nights are freezing.

When You Arrive

Park entry fees must be paid upon arrival. Be sure to get a park newspaper and brochure when you enter – they're full of useful information.

Orientation

Joshua Tree National Park is 170 miles east of Los Angeles, 200 miles (via I-15, I-215 and I-10) northeast of San Diego and 215 miles south of Las Vegas. The West Entrance Station and the North Entrance Station are both on the north side of the park (approached via Hwy 62). The South Entrance Station is approached via I-10. The towns of Joshua Tree and Twentynine Palms are the main commercial hubs.

 Sights

The park's northern half harbors most of the attractions, including all of the Joshua trees (and you've hardly visited 'JT' until you see its namesake trees).

KEYS VIEW   Lookout
From Park Blvd, it's an easy 20-minute drive up to Keys View (5185ft), where breathtaking views take in the entire Coachella Valley and extend as far as the Salton Sea and – on a good day – Mexico. Looming in front of you are Mt San Jacinto (10,800ft) and Mt San Gorgonio (11,500ft), two of Southern California's highest peaks, while down below you can spot a section of the San Andreas Fault.

DESERT QUEEN RANCH   Guided Tour
(reservations 760-367-5555; tour adult/child $5/2.50; tours 10am & 1pm daily year-round, 7pm Tue, Thu-Sat Oct-May) Anyone interested in local history and lore should take the 90-minute guided tour of this ranch that's also known as Keys Ranch after its builder, Russian immigrant William Keys. Reservations highly recommended.

OASIS OF MARA   Oasis
Behind the Oasis Park Visitor Center in Twentynine Palms, this natural oasis encompasses the original 29 palm trees for which the town is named. They were planted by members of the Serrano tribe, who named this 'the place of little springs and much grass.' The Pinto Mountain Fault, a small branch of the San Andreas, runs through the oasis, as does a 0.5-mile, wheelchair-accessible nature trail with labeled desert plants.

 **Activities**

Driving Tours

Driving around the park can be a great way to take in some of Joshua Tree's most interesting sights.

COVINGTON FLATS   Scenic Drive
Joshua trees grow throughout the northern park, including along Park Blvd, but some of the biggest trees are found in this area accessed via La Contenta Rd, south off Hwy 62 between the towns of Yucca Valley and Joshua Tree. For photogenic views, follow the dirt road 3.8 miles up the Eureka Peak (5516ft) from the picnic area.

PINTO BASIN ROAD   Scenic Drive
To see the natural transition from the high Mojave Desert to the low Colorado Desert, wind along down to Cottonwood Spring, a 30-mile drive southeast from Hidden Valley. Stop at **Cholla Cactus Garden**, where a quarter-mile loop trail leads around waving ocotillo plants and jumping 'teddy bear' cholla. Near the Cottonwood Park Visitor Center, **Cottonwood Spring** is an oasis with a natural spring that Cahuilla tribespeople depended on for centuries.

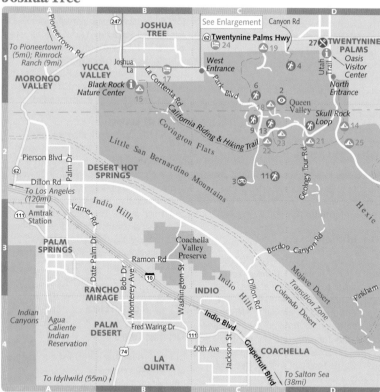

GEOLOGY TOUR ROAD   Scenic Drive

Travelers with 4WD vehicles or mountain bikes can head east of Hidden Valley on this 18-mile field trip down into and around Pleasant Valley. Here the forces of erosion, earthquakes and ancient volcanoes have played out in stunning splendor. Before setting out, pick up a self-guided tour brochure and an update on road conditions at any park visitor center.

Hiking

Staff at the visitor centers can help you match your time and fitness level to the perfect trail.

49 PALMS OASIS   Hiking

In the northernmost section of the park, this moderate, 3-mile, round-trip trail leads to a boulder-strewn oasis of fan palms in a small canyon. Beneath the canopy of fronds, small pools provide water for desert reptiles and birds, making it a great spot for bird-watching. The sight of green palm fronds hanging over the oasis is stunning.

The trailhead lies at the end of Canyon Rd, which heads south from Hwy 62, immediately west of the Indian Cove entrance. The hike has a total elevation gain of about 345ft. If you're lucky, you might spot bighorn sheep.

BARKER DAM   Hiking

Although this easy 1.1-mile loop trail is as short as they come, it offers access to one of the better areas of the park for spotting bighorn sheep – provided you get out here when there aren't loads of people. The short trail passes a site with

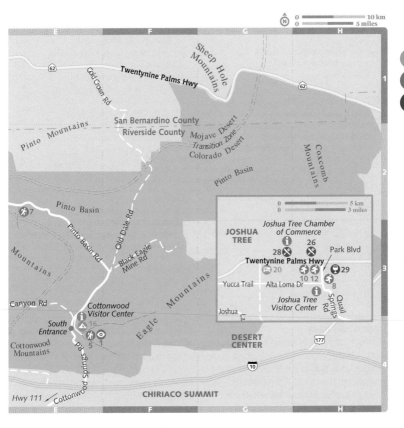

Native American petroglyphs and finally arrives at a tiny reservoir, which is surrounded by rock domes. The trailhead is at the Barker Dam parking lot, at the end of a spur off Park Blvd.

LOST HORSE MINE   Hiking

This moderate-to-strenuous trail leads to Lost Horse Mine, one of the few mines in Joshua Tree that ever produced significant quantities of gold during the California gold rush. The mine operated until 1931, and among the relics that remain is a finely preserved stamp mill, which was used to crush rock for extracting gold.

If you just go to Lost Horse Mine, the hike is 4 miles out and back. You can turn it into a 6.2 mile loop by hiking the full Lost Horse Mine Loop trail. Simply stay on the trail that continues past the short spur that branches northeast to the mine.

To get to the trailhead, head south from Park Blvd (near Hidden Valley) on Keys View Rd and swing left on Lost Horse Mine Rd. The trailhead is at the end of Lost Horse Mine Rd.

LOST PALMS OASIS   Hiking

The highlight of this moderate 7.2 mile round-trip (out and back) hike is the park's largest stand of desert fan palms, Lost Palms Oasis. The total elevation gain is only about 375ft. You can add about 1.5 miles to the hike by detouring to Mastodon Peak at the outset of the hike. As with most hikes in the park, there is very little shade on the trail, so carry plenty of water. The trail departs from the Cottonwood Spring, near Cottonwood Campground, off Cottonwood Spring Rd.

Joshua Tree

MASTODON PEAK   Hiking

Although this 3-mile round-trip hike to the top of Mastodon Peak is hardly long, it can be strenuous due to the steepness of the trail toward the top. But the rewards – views of the Eagle Mountains and the Salton Sea – from the summit of the 3371ft peak make the hike well worth it.

The trail departs from Cottonwood Spring and can be combined with the Lost Palms Oasis trail for a longer hike.

RYAN MOUNTAIN   Hiking

Strenuous, but manageable for anyone with a properly functioning cardiovascular system, this 1.5-mile one-way trail ascends Ryan Mountain and offers a beautiful bird's-eye view of the park. From the 5461ft summit, you get a 360-degree view of Joshua Tree, including Lost Horse Valley, Desert Valley and Queen Valley.

The path is well marked and departs from a trailhead on Park Blvd. Total elevation gain is about 900ft.

Backpacking

Backpacking routes, like the 16-mile, out-and-back **Boy Scout Trail** and a 35-mile

one-way stretch of the **California Riding & Hiking Trail** present a challenge because of the need to carry so many gallons of water per person per day. Overnight backcountry hikers must register at one of 13 backcountry boards located at trailhead parking lots throughout the park.

Mountain Biking

Cycling is only permitted on paved and dirt public roads; bikes are not allowed on hiking trails.

VILLAGE BICYCLE   Bicycle Rental
(☎ 760-808 4557; Hallee Rd; ⏱ 10am-6pm Mon-Fri, 9am-9pm Sat, 9am-2pm Sun) Rents basic mountain bikes for $45 per day. The owner also does repairs. Located behind Sam's in Joshua Tree.

Rock Climbing

Joshua Tree's rocks are famous for their rough, high-friction surface, and from boulders to cracks to multipitch faces, there are more than 8000 established routes, many right off the main road. The longest climbs are not much more than 100ft or so, but there are many challenging technical

Detour:
Palm Springs

The Rat Pack is back, baby, or at least its hangout is. In the 1950s and '60s, Palm Springs, about 50 miles west of Joshua Tree's South Entrance, was the swinging getaway of Sinatra, Elvis and dozens of other stars. Once the Rat Pack packed it in, though, the Coachella Valley surrendered to retirees in golf clothing. That is, until the mid-1990s, when a new generation fell in love with the city's retro-chic charms. In today's Palm Springs, retirees mix comfortably with hipsters and a significant gay and lesbian contingent.

North of downtown, the **Palm Springs Aerial Tramway** (www.pstramway.com; 1 Tram Way; round-trip adult/child $23.95/16.95; 10am-8pm Mon-Fri, 8am-8pm Sat & Sun;) is a highlight of any Palm Springs trip. It climbs nearly 6000 vertical feet through five different vegetation zones, from the Sonoran Desert floor to the San Jacinto Mountains, in less than 15 minutes.

Pampering yourself at one of the city's famous spas is a must. Try the stylish **Estrella Spa at Viceroy Palm Springs** (760-320-4117; www.viceroypalmsprings.com; 415 S Belardo Rd) or the new and unflinchingly hip **Feel Good Spa at Ace Hotel & Swim Club** (760-329-8791; www.acehotel.com/palmsprings/spa), where you can get a treatment inside a yurt.

Then lay your head down at the fabulously retro **Orbit In** (760-323-3585, 877-996-7248; www.orbitin.com; 562 W Arenas Rd; d incl breakfast $149-259;) or the luxurious **Riviera Palm Springs** (760-327-8311, 866-588-8311; www.psriviera.com; 1600 Indian Canyon Dr; r $240-260, ste $290-$540;).

routes, and most can be easily top-roped for training. Some of the most popular climbs are in the Hidden Valley area.

HIDDEN VALLEY
Rock Climbing

Some 8 miles south of the West Entrance, this whimsically dramatic cluster of rocks is a rock climber's mecca, but just about anyone can enjoy a clamber on the giant boulders. An easy 1-mile trail loops through it and back to the parking lot and picnic area.

Shops catering to climbers with quality gear, advice and tours:

JOSHUA TREE
OUTFITTERS
Rock Climbing

(760-366-1848, 888-366-1848; www.joshuatreeoutfitters.com; 61707 Twentynine Palms Hwy, Joshua Tree; usually 9am-5pm)

NOMAD VENTURES
Rock Climbing

(760-366-4684; www.nomadventures.com; 61795 Twentynine Palms Hwy, Joshua Tree;

8am-6pm Mon-Thu, to 8pm Fri & Sat, to 7pm Sun Oct-Apr, 9am-7pm daily May-Sep)

COYOTE CORNER
Rock Climbing

(760-366-9683; www.joshuatreevillage.com/546/546.htm; 6535 Park Blvd, Joshua Tree; 9am-7pm)

 Sleeping

Inside the park there are only campgrounds but there are plenty of lodging options along Hwy 62. Twentynine Palms has the bigger selection of accommodations, including national chain motels. Lodgings in Joshua Tree have more character and charm.

Camping

Of the park's nine **campgrounds** (877-444-6777; www.recreation.gov; tent & RV sites $10-15), only Cottonwood and Black Rock have potable water, flush toilets and

181

dump stations. Indian Cove and Black Rock accept reservations. The others are first-come, first-served and have pit toilets, picnic tables and fire grates. None have showers. During the springtime wildflower bloom, campsites fill by noon, if not earlier.

Along Park Blvd, Jumbo Rocks has sheltered rock alcoves that act as perfect sunset- and sunrise-viewing platforms. Belle and White Tank also have boulder-embracing views. Hidden Valley is always busy. Sheep Pass and Ryan are centrally located. Family-friendly Black Rock is good for camping novices; more remote Indian Cove has 100-plus sites. Cottonwood, near the park's South Entrance, is popular with RVs.

Lodging

HICKSVILLE TRAILER PALACE   Motel $$
(310-584-1086; www.hicksville.com; r $75-200; ⚹ 🛜 🐾) Fancy sleeping among glowing wigs, in a haunted house or in a horse stall? Check in at Hicksville, where the 'rooms' are eight outlandishly decorated vintage trailers set around a kidney-shaped saltwater swimming pool. To keep out gawkers, guests are only given directions after making reservations.

DESERT LILY   B&B $$
(760-366-4676, 877-887-7370; www.thedesertlily.com; Joshua Tree Highlands; s/d incl breakfast $140/155; 🕑closed Jul & Aug; @ 🛜) Old West meets Southwest at this three-room adobe retreat. Rooms are a bit snug, but there are also four private cabins with full kitchens should you need more elbow space. It's near the West Entrance of the park.

**SPIN & MARGIE'S
DESERT HIDE-A-WAY**   Boutique Inn $$
(760-366-9124; www.deserthideaway.com; Sunkist Rd, off Twentynine Palms Hwy; ste $125-175; ⚹ 🛜) This handsome hacienda-style inn is perfect for restoring calm after a long day on the road. The five boldly colored suites are an eccentric symphony of corrugated tin, old license plates and cartoon art. It's down the dirt Sunkist Rd, about 3 miles east of downtown Joshua Tree.

JOSHUA TREE INN   Motel $
(760-366-1188; www.joshuatreeinn.com; 61259 Twentynine Palms Hwy, Joshua Tree; incl breakfast d $95, f $110-125; ⚹ 🛜 🐾) A pleasant motel with spacious rooms behind turquoise doors leading off from a desert garden courtyard. In 1973 rock legend Gram Parsons overdosed in Room 8.

Slow: Desert Tortoise X-Ing

The Mojave Desert is the abode of the desert tortoise, which can live for up to 80 years, munching on wildflowers and grasses. With its canteenlike bladder, it can go for up to a year without drinking. Using its strong hind legs, it burrows to escape the summer heat and freezing winter temperatures, and also to lay eggs. The sex of the hatchlings is determined by temperature: cooler for males, hotter for females.

Disease and shrinking habitat have decimated the desert tortoise population. They do like to rest in the shade under parked cars (take a quick look around before driving away). If you see a tortoise in trouble, eg stranded in the middle of a road, call a ranger.

It's illegal to pick one up or even approach too closely. A frightened tortoise may urinate on a perceived attacker, possibly dying of dehydration before the next rains come.

Eating & Drinking

JT'S COUNTRY KITCHEN Breakfast, Asian $

(☎760-366-8988; 61768 Twentynine Palms Hwy, Joshua Tree; mains $4-10; ⏱6am-3:30pm) This roadside shack serves down-home cookin': eggs, pancakes, biscuits with gravy, sandwiches and... what's this? Cambodian noodles and salads? Delish.

RICOCHET GOURMET International $

(☎760-366-1898; www.ricochetjoshuatree.com; 61705 Twentynine Palms Hwy, Joshua Tree; mains $8-15; ⏱7am-5pm Mon-Sat, 8am-5pm Sun; 📶🐾) At this locally adored cafe-cum-deli, the menu bounces from breakfast frittatas to curry chicken salad and fragrant soups, all of them homemade with organic and seasonal ingredients.

RESTAURANT AT 29 PALMS INN American $$

(☎760-367-3505; www.29palmsinn.com; 73950 Inn Ave, Twentynine Palms; mains lunch $7.50-10, dinner $9-21; 📶) The well-respected restaurant has its own botanical garden and does burgers and salads for lunch and grilled meats and pastas for dinner.

SAM'S Pizza, Indian $

(☎760-366-9511; 61380 Twentynine Palms Hwy, Joshua Tree; mains $8-11; ⏱11am-9pm Mon-Sat, 3-8pm Sun; 🍴) Pizza and Indian curries.

FARMERS MARKET Market

On Saturdays mornings locals gather for gossip and groceries at the farmers market in a parking lot near Joshua Tree Health Foods, just west of Park Blvd in Joshua Tree.

ⓘ Information

Entrance Fees & Passes

Entry to Joshua Tree National Park (☎760-367-5500; www.nps.gov/jotr) costs $15

♥ If You Like...
Roadhouse Atmosphere

If you like the feel of places like JTs Country Kitchen (p183), you'll certainly feel at home at these joints.

1 Joshua Tree Saloon
(http://thejoshuatreesaloon.com; 61835 Twentynine Palms Hwy, Joshua Tree; ⏱8am-late; 📶) This watering hole with jukebox, pool tables and cowboy flair serves bar food along with rib-sticking burgers and steaks. Over 21 only.

2 Corkscrew Saloon
(☎760-786-2345; www.furnacecreekresort.com; Hwy 190, Furnace Creek Ranch, Furnace Creek, Death Valley; mains $6-23, barbecue $28-36; ⏱11:30am to midnight) Gregarious joint with darts, draft beer, dynamite BBQ and OK pub grub.

3 Toll Road Restaurant
(Stovepipe Wells Village, Hwy 190; breakfast buffet $12, dinner $12-25; ⏱7am-9:30am & 7-10pm mid-May–mid-Oct, 7am-10am & 5-9pm mid-Oct–mid-May; 📶👫) Cowboy cooking and Old West flair meet local ingredients and creative recipes.

per vehicle or $5 per pedestrian, bicycle or motorcycle.

Passes are valid for seven days and come with a map and the seasonally updated *Joshua Tree Guide*.

Opening Dates

Joshua Tree is open 24 hours a day, 365 days a year.

Tourist Information

Black Rock Nature Center (9800 Black Rock Canyon Rd, south of Hwy 62; ⏱8am-4pm Sat-Thu, noon-8pm Fri Oct-May) At the Black Rock campground.

Cottonwood Visitor Center (Cottonwood Spring Rd, north of I-10; ⏱9am-3pm) Just inside the park's South Entrance.

DANITA DELIMONT / ALAMY ©

Don't Miss **Pioneertown**

Drive 12 miles west of the Joshua Tree Visitor Center on Hwy 62 and you'll hit Pioneertown, a short jaunt into a faraway past. Looking like an 1870s frontier town, **Pioneertown** (www.pioneertown.com; admission free; 👫) was actually built in 1946 as a Hollywood Western outdoor movie set. Gene Autry and Roy Rogers were among the original investors and over 50 movies and several TV shows were filmed here in the 1940s and '50s. These days, the Pioneertown Posse stage free mock gunfights on 'Mane St' at 2:30pm on Saturdays and Sundays from April to October.

For local color, toothsome BBQ, cheap beer and kick-ass live music, drop in at **Pappy & Harriet's Pioneertown Palace** (📞760-365-5956; www.pappyandharriets.com; 53688 Pioneertown Rd; burgers $5-12, mains $16-30; ⏱11am-2am Thu-Sun, 5pm-midnight Mon), a textbook honky-tonk. Monday's open-mike nights are legendary and often bring out astounding talent.

Within staggering distance is the atmospheric **Pioneertown Motel** (📞760-365-7001; www.pioneertown-motel.com; 5040 Curtis Rd; r $50-100; ❄🛜), where yesteryear's silver-screen stars once slept during filming and whose rooms are now filled with eccentric Western-themed memorabilia; some have kitchenettes.

About 4.5 miles north, **Rimrock Ranch** (📞760-228-1297; www.rimrockranchcabins.com; 50857 Burns Canyon Rd; cabins $90-140; ❄🏊🐾) is a cluster of four vintage 1940s cabins with kitchens and private patios perfect for stargazing.

Joshua Tree Visitor Center (Park Blvd, Joshua Tree; ⏱8am-5pm) Outside the West Entrance in Joshua Tree.

Oasis Visitor Center (National Park Blvd at Utah Trail, Twentynine Palms; ⏱8am-5pm) Outside the North Entrance in Twentynine Palms.

Joshua Tree Chamber of Commerce (📞760-366-3723; www.joshuatreechamber.org; 6448 Hallee Rd, Joshua Tree; ⏱10am-4pm Tue, Thu & Sat)

Dangers & Annoyances

The desert can be a dangerous place, especially in summer when temperatures rise. Always carry plenty of water. Potable water is available at the Oasis of Mara, and Black Rock and Cottonwood campgrounds, at the West Entrance and at the Indian Cove Ranger Station.

ⓘ Getting There & Around

Air

The closest major international airports:

Los Angeles International Airport (LAX; ☏ 310-646-5252; www.lawa.org) Located 160 miles (roughly 2¾ hours) west of the park.

San Diego International Airport (SAN; ☏ 619-400-2404; www.san.org) Located 180 miles (roughly three hours) southwest of the park.

Car

Rent a car in Palm Springs or Los Angeles. From LA, the trip takes about 2½ to three hours via I-10 and Hwy 62. From Palm Springs, it takes about an hour to reach the park's West (preferable) or South Entrances.

Bus

Bus 1, operated by **Morongo Basin Transit Authority** (www.mbtabus.com), runs frequently along Twentynine Palms Hwy (one-way fares $1 to $2, day pass $3). Bus 12 to Palm Springs (one way/round-trip $7/11 from Joshua Tree & Yucca Valley) has fewer departures. Many buses are equipped with bicycle racks.

DEATH VALLEY NATIONAL PARK

The name itself evokes all that is harsh, hot and hellish – a punishing, barren and lifeless place of Old Testament severity. Yet closer inspection reveals that in Death Valley, nature is putting on a truly spectacular show: singing sand dunes, water-sculpted canyons, boulders moving across the desert floor, extinct volcanic craters, palm-shaded oases and plenty of endemic wildlife. This is a land of superlatives, holding the US records for hottest temperature (134°F, or 57°C), lowest point (Badwater, 282ft below sea level) and largest national park outside Alaska (over 5000 sq miles).

History

Native Americans have inhabited the Death Valley area for thousands of years. The Timbisha Shoshone lived in the Panamint Range (Death Valley's western mountains) for centuries before they were relocated to a small area around Furnace Creek in 1933. Mining began in 1849 but few claims were profitable, and the pursuit was mostly abandoned by the late 1920s. Death Valley became a national monument in 1933. It was designated a biosphere reserve in 1984 and finally earned national-park status with passage of the California Desert Protection Act in 1994. The same bill added more than 2000 sq miles to the park, making it the largest national park in the Lower 48.

When to Go

Peak seasons are winter and during the springtime wildflower bloom (check the park service website at www.nps.gov/deva for wildflower updates). From late February until early April, lodging within a 100-mile radius is usually booked solid and campgrounds fill before noon, especially on weekends. Heat is brutal in summer.

When You Arrive

Upon arrival, be sure to pick up a copy of the *Death Valley Visitor Guide*. It's loaded with information, including tips on how to safely deal with the heat.

Orientation

Hwy 190 runs east–west through the park and passes through Furnace Creek, the park's primary service center and home to its main visitor center. The park's second visitor center is at Scotty's Castle, accessed via Hwy 267 from Nevada. There is also a ranger station on Hwy 374.

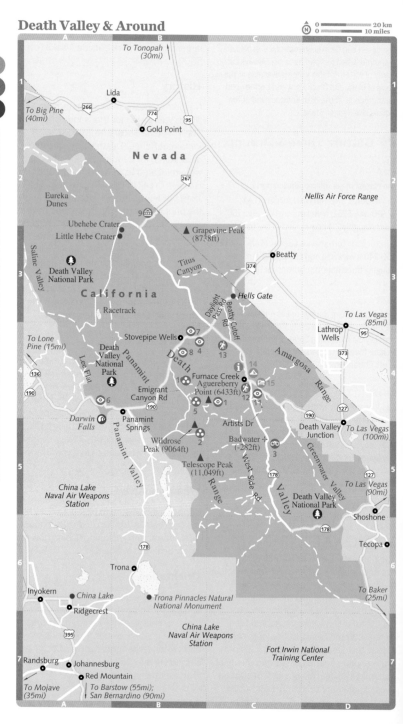

Death Valley & Around

Sights

EUREKA DUNES   Dunes

Death Valley's tallest sand dunes tower some 680ft above the desert floor in the park's remote Eureka Valley. It's possible to climb to the top of the dunes, where, if the dunes are bone dry, you can hear the sound of singing sand. The sound, caused by falling sand as it zips down the side of the highest dune, is one of Death Valley's marvels. Combined with the stunning views from the top of the dunes, it makes the drive out here well worth while.

Furnace Creek

Furnace is Death Valley's commercial hub, with a general store, park visitor center, gas station, post office, ATM, internet access, golf course, lodging and restaurants. Cleverly concealed by a date-palm grove is a solar power plant that currently generates one-third of Furnace Creek's energy needs.

BORAX MUSEUM   Museum
(⏰ 9am-9pm Oct-May, hours vary in summer)
Find out all you ever wanted to know about borax and peruse the collection of pioneer-era stagecoaches and wagons out back.

South of Furnace Creek

If possible, start out early in the morning to drive up to **Zabriskie Point** for spectacular valley views across golden badlands eroded into waves, pleats and gullies. Escape the heat by continuing on to **Dante's View** at 5000ft, where you can simultaneously see the highest (Mt Whitney) and lowest (Badwater) points in the contiguous USA. The drive there takes about 1½ to two hours round-trip.

Badwater itself, a foreboding landscape of crinkly salt flats, is a 17-mile drive south of Furnace Creek. Here you can walk out onto a boardwalk above a constantly evaporating bed of salty, mineralized water that's otherworldly in its beauty. The **Badwater Ultramarathon** (www.badwater.com) is touted as the most demanding footrace in the world: runners cover 135 miles nonstop from Death Valley to Mt Whitney in temperatures up to 130°F (55°C).

Stovepipe Wells & Around

Stovepipe Wells, about 26 miles northwest of Furnace Creek, was Death Valley's original 1920s tourist resort. Today it has a small store, gas station, ATM, motel, campground and bar. En route, look for the roadside pull-off where you can walk out onto the powdery, Sahara-like **Mesquite Flat Sand Dunes**. The dunes are at their most photogenic when the sun is low in the sky and especially magical during full moon. Across the road, look for the **Devil's Cornfield**, full of arrow weed clumps. Some 2.5 miles southwest of Stovepipe Wells, a 3-mile gravel side road leads to **Mosaic Canyon**, where you can hike over and scramble along the smooth multihued rock walls. Colors are sharpest at midday.

Along Emigrant Canyon Rd

Some 6 miles southwest of Stovepipe Wells, Emigrant Canyon Rd veers off Hwy 190 and travels south to the park's higher elevations. En route you'll pass the turnoff to **Skidoo**, a mining ghost town where the silent movie *Greed* was filmed in 1923. It's an 8-mile trip on a graded gravel road (high-clearance vehicles only) to get to the ruins and jaw-dropping Sierra Nevada views.

Further south, Emigrant Canyon Rd passes the turnoff for the 7-mile dirt road leading past the **Eureka Mines** to the vertiginous **Aguereberry Point** (high-clearance vehicles only), where you'll have fantastic views back into the valley and out to the colorful Funeral Mountains from a lofty 6433ft. The best time to visit is in the late afternoon.

Emigrant Canyon Rd now climbs steeply over Emigrant Pass and through Wildrose Canyon to reach the **charcoal kilns**, a lineup of large, stone, beehive-shaped structures historically used by miners to make fuel for smelting silver and lead ore.

Panamint Springs

About 30 miles west of Stovepipe Wells, on the edge of the park, Panamint Springs is a tiny enclave with a motel, campground, pricey gas station and small store. Several often overlooked but wonderful hidden gems are easily accessed from here. **Father Crowley Point**, for instance, peers deep into Rainbow Canyon, created by lava flows and scattered with colorful volcanic cinders.

Scotty's Castle

SCOTTY'S CASTLE   Historic Building
(adult/child $11/6; ☉grounds 7:30am-5:30pm May-Oct, to 6pm Nov-Apr) About 55 miles north of Furnace Creek, Scotty's Castle is named for Walter E Scott, alias 'Death Valley Scotty,' a gifted tall-tale teller who captivated people with his fanciful stories of gold. His most lucrative friendship was with Albert and Bessie Johnson, insurance magnates from Chicago. Despite

Left: Zabriskie Point (p187), Death Valley; **Below:** Joshua tree

(LEFT) WITOLD SKRYPCZAK / LONELY PLANET IMAGES ©; (BELOW) DAVID TOMLINSON / LONELY PLANET IMAGES ©

knowing that Scotty was a freeloading liar, they bankrolled the construction of this elaborate Spanish-inspired villa. Restored to its 1930s glory, the historic house has sheepskin drapes, carved California redwood, handmade tiles, elaborate wrought iron, woven Shoshone baskets, and a bellowing pipe organ upstairs. **Scotty's Castle Visitor Center** (☎760-786-2392, ext 231; North Hwy; ⏰8:45am-4:30pm May-Oct, 8:30am-5:30pm Nov-Apr) has exhibits from the castle's museum-worthy collection.

LIVING HISTORY TOUR   Tour
(⏰at least hourly 9:30am-4pm May-Oct, 9am-5pm Nov-Apr) Costumed guides recount Scotty's apocryphal story in colorful detail on this wacky tour. Advance tickets are available at ☎877-444-6777 or www.recreation.gov at least one day in advance. It's possible to turn up without a ticket, but expect long waits on busy weekends.

Activities

Families can pick up fun-for-all-ages **junior ranger program** activity books at the Furnace Creek Visitor Center, which has info-packed handouts on all kinds of activities, including hiking trails and mountain-biking routes.

Hiking

Avoid hiking in summer, except on higher-elevation mountain trails, which may be snowed in during winter.

**SALT CREEK
INTERPRETIVE TRAIL**   Hiking
On Hwy 190, just north of Beatty Cutoff Rd, this easy half-mile nature trail is best in late winter or early spring. During that time, rare pupfish splash in the small stream alongside the boardwalk.

GOLDEN CANYON INTERPRETIVE TRAIL
Hiking

A few miles south of Furnace Creek, a self-guided interpretive trail winds for 1 mile through Golden Canyon to the oxidized iron cliffs of **Red Cathedral**. With a good sense of orientation, you can keep going up to **Zabriskie Point** for a hardy 4-mile round-trip. To get to the Golden Canyon trailhead, park in the lot 2 miles south of Hwy 190 on Badwater Rd.

WILDROSE PEAK
Hiking

This moderate-to-strenuous trail begins near the charcoal kilns, off Wildrose Canyon Rd, and ascends to Wildrose Peak, which towers 9064ft above the park. The round-trip hike is 8.4 miles and is best in spring or fall. The elevation gain is 2200ft, but great views start about halfway up. From the top, you'll have a stunning vista of the Panamint Mountains, Badwater Basin and all of Death Valley National Park. The final mile or so below the summit is the hardest stretch.

TELESCOPE PEAK
Hiking

The park's highest and most demanding summit is Telescope Peak (11,049ft). Those who make it to the top will be rewarded with views that plummet down to the desert floor – the mountain is known for having one of the greatest direct summit-to-floor views of any mountain. The distance is akin to the depth of two Grand Canyons.

The 14-mile round-trip trail climbs 3000ft above Mahogany Flat, off upper Wildrose Canyon Rd. Summiting in winter requires an ice axe, crampons and winter-hiking experience. By June, the trail is usually free of snow and doable for fit hikers.

Other Activities

FURNACE CREEK CYCLERY
Mountain Biking

(☎760-786-3372, ext 372; www.furnacecreek resort.com; Hwy 190, Furnace Creek; 1hr/24hr $10/49; ⏰year-round) Mountain-bike rentals and tours.

FURNACE CREEK GOLF COURSE
Golf

(☎760-786-3373; Hwy 190, Furnace Creek; greens fees summer/winter $30/55; ⏰year-round) World's lowest elevation course (18 holes, par 70).

FURNACE CREEK STABLES
Horseback Riding

(☎760-614-1018; www.furnacecreek stables.net; Hwy 190, Furnace Creek; 1/2hr rides $45/65; ⏰mid-Oct– mid-May) Saddle up to see what Death Valley looks like from the back of a horse on these guided rides. The monthly full-moon rides are the most memorable.

FARABEE'S JEEP RENTALS
4WD Rentals

(☎760-786-9872; www.deathvalleyjeeprentals.com; 2-/4-door Jeep incl 200 miles

Eureka Mines (p188), Death Valley
WITOLD SKRYPCZAK / LONELY PLANET IMAGES ©

$175/195; ⏲mid-Sep-mid-May) Rents jeeps for back-road exploration. Next to the Furnace Creek Inn.

 # Sleeping

In-park lodging is pricey and often booked solid in springtime but there are several gateway towns with cheaper lodging. The closest is Beatty, but choices are more plentiful in Las Vegas and Ridgecrest.

Of the park's nine **campgrounds** (☎877-444-6777; www.recreation.gov), only Furnace Creek Campground accepts reservations and only from mid-April to mid-October. All other campgrounds are first-come, first-served. At peak times, such as weekends during the spring wildflower bloom, campsites fill by mid-morning.

Furnace Creek Ranch and Stovepipe Wells Village offer public showers ($5, including swimming-pool access).

STOVEPIPE WELLS VILLAGE Motel $$
(☎760-786-2387; www.escapetodeathvalley.com; Hwy 190, Stovepipe Wells Village; RV sites with hookups $31, r $80-155; ❄🛜🏊🐾) Newly spruced up rooms feature quality linens beneath cheerful Native American–patterned bedspreads as well as coffee-makers. The small pool is cool and the cowboy-style restaurant (mains $5 to $25) delivers three square meals a day.

FURNACE CREEK RANCH Resort $$
(☎760-786-2345; www.furnacecreekresort.com; Hwy 190, Furnace Creek; cabins $130-162, r $162-213; ❄🛜🏊🐾) Tailor-made for families, this rambling resort offers spiffy rooms swathed in desert colors with French doors leading out to porches with comfortable patio furniture.

FURNACE CREEK INN Hotel $$$
(☎760-786-2345; www.furnacecreekresort.com; Hwy 190, Furnace Creek; r $335-455, ste $440-470; ⏲mid-Oct–mid-May; ❄🛜🏊) Roll out of bed and count the colors of the desert as you pull back the curtains in your room at this elegant 1927 mission-style hotel with languid valley views.

PANAMINT SPRINGS RESORT Motel, Campground $
(☎760-482-7680; www.deathvalley.com/psr; Hwy 190, Panamint Springs; tent $7.50, RV sites with partial/full hookup $15/30, r $80-110; ❄🛜🏊🐾) Simple, clean and decent-sized rooms. Not a bad spot for launching a Death Valley exploration.

 # Eating & Drinking

Furnace Creek and Stovepipe Wells have general stores stocking basic groceries and camping supplies. Scotty's Castle has a snack bar.

WRANGLER RESTAURANT Steakhouse $$$
(Furnace Creek Ranch, Furnace Creek; breakfast/lunch buffet $11/15, dinner $28-39; ⏲6-9am, 11am-2pm & 5:30-9pm Oct-May, 6-10am & 6-9:30pm May-Oct) Furnace Creek Ranch's main restaurant serves belly-busting buffets at breakfast and lunchtime (when tour bus groups invade) and turns into a pricey steakhouse at night.

FURNACE CREEK INN International $$$
(☎760-786-2345; Hwy 190, Furnace Creek; mains lunch $13-17, dinner $24-38; ⏲7:30-10:30am, noon-2:30pm & 5:30-9:30pm mid-Oct–mid-May) Views of the Panamint Mountains are stellar from this formal dining room with a dress code (no shorts or T-shirts, jeans OK) – the menu draws inspiration from continental, southwestern and Mexican cuisine. The nicest place for sunset cocktails is the outdoor patio.

PANAMINT SPRINGS RESORT American $$
(Hwy 190, Panamint Springs; dishes from $10; ⏲breakfast, lunch & dinner; 🛜) Pizza, burgers, salads, steaks and great bottled beers.

19TH HOLE BAR & GRILL American $
(Furnace Creek Golf Course, Hwy 190, Furnace Creek; mains $8-11; ⏲lunch Oct-May) On the golf course, this place has the juiciest burgers in the park.

ℹ Information

Cell-phone reception is poor to nonexistent in the park, but there are pay phones at Furnace Creek, Stovepipe Wells Village and Scotty's Castle; phonecards are sold at the general stores in Stovepipe Wells and Furnace Creek.

Entrance Fees & Passes

Entry to Death Valley National Park (www.nps.gov/deva) costs $20 per vehicle or $10 per person if arriving by foot, bicycle or motorcycle. Passes are valid for seven days and sold at self-service pay stations throughout the park. For a free map and newspaper, show your receipt at the visitor center.

Opening Dates

Death Valley is open 24 hours a day, 365 days a year.

Tourist Information

Furnace Creek Visitor Center (📞760-786-3200; www.nps.gov/deva; Hwy 190, Furnace Creek; ⏰8am-5pm) Under construction at press time, the renovated main visitor center should have reopened by the time you're reading this.

ℹ Getting There & Away

The Furnace Creek Entrance lies 118 miles (about 2½ hours) west of Las Vegas' McCarran International Airport (LAS; 📞702-261-4636; www.mccarran.com) and roughly 300 miles (five hours) northeast of Los Angeles International Airport (LAX; 📞310-646-5252; www.lawa.org).

Gas is expensive in the park, so fill up your tank beforehand.

AROUND DEATH VALLEY

Beatty, Nevada

Around 45 miles north of Furnace Creek, this historic mining boomtown has seen better days but it still makes a reasonably inexpensive launch pad for visiting Death Valley. You'll find an ATM, 24-hour gas station, a public library with internet access and a teensy museum with artifacts from the Old West mining days all along Hwy 95 (here called Main St).

🏷 Atomic Inn (📞775-553-2250; www.atomic-inn.com; 350 S 1st St; r incl breakfast $52-60; ❄ 🐾) has deluxe rooms with

Scotty's Castle (p188), Death Valley

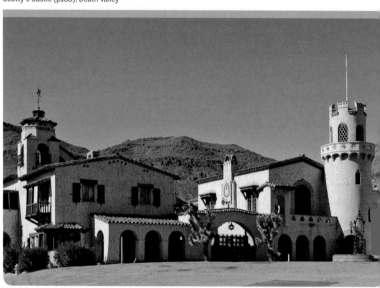

ARIADNE VAN ZANDBERGEN / LONELY PLANET IMAGES

flatscreen TVs and DVD players. There's a movie library near reception and classic movies also play in the lobby nightly. Kudos for the solar water-heating system and xeriscaped grounds.

The yummy burgers and bulging sandwiches (including vegetarian options) – on homemade bread no less! – at **KC's Outpost Saloon** (100 Main St; dishes $3.50-8; ☺10am-10pm Sun-Thu, to 11pm Fri & Sat; 🚹) have garnered rave reviews.

Shoshone

Just a blip on the desert map, Shoshone is 55 miles from Furnace Creek via Death Valley Junction, but most folks elect to follow the 20-mile longer but more scenic Hwy 178 through Badwater Basin instead. It has a gas station, store, lodging and free public wi-fi access.

Look for an old Chevy parked outside the **Shoshone Museum** (admission by donation; ☺9am-3pm), which houses quirky exhibits as well as the local **visitor center** (☎760-852-4524; www.deathvalleychamber.org; ☺10am-4pm).

Shoshone Inn (☎760-852-4335; www.shoshonevillage.com; Hwy 127; d $96-105, cabins $113; ❄🛜🏊) is a 1950s-era hotel with updated cabins and a dozen basic courtyard rooms, all with satellite TV. **Shoshone RV Park** (☎760-852-4569; RV sites with full hookups $25) is just north of town.

Cafe C'est Si Bon (Hwy 127; mains $7-10; ☺usually 8am-5pm Wed-Mon; 🛜🔌🚹) is a delightful, solar-powered place with mean espresso, gourmet baked goods, and 'flexitarian' breakfasts and lunches.

Olympic & Mt Rainier National Parks

Washington's parks are best summarized in one meteorological term: 'precipitation'.

Welcome to what are – literally – two of the snowiest and wettest places on the planet. Thanks to their end-of-the-continent location, where the damp air of the Pacific Ocean collides with the lofty mountains of the northwest coastline, both Mt Rainier and Olympic National Parks are valuable bastions of thick old-growth rainforest, landscape-altering glaciers, powerful rivers, and a green sheen more verdant than anywhere else in the US. Protected by the doyens of the American conservationist movement in the early 20th century, the parks today are studded with historic inns, ancient trees, and expansive wilderness areas little changed since the days of Columbus.

As most modern traffic arrives by car and stays close to the peripheral sights, vast stretches of the parks' interiors remain Alaskan in their solitude. Grab your walking poles, kayak or bicycle and revel in it.

Paradise (p211), Mt Rainier
RICHARD CUMMINS / LONELY PLANET IMAGES ©

Olympic & Mt Rainier Itineraries

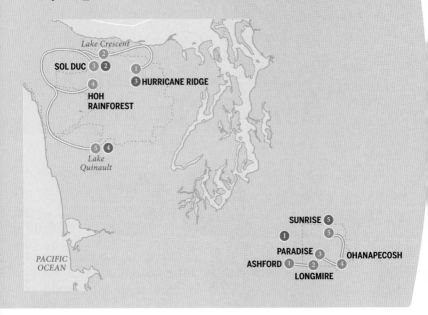

Two Days in Olympic

1 Hurricane Ridge (p199) After dropping by the Olympic National Park Visitor Center on the outskirts of Port Angeles, head 17 miles uphill to watch fickle weather roll in across this dramatic viewpoint on the cusp of the Olympic wilderness.

2 Lake Crescent (p199) If you're circumnavigating the park on US 101 you'll quickly encounter Washington's second-deepest lake heading west out of Port Angeles. Stop to stretch your legs on trails to Marymere Falls or Mt Storm King.

3 Sol Duc (p201) Home to the state's best-known natural springs, Sol Duc is reached by a side road that plunges south from US 101 into the Olympic wilderness. You'll get more out of the therapeutic hot tubs and pools if you limber up beforehand on the 6-mile Lover's Lane trail to Sol Duc Falls. Afterwards, grab a bite to eat at the

cafeteria and rest your driving arms by staying overnight in one of the comfortable cabins at the Sol Duc Hot Springs Resort.

4 Hoh Rainforest (p201) The park's most symbolic sight is a thick, wet rainforest full of moss-draped trees, some of which are older than Europe's medieval castles. It is reached by branching off US 101 south of Forks and following the Hoh River Rd east for 19 miles.

5 Lake Quinault (p202) More rainforest beckons in Quinault, where you can enjoy lunch or dinner in the historic Lake Quinault Lodge before following short paths past some of the tallest, thickest spruce and cedar trees on the continent.

⬤ **THIS LEG: 220 MILES**

Two Days in Mt Rainier

1 **Ashford** (p214) If you're staying over in Seattle, an early start will not only beat the legendary metro traffic jams, it'll also deposit you in the small settlement of Ashford just outside Mt Rainier National Park's Nisqually entrance in time for brunch.

2 **Longmire** (p210) Seven miles inside the Nisqually gate lies Longmire: a historic inn, a small museum, and a stash of short-to-medium below-the-timberline trails that offer a pleasant low-key overture for the paradisiacal sights to come.

3 **Paradise** (p210) On the days when Rainier decides to take its cloudy hat off, Paradise lives up to its ambitious name. Start by exploring the refurbished visitor center, gravitate over to the historic inn, and then venture out onto the haunting mountain slopes among strollers, day hikers and returning summiteers. Enjoy dinner in the Paradise Inn's grand dining room before disappearing upstairs to one of the cozy historic rooms for some shut-eye (reservations recommended).

4 **Ohanapecosh** (p212) Close to the park's quiet southeastern entrance you can enjoy shady tranquility amid ancient evergreens on the Grove of the Patriarchs trail.

5 **Sunrise** (p213) Tracking back to Seattle via a circuitous northern route, it would be foolish to miss lofty Sunrise, a 16-mile sidetrip off Hwy 410 where alpine flower meadows are framed by a backdrop of giant glaciers.

THIS LEG: 70 MILES

Olympic & Mt Rainier Highlights

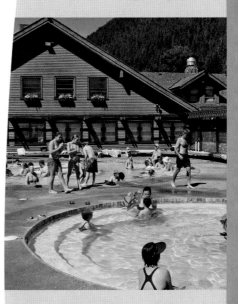

1 **Best Day Hike: Skyline Trail** (p212) Ponder the force and power of Mt Rainier in close-up from the lush domain of Paradise.

2 **Best Relaxing Activity: Sol Duc Hot Springs** (p201) Neutralize the effects of an arduous hike at Washington's coziest natural springs.

3 **Best Viewpoint: Hurricane Ridge** (p199) Meteorological geeks mix with wilderness freaks at this stormy 'balcony' over the Olympic Mountains.

4 **Best Historic Lodge: Lake Quinault Lodge** (p205) Relive the roaring '20s beside a roaring fireplace in this timeless rustic lodge in Olympic.

5 **Best Alpine Meadows: Sunrise** (p213) Flower-speckled slopes add vivacity to spectacular close-up views of Mt Rainier.

Sol Duc Hot Springs (p201), Olympic
KONRAD WOTHE / IMAGEBROKER / ALAMY ©

Discover Olympic & Mt Rainier

OLYMPIC NATIONAL PARK

The Lower 48's most westerly national park is an unblemished wilderness of the highest order with an interior redolent of Middle Earth and an end-of-the-continent coastline that makes Big Sur look positively calm. Then there's the precipitation. While nearby Seattleites whine about a little winter drizzle, the Hoh Rainforest is drowning in up to 200in of rain a year. There's an upside to all this water, of course: it's green here, 1000 verdant shades of it if you stare hard enough. And it's virgin too: untouched in over a millennium lie sapphire lakes, rarely climbed mountains, and ancient cedar and spruce trees older than most of Europe's legendary castles.

History

Native American people have inhabited Washington's Olympic peninsula for millennia, including the coast-dwelling Makah tribe whose 17th-century village preserved under a mudslide near Ozette was rediscovered in 1970. White explorers first crossed the Olympic wilderness on foot in 1889 when the *Seattle Press* newspaper sponsored an expedition and, in 1909, Teddy Roosevelt created the Olympic National Forest, ostensibly to protect the indigenous Roosevelt elk. The area was upgraded to a national park in 1938 after a personal visit by President Franklin Delano Roosevelt.

When to Go

As in most mountainous parks, late May to late September offers visitors the most reliable weather window; this is also the time when most of park's facilities are open and accessible. Olympic is one of only three parks in the US with a functioning ski area, meaning winter visits are also popular.

When You Arrive

Pay your park fee ($15 vehicles, $5 pedestrian/cyclists, valid for seven days) and pick up a free map at the Hoh and Heart o' the Hills entry booths (year-round), or the Elwha, Sol Duc and Staircase entrances (May to October). Payment is not manda-

Sol Duc Falls (p204), Olympic
JOHN ELK III / LONELY PLANET IMAGES ©

tory where there is no entrance station (ie on US 101) or when an entrance station isn't open.

Orientation

Though its interior is roadless, the park can be easily circumnavigated on US 101. Port Angeles in the northeast acts as the most convenient gateway.

Sights

Eastern Entrances

The eastern entrances to Olympic National Park are less developed than the north and west, but are handy for visitors traveling over the Hood Canal from Seattle and the 'mainland.' **Dosewallips River Valley** (⏰9am-5pm May-Oct) and **Staircase** (⏰9am-5pm May-Oct) are the two main entry points here. Both offer close proximity to some of the most rugged peaks in the Olympics.

Northern Entrances

The most popular access to Olympic National Park is from the north. Port Angeles is the park's urban hub, and other good access points are Hurricane Ridge, the Elwha Valley and Lake Crescent, the park's largest lake.

HURRICANE RIDGE   Visitor Center, Lookout

South of Port Angeles the Olympic Mountains rise up to Hurricane Ridge, one of the park's most accessible viewing points and an active ski station in the winter. Starting in Race St, the 17-mile Hurricane Ridge Rd climbs up 5300ft toward extensive wildflower meadows and expansive mountain vistas often visible above the clouds.

Hurricane Ridge is renowned for its fickle weather (storm-watchers often gather here) and is the takeoff point for a number of short summer hikes leading through meadows to vista points. The **visitor center** (⏰9:30am-5pm daily summer, Fri-Sun winter) has a snack bar, gift shop,

toilets and ski and snowshoe rentals, but no overnight accommodation or camping.

From Hurricane Ridge, you can drive a rough, white-knuckle 8-mile road to **Obstruction Peak**, laid out by the Civilian Conservation Corps (CCC) in the 1930s. From here **Wolf Creek Trail** offers an 8-mile downhill jaunt to Whiskey Bend, where it picks up the Elwha Trail.

ELWHA RIVER VALLEY   Forest

The park's largest river is today the site of the largest dam-removal scheme in US history (still ongoing as of 2011/2012). A hot-springs resort also once stood here; it too has been allowed to return to nature. The Elwha Trail leads up the main branch of the Elwha River into backcountry. Day hikers can follow it for 2 miles to the remains of the homestead-era Humes Ranch.

LAKE CRESCENT   Lake

If you're heading anticlockwise on the Olympic loop from Port Angeles toward Forks, one of the first scenic surprises to leap out at you will be expansive Lake Crescent, a popular boating and fishing area and a departure point for a number of short national park hikes. The area is also the site of the Lake Crescent Lodge, the oldest of the park's trio of celebrated lodges that first opened in 1916. The best stop-off point is in a parking lot to the right of US 101 near the **Storm King Information Station** (☎360-928-3380; ⏰9am-5pm May-Sep). Energetic hikers can climb up the side of **Mt Storm King**, the peak that rises to the east of Lake Crescent. The steep, 2.1-mile ascent splits off the Marymere Falls Trail and gains 2100ft.

SOL DUC RIVER VALLEY   Forest

The 14-mile interior road that leads off US 101 into the heart of the national park along the headwaters of the Sol Duc River is worth a turn for some great day hikes, a dip in a natural spa and a vivid glimpse of the amazing Olympic rain forest. Note how the trees along the roadside become taller and more majestic almost immediately.

As Native American legend tells it, the geological phenomenon at Sol Duc is the

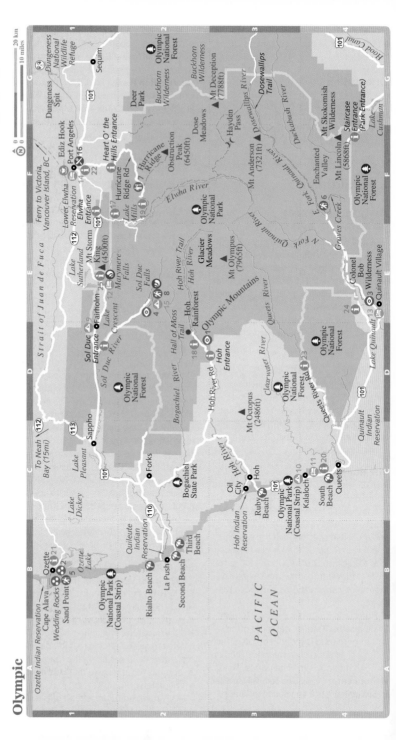

Olympic

Olympic

legacy of a battle between two lightning fish. When neither fish won the contest, each crawled beneath the earth and shed bitter tears, forming the heated mineral springs here.

SOL DUC HOT SPRINGS   Spa
(adult/child $12.25/9.25; ⊙9am-8pm Mar-Oct)
These springs have been diverted into three large tiled pools for health and recreation at Sol Duc Hot Springs Resort. There's also a standard swimming pool to cool off in, as well as a restaurant, snack bar, gift shop and overnight accommodations. Massage is available from $55 for 30 minutes.

Western Entrances
The Pacific side of the Olympics is the most remote part of the park and home to the foggy, moss-draped temperate rain forests. It is also the wettest area, receiving 12ft of rain annually, and you can expect a soaking at any time.

US 101 is the only road that accesses this vast, heavily wooded area. Paved roads penetrate the interior at the Hoh Rainforest and Lake Quinault, but are sometimes washed out.

HOH RAINFOREST   Forest
The most famous section of the Olympic rainforest, the Hoh River area offers a variety of hikes and an interpretive center. If you have room for only one stop on the western side, this should be it. The paved Upper Hoh Rd winds 19 miles from US 101 to the visitor center, passing a **giant Sitka spruce tree** along the way. This lord of the forest is 270ft high and over 500 years old.

At the end of Hoh River Rd, the **Hoh Rainforest Visitor Center** (☎360-374-6925; ⊙9am-4:30pm Sep-Jun, 9am-6pm Jul & Aug) offers displays on the ecology of the rain forest and the plants and animals that inhabit it, as well as a bookstore. Rangers lead free guided walks twice a day during summer.

If You Like…
Primeval Forests

If you like the dense foliage of the Hoh Rainforest you may also enjoy these other tree-filled wildernesses:

1 QUEETS RIVER VALLEY
Olympic's unpaved Queets River Rd follows the eponymous river for 13 miles to a campground and the gentle 3-mile Queets Campground Loop Trail in heavy old-growth rain forest.

2 CARBON RIVER AREA
Mt Rainier's wettest region protects one of the few remaining examples of temperate rainforest in the contiguous USA. Various trails lead out from the park's northwest Carbon River Entrance.

3 RIALTO BEACH
Mild mists nourish a rich coastal forest above this beach on the Olympic Coastal Strip near La Push. Below, cliffs eagles swoon over strewn drift logs.

LAKE QUINAULT   Lake
Situated in the extreme southwest of the Olympic Peninsula, the enchanting Quinault River Valley is one of the park's least crowded corners. Clustered around the deep-blue glacial waters of Lake Quinault lie forested peaks, a historic lodge and some of the oldest (and tallest) Sitka spruce, Douglas fir and western red cedar trees in the world.

The lake may be accessed from the north and the south. The south shore hosts the tiny village of Quinault, complete with the luscious Lake Quinault Lodge (p205), a **USFS office (353 S Shore Rd)**, restaurant, couple of stores, **post office (S Shore Rd)** and gas station. The North Shore Rd passes the **Quinault Ranger Station** (360-288-2444) before climbing up to the North Fork Quinault trailhead.

The Quinault region is renowned for its huge trees. Close to the village is a 191ft **Sitka spruce tree** (purported to be up

to 1000 years old), and nearby are the world's largest red cedar, Douglas fir and mountain hemlock trees.

Olympic Coastal Strip

Seventy-three miles of Washington's wild Pacific coastline is protected as part of the Olympic National Park, added in 1953. Parts of it haven't changed since pre-colonial times.

OZETTE   Archeological Site, Beach
Former home of the Makah tribe, whose ancient cliff-side village was destroyed in a mudslide in the early 18th century before being unearthed in the 1970s, Ozette is one of the most accessible slices of isolated beach on the Olympic coastal strip. Archaeologists dug up 55,000 artifacts here, many of which are on display at the Makah Museum in Neah Bay.

The Hoko-Ozette road leaves Hwy 112 about 3 miles west of Sekiu and proceeds 21 miles to **Lake Ozette Ranger Station** (☉8am-4:30pm), on Ozette Lake.

RUBY BEACH   Beach
This southernmost portion of the Olympic coastal strip, between the Hoh and Quinault Indian Reservations, is abutted by US 101, making it more accessible than the beaches further north. Be sure to stop at Ruby Beach, where a short 0.2-mile path leads down to a large expanse of wind-swept beach embellished by polished black stones and wantonly strewn tree trunks. Heading south toward Kalaloch (klay–lock), other accessible beachfronts are unimaginatively named Beach One through to Beach Six, all of which are popular with beachcombers.

 Activities

Hiking

HALL OF MOSS TRAIL   Hiking
Leading out from the Hoh Rainforest Visitor Center this easy 0.8-mile loop

leads you directly into virgin temperate rainforest, taking you through the kind of weird, ethereal scenery that even Tolkien couldn't have invented. Epiphytic club moss, ferns and lichens completely overwhelm the massive trunks of maples and Sitka spruces in this misty forest.

There is also a short wheelchair-accessible nature trail through a rainforest marsh.

HOH RIVER TRAIL
Hiking

A major entry trail into the wide, glacier-carved Hoh River Valley, this path is also the principal access route to Mt Olympus. The trail follows an easy grade for 12 miles through moss-drenched temperate rainforest, and day hikers can use it as a pleasant out-and-back excursion. Beyond this the path climbs to the flower-scattered paradise of Glacier Meadows perched at 4300ft.

The Hoh River Trail begins at the visitor center, which is at the end of the Upper Hoh Rd.

MARYMERE FALLS TRAIL
Hiking

Among the number of short 'touch-the-wilderness' hikes that leave from the Storm King Information Center on the east side of Lake Crescent is the Marymere Falls trail, a 2-mile round trip to a 90ft cascade that drops down over a basalt cliff.

ENCHANTED VALLEY TRAIL
Hiking

The Lake Quinault area's hiking highlight is this photogenic trail which climbs for 13 miles beyond the Graves Creek trailhead up to a large meadow (a former glacial lake bed) traversed by streams and springs, and resplendent with wildflowers and thickets of alders. To the north rise sheer cliff faces and peaks craning 2000ft from the valley floor; during spring snowmelt, the 3-mile precipice is drizzled by thousands of small waterfalls.

After the late-June snowmelt it is possible to lengthen this hike by continuing over 4464ft Anderson Pass (19 miles from Graves Creek) and descending to the Dosewallips trailhead on the park's eastern side.

CAPE ALVARA–SAND POINT LOOP
Hiking

From Lake Ozette on the Pacific coast, the 3.3-mile **Cape Alava Trail** leads north to the westernmost point of land in the

Marymere Falls Trail

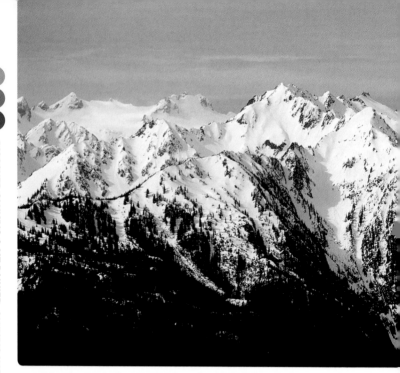

continental US and is the site of the ancient Makah village. The southern **Sand Point Trail** from Lake Ozette Ranger Station leads 3 miles to beaches below a low bluff; whale-watchers often come here in the migration season.

The two Ozette trails can easily be linked as a 9-mile-long loop by walking the 3 miles between Cape Alava and Sand Point along the beach (beware of the tides) or overland (although the trail is brushy and primitive). The high point of this hike is the **Wedding Rocks**, the most significant group of petroglyphs on the Olympic Peninsula.

LOVER'S LANE LOOP   Hiking

The most popular hike in the Sol Duc Valley is the 0.75-mile **Sol Duc Falls Trail**, where the river plummets 40ft into a narrow gorge. However you can lengthen this hike by setting out from the Sol Duc Resort along the **Lover's Lane trail** and using the 'campground trail' on the return to make a loop.

Fishing

No permits are required to fish in the park, but aspiring anglers must fill out a Washington State catch record card. Prized catches are Chinook salmon and cutthroat trout. Normal catch-and-release rules apply.

The Elwha, the largest river on the Olympic Peninsula, Lake Mills (actually a reservoir) and Lake Crescent are popular trout-fishing havens.

Lake Quinault is part of the Quinault Indian Reservation, and fishing is regulated by the tribe; check locally for tribal licenses and regulations.

Skiing

The not-for-profit **Hurricane Ridge Ski & Snowboard Area** (www.hurricaneridge. com; ⏰10am-4pm Sat & Sun mid-Dec–Mar; 🚻) has two rope tows and a lift. It is one of only two national park ski areas in the nation and the most westerly in the

Left: Mt Olympus, Olympic; **Below:** Roosevelt elk

(LEFT) ANN CECIL / LONELY PLANET IMAGES ©; (BELOW) JOHN HAY / LONELY PLANET IMAGES ©

contagious US. Though small, it gets an ample 400in of annual snow, hosts downhill and cross-country skiing and is well loved by families.

Boating

Rowboat rentals ($9/25 per hour/half day) are available at the Lake Crescent and Lake Quinault Lodges in the summer months.

 Sleeping

The park has 16 campgrounds, including Hoh, Fairholm, Sol Duc, Queets and Kalaloch, costing between $10 and $18. Twelve operate year-round. All campgrounds are first-come-first-served except **Kalaloch** (www.nps.gov/olym/planyourvisit/campgrounds.htm; ☉ Jun-Sep), which takes online reservations.

LAKE QUINAULT LODGE　　　Historic Hotel $$
(☎ 360-288-2900; www.olympicnationalparks.com; 345 S Shore Rd; r $142-259; ❄ ☒) Everything you could want in a historic national park lodge and more, the Quinault has a huge, roaring fireplace, peekaboo lake views, a manicured bowling-green-quality lawn, huge comfy leather sofas, a regal reception area and – arguably – the finest eating experience on the whole peninsula. The latter is thanks to the memorable sweet potato pancakes with hazelnut butter that are served up in the beautiful lakeside restaurant for breakfast (and are worth trying even if you're not staying here). Built in 1926, the Quinault's warmth and character are no secret and advance reservations are recommended. Trails into primeval forest leave from just outside the door.

The Best...
Fun for Kids

Sol Duc Hot Springs (p201)

Skiing at Hurricane Ridge (p199)

Gray Line Mt Rainier Bus Tour (p212)

Hall of Moss Trail (p202)

Ruby Beach (p202)

DISCOVER OLYMPIC & MT RAINIER OLYMPIC NATIONAL PARK

LAKE CRESCENT
LODGE   Historic Hotel **$$**

(☎360-928-3211; www.olympicnationalparks.com; 416 Lake Crescent Rd; lodge r with shared bath $80, cottages $126-202; ☉May-Oct; ❄🐾) Built in 1915 as a fishing resort, this venerable shake-sided building is the oldest of the Olympic National Park lodges and, along with the Lake Quinault Lodge, leads the way in style and coziness. To add star appeal, President FD Roosevelt once stayed here in 1937 – a year before he made the Olympics a national park – and the lodge's fanciest rooms are still known as the 'Roosevelt cottages.' Located lakeside and endowed with an impressive restaurant that serves up grilled duck breast and elk rib rack, the lodge is reasonably priced, fantastically placed and well known for its environmentally sustainable practices.

KALALOCH
LODGE   Historic Hotel **$$$**

(☎360-962-2271; www.olympicnationalparks.com; 157151 US 101; lodge $199-219, cabins $204-237; ❄) A little less grand than the Lake Quinault and Lake Crescent Lodges, the Kalaloch (built in 1953) nonetheless enjoys an equally spectacular setting perched on a bluff overlooking the crashing Pacific. In addition to rooms in the old lodge, there are log cabins and motel-style units, and a family-friendly restaurant and store that offer incomparable ocean views. There is an excellent ocean-side campground half a mile north of the lodge on US 101.

SOL DUC HOT SPRINGS
RESORT   Cabins **$$**

(☎360-327-3583; www.olympicnationalparks.com; RV sites $33, cabins $131-169; ☉late Mar-Oct; ❄🐾) While Sol Duc lacks the classic touches of the more luxurious Lake Quinault and Kalaloch Lodges, this well-known spa retreat packs a punch with its therapeutic spring waters and easy access to surrounding forest. Thirty-two modern but basic cabins offer private bathrooms and, in some cases, a kitchenette. Aside from the steaming waters there is also a massage service available. Day hikers and visitors can use the Spring Restaurant or poolside deli, and the pool.

Eating

The park has no specific eating outlets. However, you'll find on-site restaurants/cafeterias at the Hurricane Ridge Visitor Center, Sol Duc Hot Springs Resort, and the trio of historic park lodges: Kalaloch, Lake Crescent and Lake Quinault.

ℹ Information

Entrance Fees & Passes

Park admission fees are $15 per vehicle and $5 per pedestrian/cyclist, and are valid for seven days for park entry and re-entry. An annual 'passport' for one year's unlimited entry costs $30.

Opening Dates

Olympic National Park is open year-round and is one of the west's more accessible parks even in the winter, when the perimeter roads and ski area remain open.

Tourist Information

Olympic National Park Visitor Center (www.nps.gov/olym; 3002 Mt Angeles Rd; ☉9am-4pm) About a mile south of Port Angeles, this is the park's most comprehensive information center with maps, leaflets, exhibits, and an auditorium.

Hoh Rainforest Visitor Center (360-374-6925; 9am-4:30pm Sep-Jun, 9am-6pm Jul & Aug) At the end of Hoh River Rd.

Hurricane Ridge Visitor Center (9:30am-5pm daily summer, Fri-Sun winter)

Maps
NPS publishes a useful free map available at entry booths and visitor centers and downloadable from the park website (www.nps.gov/olym).

Dangers & Annoyances
If you are contemplating a trek along the coast, request information from the National Park Service (www.nps.gov/olym), buy good maps, learn how to read tide tables and be prepared for bad weather year-round.

Getting There & Around
The city of Seattle has the nearest international airport, Sea-tac (SEA; www.portseattle.org) and is the large gateway to the park. Olympic Bus Lines (www.olympicbuslines.com) runs a twice-daily bus from Seattle to Port Angeles ($39, three hours). Remarkably you can circumnavigate the park on public buses using the transit systems of Clallam, Jefferson, Kitsap and Gray's Harbor counties. More information is available from Washington State Department of Transportation (www.wsdot.wa.gov).

AROUND OLYMPIC NATIONAL PARK
Port Angeles
Despite the name, there's nothing Spanish or particularly angelic about Port Angeles. Propped up by the lumber industry and backed by the steep-sided Olympic Mountains, people come here to catch a ferry for Victoria, Canada, or to plot an outdoor excursion into the nearby Olympic National Park rather than for the town per se.

 Sleeping & Eating

OLYMPIC LODGE   Hotel **$$**
(360-452-2993; www.olympiclodge.com; 140 Del Guzzi Dr; r from $119; ✳ @ 🛜 ≋) There are plenty of reasons to make this your Olympic National Park HQ, including a swimming pool, on-site bistro, so-clean-they-seem-new rooms and complimentary cookies and milk.

Twilight Zone

Forks, a small lumber town on Hwy 101, was little more than a speck on the Washington state map when publishing phenomenon Stephenie Meyer set her now-famous vampire novel *Twilight* here in 2003. Ironically, Meyer – America's answer to JK Rowling – had never been to Forks when she resurrected the ghoulish legacy of Bela Lugosi et al with the first of what has become a series of insanely popular 'tweenage' books. Not that this has stopped the town from cashing in on its newfound literary fame. Forks has apparently seen a 600% rise in tourism over the last five years, spearheaded by the rise of **Dazzled by Twilight** (www.dazzledbytwilight.com; 11 N Forks Ave; 10am-6pm; 👫), which runs two *Twilight* merchandise shops in Forks (and another in Port Angeles) as well as the Forks **Twilight Lounge** (81 N Forks Ave). The company also runs four daily **Twilight Tours** (adult/child $39/25; departing 8am, 11.30am, 3pm & 6pm) visiting most of the places mentioned in Meyer's books. Highlights include the Forks High School, the Treaty Line at the nearby Rivers Resort, and a sortie out to the tiny coastal community of La Push.

BELLA ITALIA Italian $$

(118 E 1st St; mains $12-20; ⊘from 4pm) Bella Italia has been around a lot longer than Bella, the heroine of the *Twilight* saga, but its mention in the book has turned what was already a popular restaurant into an icon. Top dishes include clam linguine, chicken marsala or smoked duck breast washed down with an outstanding wine from a list featuring 500 selections.

MT RAINIER NATIONAL PARK

Emblazoned on every Washington license plate and visible throughout much of the western state, Mt Rainier (elevation 14,411ft) is the contiguous USA's fifth-highest peak and, in the eyes of many, its most awe-inspiring.

Close to Puget Sound's urban areas and unobstructed by any other peaks, the mountain's overwhelming presence, set off by its 26 glaciers, has long enraptured the millions of inhabitants who live in its shadow. Though it's an iconic peak to bag, climbing Rainier is no picnic; old hands liken it to running a marathon in thin air with crampons stuck to your shoes. Approximately 10,000 people attempt it annually.

Beneath Rainier's volatile exterior, even darker forces fester. As an active strato-volcano that recorded its last eruptive activity as recently as 1854, Rainier harnesses untold destructive powers that, if provoked, could threaten downtown Seattle with mudslides and cause tsunamis in Puget Sound. Not surprisingly, the mountain has long been imbued with myth. The Native Americans called it Tahoma or Tacoma, meaning the 'mother of waters', George Vancouver named it Rainier in honor of his colleague and friend Rear Admiral Peter Rainier, while most Seattleites refer to it reverently as 'the Mountain' and forecast the weather by its visibility.

History

Long home to the Puyallup and Nisqually Coast Salish tribes who exploited its rivers for fish, Mt Rainier was first spotted and named by Europeans in 1792. Pathfinder of the modern conservationist movement, John Muir visited and climbed Mt Rainier in 1888 and it was largely due to his efforts that it was made America's fifth national park in 1899.

When to Go

Though open year-round, the park has limited road access between October and May, meaning late spring and summer are the best times to visit.

When You Arrive

Pay your fee at the entrance booth and receive a free map and a copy of the quarterly *Tahoma News* featuring current park news (including ranger programs)

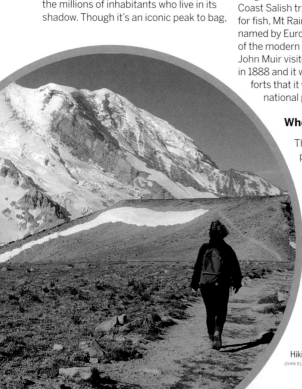

Hiking trail, Paradise (p211), Mt Rainier
JOHN ELK III / LONELY PLANET IMAGES ©

Mt Rainier

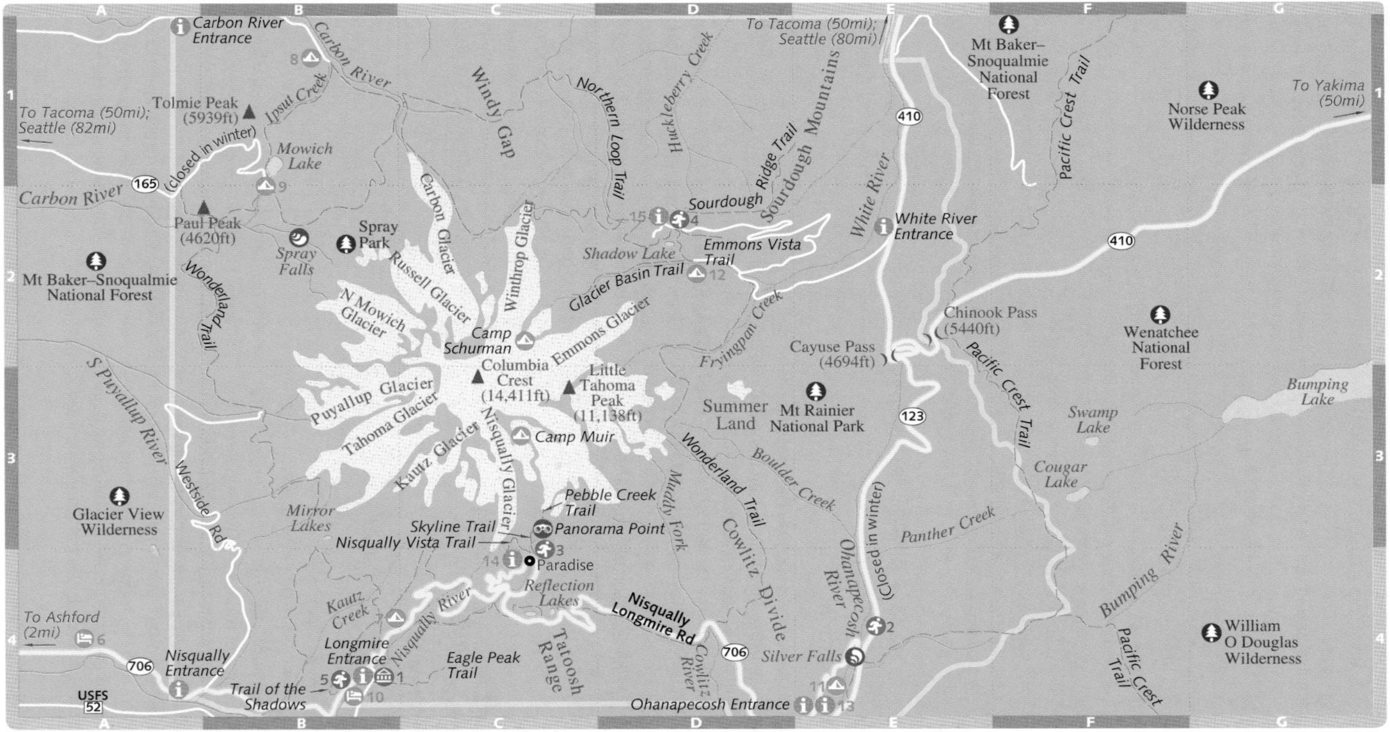

Map features and labels:

To Tacoma (50mi); Seattle (82mi)

To Tacoma (50mi); Seattle (80mi)

To Yakima (50mi)

Carbon River Entrance

Carbon River

Huckleberry Creek

Ipsut Creek

Tolmie Peak (5939ft)

Paul Peak (4620ft)

Mowich Lake

Spray Park

Spray Falls

Wonderland Trail

Northern Loop Trail

Windy Gap

Carbon Glacier

Russell Glacier

N Mowich Glacier

Tahoma Glacier

Puyallup Glacier

S Puyallup River

Westside Rd

Glacier View Wilderness

Mt Baker–Snoqualmie National Forest

To Ashford (2mi)

USFS 52

Nisqually Entrance

Trail of the Shadows

Longmire Entrance

Kautz Creek

Nisqually River

Kautz Glacier

Nisqually Glacier

Mirror Lakes

Nisqually Vista Trail

Skyline Trail

Eagle Peak Trail

Tatoosh Range

Reflection Lakes

Paradise

Panorama Point

Pebble Creek Trail

Muddy Fork

Cowlitz River

Nisqually–Longmire Rd

Ohanapecosh Entrance

Silver Falls

Cowlitz Divide

Wonderland Trail

Ohanapecosh River

Boulder Creek

Columbia Crest (14,411ft)

Little Tahoma Peak (11,138ft)

Camp Muir

Camp Schurman

Emmons Glacier

Winthrop Glacier

Glacier Basin Trail

Shadow Lake

Sourdough

Emmons Vista Trail

Sourdough Mountains

Ridge Trail

White River

White River Entrance

Fryingpan Creek

Cayuse Pass (4694ft)

Sunrise

Mt Rainier Land National Park

Chinook Pass (5440ft)

Pacific Crest Trail

Mt Baker–Snoqualmie National Forest

Norse Peak Wilderness

Wenatchee National Forest

Swamp Lake

Cougar Lake

Bumping Lake

Bumping River

Panther Creek

Pacific Crest Trail

William O Douglas Wilderness

165

410

410

123

706

706

(Closed in winter)

5 km

2.5 miles

209

Mt Rainier

as well as less perishable information on trails and wildlife.

Orientation

The park's main Nisqually entrance is in its southwestern corner on Hwy 706, about one hour 45 minutes drive southeast of Seattle. The entry booths are just past the village of Ashford and adjacent to the Nisqually River. There are seasonal entrances at Ohanapecosh in the southeast (Hwy 123), White River in the east (Hwy 410) and the more remote Carbon River in the northwest.

⊙ Sights

LONGMIRE   Visitor Center

Worth a stop to stretch your legs or gain an early glimpse of Rainier's mossy old-growth forest, Longmire, 7 miles east of the Nisqually entrance on Hwy 706, was the brainchild of a certain James Longmire, who first came here in 1883 during a climbing trip when he noticed the hot mineral springs that bubbled up in a lovely meadow opposite the present-day National Park Inn. He and his family returned the following year and established Longmire's Medicinal Springs, and in 1890 he built the Longmire Springs

Hotel. Since 1917 the National Park Inn has stood on this site – built in classic 'parkitecture' style – and is complemented by a small store, some park offices, the tiny **Longmire Museum** (admission free; ⏰9am-6pm Jun-Sep, 9am-5pm Oct-May) and a number of important trailheads.

PARADISE   Visitor Center

'Oh, what a paradise!' exclaimed the daughter of park pioneer James Longmire on visiting this spot for the first time in the 1880s. Suddenly, the high mountain nirvana had a name, and a very apt one at that. One of the snowiest places on earth, 5400ft-high Paradise remains the park's most popular draw with its famous flower meadows backed by dramatic Rainier views on the days (a clear minority annually) when the mountain decides to shrug off the clouds. Aside from hiding numerous trailheads and being the starting point for most summit hikes, Paradise guards the iconic Paradise Inn (built in 1916 and refurbished in 2008) and the informative **Henry M Jackson Visitor Center** (⏰10am-7pm daily Jun–mid-Oct, 10am-5pm Sat & Sun late Oct-Dec), completely rebuilt and reopened in 2008. Park naturalists lead free interpretive hikes from the visitor center daily in summer, and snowshoe walks on winter weekends.

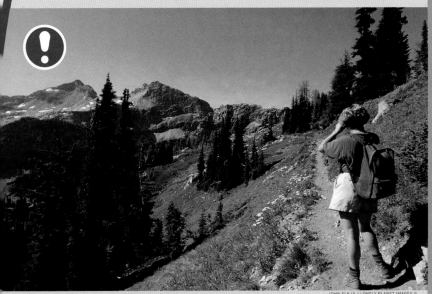

JOHN ELK III / LONELY PLANET IMAGES ©

Don't Miss **North Cascades National Park**

The wildest of all Pacific Northwest wildernesses, the lightly trodden **North Cascades National Park** (www.nps.gov/noca) has no settlements, no overnight accommodations and only one unpaved road. The names of the dramatic mountains pretty much set the tone: Desolation Peak, Jagged Ridge, Mt Despair and Mt Terror. The region contains an astounding 300 glaciers and offers some of the best backcountry adventures outside of Alaska.

The **North Cascades Visitor Center** (502 Newhalem St; ☺9am-4:30pm daily mid-Apr–Oct, Sat & Sun only Nov-Mar) in the small settlement of Newhalem on Hwy 20, 2½ hours northeast of Seattle by car, is the best orientation point for visitors and is staffed by expert rangers who can enlighten you on the park's highlights.

OHANAPECOSH ENTRANCE   Visitor Center

Shoehorned between Mt Rainier and its two southern neighbors, Mt St Helens and Mt Adams, the park's southeastern corner is a good base for travelers wanting to visit two or more of the mountains. Linked to Paradise by Hwy 706, Ohanapecosh's (o-*ha*-nuh-peh-*kosh*) roads are generally closed in the winter months due to adverse weather conditions, making it less accessible than Nisqually. There's a **visitor center** (☺9am-5pm May–mid-Oct) with displays on tree identification and the local old-growth forest.

 Activities

Climbing & Mountaineering

Approximately 10,000 climbers attempt Rainier's summit annually with a 60% success rate. The most popular route starts at Paradise and involves a brief night's rest at Camp Muir before rising between midnight and 2am to don crampons and ropes for the climb over Disappointment Cleaver and the Ingraham Glacier to the summit. All climbers going higher than Camp Muir must register at the **Paradise Ranger Station** next to the Henry M Jackson Visitor Center. Excellent four-day guided ascents are led by **Rainier Mountaineering Inc** (☎360-569-2227; www.rmiguides.com; 30205 SR 706 E; per person $926).

Hiking

TRAIL OF THE SHADOWS LOOP   Hiking
Before you hit the exposed mountain splendor of Paradise, warm up in the forests of Longmire on this 0.8-mile interpretative trail that begins across the road from the hotel and museum. The hike includes a replica homestead cabin and easily digestible information on the local plant life. It is wheelchair accessible for the first 0.4 miles.

SKYLINE TRAIL   Hiking
The Paradise area is crisscrossed with trails of all types and standards, some good for a short stroll (with the kids), others the realm of more serious hikers. For a medium-pacer, hike the 5-mile Skyline Trail, starting behind the Paradise Inn and climbing approximately 1600ft to **Panorama Point**, with good views of

Mt Rainier and the neighboring Tatoosh Range.

GROVE OF THE PATRIARCHS TRAIL   Hiking
Starting just north of the Ohanapecosh Visitor Center, this 1.5-mile trail is one of the park's most popular short hikes and explores a small island (the grove) in the middle of the Ohanapecosh River replete with craning Douglas fir, cedar and hemlock trees, some of which are over 1000 years old.

SOURDOUGH RIDGE TRAIL   Hiking
This 1-mile ridge climb heads out from the north side of the Sunrise parking area on the park's eastern side and takes you out into pristine subalpine meadows for stunning views over Washington volcanic giants: namely Mt Rainier, Mt Baker, Glacier Peak and Mt Adams.

Tours

GRAY LINE OF SEATTLE   Bus
(www.graylineseattle.com) Runs bus tours of the park mid-June to late September. The

Paradise Inn, Mt Rainier

Detour: Sunrise

Rainier's eastern White River entrance is the gateway to Sunrise, which at 6400ft marks the park's highest road. The views from Sunrise are famously spectacular and – aside from stunning close-ups of Mt Rainier itself – you can also, quite literally, watch the weather roll in over the Cascade peaks. Similarly impressive is the glistening Emmons Glacier which, at 4 sq miles in size, is the largest glacier in the contiguous USA. The **Sunrise Visitors Center** (🕐10am-6pm early Jul-early Sep) in the Sunrise Lodge has a small cafe. Numerous day hikes lead out from here.

10-hour tour (adult/child $85/65) picks up from most downtown Seattle hotels starting at 7.30am.

Sleeping

The park has five campgrounds – Ipsut Creek, Mowich Lake, White River, Cougar Rock and Ohanapecosh – open late May to early October ($12 to $15 per night). Cougar Rock and Ohanapecosh take reservations (☎877-444-6777).

PARADISE INN　　Historic Hotel $$
(☎360-569-2413; www.mtrainierguestservices. com; r with shared/private bath $109/159; 🕐mid-May–Sep) A historic 'parkitecture' inn constructed in 1916, the Paradise has long been part of the national park's fabric. Designed to blend in with the environment and constructed almost entirely of local materials, including exposed cedar logs in the Great Room, the hotel was an early blueprint for National Park Rustic architecture countrywide. Reopening in 2008 after a two-year, $30-million, earthquake-withstanding revamp, the smallish rooms (some with shared bath) retain their close-to-the-wilderness essence, while the communal areas are nothing short of regal.

NATIONAL PARK INN　　Historic Hotel $$
(☎360-569-2411; www.mtrainierguestservices. com; r with shared/private bath $112/155; ❄)

The pride of Longmire, parts of which date from 1917, goes out of its way to be rustic with no TVs or telephones in the rooms and small yet cozy facilities. But who needs HBO and the Discovery Channel when you've got fine service, fantastic surroundings and delectable complimentary afternoon tea and scones served in the comfortable dining room? Book ahead in the summer.

Eating

Aside from the two historic inns, the only eating in the park is in two cafeterias: one in the Henry M Jackson Visitor Center, the other at the Sunrise Lodge. Ashford, just outside the Nisqually entrance, has half-a-dozen options, spearheaded by the Copper Creek Inn (p214).

 Information

Entrance Fees & Passes

Park entrance fees are $15 per car and $5 for pedestrians and cyclists (those under 17 admitted free), and are valid for seven days from purchase. A $30 annual pass admits the pass-holder and accompanying passengers for 12 months from date of purchase.

Opening Dates

Mt Rainier National Park is open year-round. Only the southwest Nisqually entrance is open to road traffic in the winter when many of the park's facilities are closed.

The Best... Hikes

1 Cape Alvara–Sand Point Loop (p203)

2 Enchanted Valley Trail (p203)

3 Sourdough Ridge Trail (p212)

4 Skyline Trail (p212)

5 Marymere Falls Trail (p203)

Tourist Information

The best source of information outside the park is the **Ashford Visitors Center** (30027 SR 706; ⊙9am-8pm daily), 6 miles west of the Nisqually entrance. The official park website is www.nps.gov/mora.

Maps

The park publishes a very useful free map available at entry booths and visitor centers. **Green Trails** (www.greentrailsmaps.com) maps 269 and 270 cover the park in greater detail.

Dangers & Annoyances

The park is a natural habitat for black bears and various other wild animals; take all the normal precautions.

AROUND MT RAINIER NATIONAL PARK
Ashford

This southwestern periphery of Mt Rainier National Park is its most developed (and hence most visited) corner. Here you'll find a credible stash of accommodations options and the only year-round road in the strung-out gateway settlement of Ashford which offers plenty of useful park-related facilities.

 Sleeping & Eating

For more listings, check out the 'lodging' section of the NPS website at www.nps.gov/mora/planyourvisit/lodging.htm.

WHITTAKER'S MOTEL
& BUNKHOUSE   Hostel $
(☎360-569-2439; www.whittakersbunkhouse.com; 30205 SR 706 E; dm/d $35/85) Part of Rainier's 'furniture,' Whittaker's (in the settlement of Ashford) is the home base of legendary Northwestern climber Lou Whittaker, who first summited the mountain at the age of 19 and has guided countless adventurers to the top in the years since. Down-to-earth and comfortable, this place has a good old-fashioned youth-hostel feel with cheap sleeps available in six-bed dorms. The alluring on site **Whittaker's Café & Espresso** (⊙7am-9pm) is a fine place to hunker down for breakfast.

NISQUALLY LODGE   Motel $$
(☎360-569-8804; www.escapetothemountains.com; 31609 SR 706 E; r $95-125; ❄🛜) With an expansive lobby complete with crackling fireplace and huge well-stocked rooms, this lodge is far plusher than an average motel with an outdoor Jacuzzi and simple help-yourself breakfast. It's in Ashland, 2 miles from the Nisqually entrance

COPPER CREEK INN   Brunch $
(www.coppercreekinn.com; 35707 SR 706 E, Ashford; breakfast $6-9; ⊙7am-9pm) Forget the historic inns. This is one of the state's great rural restaurants, and breakfast is an absolute must if you're heading off for a lengthy hike inside the park. Situated just outside the Nisqually entrance, the Copper Creek has been knocking out pancakes, wild blackberry pie and its own home-roasted coffee successfully for over 50 years. The inn also offers comfy lodge and cabin accommodations close by from $150 per double per night.

ⓘ **Getting There & Around**

Seattle's **Sea-tac** (www.portseattle.org) is the nearest international airport. From here head

View from Henry M Jackson VIsitor Center (p211), Mt Rainier

RICHARD CUMMINS / LONELY PLANET IMAGES ©

south on I-5 to exit 127, then east of Hwy 512, south on Hwy 7 and east on Hwy 706 to Ashford and the Nisqually entrance.

Car-less travellers can access the park on a Gray Line coach tour (p212) from Seattle.

The only public transportation inside the park is the June-through-September **Paradise Shuttle** that links Ashford (Whittaker's Motel) with Paradise via Longmire (9:15am to 7:50pm weekends only).

Rocky Mountain National Park

Welcome to the star attraction of the northern Rockies. One of the top draws in all of Colorado, Rocky Mountain National Park offers travelers an abundance of high-mountain bliss. Over 350 miles of hiking trails crisscross alpine meadows, skirt lakes, pass waterfalls and ascend peaks that top out well over 12,000ft. Even if you were to make your way to the lowest point in the park, you'd be over 7000ft above sea level.

The park's real wonders begin above the tree line, where even non-hikers can experience the otherworldly scenery of the alpine tundra. Two breathtaking roads, including the highest continuously paved road in the country, climb above the tree line to give motorists an unimpeded view of the high country. With elk, moose, bighorn sheep, black bears, coyotes and mule deer, the park is also home to some of the best wildlife viewing in the state. Who knew having your ears pop could be so much fun?

Glass Lake, Glacier Gorge Trail (p224)
JOHN ELK III / LONELY PLANET, IMAGES ©

Rocky Mountain Itineraries

TRAIL RIDGE ROAD ③

② ALPINE VISITOR CENTER

OLD FALL RIVER ROAD

① ③ ④ ⑤ ② ESTES PARK

⑥ ⑤

Rocky Mountain National Park

LILY MOUNTAIN ⑥

⑤

④ TWIN SISTERS PEAK

① ④ LONGS PEAK ⑦ ③

WILD BASIN ⑤

INDIAN PEAKS WILDERNESS AREA ①

② NEDERLAND

Two Days

① **Old Fall River Rd** (p223) Get an early start to beat the crowds and drive up this historic, one-lane gravel road that climbs into the Rockies' heavenly high country.

② **Alpine Visitor Center** (p230) At the top of Fall River Rd, park the car and explore this outstanding visitor center with sweeping views.

③ **Trail Ridge Rd** (p227) From the visitor center, drive southwest on Trail Ridge Rd as far as Fairview Curve. Take in the views before doubling back and then descending to your starting point via the southeast leg of Trail Ridge Rd.

④ **Twin Sisters Peak** (p224) In the afternoon, put your lungs and legs to their first test, hiking 3.7 miles to the top of this 11,428ft summit. The views of Longs Peak are stunning.

⑤ **Wild Basin** (p225) On day two, pack a lunch and spend the day exploring the trails, lakes and waterfalls of Rocky Mountain National Park's painfully scenic Wild Basin area. Because it's somewhat removed from the park's main attractions, it gets fewer people.

⑥ **Ed's Cantina & Grill** (p235) Treat yourself to an excellent riverside dinner at this top-notch Mexican restaurant in Estes Park. Sure you could cook up your own campfire chili – but with food like this so close, why would you want to?

THIS LEG: 80 MILES

Four Days

1 Indian Peaks Wilderness Area (p236)
On day three, leave the crowds of Rocky
Mountain National Park and take to the trails
of Indian Peaks Wilderness. The area gets far
fewer visitors than the national park, but the
hikes are arguably just as impressive.

2 Nederland (p224) Come evening, poke
around this quirky little hippie town, find
yourself a restaurant you like and close
the evening with a meal at the foot of the
Rockies.

3 YMCA of the Rockies (p234) Return to
Estes Park and shack up at the surprisingly
wonderful YMCA. Set on 860 acres and
home to all sorts of family fun, this is not
your everyday Y.

4 Big Horn Restaurant (p235) On day
four, wake up and gorge yourself on huevos
rancheros at this Estes Park breakfast
institution. There's no better way to fuel up
for a hike.

5 Enos Mills Cabin Museum & Gallery
(p226) Head out to this outstanding
museum and learn about the history of
Rocky Mountains National Park through the
eyes of one of its staunchest advocates.

6 Lily Mountain (p224) With your recent
history lesson fresh in your mind, hike the
short trail to the top of Lily Mountain and
ponder the vastness of the scenery around
you from this easy-to-reach summit.

7 Longs Peak (p223) If you're bent on
bagging a high peak before leaving the
Rockies, here's your day-four alternative:
wake up at the crack of dawn and brave the
10- to 15-hour hike to the 14,259ft summit of
this epic peak.

➡ THIS LEG: 85 MILES

Rocky Mountain Highlights

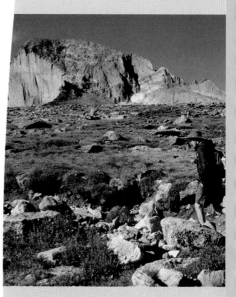

**1 Best Hotel: Shadowcliff Lodge &
Retreat Center** (p239) To really treat yourself,
check in at the Shadowcliff, a beautifully
situated resort with stunning views over Grand
Lake.

**2 Best Sandwich: DeLeo's Park Theatre
Cafe & Deli** (p235) The Dirty Harry,
Pastraminator, the Gobblefather – trust us,
these sandwiches live up to their names.

3 Best Thigh Burner: Longs Peak (p223)
Nothing can prepare you for a view like this
(not even 13 hours of hiking uphill).

4 Best Restaurant: O-A Bistro (p239)
The *prix fixe* dinner here is sublime.

5 Best Campground: Moraine Park
(p229) It may be big, but it's also beautiful
(why else would elk and moose linger
around?).

Boulder Field (p223), Longs Peak Trail
SALLY DILLON / LONELY PLANET IMAGES ©

Discover Rocky Mountain

ROCKY MOUNTAIN NATIONAL PARK

Though Rocky Mountain National Park doesn't rank among the largest national parks in the USA (it's *only* 265,000 acres), it's among one of the most popular, hosting almost three million visitors every year.

This is a place of natural spectacle on every scale, from hulking granite formations – many taller than 12,000ft, some over 130 million years old – to the yellow burst of the glacier lily, one of the dozen alpine wildflowers that explode in a short, colorful life at the edge of receding snowfields for a few days every spring.

And though it tops many travelers' itineraries and can get maddeningly crowded, the park has miles of less-beaten paths, and the backcountry is a little-explored treasure. It's surrounded by some of the most pristine wild area in the west: Comanche Peak and Neota Wilderness Areas in the Roosevelt National Forest to the north and Indian Peaks Wilderness to the south. The jagged spine of the Continental Divide intersects the park through its middle. Excellent hiking trails crisscross alpine fields, skirt the edge of isolated high-altitude lakes and bring travelers to the wild, untamed heart of the place.

History

Archeological sites within the park reveal that humans inhabited this area as far back as 12,000 years ago. More recently, the Arapaho and the Ute peoples lived here. By the late 1800s, the US government had relocated both groups to reservations outside the area. Many of the place names you'll encounter in the park today are of Arapaho origin, and both Trail Ridge Rd and Fall River Rd follow old Arapaho and Ute communication routes. The harshness of the Rockies kept most explorers and would-be settlers out of the park until the mid-1800s, when miners, prospectors, trappers and a handful of homesteaders began trickling in. In 1915, President Woodrow Wilson signed Rocky Mountain National Park into existence. Today, nearly three million people visit the park each year.

Trail to Alpine Visitor Center
CINDY MILLER HOPKINS / DANITA DELIMONT / ALAMY ©

When to Go

You can visit the park year-round, but summer is by far the best season, both for the weather and for the wildflowers. That said, it is by far the most crowded time of the year. Summer days often reach 70°F (21°C) to 80°F (26°C), yet a sudden shift in the weather can bring snow to the peaks in July. July thundershowers typically dump 2in of rain on the park, while January is the driest month. Bear Lake (9400ft) normally has a January snow base of 25in. The Continental Divide causes a pronounced rain-shadow effect: Grand Lake (west of the Divide) annually averages 20in of moisture, while Estes Park receives only about 13in.

When You Arrive

All visitors receive a free copy of the park's information brochure, which contains a good orientation map and is available in English, German, French, Spanish and Japanese.

Orientation

Trail Ridge Rd (US 34) is the only east–west route through the park; the US 34 eastern approach from I-25 and Loveland follows the Big Thompson River Canyon. There are two entrance stations on the east side: Fall River (US 34) and Beaver Meadows (US 36). The Grand Lake Station (also US 34) is the only entry on the west side. Year-round access is available through Kawuneeche Valley along the Colorado River headwaters to Timber Creek Campground. The main centers of visitor activity on the park's east side are the Alpine Visitor Center high on Trail Ridge Rd, and Bear Lake Rd, which leads to campgrounds, trailheads and the Moraine Park Museum.

 Sights

Wonders of the natural world are the main attractions here: huge herds of elk and scattered mountain sheep, pine-dotted granite slopes and blindingly white alpine tundra. However, there are a few museums and historic sites within the park's borders which are worthy of a glance and good for families.

ALPINE VISITOR CENTER   Visitor Center
(www.nps.gov/romo; Fall River Pass; ⏱10:30am-4:30pm late May–mid-Jun, 9am-5pm late Jun–early Sep, 10:30am-4:30pm early Sep–mid-Oct; 👫) The views from this popular visitor center and souvenir store – perched at 11,796ft, and right in the middle of the park – are extraordinary. You can see elk, deer and sometimes moose grazing on the hillside on the drive up Old Fall River Rd. Much of the traffic that clogs Trail Ridge Rd all summer pulls into Alpine Visitor Center, so the place is a zoo (but still worthwhile). Rangers here give programs and advice about trails. You can also shop for knickknacks or eat in the cafeteria-style dining room.

BEAVER MEADOWS VISITOR CENTER   Visitor Center
(📞970-586-1206; www.nps.gov/romo; US Hwy 36; ⏱8am-9pm late Jun-late Aug, to 4:30pm or 5pm Sep-May; 👫) This is the primary visitor center and best stop for park information if you're approaching from Estes Park. You can see a film about the park, browse a small gift shop and reserve backcountry camping sites.

KAWUNEECHE VISITOR CENTER   Visitor Center
(📞970-627-3471; 16018 US Hwy 34; ⏱8am-6pm last week May-Labor Day, 8am-5pm Labor Day-late Sep, 8am-4:30pm Oct-late May; 👫) The main visitor center on the west side of the park, Kawuneeche offers a film about the park, ranger-led walks and discussions, backcountry permits and family activities.

MORAINE PARK MUSEUM   Museum
(📞970-586-1206; Bear Lake Rd; ⏱9am-4:30pm Jun-Oct) Built by the Civilian Conservation Corps (CCC) in 1923, and once the park's proud visitors' lodge, this building has been renovated in recent years to host exhibits on geology, glaciers and wildlife.

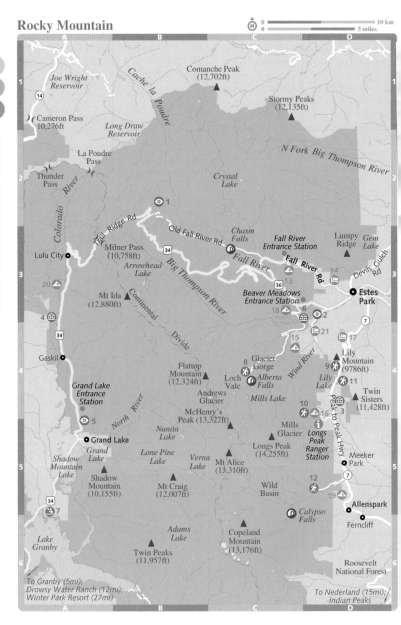

HOLZWARTH HISTORIC
SITE   Historic Village

(Never Summer Ranch; ☎ Park Headquarters 970-586-1206; Trail Ridge Rd/US 34; ⏱10am-4pm Jun-Oct; ⛟) When prohibition was enacted in 1916, John Holzwarth Sr, a Denver saloonkeeper, started a new life as a subsistence rancher. This site houses several buildings kept in their original condition, and hosts historical reenactments and ranger-led programs. The Heritage Days celebration happens in late July. The

Rocky Mountain

site lies at the end of a graded 0.5-mile path, easily accessible with strollers.

Activities

Hiking and backpacking are by far the park's most popular activities – and for good reason, offering the only access to much of the Rockie's most spectacular scenery. Cycling is also a magnificent way to see the park, but bicycles are restricted to major roads. Cross-country skiing and snowshoeing are excellent in winter.

Driving Tours

OLD FALL RIVER ROAD   Scenic Drive

With a maximum speed limit of 15mph, Old Fall River Rd offers motorists a graveled, slow-paced drive into the park's high country. Narrow, one-way (up) and without guardrails, it's also a bit hair-raising at times, and certainly not recommended for RVs. The road begins at Horseshoe Park, a short distance west of the Fall River Entrance, and winds 11 miles up to the Alpine Visitor Center at Fall River Pass – elevation, 11,796ft. From there you can head southwest (right) on Trail Ridge Rd and follow it down to Grand Lake, or take a left and loop back to Estes Park. Although Old Fall River Rd doesn't reach the dizzying heights of Trail Ridge Rd, the views of the alpine tundra and the narrowness of the road make this an equally impressive drive.

Hiking

With over 300 miles of trail, traversing all aspects of its diverse terrain, the park is suited to people of all hiking abilities. Those with the kids in tow might consider the easy hikes in the Wild Basin to Calypso Falls, or to Gem Lakes in the Lumpy Ridge area, while those with unlimited ambition, strong legs and enough trail mix will be lured by the challenge of conquering Longs Peak. Regardless, it's best to spend at least one night at 7000ft to 8000ft prior to setting out to allow your body to adjust to the elevation. Before July, many trails are snowbound and high water runoff makes passage difficult. Dogs and other pets are not allowed on the trails. All overnight stays in the backcountry require permits.

LONGS PEAK   Hiking

As the centerpiece of many a hiker's itinerary, you need not worry about getting lonesome on the 15-mile round-trip to the summit of Longs Peak (14,259ft). During summer, you're likely to find a line of more than 100 parked cars snaking down the road from the **Longs Peak trailhead**. After the initial 6 miles of moderate trail to the Boulder Field (12,760ft) the path steepens at the start of the **Keyhole Route** to the summit, which is marked with yellow and red bull's-eyes painted on the rock.

Detour:
Nederland

About an hour south of the Beaver Meadows Visitor Center, you'll find the lively, ramshackle little berg of Nederland, a mountain-town magnet for hippies looking to get off the grid. These days, Nederland has a sagging, accidental quality to its weather-beaten buildings, which are not without a certain rugged charm.

In early March, the town celebrates **Frozen Dead Guy Days**. This bizarre little festival is basically an excuse to parade through town and drink beer, all in celebration of Grandpa Bredo Morstoel, a Norwegian transplant who is cryogenically frozen and held locally in dry ice awaiting reanimation. (We kid you not.) If you're around in late August, catch **NedFest** (www.nedfest.com), an annual gathering of area folkies and jam bands.

There are several worthwhile restaurants, but for sleeps, you're better off in Estes Park or Boulder (17 miles west). For information, pop into the **Nederland Visitors Center** (303-258-3936; www.nederlandchamber.org; 4 W 1st St; 10am-4pm) downtown.

Even superhuman athletes who are used to the thin air will be slowed by the route's ledge system, which resembles a narrow cliffside stairway without a handrail. After this, hikers scramble the final homestretch to the summit boulders. The view from the top – snow-kissed granite stretching out to the curved horizon – is incredible. The round-trip hike takes anywhere from 10 to 15 hours.

Many climbers make the trail approach in early predawn hours after overnighting at Longs Peak Campground. The Keyhole Route is generally free of snow mid-July to October – otherwise you will need technical climbing skills and equipment to reach the summit. When you dial the Beaver Meadows Visitor Center, the prerecorded message will have information about the conditions on this popular route.

TWIN SISTERS PEAK   Hiking
This up-and-back hike provides an excellent warm-up to climbing Longs Peak. In addition, the 11,428ft summit of Twin Sisters Peak offers unequaled views of Longs Peak. It's an arduous walk, gaining 2300ft in just 3.7 miles. Erosion-resistant quartz rock caps the oddly deformed rock

at the summit and delicate alpine flowers (plenty of mountain harebell) fill the rock spaces near the stone hut. The **trailhead** is near Mills Cabin, 10 miles south of Estes Park on Hwy 7.

GLACIER GORGE
JUNCTION   Hiking
Accessed from the **Bear Lake trailhead,** this busy network of trails threads through pine forest and over rushing streams, offering a spectrum of difficulty. The easy stroll to Alberta Falls is good for families. Far more strenuous 5-mile options would be to hike up Glacier Gorge, past Mills Lake and many glacial erratics to Black Lake, or via Loch Vale to Andrews Glacier on the Continental Divide. The trailhead is served by the Glacier Basin–Bear Lake shuttle.

LILY MOUNTAIN   Hiking
One of the easiest climbs in the area, Lily Mountain's 1.5-mile trail ascends almost 1000ft to the hike's namesake summit, offering an outstanding panorama that includes the Mummy Range, Continental Divide, Longs Peak, Estes Park and Estes Cone. The trailhead sits on the park border, 6 miles south of Estes Park on Hwy 7.

WILD BASIN Hiking

In the park's southeast corner, Wild Basin offers several easy day hikes to cascading waterfalls, alpine lakes and swaths of wildflowers all beneath some of the parks most stunning peaks. Set out from the Wild Basin Trailhead and you'll soon reach Copeland Falls. Calypso Cascades appears in less than 2 miles; and in another mile you reach Ouzel Falls and a nearby overlook of Longs Peak. Hikers can continue another mile to a junction with the Bluebird Lake Trail that follows Ouzel Creek, or take the north branch to Thunder Lake in the upper St Vrain Creek. Both trails offer campsites and reach timberline at the 6-mile mark.

To reach the trailhead, drive 13 miles south of Estes Park on Hwy 7, and turn right on Wild Basin Rd (toward the Wild Basin Ranger Station). It's another 3 miles from the turnoff to the trailhead.

BEAR LAKE TRAILHEAD Hiking

This popular subalpine interpretive nature trail circles Bear Lake, and another 1-mile hike takes you past Nymph Lake to beautiful Dream Lake, a small gem surrounded by Englemann spruce below massive Hallett Peak. From there, one trail follows the Tyndall Glacier Gorge, crossing the terminal moraine that separates Dream Lake from Emerald Lake less than a mile upstream. The trail south from Dream Lake passes upstream of Chaos Canyon Cascades and continues to Loch Vale, past Glacier Falls and Alberta Falls, before emerging at Glacier Gorge Junction trailhead. Bear Lake is served by the Glacier Basin–Bear Lake shuttle.

FLATTOP MOUNTAIN TRAIL Hiking

Surprisingly, this is the only hiking trail in the park to link the east and west sides. Reaching the Divide on Flattop Mountain from the Bear Lake trailhead entails a strenuous 4.5-mile climb, gaining 2800ft in elevation. From the summit, you have two equidistant options for continuing to Grand Lake: Tonahutu Creek Trail or the North Inlet Trail. Both offer plenty of back-country campsites on the east side.

MILNER PASS Hiking

The Trail Ridge Rd crosses the Divide at Milner Pass (elevation 10,759ft), where trails head southeast to Mt Ida, the most accessible peak on the west side of the park. The trail climbs 2000ft in 4 miles,

Old Fall River Rd (p223)

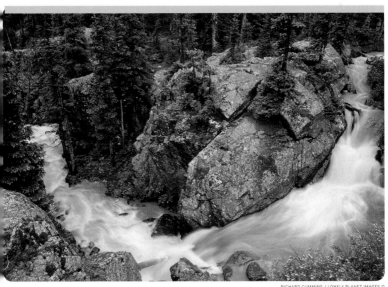

steeply at first through dense forest, before emerging onto an exhilaratingly open tundra zone with fabulous views of the valleys below. At about the 3-mile point the trail peters out, but the route is still easy to follow. Figure about three hours to the summit, and about 2½ hours to return. Because the route is so exposed, lightning can be a danger during thunderstorms.

Backpacking

Backcounty permits ($20) are required for overnight stays (May through October) outside of developed campgrounds. Reservations can be made by phone, mail or in person. Phone reservations can be made only from November to April. Reservations by mail or phone are accepted via the **Backcountry Office** (970-586-1242; www.nps.gov/romo).

Permits can be obtained in person at Beaver Meadows Visitor Center, Kawuneeche Visitor Center, and (in summer only) at the Longs Peak and Wild Basin ranger stations.

Cycling & Mountain Biking

Mountain biking and cycling have continued to gain popularity despite the park roads' heavy traffic and lack of shoulder.

It's a splendid way to see the park and wildlife, though bicycle travel is restricted to paved roads and to one dirt road, Fall River Rd. Those looking to ride technical routes on a mountain bike should go to Roosevelt National Forest.

Less daunting climbs (and climes) are available on the park's lower paved roads. A popular 16-mile circuit is the Horseshoe Park/Estes Park Loop. For a bit more of a climbing challenge you can continue to Bear Lake Rd, an 8-mile-long route that rises 1500ft to the high mountain basin.

If you are not up to climbing either Trail Ridge or Fall River Rds, Colorado Bicycling Adventures (p233) offers tours of Rocky Mountain National Park; they drive you to the top of the road, you hop on your bicycle and ride down. It also rents bicycles.

Remember that the pleasant summer weather at lower elevations can suddenly become unmercifully cold at higher altitudes – especially when descending full speed from the park's alpine peaks. Hypothermia is an emergency experienced by many unprepared cyclists each month: change into a dry shirt, full gloves and a warm, water-repellent outer shell before you get above the tree line and into the wind. The only shelter from lightning is at the Alpine Visitor Center.

History in a Cabin

Without the efforts of naturalist Enos Mills (1870–1922), there would be no Rocky Mountain National Park. At the **Enos Mills Cabin Museum & Gallery** (970-586-4706; www.enosmills.com; 6760 Hwy 7; adult/child under 12yr $5/3; 11am-4pm Tue & Wed summer;), near Estes Park, you can learn all about the man who pushed harder than anyone for the creation of what is now one of the country's greatest protected natural areas.

Mills' infectious enthusiasm and passion for nature lived on with his daughter, Enda Mills Kiley (who passed away in 2009). In the tiny cabin where Mills lived, the Mills family maintains a short interpretive nature trail, where news clippings and photographs recount Enos' advocacy to protect the wild. Reprints and vintage copies of many of Mills' 16 books are available for sale, in addition to an outstanding collection of his writings, edited by Enda, called *Adventures of a Nature Guide* (1990).

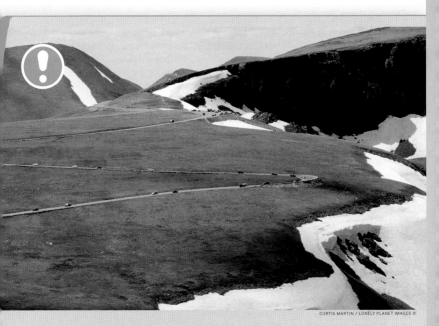

CURTIS MARTIN / LONELY PLANET IMAGES ©

Don't Miss **Trail Ridge Road**

The highest continuously paved road in the country, Trail Ridge Rd winds 48 miles between Grand Lake and Estes Park, offering motorists one of the most stunning experiences in the park. But get up and get on the road early if you want to miss the crowds.

Making its way from the aspen and pine forests of the park's lower elevations, the route climbs through dense subalpine forests of fir and spruce, ascends above the tree line at 11,500ft, winds through miles of tundra and finally tops out at a breathtaking 12,183ft. Near and above the tree line, the wildflowers are dazzling. Elk and moose are sometimes seen at lower elevations, and pikas, marmots and bighorn sheep are common sights up in the tundra.

If you were to drive the road straight through (and not have any traffic), it would only take you about 1½ hours. But there is so much to see and do, you should allow at least four hours to do the route justice.

Yet another unpleasantness is the altitude sickness and subsequent dehydration that strikes many people unaccustomed to the 12,000ft elevation reached on Trail Ridge Rd.

Snowshoeing & Cross-Country Skiing

From December into May, the high valleys and alpine tundra offer cross-country skiers unique opportunities to view wildlife and the winter scenery undisturbed by crowds. January and February are the best months for dry, powdery snow pack; spring snows tend to be heavy and wet. Most routes follow summer hiking trails, but valley bottoms and frozen stream-beds typically have more snow cover and are less challenging. In fact, most of the park should be considered 'backcountry skiing' rather than 'cross-country.' Avalanche hazards are greatest on steep, open slopes in mountainous terrain.

Overnight trips require permits, and the NPS (www.nps.gov/romo) will have a list of closed trails.

Rangers lead weekend snowshoe hikes in the east side of the park from January to April, depending on snow conditions. Trailhead locations and times are available from the park headquarters.

Snowshoe and ski rentals are available at the Estes Park Mountain Shop (p233).

Rock Climbing

Many of the park's alpine climbs are long one-day climbs or require an overnight stay on the rock face. Often the only way to accomplish a long climb and avoid afternoon thundershowers is to begin climbing at dawn – this can mean an approach hike beginning at midnight! An alternative is to bivouac (temporary open-air encampment – no tents) at the base of the climb. Free bivouac permits are issued only to technical climbers and are mandatory for all overnight stays in the backcountry.

To minimize the environmental impact of backcountry use, the **Rocky Mountain National Park Backcountry Office** (970-586-1242; www.nps.gov/romo) allows only a limited number of people to bivouac at four popular climbing areas. Phone reservations may be made March to May 20 for the following restricted zones: Longs Peak area, including Broadway below Diamond, Chasm View, Mills Glacier and Meeker Cirque; Black Lake area (Glacier Gorge), encompassing McHenry Peak, Arrowhead, Spearhead and Chiefshead/Pagoda; the base of Notchtop Peak; and the Skypond/Andrews Glacier Area, including the Taylor/Powell Peaks and Sharkstooth Peak. Reservations are not needed or accepted for other bivouacs.

For climbing gear try Estes Park Mountain Shop (p233). A small stock of climbing gear also is available from Colorado Mountain School (p232), where you can also find dormitory accommodation in the company of other climbers, shower after a climb for a few dollars or enroll in a climbing course.

Sleeping

The only overnight accommodations in the park are at campgrounds; the majority of motel or hotel accommodations are around Estes Park or Grand Lake. The closest thing the park has to the typical CCC-era lodges of parks like Yellowstone or Yosemite is the YMCA of the Rockies (p234), which is on the park's border.

The park's formal campgrounds provide campfire programs, have public telephones and a seven-day limit during summer months; all except Longs Peak take

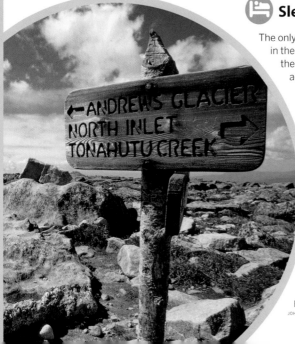

Flattop Mountain Trail (p225)

RVs (no hookups). The water supply is turned off during winter.

You will need a backcountry permit to stay outside developed park campgrounds. None of the campgrounds have showers, but they do have flush toilets in summer and outhouse facilities in winter. Sites include a fire ring, picnic table and one parking spot.

LONGS PEAK
CAMPGROUND Campground $

(970-586-1206; Mile marker 9, State Hwy 7; campsites $20) This is the base camp of choice for the early morning ascent of Longs Peak, one of Colorado's most accessible 14ers. The scenery is striking and its 26 spaces are for tents only, but don't expect much solitude in the peak of the summer.

There are no reservations, but if you're planning to bag Longs Peak after sleeping here, get here *early* one day before the climb – according to rangers the only way to ensure a site during peak season is to show up before noon.

MORAINE PARK
CAMPGROUND Campground $

(877-444-6777; www.recreation.gov; off Bear Lake Rd; campsites summer $20;) In the middle of a stand of ponderosa pine forest off Bear Lake Rd, this is the biggest of the park's campgrounds, approximately 2.5 miles south of the Beaver Meadows Visitor Center, and with 245 sites. The walk-in, tent-only sites in the D Loop are recommended if you want quiet. Reservations are accepted and recommended from the end of May through to the end of September; other times of the year the campground is first-come, first-served.

ASPENGLEN
CAMPGROUND Campground $

(877-444-6777; www.recreation.gov; State Hwy 34; campsites summer $20) With only 54 sites, this is the smallest of the park's reservable campgrounds. There are many tent-only sites, including some walk-ins, and a limited number of trailers are allowed. This is the quietest park that's highly accessible (5 miles west of Estes Park on US 34). Make reservations through the website.

OLIVE RIDGE
CAMPGROUND Campground $

(303-541-2500; campsites $14; mid-May– Nov) This well-kept USFS campground has access to four trailheads: St Vrain Mountain, Wild Basin, Longs Peak and Twin Sisters. In the summer it can get full, though sites are mostly first-come, first-served.

TIMBER CREEK
CAMPGROUND Campground $

(Trail Ridge Rd, US Hwy 34) This campground has 100 sites and remains open through the winter. No reservations accepted. It's the only established campground on the west side of the park, and is 7 miles north of Grand Lake.

Glacier Basin
Campground Campground $

(877-444-6777; www.recreation.gov; off Bear Lake Rd; campsites summer $20;) This developed campground has a large area for group camping and accommodates RVs. It is served by the shuttle buses on Bear Lake Rd throughout the summer. Make reservations through the website.

ℹ Information

The National Park Service's excellent website (www.nps.gov/romo) has information on just about everything to do with the park.

Entrance Fees & Passes

For private vehicles, the park entrance fee is $20, valid for seven days. Individuals entering the park on foot, bicycle, motorcycle or bus pay $10 each. Annual passes cost $40. Interagency and senior passes are valid.

Opening Dates

Rocky Mountain National Park is open 24 hours a day, 365 days a year. Entrance kiosks are unstaffed at night.

Tourist Information

The park has three full-service visitors centers – one on the east side, one on the west, and one in the middle. Though they all have different displays and programs, they are where you can study maps and speak with rangers about permits and weather conditions.

Peak to Peak Hwy

Snaking over 70 miles between Estes Park and the town of Black Hawk, the **Peak to Peak Scenic and Historic Byway** (aka Peak to Peak Hwy) is one of the state's most spectacular drives. Although you can drive it in about 1½ hours, you'll find so many distractions along the way – trailheads, campgrounds, lakes, scenic viewpoints – that you could easily spend the whole day exploring. If you're driving between Denver and Rocky Mountain National Park, definitely consider this route.

Alpine Visitor Center (www.nps.gov/romo; Fall River Pass; ⊙10:30am-4:30pm late May–mid-Jun, 9am-5pm late Jun-early Sep, 10:30am-4:30pm early Sep–mid-Oct; 👫) The views from this popular visitor center and souvenir store at 11,796ft, and right in the middle of the park, are extraordinary.

Beaver Meadows Visitor Center (✐970-586-1206; www.nps.gov/romo; US Hwy 36; ⊙8am-9pm late Jun-late Aug, to 4:30pm or 5pm Sep-May; 👫) The primary visitors center and best stop for park information if you're approaching from Estes Park. You can see a film about the park, browse a small gift shop and reserve backcountry camping sites.

Kawuneeche Visitor Center (✐970-627-3471; 16018 US Hwy 34; ⊙8am-6pm last week May-Labor Day, 8am-5pm Labor Day-late Sep, 8am-4:30pm Oct-late May; 👫) This is the main visitors center on the west side of the park, offering a film about the park, ranger-led walks and discussions, backcountry permits and family activities.

Park Policies & Regulations

Dogs are permitted in the park but prohibited from trails and the backcountry. Basically, you can only bring them where you can take a car.

Maps

Even though you'll get a driving map when you enter the park and some basic, non-technical photocopied maps are available at some of the most popular trail heads, high quality topographic maps are unavailable. You'll want to pick them up beforehand in Estes Park at **MacDonald Book Shop** (✐970-586-3450; www.macdonaldbookshop.com; 152 E Elkhorn Ave; ⊙8am-8pm, shorter hours in winter; 🛜) or in Boulder, at the **Boulder Map Gallery** (✐303-

444-1406; www.bouldermapgallery.com; 1708 13th St; ⊙10am-6pm Mon-Fri, to 3pm Sat).

Dangers & Annoyances

If you're in easily accessible areas during high season, the biggest annoyance in Rocky Mountain National Park will likely be the other visitors. Roads clog with RVs, garbage fills every can to the brim and screaming children seem to multiply endlessly. Brace yourself, camper: it can be annoying. But it might be more than fellow travelers giving you a headache: it could be the altitude. High elevation can play all kinds of nasty tricks here, from relatively mild problems like a pounding head and winded breathing, to fairly serious symptoms of nausea, dehydration and fatigue.

If you intend to get off the heavily beaten trail, take precautions in the spring and summer to avoid bites from wood ticks, which can transmit Colorado tick fever. Also be mindful of your food, which can attract wildlife. The park is home to black bears and mountain lions, but neither poses a serious threat to visitors.

ℹ️ Getting There & Around

Air

Denver International Airport (DIA; ✐information 303-342-2000; www.flydenver.com; 8500 Peña Blvd; @🛜) lies 75 miles southeast of Estes Park and the nearby Beaver Meadows Visitor Center. Rental cars are available or you can take the Estes Park Shuttle to Estes Park.

Car

The majority of visitors enter the park in their own cars, using the long and winding Trail Ridge Rd (US 34) to cross the Continental Divide. The most direct route from Boulder follows US 36 through

Lyons to the east entrances. Another approach from the south, mountainous Hwy 7, passes by Enos Mills' Cabin and provides access to campsites and trailheads on the east side of the divide. Winter closure of US 34 through the park makes access to the park's west side dependent on US 40 at Granby.

Park Shuttle

In summer a free shuttle bus operates from the Estes Park Visitor Center multiple times daily, bringing hikers to a park-and-ride location where you can pick up other shuttles. The year-round option leaves the Glacier Basin parking area toward Bear Lake, in the park's lower elevations. During the summer peak, a second shuttle operates between Moraine Park campground and the Glacier Basin parking area. Shuttles run on weekends only from mid-August through September.

AROUND ROCKY MOUNTAIN NATIONAL PARK

Estes Park

T-shirt shops and ice-cream parlors, sidewalks jammed with tourists and streets plugged with RVs...welcome to Estes Park,

the chaotic outpost at the edge of Rocky Mountain National Park.

There's no small irony in the fact that the proximity to one of the most pristine outdoor escapes in the USA has made Estes Park the kind of place you'll need to escape. Those expecting immediate views of the beauty of Rocky Mountain National Park may be disappointed to find themselves watching brake lights on E Elkhorn Ave, the town's artery to both park entrances. But it's not all bad. Although the strip malls and low-rise motels can be unsightly, Estes Park promises every convenience for the traveler, and during the off-season the place has a certain charm, as the streets quiet down and the prices of creekside cabins drop.

 Sights & Activities

On the doorstep of Rocky Mountain National Park and surrounded by national forest, Estes Park is one of the state's premier supply points for the mountains. With the exception of white-water rafting and skiing (better in other parts of the

Moraine Park Museum (p221)

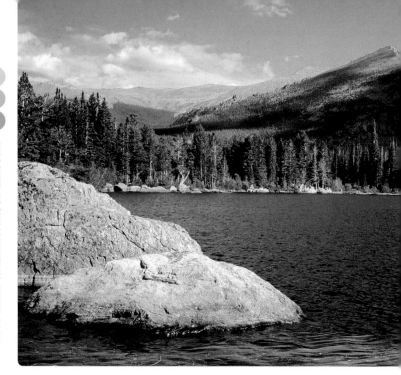

state), the area has top-notch outdoor activities of every stripe, and a stroll down Elkhorn will take you past a number of operators heading into the park via horse, jeep or hiking boots. Many of Estes Park's sights are a bit out of town and only accessible if you have a car.

ESTES PARK MUSEUM Museum

(☏970-586-6256; www.estesnet.com/museum; 200 4th St; admission free; ⊗10am-5pm Mon-Sat, 1-5pm Sun; ⍟) This ambitious community museum has a commendable rotation of exhibits on local culture. It's not only corny Ice Age mannequins either – during our last visit the main attraction was a glimpse into Estes Park's wild days in the 1960s.

ARIEL TRAMWAY Cable Car

(☏970-586-3675; www.estestram.com; 420 E Riverside Dr; adult/child/senior $10/5/9; ⊗9am-6pm Memorial Day-Labor Day; ⍟) In the time you wait to be herded aboard a tram to the top of Prospect Mountain, you could have climbed Lily Mountain on your own two feet, but the tram is a good option for those with modest ambitions who still want the view.

COLORADO MOUNTAIN SCHOOL Mountaineering

(☏303-447-2804; www.totalclimbing.com; 341 Moraine Ave; half-day guided climbs per person from $125) Simply put, there's no better resource for climbers in Colorado – this outfit is the largest climbing operator in the region, has the most expert guides and is the only organization allowed to operate within Rocky Mountain National Park. It has a clutch of classes taught by world-class instructors.

Basic courses, such as Intro to Rock Climbing, are a great way for novices to deeply experience the Rockies. There are multiday training expeditions for those with some experience. Courses are taught in an ideal setting – whether it be a towering granite peak in the park or the 10,000-sq-ft indoor climbing facility. You can also stay on-site in dorm lodging.

Left: Bear Lake (p225); **Below:** Thistle flower
(LEFT) HOLGER LEUE / LONELY PLANET IMAGES ©; (BELOW) RICHARD CUMMINS / LONELY PLANET IMAGES ©

SOMBRERO RANCH   Horseback Riding

(☎970-586-4577; www.sombrero.com; 1895 Big Thompson Ave; horse rides from $35) With affordable guided trips into the national park or through a huge private ranch in the foothills, this quality outfitter has a variety of options.

KIRKS FLYSHOP   Fishing

(☎877-669-1859; www.kirksflyshop.com; 230 E Elkhorn Ave; tours from $150; ⏰7am-7pm) This full-service fly-fishing shop offers a number of guided packages in Rocky Mountain National Park and around. It also rents equipment, guides overnight hikes and offers kayaking and fishing combos.

COLORADO BICYCLING ADVENTURES   Cycling

(☎970-586-4241, New Venture Cycling 970-231-273; 2050 Big Thompson Ave; half-day tour $60) For years this was *the* bicycle shop in town, so the staff know the surround-

ing hills like the backs of their contoured, oversized calf muscles.

GREEN JEEP TOURS   4WD

(☎970-577-0034; www.epgjt.com; 157 Moraine Ave; tours from $35;) Offerings start with 3½-hour guided tours to waterfalls in Rocky Mountain National Park and move up to all-day affairs.

🛏 Sleeping

Be warned: lodgings fill up very fast during the peak July and August period, when the prices are sky-high. You're likely to be out of luck if you travel west of Greeley without a reservation during summer. Off-season rates may be down to half that of summer prices, and many accommodations simply close for the winter. Most of the cheaper midcentury motels (which still aren't that cheap) are located east of

233

town along US 34 or Hwy 7. Most of these low-slung motels are remarkably similar: musty carpet and fairly small rooms with TV and refrigerator, though some places also boast pools, hot tubs and saunas. There are plenty of cabins to rent here too, with a concentration of them along US 66.

There are some passable budget options for those trying to save money, but the best-value accommodations, hands down, are in area campgrounds which are plentiful, easily accessible and stunning. If you didn't bring your own tent and sleeping bag, you can rent one from **Estes Park Mountain Shop** (☎970-586-6548; www.estesparkmountainshop.com; 2050 Big Thompson Ave; 2-person camping set-up $32; ⏰8am-9pm).

YMCA OF THE ROCKIES – ESTES PARK CENTER   Resort $$

(☎970-586-3341; www.ymcarockies.org; 2515 Tunnel Rd; r & d from $99, cabins from $124; ❄🛜👪) Estes Park Center is not your typical YMCA boarding house. Instead it's a favorite family vacation spot, with up-market motel-style rooms and cabins set on 860 acres of high alpine terrain. Just a few minutes outside of Estes Park (but definitely away from the hustle of town), it offers a range of activities for adults and kids. This YMCA is unapologetically outdoorsy, and most guests come to participate in the activities. Accomodations are simple and practical.

MARY'S LAKE LODGE   Lodge $$

(☎970-577-9495; www.maryslakelodge.com; 2625 Marys Lake Rd; r & cabins from $140; ❄🛜👪) This atmospheric old wooden lodge, perched on a ridge looking over its namesake lake, is an utterly romantic place to slumber. Built from polished pine logs, it reeks of Wild West ambience and has an amazing covered front porch with panoramic Rocky Mountain views. The rooms and cabins are a blend of modern and historic, and many of the latter have private hot tubs.

STANLEY HOTEL   Hotel $$

(☎970-586-3371; www.stanleyhotel.com; 333 Wonderview Ave; r from $159; 🛜✖👪) The white Georgian Colonial Revival hotel stands in brilliant contrast to the towering peaks of Rocky Mountain National Park that surround it. A favorite local retreat, the nearly-a-century-old hotel served as the inspiration for Stephen King's cult novel *The Shining*. Rooms are cozy and decorated to evoke the Old West, with period and replica antiques.

BLACK CANYON INN   Lodge $$$

(☎970-586-8113; www.black canyoninn.com; 800 MacGregor Ave, Estes Park; 1-/2-/3-bed r from $195/260/399; ❄🛜👪) A fine place to splurge is this lovely, secluded 14-acre property offering luxury suites and a 'rustic' log cabin (which comes with its own Jacuzzi).

Mountain goats

TOTAL CLIMBING LODGE
Hostel **$**

(☎303-447-2804; www.totalclimbing.com; 341 Moraine Ave, Estes Park; dm $25; @🛜) A bustling hub of climbers, lodging here is the best dorm option in town. Expect simple pine bunks, a ping-pong table and a laid-back vibe.

SILVER MOON INN
Lodge **$$**

(☎970-586-6006; www.silvermooninn.com; 175 Spruce Dr, Estes Park; d $139-159; ❄🛜♨🚹) The rooms here aren't loaded with personality, but the little things (quality continental breakfast, creekside fire pits, central location) make up for it.

DEER CREST RESORT
Lodge **$$**

(☎970-586-2324; www.deercrestresort.com; 1200 Fall River Rd; d $119-129, ste from $149; ❄🛜♨🚹) Deer Crest bests its neighboring hotels with gas grills, lots of green space for the kids and the sound of the creek shushing guests to sleep. The on-site restaurant is also excellent.

🍴 Eating & Drinking

Like lodgings, restaurants here often shift to shorter hours, close for several days of the week or shut down altogether in the snowy off-season. Another unfortunate similarity is poor value for your money. Most menus here offer only meaty American standards and humdrum pub grub, which too often come at white-tablecloth prices. If you're visiting between September and May it's wise to call ahead for reservations.

DELEO'S PARK THEATRE CAFE & DELI
Deli **$**

(☎970-577-1134; www.deleosdeli.com; 132 Moraine Ave; mains $6-10; ⊙11am-4pm; 🚹) Within one of the nation's oldest movie houses, chatty Tom DeLeo serves Estes Park's best sandwich (and according to the Food Network, one of the best in the country). Adapting its names after classic flicks (like the turkey-stacked, um, 'Gobblefather'), this place has loads of character.

BIG HORN RESTAURANT
Breakfast **$**

(☎970-586-2792; www.estesparkbighorn.com; 401 W Elkhorn; mains $6-17; ⊙6am-9pm, hours vary seasonally; 🚹) Here's the local breakfast institution – a place where you can get a side of grits and the local gossip, the best huevos rancheros (ranch eggs) and some face time with flannel-clad locals. If you get here on the way into the park, order a packed lunch with your breakfast.

PURA VIDA
Latin American **$$**

(160 1st St; mains $10-22; ⊙11am-9pm Mon-Sat, to 8pm Sun; 🚹) This place is *just* off the beaten path enough to feel like a discovery, situated away from the tourist traffic. The vibe is casual but the Latin American fare is classy – *Casado* (a plate of typical Costa Rican fare), fried yucca and a lunch buffet of fresh, inventive flavors.

LONIGANS
Pub **$$**

(☎970-586-4346; www.lonigans.com; 110 W Elkhorn Ave; ⊙kitchen closes 10pm; 🚹) This pub and grill is a place to soak up Estes Park local flavor, mostly through the sidelong glances of the good ol' boys at the bar and boozy karaoke crooners. The menu – mostly burgers and American pub basics – includes Rocky Mountain Oysters, otherwise known as bull balls.

ED'S CANTINA & GRILL
Mexican **$$**

(☎970-586-2919; www.edscantina.com; 390 E Elkhorn Ave; mains $10-25; ⊙11am-2am Mon-Fri, from 8am Sat & Sun; 🚹) With an outdoor patio right on the river, Ed's is a great place to kick back with a margarita and one of the daily $3 blue-plate specials (think flautas with shredded pork and guacamole). Serving Mexican and American staples, the restaurant is in a retro mod space with leather booth seating and a bold primary-color scheme.

ROCK INN MOUNTAIN TAVERN
Steakhouse **$$$**

(☎970-586-4116; www.rockinnestes.com; 1675 Hwy 66; mains $14-29; ⊙11am-2am; 🛜🚹) After a few days in the wilds of Rocky Mountain National Park, the rare porterhouse here seems heaven-sent (even if the country band on stage can't pass as the accompanying choir of angels).

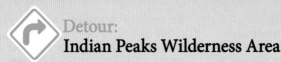

Detour:
Indian Peaks Wilderness Area

Forming the impressive backdrop to the town of Nederland, the Indian Peaks area offers many fine hiking and camping opportunities. Especially nice is the hike up to 12,000ft Arapaho Pass. It's a gentle ascent but be prepared to spend the entire day – if the altitude doesn't slow you down, the scenery should. The trail is accessed from the Fourth of July campground 9.5 miles northwest of Nederland, via Fourth of July Rd.

For more information on Indian Peaks check at the Nederland Visitors Center, which has maps and guidebooks. In Nederland's mall, **Ace Hardware** (303-258-3132; 74 Hwy 119 S; 8am-7pm Mon-Sat, 9am-5pm Sun) sells topographic and USGS maps for the Indian Peaks area and issues camping permits (required June to September 15) as well as hunting and fishing licenses.

Stick-to-the-ribs fare and a crackling fire make it ideal for hikers looking to indulge.

NEPAL'S CAFE
Nepalese $

(970-577-7035; 184 E Elkhorn Ave, Unit H; buffet $9; 10am-8pm;) Lamp-heated lunch buffets are usually a no-no, but it's worth reconsidering dropping by here. The curries are spiced just right and the *momo* (dumplings) are a filling option before or after a big hike. Come early for dinner, as the tiny place gets packed.

SMOKIN' DAVE'S BBQ & TAP HOUSE
BBQ $$

(866-674-2793; www.smokindavesbbqand taphouse.com; 820 Moraine Ave; mains $8-20; 11am-9pm Sun-Thu, to 10pm Fri & Sat;) Half-assed BBQ joints are all too common in Colorado's mountain towns, but Dave's, situated in a spare dining room, fully delivers. The buffalo ribs and pulled pork come dressed in a slightly sweet, smoky, tangy sauce and the sweet potato fries are crisply fried. Also excellent is the long, well-selected beer list.

MOLLY B RESTAURANT
American $

(970-586-2766; www.estesparkmollyb.com; 200 Moraine Ave; breakfast $5-8; 6:30am-4pm Thu-Tue;) This classic American breakfast place in town is easy to find and has a burly omelet and other greasy-spoon delights served among wood paneling and vinyl seats. Even the healthy food is

delivered jumbo size, making the 'outrageous granola' no joke.

Estes Park Brewery
Brewpub

(970-586-6409; www.epbrewery.com; 470 Prospect Village Dr; 11am-2am) Ain't nothing fancy about this brewpub – it dishes out pizza, wings and house beer in a big, boxy room that resembles a cross between a classroom and a country kitchen.

ℹ Information

Estes Park Visitors Center (970-577-9900; www.estesparkcvb.com; 500 Big Thompson Ave; 9am-8pm daily Jun-Aug, 8am-5pm Mon-Fri, 9am-5pm Sat, 10am-4pm Sun Sep-May;) Try the Estes Park Visitor Center, just east of the US 36 junction, for help with lodging; note that many places close in winter.

Post office (970-586-0170; 215 W Riverside Dr; 8:30am-4:30pm Mon-Fri, 10am-1pm Sat) Centrally located post office with a fully staffed service desk.

USFS Estes Park Visitor Center (970-586-3440; 161 2nd St) The USFS Estes Park Visitor Center sells books and maps for the Arapaho and Roosevelt National Forests and has camping and trail information for hikers and off-road cyclists. Camping permits for the heavily used Indian Peaks Wilderness Area, south of Rocky Mountain National Park, are required from June to September 15 and cost $5 per person.

ⓘ Getting There & Around

Estes Park is 34 miles west of Loveland via US 34, which you can access from I-25 exit 257. Many visitors also come up by way of Boulder along US 36, passing through Lyons. Both are spectacular drives through rugged foothills, red-rock formations and lush forest. A slower but more scenic route is the spectacular Peak to Peak Hwy.

Considering the traffic, getting around Estes Park's compact downtown is easiest on foot. Estes Park has started a free shuttle service in the summer along the town's main arteries. The routes seem to change every year, but the service operates daily from about July to August, and then weekends only through September. If you're traveling into Rocky Mountain National Park, there is a free 'Hiker Shuttle' which leaves from the Estes Park Visitors Center, making stops at Beaver Meadows Visitor Center and the park's Park & Ride lot, where you can transfer to other national park shuttles.

TO/FROM THE AIRPORT

Estes Park Shuttle (☎970-586-5151; www.estesparkshuttle.com; one way/round-trip $45/85) This shuttle service connects Denver's airport to Estes Park about four times a day. The trip takes two hours.

BICYCLE

Cycling is a great way to get around, though few visitors seem to use this mode of transport (the altitude does make for some puffing). In summer, bicycle rentals spring up in the tourist area along E Elkhorn Ave, or get some wheels from Colorado Bicycling Adventures (p233).

TAXI

Peak to Peak Taxi (☎970-586-6111) This minivan taxi service runs throughout Rocky Mountain National Park and the Front Range.

Grand Lake

As the western gateway to Rocky Mountain National Park, Grand Lake is a foil to the bustling hub of Estes Park. Sure, both are fairly inglorious tourist traps compared to the magnificent park in their shared backyard, but Grand Lake is more remote, suffers less traffic and exploits its history as an old mining town for the feel of an 'intimate' tourist trap. The namesake lake is handsome, and offers a different suite of recreational thrills in the summer. An amble along the boardwalk is pleasant, with a hodgepodge of corny souvenir

View of Longs Peak (p223) from Trail Ridge Rd

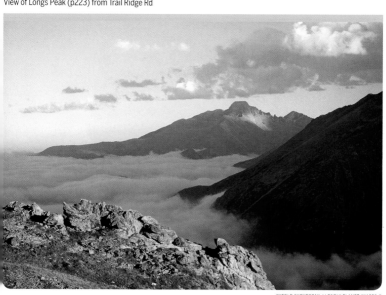

shops, decent restaurants, T-shirt stores and a few character-filled bars. Unless you're staying for a few days at the sublime Shadowcliff Lodge (p239), Grand Lake is no destination unto itself – it's more of a lunch-and-supplies stop with a handful of interesting sights and several good outfitters thrown in for fun.

Sights & Activities

Regardless of season, there's no problem keeping busy in Grand Lake; the town's bicycle and boat rentals give way to sleds and skis as the season changes. Because of its location abutting multiuse federal and state land, Grand Lake is a popular destination for snowmobiles – you can even ride in Rocky Mountain National Park. Get information about rentals and trails at the visitor center.

Several Rocky Mountain National Park trailheads are just outside the town limits, including those to the Tonahutu Creek Trail and the Cascade Falls/North Inlet Trail, both near Shadowcliff Lodge. Entering the park from these trailheads is an excellent way to dodge many of the crowds which plug up the park's eastern side.

The town is also 35 miles north of Winter Park Resort, a popular ski and mountain-bike destination.

KAUFFMAN HOUSE MUSEUM   Museum
(☎ 970-627-3351; www.kauffmanhouse.org; 407 Pitkin St; entry by donation; ☺ 1-5pm Jun-Aug; ♿) The Ezra Kauffman House is an 1892 log building that operated as a hotel until 1946. Now on the National Register of Historic Places, it contains period furniture, old skis, quilts and other dusty artifacts. Hardly hair-raising, but a nice stop for history buffs.

GRAND LAKE METRO RECREATION DISTRICT   Cycling, Hiking
(☎ 970-627-8328; www.grandlakerecreation.com; 928 Grand Ave, Suite 204; ☺ 8am-5pm Mon-Fri; ♿) With good maps and information about cycling and hiking in the Arapaho National Forest, Nordic skiing and golf, this government office serves all-season outdoor-recreation information. It can also offer dog owners guidance about getting Fido on the trail.

Fly-fishing (p233)

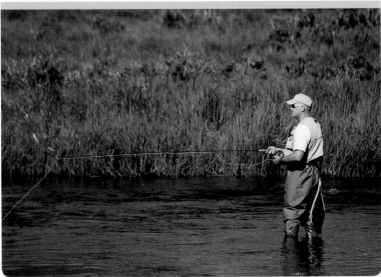

RICHARD CUMMINS / LONELY PLANET IMAGES ©

BEACON LANDING MARINA Boating

(☏970-627-3671; www.beaconlanding.us; 1026 County Rd 64; 2hr pontoon rental $75; ⏱10am-6pm Mon-Sat, from noon Sun) This marina on Granby Lake, just south of Grand Lake, can arrange pontoons, speedboats, jet skis and other waterborne machines for rent, and hosts guided fishing expeditions on the lakes.

GRAND LAKE NORDIC CENTER & GRAND LAKE GOLF COURSE Skiing, Golf

(☏970-627-8328; www.grandlakerecreation. com; County Rd 48; skiing per day $12, 9-hole golf $20; 👪) This facility, just west of town, hosts golf in the summer and a network of trails for skiing when the snow falls. The ski trails cover a range of difficulties, though they're not incredibly scenic – most of the trails are open, along the golf-course fairways.

In winter you can also rent gear and go snow tubing. Those who travel with their dog might want to try skiing here too – there's a dedicated dog loop.

SOMBRERO RANCH Horseback Riding

(☏970-627-3514; 304 W Portal Rd; rides $50; ⏱rides depart on the hour 8am-4pm Jun-Aug; 👪) The best ride with this branch of Sombrero Ranch is simply named 'The Ride.' It takes two hours and traverses some lovely Rocky Mountain vistas, fields of wildflowers in the spring and rushing streams.

 **Sleeping**

 SHADOWCLIFF LODGE & RETREAT CENTER Lodge $

(☏970-627-9220; www.shadowcliff.org; 405 Summerland Park Rd; dm/d/cabins $23/60/125; ⏱May 25-Sep 30; @🛜👪) Overlooking Grand Lake, this ecofriendly mountain resort, in a beautiful setting with a view of the lake and mountains, is among the best-value accommodations in Colorado. Rooms and dorms are simple and clean, and guests gather around the fire or grand piano in the book-lined common room downstairs.

Families and larger groups may also want to look into the Shadowcliff cabins, which are along the river. It also hosts a number of sustainability workshops, and the property abuts hiking trails into Rocky Mountain National Park. Reservations are essential. A two-night minimum stay is required for rooms.

LEMMON LODGE Cabins $$

(☏970-627-3314; www.lemmonlodge.com; 1224 Lake Ave; cabins $90-460; 🚲👪) Right on the water, these are a collection of privately owned cabins managed by one company. There's a range of prices, but quality varies widely too. This is good for a family or large group; for the best all-around stays rent either cabin 17 or 23.

Eating & Drinking

O-A BISTRO Contemporary American $$

(☏970-627-5080; 928 Grand Ave; prix fixe $25-30) Less than 10 tables fit inside this little jewel box, a favorite of Grand Lake's dining scene for made-from-scratch soups and a long, thoughtful wine list. A five- or six-course *prix fixe* is the best dining experience in the area; for lunch it has light snacks and crepes.

FAT CAT CAFE Breakfast $

(☏970-627-0900; 916 Grand Ave; mains $5-10; ⏱7am-1pm; 👪) Consider yourself lucky if you find yourself rolling into Grand Junction half-starving on a Sunday morning. The Fat Cat does its breakfast buffet ($12) and brunch with hearty expertise: biscuits and gravy, bottomless drinks, scrambled 'Scotch eggs' and omelets that come drooping off the plate.

SAGEBRUSH BBQ & GRILL Barbecue $$

(☏970-627-1404; www.sagebrushbbq.com; 1101 Grand Ave; mains $9-20; ⏱7am-9pm Mon-Thu, to 10pm Fri & Sat; 👪) Peanut shells litter the floor and bric-a-brac covers the walls of this BBQ joint, a place keenly balancing casual atmosphere with a slightly upscale menu of steak and local game dishes such as wild boar sausage. It's best when simplest though, so go for the burger.

GRAND LAKE BREWING CO Brewpub
(☎ 970-627-1711; www.grandlakebrewing.com;
915 Grand Ave; ⏱ noon-8pm Sun-Thu, to 9pm Fri
& Sat; 🌮) Patrons look over the brewing
tanks in this narrow pub, sipping pints
of Super Chicken, an ass-kicking barley
wine that's a heady 11%. The bar burgers
are well built, but the Ruben is a brilliant
disaster – stacked tall, loaded with
sauerkraut, and served on thick slices of
rye (mains $8 to $12).

Mountain Food Market Self-Catering
(☎ 970-627-3470; 400 Grand Ave; ⏱ 9am-7pm
Mon-Sat, to 5pm Sun; 🌮) This grocer, right
at the entrance to town, is a good place
to pick up supplies when heading into the
park and the best grocery store in Grand
Lake. It has a deli counter for to-go meals
and a small supply of basic camping
equipment.

ℹ Information

The Grand Lake Visitor Center (☎ 970-627-
3402; www.grandlakechamber.com; cnr West
Portal Rd & Hwy 34; ⏱ 9am-5pm Mon-Sat, 10am-
4pm Sun Jun-Aug) is at the junction of US 34 and
W Portal Rd but it has another office downtown at
928 Grand Ave (enter from the Garfield Ave side).
For information and permits for Rocky Mountain
National Park, visit the Kawuneeche Visitor Center
(p230), a bit north of town on US 34.

ℹ Getting There & Around

By car, Grand Lake is 102 miles northwest of
Denver. Take I-70 west to I-40 exit and continue
west over the Berthound Pass, which can be a
white-knuckle experience in inclement weather.
If you don't have your own wheels, Home James
Transportation Services (☎ 970-726-5060;
www.homejamestransportation.com) runs door-
to-door shuttles to Denver International Airport
($90, 2½ hours). Reservations are required.
Getting around Grand Lake by foot is easy.

Granby

At the junction of US 40 and US 34,
Granby isn't so easy on the eyes, but the
crossroads service center is a convenient stop for those heading into Rocky
Mountain National Park or several other
nearby recreation and ski areas. The **USFS
Sulphur District Ranger Office** (☎ 970-
887-4100; 62429 US 40; ⏱ 8am-5pm Mon-Fri,
plus 8am-5pm Sat & Sun summer) for the
Arapaho National Forest is at the east end
of town and has useful hiking brochures
for the Continental Divide National
Scenic Trail, the Never Summer
Wilderness Area and the Winter
Park-Fraser-Tabernash area.
It is also the place to get
permits for backcountry
camping in the Indian
Peaks Wilderness.

🛏 Sleeping & Eating

**DROWSY WATER
RANCH** Resort $$$
(☎ 970-725-3456; www.
drowsywater.com; 1454 Coun-
ty Hwy 219; weekly rates from
$1820; 🌮) If the open skies

Moraine Park
PETER PTSCHELINZEW / LONELY PLANET IMAGES ©

and mountain terrain inspire a yearning for a home on the range, put Granby's Drowsy Water Ranch on your shortlist. As an all-exclusive experience, home cookin', daily guided horseback rides and evening programs are included in the weekly price. Even though it ain't fancy, the Fosha family offer the most genuine dude-ranch experience in Colorado. The cabin accommodations are decked out in Western-themed-style coziness and it's an ideal space for families looking to escape the urban grind. Hitting the trail on horseback is the main focus; even those with no horse sense will leave with basic riding skills.

IAN'S MOUNTAIN BAKERY American $ (☏970-887-1176; www.iansmountainbakery.com; 358 E Agate Ave; mains $5-9; ☺6:30am-7pm Mon-Fri, to 2pm Sat) If you're just stopping in town for a bite, your best bet is Ian's, where Ian covers the breakfast burrito in a tangy sauce, turns out killer biscuits and gravy and chats up patrons over strong coffee.

Yellowstone & Grand Teton National Parks

There's nowhere in the world quite like Greater Yellowstone. From its raging geysers to its howling wolf packs, the land stands alone as one last pocket of a wild, primeval America. Yellowstone National Park is the crown jewel of the Greater Yellowstone Ecosystem and the destination of nearly every visitor to the region. The real showstoppers are the geysers and hot springs – nature's crowd pleasers – but at every turn this land of fire and brimstone breathes, belches and bubbles like a giant kettle on the boil.

South of Yellowstone is Grand Teton National Park, probably the most famous natural skyline in the United States and the nation's most iconic mountain range. These vertical peaks, reflected in a string of gorgeous glacial lakes, come the closest to most people's picture-postcard image of alpine splendor and will send a shiver of excitement down the spine of even the least vertically inclined.

Old Faithful (p257), Yellowstone
JASON LANGLEY / IMAGEBROKER ©

Yellowstone & Grand Teton Itineraries

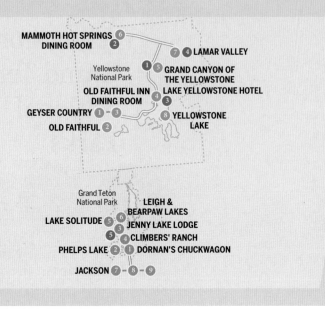

MAMMOTH HOT SPRINGS ⑥
DINING ROOM ②

Yellowstone
National Park

⑦ ④ LAMAR VALLEY

① ⑤ GRAND CANYON OF
THE YELLOWSTONE

OLD FAITHFUL INN   LAKE YELLOWSTONE HOTEL
DINING ROOM ④ ③
GEYSER COUNTRY ① – ③
OLD FAITHFUL ② ⑧ YELLOWSTONE
LAKE

Grand Teton
National Park   LEIGH &
BEARPAW LAKES
LAKE SOLITUDE ⑤ ⑥
③ JENNY LAKE LODGE
⑤ ④ CLIMBERS' RANCH
PHELPS LAKE ② ① DORNAN'S CHUCKWAGON
JACKSON ⑦ – ⑧ – ⑨

Three Days in Yellowstone

① **Geyser Country** (p257) Explore the mud pots, pools, springs and geysers of the park's geothermic center. Be sure to see Great Fountain Geyser and the Grand Prismatic Spring.

② **Old Faithful** (p257) While you're in Geyser Country, brave the crowds and witness the park's most famous sight as it blasts boiling mineral water into the air.

③ **Old Faithful Inn Dining Room** (p277) After a busy day, treat yourself to a dinner of trout cakes, antelope sausage and bison ravioli in this classic Yellowstone restaurant.

④ **Lake Yellowstone Hotel** (p274) Channel your inner romantic and spend a cozy night at this historic hotel on the shore of Yellowstone Lake.

⑤ **Grand Canyon of the Yellowstone** (p256) Start day two exploring the scenic

viewpoints and stellar hikes of Yellowstone's version of the Grand Canyon.

⑥ **Mammoth Hot Springs Dining Room** (p275) Dust off your clothes and enjoy a fine dinner at this elegant eatery. Don't be surprised to see elk outside!

⑦ **Lamar Valley** (p252) On day three, get up early – *really* early – and make for the 'American Serengeti' to spot bison, grizzlies, pronghorn, elk and trumpeter swans.

⑧ **Yellowstone Lake** (p255) Close the evening watching the sunset over this glorious alpine lake from a pullout or beach on the northeastern shore.

🠖 THIS LEG: 130 MILES

Three Days in Grand Teton

1 **Dornan's Chuckwagon** (p300) Start your first day at Grand Teton National Park with a massive plate of homemade sourdough pancakes served alfresco at this kitschy but fun outdoor restaurant.

2 **Phelps Lake** (p293) Work off your breakfast with a relaxing hike around scenic Phelps Lake. The trail is flat and suitable for most hikers, making for a great family outing.

3 **Jenny Lake Lodge** (p298) After a day on the trails, head to Jenny Lake Lodge for a delicious dinner and a quiet night's sleep. This is the oldest lodge in the park, and it oozes history.

4 **Climbers' Ranch** (p298) For something far more rustic (and less expensive) stay at this climbers'-refuge-turned-hikers-lodge, run by the American Alpine Club.

5 **Lake Solitude** (p294) On day two, stretch your hiking muscles and trek up to this stunning lake. Tack on a side trip to Inspiration Point for some of the best views in the entire park.

6 **Leigh & Bearpaw Lakes** (p293) For something less strenuous and more family friendly, amble the flat trail to these lovely lakes. The views of glacier-clad Mt Moran are sublime.

7 **Snake River Grill** (p305) Come sundown, head south to Jackson and splurge on a superb meal at this legendary fine-dining establishment.

8 **Alpine House** (p304) Spend the night in Jackson at the luxurious Alpine House, a sumptuous B&B started by two former Olympic skiers.

9 **National Museum of Wildlife Art** (p302) Spend your last day exploring the National Museum of Wildlife Art and the National Elk Refuge, two of Jackson's top sights.

THIS LEG: 80 MILES

Yellowstone & Grand Teton Highlights

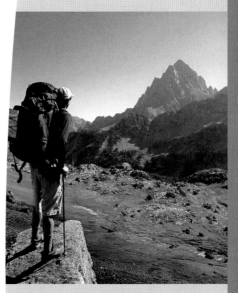

1 **Best Hike: Mt Washburn** (p266) Some of Yellowstone's best views can be had from the top of this 10,243ft peak.

2 **Best Stroll: Beaver Ponds** (p261) Animals aplenty are spotted along this gentle Yellowstone trail.

3 **Best Meal: Lake Yellowstone Hotel Dining Room** (p277) Given all the driving you've done, you owe yourself a good meal.

4 **Best Wildlife Watching: Lamar Valley** (p253) This is North America's best place to spot big mammals.

5 **Best Adventure: Grand Teton climb** (p293) Hire a guide for the non-technical climb to the top of the Tetons' mighty giant.

Hurricane Pass (p294), Grand Teton
SETH K. HUGHES / ALAMY ©

Discover Yellowstone & Grand Teton

YELLOWSTONE NATIONAL PARK

Yellowstone National Park is the crown jewel of the Greater Yellowstone Eco-system. From the steaming geysers and sublime lakes of the south to the golden canyons and wildlife-rich valleys of the north, the park has several distinct regions, and it's worth investing time to visit at least a couple to get a sense of the park's complex diversity.

Yellowstone's spectacular roadside sights are reward enough, but the park's real joys lie off the tarmac, at the end of a backcountry hiking or fishing trail, so try to fit in at least a couple of our hikes. From golden lakeshore sunsets or dawn mists rising over a steaming geyser basin, Yellowstone's beauty is both spectacular and subtle.

Our advice is not to try to pack everything into one visit. The crowds and traffic seem twice as bad if you're in a rush, and you'll appreciate the extra time if you have a surprise encounter with a moose or bison.

History

Archaeologists believe humans began inhabiting the Greater Yellowstone region 8000 to 10,000 years ago. Before that, the region was almost completely covered in ice. Between 2000 and 1500 years ago, as the climate improved and glaciers melted, the human presence in Greater Yellowstone increased dramatically.

The Tukudika (or Sheepeaters) – a Shoshone-Bannock people who hunted bighorn sheep in the mountains of Yellowstone – were the region's only permanent inhabitants before white settlement, though surrounding tribes such as the Crow/Absaroka, Shoshone, Bannock, Blackfeet/Siksikau and Gros Ventre hunted, traded and traveled seasonally through the region.

In 1807–08, an explorer and trapper named John Colter became the first white man to visit the area that is now Yellowstone, but it wasn't until the railroads began bankrolling expeditions into the region in the latter half of the century

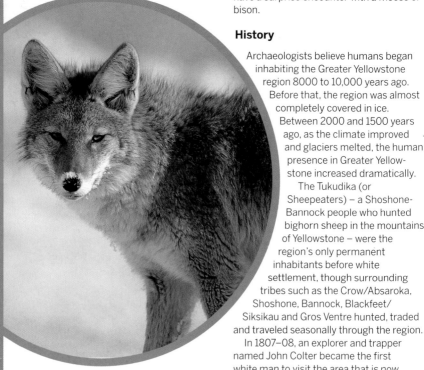

Coyote, Yellowstone
CAROL POLICH / LONELY PLANET IMAGES ©

that the area truly became known by outsiders.

In 1872 President Ulysses S Grant signed the landmark Yellowstone National Park Act, creating the world's first national park. Unfortunately, this new designation did not equal protection. What followed was a decade of rampant squatting, wildlife poaching, wanton vandalism of thermal features and general lawlessness in Yellowstone National Park. Finally, the Secretary of the Interior called in the US cavalry from nearby Fort Custer to provide protection. In the absence of park rangers, the army patrolled the park from 1886 until the hand off to the newly created National Park Service in 1918.

Until the mid-1900s, most of the park's visitors arrived by rail. But by 1940, nearly all of Yellowstone's half-million visitors entered the park in private automobiles. Today, the park is home to more than 2000 buildings, thousands of employees and tens of thousands of nightly tourists.

As the world's oldest national park, Yellowstone holds a key place in both the historical development of the US National Park Service and the spread of protected wilderness areas across the globe. This is hallowed ground to both environmentalists and tourists, and the tensions between the two form the major theme of the past, present and doubtless the future of Yellowstone and Grand Teton.

When to Go

The best time to visit Yellowstone National Park is arguably early spring or during the fall. The park is open year-round, but most roads close during winter. Yellowstone can get extremely crowded in the summer when campgrounds are packed and hotel reservations are essential.

When You Arrive

Visitors receive a free map and the *Yellowstone Today* newspaper, which has a schedule of ranger-led activities, park facilities, road closures and opening hours.

Notice boards at entrances indicate which campgrounds are full or closed.

Orientation

Seven distinct regions comprise the 3472-sq-mile park (starting clockwise from the north): Mammoth, Roosevelt, Canyon, Lake and Geyser Countries; the Norris area; and remote Bechler region in the extreme southwest corner.

The 142-mile, figure-eight Grand Loop Rd passes most of the park's major attractions. The 12-mile Norris-Canyon road divides the Grand Loop Rd into two shorter loops: the 96-mile Lower (South) Loop and the 70-mile Upper (North) Loop.

Roosevelt Country is the wildest part of the park accessible by road. Lake Country is beloved by springtime grizzlies and dominated by Yellowstone Lake. Geyser Country is home to the park's richest collection of geothermal features, including Old Faithful. The Norris Junction area is home to the park's second most impressive collection of geysers.

The Bechler region, in the far southwest, is only accessible by road from Ashton, Idaho, from the John D Rockefeller Jr Memorial Parkway to the south of Yellowstone, or by a four-day hike from the Old Faithful region.

Sights

Mammoth Country

Mammoth Country is renowned for its graceful geothermal terraces and the towering Gallatin Range to the northwest. As the lowest and driest region of the park, it's also the warmest and a good base for winter and early- or late-season activities.

The region's Northern Range is an important wintering area for wildlife, including the park's largest herds of elk, pronghorn, mule deer and bighorn sheep. Around half the park's population of elk winter here, attracted by the lower temperatures and lack of snow on many

Yellowstone

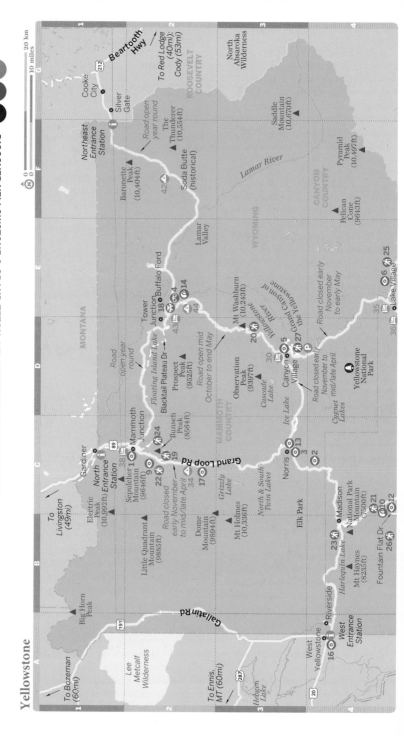

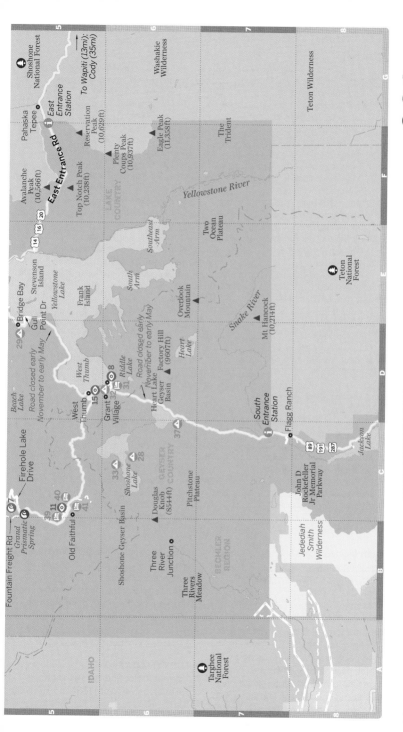

Yellowstone

south-facing slopes (due to the sun and prevailing wind).

For visitors (and most elk) the focal point of the Mammoth region is Mammoth Junction (6239ft), 5 miles south of the park's Northwest Entrance, on a plateau above Mammoth Campground. The junction contains the region's main services, including a visitor center, backcountry office, post office, gas station, medical center and even a church and courthouse. The Mammoth Hot Springs Hotel has espresso and public showers, while the Yellowstone General Store offers groceries, souvenirs, cold beer, coffee and ice cream.

Just south of the junction is Mammoth Hot Springs, the area's main thermal attraction. From here roads go south to Norris (21 miles) and east to Tower-Roosevelt Junction (18 miles).

FORT YELLOWSTONE Historic Site

Mammoth Hot Springs was known as Fort Yellowstone from 1886 to 1918, when the US Army managed the park from this collection of historic buildings. Elk regularly graze the manicured lawns of the campus-like historic and administrative centre, bringing traffic to a standstill, and the high-pitched cries of bugling elk echo around the region in fall.

MAMMOTH VISITOR CENTER MUSEUM
Museum

(☏307-344-2263; ⏰8am-7pm) Inside the Albright Visitor Center, this museum was formerly the army's bachelor quarters, but now features reproductions of 19th-century watercolors by Thomas Moran (1837–1926) and black-and-white photographs by William Henry Jackson, both of whom accompanied the 1871 Hayden expedition. Rangers give talks in front of the center at 3pm and some days also at 4pm.

MAMMOTH HOT SPRINGS HOTEL
Historic Hotel

The Mammoth Hot Springs Hotel is worth a visit even if you are not staying. Piano music echoes around the lobby from 5pm followed by video or slide presentations in the side Map Room, where you can also check out the huge wall map of the United States assembled from 15 types of wood from around the world. (Residents of Maryland will be displeased to note that theirs is the only state capital not marked.) Also worth noting is the charming antique water fountain to the left of the activities desk.

MAMMOTH HOT SPRINGS
Hot Springs

The imposing **Lower** and **Upper Terraces** of Mammoth Hot Springs are the product of dissolved subterranean limestone (itself originally deposited by ancient seas), which is continuously deposited as the spring waters cool on contact with air. As guidebooks love to say, the mountain is in effect turning itself inside out, depositing over a ton of travertine (limestone deposits) here every year. The colored runoff of the naturally white terraces is due to the bacteria and algae that flourish in the warm waters.

An hour's worth of boardwalks wend their way around the Lower Terraces and connect to the Upper Terraces Loop.

The rutting Rocky Mountain elk that sometimes lounge on Opal Terrace in fall are a favorite photo opportunity.

Surreal **Palette Springs** (accessed from the bottom parking lot) and sulfur-yellow **Canary Springs** (accessed from the top loop) are the most beautiful sites, but thermal activity is constantly in flux, so check the current state of play at the visitor center.

Mammoth to Tower-Roosevelt

The 18-mile road to Tower-Roosevelt Junction heads east from Mammoth over the Gardner River Bridge, where the Gardner River meets the Yellowstone River. By the roadside, just over 2 miles from Mammoth, is pretty three-tiered **Undine Falls**, aptly named for an alluring water nymph. For your own private views of the falls from the north side of the river, hike less than half a mile along Lava Creek trail from the nearby Lava Creek Picnic Area.

The easy 1-mile round-trip walk to **Wraith Falls** is a good family hike through pretty meadows and fire-burn patches. The trail begins at the pullout east of Lava Creek Picnic Area, 5 miles from Mammoth.

Just past **Blacktail Ponds** (good for spotting muskrats and waterfowl) is the Blacktail Trailhead, where trails lead down Rescue Creek or into the Black Canyon of the Yellowstone near Crevice Lake.

Two miles past here, the 0.5-mile **Forces of the Northern Range Self-Guiding Trail** is an accessible boardwalk that teaches kids about the environmental forces of this part of the park. Kids will get a kick from placing their hand on a wolf print.

Continue east on the main Grand Loop Rd and you'll pass **Phantom Lake** (one of three interconnected lakes that are normally dry by July) and an unsigned **scenic overview** of Hellroaring Mountain, Garnet Hill, and the Yellowstone River and Hellroaring Creek Valleys.

Mammoth to Norris

The 20-mile road from Mammoth to Norris passes the Upper Terraces and enters a jumbled landscape of **hoodoos**, formed

when the 65,000-year-old travertine deposits of nearby Terrace Mountain slipped down the hillside, breaking into boulder-like fragments. The road climbs to the cantilevered road of the Golden Gate, named after the light-colored welded rock formed from cooled ash flows. Shortly afterwards a pullout offers views of tiny **Rustic Falls**.

The peak rising to the left is **Bunsen Peak** (8564ft), a plug of solidified magma that formed inside a long-since-eroded volcanic cone. Further along on the right, delightful **Swan Lake** in the middle of Gardner's Hole offers good bird-watching (look for trumpeter swans in winter and early spring) and views of the Gallatins.

Two miles further south, turn off for the **Sheepeater Cliffs**, an amazing collection of half-million-year-old hexagonal basalt columns, stacked like building blocks.

The road passes a nice fishing spot and wintertime warming hut near **Indian Creek Campground**, then continues to a series of four pullouts at **Willow Park** and **Moose Bogs**, 2 miles further south and a good place to look for some of the park's 200 or so moose.

Obsidian Cliff, to the left of the road, exposes the interior of a 180,000-year-old lava flow. Just past here, isolated fumaroles, hot springs and other thermal features start to appear by the side of the road, heralding the approach of the thermally active Norris region.

From here the road passes pretty **North** and **South Twin Lakes** and descends to beautiful **Nymph Lake**. The lake's bubbling pools, bleached white shoreline and steaming geysers lend the area a powerfully primeval air.

Roosevelt Country

Fossil forests, the wildlife-rich Lamar River Valley, its tributary trout streams and the dramatic and craggy peaks of the Absaroka Range are the highlights in this remote, scenic and undeveloped region. The region is the birthplace of the park's current bison and wolf populations and one of the park's great wildlife-viewing areas.

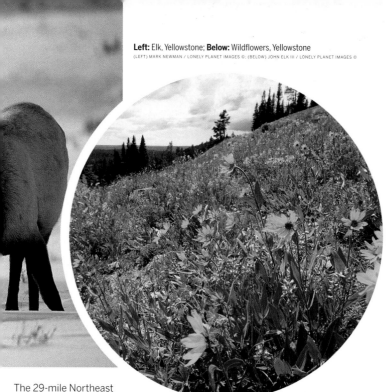

Left: Elk, Yellowstone; **Below:** Wildflowers, Yellowstone
(LEFT) MARK NEWMAN / LONELY PLANET IMAGES ©; (BELOW) JOHN ELK III / LONELY PLANET IMAGES ©

The 29-mile Northeast Entrance Rd passes from Cooke City through the Lamar Valley to Tower-Roosevelt Junction (6270ft) and then continues west for 18 miles to Mammoth Hot Springs. This is the only road in the park that remains open year-round. From Tower-Roosevelt Junction, the Grand Loop Rd heads south to Canyon Junction, over the high Dunraven Pass.

Two miles past Pebble Creek is the trailhead for the short 0.5-mile walk through fir forest and summer wildflowers to scenic **Trout Lake**, named after the abundant cutthroats that spawn here in early summer.

The road now joins the mixed sage and grasslands of the **Lamar Valley**, one of the park's premier wildlife-viewing areas. The roadside turnouts between Pebble and Slough Creek Campgrounds, particularly the stretch between Lamar River Trailhead and the Lamar Canyon, are prime places to spot wolves. Both elk and large herds of bison also make the

broad Lamar Valley their winter range, occupying separate ecological niches alongside coyotes, pronghorns and bears.

Tower Junction

CALCITE SPRINGS OVERLOOK
Lookout

This worthwhile overlook 1.5 miles south of Tower-Roosevelt Junction offers vertiginous views of a section of the Grand Canyon of the Yellowstone known as the Narrows. A short trail leads to views north of the gorge's sulfuric yellows and smoking sides.

TOWER FALL
Waterfall

Two-and-a-half miles south of Tower-Roosevelt Junction, Tower Creek plunges over 132ft Tower Fall before joining the Yellowstone River. The fall gets its name from the volcanic breccia towers around it, which are like a demonic fortress and earn it the nickname The Devil's Den. A short trail leads to a viewpoint over the falls.

Tower-Roosevelt to Canyon

It's 19 miles from Tower-Roosevelt to Canyon. The Grand Loop Rd starts to climb from Tower Fall on its way to **Dunraven Pass** (8859ft), the highest part of the Grand Loop Rd. East of the road is **Antelope Creek**, prime grizzly habitat and thus closed to visitors. Several turnouts offer popular wildlife-watching opportunities here.

Just below Dunraven Pass is the **Washburn Hot Springs Overlook**, where an interpretive sign describes the hot springs and the surrounding Yellowstone caldera, which you now enter as you continue south.

Canyon Country

The Canyon area is the second-most-heavily visited part of the park after Old Faithful, due largely to the scenic grandeur of the Grand Canyon of the Yellowstone, but also due to the junction's central location and its concentration of visitor services. The impressive canyon is the star of the show and a series of scenic overlooks and a network of trails along the canyon's rims and interior highlight its multihued beauty from a dozen angles.

CANYON VILLAGE

Canyon Village lies just east of Canyon Junction along North Rim Dr. It's the logistical base for the central part of the park and has accommodations, three restaurants, a visitor center, backcountry office, general store, outdoor gear store and ATM.

CANYON VISITOR CENTER
Visitor Center
(☎307-242-2550; ☉8am-8pm) This modern visitor center is well worth a visit for its innovative and interactive displays on Yellowstone's geology. The highlight is a room-sized relief model of the park, on which you can visualize the terrain of your upcoming hike.

Canyon to Yellowstone Lake

South of Canyon Junction, the Grand Loop Rd winds 16 miles down to Yellowstone Lake via the excellent wildlife-watching opportunities of the **Hayden Valley** and the interesting **Mud Volcano**. Hayden is the largest valley in the park and one of its premier **wildlife-viewing** areas. With patience you're likely to see coyotes, springtime grizzlies, elk and lots of bison, plus one of the largest fall ruts. Bird-watching is equally good.

The Mud Volcano area, 10 miles south of Canyon Junction and 6 miles north of Fishing Bridge, is one of the park's most geologically volatile regions. It is home to an assortment of mud pots and other gurgling sulfurous pits. Mud Volcano itself has not erupted since the 1871 Langford-Washington-Doane expedition first

Rocky Mountain bighorn sheep, Yellowstone
CAROL POLICH / LONELY PLANET IMAGES ©

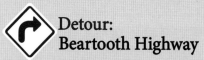

Detour:
Beartooth Highway

The breathtaking Beartooth Hwy (US 212) connects Red Lodge to Cooke City and Yellowstone's northeast entrance along a soaring 68-mile road built in 1932. An engineering feat, and the 'most beautiful drive in America' according to the late journalist Charles Kuralt, this 'All-American' road is a destination in its own right and easily the most dramatic route into Yellowstone National Park.

The highway has a short driving season and is usually closed between mid-October and late May. For information on weather conditions, hikes and bear sightings pull into the **Beartooth Ranger district office** (📞 406-446-2103), just south of Red Lodge on Hwy 212. There's gas at Red Lodge, Cooke City and, less reliably, along the highway at the Top of the World store. For more details go to www.beartoothhighway.com and www.beartoothhighway.net.

encountered it. A crater is all that remains of the original cone.

Lake Country

Yellowstone Lake (7733ft) is Lake Country's shimmering centerpiece, one of the world's largest alpine lakes, with the largest inland population of cutthroat trout in the US. Yellowstone River emerges from the north end of the lake and flows through Hayden Valley to the Grand Canyon of the Yellowstone. The lake's southern and eastern borders flank the steep Absaroka Range marking the border of the park's remote and pristine Thorofare region.

A 22-mile section of the Grand Loop Rd hugs Yellowstone Lake's shoreline between Fishing Bridge Junction to the north and West Thumb Junction to the west. Visitor centers and convenience stores are available at Fishing Bridge and Grant Village. Grant and Lake Village offer the most visitor services, including dining.

Bridge Bay Marina rents outboard motorboats and rowboats and has a fishing/grocery store, dump station, ranger station and picnic area. The busy Fishing Bridge area offers showers and laundry, as well as a gas station, groceries and camping supplies at the Yellowstone General Store.

Norris

The Norris area was a former US Army outpost. The historic log Norris Soldier Station (1908), one of only three left from the era of army control of the park, now houses the **Museum of the National Park Ranger** (📞 307-344-7353; 🕘 9am-5pm Jun-Sep), often staffed by chatty retired NPS employees. The museum's exhibits detail the evolution of the ranger profession from its military origins.

North and west of Norris Junction, the **Norris Geyser Basin** is North America's most volatile and oldest continuously active geothermal area (in existence for some 115,000 years). It's also the site of Yellowstone's hottest recorded temperatures, where three intersecting faults underlain by magma rise to within 2 miles of the surface. Barely 1000ft below the surface, scientific instruments have recorded temperatures as high as 459°F (237°C). Norris is also home to the majority of the world's acidic geysers, fed by the basin's abundant supplies of sulfur. In Norris the ground sighs, boils and rages like nowhere else on earth.

Overlooking Porcelain Basin is the tiny **Norris Museum** (📞 307-344-2812; 🕘 9am-6pm late May-Sep), which opened as the park's first in 1930. There are ranger-led walking tours of the basin at 9:30am daily and short talks at Steamboat Geyser at 2pm, 2:30pm and 3pm.

Porcelain Basin

One mile of boardwalks loop through open Porcelain Basin, the park's hottest

DOUGLAS STEAKLEY / LONELY PLANET IMAGES ©

Don't Miss Grand Canyon of the Yellowstone

After its placid meanderings north from Yellowstone Lake through the Hayden Valley, the Yellowstone River musters up its energy and suddenly plummets over **Upper Falls** (109ft) and then the much-larger **Lower Falls** (308ft), before raging through the 1000ft-deep Grand Canyon of the Yellowstone. More than 4000ft wide at the top, the canyon snakes for 20 miles as far as the Narrows near Tower-Roosevelt Junction.

On the North Rim, three popular scenic overlooks line the one-way 2.5-mile North Rim Dr: Lookout, Grandview and Inspiration Points. The less-dramatic **Upper Falls Viewpoint** is also accessible by road: the turnoff is south of Canyon Junction and Cascade Creek on the main Grand Loop Rd to Fishing Bridge.

On the South Rim, South Rim Dr passes the Chittenden Bridge and Wapiti Trailhead en route to the canyon's most spectacular overlook, at Artist Point. The 3.25-mile **South Rim Trail** follows the canyon rim from Chittenden Bridge to Point Sublime via Artist Point. **Uncle Tom's Trail** is one of the region's largest parking areas and offers the best views of the Upper and Lower Falls.

Rangers lead hikes daily at 9am from the parking lot above Uncle Tom's Trailhead, on the South Rim, and give short talks four times a day (10am for kids) at Artist Point. On the North Rim, most visitors drive between the viewpoints, but you can also hike the North Rim Trail, which connects all three. The trail parallels the road from Upper Falls Overlook to Inspiration Point. Lower Falls

exposed basin. (The name comes from the area's milky deposits of sinter, also known as geyserite.) The bleached basin boils and bubbles like some giant laboratory experiment and the ash-white ground actually pulsates in places. Check out the overviews from **Porcelain Terrace Overlook**, near the Norris Museum; views that, in the words of Rudyard Kipling, made it look 'as though the tide of desolation had gone out.'

Back Basin

Two miles of boardwalks and gentle trails snake through forested Back Basin. As you exit the museum from Porcelain Basin, take the right-hand path into Back Basin. **Emerald Spring** combines reflected blue light with yellow sulfur deposits to create a striking blue-green color.

Steamboat Geyser, the world's tallest active geyser, infrequently skyrockets up to an awesome 400ft (over twice as high as Old Faithful). The geyser was dormant for half a century until 1961 and quiet again for most of the 1990s, but erupted twice in 2002 and most recently in 2005. At the time of research the geyser was splashing with frequent but minor bursts only.

Other geysers to check out include **Cistern Spring**; the dramatic **Echinus Geyser**, the park's largest acidic geyser, which erupted every couple of hours until fairly recently; and the **Porkchop Geyser**, which exploded in 1989, blowing huge lumps of geyserite 200ft into the air.

Nearby **Pearl Geyser** is one of the park's prettiest.

Norris to Madison Junction

The 14-mile Norris to Madison Junction road quickly enters aptly named **Elk Park**, a fine place to spot elk and bison and you'll likely have to navigate a car jam here.

Just under 5 miles south of Norris Junction an easy 1-mile trail leads through burned forest to the fun mud pots and springs of **Artist Paint Pots**. The best mud pots are in the far right-hand corner.

As the road and river descends off the Solfatara Plateau, you pass **Gibbon Falls**.

Norris to Canyon

The 12-mile Norris–Canyon road connects the two parts of the Grand Loop Rd across the burnt forest and cooled lava flows of the Solfatara Plateau. Just past the junction the pleasant **Norris Meadows Picnic Area** offers some fine bird-watching over the plain of the meandering Gibbon River.

About 2 miles into the drive a one-way side road branches off past **Virginia Cascade**, which, like Gibbon Falls, lies on the caldera boundary.

Further down the Norris–Canyon road, you'll pass the Cygnet Lakes and then the Grebe Lake and Cascade Creek Trailheads, which offer an alternative route through burned forest to Grebe and Cascade Lakes.

Geyser Country

Yellowstone's Geyser Country holds the park's most spectacular geothermal features (over half the world's total), clustered in the world's densest concentration of geysers (over 200 spouters in 1.5 sq miles). It is Geyser Country that makes the Yellowstone plateau utterly and globally unique.

The majority of the geysers line the Firehole River, the aquatic backbone of the basin, whose tributaries feed 21 of the park's 110 waterfalls. Both the Firehole and Madison Rivers offer superb fly-fishing, and the meadows along them support large wildlife populations.

The most famous geysers always attract a crowd, but sometimes it's the smaller features that are the most interesting. The smaller geysers make up for their lack of size with great names, such as North Goggles, Little Squirt, Gizmo, Spanker, Spasmodic, Slurper and Bulger (aliases the seven dwarfs might adopt to form a criminal gang).

UPPER GEYSER BASIN

This heavily visited basin holds 180 of the park's 200 to 250 geysers, the most famous of which is geriatric Old Faithful. Boardwalks, footpaths and a cycling path along the Firehole River link the five distinct geyser groups, the furthest of which is only 1.5 miles from Old Faithful.

OLD FAITHFUL   Geyser

Erupting every 90 minutes or so to impatient (preliminary hand-clapping is not uncommon) visitors' delight, Old Faithful spouts some 8000 gallons of water up to 180ft in the air. Water temperature is normally 204°F (95°C) and the steam is about 350°F (176°C). It's worth viewing the eruption from several different locations – the geyserside seats, the upper-floor balcony of the Old Faithful

Inn and, our favorite, from a distance on Observation Hill.

OLD FAITHFUL VISITOR CENTER

Visitor Center

(8am-8pm mid-Apr–early Nov & mid-Dec–mid-Mar) The new, improved and environmentally friendly Old Faithful Visitor Center offers a bookstore and information booth and shows films 30 minutes before and 15 minutes after an eruption of Old Faithful. Kids will enjoy the Young Scientist displays, which include a working laboratory geyser and experiments involving elk jaw bones. The center closes at 5pm or 6pm outside of summer.

Rangers give a geology talk in front of Old Faithful eight times a day and offer an evening presentation in the theater at 7pm. There's a short talk for kids at 10am. Daily 90-minute geology walks depart at 5:30pm from Castle Geyser and at 8:30am from the visitor center, with a shorter walk around Old Faithful at 2:30pm.

BLACK SAND BASIN

This geyser basin, 1 mile northwest of Old Faithful, has a few interesting features, including the Cliff Geyser, the nearby Ragged Spring, and the exquisite Emerald Pool. Rainbow Pool is connected to nearby Sunset Lake and is one of the more colorful in the park. The black sand that gives the basin its name is derived from weathered volcanic glass (obsidian). You can access Black Sand Basin by car or, better, by foot from Daisy Geyser. Rangers lead hour-long walks here daily at 1pm.

MIDWAY GEYSER BASIN

Five miles north of Old Faithful and 2 miles south of the Firehole Lake Dr entrance is Midway Geyser Basin. The algae-tinged indigo waters of the **Grand Prismatic Spring** (p260) is the key sight here. The spring drains into Excelsior Pool, a huge former geyser that blew itself out of existence in the 1880s with massive 300ft explosions of water. The last eruptions here were in 1985, when the pool erupted almost continuously for 46 hours, before lulling itself back into a deep sleep. The pool continually discharges an amazing 4000 gallons of boiling water a minute into the Firehole River. More water is expelled here in a single day than Old Faithful releases in two months. The features are linked by a 0.5-mile boardwalk.

Black Sand Basin, Yellowstone

Geyser Strategies

The first thing to do when you arrive at Old Faithful is to check the predicted geyser eruption times at the visitor center and then plan your itinerary around these. Predictions are made for the region's six main geysers – Old Faithful, Grand, Castle, Riverside, Daisy and the Lower Geyser Basin's Great Fountain – and these are also posted at Old Faithful Lodge, Old Faithful Inn and the Madison Junior Ranger Station. You can call ahead for timings at ☎307-344-2751.

Remember, though, that geysers rarely erupt on schedule, so take some snacks and sunblock for the wait.

Budget at least half a day here to see the area around Old Faithful, and a whole day to see all the geyser basins, though you could easily spend a day or two more if you catch the geyser-gazing bug. If time is tight, concentrate on Upper and Midway Geyser Basins and skip Biscuit and Black Sand Basins.

The best loop around the Upper Geyser Basin follows the paved road one way and the boardwalk the other for a total of 3 miles. To this you can add a small hike up to Observation Point for views over the basin. There is a smaller loop around Geyser Hill, but you'll miss many of the best geysers if you limit yourself to this.

LOWER GEYSER BASIN

Separate roads access the three main sections of this sprawling thermal basin: the main Grand Loop Rd passes Fountain Paint Pot; the one-way Firehole Lake Dr loops off the main road to Great Fountain and other geysers; and Fountain Flat Dr offers access to hiking trails and minor thermal features. The latter two roads both offer the potential for a short bike ride.

FOUNTAIN PAINT
POT   Geothermal Feature

Just past pretty Silex Spring, Fountain Paint Pot is a huge bowl of plopping goop that ranks as one of the biggest in the park. The action is sloppiest in spring, with some mud pots drying up by August. The area around the thermal features is slowly being drowned in deposits, while, beyond, a grassy basin supports the park's largest bison herd.

FIREHOLE CANYON DRIVE

The one-way Firehole Canyon Dr leaves the Grand Loop Rd just south of Madison Junction. The road passes 40ft-high **Firehole Falls** at the foot of towering dark rhyolite cliffs, but the main attraction here is the lukewarm **Firehole swimming area** (no fee), one of the few locations in the park that's open for swimming.

OLD FAITHFUL TO WEST THUMB

Three miles into the 17-mile drive between Old Faithful and West Thumb is **Kepler Cascades**, where a wooden platform offers fine views of the 125ft falls. Just past the cascades turnout is the parking area for the worthwhile hike or bike ride to **Lone Star Geyser**. The road climbs past Scaup Lake, the Spring Creek Picnic Area (site of the park's biggest stagecoach robbery in 1908) and the Continental Divide Trailhead before reaching **Isa Lake** at Craig Pass (8262ft).

From the pass, the road descends to the **DeLacy Creek** Picnic Area and Trailhead and shortly afterward offers a tantalizing sliver of a view towards remote Shoshone Lake. From here the road ascends back across the Continental Divide (8391ft), before finally descending to excellent views of Yellowstone Lake and the turnoff to West Thumb.

Bechler Region

Known for its numerous waterfalls and the park's highest rainfall, the remote Bechler (*Beck*-ler) region, also known

JIM WARK / LONELY PLANET IMAGES ©

Don't Miss Grand Prismatic Spring

At 370ft wide and 121ft deep Grand Prismatic Spring is the park's largest and deepest hot spring. It's also probably the most beautiful single thermal feature in the park. Boardwalks lead around the multicolored mist of the gorgeous pool and its spectacularly colored rainbow rings of algae.

For the most dramatic photos of Grand Prismatic Spring, drive south to Fairy Falls Trailhead, walk for 1 mile, and then take a faint path up the side of the fire-burned ridge (itself a lava deposit from the west rim of the caldera). From above, the spring looks like a giant blue eye, weeping exquisite multicolored tears.

as Beckler Corner or Cascade Corner, is largely the preserve of hardy backpackers, outfitters and horseback riders who brave flooded streams, monster mosquitoes and boggy marshland to access beautiful backcountry with the park's largest waterfalls and outstanding thermal soaking springs.

Bechler is accessed via Bechler Ranger Station or Cave Falls Trailhead, both off the mostly unpaved Cave Falls Rd via US 20, 26 miles from Ashton, Idaho, itself a two-hour drive from West Yellowstone, Montana, via ID Hwy 47 and Marysville Rd. Alternative approaches include coming from Driggs, Idaho, to the south

(joining US 20) or the brutal, unpaved Grassy Lake Rd/Reclamation Rd, from the turnoff just north of Flagg Ranch, part of John D Rockefeller Memorial Parkway, 2 miles south of Yellowstone's South Entrance; allow at least two hours from Flagg Ranch.

 **Activities**

Driving Tours

There's hardly a mile of highway on Yellowstone's 142-mile Grand Loop Rd that can't be called scenic.

GEYSER TRAIL   Scenic Drive

The northern approach to Old Faithful offers lots of possible stops so don't expect to cruise this route in one hit. The drive parallels the Firehole River and there are dozens of potential fly-fishing spots along this 25-mile route.

Drive south from Madison Junction, past the junior ranger station, and after 2 miles take the Firehole Canyon Dr to the right. This 2-mile side road takes you past rhyolite cliffs and rapids, the **Firehole Falls** and the popular **Firehole swimming area**.

Back on the main road it's another 3 miles south to Fountain Flat Dr, which branches right to give access to the pleasant Nez Percé Picnic Area, the Sentinel Meadows hike, Pocket Basin backcountry geyser area and the bikeable Fountain Freight Rd.

Back on the main road, 1 mile south, the road crosses **Chief Joseph Creek**, where an interesting pullout details the flight of the Nez Percé Indians, who crossed this creek in August 1877 fleeing the US Army.

From here on you'll get your first views of the amazing thermal features ahead. A **pullout** 1 mile ahead offers a fine view of the smoking geysers and pools of Midway Geyser Basin to the right and Firehole Lake Basin on the left, as well as the meandering Firehole Valley and the occasional bison – a classic Yellowstone vista.

Just 1 mile further, take a right into Fountain Paint Pot. Another 1.5 miles south take the left on Firehole Lake Dr and make the leisurely 3-mile drive past **Great Fountain Geyser** and **Firehole Lake** to see what's on the boil.

Next up is **Midway Geyser Basin**, which is worth a stop. As you continue south, you'll see the colorful runoffs from **Excelsior Pool** flowing into the Firehole River.

Two miles further is busy Fairy Falls Trailhead, a popular starting point for hikes to Fairy Falls, views over Grand Prismatic Spring and bike rides along the gravel Fountain Freight Rd. You'll also likely see bison and fly-fishers in this vicinity.

It's a further 2 miles to the minor thermal sites of **Biscuit Basin** and **Black Sand Basin**, from where cyclists can get out and ride to **Old Faithful**, 1.5 miles away.

FIREHOLE LAKE DRIVE   Scenic Drive

Firehole Lake Dr is a one-way, 3-mile road starting 2 miles north of Midway Geyser Basin and about 1 mile south of the Fountain Paint Pot parking lot. It passes several pretty pools and large geysers, including lovely Firehole Spring and then huge Great Fountain Geyser, which soars up to 200ft in a series of wide staccato bursts every 11 hours or so. Eruption times are predicted by the visitor center at Old Faithful. The crater begins to overflow 90 minutes before an eruption and violent boiling signals an imminent eruption. Eruptions can last one hour.

Hiking

The best way to get a close-up taste of Yellowstone's unique combination of rolling landscape, wildlife and thermal activity is on foot, along the more than 900 miles of maintained trails.

MAMMOTH COUNTRY

BEAVER PONDS TRAIL   Hiking

This 5-mile loop, with gentle climbs and lots of early-morning and evening wildlife, begins between Liberty Cap and a private house next to the bus parking lot at Mammoth. The trail ascends through the fir and spruce forests along **Clematis Creek** and in 2.5 miles reaches a series of five ponds amid meadows, where beavers and moose emerge in the mornings and evenings. Black bears are also a distinct possibility.

Rangers offer free walks along the trail at 8am on Friday and Saturdays. Most families will be able to tackle this walk, as long as you bring mosquito repellent. It's an easy-to-moderate hike that takes about 2½ hours.

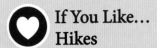

If You Like... Hikes

If you like adventurous hikes like Bunsen Peak and Avalanche Peak, you'll enjoy these trails, which get fewer people.

1 PELICAN VALLEY
(Pelican Valley Trailhead, Lake Country) Bird-watchers favor this rolling stroll through meadows and sagebrush in the heart of bear country. It's a six- to eight-hour, 16-mile loop. It's grizzly country, so hike in groups.

2 SENTINEL MEADOWS & QUEEN'S LAUNDRY GEYSER
(Freight Rd Trailhead, Geyser Country) This hike to a little-visited geyser basin is a good choice if you fancy a bit of simple off-route trailfinding and fewer people. It's a 3.2-mile hike that takes about two hours. Park at the end of Fountain Flat Dr, just off the main Grand Loop Rd, 6 miles south of Madison Junction and 13 miles north of Old Faithful.

3 MONUMENT GEYSER BASIN
(Monument Geyser Trailhead, Norris) The semi-dormant chimney-like cones of Monument Geyser Basin are among the park's tallest. The 2-mile hike to the basin is a steep but rewarding climb, with fine views over Gibbon Meadows. Great way to escape the crowds.

4 TERRACE MOUNTAIN LOOP
(Snow Pass Trailhead, Mammoth Country) This three-hour loop meanders through interesting hoodoos, and climbs high above the road for views of Rustic Falls, Mt Holmes and Swan Lake Flat. An alternative is to start at Glen Creek trailhead.

BUNSEN PEAK (& OSPREY FALLS) Hiking
Bunsen Peak (8564ft) is a popular half-day hike, and you can extend it to a more demanding day hike by continuing down the mountain's gentler eastern slope to the Bunsen Peak Rd and then *waaay* down (800ft) to the base of seldom-visited Osprey Falls. The round-trip hike is 4.2 miles (about 2½ hours) without the side trip to the falls and 10.2 miles (six to seven hours) if you visit the falls.

The initial Bunsen Peak Trail climbs east out of Gardner's Hole to the exposed summit of Bunsen Peak, offering outstanding panoramas of Mammoth, the Gallatin Range, Swan Lake Flat and the Blacktail Deer Plateau. Even if you just make it halfway up the hill you'll be rewarded with superb views.

From the Mammoth Visitor Center, head 4.5 miles south on Grand Loop Rd, cross the Golden Gate Bridge, and turn left into the unpaved parking area on the east side of the road, just beyond the Rustic Falls turnout. The parking lot is small and fills up quickly.

SEPULCHER MOUNTAIN Hiking
This is a long but varied and incredibly scenic loop hike that offers superb views over half the park and gives a secret peek at hidden thermal features of the Mammoth terraces.

The first half of this seven-hour hike is a cardio workout, gaining almost 3500ft, before descending through meadows and forest in a long but leisurely stroll back. It's a relentless climb but it's well graded, offering plenty of interest en route. The hike starts at the same trailhead as the Beaver Ponds hike so you can park anywhere in the Mammoth area. As you approach the top, look for a cairn marking the path along the ridgeline to the tomblike rocky outcrops that give Sepulcher Peak its name. At a second cairn junction take the right branch for one minute to awesome views of the Paradise Valley. The main trail and actual **summit** (9646ft) are to the left of the cairn junction, past fine views of **Electric Peak** (10,992ft) and Cache Lake below. Allow about seven hours for the difficult 11.5-mile hike. It begins at the Sepulcher Mountain Trailhead.

ROOSEVELT COUNTRY

Hikes in this region are among the first in the park to be clear of snow and are accessible by road year-round. Attractions include big rolling valley views, petrified forests, meadows of wildflowers and some of the richest wildlife in the park.

YELLOWSTONE RIVER
PICNIC AREA TRAIL   Hiking

Popular with picnickers, this scenic stroll offers fantastic views into the eroded towers and basalt formations of the Narrows and Calcite Springs, and possible glimpses of osprey and bighorn sheep: bring your binoculars. It's a good family hike but you'll need to watch the little ones because there are lots of sheer drop-offs and no guardrails. To get to the trailhead, take the Northeast Entrance Rd across the bridge from Tower-Roosevelt to the picnic area parking lot, 1.5 miles east of the junction. Park in the lot just west of the picnic area. The entire 4-mile round-trip hike takes about two hours at a leisurely pace.

Several unofficial dirt trails climb the slopes behind the picnic area but the official (signed) trail leads off from the picnic site left of the vault toilets to ascend a couple of hundred feet and deposit you puffing on the rim of the **Yellowstone Canyon**.

LOST LAKE   Hiking

A peaceful early-morning hike, this trail leads to a secluded lake and a petrified tree – perfect for families and anyone staying or dining at Roosevelt Lodge.

The Lost Lake loop trail begins directly behind Roosevelt Lodge (take the right fork), climbing about 300ft past Lost Lake to a petrified tree, from which the trail climbs onto a plateau and then descends to the Tower Ranger Station. Before you even start the hike, warm up with a quick 10-minute detour left at the trailhead to the small but pretty **Lost Creek Falls**. The easy 3.3-mile loop takes about two hours.

FOSSIL FOREST TRAIL   Hiking

A must visit for amateur geologists, this unmaintained trail climbs to several patches of petrified trees scattered

Best Places in Yellowstone to Spot Wildlife

The following places all offer an excellent chance to get a glimpse of some seriously charismatic megafauna. Maximize your chances by arriving at dawn or dusk and renting a spotting scope from Silver Gate or Gardiner.

○ **Roosevelt Country** The Lamar Valley is known as the 'American Serengeti' for its dense population of wolves, bison, grizzlies, pronghorn, elk and trumpeter swans; try also Antelope Creek for grizzlies and wolves.

○ **Mammoth Country** Elk trimming the lawns at Mammoth Junction; bighorn sheep on Everett Ridge between Mammoth and the north entrance; wildfowl at Blacktail Ponds; moose at Willow Park; bears and wolves in the backcountry Gallatin range.

○ **Lake Country** Birdlife at Sedge Bay; bison, moose, marmots and waterfowl at Storm Point; springtime grizzlies and moose at Pelican Creek; moose around Lewis Lake; grizzlies around Fishing Bridge in spring.

○ **Norris** Elk Park for, well, elk, as well as bison.

○ **Canyon Country** The Hayden Valley for bison, coyotes and bears; ospreys in the canyon; south of Mud Volcano for bison.

○ **Mt Washburn** For bighorn sheep, black bears and grizzlies.

○ **Geyser Country** The Firehole River and Madison Valley for bison.

along Specimen Ridge. Together they are thought to hold the word's largest collection of petrified trees. Paleodendrochronologists (scientists who date fossilized trees) have identified dozens of different species of trees here, including tropical avocado and breadfruit, with dozens of ancient petrified forests stacked atop even older petrified forests.

The parking area is marked 'Trailhead' and is just a few hundred yards west of the Lamar Canyon bridge, 5 miles east of Tower-Roosevelt Junction and about 1 mile southwest of the turnoff to Slough Creek Campground. Look for the wheelchair-accessible parking spot. The 3.5-mile hike takes about three hours.

CANYON COUNTRY

Though the surrounding backcountry draws far less attention than does the Grand Canyon of the Yellowstone, it is every bit as interesting.

SOUTH RIM TRAIL
& RIBBON LAKE   Hiking
Southeast of the Yellowstone Canyon's South Rim, a network of trails meanders through meadows and forests and past several small lakes. This loop links several of these and makes a nice antidote to seeing canyon views framed by the windshield of your car. It's an incredibly varied hike that combines awesome views of the Grand Canyon of the Yellowstone with a couple of lakes and even a backcountry thermal area.

Park at Uncle Tom's parking area on the Canyon's South Rim Dr and, after checking out the views of the Upper Falls and the Lower Falls from Uncle Tom's Trail, take the **South Rim Trail** east from Uncle Tom's Trail, along the rim of the canyon to **Artist Point** for some of the finest canyon views available.

From Artist Point take the trail east toward Point Sublime, then branch right past **Lily Pad Lake** for 0.3 miles to another junction. Branch left here and descend to **Ribbon Lake**, actually two conjoined ponds, with a good chance of spotting moose. For a close-up view of **Silver Cord Cascade**, continue on the path to the canyon rim, then head left along the canyon wall to the small falls. A faint path connects to the main trail at a small footbridge. This is the furthest point of the hike, 3.4 miles from the start.

Sunrise over Yellowstone Lake (p255), Yellowstone

From Ribbon Lake head back to the junction with Lily Pad Lake and instead of returning the way you came, continue straight, past several minor fumaroles and hot springs to the acidic, spring-fed waters of **Clear Lake**, 1.5 miles from Ribbon Lake. Continue along the Clear Lake Trail and at the next unsigned junction take the right branch for the final 0.7 miles back to Uncle Tom's parking area. Allow about four hours for the 6-mile loop.

CASCADE LAKE & OBSERVATION PEAK   Hiking

There's something for everyone on this trail, which starts just a couple of minutes' drive north of Canyon Village. The full hike climbs 1400ft to Observation Peak (9397ft), but the easier turnaround at Cascade Lake gives a level hike of only 4.4 miles return (2½ hours).

Cascade Lake opens to meadows on the west and backs on to the Solfatara Plateau and its ghost forest of burnt snags. The lake is worth exploring for its wildfowl and occasional moose.

The hike up to **Observation Peak**, part of the Washburn Range, takes about 1¼ hours and gains 1400ft in 3 miles. The views from the peak are superb; Cascade and Grebe Lakes sit below you, smoking Norris Geyser Basin is to the west and the Hayden Valley yawns to the south.

Start the hike at the Cascade Lake Trailhead, 1.5 miles north of Canyon Junction, or the nearby picnic area of the same name. Allow four to five hours for the full 10.4-mile hike.

LAKE COUNTRY

Lake Country is best known for its boating opportunities, but its great hikes are also worthwhile. Bear activity in the river inlets to Yellowstone Lake delays the hiking season (the Pelican Valley, Natural Bridge and Heart Lake Trails are closed until July), making it a limited early-season option. Check with a visitor center if you are coming in early summer and always hike with others.

ELEPHANT BACK MOUNTAIN   Hiking

This popular ascent is a great short-but-sweet picnic option, suitable for families with teenagers. The stunning views from the panoramic overlook (8600ft) include Yellowstone Lake and Stevenson Island, Pelican Valley and the Absaroka Range. The trailhead is 1 mile south of Fishing Bridge Junction and 0.5 miles north of the Lake Village turnoff on the Grand Loop Rd. From Lake Hotel it is 0.25 miles one way through the woods past Section J of the hotel's cabins. Allow about 2½ hours for the 3.5-mile loop.

AVALANCHE PEAK   Hiking

Relentlessly steep, this challenging peak ascent offers unparalleled views of the Absaroka Range and Yellowstone Lake.

The hike starts off steeply, gets steeper and then continues uphill (steeply) for the entire duration. Toward the top, you'll be well above the tree line and have views over glacial cirques, north to the Beartooths and south to the Tetons. The true summit (10,566ft) sits along a narrow ridge beyond a series of talus wind shelters.

The trailhead sits off the East Entrance Rd, 0.5 miles west of Sylvan Pass, 19 miles east of Fishing Bridge Junction and 8 miles west of the park's east entrance. Park in the small paved lot on the south side of the road by Eleanor Lake's west-side picnic area. Allow 3½ to five hours for the difficult hike. Check for closures; in early fall the trail is frequented by grizzlies foraging for whitebark pine nuts.

GEYSER COUNTRY

Even the short hikes described here will get you away from the crowds at Old Faithful to some spectacular backcountry waterfalls and geysers.

MYSTIC FALLS & BISCUIT BASIN   Hiking

This is a short family-friendly stroll from an interesting thermal basin to a 70ft waterfall, with the option for a longer loop hike.

The shorter, out-and-back hike to the base of the falls is relatively flat. Due to

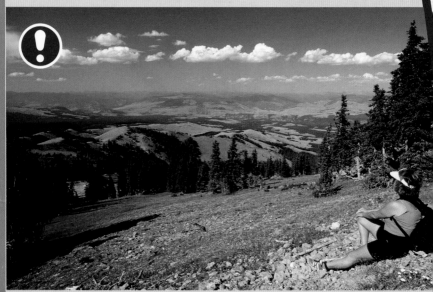

JOHN ELK III / LONELY PLANET IMAGES ©

Don't Miss Mt Washburn

Yellowstone's most popular day hike offers unsurpassed 360-degree mountaintop views, with the chance of spotting bighorn sheep and black bears.

This popular out-and-back hike climbs gradually to the fire lookout tower on the summit of 10,243ft **Mt Washburn** for some of the park's best views.

From the summit, the majestic panoramas (when the weather is clear) stretch across the Yellowstone caldera south to Yellowstone Lake, Canyon and the Hayden Valley and north to the Beartooth and Absaroka Ranges. Below you are the smoking Washburn Hot Springs. Keep your eyes peeled for marmots and bighorn sheep basking near the summit. If the crowds get too much, you can always head five minutes down the Washburn Spur Trail for some peace and quiet. From the summit return the way you came.

More than 10,000 people hike this trail annually, so head out early to avoid the crowds. The 6.4-mile hike takes about four hours. The suggested route starts from Dunraven Pass (8859ft) on the Grand Loop Rd, 4.8 miles north of Canyon and 14.2 miles south of Tower. Alternatively, begin from the larger Chittenden parking area (5 miles north of the pass) for a marginally shorter but more exposed hike (and bike trail) to the summit.

a lack of shade, the longer loop hike to the overlook is best done in the morning or late afternoon. The trail is closed from the end of the winter season until the last Saturday of May due to the presence of bears.

The Biscuit Basin turnoff is 2 miles north of the Old Faithful overpass and 14 miles south of Madison Junction, on the

west side of Grand Loop Rd. Allow about two hours for the 3.5-mile loop.

LONE STAR GEYSER Hiking

This paved and pine-lined hike is an easy stroll along a former service road to one of the park's largest backcountry geysers. It's popular with both day hikers and cyclists, yet is quite a contrast to the chaotic scene around Old Faithful. Isolated Lone Star erupts every three hours for between two and 30 minutes and reaches 30ft to 45ft in height, and it's definitely worth timing your visit with an eruption. Check with Old Faithful Visitor Center for predicted eruption times and bring a book or a packed lunch for the wait. If the parking lot at Lone Star Trailhead is full, park at the neighboring Kepler Cascades turnout.

The hike begins at the Lone Star Trailhead, above **Kepler Cascades** (where the Firehole River speeds through a spectacular gorge). The 4.8-mile round-trip walk takes 2½ hours at most.

FAIRY FALLS & TWIN BUTTES   Hiking

Tucked away in the northwest corner of the Midway Geyser Basin, 197ft Fairy Falls is a popular hike, largely because it's only a short jaunt from Old Faithful. Beyond Fairy Falls the lollipop loop trail continues to a hidden thermal area at the base of the Twin Buttes, two conspicuous bald hills severely charred in the 1988 fires. The geysers are undeveloped, and you're likely to have them to yourself – in stark contrast to the throngs around Grand Prismatic Spring.

The Fairy Falls (Steel Bridge) Trailhead is just west of the Grand Loop Rd, 1 mile south of the Midway Geyser Basin turnoff and 4.5 miles north of the Old Faithful overpass.

DELACY CREEK TRAIL   Hiking

The 6-mile DeLacy Creek Trail offers the quickest access to Shoshone Lake, one of the park's largest and loveliest lakes. The trailhead is on the Grand Loop Rd, east of Craig Pass near the DeLacy Creek Picnic Area, halfway between Old Faithful and West Thumb Junction. The parking area is on the north side of the road, the trail on the south.

June and July bring lovely wildflowers along the route but also plenty of boggy ground and biting insects, so bring bug repellent before August. Overall, it's an easy hike that takes 2½ to 3½ hours.

BECHLER REGION

Bechler boasts the highest concentration of waterfalls in Yellowstone and some of the best backcountry hot-spring soaks anywhere. Its forests also escaped the worst of the 1988 fires. The area's remoteness means it's best suited to experienced hikers taking long backcountry trips but shorter hikes are possible.

In early summer trails may be knee-deep in water, so inquire about conditions at a ranger station before driving out here.

BECHLER MEADOWS & FALLS   Hiking

Bechler Meadows' extensive wetlands are a wildlife magnet. Grizzlies and black bears as well as gray owls and great blue herons are often spotted. Add substantial cascades to an already spectacular mix by starting from the Cave Falls Trailhead.

From Bechler Ranger Station, follow the Bechler Meadows Trail 3 miles northeast past the Boundary Creek Trail junction through lodgepole pine forest to the Bechler River/Rocky Ford cutoff junction.

If it's not too boggy, hike an extra 0.5 miles north to **Bechler Meadows**. You will cross a wooden suspension bridge over Boundary Creek past campsite 9B1.

Retrace your steps to the cutoff southeast 0.7 miles past campsite 9C1 to the wide **Rocky Ford** at the Bechler River Trail junction. Instead of fording the river, trace the river's west bank south for 2 miles to the next junction, where a cutoff leads west 2 miles through forest back to the ranger station. The full 8-mile loop takes about 3½ hours.

Backpacking

There's no better way to experience the raw wildness of Yellowstone than on an overnight backpacking trip. If you don't fancy organizing a multiday trek yourself, consider a company like **Wildland Trekking Company** (www.wildlandtrekking.com), which offers backpacking trips for around $250 per day, including meals, a guide and transportation from Bozeman.

The most popular areas are the Hellroaring region of the Black Canyon of the Yellowstone in spring, Slough Creek in early summer, Shoshone Lake in August, Bechler region in August/September, and

Heart Lake throughout summer. It makes sense to include a back-up itinerary if applying for a popular region or trail in peak season.

A free backcountry-use permit, available at visitor centers and ranger stations, is required for all overnight backcountry trips (day hikes don't require permits). The backcountry-use permit is site and date specific and states the campsite where you must overnight. The park's essential *Backcountry Trip Planner* lists all campsites and is the best place to start planning and to make reservations and arrangements. Otherwise, contact the **central backcountry office** (307-344-2160; YELL_Backcountry_Office@nps.gov) in Mammoth. Outside of summer call 307-344-7381.

Around 20% of backcountry-use permits are issued no more than 48 hours (effectively three nights) in advance on a first-come, first-served, walk-in basis (no $20 fee). This means that you can leave your planning to the last minute, as long as you are flexible with your itinerary. (You may, for example, have to walk further one day than you had planned if your desired site is already booked.)

There are **backcountry offices** (8am-4:30pm) at Canyon Ranger Station, Mammoth Visitor Center, Grant Village, Bridge Bay Ranger Station, Bechler Ranger Station, Tower Ranger Station, Old Faithful Ranger Station, West Yellowstone Visitor Center and South Entrance Ranger Station.

Cycling

Cycling on Yellowstone's roads requires taking precautions. The roads are narrow and the RVs wide: in essence, you can't underestimate the threat of a rear-view mirror. For this reason, it is best to cycle on the main loops between dawn and 9am, before the traffic starts to snarl. Entering the park in the evening or leaving in the morning has you traveling against the flow of traffic.

From mid-March to the third Thursday in April park roads between West

Yellowstone and Mammoth in Yellowstone National Park are open to only nonmotorized travel, creating a vehicle-free playground for cyclists and rollerbladers.

Yellowstone has very few trails on which mountain biking is allowed; among them are the service road to Lone Star Geyser, Natural Bridge and the Bunsen Peak Rd double-track. In general bicycles are more useful for getting around campgrounds and biking on short family-friendly paved roads, rather than adventurous downhill trips.

Horseback Riding

The park concessionaire, **Xanterra** (☎ 307-344-7311; www.yellowstonenational parklodges.com), operates everything from 45-minute **stagecoach rides (adult/ child under 11yr $9.35/7.50)** to Old West **cookouts (adults $46-84, child $46-72)**, both by horseback or horse-drawn wagon. Reservations are required months in advance. Contact Xanterra for a full list of the many options.

Boating

The vast Yellowstone Lake just begs for extended kayak, boat and sailboat exploration, but it is important to plan your outing carefully.

The **Grant Village Backcountry Ranger Office** (☎ 307-242-2609; ⏰ 8am-5pm) is an excellent resource. It distributes the Backcountry Trip Planner (www.nps.gov/yell/planyourvisit/ backcountrytripplanner.htm) describing Yellowstone Lake campsites in detail, with GPS coordinates, photos and mileage from the nearest boat put-ins.

If you don't have your own vessel, head to **Bridge Bay Marina** (☎ 307-242-3880; ⏰ 8am-8pm mid-Jun–early Sep) on Yellowstone Lake, which has hourly rowboat ($10/45 per hour/day) and outboard boat ($47 per hour) rentals.

The largest backcountry lake in the Lower 48, Shoshone Lake spells paradise for hikers and kayakers. The serene lake is closed to motorized vessels and is lined with a dozen secluded boater-only campsites. On its far western edge, Shoshone Geyser Basin's pools, thermals and mud pots comprise the largest backcountry thermal area in the park.

Boating-regulation handbooks are available at all visitor centers. General boating information is at www.nps.gov/yell/plan yourvisit/boating.htm.

Fishing

Yellowstone is justly famous for its fly-fishing, and the park's gateway towns have dozens of excellent fly-fishing shops that can offer expert local advice on current flows, flies and hatches, or arrange fully guided trips. The park concessionaire, **Xanterra** (☎307-344-7311; www.yellowstonenationalparklodges.com), offers full- or half-day fly-fishing guide services, as well as rod and reel rental.

Yellowstone Lake is stocked with cutthroat trout, longnose dace, redside shiners, longnose suckers and lake chub. Popular shore or float-fishing spots include Gull Point, Sand Point Picnic Area, Sedge Bay, Mary Bay and Steamboat Point.

In Geyser Country, the Madison and Gibbon Rivers offer some of the park's best and most scenic fly-fishing. The Firehole (between Biscuit and Midway Geyser Basins), Madison and Gibbon (downstream from Gibbon Falls) Rivers are open for fly-fishing only and lots of pullouts offer access.

In Roosevelt Country, Slough Creek is the sweetest fishing spot in the northeast (closely followed by Pebble Creek and Soda Butte Creek), which is one reason why the park's Slough Creek Campground is regularly the first to fill up.

Before casting anything, pick up a copy of the park's *Fishing Regulations* pamphlet, which details Yellowstone's complex rules and regulations.

Cross-Country Skiing & Snowshoeing

The area around Old Faithful has the most trails and facilities in winter. Three-hour guided **snowshoe tours** ($25, $32 with shoe rental) depart from Old Faithful on Thursday and Sunday. Half-day guided **ski tours** ($45) leave Old Faithful on Sunday to either Fairy Falls or DeLacy Creek.

Upper and Midway Geyser Basins both make for some fine ski trips. You can ski or snowshoe from Old Faithful to Black Sand Basin via Daisy Geyser (4 miles) or to Biscuit Basin via Morning Glory and Atomizer Geyser (5 miles, with a possible extension to Mystic Falls). The Frozen Fairy Falls hike is a popular ski day trip – get dropped off at the southern end of Fountain Freight Rd, visit the falls and ski back to Old Faithful (11 miles).

The 9-mile-return Lone Star Geyser Trail takes you from Old Faithful Snow Lodge along the Mallard Lake Trail and parallel to the main road, to cross it at Kepler Cascades. A ski shuttle will allow you to take the 8-mile Spring Creek Trail (a former stagecoach road) to Lone Star Geyser.

Around the Mammoth region it's possible to ski from Indian Creek Campground to Sheepeater Cliffs and then along a backcountry trail to Bunsen Peak Trail and left to the Mammoth-Norris road (5 miles) or right down the Bunsen Peak Rd to Mammoth. There are also marked loops around Indian Creek (2.2 miles) and part way along the Bighorn Trail (5.5 miles).

 Tours

The national park's main concessionaire, **Xanterra** (☎307-344-7311; www.yellowstonenationalparklodges.com), runs a slew of daily tours in summer, all of which offer discounts for children aged 12 to 16, and are free for kids under 12. Tours include the following:

Yellowstone in a Day (☉Jun–mid-Sep) Ambitious eight-hour trip departs from Gardiner (adult/child 12-16 $73/36.50), Mammoth Hot

Springs and Old Faithful ($71/35.50) twice a week.

Circle of Fire (tour $66/33; ⏱mid-May–mid-Sep) Similar-length tour departs Old Faithful Inn, Grant Village, Lake Yellowstone Hotel, Fishing Bridge RV Park, Canyon Lodge and Bridge Bay Campground and takes in the lower loop, including the geyser basins and Canyon.

Across the Northern Range (⏱Jun–mid-Sep) Full-day trip departs Bridge Bay Campground, Lake Yellowstone Hotel and Fishing Bridge RV Park (adult/child $60/30) or Canyon Lodge ($54/27) and takes in the upper loop, including Mammoth and Norris.

Lamar Valley wildlife excursions (⏱mid-Jun–mid-Aug) A less-grueling half-day trip departs in the afternoon from Mammoth Hot Springs Hotel and Canyon Lodge (four hours, adult/child $63/31.50) and early in the morning from Canyon, Mammoth and Roosevelt (five hours, $78.50/39.25).

Sunset tours (adult/child $34/17; ⏱Jun-late Sep) Daily two-hour tour from Lake Yellowstone Hotel and Fishing Bridge RV Park along Lake Yellowstone's north shore to the Lake Butte Overlook.

Photo safaris (tour $85) Early morning trips depart daily from Lake Hotel and Old Faithful Inn.

There are dozens of other tours aboard the wonderful Old Yellow Buses, a refurbished fleet of classic convertible 19-seater touring cars that plied the park's roads between 1936 and 1956, only to return to the park in 2007. They are guaranteed to add a touch of class to your sightseeing. See the 'Things to Do' section of Xanterra's website for tour details.

Sleeping

Although competition for campsites and lodging may be fierce, there's nothing quite like falling asleep to the eerie sounds of bugling elk and howling wolves and waking to the sulfur smell of the earth erupting and bubbling in the area.

You can make reservations for park accommodations and five of the park's 12 campgrounds through the park concessionaire **Xanterra** (☎307-344-7311; www.yellowstonenationalparklodges.com; ⏱Jun-Aug 7am-6pm, Sep-May 8am-5pm). Online bookings are now possible for both hotels and campgrounds.

Camping in the Park

Most of Yellowstone's campsites are in natural junctions, areas once frequented by Native Americans as well as early trappers, explorers and the US Army. There are around 2200 formal campsites in the park, plus well over 100 backcountry sites.

Morning Glory Pool, Upper Geyser Basin (p257), Yellowstone
JOHN ELK III / LONELY PLANET IMAGES ©

Aside from backcountry campsites (which require a hike to reach), camping inside the park is allowed only in 12 designated campgrounds and is limited to 14 consecutive days from July 1 to Labor Day and 30 days the rest of the year.

The National Park Service has seven campgrounds available on a first-come, first-served basis only. Call ☎307-344-2114 for recorded NPS campsite information.

Xanterra runs five of the park's 12 campgrounds (Canyon, Madison, Fishing Bridge, Bridge Bay and Grant Village) and these are a few dollars pricier than the national park campgrounds. They feature flush toilets, cold running water and vending machines, and a couple have pay showers.

Lodging in the Park

Today's cabins and campgrounds are direct descendents of classy turn-of-the-century hotels and Wylie tent camps, the latter an affordable early option that opened up the park to budget-minded auto tours. Of the cabin options, rustic Lake Lodge is the most peaceful, and

Roosevelt Lodge offers the most authentic Western experience. Lake Yellowstone Hotel and Old Faithful Inn provide the park's most atmospheric and upscale accommodations. For reservations and information call Xanterra.

Mammoth Country

MAMMOTH CAMPGROUND   Campground $

(sites $14; ⊙year-round) The park's most exposed campground, this is a barren, sagebrush-covered area with sparse shade. On a hairpin bend in the road below Mammoth Hot Springs, it gets road noise, too.

INDIAN CREEK CAMPGROUND   Campground $

(sites $12; ⊙Jun–mid-Sep) This low-key spot is probably the park's most underused campground – most people speed by between Mammoth and Old Faithful – which is one reason we like it. Plus, it's often the last in the park to fill up. It's set in open forest on a low rise and surrounded by moose territory, and there are several hiking trails nearby. The site is 8 miles south of Mammoth Junction.

Mammoth Hot Springs (p251), Yellowstone

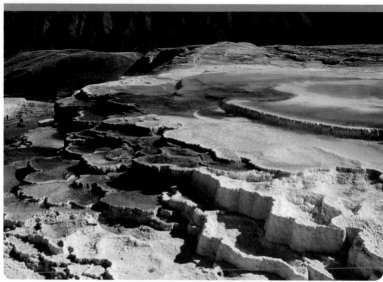

MAMMOTH HOT
SPRINGS HOTEL   Hotel, Cabins $$
(cabins without/with bath $81/112, r without/with
bath $87/120, ste $449; ☺early May–mid-Oct
& mid-Dec–early Mar) A classy vibe, a good
variety of accommodations (112 rooms)
and a useful location make this one of the
park's most popular accommodations.
The main choice is between the hotel
rooms in the main building or cabins out
back. The cheaper options come with a
sink and communal bathrooms, either
down the hall in the hotel block or in a
separate block out back by the budget
cabins.

Roosevelt Country
PEBBLE CREEK
CAMPGROUND   Campground $
(sites $12; ☺late May–late Sep) The park's
remotest campground is surrounded on
three sides by the rugged cliffs of the
Absaroka Range. It's along the banks of
a creek in grizzly habitat and is popular
with hikers and wolf-watchers, though
the sites are a bit cramped. The site is 10
miles from the Northeast Entrance at the
lower end of Icebox Canyon.

SLOUGH CREEK
CAMPGROUND   Campground $
(sites $12; ☺late May–Oct) This remote,
peaceful site, 2.2 miles up an unpaved
road, is in grizzly habitat along a prime
fishing stream. A couple of walk-in sites
are available, and there's easy access to
the Slough Creek Trail. The campsite is
10 miles northeast of Tower-Roosevelt
Junction.

TOWER FALL
CAMPGROUND   Campground $
(sites $12; ☺mid-May–late Sep) This small
single loop of 32 sites is high above Tower
Creek in an open pine forest. There are
hiking trails nearby and groceries at
nearby Tower Falls. It's 3 miles southeast
of Tower-Roosevelt Junction.

ROOSEVELT LODGE   Cabins $
(Roughrider/Frontier cabins $65/110; ☺early
Jun–early Sep) Founded in 1906 as a tented
camp, present-day Roosevelt Lodge was
built in 1919 and retains an Old West feel,

offering 80 rustic cabins, horseback rides
and a Wild West cookout in the heart of
sagebrush country.

The simple but pleasant Roughrider
cabins are among the park's greatest
bargains and come with a log-burning
stove, though the smaller ones can
be cramped. There are no en suite
bathrooms and not even running water in
the room, but the three communal wash
blocks have hot water, showers and ice.

Frontier cabins are nicely decorated
and come with private bathroom, electric
heating and two or three double beds.

Canyon Country
CANYON
CAMPGROUND   Campground $
(sites $20; ☺early Jun–early Sep) The huge
Canyon Campground is the most densely
forested in the park, but it's also the largest
(11 loops!) and one of the most cramped,
which makes staying here feel a bit like
being churned through a Pink Floyd–style
tourism meat grinder. Still, thanks to its
central location as a good base for day
trips to other parts of park, it's a very
popular campground, so book at least a
couple of days ahead in summer. Snow
can linger here well into early summer.

CANYON LODGE   Lodge, Cabins $$
(☎307-242-3900; lodge d $170, Frontier/West-
ern cabins $96/179; ☺rooms Jun–mid-Sep,
cabins close earlier) This enormous complex
has 609 rooms and is set in thick forest.
It dates from the opening of the park to
mass tourism in the 1950s and 1960s – a
drive around the multiple low-rise and
potholed loops is like a drive back in time
to a classic Middle American suburb.

The cabins date from the 1950s and
are laid out barracks-style, grouped into
blocks of four, six or eight.

Lake Country
The following campgrounds all feature
dump stations, but only Fishing Bridge
has full sewerage and electrical hookups.

BRIDGE BAY
CAMPGROUND   Campground $
(sites $20; ☺late May–mid-Sep) This mega-
complex adjacent to the marina, 3 miles

southwest of Lake Village, appeals to fishing and boating enthusiasts. Tent campers will appreciate the more desirable forested tent-only loops (I and J). Some lower sites offer lake views, but the more private ones are in the upper section.

FISHING BRIDGE RV PARK   RV Sites $
(RV sites without/with electricity $28/37; ⊙mid-May–late Sep) Along the north shore of Yellowstone Lake, 1 mile east of Fishing Bridge Junction, this place only allows hard-shelled RVs because of heavy bear activity. Rates are for up to four people and include water and sewerage hookups; all sites are back-ins, with a 40ft maximum length.

GRANT VILLAGE
CAMPGROUND   Campground $
(sites $20; ⊙late May-late Sep) Along the west shore of Yellowstone Lake, 22 miles north of the South Entrance, this is the park's biggest campground. It's an enormous forested site that has a nearby boat launch, an RV dump station and three loops of tent-only sites. Nearby facilities include showers, laundry and groceries.

LEWIS LAKE
CAMPGROUND   Campground $
(sites $12; ⊙mid-Jun–early Nov) This forested campground is at the south end of Lewis Lake, about 10 miles north of the South Entrance. A few walk-in and tent-only sites are available and generators are not allowed. Bring repellent.

LAKE YELLOWSTONE
HOTEL   Historic Hotel $$
(hotel d $207-223, standard annex d $149, Frontier cabins $130; ⊙mid-May–Sep) Right on the lake shore, this is a buttercup behemoth that sets romantics aflutter. It harks back to a bygone era, though the 296 rooms that cost $4 in 1895 have appreciated somewhat. The spacious main-building rooms feature wicker and floral designs, some sleeping up to six in three queen beds. Main lodge lakeside rooms cost extra and sell out first, but don't guarantee lake views. The comfy Frontier cabins are boxed in neat suburban rows. The

modern motel-style annex offers limited wheelchair-accessible accommodations.

LAKE LODGE   Cabins $$
(Pioneer/Frontier/Western cabins $69/106/179; ⊙early Jun-late Sep) The 186 rooms here offer a lackluster budget alternative to the Lake Yellowstone Hotel. The Western cabins are spacious and modern, and ideal for families. Cramped Pioneer cabins recall the 1920s, with propane heaters and rustic decor that could use updating. Frontier cabins are a good compromise, recently updated in 2010. In the rustic main lodge, rockers creak on the porch and fires roar inside.

GRANT VILLAGE   Motel $$
(r $152; ⊙late May-Sep) The 300 condo-like boxes with standard hotel interiors at Grant Village were once dismissed by author Alston Chase as 'an inner-city project in the heart of primitive America, a wilderness ghetto.' They do happen to be the closest lodging to the Tetons for those getting an early start.

Norris

NORRIS CAMPGROUND   Campground $
(sites $14; ⊙mid-May–late Sep) Nestled in scenic open forest on an idyllic, sunny hill overlooking the Gibbon River and bordering meadows, this is one of the park's nicest sites. There are fishing and wildlife-viewing opportunities nearby, Solfatara Creek Trailhead is in the campground and there's a 1-mile trail from near the campground (just over the bridge) to Norris Geyser Basin.

Geyser Country

MADISON
CAMPGROUND   Campground $
(sites $20; ⊙early May-late Oct) The nearest campground to Old Faithful and the West Entrance occupies a sunny, open forest in a broad meadow above the banks of the Madison River. Bison herds and the park's largest elk herd frequent the meadows to its west, making for great wildlife-watching, and it's a fine base for fly-fishing the Madison. Tent-only sites are ideally placed along the river.

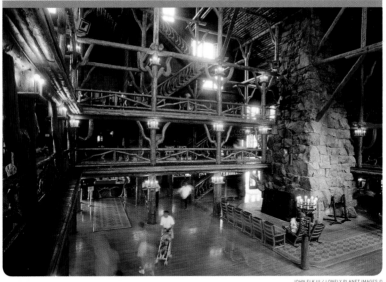

JOHN ELK III / LONELY PLANET IMAGES ©

OLD FAITHFUL INN Lodge **$$**
(ste $399-499, d $126-236, d without bath $96;
⊙ early May-early Oct) The lobby of this
historic place is a bit of a zoo during the
day, but the day-trippers quickly disappear
with the sun. The building is full of charm,
with 327 rooms, a lovely balcony, library-
style desks and century-old furniture, and
a pianist and singer at lunch and dinner. A
stay here is a quintessential Yellowstone
experience, but book well in advance or
you'll find there's no room at the inn.

**OLD FAITHFUL SNOW
LODGE** Lodge, Cabins **$$**
(lodge r $206, Frontier/Western cabins $96/149;
⊙ May-late Oct & mid-Dec-early Mar) The
park's most recent accommodations, this
place was built in 1999 in a 'New Western'
style and offers the only winter accommodations available at Old Faithful. The
main lodge has a stylish lobby decorated
in bear and elk motifs and 134 comfortable, cozy but bland modern hotel rooms,
with two double beds, a hair dryer and a
coffeemaker. Cabins are available.

OLD FAITHFUL LODGE Cabins **$**
(budget/frontier cabins $67/110; ⊙ mid-May-
mid-Sep) Glummer than its glamorous

cousins, the 132-cabin lodge was built in
1923 and has its historical roots in Yellowstone's turn-of-the century tent camps.
It's definitely a notch down in atmos-
phere, though the rooms themselves are
fine. The remodeled Frontier cabins come
with a private bathroom but no telephone.
Budget cabins have sinks with hot water,
but the toilets and showers are in outside
blocks.

 Eating & Drinking

Food in the park is split between campfire
cuisine, cafeteria food, a couple of fast-
food choices and the more pleasant
dining rooms of the park's historic inns.
The Grant Village, Old Faithful Inn and
Lake Hotel dining rooms all require dinner
reservations (☎ 307-344-7311).

Mammoth Country
**MAMMOTH HOT
SPRINGS DINING ROOM** American **$$**
(dinner $12-26; ⊙ 6:30am-10am, 11:30am-
2:30pm, 5-10pm early May-mid-Oct & mid-Dec-
early Mar) There are a few surprises in this
elegant place, including our favorite, the

delicious Thai curry mussels starter. Dinner is a more serious affair, with pistachio and parmesan-crusted trout, bison meatballs and mashed potato, or linguine with crimini and shitake mushrooms – the latter a rare vegetarian find.

MAMMOTH TERRACE GRILL Fast Food $ (mains $4-8; ⏰7:30am-9pm; 🚼) Line up for MacYellowstone-style quarter-pound burgers, chili cheese fries and ice cream, along with some breakfast foods.

Roosevelt Country

Limited groceries (as well as bear spray) are available at the small **Yellowstone General Store** (⏰8am-9:30pm).

ROOSEVELT LODGE DINING ROOM Western $$ (lunch & breakfast $10, dinner $10-20; ⏰7-10am, 11:30am-3pm & 4:30-9:30pm early Jun-early Sep) Popular for its BBQ Western-style ribs and Wyoming cheese steak, served with cornbread muffins; the meaty menu stretches to elk burgers and bison chili but has glaringly little for vegetarians.

Take a post-lunch or pre-dinner stroll up to the Lost Creek Falls, a 10-minute walk behind the lodge. The porch rockers are a fine place for a nightcap.

OLD WEST COOKOUT Western $$$ (dinner & wagon ride adult/child $57/46; ⏰depart 5pm early Jun-Labor Day; 🚼) The Roosevelt Lodge activities center offers this fun cookout, with steak, beans and the kind of cowboy coffee you have to filter through your teeth. Kids will love it. Reservations are required, preferably months in advance.

Canyon Country

Don't expect too much from Canyon's restaurants; a single kitchen prepares all meals – up to 5000 per day!

CANYON LODGE DINING ROOM American $$ (dinner $10-17; ⏰7-10am, 11:30am-2:30pm & 5-10pm Jun-late Sep) This eatery has a dated casino/steakhouse lounge feel, the kind of place where you might spot a 1970s-era Joe Pesci in a perm and a leisure suit, but it will do. Lunch features epic build-your-own burgers (including salmon burgers), but the restaurant only truly spreads its chicken wings for dinner, with bison asada and a prime rib au jus. The $10 all-you-can-eat soup and salad-bar option is low-grade but refreshing. The good wine and beer list is shared with the bar (open 3:30pm to 11pm). The breakfast menu has some lighter options, as well as a full breakfast buffet ($12).

CANYON LODGE CAFETERIA Cafeteria $ (meals $7-10; ⏰6:30-11am, 11:30am-9:30pm Jun-early Sep) Cheap and easy, serving up salads, lasagna, rice bowls, hot dogs and bison sausage sandwiches.

Lamar Valley (p253), Yellowstone

YELLOWSTONE GENERAL STORE
Diner $

(www.visityellowstonepark.com; mains $8; 🕐7:30am-8:30pm) The old-fashioned soda-fountain counter here churns out burgers, chili dogs and root-beer floats.

Geyser Country

All of the food options in Geyser Country are clustered around Old Faithful.

OLD FAITHFUL INN DINING ROOM
American $$

(📞307-545-4999; dinner $13-22; 🕐6:30-10:30am, 11:30am-2:30pm & 4:30-10pm early May-early Oct) This buzzing dining room serves good-value steaks, salads and pasta, as well as breakfast, lunch and dinner buffets ($12/14/26). Interesting starters include trout cakes and antelope sausage, while dinner mains are heavier fare, with bison ravioli and the staff-recommended pork osso bucco (pork shank in red wine).

OBSIDIAN DINING ROOM
American $$

(📞307-344-7311; mains $13-30; 🕐6:30-10:30am & 5-10:30pm May-mid-Oct, mid-Dec–early Mar, lunch winter only) A quieter affair, the dining room at the Old Faithful Snow Lodge serves up a few unexpected dishes (such as the house-made butternut squash bisque and the warm goat-cheese salad with maple pecans), alongside bison ribs braised in Moose Drool Ale.

OLD FAITHFUL LODGE CAFETERIA
Cafeteria $

(mains $8-12; 🕐11am-9pm mid-May–late Sep) It's factory-style functionality rather than fine cuisine, but this is a good-value place, churning out solid standards like meatloaf and prime rib alongside lighter fare like the chicken pesto wrap.

GEYSER GRILL
Fast Food $

(sandwiches $4-7; 🕐8am-9pm mid-Apr–early Nov & mid-Dec–mid-Mar) Burgers, breakfasts, fish and chips, bagels and beer.

YELLOWSTONE GENERAL STORES
Fast Food $

(www.visityellowstonepark.com; mains $8; 🕐7:30am-8:30pm) The two general stores

serve up snacks. The original knotted-pine Hamilton's Store near Old Faithful has a '50s-style diner counter, complete with original fountain stools, that serves up burgers, malts and sandwiches.

The modern store near the Snow Lodge offers paninis, individual pizzas, salads, breakfast biscuits and pre-packaged sandwiches in a cafeteria-style setting.

Lake Country

LAKE YELLOWSTONE HOTEL DINING ROOM
American $$$

(📞307-344-7311; breakfast buffet $14, mains $13-33; 🕐6:30-10am, 11:30am-2:30pm & 5pm-10pm late May-late Sep) Save your one unwrinkled outfit to dine in style at the dining room of the Lake Yellowstone Hotel. Lunch options include Idaho trout, a fig and proscuitto salad and sandwiches. Dinner ups the ante with starters of steamed clams and mains of bison tenderloin and rack of lamb from Paradise Valley's Wolf Ridge estate.

LAKE LODGE CAFETERIA
Cafeteria $$

(dinner mains $11-15; 🕐6:30am-2:30pm & 4:30-10pm early Jun-early Oct) This nearby affordable rustic option offers hearty breakfasts and a limited range of pre-cooked family fare like prime rib, stuffed turkey and pastas, plus lighter wraps and salads.

GRANT VILLAGE DINING ROOM
American $$

(📞307-344-7311; breakfast buffet $12, dinner $17-27; 🕐6:30-10am, 11:30am-2:30pm & 5pm-10pm late May-early Oct) The smoky BBQ aroma emanating from this place could draw a band of grizzlies, who would doubtless enjoy the house pecan-encrusted trout (but probably turn down the vegetarian quinoa cakes).

LAKE HOUSE
Cafeteria $$

(mains $8-15; 🕐6:30-10:30am & 5-10:30pm mid-Jun–late Sep) This lakeshore spot offers build-a-burger combos, dinner salads and the best lake views in the park in a casual pub-style environment. It's not open for lunch.

ℹ Information

Entrance Fees & Passes

A seven-day pass to both Yellowstone (www. nps.gov/yell) and Grand Teton (www.nps.gov/ grte) national parks costs $25/20 per vehicle/ motorcyclist or $12 for cyclists or pedestrians. An annual pass to both parks costs $50.

Opening Dates

The north entrance at Gardiner is open year-round, as is the northern Gardiner to Cooke City road via Mammoth and Roosevelt. Roads open in May on a staggered schedule. Most campgrounds, park services and visitor centers close October to May.

Tourist Information

Yellowstone's visitor centers and information stations are usually open 9am to 6pm, with extended hours from 8am to 7pm in summer. Most are closed or open reduced hours Labor Day to Memorial Day; the Albright Visitor Center in Mammoth is open year-round, and the Old Faithful Visitor Center is open in winter. Check the park newspaper for current hours of operation.

Albright Visitor Center (☎307-344-2263) Open year-round, with videos and displays on park history.

Canyon Visitor Center (☎307-242-2550; ⏱8am-8pm late May–mid-Oct) Has a backcountry office and displays on Yellowstone geology.

Fishing Bridge Visitor Center (☎307-242-2450; ⏱8am-7pm late May-late Sep) Has bird exhibits.

Grant Village Visitor Center (☎307-242-2650; ⏱8am-7pm late May-late Sep) Has exhibits on wildfires.

Madison Junior Ranger Station (⏱early Jun-late Sep)

Old Faithful Visitor Center (☎307-545-2750; ⏱8am-8pm late Apr-early Nov & mid-Dec–mid-Mar) New LEED-certified center opened in 2011. Videos and geyser predictions.

Ranger Stations (⏱8am-4:30pm) At Grant Village, Lake Village, Lewis Lake, Bechler, Canyon, Mammoth, Bridge Bay, Tower Junction, Old Faithful, Madison, Lamar Valley, and the West and South Entrances.

West Thumb Information Station (☎9am-5pm late May-late Sep)

Roosevelt Lodge Dining Room (p276), Yellowstone

West Yellowstone Visitor Information Center
(⊘ mid-Apr–early Nov & mid-Dec–mid-Mar) In the Chamber of Commerce in West Yellowstone.

Yellowstone National Park headquarters
(☏ 307-344-7381; www.nps.gov/yell; ⊘ 9am-6pm) At Fort Yellowstone in Mammoth Hot Springs. Most of the park's brochures are downloadable from its website.

Park Policies & Regulations

- It is illegal to collect plants, flowers, rocks, petrified wood or antlers in Yellowstone.

- Firearms are now allowed in the park under valid state or federal laws but are prohibited in park or concessionaire buildings.

- Swimming in water of entirely thermal origin is prohibited.

- Permits are required for all backcountry trips and activities like boating and fishing.

Maps

- **National Geographic** (www.natgeomaps.com) publishes five excellent topographical maps for Yellowstone, one covering the full park and four that cover quadrants. They are the best maps for hiking and backpacking.

- Free park maps are available at visitor centers and entry kiosks.

Dangers & Annoyances

Yellowstone is grizzly country. Bears that associate humans with food quickly become a problem, so keep all your food packed away in campgrounds or strung up on a bear pole in the backcountry. We suggest carrying bear spray on all backcountry hikes. A male hiker was killed by a grizzly in the Canyon region in 2011 – the first bear-related fatality in the park in 25 years.

For all the focus on grizzlies, more people are injured by park bison (and even moose) each year than bears. The golden rule is to keep your distance – 100yd from bears and 25yd from anything taller than a chipmunk.

ⓘ Getting There & Around

Unless you're part of a guided bus tour, the only way to get around is to drive. There is no public transportation within Yellowstone National Park, except for a few ski-drop services during winter.

Air

The nearest airport is the seasonal **West Yellowstone Airport** (WYS; ☏ 406-646-7631), operating mid-June through September only. There are also airports in Cody, WY; Bozeman and Billings, MT; and Idaho Falls, ID.

Car

The speed limit in most of the park is 45mph, dropping to 25mph at busy turnouts or junctions. In the words of writer Tim Cahill, anything faster than this is 'both illegal and silly.'

Gas and diesel are available at most junctions. Stations at Old Faithful and Canyon are open whenever the park is open to vehicles. The Roosevelt station closes at the beginning of September, Fishing Bridge in mid-September, Grant Village in late September and Mammoth in early October. Stations are manned from around 8am to 7pm and offer 24-hour credit-card service at the pump.

Dial ☏ 307-344-2114 to check road and weather conditions prior to your visit, as road construction, rock or mudslides and snow can close park entrances and roads at any time.

AROUND YELLOWSTONE

West Yellowstone

Seated a scant quarter-mile from Yellowstone National Park, the old rail terminus of West Yellowstone is the most popular gateway to Yellowstone Park. It's tiny as towns go but offers its own brand of diversity: from endless variations on the burger joint and souvenir shop to live wolves and grizzlies, RV villages, taxidermy clinics and snowmobile shops.

 Sights

GRIZZLY & WOLF DISCOVERY CENTER   Zoo
(☏ 406-646-7001; www.grizzlydiscoveryctr.org; 201 S Canyon; adult/child 5-12yr $10.50/5.50; ⊘ 8am-dusk; ⊛) Offering an afterlife to 'pest' grizzlies facing extermination, this nonprofit center offers a chance to see

Detour: Bozeman

The hip college town of Bozeman, only an hour's drive north of Yellowstone, is regularly voted one of America's best outdoor towns, and with good reason. With excellent restaurants and shops, one of the region's best museums and outdoor opportunities that beckon from every corner, the town is well worth a stop en route to the more rustic delights of the parks.

Arguably Montana's most entertaining museum, the **Museum of the Rockies** (☏406-994-3466; www.museumoftherockies.org; cnr S 7th Ave & Kagy Blvd; adult/child $13/9; ☉8am-8pm Memorial Day-Labor Day, 9am-5pm Mon-Sat & 12:30-5pm Sun rest of year; ⊞) offers some of the most jaw-dropping dinosaur displays you'll ever see, alongside displays on native cultures of the Northern Rockies, hourly planetarium shows and costumed homesteaders re-enacting 1880s life at the next-door **Living History Farm** (summer only).

There are three **USFS campsites** (☏877-444-6777; www.recreation.gov; all sites $14) southeast of town near the Hyalite Reservoir.

For a drop of Vegas in your Montana, stay at the fun, locally owned **Lewis & Clark Motel** (☏800-332-7666; www.lewisandclarkmotel.net; 824 W Main St; r $109-119; @☎). For something more sophisticated, try the excellent **Lehrkind Mansion Bed & Breakfast** (☏406-585-6932; www.bozemanbedandbreakfast.com; 719 N Wallace Ave; d incl breakfast $159-229; ☎)

Bozeman is located approximately 85 miles north of Yellowstone's North Entrance.

captive wolves and bears if you failed to see any in the park. The indoor bear exhibit is good, and there is an information wall with clippings of recent bear encounters, as well as the latest wolf-pack locations.

YELLOWSTONE HISTORIC CENTER
Museum

(☏406-646-1100; www.yellowstonehistoric center.org; 104 Yellowstone Ave; adult/child $5/3; ☉9am-9pm mid-May–mid-Oct) Housed in the 1909 Union Pacific depot, this small museum explores early stagecoach and rail travel. There are also displays on the 1988 fires and 1959 Hebgen quake, as well as good rotating exhibits.

YELLOWSTONE IMAX THEATER
Cinema

(☏406-646-4100; www.yellowstoneimax.com; 101 S Canyon; adult/child $9/6.50; ☉hourly showings 9am-9pm May-Sep, 1-9pm Oct-Apr) If it's raining head indoors for *Yellowstone*, *Lewis & Clark* and other films on a screen six stories high.

Activities

West Yellowstone is host to a range of cultural and sporting events, from summer **rodeo** (www.yellowstonerodeo.com; adult/child $12/6) and mountain-man rendezvous to the Spam Cup, a series of ski races in which the lucky winner receives a free can of preserved pork products.

FREE HEEL & WHEEL
Adventure Sports

(☏406-646-7744; www.freeheelandwheel.com; 40 Yellowstone Ave; ☉9am-7pm Sun-Thu, 9am-8pm Fri & Sat) The place for maps, gear, and bike and snowshoe rentals.

LAVA CREEK ADVENTURES
Kayaking

(☏406-646-5145; www.lavacreekadventures. com, 433 Hwy 20) Single or double kayak rental (from $49 per day) and guided sunset glides on Hebgen Lake ($65 per person).

BUD LILLY'S TROUT SHOP   Fishing
(406-646-7801; www.budlillys.com; 39 Madison Ave) Rents fishing equipment and offers one-day float and walk trips from $230 per person.

JACKLINS FLY SHOP   Fishing
(406-646-7336; www.jacklinsflyshop.com; 105 Yellowstone Ave) Offers a free weekly casting clinic Sundays at 7:30pm.

 Sleeping

Considering the number of motel signs, there is precious little variety in accommodations. Expect hefty discounts during the off-season (October, November, and mid-March to June).

Tent camping in town means cramming between rows of powered-up RVs. For more breathing space, don't forget the national forest campsites on Hebgen Lake.

**BAKERS HOLE
CAMPGROUND**   Campground $
(sites without/with electricity $16/22; mid-May–mid-Sep) The nearest forestry service campground has 73 pleasant sites on the banks of the meandering Madison River, just 3 miles north of West Yellowstone.

THREE BEAR LODGE   Lodge $$
(800-646-7353; www.threebearlodge.com; 217 Yellowstone Ave; main lodge d $219; motel d $159;) Rebuilt with reclaimed original wood after a 2008 fire, this friendly lodge once again offers spacious, stylish hotel rooms, as well as a cheaper motel option. Kids will go nuts over the 'Goldilocks and the Three Bears' themed suites ($249 to $279).

STAGE COACH INN   Hotel $$
(800-842-2882; www.yellowstoneinn.com; 209 Madison Ave; r $189-209) A longtime hub, the Stage Coach has eye-catching stuffed wildlife in the lobby, indoor hot tubs and a Mexican restaurant.

ALPINE MOTEL   Hotel $$
(406-646-7544; www.alpinemotelwest yellowstone.com; 120 Madison Ave; r $80-125, ste $159;) The friendly and well-tended Alpine has a rather cramped courtyard but remains one of the best-value places in town.

Fly-fishing (p270), Madison River, Yellowstone

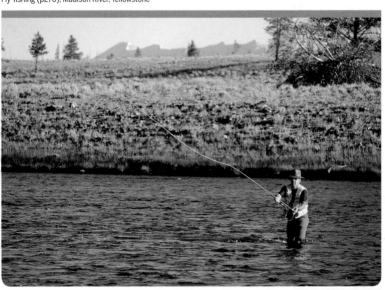

JOHN ELK III / LONELY PLANET IMAGES ©

Eating

SYDNEY'S MOUNTAIN
BISTRO Contemporary American $$
(✆406-646-7660; www.sydneysbistro.com; 38 Canyon St; mains $17-26; ✿5-10pm) An island of modern upscale cuisine in a sea of chicken-fried steak and gravy, sophisticated Sydney's is the place to turn to for a pear and walnut salad or orange Thai curry.

KIWI'S Burgers $
(cnr Hwy 20 & Electric St; mains $6-10; ✿11am-3:30pm & 5-7pm Mon-Fri) The best burgers in town and great bison meat pies.

ERNIE'S Sandwiches $
(www.erniesbakery.com; 406 Hwy 20; sandwiches $8; ✿6:30am-4pm) Popular for sandwiches and cheap breakfasts.

OLD TOWN CAFÉ Western $$
(128 Madison Ave; dinner $14-20; ✿7am-10pm) Authentic down-home beef and trout dinners.

ⓘ Information

Chamber of Commerce Information Center (✆406-646-7701; www.westyellowstonechamber.com; Canyon St; ✿8am-8pm; 🛜) Friendly traveler assistance, convenient parking and free wi-fi. There's also a ranger-staffed park desk and backcountry office, where you can buy entry permits to the park.

ⓘ Getting There & Away

Air
You can fly from Salt Lake City, UT, to West Yellowstone Airport (WYS; ✆406-646-7631) in summer only, roughly mid-June through September.

Bus
Karst Stage (✆406-556-3540; www.karststage.com) runs buses daily, December to April, from the airport to Big Sky ($51, one hour) and West Yellowstone (around $63.50, two hours); summer service is by reservation only.

Car
The following offer car rentals from $50 a day:
Budget (✆406-646-7882; www.budget-yellowstone.com; 131 Dunraven St & Yellowstone Airport)

Big Sky Car Rentals (✆800-426-7669; 415 Yellowstone Ave)

Gardiner

A quintessential gateway town founded and fed on tourism, Gardiner, Montana, is the only entrance to Yellowstone National Park open to automobile traffic year-round. The park starts just where the souvenir stores peter out at the south end of town. Mammoth Hot Springs are only 5 miles away.

Bull moose, Grand Teton

Sights & Activities

ROOSEVELT ARCH   Landmark
Gardiner's most photographed sight was
dedicated by Teddy Roosevelt himself
on April 25, 1903, and inscribed with
Congress' words 'for the benefit and
enjoyment of the people.'

**YELLOWSTONE HERITAGE
& RESEARCH CENTER**   Museum
(307-344-2664; www.nps.gov/yell/history
culture/collections.htm; library 9am-4pm Tue-
Fri) The park's abundant archives (over
five million items and growing) moved
from Mammoth to this research facility in
2004. Visitors can view the lobby displays
and peruse the library. Interesting hour-
long tours operate at 10am on Tuesday
and Thursday (Memorial Day to Labor
Day) and take you into the museum and
rare-book archives.

PARKS' FLY SHOP   Fishing
(406-848-7314; www.parksflyshop.com; 202
S 2nd St) Old-school owner Richard Parks
sells flies (specifically designed for park
waters), rents gear and offers float trips
and is the author of the much-respected
Fly Fishing Yellowstone National Park.

**YELLOWSTONE RAFT
COMPANY**   Rafting
(800-858-7781; www.yellowstoneraft.com;
111 2nd St) Offers rafting trips on the Yellowstone River; also half-day kayaking
lessons.

MONTANA WHITEWATER   Rafting
(406-848-7398; www.montanawhitewater.
com; 603 Scott St W) Rents canoes, kayaks
and float tubes, in addition to horseback-
riding combo trips in the park.

 # Sleeping

Camping & RV

ROCKY MOUNTAIN RV PARK   RV Sites $
(877-534-6931; www.rockymountain
campground.com; 14 Jardine Rd; RV sites from

$51.50, cabins $50-125; mid-Apr–mid-Oct;
) This friendly place overlooking the
river offers showers, laundry, full hookups
and fine panoramas of Yellowstone, but
little shade.

YELLOWSTONE RV PARK   RV Sites $
(406-848-7496; www.ventureswestinc.com;
117 Hwy 89; tent/RV sites $27/48;) At the
northwest end of town, this RV park has
46 fairly cramped riverside sites with full
hookups, plus showers and a laundry.

Lodging

About half of Gardiner's accommodations close between October and May;
those that remain open cut their rates by
around 50%.

ABSAROKA LODGE   Hotel $$
(800-755-7414; www.yellowstonemotel.com;
S 2nd St; r $110-125;) This modern but
surprisingly unobtrusive place offers
excellent-value doubles, some with
kitchenette and all with a fine balcony
overlooking the rushing Yellowstone River.
Book early.

YELLOWSTONE SUITES   B&B $$
(406-848-7937; www.yellowstonesuites.com;
506 S 4th St; d without/with bath $120/150;
) There's plenty of privacy in this
well-appointed, four-room 100-year-old
B&B, which makes a nice antidote to motel overload. There are cozy sitting spaces
and views of Electric Peak, but only two
rooms have attached bathrooms. Get
a deal by renting an entire floor (two
rooms).

**HEADWATERS OF THE
YELLOWSTONE B&B**   B&B $$
(406-848-7073; www.headwatersbandb.com;
9 Olson Lake Rd, 3 miles north of Gardiner; r with
breakfast $140, cabins $175-200;) For a
more personal touch, this riverside B&B
north of town offers rooms in the main
house or more private self-contained
cabins, all with fine views of Electric Peak.

HILLCREST COTTAGES   Cottages $$
(800-970-7353; www.hillcrestcottages.com;
200 Scott St W; d $78-94, 2-room cottages $120;

🕐May-Sep; 🛜) This slightly cramped mini-village features a variety of pleasant if dated cottages, most with kitchenettes, that sleep two to seven.

YELLOWSTONE RIVER MOTEL Motel $$
(📞406-848-7303; www.yellowstonerivermotel.com; 14 E Park St; d $89-110, ste $145; 🕐May-Oct; 🛜) One of Gardiner's better-run motels. Picnic tables and a BBQ area overlook the river.

YELLOWSTONE VILLAGE INN Motel $$
(📞800-228-8158; www.yellowstonevinn.com; 1102 Scott St W; d/ste from $129/199; 🛜🏊) Standing alone at the entrance to Gardiner, this locally owned motel is decent value, with a few family suites featuring a private porch.

**BEST WESTERN BY
MAMMOTH HOT SPRINGS** Motel $$
(📞406-848-7311; www.bestwestern.com/mammothhotsprings; 905 Scott St W; d $180; 🏊) Some rooms have mountain views, others have river views. Kids love the pool.

Gallatin National Forest offers three first-come, first-served primitive campgrounds just northeast of Gardiner:

Eagle Creek Campground Camping $
(campsite $7; 🕐year-round) Has 16 woodsy sites and pit toilets but no water, 2 miles of Gardiner on unpaved Jardine Rd.

Timber Camp Campground Camping $
(FR493; 🕐mid-Jun–end Oct) Further along the Bear Creek road, 10 miles from Gardiner and 4 miles past Jardine. Free dispersed camping with a toilet but no water.

Bear Creek Campground Camping $
(🕐mid-Jun–end Oct) Two miles further, free dispersed camping with a toilet but no water.

Eating

THE CORRAL DRIVE-IN Drive-In $
(711 Scott St W; burgers $8-12; 🕐11am-11pm Apr-Oct) This old-style malt-and-greasy-

Left: Hayden Valley (p255), Yellowstone; **Below:** Lower Falls (p256), Yellowstone

(LEFT) JOHN ELK III / LONELY PLANET IMAGES ©; (BELOW) JOHN ELK III / LONELY PLANET IMAGES ©

burger stand has been proudly clogging arteries since 1960. It's neither gourmet nor even cheap but really, where else are you going to dive into a half-pound elk burger followed by a huckleberry shake?

SAWTOOTH DELI Sandwiches **$**
(220 W Park St; mains $8; ⊗8am-9:30pm Tue-Sat) For a quick meal join the locals at this friendly place, which serves hot and cold subs, barbeque specials and a decent breakfast.

ⓘ Information

Chamber of Commerce (☏406-848-7971; www.gardinerchamber.com; 220 W Park St; ⊗9am-6pm Mon-Fri, 9am-5pm Sat, 1-5pm Sun) Tourist information and a public bathroom.

Cooke City

Sandwiched spectacularly between two forested ridges of the Beartooth Mountains, just 4 miles from Yellowstone's northeast entrance, this one-street Montana town gets a steady flow of summer visitors en route between the scenic splendors of the Beartooth Hwy and the national park. There's not much here in the way of shops, sights or even trailheads, but this isolated town has a backwoods feel that's more laid-back and less commercialized than the park's other gateway towns.

Sleeping & Eating

Soda Butte, Colter and Chief Joseph **campgrounds** (sites $8-9; ⊗mid-Jul–mid-Sep) are just 1.5 miles, 2 miles and 4 miles from town respectively.

ALPINE MOTEL Motel **$**
(☏406-838-2262; www.cookecityalpine.com; d $78-98, apt $120-175; ⊗year-round; 🛜)
Well-maintained and spacious rooms are the hallmark of this good-value motel,

with laundry facilities, family suites and nicely discounted winter rates.

ELKHORN LODGE
Cabins $

(☎ 406-838-2332; www.elkhornlodgemt.com; s/d $89/99, cabin $120; ☺ year-round; ☎) Choose between the six rooms in the main building with pleasant sitting area, coffee maker and fridge or the two pricier cabins with kitchenette. All are fresh and spacious.

BEARTOOTH CAFÉ
American $$

(www.beartoothcafe.com; lunch $10, dinner $16-25; ☺ 11am-10pm late May-late Sep) A bright place for lunch sandwiches (such as a buffalo burger, a 'funk burger' or lighter portobello sandwich) served on the pleasant front deck, washed down by a fine selection of 130 bottled microbrews. Dinner mains like ribs, smoked trout and hand-cut steaks are double the lunchtime prices. Breakfast is served weekends only.

❶ Information

Chamber of Commerce (☎ 406-838-2495; www.cookecitychamber.org; 206 W Main; ☎)

A helpful new visitor center with public restroom and free wi-fi.

GRAND TETON NATIONAL PARK

Rough-cut summits rising sharply from a lush valley floor, the Tetons are a sight to behold. Simply put, it is sublime and crazy terrain, crowned by the dagger-edged Grand (13,770ft), a giant in the history of American mountaineering. But there's much more, from sagebrush flats and wildflower meadows to the hundreds of alpine lakes and fragrant forests trodden by bear, moose, grouse and marmot.

While the park is dwarfed by Yellowstone, it can offer visitors a more immediate intimacy with the landscape and more varied and scenic hiking. In addition, climbers, boaters, anglers and other outdoor enthusiasts also find plenty to do. For lovers of alpine scenery, the Tetons' visual impact far exceeds that of Yellowstone. Whichever way you wander, these rock spires exercise a magnetic attraction on your gaze.

When to Go

Early summer is great for wildflowers and long days. September means fewer people, rutting elk and fall foliage. Cross-country skiing is good in winter and as late as April.

When You Arrive

Visitors receive a free orientation map and copy of the park newspaper, *Grand Teton Guide,* which details the extensive program of ranger-led activities, road closures and park news.

Rock climbing (p293), Grand Teton
JAMES KAY / SCPHOTOS / ALAMY ©

Detour: Cody

Cody is second only to Jackson as Wyoming's premier summer tourist town. Arrive at sundown and you'll find costumed gunslingers mid-brawl, flanked by Jezebels toiling under a career in false eyelashes. But Cody has more than just Wild West kitsch. The town's ultimate blessing is its proximity to Yellowstone National Park, 51 miles to the west and connected by the scenic Wapiti Valley.

Nature aside, no visit to Cody is complete without a stroll through the **Buffalo Bill Historical Center** (307-587-4771; www.bbhc.org; 720 Sheridan Ave; adult/child over 6/student/senior $18/10/13/16; 8am-6pm, closed Mon-Wed Dec-Feb), which has the slightly exaggerated nickname 'Smithsonian of the West.'

Perhaps most famously, the self-proclaimed 'Rodeo Capital of the World' draws crowds all summer long to its nightly **rodeo** (www.codynightrodeo.com; 519 West Yellowstone Ave; adult/child 7-12 $18/8; 8pm Jun-Aug;). Roping, bronco riding and barrel racing are all part of the fun.

Recently restored and stunning, the **Chamberlin Inn** (307-587-0202; www.chamberlininn.com; 1032 12th St; r/ste from $185/295; @) conjures up the mystique of the original 1904 boarding house, with French tile paintings, embossed tin ceilings, clawfoot tubs and crushed-satin bedcovers.

For information, pop into Cody's **visitor center** (307-587-2777; www.codychamber.org; 836 Sheridan Ave; 8am-6pm Mon-Fri, 9am-5pm Sat, 10am-3pm Sun).

Orientation

Just south of Yellowstone National Park, Grand Teton National Park stretches 40 miles along the compact, 15-mile-wide range.

There are three entrance stations. If you are in Jackson, the closest is the south entrance at Moose on Teton Park Rd west of Moose Junction. If you are coming from Teton Village, the southwest entrance is a mile or so north via the Moose-Wilson road. If you are driving south from Yellowstone, take the northern entrance 3 miles inside the park on US 89/191/287 north of Moran Junction.

The Teton's southern commercial hub is Moose, with a new visitor center, a gas station, accommodations, restaurants, groceries and equipment rental. The nearby Laurance S Rockefeller Preserve Center is south on the Moose-Wilson Rd.

Further north on Teton Park Rd, Signal Mountain offers accommodations, a restaurant, a gas station and grocery store. Jackson Lake Lodge has shops and restaurants.

Colter Bay hosts the highest concentration of visitor services, with a visitor center, gas station, grocery store, restaurants, laundromat, showers, campground, RV park and marina.

Sights

John D Rockefeller Jr Memorial Parkway

This NPS-managed parkway is a 7.5-mile corridor linking Yellowstone and Grand Teton National Parks. Congress recognized Rockefeller's contribution to the creation of Grand Teton National Park by designating this 24,000-acre parkway in his honor in 1972. Here, the Tetons taper to a gentle slope, and rocks from volcanic flows in Yellowstone line the Snake River. A transitional zone between the two national parks, the area combines characteristics of both, though it's less spectacular than either. Activities focus

Grand Teton

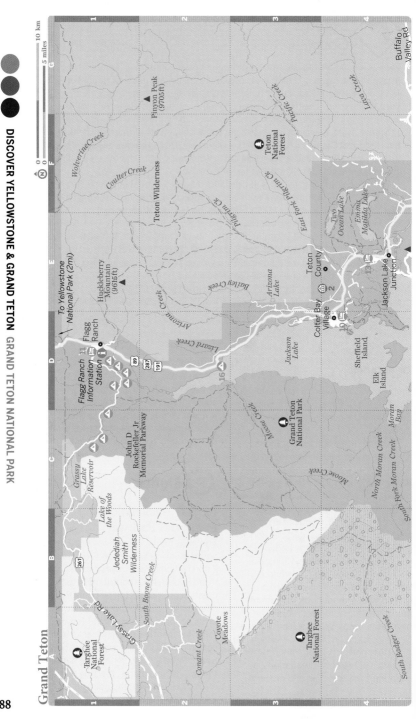

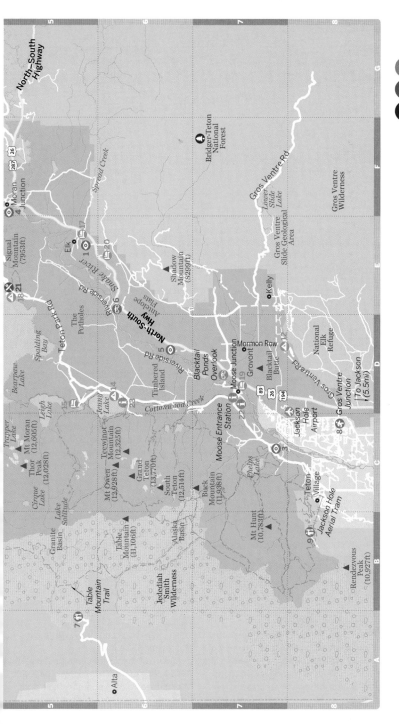

North–South Highway

Moran Junction

Signal Mountain (7953ft)

Elk

Shadow Mountain (8299ft)

Kelly

Bridger-Teton National Forest

Gros Ventre Rd

Lower Slide Lake

Gros Ventre Slide Geological Area

Gros Ventre Wilderness

Spread Creek

Snake River

Teton Park Rd

Riverside Rd

North–South Hwy

Antelope Flats

Spalding Bay

The Potholes

Bearpaw Lake

Jenny Lake

Leigh Lake

Cottonwood Creek

Timbered Island

Riverside Rd

Mormon Row

Moose Junction

Grovont

Blacktail Ponds Overlook

Blacktail Butte

National Elk Refuge

Gros Ventre Rd

Gros Ventre Junction

To Jackson (5.5mi)

Trapper Lake

Thor Peak (12,028ft)

Mt Moran (12,605ft)

Cirque Lake

Lake Solitude

Granite Basin

Mt Owen (12,928ft)

Teewinot Mountain (12,325ft)

Grand Teton (13,770ft)

South Teton (12,514ft)

Buck Mountain (11,938ft)

Moose Entrance Station

Phelps Lake

Jackson Hole Airport

Jackson Hole

Table Mountain (11,106ft)

Jedediah Smith Wilderness

Alaska Basin

Mt Hunt (10,783ft)

Teton Village

Jackson Hole Aerial Tram

Rendezvous Peak (10,927ft)

Table Mountain Trail

Alta

287 26

89

26 191

194

Grand Teton

around historic Flagg Ranch, which was established as a US Cavalry post in 1872.

North–south US 89/191/287 is the main road through the parkway.

The 52-mile, east–west **Grassy Lake Rd** links US 89/191/287 to US 20 at Ashton, Idaho, offering an infrequently used 'back way' into the national parks. This bumpy gravel road, also a good mountain-biking route, follows an old Native American trade and hunting route.

Heading west from US 89, Flagg Ranch is the first landmark on the road. Shortly after crossing the Polecat Creek Bridge, the pavement ends and the graded gravel road parallels the north bank of the Snake River. The region is peppered with lakes with great fishing options.

Colter Bay Region

The road south from Yellowstone drops off the Yellowstone plateau at the end of the Rockefeller Parkway, where a startling view of the Tetons soaring above Jackson Lake comes into play. Past Lizard Creek Campground several beaches tucked into

nooks offer some of the park's best picnic areas.

Jackson Lake is a natural glacial lake that has been dammed, so water levels fluctuate, dropping considerably toward the end of the summer. Two Ocean and Emma Matilda Lakes sit east of Jackson Lake, tucked into the hills. Visitor services are concentrated at Colter Bay Village.

COLTER BAY

At Colter Bay Visitor Center, the **Indian Arts Museum** (admission free; ⏰8am-5pm May & Sep, 8am-8pm Jun-Aug) displays artifacts from the collection of David T Vernon, including beautiful beadwork, bags and photographs. There are frequent craft demonstrations, and videos are shown all day on subjects ranging from wildlife to Native American art. The center also offers books on Native American history and lore.

South of the visitor center is the marina and trailhead for hikes to Swan Lake and Hermitage Point. A popular picnic and **swimming area** sits just north of the visitor center, though there are countless other secluded swimming and sunbathing spots dotted around Jackson Lake.

AROUND JACKSON LAKE LODGE

The elegant **Jackson Lake Lodge** is worth a stop, if only to gape at the stupendous views through its 60ft-tall windows. In cold weather the cozy fireplaces in the upper lobby are blazing. In summer you can drink in fine Teton views and a cold Snake River Lager while sitting outdoors.

About a mile north of Jackson Lake Lodge a rough dirt road branches east off the main road to a trailhead, from which it's a 1-mile walk one way (with a steep climb at the end) to **Grand View Point** (7586ft), which offers fine views of both the Tetons and Two Ocean Lake. You can also visit the viewpoint as part of the Two Ocean Lake hike.

One of the most famous scenic spots for wildlife-watching is **Oxbow Bend**, 2 miles east of Jackson Lake Junction, with the reflection of Mt Moran as a stunning backdrop. Early morning and dusk are the best times to spot moose, elk, sandhill cranes, ospreys, bald eagles, trumpeter swans, Canada geese, blue herons and white pelicans.

SIGNAL MOUNTAIN SUMMIT ROAD

This 5-mile paved road (no RVs) east of Teton Park Rd winds up to the top of **Signal Mountain** for dramatic panoramas from 800ft above Jackson Hole's valley floor. Below, the Snake River, the valley's only drainage, runs a twisted course through cottonwood and spruce. Abandoned dry channels demonstrate the changing landscape.

Views are superb at sunrise, but the best vistas are actually from three-quarters of the way up at **Jackson Point Overlook**, a short walk south from a parking area.

Eastern Slopes

Hwy 26/89/191 traverses the park's eastern flank for about 25 miles from the Moran Junction to the park's southern gate past sagebrush flats and the occasional ranch – always with the Tetons' sharp spires diverting your gaze westward. The hardscrabble lives of Jackson Hole's early homesteaders are reflected in the valley's characteristic lodgepole buck and pole fences.

MORAN TO BLACKTAIL BUTTE

Ranchers Pierce and Margaret Cunninghams, early major supporters of Grand Teton National Park, cultivated a cattle ranch at **Cunningham Cabin** in 1890, 6 miles south of Moran Junction. The property is one of the best surviving examples of a homestead cabin; a short trail elucidates local homesteading.

Four miles south, the **Snake River Overlook** offers good panoramas of the Tetons and opportunities for wildlife-watching, though forest growth means the

Teton Names

Impressions are everything... French Canadian fur trappers named the three Tetons – South, Middle and Grand – 'les Trois Tetons' (the three breasts), most likely in a lonely moment of Western wandering and reflection. Trapper Osborne Russell claimed their Shoshone moniker was 'Hoary Headed Fathers.' Teewinot means 'Many Pinnacles' in Shoshone – it now describes the range as well as Teewinot Mountain. The Snake River gets its name from the local Shoshone, or Snake, Native American tribe, though the name Snake was mistakenly given to the Shoshone when the weaving sign for the Shoshone (who called themselves the people of the woven grass huts) was confused with the sign for a snake.

photo ops aren't quite as good as when Ansel Adams immortalized the shot.

A better place for photos is **Schwabacher's Landing**, a popular rafting put-in 4 miles further south. The jagged Tetons reflected in the meandering river ranks as some of the park's most sublime scenery. Access the landing via a short dirt road.

Central Tetons

South of Signal Mountain, Teton Park Rd passes the **Potholes**, sagebrush flats pockmarked with craterlike depressions called kettles. The kettles were formed slowly by blocks of orphaned glacial ice that were stranded under the soil, left by receding glaciers. Just south is the Mt Moran turnout.

Seven miles south of Signal Mountain, the Jenny Lake Scenic Dr branches west to offer the park's most picturesque drive. The scenic heart of the Grand Tetons and the epicenter of Teton's crowds, **Jenny Lake** offers good fishing and boating opportunities, and there are shuttle services across the lake.

Just south of Jenny Lake, Teton Park Rd passes the turnoff to the Lupine Meadows Trailhead, for hikes to Surprise Lake and Garnet Canyon.

Two miles south of here, Teton Glacier turnout offers some of the best views of **Teton Glacier**, the largest in the park.

Moose-Wilson Road

Moose-Wilson Rd is a partially paved 15-mile route (its southernmost 3 miles are gravel) that connects Teton Village to Moose. RVs and trailers are not allowed on this road inside the park, which is quite narrow in sections.

Laurance S Rockefeller Preserve

For solitude and stunning views, check out this newer section of Grand Teton National Park. Once the JY Ranch, an exclusive Rockefeller family retreat, these 3100 acres around Phelps Lake were donated in 2001 by Laurance S Rockefeller. His grandfather John D Rockefeller had been an early park advocate, purchasing the first tracts of land to donate in 1927. Despite strong local opposition, by 1949 he had donated some 33,000 acres of former ranchland to Grand Teton National Park.

 **Activities**

Hiking

The Tetons' extreme verticality means the hikes in this park follow a different standard; with the steep terrain, flat and easy rambles are few. The easy-to-moderate day hikes following are suitable for families and most walkers. Hikers should adjust the distance they walk to their satisfaction.

Old barn, Grand Teton
DOUGLAS STEAKLEY / LONELY PLANET IMAGES ©

Paved wheelchair-accessible trails include the Jenny Lake shoreline, String Lake shoreline and Colter Bay Lakeshore Trail (next to the marina) and the southern edge of Jackson Lake Dam.

LEIGH & BEARPAW LAKES   *Hiking*

A fun, flat family outing skirting forest-clad, crystal-clear swimming holes.

The Leigh Lake Trailhead is at the end of the side road off Jenny Lake Dr; don't confuse it with the String Lake Trailhead. Try to get an early start on this trail, as it's very popular.

As you continue north along Leigh Lake, your surroundings open up to fine views of Mt Moran and its Falling Ice and Skillet Glaciers. Allow about 3½ hours for the 7.4 mile hike.

SURPRISE & AMPHITHEATER LAKES   *Hiking*

One of the park's oldest, this trail is a classic leg-burner and offers great views. Bring plenty of water since none is available between the trailhead and the two lakes near the top of the climb.

The well-worn trail gently winds through pine forest until it mounts a shoulder and the ascent begins in earnest. A junction with the Taggart and Bradley Lakes Trail lies atop the shoulder, 1.7 miles (40 minutes) from the start. Keep right and tackle the series of switchbacks up the flank of **Disappointment Peak**. The route offers views over Taggart Lake and Jackson Hole.

The switchbacks ease shortly before the lakes, and after 2¼ hours of solid climbing, you'll finally reach the inviting, gemstone waters of **Surprise Lake**. Set in a hollow beneath jagged white rocks and cliffs, it is a resplendent payoff for your efforts. The slightly bigger and starker **Amphitheater Lake** lies just 0.2 miles further along the trail. Return the way you came. Allow five to six hours for this difficult 9.6-mile hike. It starts at the Lupine Meadows Trailhead.

PHELPS LAKE TRAIL   *Hiking*

This is a lovely and flat forested amble around a beautiful lake. The trail leaves the Laurance S Rockefeller Preserve Center and splits. If you go left over the bridge, you will be on the **Lake Creek Trail**. Go right for the **Woodland Trail**. Before long it crosses the main road and continues in a gentle, winding ascent through pine forest and aspens, hitting the junction of the **Boulder Ridge Trail** at 0.7 miles. Continue straight; soon after, views open up and you get a glimpse of Static Peak and Buck Mountain on its right. It should take 30 or 45 minutes total to reach Phelps Lake. Go the extra 20yd to the lake viewpoint for gorgeous views of the headwall across the lake; there's benches here for resting. Allow about 3½ hours for the easy-to-moderate 7-mile loop.

Cycling

Cyclists are in less danger from motorists in the Tetons than in Yellowstone because the roads are wider and more open, but it is still best to venture out early to avoid traffic. In April, Teton Park Rd is open only to cyclists and pedestrian traffic. This is a great time to cycle if the snow has cleared.

The best spot for cycling in the park, the new multi-use **pathway** borders the Teton Park Rd between Moose and Jenny Lake (a 7.6-mile stretch). Riders can park at the lot just after the Moose entry station.

For a mellow, scenic ride, try **Mormon Row**, a 16-mile loop including terrain beyond Mormon Row, which starts and finishes in Gros Ventre Junction. While part of this ride is paved, the 3-mile Mormon Row section, bumpy and unpaved, is not great for road bikes.

Mountain bikers can ride 15 miles along the gravel Snake River Rd, beginning at the Gros River Junction. Just east of the park in Bridger-Teton National Forest, the forested **Shadow Mountain** offers a strenuous 6-mile round-trip loop. Set off along a gravel road from the parking lot at the end of paved Antelope Flats Rd.

Rock Climbing & Mountaineering

Garnet Canyon is the gateway to the most popular scrambles to Middle and South

MIKE CAVAROC / ALAMY

Don't Miss Lake Solitude

Rimmed by fir and pines and sporting ice until midsummer, Lake Solitude (9035ft) is a great spot to loll around (but probably not to swim). Due to the trail's popularity, this rewarding hike does however lack the elixir of its moniker, but still provides a challenge. Though it's a long hike with an elevation gain of 2240ft, it is not especially tough since the grade is quite gradual.

Taking the boat shuttle will shave 4 miles off. The Cascade Canyon (west) dock meets a network of trails. Head left to pass **Hidden Falls** after 0.2 miles and ascend to **Inspiration Point** in another 0.5 miles.

The Cascade Canyon Trail continues straight, past a lovely beach and a high cascade, with fine views. About two hours (4.5 miles) from the dock the valley splits. The left branch leads to South Fork and **Hurricane Pass**. Turn right and climb gently for 30 minutes to enter the **Cascade Camping Zone**, which stretches for the next 30 minutes. From the zone's end it's 10 minutes up to the lake, past a small cascade and a hitch rail marking the end of the line for horses. It's about three hours (7.2 miles) from here back to the dock.

Return to the boat dock the way you came. The terrain, shaded most of the afternoon, is all downhill, affording full views of Mt Owen and Grand Teton.

Teton and the technical ascent of Grand Teton.

The Grand Teton is cherished by climbers as a classic climb. It starts with a strenuous hike up Garnet Canyon (4000ft-plus) and making camp. Day two requires an alpine start. The Owen-Spaulding route is the most popular, but there are lots of variants from which to choose. The climb itself consists of 2700ft of elevation gain, fun scrambling, three easy 5th-class pitches and an exciting rappel from high on the mountain. Views from above are unparalleled. Ah, and then there's getting down...Very fit nonclimbers can complete the climb with an outfitter and some training beforehand.

Day climbers don't need to register, but those staying overnight need a backcountry-use permit. Call ☎307-739-3604 for recorded climbing information.

JENNY LAKE VISITOR CENTER
Rock Climbing

(☎307-739-3343; ⏰8am-6pm Jun-Sep) Ground zero for climbing information. Also sells climbing guidebooks and provides information.

CLIMBERS' RANCH
Rock Climbing

(☎307-733-7271; www.americanalpineclub.org; Teton Park Rd; ⏰summer only) An excellent resource and the spot to meet outdoor partners in crime, the American Alpine Club's ranch has been a climbing institution since it opened its doors. It also runs an inexpensive summer dormitory and rents some gear. The ranch is just south of the Teton Glacier turnout.

EXUM MOUNTAIN GUIDES
Rock Climbing

(☎307-733-2297; www.exumguides.com; Lupine Meadows) The region's oldest climbing school runs climbing courses at Hidden Falls on Jenny Lake's west shore and has a base camp at Grand Teton's Lower Saddle (11,600ft).

Horseback Riding

Colter Bay corral offers 1½- and 2½-hour trail rides around Swan Lake for $33/48. Children are charged the same rates and must be at least eight years old. Families with small children can check out the breakfast wagon rides (adult/child $37/15). Make reservations at the **activities booth** (⏰7am-8pm) next to the Colter Bay grocery store, preferably a couple of days in advance.

Jackson Lake Lodge offers guided horseback rides (two hours for $75) that loop around the local trails, as well as breakfast and dinner rides by horseback or wagon.

Flagg Ranch runs horseback-riding trips (one hour for $38) hourly from June to September.

Boating

A fun, mellow activity for families or groups is to rent a motorboat for a day and explore Jackson Lake, stopping to picnic and swim at uncrowded inlets and islands. Though they cover less terrain, canoes and kayaks are similarly great.

Signal Mountain Marina (☎307-543-2831; ⏰7am-7:30pm mid-May–early Sep) rents boats, canoes and kayaks. Reservations are accepted for larger boats only and depend on lake levels. Ten-mile **scenic floats** (adult/6-12yr $60/38) on the Snake River offer good wildlife-watching opportunities.

Busy **Colter Bay Marina** (☎307-543-2811; ⏰8am-5pm, no rentals after 3pm) provides fishing gear and licenses, as well as boat rentals.

String Lake is perfect for a family canoe trip or even just a splash about. The canoe-only put-in is at the end of a turnoff just before the Leigh Lake Trailhead parking lot.

Particularly suited to families, **Leigh Lake** offers the most scenic day and overnight paddles.

Cross-Country Skiing & Snowshoeing

The park grooms 14 miles of track right under the Tetons' highest peaks, between Taggart-Bradley Lakes parking area and Signal Mountain. Lanes are available for ski touring, skate skiing and snowshoeing. The NPS does not always mark every trail: consult at the ranger station to make sure that the trail you plan to use is well tracked and easy to follow. Rentals are available in Jackson.

For an easy snowshoeing outing, try Teton Park Rd (closed to traffic in winter). Remember to use the hardpack trail and never walk on ski trails – skiers will thank you for preserving the track!

RANGER-LED TOURS
Snowshoeing

From late December to mid-March rangers lead free 1.5-mile (two-hour) snowshoe hikes. It's also a good opportunity to study animal tracks and learn about winter ecology. Snowshoe hikes depart several times a week from the Craig Thomas Discovery & Visitor Center. Snowshoes are provided, and children over eight years old can take part.

Sleeping

Most campgrounds and accommodations are open from early May to early October, depending on the weather conditions. Camping inside the park is permitted in designated campgrounds only and is limited to 14 days (seven days at popular Jenny Lake). The NPS operates the park's six **campgrounds** (📞800-628-9988) on a first-come, first-served basis.

Demand for campsites is high from early July to Labor Day, and most campgrounds fill by 11am (checkout time). Jenny Lake fills by about 8am, followed by Signal Mountain. Colter Bay is a large site and fills later; Gros Ventre fills last, if at all.

Signal Mountain is probably the easiest place to base yourself because of its central location. Colter Bay and Jenny Lake have tent-only sites reserved for backpackers and cyclists.

John D Rockefeller Jr Memorial Parkway

The parkway is a handy place to stay en route between Yellowstone and Grand Teton National Parks.

FLAGG RANCH RESORT Cabins $$
(📞307-543-2861; www.flaggranch.com; r $189; ☻mid-May–mid-Sep; 🛜🐾) Since its occupation by the US Cavalry, this 1910 resort has been gussied up: walkways lead to prim log duplexes featuring rooms with phones, coffeemakers and patio rockers. While less rugged than a mountain hideaway, the grounds still provide solitude for a short break. Pet-friendly ($10 extra), it's popular with families and couples; most stay a night or two between parks. The lodge offers upscale dining, a minimarket and an activities desk. Shuttles go to Jackson and the Jackson Hole Airport.

FLAGG RANCH
CAMPGROUND Campground, RV sites $
(tent/RV sites $35/64; ☻May–early Oct) Among the most expensive campsites around, this campground features pull-through sites, propane for sale, 24-hour showers, laundry and a nightly campfire program. Sites are generally available the same day, but RV campers should reserve a week or more in advance.

Colter Bay Region

Jackson Lake Lodge and Colter Bay Village are operated by **Grand Teton Lodge Company** (GTLC; 📞advance reservations 307-543-3100, same-day reservations 307-543-2811; www.gtlc.com).

At campgrounds run by the Grand Teton Lodge Company, walk-in hikers and cyclists pay only $8 per person, with specific sites reserved for them.

LIZARD CREEK
CAMPGROUND Campground $
(📞800-672-6012; US 89/191/287; sites $21; ☻early Jan–early Sep) Snug in a forested peninsula along Jackson Lake's north shore, about 8 miles north of Colter Bay Junction, these secluded woodsy sites (60 total) are a great option.

SIGNAL MOUNTAIN
CAMPGROUND Campground $
(📞800-672-6012; Teton Park Rd; sites $21; ☻early May–mid-Oct) This popular campground with 86 sites looks out on lovely sunsets on Jackson Lake from 5 miles south of Jackson Lake Junction.

Some sites can be cramped, but they are convenient.

JACKSON LAKE
LODGE Lodge, Cabins $$$
(📞307-543-2811; r/ste/cottage from $229/625/229; ☻mid-May–early Oct; @🛜🏊) This lodge perches on a bluff overlooking the Tetons and Jackson Lake, 1 mile north of Jackson Lake Junction. Standard rooms have barely changed in 50 years, but aesthetics take the backseat to nature here, and the lodge gets many nostalgic returning guests. Perks include soft sheets, meandering trails and enormous

Walking trail, Jenny Lake (p292), Grand Teton

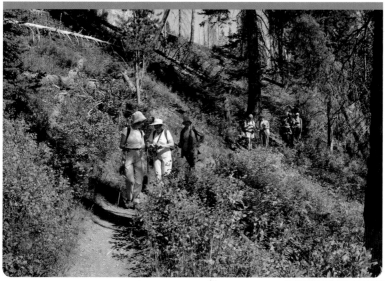

SHANNON NACE / LONELY PLANET IMAGES ©

picture windows framing the luminous peaks.

SIGNAL MOUNTAIN LODGE
Cabins, Motel $$

(☎307-543-2831; www.signalmtnlodge.com; r $175-228, cabins $132-198; ☺mid-May–mid-Oct; 📷) While these lakeside lodgings beg for a thorough update, they have one thing clear: location, location, location. Smack in the middle of the park, accommodations range from motel rooms to cabins, bungalows and lakefront retreats. All units have electric heat, while perks include self-service laundry and dryers, and a TV and games room.

COLTER BAY VILLAGE
Cabins $

(tent cabins $52, cabins without bath $65, with bath $119-165) Basic tent cabins (June to early September) and log-and-canvas structures sport all the charm of a Siberian gulag.

Eastern Slopes

TRIANGLE X RANCH
Ranch $$$

(☎307-733-2183; www.trianglex.com; 2 Triangle X Rd, Moose; weekly all-inclusive per person, double occupancy $1880, winter cabins per person $125) With the gorgeous backdrop of the jagged Tetons, this ranch on the eastern flanks of the park boasts cabins with immaculate wood interiors. Cabins have one to three bedrooms and there are loads of activities for kids and adults. One week minimum.

MOOSE HEAD RANCH
Ranch $$$

(☎307-733-3141; www.mooseheadranch.com; all-inclusive per person double occupancy $375; ☺Jun-Aug) Families rave about this ranch, which has modern log cabins, friendly young staff, a varied and tasty menu and a slew of activities for adults and kids alike. Horseback rides are for all abilities. Five-night minimum. It's located between the Tetons and Yellowstone, 18 miles north of Jackson.

Central Tetons

At the campgrounds listed, walk-in hikers and cyclists pay $8 per person, with specific sites reserved for them.

JENNY LAKE CAMPGROUND
Campground $

(Teton Park Rd; tent sites $20; ☺mid-May–late Sep) This congenial and popular tent-only campground (51 sites) sits among the evergreens and glacial boulders 8 miles north of Moose Junction. Convenient to many trailheads, it is almost always full.

GROS VENTRE CAMPGROUND
Campground $

(Gros Ventre Rd; sites $20; ⏰ late Apr–mid-Oct) This sprawling but secluded 372-site campground sits near the Gros Ventre River, 4.5 miles northeast of US 26/89/191/287 and 11.5 miles from Moose. With the tall cottonwoods for shade and nearby river, it's very attractive.

JENNY LAKE LODGE
Cabins $$$

(📞 307-733-4647; cabins incl half-board $620; ⏰ early Jun-early Oct; @ 🛜) Rife with history, this is the oldest lodge within the whole park system. Worn timbers, down comforters and colorful quilts imbue this elegant lodging off Teton Park Rd with a cozy atmosphere. Outdoor rockers welcome you to your private cabin, furnished with flannel chairs, plush quilts and down comforters. Perks include robes and remodeled baths, but no TVs or radios (phones available on request).

Reservation lines open November 1 for the following year. It's run by Grand Teton Lodge Company.

CLIMBERS' RANCH
Cabins $

(📞 307-733-7271; www.americanalpineclub.org; Teton Park Rd; dm $22; ⏰ Jun-Sep) Started as a refuge for serious climbers, this group of rustic log cabins run by the American Alpine Club is now available to hikers. Amenities include a bathhouse with showers and sheltered cook station with locking bins for coolers. Bring your own sleeping bag and pad (the bunks are bare), but it's still a great deal. The location is spectacular.

Moose

SPUR RANCH LOG CABINS
Cabins $$$

(📞 307-733-2522; www.dornans.com; cabins $175-250) Gravel paths running through a broad wildflower meadow link these tranquil duplex cabins on the Snake River in Moose. Lodgepole pine furniture, Western stylings and down bedding create a homey feel, but the views are what make it.

🍴 Eating & Drinking

Visitors dine in the park for the convenience or the stunning views, but generally not for the food.

John D Rockefeller Jr Memorial Parkway

BEAR'S DEN Western $$

(📞 800-443-2311; lunch $9-12, dinner $9-34) Hungry travelers flock to this eatery at Flagg Ranch, the area's sole dining option. Breakfast and lunches are casual, while dinner goes Western with grilled steaks, meatloaf and chicken potpie.

Rafting (p303) on Snake River, Grand Teton
CHAD EHLERS / ALAMY ©

Colter Bay Region

COLTER BAY

For the cheapest nearby picnic fixings, hit the deli counter at the Colter Bay grocery store.

LEEK'S PIZZERIA
Pizzeria $$
(📞307-733-5470; pizzas $9-21; 🕐11am-10pm) Pizza and draft beer on the patio is a fine way to end an active day.

JOHN COLTER CAFÉ
COURT PIZZA & DELI
Cafeteria $
(mains $5-9; 🕐11am-10pm) An airy, plain cafeteria offering salads, burritos, picnic takeout and grill staples.

RANCH HOUSE
Western $$
(breakfast buffet adult/child $13/7, dinner $13-25; 🕐7:30am-9pm May-Sep; 🍴) Serving wild game, salmon and flank steak, this Western dining room with a branded bar offers a more formal setting. Vegetarians are appeased (but barely) with veggie burgers or tofu lo mein. The all-you-can-eat breakfast buffet is a pre-hike institution.

JACKSON LAKE LODGE MURAL
ROOM
Contemporary American $$$
(📞307-543-3100; Jackson Lake Lodge; meals $18-28) In addition to stirring views of the Tetons and moose ambling in the willow flats, the dining-room walls are adorned with the romantic Rendezvous Murals, depictions of 19th-century life by Carl Roters. Gourmet selections include game dishes and imaginative creations like trout wrapped in sushi rice with sesame seeds. Breakfasts are very good.

PIONEER GRILL
Diner $$
(Jackson Lake Lodge; mains $7-15; 🕐6am-10:30pm) A casual classic diner with leatherette stools lined up in a maze, the Pioneer serves up wraps, burgers and salads. Pioneer has a takeout window, boxed lunches (order before 9pm for the next day) and room-service pizza for pooped hikers (5pm to 9pm).

POOLSIDE BARBECUE
BBQ $$$
(📞307-543-2811; Jackson Lake Lodge; adult/child $23/12; 🕐6-8pm Sun-Fri Jul & Aug) Reservations are required for this all-you-can-eat BBQ buffet (think brisket, burgers, chicken, grilled veggies and lots of sides) with live music.

SIGNAL MOUNTAIN

THE PEAKS
Contemporary American $$$
(📞307-543-2831; Signal Mountain Lodge; meals $18-28) At Signal Mountain Lodge, dine on selections of cheese and fruit, local free-range beef and organic polenta cakes. Small plates, like wild game sliders, are also available. Patio seating gets snapped up early.

TRAPPER GRILL
Cafe $$
(📞307-543-2831; Signal Mountain Lodge; mains $5-16) With an encyclopedic menu, the Trapper Grill should please each picky member of the family, offering a range from grass-fed burgers and Mexican to gourmet sandwiches and ribs.

Central Tetons

JENNY LAKE LODGE DINING
ROOM
Contemporary American $$$
(📞307-733-4647; breakfast dishes $19, lunch mains $10-30, dinner mains $60) A five-course meal in the wilderness. Leave your hiking boots in the car; men must wear jackets at the park's premier restaurant. Pasta, an excellent wine list and strip steak in soy glaze are some of the offerings. Dinner reservations are required.

Moose

PIZZA PASTA COMPANY
Pizzeria $$
(mains $9-16; 🕐noon-9pm) Packed with crowds nightly, this unpretentious pizza parlor is simple yet so satisfying.

DORNAN'S GROCERY
STORE
Market, Deli $
(📞307-733-2415; Moose Village) The park's best-quality selection, with an excellent deli with imported cheeses, sandwiches, espresso counter and a wildly popular frozen-yogurt machine.

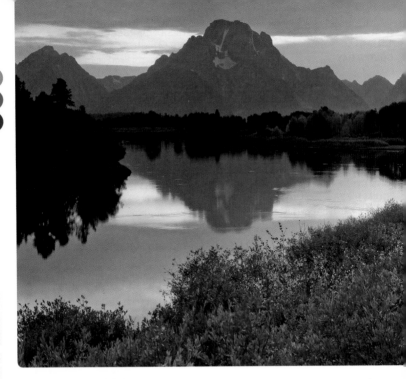

DORNAN'S CHUCKWAGON   BBQ **$$**
(☎ 307-733-2415 ext 213; Moose Village;
dinner $17; ⊙ 7:30-11am, 11:30am-3pm & 5-9pm
Jun–mid-Sep, closed Fri & Sat evening) Dinner
doesn't get any more casual than these
picnic tables scattered in the open air, but
the views are simply grand. At this family
favorite, breakfast means sourdough
pancakes and eggs off the griddle while
lunchtime means light fare and
sandwiches.

🛈 Information

Entrance Fees & Passes

Entrance to Grand Teton National Park (www.
nps.gov/grte) costs $25 per vehicle, $20 per
motorcyclist and $12 for cyclists or hikers on
foot. Winter day use costs $5. An annual pass to
both Yellowstone and Grand Teton National Parks
costs $50.

Opening Dates

The park is open year-round, though most of
Teton Park Rd is closed to vehicles in winter. Most
campgrounds and visitor centers (except the
Craig Thomas Discovery & Visitor Center) close
October to May.

Tourist Information

Colter Bay Visitor Center (☎ 307-739-3594;
⊙ 8am-5pm early May–mid-May & Sep-early
Oct, 8am-7pm Jun-early Sep) On US 89/191/287,
6 miles north of Jackson Lake Lodge. Issues
backcountry permits and offers crafts
demonstrations and tours of its Indian Arts
Museum.

Craig Thomas Discovery & Visitor Center
(☎ 307-739-3300; ⊙ 8am-5pm year-round,
8am-7pm peak summer season, closed Christmas
Day) Inaugurated in 2007, this $21-million center
on Teton Park Rd, half a mile west of Moose
Junction, is open year-round. Backcountry,
climbing and boating permits are available
here, as is information on weather, road and
avalanche conditions. Excellent interactive
displays.

Flagg Ranch Information Station (☎ 307-
543-2327; ⊙ 9am-4pm Jun-early Sep, closed for
lunch) Provides park information, rest rooms

Left: Oxbow Bend and Mt Moran (p291), Grand Teton;
Below: Bison, Grand Teton

and a small bookstore. Located 2.5 miles from Yellowstone's South Entrance.

Grand Teton National Park Headquarters (307-739-3600; www.nps.gov/grte) Shares the building with the Craig Thomas Discovery & Visitor Center. For general visitor information call 307-739-3300.

Jenny Lake Visitor Center (307-739-3343; 8am-4:30pm Sep-May, 8am-7pm Jun-Aug) On Teton Park Rd, 8 miles north of Moose Junction. Facilities include a store, lockers, exhibits, rest rooms and information on backpacking and trails.

Park Policies & Regulations

Anglers must carry a valid Wyoming fishing license. Boaters with their own craft must obtain permits (see www.nps.gov/grte/planyourvisit/boat.htm for details).

Maps

National Geographic (www.shopnational geographic.com) publishes excellent trail and road maps for the park. Winter and summer park maps are available at visitor centers and entrance kiosks.

Dangers & Annoyances

Though people are the greater nuisance, black bears and a growing population of grizzlies live in the park.

Mid-October to early December is elk-hunting season in areas east of US 26/89/191, west of US 26/89/191 along the Snake River between Moose and Moran Junctions, and the Rockefeller Memorial Parkway. If you must venture into these areas during hunting season, exercise caution.

Getting There & Around

Air

The nearest airport is **Jackson Hole Airport** (307-733-7682; www.jacksonholeairport.com; @). It's within the park borders.

Bus

Alltrans Park Shuttle (☎307-733-3135; www.
alltransparkshuttle.com; daily pass to/from park
$12; ⊘7am-7pm Jun-Sep) Operates several buses
a day in summer between Jackson, Moose, Jenny
Lake Lodge, Signal Mountain Lodge, Jackson Lake
Lodge and Colter Bay. Riders can pay with cash
or credit cards. Rides are unlimited on the daily
pass. Call for airport shuttle service (one way from
Jackson is $16).

Car

The speed limit on US 26/89/191 is 55mph;
elsewhere it's generally 45mph. Gas stations are
open year-round at Moose (24 hours, credit card
only 8pm to 8am) and Flagg Ranch Resort, and
summers only at Colter Bay, Signal Mountain and
Jackson Lodge.

AROUND GRAND TETON NATIONAL PARK

Posh and popular Jackson serves as the
regional hub and base camp, where you
can browse for Western baubles, down
pints of fresh organic lager or wrap yourself in honey and rose petals.

Jackson

Once a diamond in the rough, Jackson is
now a haven for millionaires as much as for
ranchers. Throw in a cadre of rhinestone
cowboys, sporty mountain athletes and
an army of service workers and you have
Jackson today, an evolving community
that buzzes with life. Trails and outdoor opportunities abound, fresh sushi is flown in
daily and generous purse strings support
a vigorous cultural life. When it becomes
a little much, just skip the souvenir shops
and dwell in the glorious backyard called
Grand Teton National Park.

◉ Sights

**NATIONAL MUSEUM OF
WILDLIFE ART** Museum
(☎307-733-5771; www.wildlifeart.org; 2820
Rungius Rd; adult $10, child free with adult;
⊘9am-5pm; 👪) If you visit only one area
museum, make it this one, with major
works by Bierstadt, Rungius, Remington
and Russell that will make your skin
prickle.

**NATIONAL ELK
REFUGE** Nature Reserve
(☎307-733-9212; 675 E Broadway;
⊘daylight hours Oct-May) About
7000 Rocky Mountain 'wel-
fare' elk (and a few hungry
wolves) winter on alfalfa
hay pellets here when
snow covers the native
grasses. Access these
25,000 acres northeast
of Jackson via Elk
Refuge Rd, an exten-
sion of E Broadway.
Bundle the kids up for
the refuge's one-hour
winter **sleigh ride** (adult/
child 5-12 $16/12), departing

Canoeing on Leigh Lake (p295),
Grand Teton
JOHN ELK III / LONELY PLANET IMAGES ©

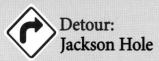

Detour: Jackson Hole

Dubbed the 'hole' by early European visitors, the broad Jackson Hole valley is one of the most breathtaking destinations in the country. Moose, elk and bison roam the valley floor against the rugged backdrop of the Tetons. Eagles and osprey fish the cold, crystalline streams and lakes. Surrounding the valley, the mountainous 3.4-million-acre Bridger-Teton National Forest is the second-largest forest in the Lower 48. The communities of Jackson, Teton Village, Kelly, Moose and Wilson, as well as much of south Grand Teton National Park, lie within the Hole.

One of the region's most famous attractions is **Jackson Hole Mountain Resort** (☏307-733-2292; www.jacksonhole.com; ☉Dec-Mar), one of the world's top ski resorts, boasting a continuous vertical rise of 4139ft. The resort has 2500 acres of ski terrain blessed by an average of 380in of snow annually.

For information on activities and tours, and to pick up a free *Jackson Hole Mountain Map & Guide*, head to **Jackson Hole Guest Services** (☏307-739-2753; Clock Tower Bldg) in Teton Village. For help with lodging reservations, contact **Jackson Hole Central Reservations** (☏888-838-6306; www.jacksonholewy.com).

from the National Museum of Wildlife Art mid-December through early April.

 Activities

The cowboy myths may have gone to pasture, but Jackson remains paradise for outdoor enthusiasts. Options are only limited by your lack of gear or imagination, so consult the following shops for rentals or trip suggestions.

MILL IRON RANCH　　Horseback Riding
(☏307-733-6390; www.millironranch.net; 5 US Hwy 89; 2hr ride $50) This fourth-generation operation of a Wyoming ranch family is the real deal. Climbing 2000ft, its two-hour ride in the Bridger Teton National Forest is rated the number-one trail ride in the US. It also offers dinner rides, sleigh rides and barn dances. To get here, drive south from Jackson on Hwy 89.

SNOW KING RESORT　　Snow Sports
(☏307-733-5200; www.snowking.com; 400 E Snow King Ave; adult/child $42/32; ☉Thanks-giving-Mar) Sling the skis over your shoulder and walk to this tiny 400-acre resort from downtown. Three lifts serve ski and snowboard runs with a vertical drop of 1571ft (15% beginner, 25% intermediate, 60% advanced). This north-facing slope catches less snow than other resorts but is convenient and well suited to children and families.

JACK DENNIS OUTDOOR SHOP　　Fishing
(☏307-734-8103; www.jackdennis.com; 70 S King St, Jackson) A pro fly shop offering guided fly-fishing and casting instruction.

BARKER-EWING RIVER TRIPS　　Rafting
(☏307-733-1000; www.barker-ewing.com; 45 W Broadway) Reputable outfitter offering rafting trips on the Snake River.

DAVE HANSEN WHITEWATER　　Rafting
(☏307-733-6295; www.davehansenwhitewater. com; 515 N Cache St) Gets rave reviews from families.

SOLITUDE FLOAT
TRIPS
Rafting

(📞 888-704-2800, 307-733-2871; www.solitude floattrips.com; Moose) Runs Deadman's Bar–Moose trips and sunrise trips, plus shorter 5-mile floats on Snake River.

TRIANGLE X FLOAT
TRIPS
Rafting

(📞 888-860-0005; www.jackson-hole-river -rafting.com) Offers dawn, daytime and sunset floats on Snake, plus a four-hour early evening float and cookout.

Sleeping

Budget lodgings in Jackson have gone the way of the stagecoach, but deals can be found during the shoulder seasons (from October 1 until the opening of ski season in late November and after spring snowmelt in early April until Memorial Day). For more lodging options, contact **Jackson Hole Central Reservations** (📞 888-838-6806; www.jacksonholewy.com), which has listings for the town of Jackson as well as for Teton Village.

CURTIS CANYON
CAMPGROUND
Campground $

(sites $12; 🕙 late May-Sep 30) Conveniently located, this popular 12-site campground, on gravel USFS Rd 30440 (off Elk Refuge Rd), sits 7 miles northeast of Jackson at 6900ft, with splendid views of the Tetons.

ALPINE HOUSE
B&B $$$

(📞 307-739-1570; www.alpinehouse.com; 285 N Glenwood St; d incl breakfast $185-225; @ 🛜) Two former Olympic skiers infused this eco-certified downtown home with sunny Scandinavian style and personal touches like great service and a cozy mountaineering library. Amenities include brushed cotton robes, down comforters, a shared Finnish sauna and an outdoor Jacuzzi.

RUSTY PARROT
LODGE AND SPA
Lodge $$$

(📞 888-739-1749; www.rustyparrot.com; 175 N Jackson St; r incl breakfast $360-595) With a collection of Remington sculptures and amazing Western art, this elegant lodge is excruciating in its luxury. Service is top-notch and rooms pamper with well-tended bedroom fireplaces and a plush teddy bear posed on the bed.

Wildflowers, Grand Teton

BUCKRAIL LODGE
Motel $$

(☎307-733-2079; www.buckraillodge.com; 110 E Karnes Ave; r $143; ❄ @ 🛜) Spacious and charming log-cabin-style rooms, this steal is centrally located, with hanging flower baskets and rockers outside each room and an outdoor Jacuzzi. With a sprawling lawn and wooden swing, it's a good bet for families.

INN ON THE CREEK
Inn $$$

(☎307-739-1565; www.innonthecreek.com; 295 N Millward St; r incl breakfast $179-599; @) Elegant and intimate, this stone inn offers nine handsome rooms.

PONY EXPRESS
Motel $$

(☎307-733-3835, www.ponyexpresswest.com; 1075 W Broadway; r $149; ❄ 🛜 🏊) A proud little motel hidden behind the gas station.

 Eating & Drinking

Jackson's fare boasts sophistication – even if that means garnishing your burger with a basil leaf. Pick up a free *Jackson Hole Dining Guide,* found in shops and hotel lobbies, for menus.

SNAKE RIVER
GRILL
Contemporary American $$$

(☎307-733-0557; 84 E Broadway; mains $21-52; ⏰from 5:30pm) With a roaring stone fireplace, an extensive wine list and snappy white linens, this grill creates notable American haute cuisine. The crispy pork falls off the bone, and grilled elk chops show earthy goodness.

RENDEZVOUS
BISTRO
Contemporary American $$$

(☎307-739-1100; www.rendezvousbistro.net; 380 S Broadway; mains $15-29; ⏰5:30-10pm) A sure bet for sophisticated bistro food. The happy-hour menu hits the mark with well-priced sophisticated small plates, like oyster shooters, foie gras with fig jam and a creamy chipotle corn dish that's out of this world.

SNAKE RIVER BREWING CO
Brewpub $$

(☎307-739-2337; 265 S Millward St; mains $6-15; ⏰11:30am-midnight) With an arsenal of 22 microbrews made on spot, some award-winning, it is no wonder that this is a favorite rendezvous spot. Happy hour is from 4pm to 6pm.

PICA'S MEXICAN TAQUERIA
Mexican $$

(1160 Alpine Lane; mains $7-15; ⏰11:30am-9pm Mon-Fri, 11am-4pm Sat & Sun) Cheap and supremely satisfying Mexican food.

DOG
Breakfast $

(25 S Glenwood; burrito $6; ⏰7am-2pm) Excellent giant breakfast burritos.

❶ Information

Jackson Hole & Greater Yellowstone Visitor Center (☎307-733-3316; www.jacksonholechamber.com; 532 N Cache St; ⏰8am-7pm summer, 8am-5pm winter) Provides information, books, restrooms, an ATM and a courtesy phone for free local calls.

❶ Getting There & Away

AIR Actually within Grand Teton National Park, **Jackson Hole Airport** (☎307-733-7682; www.jacksonholeairport.com; @) is 7 miles north of Jackson off US 26/89/191. It's always packed, and the airport yearns to expand but is limited by a 50-year agreement with the National Park Service (NPS).

SHUTTLE Alltrans' Jackson Hole Express (☎307-733-1719; www.jacksonholebus.com) goes daily from Jackson to Salt Lake City (one way $70, 5½ hours) and points in between. Reservations are recommended. Jackson pickup is at Exxon service station, on the corner of Hwy 89 S and S Park Loop Rd.

Yosemite National Park

Yosemite has a way with humans. Its beauty – which is utterly overwhelming – gave birth to the idea of setting aside land as a protected park. It inspired writers and artists like John Muir and Ansel Adams to produce their finest work. To the indigenous Miwok, it was a land of forest and river spirits and of thousands of years of ancestral history.

Today, Yosemite is a very different place, and some visitors find themselves bemoaning the crowds and commercialism in Yosemite Valley. But don't let the numbers deter you. Visit in spring, when the dogwoods are blooming and the waterfalls are roaring, and you'll find a Yosemite worthy of the same adoration bestowed upon it by its earliest admirers. In summer, take to the Tuolumne high country and, instead of crowds, you'll find alpine meadows, glacial lakes, granite peaks and Sierra breezes that will lull you into a blissful stupor.

Half Dome (p316) at sunset
DOUGLAS STEAKLEY / LONELY PLANET IMAGES ©

Yosemite Itineraries

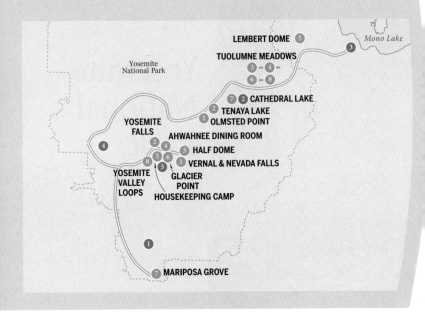

LEMBERT DOME ⑤

TUOLUMNE MEADOWS
③ – ④ –
⑥ – ⑧

Mono Lake ③

Yosemite
National Park

⑦ ② CATHEDRAL LAKE

② TENAYA LAKE
① OLMSTED POINT

YOSEMITE
FALLS

AHWAHNEE DINING ROOM

② ④ ③ HALF DOME
⑤ ⑥ ① VERNAL & NEVADA FALLS
⑧ ⑤
GLACIER
POINT
HOUSEKEEPING CAMP

YOSEMITE
VALLEY
LOOPS

④

① MARIPOSA GROVE ⑦

Two Days

① **Vernal & Nevada Falls** (p332) Climb the mist-moistened granite steps to Vernal Fall and continue up the trail to Nevada Fall. Both falls plunge nearly 600ft over granite cliffs.

② **Yosemite Falls** (p317) In the afternoon, walk to the base of North America's highest waterfall and marvel at the water tumbling 2425ft over the cliff above. With more time on your hands, you can hike the grueling switchbacks to the top of the falls.

③ **Half Dome** (p316) Walk over to the beach in front of Housekeeping Camp, on the Merced River, and watch the setting sun light up Half Dome's granite face.

④ **Ahwahnee Dining Room** (p346) Treat yourself to an exquisite meal beneath a 34ft-high beamed ceiling inside one of the national park's most beautiful lodges.

⑤ **Housekeeping Camp** (p342) Join the families who've been visiting this mishmash of tent cabins for generations and sleep beneath a canvas roof.

⑥ **Glacier Point** (p320) On day two, drive or hike up to Yosemite Valley's most famous viewpoint and take in the astonishing views.

⑦ **Mariposa Grove** (p321) Drive out to this grove of giant sequoias. The famous grove includes the Grizzly Giant, a 2700-year-old behemoth, and the California Tunnel Tree.

⑧ **Yosemite Valley Loops** (p329) Head back to Yosemite Valley and close the afternoon wandering this relaxing loop trail. The mostly paved paths meander for 12 miles around the valley, but you can walk sections of them for shorter strolls.

⮕ **THIS LEG: 60 MILES**

Four Days

1 **Olmsted Point** (p324) On day three, wake up early and drive up Hwy 120 (Tioga Rd) to Olmsted Point. With its mind-blowing views down Tenaya Canyon to the backside of Half Dome, it's one of the best viewpoints in the entire park.

2 **Tenaya Lake** (p323) Continue up Hwy 120 to this gorgeous lake, set in a bowl of granite and ringed with beaches. If it's warm enough, take a dip in its icy waters.

3 **Tuolumne Meadows Campground** (p341) Check into your campsite at this big but beautiful campground in the high country.

4 **Tuolumne Meadows** (p345) Wander leisurely around the largest alpine meadow in the Sierras while pondering the Cathedral Range above and the wildflowers at your feet.

5 **Lembert Dome** (p325) Hike to the top of Tuolumne's iconic granite dome. After wandering the massive slab of granite up top, take in the sunset over the meadow below.

6 **Tuolumne Meadows Lodge** (p348) On day four, wake up early and grab a 7am breakfast at the communal tables of this down-home lodge. The conversation is always tops.

7 **Cathedral Lake** (p334) Hike up to this spectacular alpine lake that sits within a massive glacial cirque beneath the towering spire of Cathedral Peak. Be sure to walk around the lake and take in the views.

8 **Tuolumne Meadows Grill** (p348) Close the day with a burger and fries, which you order from a window beside the Tuolumne Meadows Store. Devouring them in the parking lot out front is a Yosemite rite of passage.

THIS LEG: 57 MILES

Yosemite Highlights

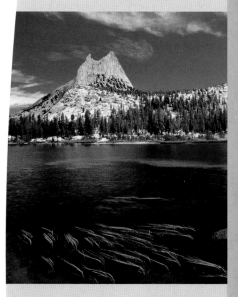

1 **Best Little-Known Falls: Chilnualna Falls** (p332) Too busy ogling falls in Yosemite Valley, most visitors miss this lovely spot.

2 **Best Hike: Cathedral Lakes** (p334) These glacial lakes give you the best of Yosemite's high country.

3 **Best Lunch: Whoa Nellie Deli** (p355) Gourmet food at a gas station? Yep. This roadside stop is worth the journey outside the park.

4 **Best Campground: Tamarack Flat** (p344) This serene campground seems worlds away from the mayhem of the Valley campgrounds.

5 **Best Adventure: Yosemite Mountaineering School** (p337) Learn to rock climb at this world-famous school of rock.

Cathedral Lakes (p334)
DOUGLAS STEAKLEY / LONELY PLANET IMAGES ©

Discover Yosemite

YOSEMITE NATIONAL PARK

The jaw-dropping head turner of USA national parks, Yosemite (yo-*sem*-it-tee) garners the devotion of all who enter. From the waterfall-striped granite walls buttressing emerald-green Yosemite Valley to the skyscraping giant sequoias catapulting into the air at Mariposa Grove, you feel a sense of awe and reverence that so much natural beauty exists in one place. It is a Unesco World Heritage Site that makes even Switzerland look like God's practice run. As far as we can tell, America's third-oldest national park has only one downside: the impact of the four million visitors annually who wend their way here. But lift your eyes ever so slightly above the crowds, seek out the park's serene corners or explore its miles of roadless wilderness and you'll feel your heart instantly moved by unrivaled splendors.

History

History unfolds here at varying rates of speed: the timelessness of the physical landscape; the presence of its first people, Native American tribes who still call it home; the decomposing ghost towns left behind by California's early settlers and miners; and the record-setting feats of modern rock climbers and mountaineers have all left their mark. The names you'll encounter as you explore – Tenaya, Whitney, Ahwahnee, Muir – tell the story of the park's peopled past.

During the gold rush era, conflict between miners and Native American tribespeople escalated until the Mariposa Battalion marched into Yosemite in 1851, finally forcing the capitulation of Chief Tenaya and his Ahwahneechee people. In 1855 San Francisco entrepreneur James Hutchings guided the first tourists to Yosemite Valley, and before long tourist inns and roads began springing up.

Alarmed by tourist development, conservationists petitioned Congress to protect the area – with success. In 1864 President Abraham Lincoln signed the Yosemite Grant, which ceded Yosemite Valley and the Mariposa Grove of giant

Bridalveil Fall (p318)
CAROL POLICH / LONELY PLANET IMAGES ©

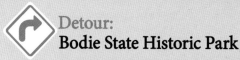

Detour:
Bodie State Historic Park

For a time warp back to the gold rush era, drive out to **Bodie** (☎760-647-6445; www.parks.ca.gov; Hwy 270; adult/child $7/5; ⏱9am-6pm Jun-Aug, 9am-3pm Sep-May), one of the West's most authentic and best preserved ghost towns. Gold was first discovered here in 1859, and within 20 years the place grew from a rough mining camp to an even rougher boomtown with a population of 10,000 and a reputation for unbridled lawlessness.

Fights and murders took place almost daily, the violence no doubt fueled by liquor dispensed in the town's 65 saloons, some of which did double duty as brothels, gambling halls or opium dens. The hills disgorged some $35 million worth of gold and silver in the 1870s and '80s, but when production plummeted, so did the population and eventually the town was abandoned to the elements.

About 200 weather-beaten buildings still sit frozen in time in this cold, barren and windswept valley heaped with tailing piles. The former Miners' Union Hall now houses a **museum and visitor center** (⏱9am-1 hour before park closes). Rangers conduct free general tours. In summertime, they also offer tours of the landscape and the cemetery; call ahead for details.

Bodie is about 13 miles east of Hwy 395 via Rte 270; the last 3 miles are unpaved. Although the park is open year-round, the road is usually closed in winter and early spring, so you'd have to don snowshoes or cross-country skis to get there.

sequoias to California as a state park. This landmark decision eventually paved the way for the US national park system, of which Yosemite became a part in 1890, thanks in part to efforts by conservationist John Muir.

The park's popularity as a tourist destination soared throughout the 20th century. By the mid-1970s, traffic and congestion had draped it in a smoggy haze, however. Today, national park managers struggle to balance the needs of visitors with the preservation of the natural beauty that draws them here in the first place.

When to Go

Although summer is jam-packed in Yosemite Valley, it's the only time of year when Tioga Pass and the Tuolumne high country are open. The rest of the year, they're covered in snow. May and June, when the snowmelt fills Sierra creeks and rivers to their fullest, is waterfall season and an outstanding time to visit the

Valley. Winter in Yosemite Valley is a truly magical experience.

When You Arrive

Entrance fees are valid for one week; keep your receipt if you plan to exit and enter the park during your stay. You'll receive a park map and the seasonal *Yosemite Guide* newspaper with information on activities, campgrounds, lodging, shuttles, visitor services and more.

Orientation

The most popular (and crowded) region of the park is Yosemite Valley, a relatively small sliver of the park at the heart of Yosemite. Along with spectacular scenery, you'll find the largest concentration of visitor services, including lodges, campgrounds, stores and restaurants.

About 55 miles northeast of the Valley, near the east end of Tioga Rd, is Tuolumne Meadows (elevation 8600ft), the focal point of Yosemite's high country

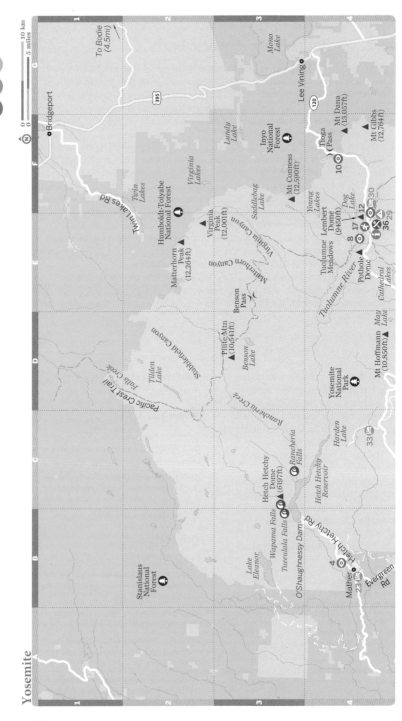

DISCOVER YOSEMITE YOSEMITE NATIONAL PARK

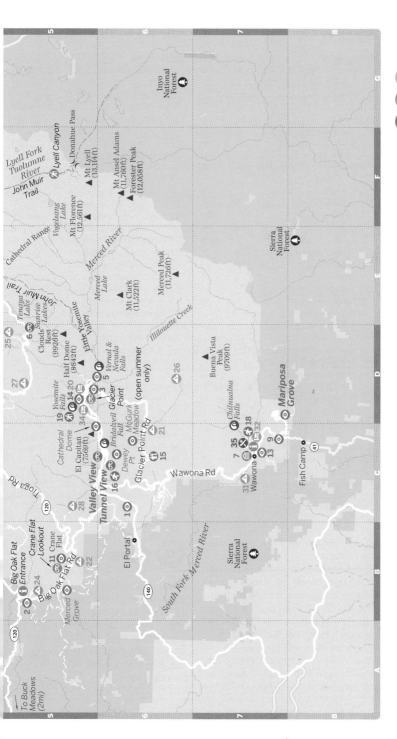

Inyo National Forest

Lyell Fork Tuolumne River
John Muir Trail

Donahue Pass

Lyell Canyon

Mt Lyell (13,114ft)

Mt Ansel Adams (11,760ft)
Forester Peak (12,058ft)

Mt Florence (12,561ft)

Vogelsang Lake

Cathedral Range

Merced River

Sierra National Forest

Merced Lake

Mt Clark (11,522ft)

Merced Peak (11,726ft)

Tenaya Lake

John Muir Trail

Clouds Rest (9926ft)

Sunrise Lakes

Half Dome (8842ft)

Little Yosemite Valley

Illilouette Creek

Yosemite Falls

Vernal & Nevada Falls

Buena Vista Peak (9709ft)

Cathedral Dome

El Capitan (7569ft)

Bridalveil Fall

Glacier Point

McGurk Meadow

Dewey Pt

Glacier Point Rd (open summer only)

Valley View

Tunnel View

Wawona Rd

Chilnualna Falls

Mariposa Grove

Tioga Rd

Big Oak Flat Entrance

Crane Flat Lookout

Crane Flat

Big Oak Flat Rd

Merced Grove

El Portal

Wawona

Fish Camp

Sierra National Forest

South Fork Merced River

To Buck Meadows (2mi)

313

Yosemite

and summertime home to a small hub of visitor services.

Crane Flat sits at the junction of Tioga and Big Oak Flat Rds. You'll find limited visitor services here and to the north at the park's Big Oak Flat Entrance. To the west, a short drive from the Big Oak Flat Entrance, is Hetch Hetchy Reservoir.

Thirty-six miles south of Yosemite Valley is Wawona, home to a historic hotel and other services for those visiting the giant sequoias of nearby Mariposa Grove.

 Sights

Yosemite Valley

Yosemite Valley is the park's crown jewel. It's home to what most people think of when they imagine Yosemite: Half Dome, Yosemite Falls, El Capitan, the Royal Arches – all those mind-boggling sights that draw over four million people to the park each year.

YOSEMITE VILLAGE Historic Center

Regardless of your feelings toward commercial development in one of the world's natural wonders, you'll probably wind up here at one point or another, as the village offers just about every amenity – from pizzas and ice cream to firewood and wilderness permits.

Commercial development began in the Valley almost as soon as the public became aware of the park. Quite a few hotels opened around the turn of the 20th century, and by the 1920s a collection of businesses – including hotels, photo studios, a dance pavilion and even a cinema – had risen just south of the river near Sentinel Bridge. This was the original Yosemite Village. By the 1950s, however, it was downgraded to the 'Old Village,' as businesses moved north of the river. The site of the Old Village has since reverted to meadow (look for road marker V20), though the chapel remains, albeit in a slightly different spot. A few buildings were moved to the Pioneer Yosemite History Center in Wawona, and Best's Studio was moved to the present-day village and eventually renamed the Ansel Adams Gallery.

YOSEMITE VALLEY
VISITOR CENTER Visitor Center

(✆ 209-372-0299; ⏱ 9am-7:30pm summer, shorter hours rest of year) Rarely do visitors spend much time in the Valley without a stop at the park's main visitor center. If you've never been to Yosemite, it's an excellent place to load up on information, ask questions, pick up maps, and check weather reports and trail conditions.

YOSEMITE THEATER Theater

(performances adult/child $8/4; ⏱ 9am-7:30pm summer, shorter hours rest of year) Behind the visitor center stands this theater, which screens the painfully dramatic, but beautifully photographed, 22-minute film *Spirit of Yosemite*. The movie starts every half-hour or so between 9:30am and 5:30pm, and offers a free, air-conditioned respite from the summer heat. On Sundays, the first screening is at noon.

In the evening, take your pick from a rotating cast of performers, including Wawona Hotel pianist Tom Bopp, the fascinating life and philosophy of John Muir as portrayed by actor Lee Stetson, and park ranger Shelton Johnson recreating the experiences of a buffalo soldier. There are also children's shows.

YOSEMITE MUSEUM Museum

(admission free; ⏱ 9am-4:30pm or 5pm) Next to the visitor center, the Yosemite Museum features a series of cultural and historical exhibits on the Valley's native Miwok–Ahwahneechee and Paiute people, covering the period from 1850 to today. It's worth a visit just to see the giant, intricately woven **Miwok–Paiute baskets** dating from the 1920s and '30s. The baskets were woven (some over periods as long as three years) by famous weavers such as Lucy Telles, Carrie Bethel and Alice Wilson. A basket by Telles, the largest in the collection, took four years to make. She later declined an offer by Robert Ripley (of *Ripley's Believe It or Not!*) to purchase the basket.

Behind the museum, a free, self-guided interpretive trail winds through the **Indian Village of Ahwahnee**, where you can peek inside full-size, reconstructed Miwok buildings, including a traditional roundhouse. The building and the sweat lodge behind it are used for ceremonial purposes by the Miwok.

ANSEL ADAMS GALLERY Gallery

(✆ 209-372-4413; www.anseladams.com; admission free; ⏱ 9am-6pm summer, to 5pm rest of year) Located east of the visitor center, this is a privately run art gallery that showcases a few Ansel Adams photographs and plenty of work by other contemporary artists. It also houses a great selection of art and ecology books and other gift items.

YOSEMITE ART
& EDUCATION CENTER Art Center

(✆ 209-372-1442; ⏱ 9am-noon & 1-4:30pm) In summer and fall, this center in Yosemite Village holds **art classes** (suggested donation $5; ⏱ 10am-2pm Tue-Sat Apr-Oct) that feature a different artist and medium (watercolor,

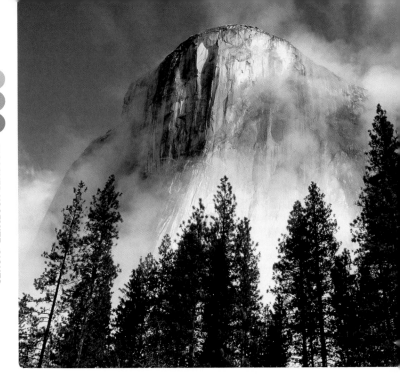

pastel, acrylic etc) each week. Classes usually take place outside, and students must bring their own supplies or purchase them at the center. No experience is necessary. Children under 12 must be accompanied by an adult. Sign up at least a day ahead to get a spot.

CURRY VILLAGE   Historic Center

Lying directly below Glacier Point, Curry Village is home to the Valley's second-biggest collection of restaurants, stores and overnight accommodations. Originally called Camp Curry, it was founded in 1899 by David and Jennie Curry as a place where everyday visitors could find 'a good bed and a clean napkin at every meal.' Starting with just a handful of tents, the camp quickly grew, thanks in large part to David Curry's entrepreneurial drive and booming personality.

More than 100 years later, the Camp Curry sign still hangs over the entrance, but this sprawling complex retains few traces of its turn-of-the-century roots. From the parking lot, a sea of tent cabins

fans out toward the base of Glacier Point, radiating from a central cluster of stores and snack bars – not exactly a vision of rustic glory. Still, it's pleasant to settle in for pizza and beer on the patio that faces the amphitheater out back. There's even a small cocktail bar.

HALF DOME   Rock Formation

Rising 8842ft above sea level, and nearly a mile above the Valley floor, Half Dome serves as the park's spiritual centerpiece and stands as one of the most glorious and monumental (not to mention best-known) domes on earth.

Its namesake shape is, in fact, an illusion. While from the Valley the dome appears to have been neatly sliced in half, from Glacier or Washburn Points you'll see that it's actually a thin ridge with a back slope nearly as steep as its fabled facade.

Half Dome towers above Tenaya Canyon, a classic, glacially carved gorge. Across this canyon rise **North Dome** and **Basket Dome**, examples of fully intact

Left: El Capitan (p318); **Below:** Campsite at dusk
(LEFT) DOUGLAS STEAKLEY / LONELY PLANET IMAGES ©; (BELOW) WOODS WHEATCROFT / LONELY PLANET IMAGES ©

domes. In contrast, Half Dome's north face shattered along cracks as a small glacier undercut the dome's base. The resulting cliff boasts a 93% vertical grade (the sheerest in North America), attracting climbers from around the world. Hikers with a permit can reach its summit from the Valley via a long series of trails. The final 45-degree stretch to the top was first made accessible by George Anderson, a local blacksmith who drilled holes in the granite in 1875 and installed a rope system (later replaced by the steel cables in use today).

YOSEMITE FALLS   Waterfall

One of the world's most dramatic natural spectacles, Yosemite Falls is a marvel to behold. Naturalist John Muir devoted entire pages to its changing personality, its myriad sounds, its movement with the wind and its transformations between the seasons. No matter where you are when you see it (and it regularly pops into view

from all over the Valley), the falls will stop you in your tracks.

In spring, when snowmelt gets Yosemite Creek really pumping, the sight is astounding. On those nights when the falls are full and the moon is bright, you might spot a 'moonbow.' In winter, as the spray freezes midair, an ice cone forms at the base of the falls.

Dropping 2425ft, Yosemite Falls is considered the tallest in North America. Some question that claim, however, as Yosemite Falls comprises three distinct tiers: towering 1430ft Upper Yosemite Fall, tumbling 675ft Middle Cascade and the final 320ft drop of Lower Yosemite Fall. The easternmost route of the loop trail is wheelchair-accessible.

To get to the base of Lower Yosemite Fall, get off at shuttle stop 6 (or park in the lot just north of Yosemite Lodge) and join the legions of visitors for the easy quarter-mile stroll. Note that in

Summiting Half Dome

For many visitors, the 17-mile round-tip trek to the top of Half Dome and back is the ultimate Yosemite hike. The stand-alone summit of this glacier-carved chunk of granite offers awesome 360-degree views, and peering down its sheer 2000ft north face offers a thrill you'll remember the rest of your life.

Ideally, Half Dome is best tackled in two days, allowing you more time to rest up and enjoy the gorgeous surroundings. But since it's so popular, you'll have a hard time getting a wilderness permit, which is required to sleep overnight at the limited legal camping areas on the route (the most popular being Little Yosemite Valley). If you do attempt this hike in a single day (and many people do), and have a coveted permit, be ready for some serious exertion. Get an early start (like 6am, though the shuttle doesn't start until 7am), pack lots of water and bring a flashlight, because you may wind up hiking home in the dark.

Climbing gear is unnecessary. Instead, hikers haul themselves up the final 650ft to the summit between two steel cables. Climbing this stretch is only allowed when the **cable route** is open, usually late May to mid-October, depending on snow conditions. If planning an early-season or late-season trip, confirm ahead that the cables are in place.

MANDATORY HALF DOME PERMITS

To stem lengthy lines (and increasingly dangerous congestion) on the vertiginous cables of Half Dome, the park now requires that all day hikers obtain an advance **permit** (☏ 877-444-6777; www.recreation.gov; fee per person $1.50) to climb the cables or go beyond the base of the subdome. Permits go on sale four months in advance, and the 300 available per day sell out almost immediately. Overnight hikers must have a wilderness permit (see p349).

midsummer, when the snowmelt has dissipated, both the upper and lower falls usually dry up – sometimes to a trickle, other times stopping altogether.

BRIDALVEIL FALL   Waterfall

At the southwest end of the Valley, Bridalveil Fall tumbles 620ft. The Ahwahneechee people call it Pohono (Spirit of the Puffing Wind), as gusts often blow the fall from side to side, even lifting water back up into the air. This waterfall usually runs year-round, though it's often reduced to a whisper by midsummer. Bring rain gear or expect to get soaked when the fall is heavy.

Park at the large lot where Wawona Rd (Hwy 41) meets Southside Dr. From the lot, it's a quarter-mile walk to the base of the fall. The path is paved, but probably too rough for wheelchairs, and there's a

somewhat steep climb at the very end. Avoid climbing on the slippery rocks at its base – no one likes a broken bone.

If you'd rather walk from the Valley, a trail (part of the Loop Trails) follows Southside Dr, beginning near the LeConte Memorial Lodge and running about 3.8 miles west to the falls.

EL CAPITAN   Rock Formation

At nearly 3600ft from base to summit, El Capitan ranks as one of the world's largest granite monoliths. Its sheer face makes it a world-class destination for experienced climbers, and one that wasn't 'conquered' until 1958. Since then, it's been inundated. Look closely and you'll probably spot climbers reckoning with El Cap's series of cracks and ledges, including the famous 'Nose.' At night, park along the road and dim your headlights; once your eyes adjust, you'll easily make out the pinpricks of headlamps dotting the rock face. Listen, too, for voices.

The road offers several good spots from which to ogle El Capitan. The Valley View turnout is one. For a wider view, try the pullout along Southside Dr just east of Bridalveil Fall. You can also park on Northside Dr, just below El Capitan, perhaps the best vantage point from which to see climbers, though you'll need binoculars for a really good view. Look for the haul bags first – they're bigger, more colorful and move around more than the climbers, making them easier to spot. The **Yosemite Climbing Association** (www.yosemiteclimbing.org) began an 'Ask-a-Climber' program in 2011, where it sets up a telescope at El Capitan Bridge for a few hours a day (mid-May through mid-October) and answers visitors' questions.

AHWAHNEE HOTEL   Historic Hotel
Almost as iconic as Half Dome itself, the elegant Ahwahnee Hotel has drawn well-heeled tourists through its towering doors since 1927. Of course, you needn't be wealthy in the least to partake of its many charms. In fact, a visit to Yosemite Valley is hardly complete without a stroll through the **Great Lounge** (aka the lobby), which is handsomely decorated with leaded glass, sculpted tiles, Native American rugs and Turkish kilims. You can relax on the plush but aging couches and stare out the 10 floor-to-ceiling windows, wander into the **Solarium**, or send the kids into the walk-in fireplace (no longer in use) for a photo. You can even sneak up the back stairs for a peek into the private **Tudor Room**, which has excellent views over the Great Lounge.

The Ahwahnee was built on the site of a former Ahwahnee–Miwok village. In order to promote the relatively young national park, National Park Service (NPS) director Stephen Mather dreamed up the idea of a majestic hotel to attract wealthy guests. The site was chosen for its exposure to the sun and its views of Half Dome, Yosemite Falls and Glacier Point. The hotel was designed by American architect Gilbert Stanley Underwood, who also designed Zion Lodge, Bryce Canyon Lodge and Grand Canyon North Rim Lodge. If the Ahwahnee's lobby looks familiar, even if you have never been there, perhaps it's because it inspired the lobby of the Overlook Hotel, the ill-fated inn from Stanley Kubrick's *The Shining*.

YOSEMITE VALLEY CHAPEL   Church
(www.yosemitevalleychapel.org) Built in 1879, this chapel is Yosemite's oldest structure that still remains in use. The church originally stood near the base of Four Mile Trail, and in 1901 was moved about a

Ansel Adams Gallery (p315)
SPRING IMAGES / ALAMY ©

mile to its present site. Sunday morning services are nondenominational.

LECONTE MEMORIAL LODGE
Historic Building

(☎209-372-4542; www.sierraclub.org/ education/leconte; ⊗10am-4pm Wed-Sun May-Sep) Built by the Sierra Club in 1903, this small, rustic granite-and-wood lodge offers a glimpse into a relatively unknown chapter of California architecture. Designed by Berkeley architect John White, the building sits firmly within a style known as the First Bay Tradition, a movement that was intimately linked with the 20th-century Arts and Crafts Movement. The First Bay Tradition placed great importance on reflecting the natural world and insisted each work of architecture be specific to its surroundings. The Sierra Club built the lodge in honor of Joseph LeConte (1823–1901), a University of California Berkeley geologist and a cofounder of the Sierra Club.

NATURE CENTER AT HAPPY ISLES
Nature Center

(⊗9:30am-4pm May-Sep; 🚼) Happy Isles lies at the Valley's southeast end, where the Merced River courses around two small islands. The area is a popular spot for picnics, swimming and short strolls in the woods. It also marks the start of the John Muir Trail and Mist Trail, where hikers begin treks to Vernal Fall, Nevada Fall, and Half Dome.

On the site of a former fish hatchery, the nature center features great hands-on exhibits that will enthrall kids and adults alike. Displays explain the differences between the park's various pinecones, rocks, animal tracks and (everyone's favorite subject) scat. Out back, don't miss an exhibit on the 1996 rock fall, when an 80,000-ton rock slab plunged 2000ft to the nearby valley floor, killing a man, felling about 1000 trees and seriously damaging the nature center.

Happy Isles is about a mile from Curry Village. The road is closed to cars (except those with disabled placards); instead, reach it by either an easy walk, bike ride or the free shuttle bus.

GLACIER POINT
Lookout

If you drove up here, the views from 7214ft Glacier Point can make you feel like you cheated somehow – a huge array

Sentinel Dome (p331)

JOHN ELK III / LONELY PLANET IMAGES ©

of superstar sights present themselves without any physical effort. A quick mosey up from the parking lot and you'll find the entire eastern Yosemite Valley spread out before you, from Yosemite Falls to Half Dome, as well as the distant peaks that ring Tuolumne Meadows. Half Dome looms practically at eye level, and if you look closely you can spot ant-sized hikers on its summit.

To the left of Half Dome lies the glacially carved Tenaya Canyon, and to its right are the wavy white ribbons of Nevada and Vernal Falls. On the Valley floor, the Merced River snakes through green meadows and groves of trees. Sidle up to the railing, hold on tight and peer 3200ft straight down at Curry Village. Basket Dome and North Dome rise to the north of the Valley, and Liberty Cap and the Clark Range can be seen to the right of Half Dome.

Almost from the park's inception, Glacier Point has been a popular destination. It used to be that getting up here was a major undertaking. That changed once the Four Mile Trail opened in 1872. A wagon road to the point was completed in 1882, and the current Glacier Point Rd was built in 1936.

At the tip of the point is **Overhanging Rock**, a huge granite slab protruding from the cliff edge like an outstretched tongue, defying gravity and once providing a scenic stage for daredevil extroverts. Through the years, many famous photos have been taken of folks performing handstands, high kicks and other wacky stunts on the rock. The precipice is now off-limits.

Wawona

Wawona, Yosemite's historical center, was home to the park's first headquarters and tourist facilities. The latter was a simple wayside station run by Galen Clark, who homesteaded in Wawona in 1856. A decade later, Clark was appointed state guardian of the Yosemite Grant, which protected Yosemite Valley and the Mariposa Grove. In 1875 he sold his lodge to the Washburn brothers, who built what's known today as the Wawona Hotel.

The Washburns also renamed the area Wawona – thought to be the local Native American word for 'big trees.'

Wawona lies on Hwy 41 (Wawona Rd), 4 miles north of the park's South Entrance, which is about 63 miles north of Fresno. Yosemite Valley is a 27-mile drive north.

WAWONA HOTEL   Historic Building
A blend of Victorian elegance and utilitarian New England charm, the Wawona Hotel is the commercial hub of the area. The unassuming white wooden building sits behind a large, manicured green lawn and a fountain inhabited by very vocal frogs.

Across Hwy 41, there's the Wawona Golf Course and the expansive Wawona Meadow, which doubled as the local airport in the early 20th century. To the north is the Pioneer Yosemite History Center, which includes some of the park's oldest buildings, relocated from various points including 'Old Yosemite Village.' The center also features a nice collection of horse-drawn stagecoaches and buggies that brought early tourists to Yosemite.

WAWONA INFORMATION STATION   Visitor Center
(☎ 209-375-9531; ⏰ 8:30am-5pm late May-early Oct) Wawona's visitor center is located inside Hill's Studio, a historic 1886 building (it was the studio of landscape painter Thomas Hill) adjacent to the Wawona Hotel. Small exhibits in the studio include reproductions of his work. It also doubles as the area's wilderness center and issues wilderness permits.

MARIPOSA GROVE   Forest
Some 6 miles southeast of Wawona stands the Mariposa Grove of giant sequoias, the park's largest sequoia grove. With their massive stature and multi-millennium maturity, the chunky high-rise sequoias will make you feel rather insignificant. There are approximately 500 mature trees towering over 250 acres, with a number of mammoths right in the parking lot. A few walking trails

wind through this very popular grove, and you can usually have a more solitary experience if you come during the early evening in summer or anytime outside of summer. The Mariposa Grove Rd closes to cars from about November to April, but you can always hike in (2 miles, 500ft of elevation gain) and experience it in its quiet hibernation.

Walk a half-mile up to the 2700-year-old **Grizzly Giant**, a bloated beast of a tree with branches that are bigger in circumference than most of the pines trees in this forest. The walk-through **California Tunnel Tree** is close by, and the favored spot for 'I visited the tall forest' photos. Incredibly, this tree continues to survive, even though its huge portal was hacked out back in 1895. The more famous **Fallen Wawona Tunnel Tree**, however, fell over in a heap in 1969 – its 10ft-high hole gouged from a fire scar in 1881. Other notable specimens include the **Telescope Tree** and the **Clothespin Tree**. Three miles from the parking lot, the wide-open overlook at **Wawona Point** (6810ft) takes in the entire area. It's about a mile round-trip from the Fallen Wawona Tunnel Tree.

The upper grove is home to the **Mariposa Grove Museum** (⊙10am-4pm May-Sep), a small building further dwarfed by the scale of the surrounding trees. The museum has exhibits on sequoia ecology.

Parking can be very limited, so come early or late, or take the free shuttle bus from the Wawona Store or the park entrance. You can also explore the grove on a one-hour guided tour aboard a noisy open-air **tram** (🖉209-375-1621; adult/child $25/18; ⊙usually May-Sep) that leaves from the parking lot.

PIONEER YOSEMITE HISTORY CENTER Historic Site
(admission free; ⊙24hr) In the 1960s, a large number of Yosemite's historic wooden buildings – including some from the original site of Yosemite Village – were transferred to the Pioneer Yosemite History Center, forming a period village along the South Fork of the Merced River just north of the Wawona Hotel. Mostly furnished, the buildings include a Wells Fargo office, a jail and the Hodgdon homestead cabin. An evocative covered bridge crosses the river, and a barn south of the river holds a collection of vintage stagecoaches. In a reminder of daffy past land-management practices, there's also a 'mosquito wagon' that once sprayed oil on Tuolumne Meadows ponds to control bugs!

Big Oak Flat Road & Tioga Road

Those arriving on Hwy 120 first encounter this section of the park. While not the most spectacular part of Yosemite, it has a steady flow of visitors. Though many just pass through, the campgrounds at Hodgdon Meadow and Crane Flat keep the area humming with people.

Big Oak Flat Rd was the second route into the park, completed in 1874, just a month after Coulterville Rd. Both were toll roads. Today, Big Oak Flat Rd (Hwy 120) follows a modified route into the Valley, though a portion of the old road remains open to cyclists and hikers headed for **Tuolumne Grove**, a smaller, less visited grove of giant sequoias (compared to the Mariposa Grove). In winter the road is popular with cross-country skiers.

Going east on Big Oak Flat Rd past the Big Oak Flat Entrance, you'll find the **Big Oak Flat Information Station** (🖉209-379-1899; ⊙8am-5pm May-Sep). It serves as a mini visitor center, with a good variety of books, maps and postcards for sale.

At **Crane Flat**, the **Crane Flat Service Station & General Store** (⊙8am-8pm summer, approx 9am-5pm winter) sells firewood, ice, beer and a smattering of groceries and last-minute camping supplies. Perhaps most importantly, it also has decent fresh coffee. Hurrah!

From the entrance station, Big Oak Flat Rd descends southeast into the Valley, passing through several tunnels that offer great overlooks of the Merced River Canyon.

JOHN ELK III / LONELY PLANET IMAGES ©

DISCOVER YOSEMITE SIGHTS

CRANE FLAT FIRE LOOKOUT   Lookout
It's easy to miss the turnoff for this fire lookout, so keep your eyes peeled to the north between Crane Flat campground and the Merced Grove parking area. At the top of a 1.5-mile spur road (RVs and trailers should not attempt the climb), a short walk from the parking area leads to the lookout, offering fantastic 360-degree views of the park, including the jagged peaks of the Clark Range to the south and (on cloudless days) the San Joaquin Valley to the west. The historic 1931 building is open to the public and contains an Osborne Firefinder, the circular map and plotting device used to pinpoint fires. The adjacent building houses the park's crack search-and-rescue and fire crews, and a working heliport sits a bit lower down.

Along Tioga Road

The only road that bisects the park is Tioga Rd, a 56-mile scenic highway that runs between Crane Flat in the west (starting from Crane Flat junction) and Hwy 395 at Lee Vining, about 12 miles east of Tioga Pass, the park's eastern-most gate. Along the way it traverses a superb High Sierra landscape. Be prepared to pull over regularly to gawk at sights such as glorious Tenaya Lake, mighty Clouds Rest and Half Dome from Olmsted Point.

TENAYA LAKE   Lake
Just east of Olmsted Point, Tenaya Lake (8150ft) takes its name from Chief Tenaya, the Ahwahneechee chief who aided white soldiers, only to be driven from the land by white militias in the early 1850s. Tenaya allegedly protested use of his name, pointing out that the lake already had a name – Pywiack, or 'Lake of Shining Rocks,' for the polished granite that surrounds it. The lake's shiny blue surface looks absolutely stunning framed by thick stands of pine and a series of smooth granite cliffs and domes. Dominating its north side is **Polly Dome** (9806ft). The face nearest the lake is known as **Stately Pleasure Dome**, a popular spot with climbers – you may see them working their way up from the road. Sloping up from the lake's south shore are Tenaya Peak (10,301ft) and Tresidder Peak (10,600ft).

323

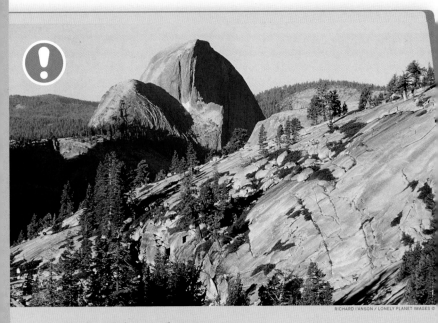

RICHARD I'ANSON / LONELY PLANET IMAGES ©

Don't Miss **Olmsted Point**

This 'honey hit the brakes!' viewpoint is a lunar landscape of glaciated granite with a stunning view down Tenaya Canyon to the backside of Half Dome. Midway between the May Lake turnoff and Tenaya Lake, the point was named for Frederick Law Olmsted (1822–1903), who was appointed chairman of the first board of commissioners to manage the newly established Yosemite Grant in 1864. Olmsted also helped to design Central Park in New York City and did some landscaping for the University of California and Stanford University.

Looming over the canyon's eastern side is 9926ft **Clouds Rest**, a massive mountain comprising the largest exposed chunk of granite in Yosemite. As its name implies, clouds often settle atop the peak. Rising 4500ft above Tenaya Creek, it makes a strenuous but rewarding day hike.

To experience an even better view, and without the company of your awestruck compatriots, stroll a quarter-mile down to the overlook, where you can get past the tree cover and see even deeper into the canyon. Because of extreme avalanche hazards, Olmsted Point is the last area of Hwy 120 to be plowed before the road opens.

Tuolumne Meadows

Arriving at Tuolumne (too-*ahl*-uh-mee) Meadows after the drive up from the Valley is like stepping into another world, even though the two areas are only about 55 miles apart. Instead of being surrounded by waterfalls and sheer granite walls, you emerge in a subalpine wonderland marked by jagged peaks, smooth granite domes, brilliant blue lakes and the meadows' lush grasses and wildflowers. The flowers, which peak in July, are truly a highlight of any visit to Yosemite.

Flowing from the Sierra Crest, the Lyell and Dana Forks of the Tuolumne River – not to mention creeks such as Budd, Unicorn and Delaney – all converge at Tuolumne Meadows (8600ft elevation). At 2.5 miles long, the main flat cradles the Sierra's largest subalpine meadow. The surrounding peaks and domes make Tuolumne a paradise for climbers and hikers, with trails stretching in all directions.

Lying deep in the high country of the Sierra, the Tuolumne Meadows region enjoys a brief but glorious summer and, depending on weather conditions, is only accessible roughly between June and November. Despite the short season, Tuolumne is far quieter than the Valley, although the area around the store, campground and visitor center can get crowded, especially on midsummer weekends. Many hiking trails, such as Dog Lake, are also well traveled, but with a little effort you'll quickly find solitude.

TUOLUMNE MEADOWS
VISITOR CENTER   Visitor Center
(209-372-0263; 9am-6pm Jul & Aug, to 5pm spring & fall) Rangers answer questions, sell books and hiking maps, and have helpful handouts describing local trails. There are a few good displays that explain common glacial features. Especially handy is the wildflower display, which will help you identify what you see on your hikes. It also has a wilderness center for backcountry permits.

MAIN MEADOW   Meadow
Stretching nearly 3 miles from Pothole Dome in the west to Lembert Dome in the east, Tuolumne's main meadow is a beautiful sight to behold, especially during sunset, when golden light ripples across the green grass and lashes up the sides of distant peaks into the still blue sky. Grab a fishing pole and dip into the gently rolling **Tuolumne River** as the sunlight drifts away, or just find a quiet spot to sit and stare at the landscape as the mood shifts and the colors shimmer.

The meadow is a perfect place for quiet contemplation, but there's actually a lot of activity going on here. Blanketed in snow for most of the year, the meadow explodes to life in summer, when the wildflowers, taking full advantage of the short growing season, fill the grassy expanse with color. For an explanation of what's happening beneath the meadow's deceptively still surface, check out the interpretive signs that line the dirt road between the stables and Soda Springs.

POTHOLE DOME   Rock Formation
Pothole Dome marks the west end of Tuolumne Meadows. It's small by Yosemite standards, but the short, 200ft climb to the top offers great views of the meadows and surrounding peaks – especially, of course, at sunset. Park along Tioga Rd, then follow the trail around the dome's west side and up to its modest summit. It's a fairly quick trip and well worth the effort.

LEMBERT DOME   Rock Formation
Prominently marking the eastern end of the main meadow, Lembert Dome towers about 800ft above the Tuolumne River. Its summit, which chalks in at 9450ft above sea level, is easily one of the finest places to watch the sunset in Yosemite. Its steep western face is a de facto granite playground for everyone from kids (who stick around the gently sloping bottom) to climbers (who rope up and head to the top). Nonclimbers can reach the summit by hiking up the backside. The dome was named for 19th-century shepherd Jean-Baptiste Lembert, who homesteaded in Tuolumne Meadows.

SODA SPRINGS & PARSONS
MEMORIAL LODGE   Historic Site
Above the northern shore of the Tuolumne River, carbonated mineral water burbles silently out of Soda Springs, a small natural spring that turns its surroundings into a cluster of mineral-crusted, rust-red puddles. People (and animals) used to drink the stuff, though the park service now discourages the practice due to possible surface contamination – no big deal as it's not exactly an appealing method for quenching your thirst anyway.

Nearby stands Parsons Memorial Lodge, a simple but beautifully rugged cabin built in 1915 from local granite. It initially served as a Sierra Club meeting room and was named for Edward Taylor Parsons (1861–1914), an adventurer and active Sierra Club member who helped found the club's outings program. Today, it opens as a shelter during thunderstorms (there's a huge fireplace inside), as well as for special events, ranger talks and other programs. See *Yosemite Guide* for the current schedule.

CATHEDRAL RANGE   Mountain Range
Dominating the views to the south of Tuolumne Meadows, the jagged Cathedral Range runs roughly northwest from the Sierra Crest, marking the divide between the Tuolumne and Merced Rivers. Its granite pinnacles are immediately striking, in particular **Cathedral Peak** (10,911ft), visible from numerous spots in the region, including along Tioga Rd. At certain angles, its summit appears to be a near-perfect pinpoint, though in reality it's a craggy, double-pronged affair. Other mountains in the range include Tresidder Peak, Echo Peaks, the Matthes Crest and Unicorn Peak (10,823ft), another stand-out with a horn-shaped protuberance, just east of Cathedral Peak.

TIOGA PASS   Scenic Road
East of Tuolumne Meadows, Tioga Rd (Hwy 120) climbs steadily toward Tioga Pass, which at 9945ft is the highest auto route over the Sierra. The short ride by car or free shuttle bus from Tuolumne Meadows takes you across dramatic, wide-open spaces – a stretch of stark, windswept countryside near the timberline. You'll notice a temperature drop and, most likely, widespread patches of snow.

Tioga Rd parallels the Dana Fork of the Tuolumne River, then turns north, where it borders the beautiful Dana Meadows all the way to Tioga Pass. To the east you'll see great views of Mt Gibbs (12,764ft) and 13,053ft Mt Dana, the park's second-highest peak after Mt Lyell (13,114ft).

Hetch Hetchy

No developed part of the park feels as re-moved from the rest of the park as Hetch Hetchy. Despite the fact that 'Hetchy's' soaring waterfalls, granite domes and sheer cliffs rival its more glamorous counterparts in Yosemite Valley, Hetch Hetchy receives but a fraction of the vis-itors that the Valley does. This is mainly because Hetch Hetchy Valley is filled with water – the Hetch Hetchy Reservoir – and because, save for a couple of drinking fountains, a parking lot and a backpacker

Tuolumne Meadows (p324)

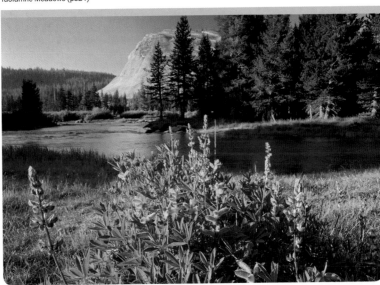

Dam!

Hetch Hetchy Valley was filled with water only after a long political and environmental battle that lasted a dozen years during the early 20th century. Despite the best efforts of John Muir, who led the fight against it, the US Congress approved the 1913 *Raker Act*, which allowed the city of San Francisco to construct O'Shaughnessy Dam in the Hetch Hetchy Valley. This blocked the Tuolumne River and created Hetch Hetchy Reservoir. Muir's spirit was crushed, and he died a year later, supposedly of a broken heart.

campground, there are practically no visitor services. Hetch Hetchy is a magical place, and is definitely worth the detour north from the much busier Big Oak Flat Entrance.

Hetch Hetchy is a 40-mile drive from Yosemite Valley. From the park's Big Oak Flat Entrance, drive a mile or two west on Hwy 120 and look for the signed turnoff to Hetch Hetchy along Evergreen Rd; turn right (north), drive 8 miles to Mather and turn right (east) on Hetch Hetchy Rd. The **Hetch Hetchy Entrance** (☏209-379-1922; ⊘7am-9pm summer, 8am-5pm winter) is just a mile beyond the junction; here backpackers can pick up wilderness permit and rent bear canisters.

The road to Hetch Hetchy is only open during daylight hours – approximately 7am to 9pm in summer, 8am to 7pm in spring and fall, and 8am to 5pm in winter.

 **Activities**

Driving Tours

Driving is hardly the proper way to see Yosemite Valley (unless you enjoy craning your neck in traffic to see the sights otherwise blocked by your roof), but it's an undeniably superb way to experience the high country – and beyond – via the spectacular Tioga Rd. This is the only road that bisects the park between its eastern and western borders. All park roads, however, are lined with beautiful scenery, so really you can't go wrong. If you're going to drive within Yosemite Valley, try to avoid doing it on weekends.

YOSEMITE VALLEY   Scenic Drive

The only driving route in Yosemite Valley takes you past the Valley's classic sights and viewpoints, including **Bridalveil Fall** and **Yosemite Falls**. Most of this route is covered by the free Valley and El Capitan shuttles (the latter goes as far west as the El Capitan Bridge), so consider parking the car, freeing up your hands, and doing this by public transport.

The 12.5-mile loop follows the only two roads in and out of Yosemite Valley: **Northside Drive** and **Southside Drive**. Each is (mostly) one way and, as their names suggest, they sit on either side of the Merced River. Without traffic, you can easily drive the loop in less than an hour, but budget more time as you'll want to stop frequently. Despite the fact that the park service has tried to limit the number of cars in the Valley, it remains a popular driving tour.

TIOGA ROAD TO MONO LAKE   Scenic Drive

Get ready to ascend over 3500ft as you drive over dizzying Tioga Pass (elevation 9945ft) before zigzagging down the steep eastern side to surreal Mono Lake. Without a doubt, this 60-mile round-trip journey is one of California's ultimate drives.

From Crane Flat, the tour follows Tioga Rd up through the trees to **Olmsted Point**, **Tenaya Lake** and **Tuolumne Meadows**. It then flanks beautiful **Dana**

JOHN ELK III / LONELY PLANET IMAGES ©

Don't Miss **Two Classic Roadside Views**

For two of the very best views over Yosemite Valley, you don't even have to stroll far from your car. The best all-around photo op of the Valley can be had from **Tunnel View**, a large, busy parking lot and viewpoint at the east end of Wawona Tunnel, on Hwy 41. It's just a short drive from the Valley floor. The vista encompasses most of the Valley's greatest hits: El Capitan on the left, Bridalveil Fall on the right, the green Valley floor below, and glorious Half Dome front and center. This viewpoint is often mistakenly called Inspiration Point. That point was on an old park road and is now reachable via a steep hike from the Tunnel View parking lot.

The second view, known as **Valley View**, is a good one to hit on your way out. It offers a bottom-up (rather than top-down) view of the Valley and is a lovely spot to dip your toes in the Merced River and bid farewell to sights like Bridalveil Fall, Cathedral Rocks and El Capitan. Look carefully to spot the tip-top of Half Dome in the distance. As you head west out of the Valley on Northside Dr, look for the Valley View turnout (roadside marker V11), just over a mile past El Capitan Meadow. Yosemite Valley as seen from Tunnel View

Meadows before crossing the dizzying **Tioga Pass**. You can either turn around here or, if you have enough time, continue down the precipitous eastern side of the Sierra Crest to the town of Lee Vining and beautiful Mono Lake. The scenery along this route – the spiky peaks of the Cathedral Range, the granite domes around Tuolumne Meadows, the stunted subalpine forests, the meandering creeks and shimmering lakes – will give you whiplash harder than driving into a giant sequoia.

Tioga Rd is only open during summer and fall, usually from mid-June to late October. From Yosemite Valley, it's only about 1½ hours to Tuolumne Meadows, but that's not including stops for views (Olmsted Point is a must), hikes or lunch at the Tuolumne Meadows Grill. From Tioga Pass, it's another half-hour east to Hwy 395 and Mono Lake. While you could easily make the drive in about two hours, it's best to take all day.

WAWONA ROAD
& GLACIER POINT ROAD   Scenic Drive

Some of the best park views are along this 52-mile route south of Yosemite Valley. The Tunnel View and Glacier Point overlooks give excellent Valley views from different angles.

Start your expedition from the east side of the **Wawona Tunnel** in the spectacular pull-off point of **Tunnel View**. No, you will not be staring slack-jawed at a dark traffic structure, but at the magnificent landscape to the east. Best in the spring when snowmelt has it gushing, 620ft **Bridalveil Fall** leaps off a plateau. The sheer wall of El Capitan rises to the north side of the Valley, and Half Dome pops out in the background past deep green forest.

Buckle up and proceed west through Wawona Tunnel, the longest one in the park at almost a mile. Two miles after your return to daylight, you approach **Turtleback Dome**, a slab of exfoliating granite that looks like it's been sliced horizontally into pieces of crumbling bread.

In six more miles you'll come to the **Chinquapin** junction; turn left onto Glacier Point Rd to begin the forested 16-mile stretch to Glacier Point. In 2 miles is the wide western view of **Merced Canyon**, which descends 4500ft below you. The **Badger Pass Ski Area** appears in three more miles, though the lifts and lodge will be deserted in warm weather. In winter, the road is closed beyond here. Pass Bridalveil Creek campground, with nearby views of the Clark Range to the east.

The road turns abruptly north near **Mono Meadow**, reaching **Pothole Meadows**, where strangely small bowls of water collect during wet months. A quarter-mile more lands you at **Sentinel Dome** (8122ft), one of the park's easiest-to-hike granite domes. Switchbacks descend through red fir forest to **Washburn Point**, which has views *almost* as good as those from Glacier Point.

Winding through into Glacier Point, the peak of **Half Dome** parades before you.

Retrace your route back to the Chinquapin junction, and turn left to continue south on the Wawona Rd (Hwy 41). The final 12-mile stretch passes the turnoff for Yosemite West, a private community that's accessible only through the park, and crosses the South Fork of the Merced River before reaching the **Wawona Hotel**, a landmark lodging dating from 1879. Allow at least two hours.

Hiking

There is no better way – and often no other way – to see Yosemite than by hiking into it. It's impossible to say one area of the park is better for hiking than another. Really, it depends on the hiker's ability and interests and the time of year. For example, the vast wilderness surrounding Tuolumne Meadows is a hikers' mecca, but it's accessible only when Tioga Rd is open (usually late May through mid-November). Many of Yosemite's easiest hikes – some might call them strolls – are along the mostly flat floor of Yosemite Valley. It's a lovely place to wander, especially in the evenings, when the day-trippers are gone and Half Dome glows against the sunset. Nearly all day hikes *up* from Yosemite Valley require some ascent.

YOSEMITE VALLEY LOOPS   Hiking

(Yosemite Valley) Whether you want to plot a route from your campsite to the nearest hot shower, or take in the views from the meadows and bridges around the valley floor, the vaguely defined loop trails are an undeniably great way to get to know Yosemite Valley. Parts are even wheelchair- and stroller-friendly, and they connect the valley's most important historic and natural features. In some places the trail joins the road, in other places it peters out only to reappear later. Generally, it follows alongside Northside and Southside Drives, and it's nearly impossible to get lost.

For the ambitious, a well-marked path leads up and down the entire Valley, but it's easily broken into segments, making the journey manageable for just about any level of hiker.

You can walk a 2.6-mile loop around the eastern end of the Valley by starting at **Curry Village**. From here, head east along the edge of the day-use parking area, with the tent cabins on your right. When you hit the shuttle road, turn right and follow the road into and through the trailhead parking area. Southeast of the parking lot, two trails lead to **Happy Isles**: one skirts the shuttle road, and another leads into the trees and across a delicate meadow area known as **The Fen**. After visiting the Nature Center at Happy Isles, cross the Merced River and follow the trail alongside the road, veering left when you can to stay along the banks of the river. Just before you reach the **stables**, head left (southwest) on the road across the river, past the entrances to Lower and Upper Pines Campgrounds. Then look for the sign pointing to Curry Village.

Further removed from the Valley's central commercial district, the 6.5-mile loop on the west end of the Valley passes good swimming spots on the Merced and offers fabulous views of El Capitan and Bridalveil Fall. The trail basically follows Northside and Southside Drs between the base of El Capitan and **Pohono Bridge**, the westernmost bridge over the Merced River.

MIRROR LAKE
Hiking

(Yosemite Valley) Formed when a rockfall dammed a section of Tenaya Creek, Mirror Lake has been slowly reverting to 'Mirror Meadow' ever since the park service stopped dredging it in 1971. Only folks who visit in spring and early summer get the splendid sight that Mirror Lake is named for: Mt Watkins and Half Dome reflected on its tranquil surface.

By midsummer, it's just Tenaya Creek, and by fall, the creek has sometimes dried up altogether. Spring is also a marvelous time to visit for other reasons: the dogwoods are in full bloom and Tenaya Creek becomes a lively torrent as you venture further up the canyon. The Ahwahneechee called Mirror Lake Ahwiyah, meaning 'quiet water.'

From the **Mirror Lake Trailhead**, near shuttle stop 17, follow the Mirror Lake road to **Tenaya Bridge**. Cross Tenaya Creek and follow the partially paved trail 0.9 miles to **Mirror Lake**, where interpretive signs explain the area's natural history. From here you can return to the shuttle stop along the Mirror Lake road (for the sake of looping), or journey up Tenaya Canyon for a little solitude.

INSPIRATION POINT
Hiking

(Yosemite Valley) Some of the best vistas in all Yosemite are granted to those who hike the steep, 1.3-mile trail up to this classic viewpoint. Inspiration Point used to be a viewpoint along an old road into Yosemite Valley. The

Mist Trail (p332), Vernal Fall

roadbed still exists, but this hike (actually the western end of the Pohono Trail) is now the only way to reach the point. You'll start by climbing a series of switchbacks from the upper **Tunnel View parking lot** (which is on Hwy 41 immediately east of the Wawona Tunnel). Almost immediately the view improves, with fewer trees and no bus tourists to battle for camera positions. Short spur trails lead to open viewpoints.

The climb is steep and steady but, thankfully, fairly short. The view from Inspiration Point itself, a large open area, isn't as spectacular as what you get on the way up, but it's a worthy destination nonetheless, quiet and perfect for a picnic. If you've got the energy, continue up the trail 2.5 miles further to **Stanford Point** and even on to **Crocker Point**. Both offer epic views. The Inspiration Point trail is often doable in winter. The full 2.6-mile round-trip hike takes 1½ to 2½ hours.

YOSEMITE FALLS   Hiking

(Yosemite Valley) This classic hike along one of the park's oldest trails leads from the Valley floor to the top of the falls. The stiff ascent (and equivalent descent) makes it a real thigh-burning, knee-busting haul. The full 6.8-mile trek takes five to six hours.

The heart-stopping views from atop Upper Yosemite Fall will make you quickly forget any pain endured on the hike up. If it seems a bit much, you can always hike just the first mile (and 1000 vertical feet) to **Columbia Rock** (5031ft), a justifiably classic viewpoint.

From the northeastern side of Camp 4, the trail begins at the **Yosemite Falls Trailhead** and immediately starts in on the four dozen short switchbacks that zigzag up a talus slope through canyon live oaks. After 0.8 miles, the grade eases as the trail follows more switchbacks east to Columbia Rock. Some people stop here.

In another 0.4 miles, the trail approaches the top of **Lower Yosemite Fall**, where breezes may shower you with a fine, cooling mist. After admiring the view of Upper Yosemite Fall, brace yourself for the numerous switchbacks that run steadily up a rocky cleft to the Valley rim. The falls once ran down this cleft.

The trail tops out 3.2 miles from the trailhead and bends east. At the junction, the trail going straight leads to **Eagle Peak** (7779ft). Turn right at this junction and follow the trail 0.2 miles to the brink of Upper Yosemite Fall at the **Yosemite Falls Overlook** (6400ft). The view of the falls is impressive, but views of El Capitan and Half Dome are obscured. For a wider perspective, go the extra 1.6 miles (and nearly 600ft more in elevation gain) to **Yosemite Point** (6936ft), where you'll get incredible views of Half Dome, North Dome, Clouds Rest, Glacier Point, Cathedral Rocks and Lost Arrow.

Keep in mind that the falls are often dry by midsummer, so late May and June (after the snow has cleared) are the best months to catch the scene in all its frothy glory. When you're done, retrace your steps to the trailhead.

SENTINEL DOME   Hiking

(Glacier Point Area) The hike to **Sentinel's summit** (8122ft) is the shortest and easiest trail up one of Yosemite's granite domes. For those unable to visit Half Dome's summit, Sentinel offers an equally outstanding 360-degree perspective of Yosemite's wonders, and the 2.2-mile round-trip hike only takes about an hour. A visit at sunrise, sunset or during a full moon is spectacular. You can also combine a trip up Sentinel Dome with a walk to Taft Point and the Fissures, an equidistant hike from the same trailhead, or combine the two to form a loop via the solitary **Pohono Trail**.

Park in the Sentinel Dome/Taft Point lot on the north side of Glacier Point Rd, about 13 miles from Chinquapin. From the roadside parking lot, take the trail's gently rising right fork. After 20 minutes, it heads northwest across open granite slabs to the dome's base. Skirt the base to an old service road, which leads to the

JOHN ELK III / LONELY PLANET IMAGES ©

Don't Miss Vernal & Nevada Falls

If you can only do a single day hike in Yosemite (and it happens to be springtime) make this the one. Not only are Vernal and Nevada Falls two of Yosemite's most spectacular waterfalls, but Yosemite Falls and Illilouette Fall both make appearances in the distance from select spots on the trail.

From the Happy Isles shuttle stop, follow the trail up the Merced River. After 0.8 miles you arrive at the **Vernal Fall footbridge**. Shortly beyond the footbridge (just past the water fountain and restrooms), you'll reach the junction of the **John Muir Trail** and **Mist Trail**. To do the trail clockwise, hang a left and shortly begin the steep 0.3-mile ascent to the top of **Vernal Fall** by way of the Mist Trail's granite steps. If it's springtime, prepare to get drenched in spray. Above the falls, the Merced whizzes down a long ramp of granite known as the **Silver Apron** and into the deceptively serene Emerald Pool before plunging over the cliff. No matter how fun the apron looks on a hot day, *don't enter the water*: underwater currents have whipped many swimmers over the falls.

From above the apron, it's another 1.3 miles via granite steps and steep switchbacks to the top of the Mist Trail, which meets the John Muir Trail. Shortly after joining the John Muir Trail, you'll cross a **footbridge** (elevation 5907ft) over the Merced. Beneath it, the river whizzes through a chute before plummeting 594ft over the edge of **Nevada Fall**.

There are two ways to hike this loop: up the Mist Trail and down the John Muir Trail (in a clockwise direction), or vice versa. It's much easier on the knees to climb the granite steps along the Mist Trail, so go for the clockwise route, as described above.

Mist Trail, Vernal Fall

dome's northeast shoulder. From here, head up the gentle granite slope to the top (wear good hiking shoes), where you'll have views of the entire park.

CHILNUALNA FALLS Hiking
(Wawona area) Chilnualna Creek tumbles over the north shoulder of forested Wawona Dome in an almost continuous

series of cascades. The largest and most impressive of these, Chilnualna Falls thunders into a deep, narrow chasm. Unlike its valley counterparts, this fall is not free-leaping, but its soothing, white-water rush makes it an attractive day hike without lots of company. Carry lots of water or a filter, as the route can be hot. The top is a nice picnic spot. Like all Yosemite waterfalls, Chilnualna Falls is best between April and June when streams are at their fullest. July and August are often too hot for an afternoon hike, and by September the fall is limited by low water.

The **Chilnualna Falls Trailhead** is at the eastern end of Chilnualna Falls Rd. Follow Hwy 41 (Wawona Rd) a quarter-mile north of the Wawona Hotel and store, and take a right just over the bridge on Chilnualna Falls Rd; follow it for 1.7 miles. The parking area is on the right, and the trailhead is marked.

The hike is 8.6 miles round-trip and takes four to five hours (not counting relaxation time at the top).

TENAYA LAKE   Hiking

(Tioga Rd) A pleasant one-hour stroll, this lovely 2-mile loop skirts the south shore of one of the park's biggest natural lakes. Begin from the parking lot on the lake's east end, adjacent to the popular sandy beach. Walk south along the beach, and look for the trail amid the trees just ahead. As the path traces the shore, small spurs lead down to the water. Though the shoreline is rocky, there are several nice spots for a picnic. When you reach the west end (and the Sunrise Trailhead), it's best to either wait for the free shuttle bus back to the parking lot or simply return the way you came.

CLOUDS REST   Hiking

(Tioga Rd) A fair amount of effort and distance is required for this classic hike, but you'll be amply rewarded with phenomenal 360-degree views from one of the park's best vantage points. Yosemite's largest granite peak, **Clouds Rest** (9926ft) rises 4500ft above Tenaya Creek, with spectacular views from the summit and along the trail. More than

1000ft higher than nearby Half Dome, Clouds Rest may well be the park's best panoramic viewpoint. The hike involves a strenuous ascent and equally significant descent (make sure you have a cold drink waiting for you!), but getting here is definitely worth the effort.

Start from the **Sunrise Lakes Trailhead** at the west end of Tenaya Lake. Trailhead parking is limited, and the lot fills early. The 14.4-mile round-trip hike takes six to seven hours.

LEMBERT DOME   Hiking

(Tuolumne Meadows) The short hike (and scramble) to the top of Tuolumne's most iconic dome offers fun on granite and fantastic views in all directions, especially at sunset. Lembert Dome (9450ft) rises from the meadows' east end, opposite the campground. Scrambling around the base of the dome's steep southwest face is a favorite Tuolumne pastime, but the real pleasure is hiking up the backside and standing atop the summit, where the views are staggering. Mt Dana, the Cathedral Range, Tuolumne Meadows, Pothole Dome, Fairview Dome and the Lyell Fork Tuolumne are all visible from the top. To the east, the Sierra Crest stretches from Mt Conness to the Kuna Crest. It's magical just before sunset.

This 2.4-mile round-trip hike is doable for most walkers, but reaching the summit requires scrambling up the granite at the end – not recommended for the slippery-footed or faint at heart. Once you're on top, however, you can picnic upon a ledge or walk the ridge. The entire hike takes two to three hours.

Two similarly named trails lead to Lembert Dome. The one from the Lembert Dome parking lot, at the very base of the dome, is a steep, borderline-unpleasant trail that's been damaged by storms. To reach the preferred **Dog Lake Trail** by car, drive east from the Tuolumne Meadows campground and turn right onto the road leading to Tuolumne Meadows Lodge. Park in the Dog Lake parking lot, about a half-mile up this road. From the north side of the lot, follow the

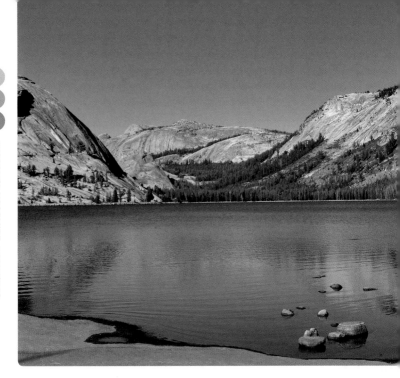

signed Dog Lake/Young Lakes trail up and across Tioga Rd.

This trail, almost entirely shaded in pine forest, is the quickest way up the backside of the dome. From the top of the trail, you can scramble up the granite to the dome's summit.

CATHEDRAL LAKES   Hiking

(Tuolumne Meadows) If you can only manage one hike in Tuolumne, this should probably be it. **Cathedral Lake** (9588ft), the lower of the two lakes, sits within a mind-blowing glacial cirque, a perfect amphitheater of granite capped by the iconic spire of nearby **Cathedral Peak** (10,911ft). From the lake's southwest side, the granite drops steeply away, affording views as far as Tenaya Lake, whose blue waters shimmer in the distance. Although it's only about two hours to the lower lake, you could easily spend an entire day exploring the granite slopes, meadows and peaks surrounding it. Continuing to the **upper lake** (9585ft) adds less than an hour to the hike and puts the round-

trip walk at 8 miles (five to seven hours total), including the stop at Cathedral Lake. Admittedly, the upper lake is less spectacular when measured against the lower lake, but by all other standards it's utterly sublime.

Parking for the **Cathedral Lake Trailhead** is along the shoulder of Tioga Rd. Due to the popularity of this hike, parking spaces fills up fast, so arrive early or take the free shuttle. Camping is allowed at the lower lake (despite what some maps show), but be absolutely certain you're 100ft from the water *and* the trail.

From the Cathedral Lake Trailhead on Tioga Rd, the hike heads southwest along the John Muir Trail. Almost immediately, it begins to climb through forest of lodgepole pine, mountain hemlock and the occasional whitebark pine. After ascending over 400ft, the trail levels out and a massive slab of granite – the northern flank of Cathedral Peak – slopes up from the left side of the trail. Soon

you'll see Fairview Dome (9731ft) through the trees to your right.

Before long, the trail begins its second ascent, climbing nearly 600ft before leveling off and affording outstanding views of Cathedral Peak. Three miles from the trailhead, you'll hit the junction that leads 0.5 miles southwest to Cathedral Lake. This trail crosses a stunning **meadow** (turn around as you cross it for the head-on view of Cathedral Peak) before arriving at the granite shores of the lake. Be sure to follow the trail around the lake and take in the views from the southwest side.

To visit the upper lake, backtrack to the main trail, turn right (southeast) and, after about 0.5 miles, you'll hit the lake. If you wish to stretch the hike out even further, you can continue past the upper lake to **Cathedral Pass** (9700ft), where you'll be rewarded with a stellar side-view of Cathedral Peak and Eichorn Pinnacle (Cathedral's fin-like west peak). This side trip adds about 0.6 miles to the trip.

Backpacking

Backcountry hiking and sleeping beneath the stars is one of Yosemite's finest adventures. The vast majority of the almost four million people who visit Yosemite every year never leave the Valley floor, meaning the park's 1101 sq miles of wilderness is, for the most part, empty. There are a few painless bureaucratic hurdles to jump before heading out, however, but a little planning will make your trek a triumph.

Half Dome is the park's classic overnighter, but there are countless other backcountry trips that have a fraction of the crowds and just as much scenic punch. They include **Lyell Canyon** (near Tuolumne Meadows); the two-day walk from **Tenaya Lake to Yosemite Valley** (a downhill hike); the steep, two-day hike up to **Young Lakes** and the three-day semi-loop **Vogelsang** trek. Information on all these hikes, as well as topographical maps, can be found at the park's visitor centers.

Wilderness permits are required for all overnight backcountry trips (not for day hikes). To stem overuse of the backcountry, a quota system is in effect for each trailhead. You must spend your first night in the area noted on your permit – from there, you're free to roam. Permits are available either in advance (between 24 weeks and two days ahead) or on a first-come, first-served basis from the nearest wilderness center (p349). The park reserves 40% of its wilderness permits for walk-ups; these become available at 11am one day before the hike-in date.

Reserving a **permit** (📞 209-372-0740; fax 209-372-0739; www.nps.gov/yose/planyourvisit/wpres.htm; advance reservation fee $5, plus per person $5; ⏰8:30am-4:30pm Mon-Fri late Nov-Oct) is the best way to ensure you get one, and you can do so by fax, phone, or through the mail.

Cycling

Bikes are prohibited from all hiking trails within Yosemite, so break out that road bike or beach cruiser if you want to do any pedaling in the park. Moderate-level bike rides within Yosemite, which is dominated by steep grades except in Yosemite Valley, are few and far between. Generally it's either easy (ie the Valley) or demanding (everywhere else).

Many people bicycle along formidable **Tioga Rd**, though it's not a route for the casual cyclist. **Glacier Point Rd**, a 32-mile round-trip from the Chinquapin junction, is another option for a longer ride. The pavement's smooth, the traffic is usually not too heavy and the vistas at Glacier Point are worth the climbs.

The best riding for most people will be the relaxed **Yosemite Valley Loops**, which are a wonder to ride at slow pace while taking in the marvelous views from the Valley floor.

Bike-rental stands at Yosemite Lodge at the Falls and Curry Village rent single-speed beach cruisers (per hour/day $10/28) or bikes with an attached child trailer (per hour/day $16.50/54). You're required to leave either a driver's license or credit card for collateral.

Backpackers, Lyell Canyon (p335)

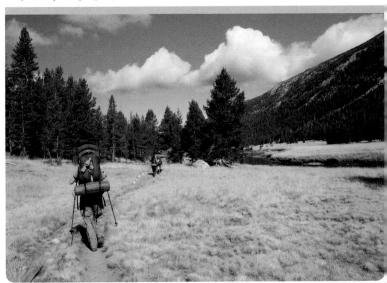

Rock Climbing & Bouldering

When it comes to rock climbing, Yosemite National Park reigns supreme. While covering Yosemite's climbing routes is beyond the scope of this book (try something by Don Reid), at least we can point the first-time climber or visitor in the right direction. If you're new to climbing, consider taking a class at the Yosemite Mountaineering School.

First, know this: all ropes lead to **Camp 4**. Most of the Valley's climbing activity revolves around this walk-in campground and historic hangout for climbing's most legendary figures. Camp 4 is where you go when you want to stop reading and start asking real people questions about where to climb, what to carry and what to expect. It's also where you find climbing partners, pick up used gear (among other things) and find the car keys you left sitting at the base of the climb.

As for bouldering, the possibilities are limitless. Popular areas include the west end of Camp 4, **Sentinel Rock**, the **Four Mile Trail Trailhead**, and the rocks near **Housekeeping Camp** and around **Mirror Lake**, to name only a few.

YOSEMITE MOUNTAINEERING SCHOOL
Rock Climbing

(📞 209-372-8344; www.yosemite mountaineering.com) Since 1969, Yosemite Mountaineering School has been teaching and guiding rock climbers, mountaineers and back-country skiers of all levels. Whether you're a 12 year old who wants to learn the basics of climbing, belaying and rappelling or a sport climber who wants to learn the art of big walls, you'll find this school a gold mine of opportunity. Beginners over the age of 10 can sign up for the Go Climb a Rock seminar ($148 per person), which is pretty much guaranteed to inspire participants to go on for more. For parents, it's a great and constructive way to turn

If You Like... Stunning Hikes

If you like Vernal and Nevada Falls (p332) and the hike to Cathedral Lakes (p334), you'll love these other spectacular hikes.

1 FOUR MILE TRAIL
(9.2 miles round-trip; Four Mile Trailhead) Fulfilling day hike from Yosemite Valley that ascends the Valley's southern wall to Glacier Point, the park's most famous viewpoint. The reward for the grunt is one of the finest vistas in the entire country.

2 PANORAMA TRAIL
(8.5 miles one way; starts at Glacier Point) Picture-postcard views accompany this trail and eye-popping sight lines of Half Dome are a highlight. Visit Nevada Fall as you descend down, down, down to the Valley floor.

3 GAYLOR LAKES
(3 miles round-trip; Gaylor Lakes Trailhead, Tuolumne Meadows) This spectacular and popular high-altitude trail climbs gently up to Gaylor Lakes, set in pristine alpine territory just inside the park boundary near Tioga Pass.

4 MONO PASS
(7.4 miles round-trip; Mono Pass Trailhead, 1.4 miles south of Tioga Pass) This outrageously scenic, high-altitude hike from Dana Meadows starts at 9689ft and follows an ancient Native American trail past meadows and through open forest to the vast, lake-crowned Mono Pass.

5 MT DANA
(5.8 miles round-trip; unmarked trailhead immediately east of Tioga Pass Entrance) Starting at 9945ft, this strenuous hike is a leg-working, lung-busting climb to the top of Yosemite's second-highest peak, which, at 13,057ft, offers stunning views in every direction.

6 ELIZABETH LAKE
(5.2 miles round-trip; Elizabeth Lake Trailhead, Tuolumne Meadows Campground) At the foot of jagged Unicorn Peak, this easily reached alpine lake offers spectacular views and plenty of opportunity for exploration beyond the lake itself.

the kids loose for a day. Numerous other classes are on offer.

The school is based out of the Curry Village Mountain Shop from April to November; it relocates to Badger Pass in winter. From late June to early September (when Tioga Rd is open) it also maintains a branch at the Tuolumne Meadows Sport Shop. At all locations, the knowledgeable staff will offer suggestions based on your skill level and objectives.

Horseback Riding

There's ample opportunity to ride in Yosemite, but unless you bring your own horse you'll probably be on the back of a mule. For kids, it's a great way to take in the scenery, breathe some dust and have a little fun. Guided mule rides are offered at three stables within the park from roughly spring through fall.

Yosemite Valley Stables Horseback Riding
(☏209-372-8348) Located near North Pines Campground, with rides to Mirror Lake and Clark's Point (for views of Vernal Fall).

Tuolumne Meadows Stables Horseback Riding
(☏209-372-8427) Has some of the park's most scenic riding trips, including part of the Young Lakes trail and along the Tuolumne River.

Wawona Stables Horseback Riding
(☏209-375-6502) Located behind the Pioneer Center, it offers rides around Wawona Meadow and to Chilnualna Falls.

Yosemite Trails Pack Station Horseback Riding
(☏559-683-7611; www.yosemitetrails.com) Just outside the park's South Entrance, this station offers rides to the Mariposa Grove of big trees ($140 per person for half-day), and sleigh rides (adult/child $30/20) in winter.

Yosemite High Sierra Camps Saddle Trips Horseback Riding
(☏801-559-4909, freight 209-372-8427; www.yosemitepark.com; adult/child from $1018/856)

These are far and away the most popular (though definitely not the cheapest) way to see the park from a saddle, with mules schlepping you and all the supplies. The four- to six-day trips include all meals and depart from the Tuolumne Stables for the spectacular High Sierra Camps circuit. It books up months in advance.

Rafting & Kayaking

Bad news first: there are no rapids to ride within the park – you'll have to head outside Yosemite for that. The good news is that the Merced River flows lazily through Yosemite Valley, offering rafters and kayakers a marvelous way to take in the scenery on a hot summer day. That said, you do have to share the water with a plethora of other boats, but with the right sense of humor and a little Merced River water running down your face, it's undeniably fun.

Rafts, kayaks, air mattresses and inner tubes (or whatever strange, nonmotorized flotation device you're using) are allowed only along the 3-mile stretch between Stoneman Bridge (near Curry Village) and Sentinel Beach. The waters are gentle enough for children, and **raft rentals** (☏209-372-4386; per adult/child over 50 lbs $26/16; ☉approx late May-Jul) for the 3-mile trip are available at Curry Village.

Swimming

River swimming throughout Yosemite is best mid- to late summer, when the water levels are low and the current gentler. The Merced River is Yosemite's biggest killer, so never swim where you're not certain the current is safe.

On a hot summer day in Yosemite Valley, nothing beats the heat like lounging in the gentle Merced River. Provided you don't trample the riparian life on your way, you can jump in just about anywhere, but there are several locations proving particularly good: at the beach just behind Housekeeping Camp; on the stretch behind Yosemite Lodge; and at the Cathedral Beach and Devil's Elbow areas opposite the El Capitan Picnic Area. The beach immediately below Swinging Bridge is hugely popular

LEE FOSTER / LONELY PLANET IMAGES ©

and, thanks to calm waters, great for families. Tenaya Creek offers good swimming as well, especially near the bridge leading toward Mirror Lake.

Skin too thin? Curry Village and Yosemite Lodge provide public outdoor **swimming pools (adult/child $5/4)**. The price includes towels and showers.

Fishing

Yosemite may not be the sort of place you go to catch whopping trophy trout, but the setting is fabulous, and wettin' a line in the Merced or Tuolumne River is pretty darn satisfying. Stream and river fishing is permitted only from the last Saturday in April until mid-November; lake fishing is okay year-round.

The park's most satisfying fishing, especially for fly casters, is undoubtedly in Tuolumne Meadows. Although the fish aren't big, they're fun, and the setting is unbeatable. In Wawona, the South Fork of the Merced offers some of the best stream fishing in the park. In and around the Valley, you can fish the Merced River between Vernal and Nevada Falls and above Washburn Lake, although if you catch a rainbow trout, you'll have to throw

it back. In Yosemite Valley, you're only allowed five brown trout per day, and bait is prohibited (artificial lures or barbless flies only).

Campfire & Public Programs

There's something almost universally en-joyable about group campfire programs. Pull a bench around a roaring bonfire, with stars above, big trees behind you and lots of friendly folks all around, and it's as if you've left the world's troubles behind.

During the summer, free campfire programs are held at the following Yosemite campgrounds: Tuolumne Meadows, Wawona, Bridalveil Creek, Crane Flat, White Wolf and Lower Pines. Check the *Yosemite Guide* for the week's programs and times. Rangers, naturalists and other park staff lead the programs, and topics include the history, ecology and geology of the local region, a few tips on dealing with bears, and maybe some stories and songs. They're geared toward families and people of all ages.

Similar evening programs are also held at amphitheaters behind Yosemite Lodge and Curry Village – even in the absence of an actual campfire, the mood remains the same. These programs include general talks about the area, with occasional slide shows and films.

The Sierra Club's LeConte Memorial also hosts programs each week. A little more in-depth than the average campfire talk, these cover such topics as the founding of the John Muir Trail and the history of Hetch Hetchy.

Glacier Point rangers lead weekly programs at a lovely stone amphitheater near the snack bar, and sometimes offer sunset talks along the railing overlooking the Valley. Over at Tuolumne Meadows, talks take place at Parsons Memorial Lodge, reachable via an easy half-mile hike.

The busiest time is, of course, during the summer, usually June to September. Limited programs are offered in the off-season, and they're held during cold weather at indoor locations such as Yosemite Lodge and the Ahwahnee Hotel.

Cross-Country Skiing

Twenty-five miles of groomed track and 90 miles of marked trails fan out from Badger Pass. From here, you can schuss out to the Clark Range Vista and Glacier Point, an invigorating 21-mile round-trip. There are also trails in Wawona and in the Big Oak Flat Rd area. Pick up a trail map or download one from the Yosemite website.

YOSEMITE CROSS-COUNTRY SKI CENTER Ski Tours & Rental
(☎209-372-8444) Offers learn-to-ski packages ($46), guided tours (from $102 per person), telemark instruction ($49), private lessons (starting at $37), and equipment rental ($23 for skis, boots and poles). It also leads very popular over-night trips to the Glacier Point Ski Hut.

GLACIER POINT SKI HUT Ski Hut
(☎209-372-8444; www.yosemitepark.com) In winter, the concession stand at Glacier Point fills with bunk beds and becomes the Glacier Point Ski Hut. It's reached by way of a 10.5-mile trip on an intermediate trail.

OSTRANDER LAKE SKI HUT Ski Hut
(www.yosemiteconservancy.org; bunk weekday/weekend $32/52) This handcrafted stone hut can accommodate up to 25 skiers in a gorgeous lakeside spot beneath Horse Ridge. Cooking facilities are provided, but you must ski in with all of your supplies. The 10-mile trip requires experience and a high fitness level.

Downhill Skiing & Snowboarding

California's oldest ski slope, **Badger Pass Ski Area** (☎209-372-8430; www.badgerpass.com; adult/child/youth lift tickets $42/23/37; ☺mid-Dec–early Apr; 🚡) sits at 7300ft on Glacier Point Rd, about 22 miles from the Valley. Known as a family-friendly mountain

Lembert Dome (p325)
JOHN ELK III / LONELY PLANET IMAGES ©

geared toward beginners and intermediates, it features an 800ft vertical drop, nine runs, two terrain parks, five lifts, a full-service lodge and equipment rental ($31 for a full set of gear).

Snowshoeing

It wouldn't be difficult to argue that Yosemite Valley is at its very best just after a fresh snowfall. Snowshoeing around the Valley, past icy monoliths, frozen waterfalls and meadows blanketed in snow, is a truly magical activity. The John Muir Trail, which begins at Happy Isles, is a popular destination.

You can rent snowshoes ($18.50/22.50 per half-/full day) at Badger Pass (and sometimes at the Curry Village Ice Rink), where rangers lead two-hour naturalist treks that are informative, fun and almost free ($5). Check the *Yosemite Guide* for schedules. From January to March, rangers offer two-hour 'Full Moon Snowshoe Walks' ($18.50 with equipment rental, $5 without) on nights of, and leading up to, a full moon. Sign up at the Yosemite Lodge Tour Desk or by calling ☏209-372-1240.

Ice-Skating

A delightful way to spend a winter's afternoon is twirling about on the large outdoor **Curry Village Ice Rink** (2½hr session adult/child $8/6, skate rental $3; ⊙Nov-Mar). Daily sessions begin at 3:30pm and 7pm, with additional sessions at 8:30am and noon on weekends and holidays.

 Sleeping

During the height of summer, visitors fill the smattering of open campsites, hotel rooms and tent cabins faster than blue jays descend on a picnic. Unless you want to take your chances on a first-come, first-served site, reservations are a must from spring through fall.

Reservations for all campgrounds within the park are handled by **Recreation.gov** (☏877-444-6777, 518-885-3639; www.recreation.gov; ⊙7am-7pm Nov-Feb, to 9pm Mar-Oct). Sites regularly book out within minutes of becoming available.

If you arrive at Yosemite without reservations, you can try your luck at Camp 4, the only first-come-first served campground in the Valley. Otherwise head straight to one of the following reservation offices, where you can line up a campsite if there are cancellations.

If you still have questions regarding the whole process or simply wish to speak with a human being in Yosemite, call the Yosemite Valley Campground Reservation Office.

Yosemite Valley Campground Reservation Office (☏information only 209-372-8502; ⊙8am-5pm) In the day-use parking lot near Camp Curry.

Wawona (☏209-375-9535; ⊙8am-5pm late May-early Oct) On Chilnualna Falls Rd.

Big Oak Flat (☏209-379-2123; ⊙8am-5pm mid-Apr–mid-Oct) At the Big Oak Flat Entrance; no waiting list so be here when it opens to scoop up cancellations.

Tuolumne Meadows (☏209-372-4025; ⊙8am-5pm Jul-Sep) Near the campground entrance.

Nearly all the other lodging in Yosemite National Park – from tent cabins and High Sierra Camps to the Ahwahnee Hotel – is managed by **DNC Parks & Resorts** (☏801-559-4884; www.yosemitepark.com). Reservations are available through DNC 366 days in advance of your arrival date. If you roll into the park without a room reservation, the Yosemite Valley Visitor Center and all the lodging front desks have courtesy phones so you can inquire about room availability throughout the park. That said, it's important to remember that rooms rarely become available midsummer.

Yosemite Valley

While Yosemite Valley campgrounds are convenient to many of the park's major sights and activities, they're also very crowded, often noisy and definitely lacking in privacy. Don't camp here expecting to get away from it all – for solitude, you're better off in less-visited areas of the park.

CAMPING

UPPER PINES
Campground $

(campsites $20; ⊙year-round; 🐾) With 238 sites spread under a forest of pine, Yosemite's second-largest campground is close-quarters camping at its finest. It sits along the bus and pedestrian road to the Nature Center at Happy Isles and trailhead, only a short walk away from Curry Village.

LOWER PINES
Campground $

(campsites $20; ⊙Mar-Oct; 🐾) Directly west of North Pines, Lower Pines is smaller but almost identical to Upper Pines, set amid the trees on the south shore of the Merced River. It has 60 sites.

NORTH PINES
Campground $

(campsites $20; ⊙Apr-Sep; 🐾) Across the Merced River from Lower Pines, the 81-site North Pines campground is probably the quietest of the Valley's campgrounds. Although most of its sites are similar to those at the other Pines, it boasts a handful of riverside sites that are comparatively outstanding.

CAMP 4
Campground $

(tent sites per person $5; ⊙year-round) Formerly known as Sunnyside, legendary Camp 4 is Yosemite's only first-come, first-served campground and, for over half a century, has been hub and home for Valley climbers. The check-in kiosk opens at 8:30am; from Thursday through Saturday in summer, be in line by 6:30am.

LODGING

Yosemite Valley offers a fair range of accommodations, from simple tent cabins to standard motel units to luxurious accommodations at the historic Ahwahnee. Tent cabins at Curry Village and Housekeeping Camp are great for families who wish to avoid both exorbitant hotel costs and the labor of setting up camp.

AHWAHNEE HOTEL
Historic Hotel $$$

(☎209-372-1407; r from $449; ❄@☎🐾) A National Historic Landmark, the Ahwah-

nee has been offering its guests the royal treatment since 1927. A stunning work of architecture, the hotel is by far the most luxurious place in the park. The 99 rooms, all tastefully decorated with Native American touches, boast great views and supremely comfortable beds. Other options include 24 cottages out back and a handful of suites. Tucked away in its own quiet, secluded corner of the Valley, the Ahwahnee is worth a visit even if you're not staying overnight. The hotel features an upscale restaurant, a cafe and friendly bar, a swimming pool, occasional evening programs and an amazing series of public common rooms.

YOSEMITE LODGE AT THE FALLS
Motel $$

(☎209-372-1274; r $191-218; @☎🐾) Located a short walk from the base of Yosemite Falls, the modest and meandering Yosemite Lodge makes for great family accommodations, thanks to its giant swimming pool, an array of hosted activities, tours, bike rentals, a small amphitheater, a store and 226 spacious 'lodge' rooms and a few bigger 'family' rooms. Its 19 'standard' rooms are comfy for couples but about as exciting as a Motel 6 in Barstow, California. There are also restaurants and a bar on the premises. Despite the number of rooms, the place fills up a year in advance (so plan ahead).

HOUSEKEEPING CAMP
Tent Cabins $

(4-person tent cabins $93; ⊙Apr-Oct) A 10-minute walk from Yosemite Village, Housekeeping Camp is a conglomeration of 266 tent cabins grouped tightly together on the southern shore of the Merced River. Each cabin has concrete walls, a canvas roof, an electrical outlet, cots, an enclosed outdoor table and a fire pit. Our tip – expect noise and bring your sense of humor.

CURRY VILLAGE
Cabins, Motel $$

(tent cabins $112-120, cabins without/with bath $127/168, r $191; 🐾) Resembling a cross between a summer camp and a labor camp, the vast, crowded and historic Curry Village offers several types of accommodations. The 319 canvas tent cabins sleep up to five people each and include linens but lack heating, electrical outlets and fire pits. Cars must park outside the cabin area, however, which cuts down on the noise. Some tents have propane heaters that can be used during winter. The wooden cabins are a bit nicer: some share central bathroom units and have propane heaters but are still crowded together; and some boast private bathrooms, electric heat and outlets, plus more spacious and cozy quarters. Its Stoneman House also contains 18 straightforward motel-style rooms (including a loft suite sleeping up to six) without televisions or phones.

Glacier Point & Badger Pass

BRIDALVEIL CREEK   Campground $
(Glacier Point Rd; campsites $14; ⊗ Jul–early Sep; 🐾) If the Valley's stewing through a summer heat wave, remember that the altitude here (7200ft) keeps things much cooler. Tucked 25 miles (a mere 40 minutes) away from the Valley buzz, this 110-site campground is the only developed place to stay in the Glacier Point Rd area. It's first-come, first-served, and has drinking water and flush toilets.

Wawona

WAWONA   Campground $
(campsites $20; ⊗ year-round; 🐾) The south fork of the Merced River cuts through this southernmost section of Yosemite, and this campground includes some sites situated right alongside its banks. It's a pleasant place to set up your tent or RV, though some of the nicer 93 spots are in the back section and are only open during summer (approximately May to September), when the whole campground goes on the reservation system. The rest of the year it's first-come, first-served.

WAWONA HOTEL   Historic Hotel $$
(☎ 209-375-6556; r without/with bath incl breakfast $147/217; ⊗ mid-Mar–Dec; 🎧📶♿) This National Historic Landmark, dating from 1879, is a collection of six graceful, New England–style buildings, each painted white and lined with wide porches. The 104 rooms come with Victorian furniture and other period items, and most open up onto a veranda. About half the rooms share bathrooms, and nice robes are provided for the walk there. Rooms with private facilities are a bit larger, and most rooms can be configured to connect to

Ahwahnee Hotel

others, which is handy for families. None has a TV or phone. The grounds are lovely, with tennis courts and a spacious lawn dotted with Adirondack chairs. There's an excellent restaurant in the main building, as well as bar service nightly in the lobby lounge or out on the porch.

Big Oak Flat Road & Tioga Road

If you're in the mood for some solitude and crisper evening air, you'll find a number of options along Tioga Rd (Hwy 120) as it heads east from Crane Flat to Tuolumne Meadows. Four campgrounds along Tioga Rd operate on a first-come, first-served basis, and two of them are the most rugged, quiet and beautiful in the park. White Wolf offers flush toilets, while the other three are primitive, with only vault toilets and no water tap, so be sure to bring your own water or be prepared to purify it from adjacent streams.

HODGDON MEADOW   Campground $
(campsites $14-20; ☼year-round; 🐾) Just east of the Big Oak Flat Entrance, this popular campground has 105 decent sites; a few of the nicer ones are walk-ins, though

you won't have to go more than 20yd. All campsites here must be reserved during summer (mid-April to mid-October) but are first-come, first-served the rest of the year.

CRANE FLAT   Campground $
(campsites $20; ☼Jun-Sep; 🐾) Around 8 miles east of the Big Oak Flat Entrance (at 6192ft) is this campground, which sits near the Crane Flat store and the junction with Tioga Rd. Sites lie along five different loops, most in the trees and some very nicely dispersed (there's 166 in total). The central location between Tuolumne Meadows and Yosemite Valley is great. Reservations are required year-round; can open late during high snow years.

TAMARACK FLAT   Campground $
(campsites $10; ☼Jul-Sep) One of the most serene and spacious places in the park to set up your tent is 3 miles down a rough, barely paved road that's as steep and narrow as it is woodsy and beautiful. Expect about a 15-minute drive off Tioga Rd; RVs and trailers aren't recommended. The 52 tent-only sites are well dispersed among trees, with some near a creek – which lends the campground a very open feel, with lots of

High Sierra Camp (p341)

sun and sky. The parts of the park accessible by road are rarely this quiet.

WHITE WOLF Campground $
(campsites $14; ☺ Jul–early Sep; 📷) Don't feel like cooking over the ol' Coleman every night but don't want to deal with Valley throngs? Located north of Tioga Rd on a mile-long spur road, this 74-site campground, adjacent to the White Wolf Lodge and store, enjoys a relaxed setting among pine trees and granite boulders beside a lazy stream.

PORCUPINE FLAT Campground $
(campsites $10; ☺ Jul–Sep) If you want easy access to Tioga Rd and don't mind treating or bringing your own water, try this 52-site campground, which sits about halfway between Crane Flat and Tuolumne Meadows, the latter only a 20-minute drive away. The sites up front can handle RVs and campers, but the quieter and more rustic back half is for tents only. There's some road noise in the daytime, but it dissipates after dark. At 8100ft, it's the second-highest developed campground in the park, and a good place to spend the night acclimatizing before hitting the high country.

WHITE WOLF LODGE Cabins $$
(tent cabins $99, cabins with bath $120; ☺ Jul–mid-Sep) This complex enjoys its own little world a mile up a spur road, away from the hubbub and traffic of Hwy 120 and the Valley. It also features nice hiking trails to Lukens and Harden Lakes. There are 24 spartan tent cabins and four very in-demand hard-walled cabins housed in two duplex buildings. There's also a dining room and a tiny counter-service store. The four-bedded tent cabins include linens, candles and wood stoves with wood, but have no electricity; they share central bathrooms.

Tuolumne Meadows

TUOLUMNE MEADOWS Campground $
(campsites $20; ☺ Jul-Sep; 📷) This is the largest campground in the park, with 304 sites for tents or RVs (35ft limit). Despite its size, many of the sites are tucked into the trees, making the place feel far less crowded than other park campgrounds.

Half the sites here are on the reservation system, while the other half are kept first-come, first-served.

TUOLUMNE MEADOWS LODGE Tent Cabins $$
(📞 information 209-372-8413; tent cabins $107; ☺ mid-Jun–mid-Sep) Don't let the name confuse you. This 'lodge' consists of 69 wood-framed, canvas-covered tent cabins, each set on a cement floor and boasting a prehistoric wood-burning stove, card table, roll-up canvas window and candles (no electricity). The lodge complex – which is part of the original High Sierra Camp loop – also includes a dining hall serving great breakfasts, box lunches and dinner. Bathrooms and showers are shared.

Hetch Hetchy

The only place to stay in this area is the **Backpackers' Campground** (campsites per person $5), which is one of the park's nicest. But it's brutally hot in summer and available only to holders of valid wilderness permits for Hetch Hetchy.

Once you leave the park, you can drive down any of the dirt Forest Service roads and camp for free wherever you wish. The nearest official campground is the pleasant **Dimond O Campground** (📞 877-444-6777; www.recreation.gov; Evergreen Rd; sites $21; ☺ May–mid-Sep), which lies 6 miles north of Hwy 120 on Evergreen Rd, in the Stanislaus National Forest. Some can be reserved; others are first-come, first-served.

There is no park lodging in Hetch Hetchy. The nearest accommodations are at the lovely **Evergreen Lodge** (📞 209-379-2606; www.evergreenlodge.com; 33160 Evergreen Rd; tents $75-110, cabins $175-350; ☺ closed Jan; @ 📶 📶), about 1.5 miles outside the park border, just south of Camp Mather.

⚒ Eating & Drinking

With the exception of dining at the Mountain Room Restaurant or the Wawona and Ahwahnee Hotels, Yosemite is hardly defined by its culinary wonders – except, of course, when setting comes into play. As for the food, content yourself with reliably prepared, fill-the-stomach type meals that are slightly overpriced but certainly do the trick after a good hike. All restaurants (except dinner at the Ahwahnee) are child-friendly.

Yosemite Village and Curry Village are the best options for relatively cheap eats and to-go items.

Yosemite Lodge at the Falls

Near the base of Yosemite Falls, this 'lodge' is not a single rustic building but rather a cluster of contemporary condo-type hotel units, gift shops and restaurants.

MOUNTAIN ROOM RESTAURANT   Contemporary $$
(mains $17-35; ☺5:30-9:30pm, shorter winter hrs; ⚑⛹) Dig into a plate of Southwestern chicken, seafood pasta, halibut, mahi-mahi or one of several cuts of deliciously grilled beef at the lodge's classy yet casual restaurant. Views of Yosemite Falls

compete with the food – arguably the best in the park – for diners' attention. Great cocktails, and no reservations unless your group has eight or more.

YOSEMITE LODGE FOOD COURT   Cafeteria $
(mains $7-12; ☺6:30am-8:30pm Sun-Thu, to 9pm Fri & Sat; ⚑⛹) The lodge's cheapest option is this self-service cafeteria, just behind the hotel's main lobby. Sauntering over from Camp 4 for breakfast and coffee before the climb is a Valley tradition. Dinner choices include burgers, pizza, salads and pasta, with vegetarian and gluten-free options available.

MOUNTAIN ROOM LOUNGE   Bar
(☺4:30-11pm Mon-Fri, noon-11pm Sat & Sun; ⛹) Across the courtyard from the restaurant, the Mountain Room Lounge is an undeniably fine place to knock back a couple of cocktails, thanks to the spacious interior and big windows. In winter, order a s'mores kit (graham crackers, chocolate squares and marshmallows) to roast in the open-pit fireplace. Kids welcome until 9pm.

Ahwahnee Hotel

⚐AHWAHNEE DINING ROOM   Californian $$$
(☏209-372-1489; breakfast $7-16, lunch $16-23, dinner $26-46; ☺7-10:30am, 11:30am-3pm & 5:30-9pm) Sit by candlelight beneath the 34ft-high beamed ceiling and lose yourself in the incredible scenery, viewed through massive picture windows – it's nothing less than spectacular. The food is excellent, though compared with the surroundings it may come in second. There's a dress code at dinner, but you can wear shorts and sneakers at breakfast and lunch. The outrageously decadent

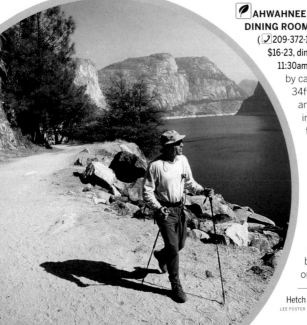

Hetch Hetchy (p326)
LEE FOSTER / LONELY PLANET IMAGES ©

Sunday brunch ($39.50) is a classic Yosemite experience. Reservations highly recommended for brunch and dinner.

AHWAHNEE BAR Bar $$
(mains $9.50-23; ⏱11:30am-11pm) Pinching pennies? Worry not – you can still experience the Ahwahnee's charms at the casual Ahwahnee Bar. Drinks aren't exactly cheap, but the atmosphere on the patio is splendid. The food (salads, wraps, sandwiches, cheese-and-fruit plates and the like) is affordable and quite good, making it an excellent choice for a light dinner.

Glacier Point & Badger Pass
When the road is open, the unexciting **snack bar** (⏱9am-5pm) at Glacier Point is your only food option.

In the wintertime (until 4pm), Badger Pass Ski Area runs a **fast food grill** (mains $3-8) serving pizza, burgers, nachos and chicken strips. On weekends and holidays, the **Snowflake Room** (mains under $10; ⏱11am-4pm) has a cozy wood-beamed room offering sandwiches and salads, a bar and a view of the lifts. Its walls are covered with cool old ski photos and pieces of vintage ski equipment.

Wawona
The Wawona General Store, a short walk from the Wawona Hotel, offers a few picnic and camping items but focuses more on snacks and gifts.

**WAWONA HOTEL
DINING ROOM** American $$
(☎209-375-1425; breakfast & lunch $11-15, dinner $19-30; ⏱7:30-10am, 11:30am-1:30pm, 5:30-9pm Easter-Dec; ✎👪) Inside the historic 1879 Wawona Hotel, this old-fashioned white-tablecloth dining room is lit by beautiful painted lamps, and the Victorian detail makes it an enchanting place to have an upscale (though somewhat overpriced) meal. 'Tasteful, casual attire' is the rule for dinner dress. Seating is first-come, first-served.

PINE TREE MARKET Market $
(7995 Chilnualna Falls Rd; ⏱8am-8pm summer, 8:30am-6:30pm rest of year) This tiny and superfriendly market sells groceries and

Quick Eats
If you need a quick, hearty meal to fill the void after a long hike, you'll like these stand-bys in Yosemite Village and Curry Village.

○ **Village Store** (Yosemite Village; ⏱8am-10pm summer, to 8pm rest of year) The biggest and best grocery store in the park is located smack in the center of Yosemite Village.

○ **Degnan's Deli** (Yosemite Village; sandwiches $6-8; ⏱7am-5pm) Fresh sandwiches to go, soups and lots of snacks and beverages.

○ **Degnan's Cafe** (Yosemite Village; sandwiches & salads $5-10; ⏱11am-6pm Apr-Sep) Beside the deli, Degnan's Cafe serves espresso drinks, smoothies and pastries.

○ **Degnan's Loft** (Yosemite Village; mains $8-10; ⏱5-9pm Mon-Fri year-round, plus Sat & Sun Apr-Oct) Upstairs from the cafe, this no-frills pizza parlor has a totally unadorned, ski-lodge feel. Great spot for pizza.

○ **Village Grill** (Yosemite Village; burgers $5-7; ⏱11am-5pm Apr-Oct) Standard fast-food counter with patio seating and subpar burgers, chicken sandwiches and the like. Good fries!

○ **Curry Village Taqueria** (Curry Village; mains $5-10; ⏱11am-5pm mid-Apr–Oct) Walk-up taco stand with tasty, vaguely Mexican fast food.

○ **Pizza Patio** (Curry Village; pizzas from $8; ⏱noon-10pm, shorter winter hrs) Mediocre pizzas, chili dogs and 'veggie bowls' taste amazing with a pint of beer from the bar next door.

○ **Curry Village Dining Pavilion** (Curry Village; adult/child breakfast $12/8, dinner $15/8; ⏱7-10am & 5:30-8pm Apr-Oct) All-you-can-eat breakfasts and dinners draw ravenous families to Curry Village's giant cafeteria.

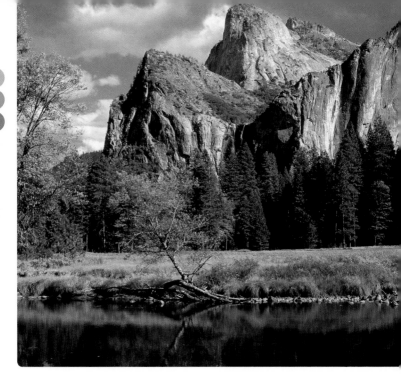

bags of divine locally roasted coffee, and in summer it sells seasonal fruit grown by regional farmers. It's located a mile east of Hwy 41 amid the Redwoods in Yosemite; turn east off Chilnualna Falls Rd, which is just north of the Pioneer History Center.

Tuolumne Meadows

As with everything else along the Tioga Rd, the eating establishments in Tuolumne Meadows are open roughly late June to mid-September only. Exact dates depend on snowfall.

TUOLUMNE MEADOWS GRILL   Fast Food $
(mains $4-9; ⊙8am-5pm; ⌗) You can hardly say you've visited Tuolumne without smacking down a burger and a basket of fries in the parking lot in front of the Tuolumne Grill. The soft-serve ice-cream cones and hearty breakfasts – not to mention the people-watching – are equally mandatory.

TUOLUMNE MEADOWS LODGE   American $$
(☎209-372-8413; breakfast $7-13, dinner $10-$26; ⊙7-9am & 5:45-8pm; ⌗) For yet another classic Yosemite experience, make a dinner reservation (for breakfast, just show up) at the Tuolumne Meadows Lodge. The place is as basic-looking as they come, but the breakfasts are hearty and the dinners are good.

TUOLUMNE MEADOWS STORE   Market $
(⊙8am-8pm) Stocks just about every necessity item you could have possibly forgotten.

ⓘ Information

Entrance Fees & Passes

Entry to Yosemite National Park (www.nps.gov/yose) costs $20 per vehicle or $10 per pedestrian, bicycle or motorcycle; passes are valid for one week. An annual Yosemite Pass costs $40, and interagency and senior passes are valid. All can be purchased at entrance stations and visitor centers.

Left: View of Cathedral Rocks from Valley View (p328);
Below: Yosemite Valley Chapel (p319)

(LEFT) GLENN VAN DER KNIJFF / LONELY PLANET IMAGES ©; (BELOW) DOUGLAS STEAKLEY / LONELY PLANET IMAGES ©

Opening Dates

Yosemite Valley and Wawona are open 24 hours a day, year-round. Tuolumne Meadows is open only in summer (dates depend on snowmelt).

Tourist Information

Big Oak Flat Information Station (☎209-379-1899; ⏰8am-5pm May-Sep)

Tuolumne Meadows Visitor Center (☎209-372-0263; ⏰9am-6pm late spring-early fall)

Wawona Information Station (☎209-375-9531; ⏰8:30am-5pm May-Sep) Located inside the Hill's Studio building next to the Wawona Hotel.

Yosemite Valley Visitor Center (☎209-372-0299; ⏰9am-7:30pm in summer, shorter hours rest of year) The park's main visitor center.

Wilderness Centers

Yosemite's two main wilderness centers are in Yosemite Valley and Tuolumne Meadows. At both, hikers can buy maps and guidebooks,

check current weather and trail conditions, get helpful tips on planning and packing, and – most importantly – obtain wilderness permits. You can also rent the all-important bear-proof food canisters ($5 per week).

There are wilderness centers inside the Yosemite Valley Visitor Center, the Tuolumne Meadows Visitor Center, the Wawona Information Station, the Hetch Hetchy Entrance Station and the Big Oak Flat Information Station.

Park Policies & Regulations

As in all national parks, feeding any animals is illegal. Wood and kindling gathering is illegal in the Valley, so you'll have to buy firewood.

Black bears are everywhere in Yosemite, and they regularly break into cars for food. Put all food, gum and scented non-food products such as sunblock or lotions in the park's ubiquitous food lockers. Bears also recognize coolers and grocery bags, so even if these are empty and clean, at least cover them with a blanket. Failure to follow these rules can lead to a citation (or the trashing of your car). Anyone sleeping in the

349

backcountry must store food in a bear vault or other bear-proof canister; hanging your food is not allowed in Yosemite.

Maps

National Geographic (www.nationalgeographic.com) publishes five outstanding hiking maps for Yosemite under its Trails Illustrated series. The park newspaper has an excellent map for locating trailheads and services.

Dangers & Annoyances

With its exposed granite peaks, lightning can be a danger for people heading up high. Before starting a hike, check the weather forecast at a visitor center or ranger station.

Getting There & Around

Air

Fresno Yosemite International Airport (**FAT**; ☎559-621-4500; www.flyfresno.org) The closest regional airport; approximately 90 miles southwest of Yosemite.

Major nearby international airports are:

Los Angeles International (**LAX**; ☎310-646-5252; www.lawa.org)

Mineta San Jose International (**SJC**; ☎408-277-4759; www.sjc.org)

Oakland International (**OAK**; ☎510-563-3300; www.flyoakland.com)

Sacramento International (**SMF**; ☎916-929-5411; www.sacairports.org)

San Francisco International (**SFO**; ☎650-821-8211; www.flysfo.com)

Bicycle

Twelve miles of mostly flat, paved bicycle trails run up and down Yosemite Valley, making cycling a fantastic way to get around the Valley.

Car & Motorcycle

Car is the easiest way to get to the park, but the traffic can be horrendous in summer. You'll find gas stations in Crane Flat, Wawona and (in summer) Tuolumne Meadows. Gas is not available in Yosemite Valley; the closest gas station to the Valley is in El Portal.

Most trailheads have free parking areas where you can leave your vehicle for several days. Day-use visitors can use the day-use parking lots either at Curry Village or near Yosemite Village, and take the free shuttle bus around the Valley.

Free Shuttles

Yosemite offers good public transportation within Yosemite Valley and hikers' buses along Tioga Rd to Tuolumne Meadows. For information, schedules and departure points, check the free *Yosemite Guide* or the park's website at www.nps.gov/yose/planyourvisit/bus.htm.

To get from the Valley to Tuolumne and other points along Tioga Rd, you can also ride the **Yosemite Area Regional Transport System** (YARTS; www.yarts.com) buses heading to Mammoth Lakes.

Rock climbing on Half Dome (p318)
MICHAEL MALONEY / SAN FRANCISCO CHRONICLE / CORBIS ©

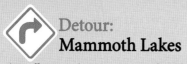

Detour:
Mammoth Lakes

A small mountain resort town endowed with larger-than-life scenery, Mammoth Lakes is dominated by the dizzying 11,053ft Mammoth Mountain. Skiers and snowboarders carve up its powdery slopes all winter. Come summer, the area transforms into an outdoor wonderland of mountain-bike trails, excellent fishing, endless alpine hiking and blissful hidden spots for hot-spring soaking.

Mammoth Mountain (📞760-934-2571, 24hr snow report 888-766-9778; www. mammothmountain.com; lift tickets adult/senior & child $92/46) is a snow junkie's dream resort, with sunny skies, a reliably long season (roughly November to June) and over 3500 acres of fantastic tree-line and open-bowl skiing.

In business since 1924, the cozy old **Tamarack Lodge & Resort** (📞760-934-2442; www.tamaracklodge.com; lodge r $99-169, cabins $169-599; @ 🛜) is a comfy place to bed down.

About 15 **USFS campgrounds** (📞877-444-6777; www.recreation.gov; campsites $20-21; 🕑approx mid-Jun–mid-Sep) are scattered in and around Mammoth Lakes, all with flush toilets but no showers.

Mammoth Lakes lies 50 miles southeast of Tuolumne Meadows, via Hwy 120, Hwy 395 and, finally, Hwy 203. The **Mammoth Lakes Welcome Center** (📞760-934-2712; www.visitmammoth.com; 🕑8am-5pm) and the **Mammoth Lakes Ranger Station** (📞760-924-5500; www.fs.fed.us/r5/inyo; 🕑8am-5pm) share a building on the north side of Hwy 203.

AROUND YOSEMITE

Heading to Yosemite by car or bus, you'll travel along one of four primary approaches. To the west, Hwys 120 and 140 provide the main access routes, with wonderful little gold rush–era towns and groovy old-time saloons. To the south, Hwy 41 passes through pastoral fishing lakes and mountain roads, and the eastern route over Tioga Pass is the highest auto pass in California.

El Portal

Once the terminus of the Yosemite Valley Railroad, El Portal is now home to a collection of gateway services (including a pricey gas station), housing for park staff and park administrative offices. Just west of the Arch Rock Entrance and about 14 miles west of Yosemite Village, the town stretches 7 miles alongside the Merced River.

YARTS (📞877-989-2787; www.yarts. com) buses run from Cedar Lodge and Yosemite View Lodge to Yosemite Valley (one hour, adult/child round-trip $7/5).

 Sleeping & Eating

YOSEMITE VIEW LODGE Lodge $$$
(📞209-379-2681; www.stayyosemiteviewlodge. com; 11136 Hwy 140; r $164-254, ste $304-714; ❄️ 🛜 ⛵ 🐾) Less than 2 miles from the park entrance is this big, modern complex with hot tubs and four pools. All the 336 rooms feature kitchenettes, some have gas fireplaces and views of the Merced River, and the ground-floor rooms have big patios. The souped-up 'majestic suites' are massive, with crazy-opulent bathrooms featuring waterfall showers and plasma TV entertainment centers.

There's an on-site **pizzeria** (pizzas & sandwiches from $8; 🕑5-9:30pm Apr-Nov), plus a **restaurant** (dinner $14-23; 🕑7-11am & 5:30-10pm; 📞) offering pasta and seafood dishes and meaty mains.

CEDAR LODGE
Lodge $$

(📞209-379-26121; www.stayyosemitecedar lodge.com; 9966 Hwy 140; r $119-200; ❄🛜⊠) Approximately 9 miles west of the Arch Rock Entrance, the Cedar is a sprawling establishment with more than 200 adequate rooms, an indoor and a seasonal outdoor pool, and a couple of restaurants. A **grill** (mains $10-13; ⏲11am-10pm; 🚻) offers food and cocktails in a room that looks like an overeager cross between a sports bar and a 1950s diner, while steaks, pasta and chicken are on hand in the adjacent **restaurant** (breakfast buffet $11, dinner $14-24; ⏲7-11am & 5:30-10pm).

INDIAN FLAT RV PARK
Camping, Tent Cabins $

(📞209-379-2339, www.indianflatrvpark.com; 9988 Hwy 140; tent sites $25, RV sites $37-42, tent cabins $59, cottages $109; ⏲year-round; ❄) This private campground has a number of interesting housing options, including two pretty stone cabin cottages with air-conditioning. Guests can use the pool and wi-fi at the Cedar Lodge next door, and nonguests can pay to shower.

SAL'S TACO TRUCK
Mexican $

(mains under $10; ⏲approx 5-9pm, every other Thu) The local's favorite food spot, Sal's biweekly arrival conveniently coincides with payday for government employees. Look for the line next to the post office.

Buck Meadows & Around

A former stagecoach stop en route to Yosemite, the blink-and-you'll-miss-it settlement of Buck Meadows is only 20 minutes' drive from the park entrance, and a good alternative to staying inside the park.

 Sleeping & Eating

YOSEMITE WESTGATE LODGE
Lodge$$$

(📞209-962-5281; www.yosemitewestgate.com; 7633 Hwy 120; r $189-299; ❄@🛜⊠🚻) In Buck Meadows proper, this generic lodge features better-than-average motel rooms with modern amenities overlooking a large parking lot and a pool.

Hikers, Tuolumne Meadows (p324)

Detour:
Groveland

About 25 miles west of Yosemite's Big Oak Flat Entrance, Groveland is a picture-perfect old Sierra mining town. It's as if Hwy 120 rolled right into a spaghetti western, taking you with it. After two blocks of exceptionally well-preserved gold rush–era buildings, you're back in the foothills.

Having the complete Groveland experience is relatively straightforward. Check into the historic **Groveland Hotel** (☎209-962-4000; www.groveland.com; 18767 Main St; r incl breakfast $135-349; ✿@☎), which was built in 1850 and has 17 quaint, lovingly decorated rooms.

Then, eat dinner (and stay for a drink) at the classic **Iron Door Saloon** (www.iron-door-saloon.com; 18761 Main St; mains $8-21; ☺11am-late; ☎), which, contrary to its name but appropriate for the atmosphere, has swinging doors. They say it's the oldest bar in the state.

Finally, make the obligatory visit to **Mountain Sage** (www.mountainsagemusic.org; 18653 Main St; snacks $4-5; ☺8am-5pm Sun, 7am-6pm Mon-Thu, to 7pm Fri & Sat, closed Mon & Tue winter; @☎), the community hub, cafe, store, nursery and live-music venue all rolled into one.

BLACKBERRY INN BED & BREAKFAST
B&B $$$
(☎209-962-4663, 888-867-5001; www.blackberry-inn.com; 7567 Hamilton Station Loop; r $195-215; ✿@☎) Also in town, and owned by a local Yosemite expert (need info, she's got it).

STANISLAUS NATIONAL FOREST
Campgrounds $
(☎209-962-7825; www.fs.usda.gov/stanislaus) A number of first-come, first-served campgrounds can be found in this nearby forest:

The Pines (campsites $16)

Lost Claim (campsites $16; ☺May-early Sep)

Sweetwater (campsites $19; ☺May-early Sep)

Fish Camp

Fish Camp is practically just a bend in the road, a tiny pretty place with a small general store, a post office, and a handful of lodges and worthwhile B&Bs. The town is only 2 miles from Yosemite's southern-most entrance, so it makes a good base for visiting the park.

 Sleeping & Eating

NARROW GAUGE INN
Inn $$
(☎559-683-7720; www.narrowgaugeinn.com; 48571 Hwy 41; r incl breakfast Nov-Mar $79-109, Apr-Oct $120-220; ✿☎⛵🐾) Adjacent to the popular Sugar Pine Railroad, this beautiful, friendly and supremely comfortable 26-room inn has a hot tub, small bar and a fine **restaurant** (☎559-683-6446; dinner $19-37; ☺5:30-9pm Wed-Sun Apr-Oct).

BIG CREEK INN B&B
B&B $$$
(☎559-641-2828; www.bigcreekinn.com; 1221 Hwy 41; r incl breakfast $219-259; @☎) Each of the three white-palette rooms has peaceful creek views and a private balcony, and two have gas fireplaces. From the comfortable rooms or the bubbling hot tub, you can often spot deer and beavers, or hummingbirds lining up at the patio feeder. Amenities include in-room DVD players and a large movie library, plus kitchenette use.

Detour:
Mono Lake

North America's second-oldest lake is a quiet and mysterious expanse of deep blue water whose glassy surface reflects jagged Sierra peaks, young volcanic cones and the unearthly tufa (*too*-fah) towers that make Mono Lake so distinctive. Jutting from the water like drip sand castles, the tufas form when calcium bubbles up from subterranean springs and combines with the carbonate in the alkaline lake waters.

Make the **Mono Basin Scenic Area Visitors Center** (☎760-647-3044; www.fs.usda.gov/inyo; Hwy 395, ◷8am-5pm mid-Apr–Nov), half a mile north of Lee Vining, your first stop. Here you can pick up maps, peruse interpretive displays and a good bookstore, and watch a 20-minute movie about Mono Lake.

Tufa spires ring the entire lake, but the biggest grove is the **South Tufa Reserve** (☎760-647-6331; adult/child $3/free), on the lake's south rim. To get to the reserve, head south of Lee Vining on Hwy 395 for 6 miles, then east on Hwy 120 for 5 miles to the dirt road leading to a parking lot.

From late June to early September, the Mono Lake Committee operates one-hour **canoe tours** (☎760-647-6595; www.monolake.org/visit/canoe; tours $25; ◷8am, 9:30am & 11am Sat & Sun) around the tufas. Half-day kayak tours along the shore or out to Paoha Island are also offered by **Caldera Kayaks** (☎760-934-1691; www.calderakayak.com; tours $75; ◷mid-May–mid-Oct). Both places require reservations.

Mono lake is immediately north of Lee Vining, off Hwy 395.

SUMMERDALE CAMPGROUND   Campground $

(☎877-444-6777; www.recreation.gov; campsites $21; ◷May-Sep; ☻) The closest campground to the park, this pleasant spot along Big Creek has 28 well-dispersed sites in an area of grassy meadow and trees.

Tioga Pass

The campground closest to Tioga Pass is at **Tioga Lake** (Hwy 120; sites $19; ☻), which has a handful of sunny, exposed sites right on the lake but visible from the road.

Founded in 1914, **Tioga Pass Resort** (tiogapassresortllc@gmail.com; r $125, cabin $160-240) justifiably attracts a loyal clientele with its 10 rustic cabins tucked into the rocks and trees beside Lee Vining Creek, just 2 miles east of Tioga Pass. The cabins are basic but cozy, and each includes a kitchen, porch, bathroom and linens. Book via email. Although the attached **diner** (breakfast & lunch $8-9, dinner $15; ◷7am-9pm) has only a small

counter and two tables, the intimate, old-time character makes for a superb setting. The lodge is open roughly from late May to mid-October, depending on snow. During the winter the lodge serves as a base camp for backcountry skiing forays into the surrounding wilderness. Winter visitors approach from Lee Vining and park their cars along Hwy 120. From there, they ski more than 6 miles to the resort.

In September, check out the **Tioga Pass Run** (www.tiogapassrun.com), a footrace from Lee Vining to Tioga Pass: 12.4 miles – and only one (3100-foot) hill!

Lee Vining

Hwy 395 skirts the western bank of Mono Lake, rolling into this gateway town where you can eat, sleep, gas up (for a pretty penny) and catch Hwy 120 to Yosemite National Park when the road's open. A superb base for exploring Mono Lake, Lee Vining is only 12 miles (about a 30-minute drive) from Yosemite's East Entrance. Lee

Vining Canyon is a popular location for ice climbing.

Before you leave town, take a quick look at the **Upside-Down House**, a kooky tourist attraction created by silent film actress Nellie Bly O'Bryan. Originally situated along Tioga Rd, it now resides in a park in front of the tiny **Mono Basin Historical Society Museum** (www. monobasinhs.org; donation $2; ⏰10am-4pm Thu-Sat & Mon, noon-4pm Sun, mid-May–early Oct). To find it, turn east on 1st St and go one block to Mattley Ave.

 Sleeping & Eating

All of Lee Vining's modest, family-run motels are along Hwy 395. Rates drop when Tioga Pass is closed.

EL MONO MOTEL   Motel $
(📞760-647-6310; www.elmonomotel.com; 51 Hwy 395; r $69-99; ⏰May-Oct; 📶) Grab a board game or soak up some mountain sunshine in this friendly flower-ringed place attached to an excellent cafe serving organic coffee, espresso drinks and muffins. It has been in operation since 1927, and is often booked solid. Each of its 11 simple rooms (a few share bathrooms) is unique, decorated with vibrant and colorful art and fabrics.

YOSEMITE GATEWAY MOTEL   Motel $$
(📞760-647-6467; www.yosemitegatewaymotel. com; Hwy 395; r $169; 📶) Think vistas. This is the only motel on the east side of the highway, and the views from some of the rooms are phenomenal.

HISTORIC MONO INN   Californian $$
(📞760-647-6581; www.monoinn.com; 55620 Hwy 395; dinner $8-25; ⏰11am-9pm May-Dec) A restored 1922 lodge owned by the family of photographer Ansel Adams, it's now an elegant lakefront restaurant with outstanding California comfort food, fabulous wine and views to match it all. Browse the 1000-volume cookbook collection upstairs, and stop in for music on the creekside terrace. It's located about 5 miles north of Lee Vining. Reservations recommended.

WHOA NELLIE DELI   Deli $$
(www.whoanelliedeli.com; near junction of Hwys 120 & 395; mains $8-19; ⏰7am-9pm mid-Apr–Oct) Chef Matt 'Tioga' Toomey feeds delicious fish tacos, wild buffalo meatloaf and other tasty morsels to locals and clued-in passersby inside a gas station minimart. Portions are huge, the prices fair and the views great.

Zion & Bryce Canyon National Parks

On first impression, this is a puzzling and forbidding landscape. Standing atop wind-whipped Angels Landing in Zion Canyon, or staring out at the ancient hoodoos of Bryce Canyon's Silent City, one can only wonder what to make of it all. Indeed, this is no orderly garden, but a scorched and broken land that extends as far as the disbelieving eye can see.

Frankly, it's a wonder humans ever came here at all. That they still do, and at times in droves, is testament to the sheer joy and amazement that this red-rock desert inspires. The vast and unfathomable rock formations here contain not one epiphany, but thousands.

Fortunately, much of this red-rock wilderness has been preserved nearly as it was centuries ago. In nature's temple, Zion and Bryce remain spiritual experiences of the highest order.

Court of the Patriarchs (p365), Zion

Zion & Bryce Canyon Itineraries

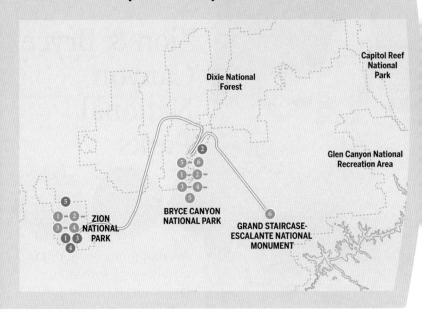

Three Days

1 **Zion Canyon Scenic Drive** (p364) Hop on a shuttle outside the Zion Canyon Visitor Center and wind your way between the towering red cliffs of Zion Canyon. The shuttle stops at every major trailhead on the way.

2 **Zion Lodge** (p375) Close the evening by wandering the grounds of this historic lodge before treating yourself to dinner at its prized Red Rock Grill.

3 **Angels Landing** (p371) Get up early and put your thighs to the ultimate test by hiking up to Angels Landing. The 360-degree views from the top make this 5.4-mile trail well worth the effort.

4 **Watchman Trail** (p373) After a leisurely afternoon, once your thighs have rested and the heat has waned, follow this trail along the Virgin River up to the foot of Bridge Mountain. The overlooks up here are the best places to watch the sunset in Zion.

5 **Bryce Canyon** (p381) On day three, drive out to Bryce Canyon National Park, situate yourself and spend the day exploring the sights and views along Bryce Canyon Scenic Dr.

6 **Rim Trail** (p390) Toward the end of the day, make your way back to the north end of the canyon and hike part or all of the Rim Trail. The mostly gentle path leads from Fairyland Point to Bryce Point and passes some of the most spectacular views in the park.

THIS LEG: 170 MILES

Five Days

1 Peek-a-boo Loop Trail (p391) On day four, rest your legs and take to horseback for a clop down this stunning 5.5-mile trail. It boasts some of the finest and most varied views in the park.

2 Bryce Canyon Lodge (p395) In the afternoon, wander around the majestic Bryce Canyon Lodge and treat yourself to a succulent bison burger dinner in the lodge's excellent restaurant.

3 Paria View (p385) After dinner, drive out to Paria View, where you can watch hoodoos glow red against the setting sun. This is one of the only west-facing amphitheaters in Bryce, making it the best place to watch the sunset.

4 Inspiration Point (p391) Once the sun goes down, make the short drive from Paria View to Inspiration Point, a superb and easily accessible place to stargaze. On clear nights you can see stars over 2.2 million miles away.

5 Bryce Point (p386) On day five, wake up early (*really* early) and prepare yourself for one of the Southwest's most astonishing sights – sunrise from Bryce Point. Below you, the hoodoos of Bryce Amphitheater's Silent City light up in the morning sunlight and glow fiery red.

6 Grand Staircase-Escalante National Monument (p384) After Bryce Point's spectacular sunset, drive 1½ hours northeast to Grand Staircase National Monument, the largest park in the Southwest.

⬤ **THIS LEG: 140 MILES**

Zion & Bryce Canyon Highlights

1 Best Hike: The Narrows (p370) Zion's quintessential hike follows the Virgin River into a narrow slot canyon.

2 Best View: Bryce Point (p386) Bryce Canyon's famous viewpoint overlooks a sea of hoodoos in the Southwest's most magnificent natural amphitheater.

3 Best Place to Cool Off: Riverside Walk (p369) Shaded by towering canyon walls, this gentle path meanders past seeps, hanging gardens and wading spots.

4 Best Burger: Oscar's Café (p377) The Murder Burger, topped with chipotle-and-garlic aioli, is to die for.

5 Best Campground: Lava Point (p375) Ditch the crowds and nab a spot at this remote six-site Zion campground.

Bryce Point (p386), Bryce Canyon
LEE FOSTER / LONELY PLANET IMAGES ©

Discover Zion & Bryce Canyon

ZION NATIONAL PARK

Utah's southernmost national park protects a world of narrow, maze-like canyons, weeping rocks, sandstone grottos and lush hanging gardens. The presence of water defines this park, in comparison to other desert parks in southern Utah, and verdant riverbanks support trees and grasses that add splendid colors to Zion's already dazzling desert palette. Wading up the Virgin River, which is bound by the slot-like walls of the Zion Narrows, is the park's quintessential experience. But it's the park's centerpiece, spectacular Zion Canyon, that attracts 2.7 million visitors every year. You can leisurely explore the canyon floor by bike, foot or shuttle, or put your body (and mind) to the test by hiking the hair-raising, cliff-side trail to Angels Landing. Those who make it to the top of Zion's most famous hike will be rewarded with a heart-stopping 360-degree view of Zion Canyon. No matter how you experience this national park, you won't leave unfazed.

History

Zion's mysterious rock art – petroglyphs and pictographs created by Ancestral Puebloans and, later, the Fremont people – makes it clear that humans inhabited this area for thousands of years. When Spanish explorers entered the region in the late 18th century, they encountered the Kaibab Paiutes, who, until then, had lived mostly in peace. By the mid-1800s, European smallpox and measles had decimated the indigenous population.

The first non-Native American to enter Zion Canyon was Nephi Johnson, a Mormon pioneer who ventured south in 1854 on a mission to convert Native Americans. In 1916, Methodist minister Frederick Vining Fisher and a Mormon bishop toured the canyon, giving names to many of the famous rock formations, including Angels Landing and the Great White Throne. Zion became a national park in 1919.

In 1930 the Zion–Mt Carmel Hwy and its tunnel were completed, offering a paved route into and through Zion, bringing in over 55,000 tourists that year. Over the years, the park became so popular that, in 2000, a mandatory shuttle system was instituted

Angels Landing (p371), Zion
DLILLC / CORBIS ©

to relieve congestion in the canyon. Today the park gets some 2.7 million visitors every year.

When to Go

Fall is arguably the best season to visit Zion. September is still hot, but the days are usually clear, the water remains warm and foliage at high elevations begins to change color. Crowds are thinner than during summer, too. Winter visitation drops so low that many businesses around the park curtail their hours or close altogether. Spring weather is unpredictable, bringing both rain and sun. Spring wildflowers begin to bloom in April at lower elevations, continuing into July at high elevations. By June, the average daytime temperatures already tops 90°F (32°C). The July and August 'monsoon' season often brings sudden, short afternoon thunderstorms.

When You Arrive

Upon entry, be sure to pick up a copy of the park's free newspaper, the *Zion National Park Map & Guide*. It's loaded with information, including shuttle schedules, park events and happenings, maps, safety tips and more.

Orientation

Zion National Park spans 147,000 acres between I-15 and Hwy 9 in southwestern Utah. The main section of the park, encompassing Zion Canyon, is closest to the South Entrance on Hwy 9 outside the town of Springdale. You can also get to the canyon from the East Entrance, which is 14 serpentine, uphill miles east toward Mt Carmel Junction. Springdale is an outdoorsy community of eclectic restaurants, galleries, motels and such that provide the majority of services in the area.

 Sights

It's hard to do Zion justice in fewer than three days, but if you're short on time, you can come close by touring Zion

The Best...
Viewpoints

Canyon Scenic Dr and hiking to the top of Observation Point. Be sure to start at the visitor center, the best place to orient yourself to the park.

ZION CANYON VISITOR CENTER　　　　Visitor Center
(☎435-772-3256; www.nps.gov/zion; ⊘8am-7:30pm Jun-Aug, 8am-6pm Sep-May)
In addition to being the font for all park information, the visitor center is a model of functional and attractive environmental architecture. Despite its lack of air-conditioning or heating units, the building remains pleasant year-round. Cooling towers harness summer winds to cool water and funnel colder, heavier air into the building, while passive solar walls are positioned to catch the winter sun. This is also the best place to familiarize yourself with the park before setting out to explore it on your own. Rangers answer questions, and outdoor exhibits explain the natural history of the canyon. One of the center's highlights is the **Zion Natural History Association** (☎800-635-3959; www.zionpark.org), which runs an excellent bookstore, selling area and activity guides, history and children's books, maps and more.

HUMAN HISTORY MUSEUM　　Museum
(☎435-772-0168; admission free; ⊘9am-7pm late May-early Sep, 10am-5pm early Mar-late

Zion

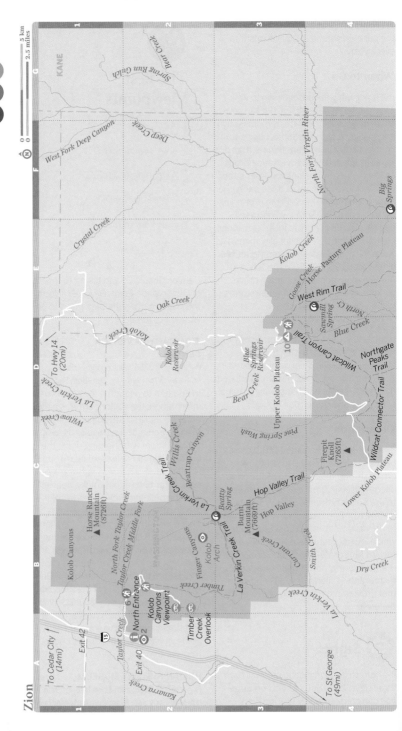

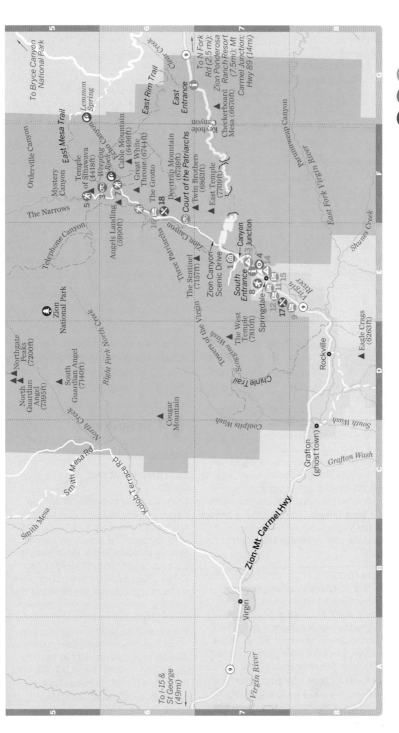

To Bryce Canyon National Park

Lemmon Spring

East Mesa Trail

East Rim Trail

Clear Creek

9

To N Fork Rd (2.5mi); Zion Ponderosa Ranch Resort (7.5mi); Mt Carmel Junction: Hwy 89 (14mi)

East Entrance

1

Keyhole Canyon

Checkerboard Mesa (6670ft)

Orderville Canyon

Mystery Canyon

Temple of Sinawava

Echo Canyon

Weeping Rock

Cable Mountain (6496ft)

Great White Throne (6744ft)

The Grotto

Deertrap Mountain (6739ft)

Court of the Patriarchs

Twin Brothers

East Temple (7709ft)

Temple (6863ft)

The Narrows

5 3 7

18

Angels Landing (5990ft)

Three Patriarchs

Zion Canyon

Telephone Canyon

The Sentinel (7157ft)

Zion Canyon Scenic Drive

Canyon Junction

South Entrance

Zion National Park

Right Fork North Creek

The West Temple (7810ft)

Towers of the Virgin

Pine Creek

9

Virgin River

2 4
8 13
12 11 15
17

Springdale

Northgate Peaks (7200ft)

North Guardian Angel (7395ft)

South Guardian Angel (7140ft)

North Creek

Cougar Mountain

Coalpits Wash

Chinle Trail

Scoggins Wash

East Fork Virgin River

Shunes Creek

Paunwecep Canyon

Eagle Crags (6263ft)

Rockville

Grafton (ghost town)

South Wash

Grafton Wash

Smith Mesa

Smith Mesa Rd

Kolob Terrace Rd

Zion-Mt Carmel Hwy

Virgin

9

Virgin River

To I-15 & St George (49mi)

363

Zion

May & early Sep-Nov, closed Nov-early Mar)
Inside this air-conditioned oasis, exhibits cover the geology and human history of Zion Canyon, as well as its creation and management as a national park. The building itself is part of an original Mormon homestead settled by the Crawford family. Make sure to see the 22-minute film, screened every half-hour; it's a beautiful – and accurate – introduction to the park. Outside the museum, look for the interpretive signs that point out the park's tallest sandstone cliffs, including the **West Temple** (7810ft) and the **Towers of the Virgin**. Look for the natural arch near the peak of **Bridge Mountain** to the south.

ZION LODGE   Historic Building
(☏ 435-772-7700; www.zionlodge.com; Zion Canyon Scenic Dr) Whether you plan to stay at the Zion Lodge or not, a visit to this historic lodge, smack in the middle of Zion Canyon, is a must. Although the architecture itself pales in comparison to some of its counterparts in other national parks, its location is incomparable. Stunning red-rock cliffs surround you on all sides, and views of Lady Mountain, Heaps

Canyon and the Virgin River are simply stunning. Evening nature programs and talks are also hosted on the grounds. For lodging information see p375.

 **Activities**

Driving Tours

ZION CANYON SCENIC
DRIVE   Scenic Drive
Snaking its way between the vertical red stone walls that form Zion Canyon, this spectacular drive is by far the park's most famous. First stop is the **Human History Museum**, where exhibits explain the natural and human history of Zion Canyon. Just past the museum are a few turnouts that overlook the **Streaked Wall**. In spring, with binoculars, scan the rim for nesting peregrine falcons. Officially, the scenic drive begins where you turn north, and cars are restricted, at **Canyon Junction** (where Zion–Mt Carmel Hwy meets Zion Canyon Scenic Dr). This stop marks one end of the **Pa'rus Trail**, which accesses wading spots along the Virgin River.

Continuing up the canyon, you'll pass the **Sentinel Slide** on the left. About, oh, 4000 years ago or so, a big chunk of the cliff face sloughed off and blocked the water flow, turning the canyon into a big lake. (That's why the up-canyon features you see are more rounded and sculptural than in a typical river-cut gorge like the Grand Canyon.) The water eventually carved its way through the blockage and carried on. The slide became active again in 1995, when it covered the road and trapped tourists at the Zion Lodge for three days, and again in 1998 when the road washed away. It's all been properly reinforced now, but you'll notice that the rock looks a lot more loose and crumbly here than in other areas.

Next, the **Court of the Patriarchs** stop fronts the shortest trail in the park, a 50yd, staircase-like walk uphill to a view of the namesake peaks. Named by a Methodist minister in 1916, from left to right are Abraham, Isaac and Jacob, while crouching in front of Jacob is Mt Moroni (named for a Mormon angel).

Ahead on your right, **Zion Lodge** houses the park's only cafe and restaurant. The lodge was first built in the 1920s, but burnt down in 1966. The rebuilt lodge is not as grand as those in other states, but the wide grassy front lawn – shaded by a giant cottonwood tree – is a favored place for a post-hike ice cream and nap. Across the road from the lodge is the corral for **horseback rides** and the trailhead for the **Emerald Pools**.

The **Grotto**, barely a half-mile north, is a large, cottonwood-shaded picnic area with plenty of tables, restrooms and drinking water. From the picnic area, the Grotto Trail leads south to Zion Lodge. Across the road from the picnic area, the **West Rim Trail** leads north toward **Angels Landing**. Those who'd rather admire Angels Landing than climb it should stroll the first flat quarter-mile of the West Rim Trail to a stone bench for the perfect vantage point.

Make sure you spend some time at **Weeping Rock**, a short distance further on. There's a lot to see at this bend in the river, a great example of an 'incised meander.' Pause to admire Angels Landing, the Organ, Cable Mountain, the Great White Throne and looming Observation Point. A short detour up the bucolic **Weeping Rock Trail** to a sheltered alcove and hanging garden is a worthwhile driving diversion. Two other great trails are accessed from here: the chain-assist **Hidden Canyon Trail** and the Papa Bear of workouts, **Observation Point**.

There are no trailheads at **Big Bend**, but rock climbers get out here on their way to some of Zion's famous walls. Others just soak up the view, which is a different vantage of the features seen from Weeping Rock. It's a good place to bring binoculars and scan the skies for California condors.

If you're using the shuttle, the only way to the next two sights is to walk. As

It's a Bird, It's a Plane, It's a Condor!

With a wingspan of up to 10ft, the endangered California condor is the largest feathered flyer in North America. In recent years, captive-bred birds released around the Grand Canyon have moved north. In Zion they seem to like circling above Angels Landing and other tall park features. The Big Bend shuttle stop is a particularly good vantage point from which to spot them. (Be sure to bring binoculars.) Condors are basically big vultures, and they can be hard to differentiate from the common variety. To identify the real thing, look for all-black wings with a triangle of white at the tip underneath, visible when they fly.

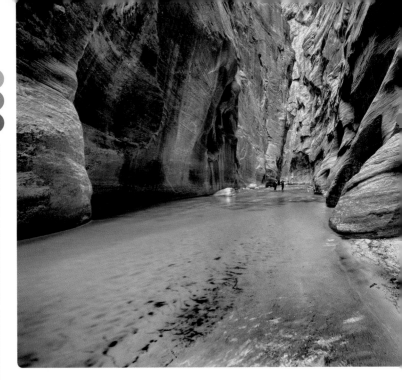

you continue north, on a ledge up to the right look for a reconstructed **granary**. Although ancient Native American in origin it was rebuilt in the 1930s by the Boy Scouts. After about a half-mile, you get to **Menu Falls**, so-named because it was pictured on Zion Lodge's first menu cover. The multilevel deck with overlook is the most popular place to get married in the park. From there it's easier to backtrack to Big Bend shuttle than to hoof it all the way up to the last stop. The canyon narrows near the 4418ft cliff face that forms a natural amphitheater known as the **Temple of Sinawava** at the road's end. Across the road the rock called the **Pulpit** does indeed look a bit like a giant lectern. From here you can take the popular **Riverside Walk** to **The Narrows**. Interpretive signs explain how the seemingly soft and gentle Virgin River could have carved this 1500ft gash.

From April through October, all visitors wishing to tour the road by vehicle must ride the **Zion Park Shuttle** (p380). The rest of the year, cars can drive freely up the spur road that leads just over 6 miles to the Temple of Sinawava. The drive can also be done as an excellent bike ride (even better if you shuttle your bicycle up to the top and coast down). Shuttle riders usually start at the visitor center.

ZION–MT CARMEL HWY Scenic Drive
Open to private vehicles year-round, this 12-mile stretch of Hwy 9 traverses Zion National Park between South Entrance and East Entrance, twisting and turning its way up to Zion–Mt Carmel Tunnel and on to the evocative slickrock covering the park's east side.

From the ranger-staffed **South Entrance** gate, where you pay your fees and get your maps, the turnoff to **Zion Canyon Visitor Center** is immediately on your right. A quarter-mile further is the signed turnoff for South Campground and the summer-only **Zion Nature Center**, home to many of Zion's children's programs. The gym-like building houses flora and fauna exhibits and sits beside a grassy riverside picnic area that makes

Left: Virgin River (p369), Zion; **Below:** Checkerboard Mesa, Zion
(LEFT) DENIS CORRIVEAU / LONELY PLANET IMAGES ©; (BELOW) WITOLD SKRYPCZAK / LONELY PLANET IMAGES ©

a great place to chill out during the midday heat.

Also just off the highway is the **Human History Museum**. Past Canyon Junction, Hwy 9 climbs a 3.5-mile series of long, steep switchbacks. This scenic stretch offers windows full of red rock and amazing views of the **Great Arch**.

Make sure to stop at one of the several large turnouts before you get to the engineering marvel that is **Zion– Mt Carmel Tunnel**. At the time of its completion, the 1.1-mile tunnel was the longest in the United States. Engineers had to construct an aerial tramway just to create a workers' base camp. During the three years of construction (from 1927 to 1930), more than 146 tons of dynamite were used to move 72,000 cubic yards of stone. Much of it was thrown out of the six 'galleries' you see as you drive through; the remainder was used to fill in the roadway below.

At the tunnel's east entrance is a small parking lot with pit toilets and the trailhead for the **Canyon Overlook**, an unchallenging cliff-hugging detour with an interesting perspective. From here the road passes vast undulating fields of pale beige and yellow slickrock (not red!). Here the fracture lines make the sandstone look liquid, and brittle slabs ooze right up to the road. After about 3.5 miles, you get your first glimpse of **Checkerboard Mesa**, a huge sloping face of light slickrock etched like a giant checkerboard.

It's another mile to the official Checkerboard Mesa viewpoint, your last must-see stop. About a quarter-mile further on is the **East Entrance**, beyond which is the park boundary.

KOLOB CANYONS ROAD Scenic Drive
The saying 'short but sweet' has never been more aptly applied than to the Kolob Canyons Rd scenic drive. It's only 5 miles long, but around every curve looms a stunning red-rock vista. One-tenth the number of visitors come here as compared to Zion Canyon. That's a shame, at

367

If You Like...
Guided Adventure

If you like adventure and love to leave the logistics to someone else, try one of these local tour operators:

1 MOUNTAIN BIKE BUDDIES
(☎800-860-6460; www.mountainbikebuddies. com; 642 N Bandolier Ln, Washington, UT) This outfitter arranges do-it-yourself bike tours that include hotel pick-up, bike rental and shuttle to and from trailheads around Zion, St George and Cedar City.

2 ZION ADVENTURE COMPANY
(☎435-772-1001; www.zionadventures.com; 36 Lion Blvd, Springdale) Rent an inner tube and float 2 miles down a stretch of the Virgin River outside the park, before getting shuttled back to base.

3 ZION OUTBACK SAFARIS
(☎866-946-6494; www.zionjeeptours.com) Hop in a 'safari vehicle' and journey by backroad to Smithsonian Buttes and the ghost-town of Grafton. Sunset trips available too.

4 MILD TO WILD RHINO TOURS
(☎435-216-8298; www.mildtowildrhinotours. com; 839 Lion Blvd, Springdale) Guides teach you to use the four-seat, open-air Yamaha Rhino utility vehicle and then lead you around BLM lands. It's 'mild' if you drive, 'wild' if they do.

least for drivers, since the overlooks pack such up-close, visual punch. Late May through June abundant upcountry wildflowers bloom; in winter, the road remains plowed, but may shut temporarily for snow. Forty miles from Springdale and 20 miles from Cedar City, just off I-15, pay your fee or show your receipt or pass at the tiny **Kolob Canyons Visitor Center**. From there the road is wonderfully steep, ascending from a beginning elevation of 5350ft. (It's a great drive, but not a favorite cycling route.) All along the way there are pullouts and interesting interpretive signs.

After 1.8 miles you'll reach the trailhead to the **Taylor Creek Middle Fork**, along with your first good views of the **finger canyons** and Zion's highest point, **Horse Ranch Mountain** (8726ft). As the road affords a high vantage point, the rough-hewn cliffs appear shorter than those in Zion Canyon, but they are every bit as tall and have just as much dramatic flair.

At **Lee Pass**, you'll find the trailhead for the hardcore **La Verkin Creek Trail** to Kolob Arch. About a mile further is the end of the road, marked by a large parking area and pit toilets. To the west you can see the **Hurricane Cliffs** and the **Pine Valley Mountains**. You have to climb up the mile-long **Timber Creek Overlook** to see the finger canyons from here. About 100yd along the trail, a picnic area in the scrub forest provides a good spot for a rest or lunch.

Hiking

Zion seems to have been cut and crafted with hikers in mind. Its wealth of experiences and scenery rivals that of any national park, and most of it is accessible on day hikes. Even back-country routes like the West Rim and The Narrows trails are doable in a single (admittedly long and challenging) day.

Though each of Zion's areas offers hikes, Zion Canyon boasts the lion's share of trails, and they tend to be the most crowded. Most canyon trails are paved to some degree, even the steepest; route-finding is barely an issue. Every trailhead features a signboard with a map and all are near Zion Park Shuttle stops. Bus drivers usually announce the trails at each stop. Remember that off-season you will have to make round-trip hikes in order to get back to your car.

PA'RUS TRAIL
Hiking

Although the Pa'rus (PAH-roos) trail is one of Zion's busiest, this 1.7-mile (one way) path still makes for a pleasant mid-canyon stroll along the **Virgin River**. Here the widely spread canyon walls are stately and majestic rather than awesome and overpowering. The paved, wheelchair-accessible trail is the only trail in the park open to bikes and dogs, and is the perfect place to contemplate the **Towers of the Virgin**, the **Streaked Wall**, **Bridge Mountain** and the **Watchman**. Four footbridges along the way crisscross the river, and numerous dirt paths lead down to the water where you can play. At trail's end, Canyon Junction, you can turn around or hop on a return shuttle. Allow about 1½ hours for this easy walk. The trail begins at the Zion Canyon Visitor Center.

RIVERSIDE WALK   Hiking
Shadowed from the slanting sun by towering walls, this fun and easy 2-mile walk (a kids' favorite) parallels the slippery cobblestones of the **Virgin River**, accessing seeps, hanging gardens and wading spots. Interpretive signs explain the geology and ecology of the corridor, and various mini-spur trails lead to the river itself. The water is a great place to play from mid-June through August. The trail starts at the Temple of Sinawava, at the end of Zion Canyon Rd, and the hike takes about an hour (round-trip).

TAYLOR CREEK MIDDLE FORK   Hiking
From its start at Kolob Canyons Rd, this moderate, paved 5-mile trail crisscrosses Taylor Creek, passing through juniper, sage and piñon to get to two historic cabins. After undulating up and down over roots and in and around water-carved alcoves, the trail ends with splendid views of **Double Arch Alcove**, a natural amphitheater. Here, **The Narrows** begin, at a raised cul-de-sac with benches, and steps lead down to a rocky fan at the river's edge. Wear shoes you don't mind getting wet; the river is irresistible.

You can hike this in three hours (round-trip).

WEEPING ROCK TRAIL   Hiking
For a trail that's over almost before it's begun, this easy-to-moderate half-mile jaunt is surprisingly memorable. The enormous, cool alcove at trail's end contains the park's largest hanging garden and an incredible amount of plant diversity. Interpretive signs explain much of the blooming foliage. The popular, mostly paved trek climbs 100ft to a romantically framed view of the **White Throne** and **Zion Canyon**. When the water is really running, it forms a veil from above; in all temperate seasons, expect to get a bit damp. In winter the weep can form giant icicles that may cause trail closure.

EMERALD POOLS & KAYENTA TRAILS   Hiking
This extremely popular sequence of trails links to a series of bucolic ponds, stunning desert-varnished rocks and a surprisingly verdant desert oasis. Water seeps from sandstone and colorful pools

Weeping Rock (p365), Zion
CAROL POLICH / LONELY PLANET IMAGES ©

are rimmed with life; wildflowers spring up in May and autumn leaves turn in October.

From Zion Lodge, cross the road and bridge to get to the trailhead. The **Middle Pools** path heads left (take it if you don't mind going up steeply at first and want to be traveling against the crowds). The **Lower Pools** trail, to the right, leads to the same pools. Follow this paved path, which gradually rises and falls for less than a mile before reaching the **Lower Pool**. Here waterfalls cascade down a multicolored, mineral-stained overhang in a long arc, misting the trail (and you) as you pass beneath. From here, the trail ascends 150ft to the two, less dramatic, **Middle Pools** that feed the waterfalls below.

From between the ponds, a steep, rocky half-mile one-way spur requires a little scrambling to get to the **Upper Pool**. This, the loveliest grotto of all, is surrounded by the sheer-walled skirts of **Lady Mountain**.

The round-trip hike is roughly 3 miles and takes about 2½ hours. Difficulty is moderate.

THE NARROWS: FROM THE BOTTOM   Hiking

Hiking through a rocky river in ankle- to chest-deep water, as the canyon walls seem to grow and press in on you, The Narrows is a quintessential Zion walking experience. The 'trail' (which is the Virgin River itself) begins at the **Temple of Sinawava**, at the end of the **Riverside Walk**. Here, you enter the river and start hiking upstream. Around the first bend is **Mystery Falls**, the exit point for Mystery Canyon. As you hike, each alcove, bowl, hollow, crack and arch seems its own secret place. Ravens glide low over the water, and you can sometimes hear waterfalls spilling down from inside the rock.

It's about 2.5 miles to the junction with **Orderville Canyon**. Beyond that, you'll enter **Wall Street**, where the sheerness, nearness and height of the cliffs shatter whatever remains of your perspective. After this section, the canyon opens slightly again, the water gets periodically deeper (usually requiring swimming), and your fellow hikers thin out.

After the 4-mile point, you'll negotiate a series of huge boulders, and the canyon, though gorgeous, becomes somewhat

East Temple, Zion

less otherworldly. At 5 miles you come to **Big Springs**, a fern-fringed rush of water much larger than anything so far. Here day hikers are required to turn around.

While it can take up to eight hours to do the full 10-mile round-trip to Big Springs, set aside a minimum of five hours so you'll at least have time to reach memorable Wall Street. Always check conditions with a ranger before hiking this difficult 'trail'. When the river is running more than 120 cubic feet per second (usually in April and May), The Narrows is closed. In winter, wet or dry suits are required, and specialized footwear (all available for rent at local outfitters) is always recommended.

ANGELS LANDING   Hiking

'How far did you get?' is the question asked every morning at coffee shops all over Springdale, as hikers compare notes on Angels Landing. This strenuous four-hour, 5.4-mile (round-trip) hike is not just a physical challenge, but a mental one for those with a fear of heights.

From the trailhead, across the road from the Grotto picnic area, the trail meanders along the desert floor then ascends gradually but relentlessly, becoming steeper as you begin long, paved switchbacks up the canyon wall. The last switchback crosses beneath a rock overhang. Beyond it, the trail levels out a little, and runs deep into narrow, slightly cooler **Refrigerator Canyon**.

Once through the canyon, you'll ascend a few more switchbacks before reaching **Walter's Wiggles**, one of the park's engineering marvels. This set of 21 short, steep, stonework zigzags is named after the early superintendent of Zion who imagined them. You emerge atop **Scout Lookout** at a sandy bench with a pit toilet and a turnoff for the West Rim. (Tip: those who don't like chains and narrow footways could continue up the strenuous West Rim Trail to panoramic overlooks.)

If you've made it this far, you should really continue at least the next 70ft or so

If You Like…
Quiet Hikes

If you like hikes, but want to escape the crowds of Zion Canyon, head to the Kolob Canyon area (to the northwest sector of the park) or East Zion.

1 CANYON OVERLOOK
(Trailhead east of Zion-Mt Carmel Tunnel, Kolob Canyons) A convenient stop off Hwy 9, Canyon Overlook is a quick 1-mile hike that rewards with intimate canyon experiences and ends in much-photographed panoramic vistas. Difficulty: easy to moderate.

2 NORTHGATE PEAKS TRAIL
(Wildcat Canyon trailhead, Kolob Terrace Rd) On this overlooked, 4.4-mile west-side gem, traipse through sage meadows and pine forest to reach a lava outcrop with a view of 7000ft-plus peaks. Access via Kolob Terrace Rd. Difficulty: easy to moderate.

3 TIMBER CREEK OVERLOOK
(Trailhead at end of Kolob Canyon's Rd, Kolob Canyons) Follow this 1-mile dirt trail to a promontory with 270-degree views of canyons and mountains. The track gets a bit steep and rocky, but unless elevation affects you, it isn't too hard. Difficulty: easy to moderate.

4 CABLE MOUNTAIN TRAIL
(Trailhead off West Pine Rd, inside Zion Ponderosa Ranch Resort, East Zion) This 6.2-mile upcountry hike has little elevation change and leads through ponderosa pines to your choice of Zion Canyon overlooks. Difficulty: moderate.

5 EAST MESA TRAIL
(Trailhead at Zion Ponderosa Ranch, Beaver Rd, East Zion) This sneaky, backcountry approach to Observation Point starts off on a 4WD road on the east side of Zion and traverses upcountry ecosystems before dropping down to the overlook. Difficulty: moderate.

to see the incredible views. To do so, you'll have to brave the first part of the scary stuff – a cliff-face climb using carved-out footholds and anchor-bolted chains.

Afterwards, you get your first good look at **Angels Landing**. Seeing the thin saddle you have to cross – at times just 5ft wide and with a drop of 1000ft to the canyon floor on either side – stops many people in their tracks. Once across, the last 0.5 miles of the trail, such as it is, gets much steeper and rockier. Chains are bolted into the rock for much of the way. Trail's end, a sloping 30ft-wide flat rock surface at the top, is abundantly clear. Sit and take in the stunning 360-degree view of nearly all of Zion Canyon. You've earned it.

OBSERVATION POINT *Hiking*

Yeah, we know, we know – you want to climb Angels Landing. That's great, but for effort spent, Observation Point is a much better trail: fewer people, an incredible hanging-chasm slot canyon and the best views in the park at day's end. Be warned though, this 8-mile, five-hour hike (round-trip) is one of the most difficult in Zion, rising 2150ft in total. On the positive side, the exposed parts of the trail are wider than their counterparts on the Angels Landing trail and therefore less frightening.

Starting from the Weeping Rock stop, the first half-mile of the trail is the same as that for Hidden Canyon, ascending long, steep, leg-burning switchbacks. These continue to **Echo Canyon**, a beautiful hanging chasm, where the trail levels out briefly, hugging the serpentine cliff as the water-eroded chasm yawns below. Towering above, the flat face of **Cable Mountain** is truly a sight to behold. Further up, a long series of tough switchbacks draw you up the mountain. The trail is exposed to a long drop, but it's wide, and no chains are necessary. Finally, you'll reach the mesa top, and the trail is fairly level as it skirts the rim.

For the final half-mile, you'll traverse a sandy piñon-juniper forest to **Observation Point**. From this perch at 6508ft, you can peer 600ft *down* to the knife-edge of **Angels Landing** and 2150ft to the **Virgin River** – an incredible perspective on an infamous hike. The raven's-eye view down the canyon also includes a nice perspective of **Red Arch Mountain**. To the west, you're level with white **Cathedral Mountain** as the whole Zion world seems to spread out before you.

Backpacking

Despite its accessibility, Zion's backcountry sees relatively little use compared to other major national parks. Thus hikers can enjoy the park's ethereal and overwhelming beauty in near solitude, even on summer weekends when the Zion Park Shuttle is standing-room only.

One reason the Zion backcountry is so quiet is that it can be a hot, dry, extremely remote place – preparation is essential. The **Backcountry Desk** (☏ 435-772-0170; www.nps.gov/zion; ☉7am-7:30pm late May-early Sep, reduced hours rest of year) in the Zion Canyon Visitor Center serves as your main information resource and permit vendor. Backcountry permits cost $10 for one to two people and $15 for three to seven. Permits can be reserved by phone or online.

Cycling

In the park, cycling is allowed on roads and on the **Pa'rus Trail**, both of which are very pleasant and popular. In fact, the lack of cars from April through October makes cycling a great way to see the canyon. We recommend that you shuttle your bike up to the Temple of Sinawava and follow our **Zion Canyon Scenic Dr** (p364) in reverse. It's all downhill. Do note that the park requires that you pull over and let shuttles pass.

Enthusiasts can also ride quite comfortably along Hwy 9 through Springdale to the Zion Canyon drive. Speed limits are low and cars usually crawl along the super-flat stretch. Note that east of the Zion Canyon turnoff the road climbs precipitously, and bicycles are not allowed in the Zion–Mt Carmel Tunnel.

As at all national parks, mountain biking is prohibited, but nearby areas provide trails on a par with any in southern Utah – even Moab. Technical slickrock, with audacious obstacles, and genuine singletrack make **Gooseberry**

DENIS CORRIVEAU / LONELY PLANET IMAGES ©

Don't Miss **Watchman Trail**

Zion's sunset trail of choice ascends a mere 400ft, but its end point provides stunning views of the park's sandstone formations as they glow against the setting sun. Wait until the midday heat has waned, then start off at the trailhead, across the road from the Zion Canyon Visitor Center. After following the Virgin River, the trail gently ascends to a small canyon at the base of **Bridge Mountain**. Continue your ascent on several long switchbacks past moderate drop-offs to the top of a foothill, where the trail emerges to wide views. At the end, a 0.3-mile loop trail skirts the foothill, leading to several prime overlooks of the **Towers of the Virgin** and the town of **Springdale**. Rising alone to the south you'll see the ragged **Eagle Crags**. The angular **Watchman** is the last formation to catch the fading light of sunset. Bring a flashlight for the return hike.

The facts: distance 2.7 miles round-trip; duration 1½ to two hours; difficulty easy-moderate; start/finish Zion Canyon Visitor Center. Watchman Peak

Mesa, off Smithsonian Buttes Rd south of Rockville, one of the most popular trails. Occasional sweeping views of Zion's panorama make it all the more attractive. Also try **Hurricane Cliffs**, outside Kolob Canyons, and **Rockville Bench**, southwest of Zion Canyon. Springdale bike shops can provide directions and point you to all the trails. Just remember, summer is hot, hot, hot; spring and fall are the most enjoyable times for biking.

There are two full-service bike shops in Springdale. Both shops offer bike tours and rent road, mountain and hybrid bikes ($35 to $50 per day); and kids' bikes, trailers and car racks (all $15 per day).

ZION CYCLES   Cycling
(☎435-772-0400; www.zioncycles.com; 868 Zion Park Blvd, Springdale; ☺9am-7pm) Set back behind Zion Pizza & Noodle, next to Orange Frozen Yogurt. It offers half- and full-day bike tours outside the park in conjunction with Zion Adventure.

BIKE ZION
Cycling

(☏ 435-772-3303; www.bikingzion.com; 1458 Zion Park Blvd, Springdale; ⊙ 8am-8pm Mar-Oct, hours vary Nov-Feb) In the same building as Zion Rock & Mountain Guides. In addition to day trips, it also offers multiday and multisport tours (hiking, biking, canyoneering and/or climbing).

Canyoneering

If there's one sport that makes Zion special, it's canyoneering. Rappelling 100ft over the lip of a sandstone bowl, swimming icy pools, tracing a slot canyon's sculpted curves, staring up at a ragged gash of blue sky – canyoneering is beautiful, dangerous and sublime all at once. And it's not terribly hard to learn.

As such, canyoneering has become the fastest-growing activity at Zion. The park service sets day-use limits to protect many routes, and permits are required for all. None of the canyons should be taken lightly; classes are available from area outfitters. Even if you've never considered canyoneering before, a half-day guided trip (no experience required) might be the highlight of your visit to Zion.

Guided canyoneering is prohibited in the park, but two Springdale outfitters offer half-day to multiday training – and highly recommended half- and full-day guided trips – on the every-bit-as-beautiful public lands surrounding. (Rates start at $150 per person for a half-day.) Both companies have excellent reputations and tons of experience.

ZION ROCK & MOUNTAIN GUIDES
Canyoneering

(☏ 435-772-3303; www.zionrockguides.com; 1458 Zion Park Blvd; ⊙ 8am-8pm Mar-Oct, hours vary Nov-Feb) Super-knowledgeable guides are long-term area residents. All classes and trips are private, for your group alone. Zion Rock is the only place that rents static canyon ropes.

ZION ADVENTURE COMPANY
Canyoneering

(☏ 435-772-1001; www.zionadventures.com; 36 Lion Blvd; ⊙ 8am-8pm Mar-Oct, 9am-noon & 4-7pm Nov-Feb) Provides a bit more hand-holding, with introductory videos and life-size pictures of the rappels. You may get a rappel or two fewer, but you'll have just as much fun.

Kids' Activities

Late May through late August, Zion National Park offers a series of children's programs for various age groups. Many are based at **Zion Nature Center** (☏ 435-772-3256; South Campground, off Hwy 9; admission free; ⊙ noon-5pm late May-late Aug), but some take place at Zion Lodge or on trails. You might hunt for animal habitats along the Virgin River or hear stories about the life of the first pioneer settlers in the area. For schedules check

California condor, Zion
YVA MOMATIUK & JOHN EASTCOTT / MINDEN PICTURES / GETTY ©

online (www.nps.gov/zion) or in the summer park newspaper.

Sleeping

Zion proper boasts just one lodge and three basic campgrounds, which fill up quickly on weekends and in summer. Reservations can be made at Watchman Campground only. Thankfully, lodging-rich Springdale is right outside the park's front door.

Just inside Zion's South Entrance are the park's two main campgrounds, Watchman and South. They are adjacent to each other and to the visitor center. Neither has showers, laundry facilities or a general store; these are available in Springdale. At both, there is a maximum stay of 14 days from March through October, 30 days the rest of the year.

Zion Canyon & Kolob Terrace Road

ZION LODGE
Park Lodge $$

(📞 lodge 435-772-7700, reservations 888-297-2757; www.zionlodge.com; Zion Canyon Scenic Dr; r $165-190, cabins $180; @ 📶) Stunning red-rock cliffs surround this historic lodge on all sides and, for many, the location in the middle of Zion Canyon is enough. 'Western cabins' (actually duplexes and four-plexes) have gas fireplaces, wood floors and elaborate headboards, but they also have paper-thin walls. For the best views, request a 2nd-floor motel room in Building A, overlooking the lawn and canyon.

WATCHMAN CAMPGROUND
Campground $

(📞 435-772-3256, reservations 877-444-6777; www.recreation.gov; Zion Canyon Visitor Center, Hwy 9; tent sites $16, RV sites $18-20; 🕐 year-round; 🚻 👶) Towering cottonwoods provide fairly good shade for Watchman's 165 well-spaced sites, some of which are on the Virgin River. Facilities include restrooms (but no showers), drinking water, picnic tables, fire grates, a dump station and recycling bins. Some have electricity; generators are prohibited. Sites are

by reservation from early March through late October; the rest of the year it's first-come, first-served.

SOUTH CAMPGROUND
Campground $

(📞 435-772-3256; Zion Canyon Visitor Center, off Hwy 9; campsites $16; 🕐 Mar-Oct; 👶) Also on the Virgin River, this first-come, first-served campground sits beside the busy Pa'rus Trail, so it has a bit more company than Watchman. It has no hookups; generator use is allowed from 8am to 10am and 6pm to 8pm. Facilities are similar to Watchman.

LAVA POINT CAMPGROUND
Campground $

(📞 435-772-3256; Lava Point Rd, off Kolob Terrace Rd; tent sites free; 🕐 Jun-Oct; 👶) An attractive loop of six primitive first-come, first-served campsites sits off Kolob Terrace Rd at 7900ft. There's a pit toilet, picnic tables and fire grates, but no water. The campground is rarely full, as it's an hour from the South Entrance and Springdale.

Springfield & Around

ZION CANYON B&B
B&B $$

(📞 435-772-9466; www.zioncanyonbandb.com; 101 Kokopelli Circle; r $115-185; ❄ @ 📶) Everywhere you turn there's another gorgeous red-rock view framed perfectly in an oversized window. Deep canyon wall colors – magenta, eggplant, burnt sienna – compliment not only the scenery, but the rustic Southwestern decor. Think gourmet dishes, like German puff pancakes, for breakfast.

RED ROCK INN
B&B $$

(📞 435-772-3139; www.redrockinn.com; 998 Zion Park Blvd; cottages $122-192; ❄ 📶) The five romantic rooms here are all little B&B cottages, each with a whirlpool or hot tub. In the morning an egg and pastry breakfast basket arrives at your door, to be enjoyed on your small terrace or up the hill in a desert garden.

UNDER-THE-EAVES BED & BREAKFAST
B&B $$

(📞 435-772-3457; www.under-the-eaves.com; 980 Zion Park Blvd; r $85-125, ste $165-185;

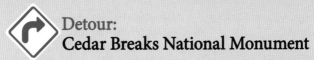

Detour:
Cedar Breaks National Monument

In Cedar Breaks' wildly eroded natural amphitheater, sculpted cliffs and hoodoos form a kaleidoscope of magenta, salmon, plum, rust and ochre. Think of the park as the icing on the Grand Staircase cake – it contains the same geologic layers as Bryce but is more than 1000ft higher, rising to 10,450ft atop the Markagunt Plateau.

The compact park (www.nps.gov/cebr) lies 22 miles east and north of Cedar City, off Hwy 14, about 60 miles from Bryce and 70 miles from Zion's East Entrance. Snow typically limits access to the park between October and late May (at least). In season, rangers hold geology talks and star parties at the small **visitor center** (☏435-586-9451, ext 4031; ⏰9am-6pm Jun–mid-Oct). Park entrance is $4 per person, and national park passes are accepted. The pretty, first-come, first-served 28-site **campground** (sites $14; ⏰late Jun-Aug) provides water and restrooms but no showers. It's rarely full and opening dates fluctuate. Summer temperatures range from 40°F (4°C) to 70°F (21°C), and brief storms can drop rain, hail and even snow. Including **Point Supreme** at the visitor center, the five viewpoints off Hwy 148 are the park's must-sees.

❄🛜) From colorful tractor reflectors to angel art, the owners' collections enliven every corner of this 1930s bungalow. Most rooms are snug, but there's plenty of space to hang out in the Craftsman living room or on Adirondack chairs in the gardens. Breakfast (included) is at a local restaurant.

DESERT PEARL INN   Hotel $$
(☏435-772-8888; www.desertpearl.com; 707 Zion Park Blvd; r $119-178, ste $209-298; ❄@🛜⛱) What a naturally stylish inn: twig art decorates the walls, sculptural metal headboards resemble art and full granite showers surround you with luxury. Outside, terraces and expert landscaping eclipse the pool's near-road location. Opt for a spacious riverside king suite to get a waterfront patio.

DRIFTWOOD LODGE   Hotel $$
(☏435-772-3262; www.driftwoodlodge.net; 1515 Zion Park Blvd; r $120-199; ❄🛜⛱🐾) Having the top restaurant in town (Parallel 88, p378) on-site is enough reason for some to stay in the upscale rooms here. Request a Watchman suite and you get pastoral sunset views of field, river and mountain beyond.

PIONEER LODGE   Hotel $$
(☏435-772-3233; www.pioneerlodge.com; 838 Zion Park Blvd; r $135-165; ❄@🛜⛱) This rustic hotel, restaurant and cafe always seems to be bustling in the center of town. Pine-log beds carry the Western theme along. The popular 2nd-floor 'Canyon view' rooms share a massive deck.

ZION CANYON CAMPGROUND & RV RESORT   Campground $
(☏435-772-3237; www.zioncamp.com; 479 Zion Park Blvd; tent sites $30, RV sites $35; ⏰year-round; 🛜⛱🐾) Excellent amenities at this 200-site campground on the Virgin River include a heated pool, showers, laundry, camp store, restaurant, playground, river access and tubing.

 Eating

Zion Lodge is the only place within the park that serves or sells food, but the quality does not match the unparalleled surroundings. Thankfully, Springdale offers a handful of really good options – and some so-so ones that take advantage of the fact they will probably only ever see tourist patrons once.

There are no stand-alone bars in Springdale, but a few area eateries have bar sections. For a laid-back local vibe try the beer and wine at the Bit & Spur. Switchback Jack's Sports Grille, with a full liquor menu, has super-comfy club chairs and a sports-bar feel to it. Even though Utah's alcohol laws have eased a little, you'll still have to buy at least chips and salsa to drink.

Zion Canyon

RED ROCK GRILL American $$$
(435-772-7760; Zion Lodge; breakfast $6-8, lunch $7-10, dinner mains $15-29; 6:30-10:30am, 11:30am-3pm & 5-10pm) The lodge's main restaurant is on the 2nd floor, and the best thing about it is the spacious deck, where you can soak up the magnificent red-cliff views. Breakfast is a basic buffet, and lunch choices are mainly sandwiches, burgers and wraps. Though the dinner menu touts its sustainable-cuisine stance for dishes like roast pork loin and flatiron steak, the results are decidedly hit-or-miss. Reservations are required. It has a full bar.

CASTLE DOME CAFE American $
(435-772-7700; Zion Lodge; mains $5-7; 10:30am-6:30pm, till 5:30pm Apr & Sep, closed Oct-late Mar;) The quick cafe serves sandwiches, burgers, pizza and salads. Most importantly, it sells ice cream, which you can enjoy under the lodge's giant cottonwood tree.

Springdale

WHIPTAIL GRILL Mexican $$
(435-772-0283; 445 Zion Park Blvd; mains $11-20; noon-10pm Apr-Oct, closed Nov-Mar) The old gas-station building isn't much to look at, but man, you can't beat the fresh tastes here – pan-seared tilapia tacos, chipotle chicken enchiladas, organic beef Mexican pizza... There are numerous vegetarian options as well.

OSCAR'S CAFÉ Southwestern $$
(435-772-3232; 948 Zion Park Blvd; breakfast & sandwiches $8-12, mains $9-20; 7:30am-10pm) From green chili–laden omelets to pork verde burritos, Oscar's has the Southwestern spice going on. But it also does smoky ribs, shrimp and garlic burgers well. In the evening, the living-room-like,

Autumn in Zion

Mexican-tiled patio with twinkly lights (and heaters) is a favorite hangout.

BIT & SPUR RESTAURANT
& SALOON   Mexican $$$
(☏ 435-772-3498; www.bitandspur.com; 1212 Zion Park Blvd; mains $18-25; ☺5pm-10:30pm, bar to midnight) Sweet-potato tamales and chile-rubbed rib eyes are two of the classics at this local institution. Inside the walls are wild with local art; outside it's all about the red-rock sunset.

PARALLEL 88   Contemporary $$$
(☏ 435-772-3588; www.paralleleighty-eight restaurant.com; Driftwood Lodge, 1515 Zion Park Blvd; breakfast $8-12, dinner mains $16-30; ☺7-10:30am & 5pm-close) Chef Jeff Crosland has mastered 'casually elegant' with a top-notch seasonal menu, gorgeous red-cliff views and friendly service. Most nights he can be seen chatting with guests on the patio as they nosh on impossibly tender green-apple pork loin or vegetable terrine.

FLYING MONKEY   Italian American $
(☏ 435-772-3333; 975 Zion Park Blvd; mains $6-13; ☺11am-9:30pm) Wood-fired goodness at great prices. Expect interesting ingredients like fennel and yellow squash on your

roast veggie pizza, or Italian sausage with prosciutto on your oven-baked sandwich. Burgers, salads and pastas are on the menu too.

🍃SPRINGDALE FRUIT
COMPANY MARKET   Market $
(☏ 435-772-3222; www.springdalefruit.com; 2491 Zion Park Blvd; ☺8am-8pm Apr-Oct, closed Nov-Mar; 🛠) The selection of high-quality organic, vegan and gluten-free foodstocks here is great. On-site orchards produce peaches and apples in summer. The store also makes focaccia sandwiches and fruit smoothies, best enjoyed on the shady tables outside in the parklike surrounds.

MEAN BEAN COFFEE HOUSE   Cafe $
(☏ 435-772-0654; 932 Zion Park Blvd; breakfast & sandwiches $6-11; ☺7am-5pm Jun-Aug, 7am-2pm Sep-May; 🛜) Probably the town's best brew. Take your breakfast burrito or panini up to the roof deck.

ℹ Information

Entrance Fees & Passes
Entry to Zion National Park cost $25 per vehicle or $12 per pedestrian, bicycle or motorcycle; passes

Slickrock along the Zion–Mt Carmel Hwy (p366)

are valid for one week. An annual Zion Pass costs $50, and interagency and senior passes are valid. All can be purchased at entrance stations and visitor centers.

Opening Dates

Zion is open 24 hours a day, 365 days a year. Entrance kiosks are unstaffed at night.

Tourist Information

Kolob Canyons Visitor Center (☏435-586-0895; Kolob Canyons Rd, off I-15; ☺8am-6pm late May–early Sep, 8am-5pm late Apr–late May & early Sep–mid-Oct, 8am-4:30pm mid-Oct–late Apr) Small, secondary visitor center in the northwest section of the park.

Zion Canyon Backcountry Desk (☏435-772-0170; www.nps.gov/zion; Zion Canyon Visitor Center; ☺7am-8pm late May–early Sep, 7am-6pm late Apr–late May & early Sep–mid-Oct, 8am-4:30pm mid-Oct–late Apr) Issues backcountry trail and camping permits.

Zion Canyon Visitor Center (☏435-772-3256; www.nps.gov/zion; ☺8am-8pm late May–early Sep, 8am-6pm late Apr–late May & early Sep–mid-Oct, 8am-5pm mid-Oct–late Apr) Main visitor center.

Park Policies & Regulations

○ As at all national parks, you are not allowed to feed wildlife or to touch or deface any cultural artifact or site. Pets are not permitted on park shuttles, in the backcountry, on trails or in park buildings. Bicycles and pets are allowed on one trail, the Pa'rus Trail. Bicycles are welcome on park roads but may not be ridden through the Zion–Mt Carmel Tunnel.

○ Campfires are allowed only in fire grates in Watchman and South Campgrounds. Wood gathering is not permitted in the park; buy all firewood in Springdale. When fire danger is high, all campfires may be banned. Fireworks are prohibited in the park.

○ People are not allowed in the Virgin River when it is flowing in excess of 120 cubic feet per second.

Maps

National Geographic (www.natgeomaps.com) puts out a colorful, waterproof *Trails Illustrated* map (No 214) for Zion. The less snazzy park map from **Zion Natural History Association**

(www.zionpark.org) also gets the job done. Both are available at park visitor centers.

Dangers & Annoyances

Before you hike any narrow canyon, check the weather. Flash floods are a real danger. Do not enter narrow canyons if storms threaten. Even if the weather seems good, watch for signs of a flash flood. These include sudden changes in water clarity, rising water levels and/or floating debris, and a rush of wind, the sound of thunder or a low, rumbling roar. If you notice any of these, immediately get to higher ground (even a few feet could save your life). Zion gets extremely hot in summer, so always bring plenty of water with you.

❶ Getting There & Around

Air

Las Vegas' **McCarran International Airport** (LAS; ☏702-261-5211; www.mccarran.com) is the closest international airport to Zion. You can fly there and rent a car for the 170-mile drive to the park.

Salt Lake City International Airport (SLC; ☏801-575-2400; www.slcairport.com) is the next closest major international airport, 315 miles north.

The closest regional airports are SGU **Municipal Airport** (☏435-673-3451; www.flysgu.com) in St George and **Cedar City Regional Airport** (☏435-867-9408; www.cedarcity.org) in Cedar City. The former is 49 miles away, and the latter is 60 miles away. Both airports have rental cars.

Bus

The closest **Greyhound** (☏800-231-2222; www.greyhound.com) bus stations are in St George and Cedar City.

Car & RV

○ Zion has two main entrances, a southern entrance via Hwy 9 and a northern entrance via I-15. Zion Canyon is accessed from Hwy 9.

○ Between April and October, no passenger cars are allowed to tour Zion Canyon Scenic Dr; to access it you will have to take the Zion Park Shuttle or ride a bike. Personal vehicles are permitted between November and March, when the shuttle does not operate. During shuttle season, it's still possible to drive through the southern section of Zion on Hwy

9, which connects Springdale with Mt Carmel Junction. Year-round you can drive on Kolob Canyons Scenic Dr. Kolob Terrace Rd becomes impassable when snows set in (roughly December into May).

○ RV drivers: Zion–Mt Carmel Tunnel has vehicle size restrictions. Vehicles larger than 7ft, 10in wide or 11ft, 4in high must pay a $15 escort fee and can only travel through the tunnel during daytime hours. Pay fees at the east or south entrance stations.

Park Shuttle

For the most part, private vehicles are prohibited in Zion Canyon from April 1 to October 31, during which time the Zion Park Shuttle is the only way to get around. The shuttle makes nine stops along the Zion Canyon Scenic Dr, from the visitor center to the Temple of Sinawava (a 90-minute round-trip).

Outside the canyon, the optional Springdale Town Shuttle makes six regular stops and three flag stops at hotels and businesses along Hwy 9. Most hotels in Springdale are near shuttle stops, and you'll find tons of free shuttle parking along the town's main road.

The *Zion National Park Map & Guide* (available at visitor centers and entrance stations) contains a route map and timetable and is indispensable for shuttle travel.

BRYCE CANYON NATIONAL PARK

Proving, yet again, to be nature's finest artist, erosion has sculpted southern Utah's Paunsaugunt Plateau into a bizarre landscape of sand-castle spires, slot canyons, limestone arches, fins and windows. Not actually a canyon at all, Bryce Canyon National Park is composed of a series of natural amphitheaters whittled into the edge of an 18-mile plateau. The park's Pink Cliffs mark the top step of the Grand Staircase, a giant geologic terrace that drops all the way to the Grand Canyon. Hiking and horse trails descend into Bryce's 1000ft amphitheaters through a maze of towering stone daggers called hoodoos. At the bottom of Bryce lies the same layer of rock that forms the geological roof of nearby Zion.

Because Bryce is higher than Zion, the air is cleaner and drier, which makes for excellent visibility. On clear nights views reach all the way into the Andromeda galaxy, some 2.2 million miles away. And during the day, with your gaze toward the earth from a Bryce Canyon viewpoint, the landscape seems endless. You'd never know this is the smallest national park in southern Utah.

When to Go

As with Zion, spring and fall can be the nicest times to visit Bryce because you avoid the crowds. However, Bryce's average elevation is several thousand feet higher than Zion's,

Rock formation, Mossy Cave Trail (p387), Bryce Canyon

The Grand Staircase

Along the Colorado Plateau's western edge, a line of high, forested plateaus tower 3000ft above the desert lowlands and valleys that spread out below. Nicknamed the High Plateaus by geologist Clarence Dutton in 1880, the term encompasses the flat-topped mesas of Zion and Bryce Canyon National Parks and also Cedar Breaks National Monument.

From an aerial perspective, these lofty plateaus and cliffs form a remarkable staircase that steps down from southern Utah into northern Arizona. Topping this so-called '**Grand Staircase**' are the Pink Cliffs of the Claron Formation, so extravagantly exposed in Bryce Canyon. Below them jut the Gray Cliffs of various Cretaceous formations. Next in line are the White Cliffs of Navajo sandstone that make Zion Canyon justly famous. These are followed by the Vermilion Cliffs near Lees Ferry, Arizona, and finally come the Chocolate Cliffs abutting the Kaibab Plateau and Grand Canyon.

Another way of understanding the Grand Staircase is to visualize that the top layers of exposed rock at the Grand Canyon form Zion's basement, and that Zion's top layers in turn form the bottom layers of Bryce Canyon National Park. Geologically speaking, one can imagine the parks as being stacked on top of each other. Hypothetically, a river cutting a canyon at Bryce would eventually form another Zion Canyon, and then over time create another Grand Canyon.

so it can be much cooler. May through September, the park's sole paved road and scenic overlooks get pretty crowded, but you can still find solitude by hiking off-hours or seeking out less-traveled trails under the rim. In winter, the park is practically deserted, but the park service keeps the road and turnouts plowed.

When You Arrive

At the entrance kiosk you'll receive a park brochure that includes a good driving map, general information about facilities, and details about the park's geology and wildlife. You'll also get a copy of the park newspaper, *The Hoodoo*, which gives up-to-date information about opening hours, ranger-led activities, hiking trails, backpacking and shuttle information.

Orientation

Compared with the vast landscape that surrounds it, Bryce is small – only 56 sq miles. Shaped somewhat like a seahorse, the long, narrow park is an extension of the sloping Paunsaugunt Plateau and runs north–south, rising from 6600ft on the canyon floor to 7894ft at the visitor center and 9115ft at Rainbow Point, the plateau's southernmost tip.

Bryce's sole vehicle entrance is 3 miles south of Utah Hwy 12, via Hwy 63. The park has one paved road, which is 18 miles long and dead ends at the south end of the plateau. The route gets jammed on summer weekends. To alleviate congestion between mid-May and late September, the park employs a system of voluntary shuttles, which you can board either inside the park or 2 miles north of the entrance station, at the southern end of Bryce Canyon City.

Aside from lodging and dining at Bryce Canyon Lodge, and camping supplies and groceries at the general store (both near Sunrise Point), the park lacks commercial services.

 Sights

Bryce Canyon's major sights, described here, are easily accessible along the 17-mile **Bryce Canyon Scenic Dr**. The road winds south from along the canyon rim,

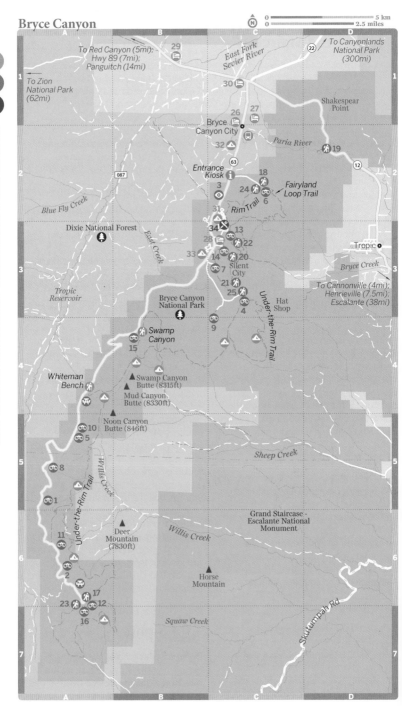

Bryce Canyon

climbing from 7894ft at the visitor center to 9115ft at Rainbow Point, the plateau's southern tip at road's end.

If you're tight on time, be sure to see Sunrise, Sunset and Inspiration Points (all 2 miles from the visitor center) and Bryce Point (4 miles). As all viewpoints lie on the east side of the road (the left side as you drive south), you may want head directly to Rainbow Point (the drive from the visitor center takes about 35 minutes), then work your way back, stopping at the scenic overlooks and turnouts as you reach them.

VISITOR CENTER Visitor Center
(☎435-834-5322; www.nps.gov/brca; Hwy 63; ⊗8am-8pm May-Sep, to 6pm Oct & Apr, to 4:30pm Nov-Mar; ☎) At Bryce's sole visitor center, digital information screens list everything from campground availability to atmospheric conditions (including sunrise and moonrise), schedules of ranger-led programs, hiking-trail descriptions, and a calendar of events. Interpretive exhibits show plant and animal life, as well as geologic displays that explain how Bryce connects with the Grand Canyon and Grand Staircase. The visitor center also screens the excellent 20-minute orientation video, *Bryce Canyon: Shadows of Time*.

Also inside the visitor center, the nonprofit **Bryce Canyon Natural History Association** (☎435-834-4782; www.brycecanyon.org) aids the park service with educational, scientific and interpretive activities. It operates the bookstore, and trained staff members are on duty to answer questions. It also runs an excellent online shop that sells books, maps, videos, music and trip-planning packets tailored to individual travelers' needs.

RAINBOW POINT Lookout
On a clear day you can see more than 100 miles from this overlook at the southernmost end of Bryce Canyon Scenic Drive. The viewpoint provides jaw-dropping views of canyon country. Giant sloping plateaus, tilted mesas and towering buttes jut above the vast landscape, and

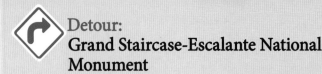

Detour:
Grand Staircase-Escalante National Monument

Nearly twice the size of Rhode Island, **Grand Staircase-Escalante National Monument** (GSENM; entry free) is by far the largest park in the Southwest, yet its spectacular scenery is some of the least visited. Here, a 150-mile-long series of geological strata begins at the bottom of the Grand Canyon and rises, like a staircase, 3500ft to Bryce Canyon and the Escalante River canyons. Together the layers of rock reveal 260 million years of history in a riot of color. Most of the monument lies off the beaten path, so solitude is almost guaranteed.

The most immediately gratifying, dramatic drive is the **Burr Trail**, a paved road that heads east from **Boulder**, crosses GSENM's northeast corner and, after 30 miles, arrives at Capitol Reef National Park, where the road turns to gravel. The road passes several trailheads, including the starting point for the **Escalante River Natural Bridge Trail**, 15 miles east of Escalante. The mostly level, 4.4-mile trail crisscrosses the river seven times before reaching a large natural bridge and arch beyond.

The park has two first-come, first-served campgrounds, but **Calf Creek Campground** (435-335-7382; Hwy 12; campsites $7; year-round;) is the only one with running water. The 14-site campground is surrounded by red-rock canyons and straddles a year-round creek, 15 miles east of Escalante. For information, visit the **Cannonville Visitor Center** (435-826-5640; 10 Center St, Cannonville; 8am-4:30pm Apr-Nov), which is only 14 miles from Bryce Canyon City via Hwy 12.

interpretive panels explain the sights. On the northeastern horizon look for the Aquarius Plateau – the very top step of the Grand Staircase – rising 2000ft higher than Bryce. The viewpoint is reached on a short, paved, wheelchair-accessible path at the far end of the parking lot.

YOVIMPA POINT   Lookout
Accessed by a paved path from the same parking lot as Rainbow Point, Yovimpa Point is one of the park's windiest spots. The southwest-facing view reveals more forested slopes and less eroding rock. Look for Molly's Nipple, an eroded sandstone dome often mistaken for a volcano. Dipping below the horizon is the Kaibab Plateau, marking the Arizona border and the Grand Canyon.

BLACK BIRCH CANYON OVERLOOK   Lookout
Just north of mile 16, at 8750ft, the small **Black Birch Canyon** overlook demonstrates just how precipitously the cliffs

drop from the road. It also offers an up-close look at hoodoos – though these are modest in comparison to those at Bryce Amphitheater.

PONDEROSA CANYON   Lookout
Ponderosa Canyon offers long vistas over giant ponderosa pines and a small amphitheater of hoodoos and burnt-orange cliffs which are especially breathtaking in morning light. If you're feeling ambitious, descend a stretch of the moderately strenuous **Agua Canyon Connecting Trail**, a lightly traveled, steep trail that drops past woods into a brilliant amphitheater of hoodoos before joining the Under-the-Rim Trail after 1.6 miles.

AGUA CANYON VIEWPOINT   Lookout
One of the best stops at the southern end of the park, the **Agua Canyon** viewpoint overlooks two large formations of precariously balanced, top-heavy hoodoos that could – quite literally – fall at any time. That you can only see the tops of these

giant spires, not their bases, ought to give you an idea of the precipitous drop-off at your feet. On the ridge above, note the distinct sedimentary lines between iron-rich red rock and white limestone. Clear days promise mesmerizing vistas of the purple and blue horizon.

NATURAL BRIDGE Landmark

Natural Bridge is an extremely popular stop, and with good reason: a stunning span of eroded, red-hued limestone juts from the edge of the overlook. Though called a bridge, it's technically an arch. A bridge forms when running water, such as a stream, causes the erosion. In this case, freezing and thawing of water inside cracks and crevices, combined with gravity, shattered rock to create the window. Even if you're tight on time, squeeze this stop onto your agenda.

FAIRVIEW POINT Lookout

As its understated name suggests, the stop at Fairview Point offers a grand view of the tree-studded rises and benches, giant plateaus, blue-hued mesas and buttes that extend from the skirts of Bryce into the Grand Staircase, as far as the eye can see. Navajo Mountain lies 80 miles away on the Arizona border, but even that's not the furthest visible point. On clear days you can see 160 miles to Arizona's Black Mesas. A short walk from here leads to another overlook at **Piracy Point**, and though it's not much different, the walk among the deep-green, vanilla-scented pines is a great chance to stretch your legs before getting back in the car. You'll also find toilets here, but no running water.

SWAMP CANYON Lookout

The overlook at Swamp Canyon sits in a forested dip between two ridge-lines that extend into the canyon as fins, dropping to hoodoo formations. From the turnout you can take a short walk through the trees and descend to towering pink-orange cliffs of crumbling limestone, one of the more intimate views along the drive. Trees extend from the rim into the canyon, as does red-barked greenleaf manzanita. Nature lovers like the variety of plant and animal life here; kids like the steep trail into the canyon. This is also the jumping-off point for the **Swamp Canyon Connecting Trail**, which drops into the canyon and follows a series of switchbacks for about a mile to the Under-the-Rim Trail (to do this hike, bear right at the fork in the trail below the parking area).

PARIA VIEW Lookout

Three miles north of Swamp Canyon, signs point to the Paria View viewpoint, which lies 2 miles off the main road. If you're tired of RVs and buses, you'll be pleased to learn that this small overlook is for cars only – though it's reserved for cross-country skiers in winter, when the access road isn't plowed. This is *the* place

Agua Canyon, Bryce Canyon
DAVID MUENCH / CORBIS ©

ROBERTO GEROMETTA / LONELY PLANET IMAGES ©

Don't Miss **Inspiration Point**

This overlook into Bryce Amphitheater may sit lower than the popular Bryce Point overlook – and, in many ways, provides much the same view – but seen from here, the hoodoos of the Silent City below are more compelling than from any other rim-top viewpoint. They feel closer, and you can make out more details on the canyon floor below. Inspiration Point is also a great place to return to for stargazing. Although Bryce Point is higher, it sits in view of the too-bright lights of Bryce Canyon City and the town of Tropic, an unfavorable position which dims the starlight.

Two miles south of the visitor center, an easy, short, paved path accesses the lower overlook. From there, a trail deemed 'dangerous' by the park leads 0.25 miles to the middle and upper overlooks; hike this stretch at your own risk.

to come for sunsets. Most of the hoodoo amphitheaters at Bryce face east, making them particularly beautiful at sunrise, but not sunset. The amphitheater here, small by comparison but still beautiful, faces west toward the Paria River watershed.

BRYCE POINT   Lookout
If you stop nowhere else along the scenic drive, be sure to catch the stunning views from Bryce Point. You can walk the rim above **Bryce Amphitheater** for awesome views of the **Silent City**, an assemblage of hoodoos so dense, gigantic and hypnotic

that you'll surely begin to see shapes of figures frozen in the rock. Be sure to follow the path to the actual point, a fenced-in promontory that juts out over the forested canyon floor, 1000ft below. The extension allows a broad view of the hoodoos. This rivals any overlook in the park for splendor and eye-popping color. An interpretive panel tells the story of Ebenezer Bryce, the Mormon pioneer for whom the canyon was named, and his wife Mary.

Bryce Point marks the beginning of the 5.5-mile Rim Trail. The Peek-a-boo Loop

Trail also begins here. There is a chemical toilet.

SUNSET POINT   Lookout

Views into Bryce Amphitheater at Sunset Point are as good as you'll find, but don't expect solitude. You're at the core of the park here, near campgrounds, the lodge and all visitor services. Aside from great views of the Silent City, this point is known for **Thor's Hammer**, a big square-capped rock balanced atop a spindly hoodoo. Just left of the point, it stands apart from the other hoodoos and makes a great picture. This is the starting point for the Navajo Loop Trail, the park's most popular hike. You'll also find restrooms, drinking water and picnic tables. Don't be fooled by the name of this point; because it faces east, sunrises are better here than sunsets.

SUNRISE POINT   Lookout

Marking the north end of Bryce Amphi-theater, the southeast-facing Sunrise Point offers great views of hoodoos, the Aquarius Plateau and the Sinking Ship, a sloping mesa that looks like a ship's stern rising out of the water. Keep your eyes peeled for the **Limber Pine**, a spindly pine tree whose roots have been exposed through erosion, but which remains an-chored to the receding sand nonetheless. Within walking distance or a one-minute drive are the Bryce Canyon General Store, drinking water, restrooms, picnic tables and a snack bar; head north toward the campground on the loop road.

FAIRYLAND POINT   Lookout

Because it's a few miles off Bryce Canyon Scenic Dr, Fairyland is a less-visited spot. From the viewpoint, you can see wooded views north toward the Aquarius Plateau and hoodoos at all stages of evolution, from fin to crumbling tower. This also marks the start of the Fairyland Loop Trail. To reach the point, drive a mile north of the entrance gate, then a mile east of the main road (the turnoff is marked only to northbound traffic – you won't see it on your way into the park).

 **Activities**

Hiking is the park's most popular activity. Though you can see many of Bryce's spectacular rock formations from turnouts along the scenic drive, the best way to appreciate hoodoos is from the canyon floor, as they tower above and around you. The best – and, for the most part, only – way to do this is to hike down to the canyon floor yourself. Come win-tertime, Bryce's exceptionally dry snow makes for outstanding cross-country skiing and snowshoeing.

Hiking

Bryce is a relatively small park and most trails are day hikes around and into Bryce Amphitheater, home to the highest concentration of hoodoos. Hikes range from easy walks on paved paths along the rim (with some stretches suitable for wheelchairs) to steep switchbacks up and down sometimes muddy, sometimes dusty, packed-earth trails. Further south or north on the plateau, you won't see as many hoodoos – or as many people.

Whenever hiking in Bryce, carry lots of water and don't expect to find any along trails. Though temperatures are often comfortable, remember you're at 8000ft in a high desert. The sun is stronger at altitude and it's easy to get dehydrated. Until you're acclimated to the elevation, you may get winded quickly. Take it slow and pace yourself, especially ascending out of the canyon.

Check ahead with rangers for trail-closure information, particularly after winter.

MOSSY CAVE TRAIL   Hiking

If you're visiting Bryce in the heat of sum-mer, you can cool off beside a year-round waterfall off Hwy 12 at the north end of the park, and check out a small, damp cave with permanent moss – a rarity in this dry climate. The streamside hike is only 0.8 miles (round-trip) and its gentle grades and minimal elevation changes make for easy to moderate hiking.

Though within the park, the trail lies outside the section requiring an entrance fee. From the Hwy 12/63 junction north of the park, turn east on Hwy 12 and drive just past ile 17 (about 3.5 miles) to a small parking area on the right. A placard at the trailhead shows the route. Restrooms flank the trailhead.

Skirting the **Tropic Ditch**, the main water channel for the town of Tropic, the route takes you across two wooden footbridges into small Water Canyon. Take the right fork to reach the **waterfall** or the left fork to reach **Mossy Cave**; both are 0.4 miles from the parking lot.

Don't attempt to climb down the small cliffs to the base of the falls. Instead, at the second footbridge, hop off the path and walk up the wash alongside the creek. Beware of flash floods following rainstorms. Above the falls you can cross the creek and scramble up a short, steep trail to the small arches and windows in the salmon-colored rock.

Mossy Cave may be a slight disappointment for serious cave enthusiasts, since it's more overhang than cave. Stay behind the railing at the cave to avoid unsafe footing and to avoid trampling the fragile mosses. If the trail is passable in winter, Mossy Cave is hung with icicles, which makes a dramatic sight.

BRISTLECONE LOOP TRAIL   Hiking

If driving to Rainbow Point, this easy 1-mile round-trip hike is a must. Starting at 9115ft at the south tip of the Paunsaugunt Plateau, it's Bryce's highest trail. The loop spans fir forests to high cliffs, revealing how Bryce Canyon – the top step of the Grand Staircase – fits into the surrounding landscape and larger Colorado Plateau.

Along the trail are places to rest and take in the marvelous vistas – on clear days you can see as far as 200 miles. Though you'll spot hoodoos rising from the forested canyon floor, first from the trailhead and again at the tip of the plateau, they are not the focus of this walk.

To access the path, park at the Rainbow Point lot, 17 miles from the visitor center. From the overlook kiosk, the well-marked trail ducks into the woods. Bear left at the beginning of the loop. You'll quickly descend below the rim,

Winter in Bryce Canyon

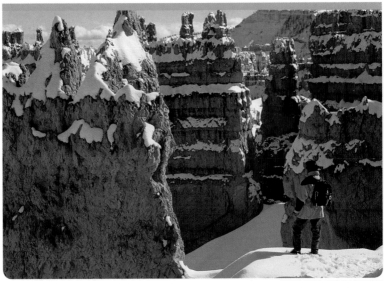

CHEYENNE ROUSE / LONELY PLANET IMAGES ©

Hoodoos

Bryce Canyon is famous for its hoodoos: narrow spires of rock that stand hundreds of feet high and create an utterly surreal landscape. The bizarre formations are formed as runoff over the canyon rim carves parallel gullies with narrow rock walls, known as fins. These fins ultimately erode into columns.

The layers of earth in and around Bryce are so soft that in heavy rains they would quickly dissolve the fins into muddy little mounds, except that siltstone layers alternating with resilient limestone bands give them strength as they erode into towering hoodoos. Many hoodoos end up with a cap of harder limestone at their apex, protecting the softer material underneath. The hoodoo known as Thor's Hammer is a perfect example. Bryce's most impressive conglomeration of Hoodoos is called the Silent City, and it is best viewed from Bryce Point (p386) or Inspiration Point (p391).

cross the Under-the-Rim Trail and enter pine stands. Interpretive panels along the route discuss forest ecology.

At the tip there's a gazebo to get out of the sun (or escape a summer thunderstorm). Enjoy the view before continuing west to see the ancient **bristlecone pines**. This is the breeziest spot in the park, so carry a windbreaker and hold on to your hat. A short ascent leads back to the parking lot, but bear left when you reach the paved path to Yovimpa Point, a fenced-in overlook at the edge of sheer drop-offs.

Though the trail isn't wheelchair accessible, the spur to adjacent Yovimpa Point is.

NAVAJO LOOP TRAIL　　　Hiking
Short, spectacular and sometimes very steep, this popular 1.3-mile trail passes alongside Thor's Hammer, the park's most famous rock formation. It also passes beneath Two Bridges, a pair of small water-carved arches and through Wall Street, a narrow canyon with steep rock walls that reveal only a sliver of sky above.

From the wide, fenced-in viewing area at Sunset Point, follow signs for the Navajo Loop. The trail drops immediately into a switchback, then forks about 100yd ahead. Take the left fork, which leads past **Thor's Hammer** down a long slope to the canyon floor. Entering the canyon, you can follow the sign on your left to see Two Bridges.

At the canyon floor, turn right to continue the loop and ascend back to the rim. Sometimes closed due to rockfall (check ahead with rangers), **Wall Street** features 100ft walls which block much of the sunlight, keeping the canyon shady and cool. The giant Douglas fir trees towering between the walls are more than 750 years old.

To the left of the Wall Street trail, the **Silent City** looms large. If the spur trail through the tunnel on your left is open, take a quick jaunt to look down on these eerie pinnacles. The trail finishes with a steep ascent and some 30 switchbacks that lead to the rim.

The Navajo Loop is a strenuous ascent and descent, but the trail is clearly marked and fairly wide. Those in reasonably good shape won't have a problem. Rangers strongly recommend hiking it clockwise to avoid a steep descent through Wall Street, a notorious ankle-buster. To lengthen your hike by 30 minutes to an hour, you could also start at Queen's Garden Trail.

QUEEN'S GARDEN TRAIL　　　Hiking
Good for kids, the easiest trail into the canyon makes a gentle descent over sloping erosional fins. The moderate 1.8-mile

out-and-back hike passes elegant hoodoo formations but stops short of the canyon floor.

Views of the amphitheater as you descend are superb – a maze of colorful rock spires extends to Bryce Point, and deep-green pines dot the canyon floor beneath undulating slopes seemingly tie-dyed pink, orange and white. As you drop below the rim, watch for the stark and primitive **bristlecone pines**, which at Bryce are about 1600 years old (specimens in California are 5000 years old). These ancient trees' dense needles cluster like foxtails on the ends of the branches.

After a series of switchbacks, turn right and follow signs to Queen's Garden. The short spur from the main trail passes through a tunnel and emerges among exceptionally beautiful hoodoo castles in striking whites and oranges amid rich-green pines. After looping around a high wall and passing through two more tunnels, bear right and follow signs to **Queen Victoria**. The trail's namesake monarch peers down from a white-capped rock, perched atop her throne, lording over her kingdom.

The trail is accessed from Sunrise Point, where you follow signs to the trailhead off the Rim Trail. On your return hike, you can follow the same route back to the rim or link up with the Navajo Loop via the Queen's Garden Connecting Trail, which drops to the canyon floor.

NAVAJO LOOP–QUEEN'S GARDEN COMBINATION   Hiking

Bryce's most popular trail is fairly gentle, though sometimes quite steep, and hits Bryce's signature features in a relatively short amount of time. Start at Sunrise Point and follow the Queen's Garden Trail description. Follow signs for the Queen's Garden Connecting Trail, which descends to the garden of spires and follows the canyon floor. A major advantage of taking this trail is that it provides extra time spent on the canyon floor, where tall pines provide shade and offer perspective on oversized hoodoos. The final push, a steep ascent through **Wall Street** and past the **Silent City**, is the more visually stunning of the two trails. If Wall Street is closed due to rockfall, opt to ascend to the rim via the Two Bridges side of the Navajo Loop Trail.

Before you top out on the rim, detour right a short distance to see **Thor's Hammer**. Then stroll back to Sunrise Point along the Rim Trail, gazing into the canyon for yet another perspective on the hoodoos. The full loop is 2.9 miles.

RIM TRAIL   Hiking

Skirting the canyon rim for 5.5 miles, the aptly named Rim Trail stretches from the south end of Bryce Amphitheater at Bryce Point all the way to Fairyland Point, near the northern park boundary. Sections of this trail are

A natural arch, Bryce Canyon

level, particularly between Sunrise and Sunset Points, where the path is paved and wheelchair accessible. Log rail fences mark vertical drop-offs in many places. In other spots you'll ascend moderately steep, wooded rises to seek shade beneath the pines, watch wildlife or soak up vibrant displays of spring wildflowers. The colors in the rock pop out most when lit by the morning or afternoon sun.

You can join the trail anywhere along its route – just keep in mind that unless the shuttle is running or you arrange to be picked up, you'll have to walk back. If you plan on taking the shuttle, note that buses don't stop at Fairyland.

You'll find restrooms and drinking water at Sunset Point, and the general store and snack bar (both open spring through fall) near Sunrise Point, the approximate midpoint of the hike. You can also duck into Bryce Canyon Lodge for lunch, restrooms and drinking water.

Remember that Bryce sits atop a sloping plateau. The north end of the Rim Trail is lower than the south end, so it's downhill to walk from Bryce Point to Fairyland Point, though the trail rises and falls in a few spots, particularly on the climb from Sunrise Point to North Campground.

During the walk, you'll leave behind Bryce Amphitheater and arrive above Campbell Canyon and Fairyland Amphitheater. You'll find fewer formations at this end of the park, but giant Boat Mesa and her high cliffs rise majestically to the north.

From Bryce Point to Inspiration Point the trail skirts the canyon rim atop white cliffs, revealing gorgeous formations, including the **Wall of Windows**. After passing briefly through trees, it continues along the ridgetop to the uppermost level of **Inspiration Point**, 1.3 miles from Bryce Point.

The leg to Sunset Point drops 200ft in 0.75 miles, winding its way along limestone-capped cliffs that yield to orange sandstone fins. Below the rim the **Silent City** rises in all its hoodoo glory; the lower you go, the higher the rock spires rise up beside you.

At **Sunset Point** you may wish to detour along the Navajo Loop Trail for a taste of the canyon; you can reemerge on the Rim Trail further ahead by adding the Queen's Garden Connecting Trail. Otherwise, stay the course and look for **Thor's Hammer** as you continue the 0.5-mile stroll along a paved path to **Sunrise Point** – the most crowded stretch of trail in the entire park. The views are worth it.

Past Sunset Point, crowds thin as the trail climbs 150ft toward North Campground. Fork left at the Fairyland Loop Trail junction, unless you'd like to follow the moderately difficult, 3-mile round-trip spur into the canyon (950ft elevation loss) to see the window-laced **China Wall** and **Tower Bridge**, twin arches between chunky rock spires. Otherwise, watch for these features from the Rim Trail.

Topping out near North Campground, the path ambles across gently rolling hills on the forested plateau before rejoining the canyon rim at **Fairyland Point**, 2.5 miles from Sunrise Point.

PEEK-A-BOO LOOP TRAIL   Hiking

An ideal day hike, the strenuous Peek-a-boo Loop Trail sees the most variety of terrain and scenery in Bryce, with 1500ft to 1800ft of cumulative elevation changes. Views are among the best in the park, particularly of the Wall of Windows, the Silent City and the Fairy Castle. You'll also find shady spots to rest, a picnic area and pit toilets (the latter are on the loop, just west of its intersection with the connecting trail to Bryce Point).

From **Bryce Point** follow signs to the Peek-a-boo Connecting Trail, just east of the parking area. Bear left at the fork where you'll descend 1.1 miles down the connecting trail. You'll pass through mixed conifers, then swoop out along a gray-white limestone fin beneath the Bryce Point overlook. Further down the trail, hoodoo columns take on a bright-orange hue. After passing through a man-made tunnel, look for the **Alligator** in the white rock ahead. As you work your way down the switchbacks, watch for the **Wall of Windows**, which juts above bright-orange hoodoos atop a sheer vertical cliff face perpendicular to the canyon rim. The windows line the top of this wall.

At the loop trail junction, bear right. As you pass beneath healthy fir and spruce trees, you'll spot a few blackened snags – victims of electrical storms, not forest fires. The plateau's high elevation and isolated trees attract lightning. Also look for ancient bristlecone pines; an inch of these trees' trunks represents 100 years' growth.

Climbing a saddle, you'll rise to eye level with the hoodoo tops before dropping over the other side to the cluster of delicate red spires at **Fairy Castle**. Midway around, just past the turnoff for the Navajo Loop, the trail climbs again to spectacular views of the Silent City and passes beneath the **Cathedral**, a majestic wall of buttresslike hoodoos. The rolling trail skirts the Wall of Windows, threads through a tunnel and switchbacks down. Notice the rapidly changing views as you pass the huge Wall of Windows. The trail turns west and climbs, then drops again amid more hoodoos. As you approach the Bryce Point trail, take the spur on your right to the lush green rest area near the horse corral for a cooldown or picnic before climbing out of the canyon.

Hiked from Bryce Point, as described here, the trail is 5.5 miles long (if starting from Sunrise Point it's a 6.6-mile hike; from Sunset Point it's 5 miles). It rises and falls many times, so be prepared for a workout. If you're afraid of heights, be forewarned that in places you'll pass sheer drops, though the trail is wide. The Peek-a-boo Loop Trail is also a horse trail, so expect to see occasional teams. They move slowly, so you'll have plenty of advance warning. Stock animals have right of way. If you don't want to navigate around horse droppings, consider another route.

FAIRYLAND LOOP TRAIL   Hiking

This difficult 8-mile loop begins at Fairyland Point and circles the majestic cliffs of flat-topped, 8076ft Boat Mesa, emerging on the rim near Sunrise Point. It's a great day hike and a good workout, with multiple elevation changes. Compared to Bryce Amphitheater, there are fewer hoodoos, but there are also fewer people. The last 2.5 miles of the loop follow the Rim Trail back to the trailhead. (Note that the park shuttle doesn't stop at Fairyland.)

This trail is difficult primarily because it meanders – in and out of the hoodoos, down into washes, up and over saddles and so on. Carry plenty of water, and pace yourself.

From the point, the trail dips gradually below the rim – watch your footing on the narrow sections. To the south, Boat Mesa stands between you and views of the park. A short walk leads past ancient **bristlecone pines**, some clinging precariously to the ragged cliffs, their 1000-plus-year-old roots curled up like wizened fingers. Looping around hoodoos that rise like castle turrets and towers, the trail soon drops to the canyon floor and a seasonal wash. Much of the north-facing terrain here holds its snowpack until May, sometimes June.

At **Fairyland Canyon**, 600ft below your starting point, towers of deep-orange stone rise like giant totem poles. The trail rises and falls before traversing a ridge toward **Campbell Canyon**. As you walk beneath Boat Mesa's great cliffs, notice how the formation comes to a point like the bow of a ship – you'll quickly understand how it got its name.

Zigzagging up and down, the trail eventually reaches a seasonal wash on the floor of Campbell Canyon. Keep an eye out for **Tower Bridge**, which connects three spires to two windows. To reach the base of the formation, take the clearly marked dead-end spur from the wash. From Tower Bridge it's a 950ft climb in 1.5 miles to the Rim Trail, some of it strenuous. En route, to your left, look for the long, white **China Wall** and its little windows. A look back at Boat Mesa shows the changing vistas of canyon country.

Backpacking

Only 1% of park visitors venture into the backcountry, virtually guaranteeing those who do a peaceful hike. That said, the

Thor's Hammer (p389), Bryce Canyon

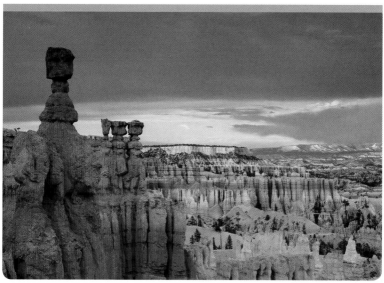

DAVID EVANS / LONELY PLANET IMAGES ©

backcountry trails were originally made as boundary and fire-control routes, not for the landscape itself. If you come here, it's for the solitude.

Bryce features two backcountry trails: the **Under-the-Rim Trail** and the **Riggs Spring Loop Trail**. Due to its length and diverse terrain, the Under-the-Rim Trail is the premier overnight hike. This one-way trail, 500ft to 1000ft beneath the rim, roughly parallels the scenic drive. You'll neither hear nor see the road until you return to the rim.

The park's southernmost trail, the Riggs Spring Loop, can be done as a day hike from Rainbow or Yovimpa Points, offering an excellent backcountry sampler. Because of the trail's great elevation loss, however, most hikers make this an overnight hike. A slower trip also lets you enjoy the transition from spectacular Pink Cliffs to rolling green hills and canyons.

A backcountry permit costs $5 to $15 for up to 14 days, depending on the number of hikers in your party. Permits are only available at the visitor center between 8am and one hour prior to the center's closing time. You cannot place an advance order by telephone or email, but you can make reservations in person up to 48 hours in advance. Hikers may camp only at designated backcountry campsites. Weather-wise, June and September are ideal; in July and August you'll have to contend with thunderstorms.

Horseback Riding

Horses are permitted in the park on specific trails, most notably the Peek-a-boo Loop Trail. If you don't have the energy to hike this fantastic trail, or if you have little ones who can't walk that far, book a half-day trail ride. Alternatively, you can descend the canyon on a two-hour round-trip ride below the Queen's Garden Trail. There are no overnight backcountry tours within the park.

Try the excellent **Canyon Trail Rides** (435-679-8665; www.canyonrides.com; PO Box 128, Tropic, UT 84776; 2hr/half-day ride $50/75), which operates out of Bryce Canyon Lodge. It uses both horses and mules (mules offer a smoother ride).

393

Watching Wildlife

Bryce Canyon is home to 59 mammal species, 11 reptile species, four amphibian species and more than 1000 insect species. As many as 175 bird species pass through annually, though large, highly adaptable ravens are among the few birds found year-round in the park. If you're lucky, you might also spot California condors or a peregrine falcon. Keep an eye to the ground for the threatened Utah prairie dog.

For more information, pick up books and wildlife charts at the visitor center, or visit www.nps.gov/brca/naturescience/animals.htm.

Winter Activities

In winter, Bryce's rosy rock formations and pine forests wear a blanket of fresh powder. Though nighttime temperatures can drop below freezing for more than 200 consecutive nights, days are often mild and sunny, perfect for snowshoeing or cross-country skiing. Snowfall averages 100in per winter. Visitors become scarce, and the dry, light powder is perfect for snowshoeing and cross-country skiing. Ten miles of Bryce's dedicated ski trails (ungroomed) connect with 20 additional miles of groomed trails through Dixie National Forest. Trail use in the national forest is free, though snowmobiles are also granted access, so keep watch for traffic. Rent skis, snowshoes and snow boots (half-day $7, full day $10) at Best Western Ruby's Inn; it also has trail maps and you can ski from here.

When snow and staff are sufficient, rangers offer guided snowshoe hikes along the plateau top. Inquire at the visitor center.

Every Presidents Day weekend in February, the **Bryce Canyon Winter Festival** is hosted at Ruby's Inn. In addition to races, there are free ski and photography clinics, kids' races and snow sculptures.

Sleeping

Because Bryce has only two campgrounds and a lodge, most visitors sleep just north or west of the park, or 11 miles east, in the town of Tropic. If nearby

Silent City (p386), Bryce Canyon

ROBERTO GEROMETTA / LONELY PLANET IMAGES ©

lodgings are full, consider staying in or around Panguitch, 24 miles west of the park, or Kodachrome Basin State Park, 19 miles east. Dixie National Forest, which surrounds Bryce Canyon, offers several campgrounds within a short drive of the park. The ranger stations in Panguitch and Escalante can provide maps and information.

In the Park

BRYCE CANYON LODGE   Lodge $$
(☏435-834-8700; www.brycecanyonforever. com; r $130-180, cabins $175; ☉Apr-Oct) Built in the 1920s, this lodge is the essence of old Western park grandeur. The only lodge still standing in its original form from the parks' railroad boom, it exudes rustic mountain charm. Flanked by hickory rocking chairs, a stone fireplace dominates the lobby, where orange-hued, wood-paneled walls and ceiling echo the color of canyon hoodoos. Accommodations range from modern hotel units to freestanding cabins, and decor within the rooms is significantly dated but pleasant enough. Hotel rooms are in discrete, two-story wood-and-timber buildings and feature private balconies or porches and bathrooms tiled in attractive stone.

NORTH CAMPGROUND   Campground $
(☏reservations 877-444-6777; www.recreation. gov; campsites $15; ☉year-round) Sites vary at this enormous and popular campground, which accommodates tents and RVs. Some sites sit up high amid tall trees, while others are close to the canyon rim. All include campfire rings, and a short walk from the campground takes you to showers, a coin laundry and a general store (open April through October). Reservations are accepted early May through late September.

SUNSET CAMPGROUND   Campground $
(☏reservations 877-444-6777; www.recreation. gov; campsites $15; ☉late spring-fall) Just south of Sunset Point, this 102-site campground offers more shade than North Campground but has few amenities beyond flush toilets. Sites vary between shady and sunny, and the best are on the outer ring. Loop A allows RVs, though it has few pull-through spots. Twenty sites can be reserved May through September.

Bryce Canyon City

The village of Bryce Canyon City is located just outside the park. Not an actual town, it is a growing tourist center with minimarts, outfitters, a gas station and hotels.

If you're unable to secure a reservation, and don't arrive early enough to get a site in the park, you could spend a night at a Bryce Canyon City campground and return early in the morning to grab a spot in the park.

Except for a few notable exceptions, lodgings at Bryce are nothing special. Expect motel rooms with fiberglass tub-shower combinations and plastic drinking cups by the sink. A coffeemaker is a luxury. For more character, book a B&B in a nearby town. Rates drop in the fall and spring; most properties close in winter.

BEST WESTERN RUBY'S INN   Hotel $$
(☏435-834-5341; www.rubysinn.com; 1000 S Hwy 63; r $135-169; ✳@🛜🐾) A gargantuan motel complex 1 mile north of the park entrance, Ruby's has 369 standard rooms with amenities like coffeemakers, hair dryers, ironing boards and irons. The facilities are the major attraction. Open to nonguests, the sprawling property includes a grocery store, two gas stations, a post office, coin laundry, a pool and hot tub, showers, a foreign-currency exchange, gift shops, email kiosks, wi-fi, bike rentals, tour desk and a liquor store. In summer there's even a nightly rodeo (except Sunday).

RUBY'S CAMPGROUND   Campground $
(☏435-834-5301; www.brycecanyoncamp grounds.com; Hwy 63; tent sites $28 plus $2 per person, RV sites $46; ☉Apr-Oct; 🐾) This crowded campground just outside Bryce, 3 miles north of the visitor center, boasts lots of amenities, including flush toilets, showers, drinking water, a coin laundry, electrical hookups, a dump station, restaurant, general store and a hot tub.

Both cabins and tepees use shared camp bathroom facilities.

BRYCE CANYON RESORT   Resort $$
(📞435-834-5351; www.brycecanyonresort.com; cnr Hwys 12 & 63; r $80-155, cottages $150-190, cabins $120-160; ❄ 🛜 🏊 🐾) Four miles from the park, this is a great alternative to Ruby's Inn. Remodeled rooms include newer furnishings and extra amenities, while economy rooms are standard. Some units have kitchenettes. Cottages have kitchenettes and sleep up to six. There's also a small campground and restaurant.

BRYCE CANYON GRAND HOTEL   Hotel $$
(📞866-866-6634; www.brycecanyongrand. com; 30 N 100 East; r $125-199; ❄ 🛜 🏊) Opened in 2009, this Best Western hotel is the best digs in the area, with stylish, ample rooms, wi-fi in the rooms and a free breakfast bar. It's operated by the same family who owns Ruby's Inn, so all the amenities at Ruby's are available to guests of the Grand Hotel.

Eating

Food around Bryce isn't nearly as good as the scenery. Service may be poky, coffee watered-down and vegetables possibly limited to the speck of garnish alongside your chicken-fried steak. Particularly for vegetarians, it's worth traveling with a cooler of fresh fruit and vegetables.

In the Park

BRYCE CANYON LODGE   American $$
(📞435-834-8700; breakfast mains $6-10, lunch $9-13, dinner $12-25; ⏰6:30-10:30am, 11:30am-3pm & 5-10pm Apr-Oct) This is the best restaurant in the region. Be warned, service may be slow but meals deliver, with excellent regional cuisine, ranging from fresh green salads to bison burgers, braised portobellos and steak. All food is made on site and the certified green menu offers only sustainable seafood. Best of all, the low-lit room is forgiving if you come covered in trail dust.

BRYCE CANYON GENERAL STORE & SNACK BAR   Market & Deli $
(📞435-834-5361; snacks $3-5; ⏰8am-8pm summer, to 6pm spring & fall, closed Nov-Mar) In addition to foodstuff and sundries, the general store near Sunrise Point sells hot dogs, cold drinks, packaged sandwiches, chili, soup and pizza.

Bryce Canyon City

BRYCE CANYON PINES   American $
(📞435-834-5441; Hwy 12; mains $6-20; ⏰6:30am-9:30pm Apr-Oct) This supercute diner is classic Utah, with wait staff that dotes, Naugahyde booths and even a crackling fire on cold days. Expect hearty plates of potatoes and

Grand View Point

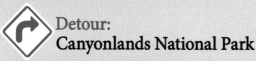

Detour:
Canyonlands National Park

Some 300 miles northeast of Bryce Canyon, in the center of the Colorado Plateau, lies Utah's spectacular Canyonlands National Park. Surprisingly, this labyrinth of stone amphitheaters, rock arches, natural bridges, towering spires and surreal tabletop buttes is also the Southwest's least-visited national park. Those who do make the journey, however, will be richly rewarded by a high-desert wilderness carved into vast serpentine canyons by the Colorado and Green Rivers.

The most popular sector of the park is the **Island in the Sky** district, which is accessible via Hwy 313. Island in the Sky is a wide sandstone mesa hemmed by precipitous cliffs that drop over 1000ft to the floor below. The **Island in the Sky Visitor Center** (435-259-4712; www.nps.gov/cany/planyourvisit/islandinthesky. htm; Hwy 313; 9am-4:30pm) sits atop the mesa about 2 miles beyond the park entrance station. From the visitor center, the road heads 12 miles south to **Grand View Point**. About halfway to the point, a paved spur leads northwest 5 miles to **Upheaval Dome**. A number of overlooks and trails line each road.

The only other paved entrance to the park is via Hwy 211, which leads to the **Needles** district in the southeast corner of the park. Here, you will find the **Needles Visitor Center** (435-259-4711; www.nps.gov/cany/planyourvisit/needles.htm; Hwy 211; 9am-4:30pm).

Canyonlands lacks hotels and restaurants and has only one campground, **Willow Flat Campground** (435-719-2313, 435-259-4712; www.nps.gov/cany; sites $10; year-round), which is accessed via a mile-long dirt spur from the road to Upheaval Dome.

meat, perfect BLTs and meal-size soups. While mains feel run-of-the-mill, locals come for towering wedges of homemade pie, such as the banana blueberry creme.

**EBENEZER'S
BARN & GRILL**   Southwestern $$$
(800-468-8660; 1000 S Hwy 63; dinner show $25-32; 8pm nightly May-Oct) Sidle in for a kitschy but good-natured evening of country-and-western music with the Bar G Wranglers and your choice of four main courses, including Cowboy Chicken, rib-eye and a BBQ plate (soft drinks included). Reservations are necessary. It's run by Ruby's and located across the street.

ℹ Information

Radio station AM 1590 broadcasts current general park information.

Entrance Fees & Passes

Admission, good for seven days, costs $25 per car or $12 per person arriving by motorcycle, bicycle or foot. A Bryce Canyon National Park Annual Pass costs $30, and interagency and senior passes are valid. All can be purchased at entrance stations and visitor centers.

Opening Dates

Bryce Canyon is open 24 hours a day, 365 days a year. Entrance kiosks are unstaffed at night.

Tourist Information

Bryce Canyon Visitor Center (435-834-5322; www.nps.gov/brca; Hwy 63; 8am-8pm May-Sep, to 6pm Oct & Apr, to 4:30pm Nov-Mar;)

Park Policies & Regulations

It's particularly important not to feed wild animals. Pets must be kept on a leash and are only allowed on paved surfaces in the park (roads, parking lots, paved scenic overlooks and the section of Rim Trail between Sunset and Sunrise Points). They are not allowed on unpaved trails or in public buildings.

Dangers & Annoyances

Due to Bryce's high elevation, some visitors may experience altitude sickness. Lightning strikes are very common at Bryce. If caught at an overlook during a sudden thunderstorm, immediately take shelter. The safest retreat is inside your vehicle.

❶ Getting There & Around

Air

The closest international airport is McCarran International Airport (LAS; ☎702-261-5211; www.mccarran.com) in Las Vegas, 255 miles away. Salt Lake City International Airport (SLC; ☎800-595-2442; www.slcairport.com) is 270 miles away. The closest regional airports are Cedar City Regional Airport (☎435-867-9408; www.cedarcity.org/airport.html) in Cedar City; and SGU Municipal Airport (☎435-627-4080; www.sgcity.org/airport) in St George. The former is 80 miles away, the latter 125 miles away. All four airports have rental cars.

Bus

The closest Greyhound (☎800-231-2222; www.greyhound.com) bus stations are in Cedar City and St George.

Car & RV

Unless you're on an organized tour, the only way to get around the park from fall through spring is in a private vehicle. The park's main road is easily navigable and well maintained, with turnouts and parking areas clearly marked in the brochure you receive upon paying your fee. It is plowed throughout winter and closes only briefly after snowstorms. The closest gas stations are 3 miles north, in Bryce Canyon City.

Trailers are not permitted up to Bryce Point or Paria View. You can park them at the trailer turnaround lot in summer or the visitor center parking lot in winter.

Park Shuttle

If visiting during a peak period, such as a summer weekend, seriously consider riding the free shuttle bus into the park, as parking lots at the major overlooks and visitor center fill up fast. Leave your car in the large lot at the shuttle staging area, 2 miles north of the park's entrance station, at the south end of Bryce Canyon City.

Service is available from May through early October, about every 10 to 15 minutes from 8am to roughly 8pm. *The Hoodoo* newspaper lists routes and schedules. Buses run from the shuttle staging area north of the park to the visitor center and the major Bryce Amphitheater overlooks as far south as Bryce Point. The free Rainbow Point bus tour hits the highlights daily, with a morning departure and an afternoon departure; times change, so inquire inside the visitor center or at the shuttle staging area. Both shuttles stop at most trailheads.

Best of the Rest

Arches (p400)
Home to more rock arches than anywhere else on earth.

Big Bend (p402)
Protects the Chisos Mountains, the Chihuahuan Desert and the Rio Grande.

Capitol Reef (p404)
Arches, domes and monoliths decorate a 100-mile buckle in the earth's crust.

Denali (p406)
North America's highest mountain stands in this remote Alaskan park.

Haleakalā (p408)
With volcanic craters and cinder cones, fern-clad gorges and bamboo forests.

Hawaii Volcanoes (p410)
Home to two active volcanoes.

Sequoia & Kings Canyon (p412)
Has some of the world's largest trees and some of the Sierra's mightiest mountains.

Top: Lava flow, Hawaii Volcanoes (p410);
Bottom: Delicate Arch (p401), Arches

Arches National Park

HIGHLIGHTS

1. **Delicate Arch** See Utah's most famous rock formation, a massive 52ft-tall freestanding arch.
2. **Fiery Furnace** Explore the slot canyons and eroded fins on this guided hike.
3. **Windows Trail** Take the best photo of your trip through windows in rock.

Partition Arch
PHOTOGRAPHER: JOHN ELK III / LONELY PLANET IMAGES ©

Arches National Park

Arches National Park boasts the highest density of rock arches anywhere on earth – more than 2500 in a 116-sq-mile area. You'll lose perspective on size at some, such as the thin and graceful Landscape Arch, which stretches more than 300ft across (it's one of the largest in the world). Others are tiny – the smallest only 3ft across. Once you train your eye, you'll spot them everywhere (like a game of 'Where's Waldo?'). An easy drive makes the spectacular arches accessible to all. Fiery Furnace is a not-to-be-missed guided-tour-only area of the park, where you weave your way through narrow canyons and soaring finlike rocks.

👁 Sights & Activities

Arches is geared more to drivers than hikers, with most of the main sights within a mile or two of paved roads. There are a few exceptions, but you won't find an extensive system of trails as at other national parks. Still, you can enjoy several hikes that will take you away from the sound of traffic, at least for a few hours.

Arches' main sights lie along the park's eponymous scenic drive. Visible from the road are towering rock walls and rounded formations, sandstone fins, red-rock arches and windows. Far in the distance, look for the snow-covered La Sal Mountains to the east.

ARCHES SCENIC DRIVE   Scenic Drive
Hitting all the highlights, this paved drive visits Arches' strange forms and flaming desert landscapes. It's packed with photo ops and short walks to arches and iconic landmarks. From the visitor center, the steep road ascends Navajo sandstone, once ancient sand dunes. Stop at the **Moab Fault Overlook**, then continue to **Park Avenue**, where you can walk to a giant rock fin that calls to mind a row of New York City skyscrapers. The full 43-mile drive (including spurs) takes two to three hours if you're not taking any hikes.

WINDOWS TRAIL Hiking

Tight on time? The **Windows Section** of the park has stunning arches that take little effort to reach. The 0.6-mile round-trip Windows Trail brings you up to the most famous formations. Stand beneath North Window and look out to the canyon views beyond, or frame North Window within South for a stunning picture. Don't forget Double Arch, right across the parking lot.

FIERY FURNACE Hiking

Book ahead for a Fiery Furnace guided hike, so you can explore the maze of spectacularly narrow canyons and giant fins. Buy tickets in person (adult $10, child $5) at the visitor center. Reserve at the visitor center up to seven days in advance for the two- to three-hour walks, offered morning and afternoon, April to October.

DELICATE ARCH Hiking

The park's most famous hike is to Delicate Arch. You've seen this one before: it's the unofficial state symbol and is pictured on just about every piece of Utah tourist literature out there. To get there, drive 2.5 miles beyond **Balanced Rock**, a 3577-ton boulder sitting atop a spindly pedestal. From there a spur road leads 2 miles to **Wolfe Ranch**, a well-preserved 1908 pioneer cabin. A footbridge crosses **Salt Wash** and marks the beginning of the moderate, 3-mile round-trip trail to Delicate Arch. The trail ascends slickrock, culminating in a wall-hugging ledge.

PARK AVENUE Hiking

Many short hikes originate near the main park road. Just over 2 miles from the entrance is Park Avenue, a mile-long trail past a giant fin of rock reminiscent of a New York skyline. Kids love running through the **Sand Dune Arch** (0.4-mile round-trip); from the same trailhead, walk across grassland for 1 mile to reach 60ft **Broken Arch.**

DEVILS GARDEN Hiking

Nineteen miles from the visitor center, at the end of the paved road, Devils Garden marks the beginning of several hikes, from 2- to 7-mile round-trips, that pass nearly a dozen arches. The easy mile to **Landscape Arch** gets busy, but ahead, the trail gets less crowded and grows rougher.

Sleeping & Eating

No food is available in the park. For eats, head to Moab.

**DEVILS GARDEN
CAMPGROUND** Campground $
(518-885-3639; www.recreation.gov; campsites $15) Don't expect much shade, just red rock and scrubby piñon trees at the park's only campground, 18 miles from the visitor center. From March to October, half the sites are available by reservation only; for same-day availability, check at the visitor center, not the campground. No showers.

Information

A seven-day admission to Arches National Park (www.nps.gov/arch; ☉year-round) costs $10 per vehicle or $5 per pedestrian, cyclist or motorcycle.

Check ranger-led activity schedules, reserve your tickets for a Fiery Furnace hike and buy maps at the visitor center (☏435-719-2299; www.nps. gov/arch; ☉7:30am-6:30pm Apr-Oct, 8am-4:30pm Nov-Mar)

ⓘ Getting There & Around

The park entrance station lies off Hwy 191, 5 miles northwest of Moab. Arches has no shuttle system and no public buses run to the park. In other words, you need your own wheels.

Big Bend National Park

HIGHLIGHTS

1. **Rio Grande** Float the US–Mexico border on one of the country's best river-rafting trips.

2. **Lost Mine Trail** Ascend into the Chisos Mountains and take in the stellar views.

3. **Castolon Historic District** Pretend you're in a David Lynch movie in this abandoned farming town.

Santa Elena Canyon
PHOTOGRAPHER: WITOLD SKRYPCZAK / LONELY PLANET IMAGES ©

Big Bend National Park

Everyone knows Texas is big. But you can't really appreciate just how big until you visit Big Bend. It's a land of incredible diversity, vast enough to allow a lifetime of discovery, yet laced with enough well-placed roads and trails to permit short-term visitors to see a lot in a few days.

Like many popular US parks, Big Bend has one area – the Chisos Basin – that absorbs the overwhelming crunch of traffic. The Chisos Mountains are beautiful, but any visit to Big Bend should also include time in the Chihuahua Desert, home to curious creatures and adaptable plants, and on the Rio Grande.

 Sights

If you're short on time, the park has three scenic drives – **Maverick Dr** (22 miles), **Ross Maxwell Scenic Dr** (30 miles) and **Rio Grande Village Dr** (20 miles) – that make seeing the park easy.

CASTOLON HISTORIC DISTRICT   Historic Site
Dwarfed by the looming Sierra Ponce, the cluster of buildings that make up the Castolon Compound were built in 1920. A half-mile historic stroll offers a brief look at life on the frontier.

 Activities

Hiking

Big Bend has 150 miles of trails amid the largest area of roadless public land in Texas. The *Hiker's Guide to Trails of Big Bend National Park* ($1.95 at park visitor centers) gives descriptions of 36 trails.

LOST MINE TRAIL   Hiking
On this Chisos Mountains hike, it's all about the views, which, as you climb over 1000ft in elevation, just get better and better. You'll be right up there with Casa Grande, Lost Mine Peak and, from the highest point, the Sierra del Carmen. It's 4.8 miles total, but you can get a partial payoff by catching the

views from about a mile in then turning around and coming back.

SANTA ELENA CANYON TRAIL   Hiking
A hike on this riverside trail is a must if you don't have time to float the Rio Grande. The 1.7-mile round-trip trek from the end of Ross Maxwell Scenic Dr takes hikers upriver into the amazingly steep, narrow Santa Elena Canyon. The trail crosses Terlingua Creek near its start, so pack along some old shoes in case you need to wade.

Rafting

Rio Grande has earned its place among the top North American river trips for both rafting and canoeing. Rapids up to Class IV alternate with calm stretches that are perfect for wildlife-viewing, photography and just plain relaxation. The following outfitters offer multihour to multiday floats.

Guided floats cost about $120 per person per day, including all meals and gear (except a sleeping bag for overnighters, and your personal effects). Three companies offer guided river rafting trips in and around Big Bend. All have have solid reputations.

BIG BEND RIVER TOURS   Rafting
(☎432-424-3219; www.bigbendrivertours.com; Terlingua)

DESERT SPORTS   Rafting
(☎432-371-2727; www.desertsportstx.com; Terlingua) Well-regarded for its for its reputable guides.

FAR FLUNG ADVENTURES   Rafting
(☎432-371-2489; www.farflung.com; Terlingua) Known for creative trips, such as its 'Paddle and Saddle' or 'Rock and Raft' trips.

Sleeping & Eating

For tent campers or smaller RVs that don't require hookups, there are three main campgrounds.

CHISOS MOUNTAINS LODGE   Lodge $$
(☎432-477-2291, reservations 877-386-4383; www.chisosmountainslodge.com; d $110-150, cottages $137) This complex in the basin offers decent accommodations and food. You can do better on both counts if you stay outside the park, but the scenery here is better, and it offers easy access to trails. It's also nice to know that you can go straight to your room posthike.

**CASA GRANDE LODGE
& RIO GRANDE MOTEL**   Motel $$
(d $108-113) Modest, motel-style rooms with private balconies and views of the basin and surrounding mountains. The lodge **dining room** (breakfast $2-7, dinner $5-10; ◷7-10am, 11am-4pm & 5-8pm) has decent food.

**CHISOS BASIN
CAMPGROUND**   Campground $
(☎reservations 877-444-6777; sites $14) The most centrally located of the main campgrounds is a 60-site campground that has sites with stone shelters and picnic tables.

**COTTONWOOD
CAMPGROUND**   Campground $
(no reservations; sites $14) Set beneath cottonwood trees near Castolon. Over 30 sites provide a subdued and shady environment along the river.

**RIO GRANDE VILLAGE
CAMPGROUND**   Campground $
(☎reservations 877-444-6777; sites $14) Offers 100 sites with water and flush toilets.

❶ Information

Seven-day admission to **Big Bend National Park** (☎432-477-2251; www.nps.gov/bibe; ◷year-round) costs $20 per vehicle or $10 per pedestrian, cyclist or motorcycle.

In addition to the main **visitor center** (park headquarters; ☎432-477-2251; www.nps.gov/bibe; ◷8am-6pm) at Panther Junction, visitor centers are found in Chisos Basin and at Persimmon Gap. There are also seasonal visitor centers at Castolon and the Rio Grande Village.

❶ Getting There & Away

There is no public transportation to, from or within the park. The closest buses and trains run through Alpine, 108 miles northwest of Panther Junction. The nearest major airports are in Midland (230 miles northeast, with shuttle service available to Alpine) and El Paso (325 miles northwest).

Capitol Reef National Park

HIGHLIGHTS

① **Fruita Historic District** Pick apples, cherries, plums and pears at this ghost-town orchard.

② **Scenic Drive** Explore the arches, hoodoos, canyons and trails of Waterpocket Fold, a vast buckle in the Earth's crust.

③ **Hickman Bridge Trail** Hike this short-but-sweet trail through a canyon to a natural bridge.

Cathedral Valley & Temple of the Sun
PHOTOGRAPHER: CAROL POLICH / LONELY PLANET IMAGES ©

Capitol Reef National Park

Giant slabs of chocolate-red rock and sweeping yellow sandstone domes dominate the landscape of Capitol Reef, which Fremont Indians called the 'Land of the Sleeping Rainbow.' The park's centerpiece is Waterpocket Fold, a 100-mile-long monocline – a buckle in the earth's crust – that blocked explorers' westward migrations like a reef blocks a ship's passage. Known also for its enormous domes, one of which resembles Washington DC's Capitol Dome, the park has fantastic desert hiking trails, 800-year-old petroglyphs and a verdant 19th-century Mormon settlement with prolific fruit trees.

Sights

The narrow park runs north–south along Waterpocket Fold. Hwy 24 traverses its northern section. Capitol Reef's central region is the Fruita Historic District. To the far north lies Cathedral Valley, the least-visited section.

FRUITA HISTORIC DISTRICT   Historic Site

Fruita (*froo-tuh*) is a cool green oasis where shade-giving cottonwoods and fruit-bearing trees line the Fremont River's banks. The first Mormon homesteaders arrived in 1880; Fruita's final resident left in 1969. Among the historic buildings, the NPS maintains 2700 cherry, apricot, peach, pear and apple trees planted by early settlers. Visit between June and October, and pluck ripe fruit from the trees, for free, from any unlocked orchard. Near the orchards is a wonderful picnic area, with roaming deer and birds in the trees, a desert rarity.

Across the road from the blacksmith shop is the **Ripple Rock Nature Center** (☽usually noon-5pm daily late May-Jun, 10am-3pm Tue-Sat Jul-early Sep), a family-oriented learning center. The **Gifford Homestead** (☽10am-3pm Mar-Oct) reveals the day-to-day world of pioneer homesteads.

PETROGLYPHS
Historic Site

East of the visitor center on Hwy 24, look for the freely accessible roadside petroglyphs; these are the carvings that convinced archaeologists that the Fremont Indians were a distinct group.

 **Activities**

SCENIC DRIVE
Scenic Drive

(per vehicle $5) This rolling, mostly paved drive along the **Waterpocket Fold** is a geology diorama come to life, with arches, hoodoos, canyon narrows and other unique features easily within view, plus day-hiking opportunities, too. The best of the route is its last 2 miles between the narrow sandstone walls of Capitol Gorge. It'll knock your socks off. To continue south past Pleasant Creek, a 4WD vehicle is advised.

The 9.3-mile road starts at the Scenic Dr fee station, just south of Fruita Campground. Pick up a self-guided driving-tour brochure ($2) or audio CD ($6); for a free printout, visit www.nps.gov/care/planyourvisit/scenicdrive.htm.

HICKMAN BRIDGE TRAIL
Hiking

If you only have time for one hike, make it the Hickman Bridge Trail. It's a moderate 1-mile walk that leads through both a canyon and desert-wash walk to a natural bridge. It offers long sky views and spring wildflowers to boot. Mornings are coolest, and cairns mark some of the route. Pick up a self-guided Hickman Bridge nature trail brochure at the trailhead, about 2 miles east of the visitor center.

COHAB CANYON
Hiking

Often overlooked, this moderate 1.7-mile trail deters crowds with a steep climb at the beginning, but exploring a hidden canyon and the views from atop Capitol Reef are worth every sweaty step. Starting across the road from Fruita Campground, just south of the Gifford Homestead, the trail makes a steep 0.25-mile ascent atop a rocky cliff. From there it levels out though a desert wash, beside small slot canyons. You'll pass more striking geologic features on your way through Cohab Canyon itself.

 Sleeping & Eating

There's no lodging or food in the park, except for the park's pick-your-own fruit orchards and the baked goods sold at the Gifford Homestead. Torrey is the nearest place to get a hotel room or eat.

Free primitive camping is possible year-round at Cathedral Valley Campground, at the end of River Ford Rd, and at Cedar Mesa Campground, about 23 miles south along Nottom-Bullfrog Rd.

FRUITA CAMPGROUND
Campground $

(☏ 435-425-3791; www.nps.gov/care; Scenic Dr; ⊙year-round; 🚻) The terrific 71-site Fruita Campground sits alongside the Fremont River, surrounded by orchards. First-come, first-served; water, no showers. In the summer high season, sites fill up early. It's 1.2 miles south of the visitor center.

 Information

Admission to Capitol Reef (www.nps.gov/care; ⊙year-round) is free.

Just south of Hwy 24, the visitor center (☏ 435-425-3791; www.nps.gov/care; 52 Scenic Drive, Torrey; ⊙8am-4:30pm Sep-May, to 6pm Jun-Aug) is also the park's headquarters. It's the only source of information in the park.

Getting Around

Capitol Reef National Park is southwest of I-70, 107 miles from Green River. All services – food, gas, medical – are based out of Torrey, 11 miles west, and Hanksville (37 miles east). The park lacks public transportation.

In summer you can drive most dirt roads in a regular passenger car. In remote regions like Cathedral Valley, you'll likely need a high-clearance 4WD.

Bicycles are allowed on all park roads, paved or dirt, but are prohibited on hiking trails. Cyclists and hikers can arrange shuttle services (from $25) with Hondoo Rivers & Trails (☏ 435-425-3519; www.hondoo.com; 90 E Main St, Torrey).

Denali National Park

HIGHLIGHTS

1 **Park Rd** Jump on a shuttle and journey into the heart of this vast and wild park.

2 **Savage River** Hike the banks of the Savage River and ponder Alaska's great expanses.

3 **Denali Mountain Morning Hostel** Get friendly with fellow adventurers at this fabulous hostel.

Mt McKinley
PHOTOGRAPHER: LEE FOSTER / LONELY PLANET IMAGES ©

Denali National Park

For many travelers, Denali National Park is the beginning and end of their Alaskan adventure. This is probably your best chance in the interior (if not in the entire state) of seeing a grizzly bear, a moose, a caribou and maybe even a fox or wolf.

 Sights & Activities

For a day hike, just ride the shuttle bus and get off at any valley, riverbed or ridge that grabs your fancy. The park has few trails; most hiking is cross-country over open terrain.

PARK ROAD   Scenic Road

A straight shot into the heart of Denali, Park Rd is also the jumping-off point for most hikes. It begins at George Parks Hwy and winds 92 miles through the heart of the park, ending at Kantishna, the site of several wilderness lodges.

Mt McKinley, the highest mountain in North America and the park's centerpiece, are first visible between Mile 9 and Mile 11. After that the road passes the **Savage River** (Mile 14) – which has an established trail alongside the river – and then dips into the **Sanctuary and Teklanika River valleys**. Both these rivers are in excellent hiking areas, and three of the five backcountry campgrounds lie along them.

Park Rd continues for another 78 miles, past rivers, backcountry campgrounds, overlooks and mountain passes that afford stunning views on those rare clear days.

Eielson Visitor Center (Mile 66; ⏱9am-7pm), on the far side of Thorofare Pass (3900ft), is the most common turning-around point for day-trippers taking the shuttle (an eight-hour round-trip affair). The 7400-sq-ft facility cost around $9.2 million to build, and features several 'green' design elements, including solar and hydroelectric power.

Kantishna (Mile 90) is mainly a destination for people staying in the area's private lodges. The buses turn around here, and begin the long trip back to the Wilderness Access Center.

MT HEALY OVERLOOK · Hiking

This is the longest maintained trail in the entrance area, and the only one in the vicinity that truly lets you escape the crowds. Plan on three to five hours for the hike.

SAVAGE RIVER LOOP · Hiking

You can get to this trailhead by car (Mile 14), but you are better off taking the Savage River Shuttle Bus as the small parking lot here often fills up. The 2-mile loop is wheelchair accessible for the first half a mile and runs north from Park Rd on either side of the river.

 Tours

ARAMARK · Natural History, Wildlife

(☏ 866-761-6629; www.reservedenali.com) Offers a variety of natural-history and wildlife tours throughout the park.

DENALI AIR · Scenic Flights

(☏ 907-683-2261; www.denaliair.com) Charges around $325/$165 per adult/child for a narrated flight of about an hour around Mt McKinley.

DENALI OUTDOOR CENTER · Rafting

(☏ 907-683-1925; www.denalioutdoorcenter. com; Mile 240.5 & Mile 247 George Parks Hwy) Universally considered the finest river-rafting outfit around. Offers floats on the Nenana River.

 Sleeping & Eating

Campsites inside the park cost between $9 and $20, and most can be reserved for a $4 fee. Most are along Park Rd, including the **Wonder Lake** (Mile 84 Park Rd; campsites $16), overlooking Mt McKinley, and **Sanctuary River** (Mile 23 Park Rd; campsites $9), which makes a great base for day hikes.

DENALI MOUNTAIN MORNING HOSTEL · Hostel $

(☏ 907-683-7503; www.hostelalaska.com; dm $32, d $75-95; ☺summer only; @) Perched lovingly beside the gurgling Carlo Creek, this is the area's only true hostel. And, lucky for indie travelers, it is one of the best in all Alaska.

DENALI BACKCOUNTRY LODGE · Lodge $$$

(☏ 907-376-1992; www.denalilodge.com; per person $450-530) The last lodge on this end of the road, this place on the banks of Moose Creek has comfortable cabins and common areas.

CAMP DENALI · Lodge $$$

(☏ 907-683-2290; www.campdenali.com; cabin 3-night minimum per person $1425) Verging on legendary, Camp Denali has been the gold standard among Kantishna lodges for the last half-century.

OVERLOOK BAR & GRILL · American $$$

(☏ 907-683-2641; Mile 238.5 George Parks Hwy; sandwiches & burgers $9-18; ☺11am-11pm) Up on the hill over Glitter Gulch, the 'Big O' does steak, seafood, pasta and poultry. It's a good nightlife spot and gets raves for its view and beer list.

❶ Information

Seven-day admission to **Denali National Park** (www.nps.gov/dena; ☺year-round) is $20 per vehicle, $10 per pedestrian, motorcycle or cyclist.

Denali Visitor Center (☏ 907-683-2294; www. nps.gov/dena; Mile 1.5 Park Rd; ☺8am-6pm)

Wilderness Access Center (WAC; ☏ 907-683-9274; Mile 0.5 Park Rd; ☺5am-8pm) Transport hub and campground reservation center.

Wrangell-St Elias National Park Headquarters & Visitor Center (☏ 907-822-5234; www.nps.gov/wrst; Mile 106.8 Richardson Hwy; ☺8am-6pm)

❶ Getting There & Around

Alaska Railroad (☏ 907-265-2494; www. alaskarailroad.com) The most enjoyable way to arrive or depart from the park.

Alaska/Yukon Trails (☏ 800-770-7275; www. alaskashuttle.com) Buses to Anchorage and Fairbanks.

Park Connection (☏ 800-266-8625; www. alaskacoach.com) Buses to Anchorage and Fairbanks.

Talkeetna Aero Services (☏ 907-683-2899; www.talkeetnaaero.com) Offers air transportation to/from Talkeetna.

Haleakalā National Park

HIGHLIGHTS

1. **Waimoku Falls** Hike into the 'Ohe'o Gulch to see one of Hawaii's most beautiful waterfalls.

2. **Haleakalā Visitor Center** Stare down into a massive volcanic crater from the summit of Haleakalā.

3. **Kuloa Point Trail** Dip into freshwater pools linked by tumbling cascades beside this classic trail.

Lower Pools

Haleakalā National Park

No trip to Maui is complete without visiting this sublime **national park** (☎808-572-4400; www.nps.gov/hale; 3-day entry pass per car $10, per person on foot, bicycle or motorcycle $5), containing East Maui's mighty volcano, Haleakalā. From the towering volcano's rim near the summit, there are dramatic views of a lunarlike surface and multicolored cinder cones. This is the **Summit Area** of the park.

But there's more to Haleakalā National Park than the cindery summit. The park extends down the southeast face of the volcano all the way to the sea. The crowning glory of the **Kipahulu Area** of the park is **'Ohe'o Gulch**, with its magnificent waterfalls and wide pools, each one tumbling into the next one below. When the sun shines, these cool, glistening pools make the most inviting swimming holes on Maui.

Sights & Activities

Summit Area

HALEAKALĀ VISITOR CENTER
Visitor Center

(☉sunrise-3pm) Perched on the rim of the crater, the visitor center, at 9745ft, is the park's main viewing spot. And what a magical sight awaits. The ever-changing interplay of sun, shadow and clouds reflecting on the crater floor creates a mesmerizing dance of light and color. Sunrises here are astounding.

PU'U'ULA'ULA (RED HILL) OVERLOOK
Lookout

Congratulations! The 37-mile drive from sea level to the 10,023ft summit of Haleakalā you've just completed is the highest elevation gain in the shortest distance anywhere in the world. Sitting atop Pu'u'ula'ula, Maui's highest point, the **summit building** provides a top-of-the-world panorama from its wraparound windows. On a clear day you can see the Big Island, Lana'i, Moloka'i and even O'ahu.

SLIDING SANDS (KEONEHE'EHE'E) TRAIL Hiking

This trail starts at the south side of the Haleakalā Visitor Center at 9740ft and winds down to the crater floor. The path descends gently into an unearthly world of stark lava sights and ever-changing clouds. The full trail leads 9.2 miles to the Paliku cabin and campground, passing the Kapalaoa cabin at 5.6 miles after roughly four hours.

HOSMER GROVE TRAIL Hiking

Anyone who is looking for a little greenery after hiking the crater will love this shaded woodland walk, and birders wing it here as well. The half-mile loop trail starts at Hosmer Grove campground, 0.75 miles south of the Park Headquarters Visitor Center.

Kipahulu Area ('Ohe'o Gulch)

LOWER POOLS Freshwater Pools

Even if you're tight on time, take this 20-minute stroll. The **Kuloa Point Trail**, a half-mile loop, runs from the Kipahulu Visitor Center down to a series of large freshwater pools terraced one atop the other and connected by gentle cascades. They're usually calm and great for swimming, and their cool waters refreshingly brisk. Beware flash floods.

WATERFALL TRAILS Hiking

The **Pipiwai Trail** runs up the 'Ohe'o streambed, rewarding hikers with picture-perfect views of waterfalls. The trail starts on the *mauka* (inland) side of the Kipahulu Visitor Center and leads up to **Makahiku Falls** (0.5 miles) and **Waimoku Falls** (2 miles). Along the path, you'll pass large mango trees, patches of guava, old banyan trees and a bamboo forest before finally reaching Waimoku Falls.

Sleeping

To spend the night at Haleakalā is to commune with nature. All of the camping options are primitive; none has electricity or showers. Sites are first-come, first-served.

HOSMER GROVE CAMPGROUND Camping $

(Summit Area; campsites free) Wake up to the sound of birdsong at Hosmer Grove, the only drive-up campground in the mountainous section of Haleakalā National Park. It's surrounded by lofty trees and adjacent to one of Maui's best birding trails.

KIPAHULU CAMPGROUND Camping $

(Kipahulu Area; campsites free) This Kipahulu campground enjoys an incredible setting on oceanside cliffs amid the stone ruins of an ancient Hawaiian village. Facilities include pit toilets, picnic tables and grills, but there's no water. The campground is 0.25 miles southeast of the Kipahulu Visitor Center.

HALEAKALĀ WILDERNESS CABINS Cabins $

(Summit Area; ☎808-572-4400; https://fhnp.org/wcr; cabin 1-12 people per night $75) Three rustic cabins, which date from the 1930s, lie along trails on the crater floor at Holua, Kapalaoa and Paliku. Each has a wood-burning stove, two propane burners, cooking utensils, 12 bunks with sleeping pads (but no bedding), pit toilets and a limited supply of water and firewood. Reserve up to 90 days in advance.

Information

All three visitor centers have books, maps and natural-history exhibits.

Haleakalā Visitor Center (dawn-3pm)

Kipahulu Visitor Center (☎808-248-7375; 8:30am-5pm)

Park Headquarters Visitor Center (7am-3:45pm)

Getting There & Around

Paved Haleakalā Crater Rd (Hwy 378) twists and turns for 11 miles from Hwy 377 near Kula up to the park entrance, then another 10 miles to Haleakalā summit.

The drive to the summit takes about 1½ hours from Pa'ia or Kahului, two hours from Kihei and a bit longer from Lahaina. No services on Haleakalā Crater Rd.

Hawaii Volcanoes National Park

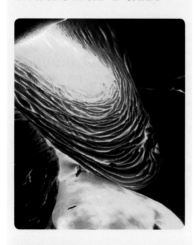

HIGHLIGHTS

1. **Thurston Lava Tube** Confront your fear of the dark in the depths of this giant lava tube.

2. **Kilauea Iki Trail** Hike through ohia forest and across a volcanic crater.

3. **Chain of Craters Rd** Motor through ever-changing tropical scenery on this descent down Kilauea Volcano.

Lava flow, Kilauea
PHOTOGRAPHER: KARL LEHMANN / LONELY PLANET IMAGES ©

Hawaii Volcanoes National Park

Even among Hawaii's many natural wonders, this park stands out: its two active volcanoes testify to the ongoing birth of the islands. Majestic Mauna Loa (13,677ft) looms like a sleeping giant, while young **Kilauea** – the world's most active volcano – has been erupting almost continually since 1983. With luck, you'll witness the primal event of molten lava tumbling into the sea. But the park contains much more too, including overwhelming lava deserts, steaming craters, lava tubes and ancient rainforests.

◎ Sights & Activities

Shifting eruptions can cause unexpected road and trail closures.

CRATER RIM DRIVE   Scenic Drive
The 11-mile Crater Rim Dr circles Kilauea Caldera, offering almost nonstop views of the goddess Pele's scorched, smoldering home. Sections of this road close at times due to high sulfur dioxide levels. For updates on closures, contact the park's main visitor center or check the park website at www.nps.gov/havo.

THURSTON LAVA TUBE   Lava Tube
This popular half-mile loop starts in ohia forest and passes through an impressive lava tube. Dating back perhaps 500 years, Thurston Lava Tube is a massive tunnel, almost big enough to run a train through. Bring a flashlight and you can explore the 300yd unlit extension, an eerie dive into the unknown where few tourists dare to tread.

KILAUEA VISITOR CENTER   Visitor Center
(☎808-985-6017; Crater Rim Dr; ⏰7:45am-5pm) The park visitor center screens a 25-minute Kilauea Volcano **documentary** (admission free; ⏰hourly 9am-4pm). Ranger-led **guided walks** leave daily from here; see the bulletin board for what's on. Get your backcountry permits here.

JAGGAR MUSEUM
Museum

(☎808-985-6049; Crater Rim Dr; ⏰8:30am-8pm) Inside this one-room museum, seismographs and tiltmeters record earthquakes within the park. Head around back for an excellent view of Pele's house, at smoking **Halema'uma'u Crater**. When the crater began erupting in 2008, the real show moved from the museum to the viewpoint outside, replete with a telescope trained 24/7 on the lava lake in the crater's center.

KILAUEA IKI CRATER
Lookout

In 1959, Kilauea Iki (Little Kilauea) burst open in a fiery inferno, turning the crater into a roiling lake of molten lava and sending 1900ft fountains of lava into the night sky. At its peak, it gushed out 2 million tons of lava an hour and the island glowed an eerie orange for miles. From the **overlook** there's a good view of the steaming mile-wide crater below.

CHAIN OF CRATERS ROAD
Scenic Drive

Chain of Craters Rd winds 20 miles and 3700ft down the southern slopes of Kilauea Volcano, ending abruptly at the East Rift Zone on the Puna Coast. This scenic drive takes in an impressive array of sights along a paved two-lane road.

KILAUEA IKI TRAIL
Hiking

If you can only do one day hike, make it this one. Head out early to beat the rest of the day-trippers. The 4-mile loop, beginning near the Thurston Lava Tube parking lot, takes you through a microcosm of the park, quickly descending 400ft through fairytale ohia forest and then cutting across the mile-wide crater, passing close to the main vent. The hike northwest across the crater floor is hot, but short (about 1.5 miles) and marked by stone cairns.

Sleeping & Eating

The national park has two free, drive-up campgrounds (no reservations). The nearby village of Volcano has B&Bs, rainforest cottages and vacation homes. **Volcano Gallery** (☎800-967-8617; www.volcanogallery.com) is a locally managed rental agency.

KILAUEA LODGE
Inn $$

(☎808-967-7366; www.kilauealodge.com; 19-3948 Old Volcano Rd; r incl breakfast $170-205; 🛜) With a variety of country-cozy B&B rooms, this rambling lodge is an appealing choice. Plus, it runs the area's only fine-dining restaurant, serving hearty chophouse staples (*hassenpfeffer*, anyone?).

VOLCANO COUNTRY COTTAGES
Inn $$

(☎808-967-7690; www.volcanocottages.com; 19-3990 Old Volcano Rd; cottages incl breakfast $105-135) For your own private rainforest retreat, these lovingly restored plantation cottages have everything a hideaway needs, from airy lanai to Hawaiian CDs and books. DIY breakfast fixings provided.

HOLO HOLO INN
Hostel $

(☎808-967-7950; www.volcanohostel.com; 19-4036 Kalani Honua Rd; dm $25, r $65-80; @🛜) Make yourself right at home inside this small, friendly hostel, an acceptable budget choice.

THAI THAI RESTAURANT
Thai $$$

(☎808-967-7969; 19-4084 Old Volcano Rd; mains $15-26; ⏰noon-9pm Thu-Tue) Inspired by Pele, perhaps, the superior Thai cuisine here is satisfyingly hot and fairly authentic, if overpriced.

 Information

The **park** (☎808-985-6000; www.nps.gov/havo; 7-day pass per car $10, per person on foot, bicycle or motorcycle $5) never closes, allowing all-night views of the spectacular stars and lava flows.

Overnight camping permits must be obtained in person at the **Kilauea Visitor Center** (☎808-985-6017; Crater Rim Dr; ⏰7:45am-5pm) no more than 24 hours before you intend to hike.

Getting There & Around

The park is 29 miles (45 minutes) from Hilo and 97 miles (two hours) from Kailua-Kona via Hwy 11. Volcano village is a couple of miles east of the park entrance.

The **Hele-On bus** (☎808-961-8744; www.heleonbus.org) leaves three times a day from Hilo and arrives at the park visitor center an hour later before continuing on to Ka'u.

Sequoia & Kings Canyon National Parks

HIGHLIGHTS

1. **Zumwalt Meadow** Take in the sweeping Sierra Nevada views from beside the Kings River.

2. **Giant Forest** Be dwarfed by the largest living things on the planet, giant sequoias.

3. **Moro Rock** Climb the quarter-mile staircase to this viewpoint and marvel at the Great Western Divide.

Sequoia trees, Sequoia
PHOTOGRAPHER: CAROL POLICH / LONELY PLANET IMAGES ©

Sequoia & Kings Canyon National Parks

In these neighboring parks, the famous rust-red giant sequoia trees are bigger and more numerous than anywhere else in the Sierra Nevada. Tough and fire-charred, they'd easily swallow two freeway lanes each. Giant, too, are the mountains – including **Mt Whitney** (14,505ft), the tallest peak in the Lower 48 states. Finally, there is the giant Kings Canyon, carved out of granite by ancient glaciers and a powerful river.

 Sights & Activities

Sequoia National Park

GIANT FOREST Forest
We dare you to try hugging the trees in this 3-sq-mile grove protecting the park's most gargantuan specimens. The world's biggest is the **General Sherman Tree**. Lose the crowds by venturing onto any of the many forested trails.

MORO ROCK Natural Feature
A quarter-mile staircase climbs over 300ft to the top of Sequoia's iconic granite dome, offering views of the Great Western Divide. Running north to south through the center of the park, the Divide splits the watersheds of the Kaweah River to the west and the Kern River to the east.

GIANT FOREST MUSEUM Museum
(559-565-4480; Generals Hwy; 9am-7pm, reduced hours outside summer;) For a primer on the intriguing ecology and history of giant sequoias, this pint-sized museum will entertain both kids and adults.

MINERAL KING Scenic Area
Perched at 7500ft, this giant, gorgeous and glacially sculpted valley ringed by massive mountains, including jagged **Sawtooth Peak** (12,343ft), is a supremely good place to find solitude. The valley is reached via narrow, twisting 25-mile Mineral King Rd, which heads east from Hwy 198 south of the park's Ash Mountain Entrance.

CRYSTAL CAVE Cave

(📞559-565-3759; www.sequoiahistory.org; Crystal Cave Rd; tours adult/child 5-12yr/senior from $13/7/12; ⏰regular tours 10:30am-4:30pm mid-May–late Oct) Inside this massive cave, stalactites hang like daggers from the ceiling, and milky white marble formations take the shape of ethereal curtains, domes, columns and shields. Purchase tickets in advance at the Lodgepole or Foothills Visitor Centers.

Kings Canyon National Park

North of Grant Grove Village, **General Grant Grove** brims with majestic giants. Beyond here, Hwy 180 begins its 35-mile descent into **Kings Canyon**, serpentining past chiseled rock walls laced with spring waterfalls. The road meets the **Kings River**, its roar ricocheting off granite cliffs soaring over 4000ft high, making this one of North America's deepest canyons.

ZUMWALT MEADOW Natural Feature

This verdant meadow, bordered by the Kings River and soaring granite canyon walls, offers phenomenal views. Taking the partly shaded nature loop trail gives you a quick snapshot of the canyon's beauty.

BOYDEN CAVERN Cave

(📞559-965-8243; www.boydencavern.com; Hwy 180; 45min tour adult/child $13/8; ⏰May–mid-Nov; 👶) While smaller than Crystal Cave in Sequoia National Park, the beautiful and whimsical formations here require no advance tickets.

MIST FALLS Hiking

This long walk along the riverside and up a natural granite staircase highlights the beauty of Kings Canyon. The trail begins just past the Road's End wilderness permit station, winds through forest and works its way up the Kings River before finally reaching Mist Falls.

 Sleeping & Eating

Outside Sequoia's southern entrance, several motels line Hwy 198 through Three Rivers town. Camping **reservations**

(📞518-885-3639; www.recreation.gov) are accepted only at Lodgepole and Dorst in Sequoia. The parks' dozen other campgrounds are first-come, first-served.

JOHN MUIR LODGE & GRANT GROVE CABINS Lodge, Cabins $$

(📞559-335-5500; www.sequoia-kingscanyon.com; Hwy 180, Grant Grove Village; d $69-190; 📶) The woodsy lodge has good-sized, if generic, rooms and a cozy lobby with a stone fireplace and board games. Also thin-walled canvas tents or furnished historical cottages with private baths.

CEDAR GROVE LODGE Motel $$

(📞559-335-5500; www.sequoia-kingscanyon.com; Hwy 180, Cedar Grove Village; r $119-135; ⏰mid-May–mid-Oct; 📶) The 21 motel-style rooms with common porches overlooking Kings River are simple, but the best option in the canyon.

🛈 Information

The two **parks** (📞559-565-3341; www.nps.gov/seki; ⏰year-round) operate as one unit with a single admission fee (valid for seven days) of $20 per car, $10 on motorcycle, bicycle or foot.

The following visitor centers maintain reduced hours outside the summer hours listed here.

Cedar Grove Visitor Center (📞559-565-3793; ⏰9am-5pm) In Cedar Grove Village.

Foothills Visitor Center (📞559-565-3135; ⏰8am-4:30pm) One mile north of Ash Mountain Entrance.

Kings Canyon Visitor Center (📞559-565-4307; ⏰8am-7pm) In Grant Grove, 3 miles east of the Big Stump Entrance.

Lodgepole Visitor Center (📞559-565-4436; ⏰7am-6pm) In Lodgepole Village.

🛈 Getting There & Around

In summer, free shuttle buses cover the Giant Forest and Lodgepole Village areas of Sequoia National Park, while the **Sequoia Shuttle** (📞877-287-4453; www.sequoiashuttle.com) connects the park with Three Rivers and Visalia (round-trip $15), with onward connections to Amtrak; reservations required. Currently, there is no public transportation into Kings Canyon National Park.

The Parks

In Focus

View from Highline Trail (p76), Glacier
PHOTOGRAPHER: SHANNON NACE / LONELY PLANET IMAGES ©

The Parks Today

Crater at Stovepipe Wells (p187), Death Valley

> *Congestion and crowds remain a constant source of concern*

seasonal visitation
(% of visitors)

42	24	24	10
Summer	Autumn	Spring	Winter

if 100 people stayed overnight in a National Park

42 camped
36 stayed in an RV
22 stayed in a hotel

visitors per sq mile

♦ ≈ 190 people

Death Valley   Yosemite   Great Smoky Mountains

State of the National Parks

Since Yellowstone was created in 1872, the national park system has grown to encompass 395 parks and 84 million acres. The parks today protect many of the continent's most sensitive ecosystems, some of the world's most remarkable landscapes and America's most important historical and cultural landmarks. Over the years, more than 11 *billion* people from the US and around the world have visited them. They are the country's greatest treasure. Yet today they still face a variety of threats and obstacles.

In 2011, the National Parks Conservation Association (NPCA) published a document titled *The State of America's National Parks*, based on a decade of research. It identifies the greatest threats our parks face today. The list is staggering: 'loss of biodiversity, degradation of cultural resources, declining air and water quality, landscape fragmentation, climate disruption, and insufficient funding' get top mention. These are the topics you'll hear heatedly discussed around the parks today.

WITOLD SKRYPCZAK / LONELY PLANET IMAGES ©

Budget Cuts & Freezes

While conservationists, policy makers and the NPS debate how to protect the parks, nearly everyone agrees the parks need money. In 2010, the NPS faced an annual operating shortfall of $600 million and 'a backlog of maintenance projects totaling nearly $11 billion,' according to the NPCA. When controlled for inflation, the National Park Service budget today is $385 million below where it was a decade ago, while the fixed cost of running the parks has gone up. While this deficit may not be immediately visible to someone wandering the backcountry, it is quickly becoming apparent to those in the frontcountry where visitor center hours in some parks have been reduced, interpretive programs face cuts, staff positions have gone unfilled, infrastructure remains unimproved, and, in some parks, historic structures desperately need facelifts. However, the needed funds are unlikely to come any time soon. In 2011, the NPS budget was cut by $140 million, and with the current US deficit and the budget-cutting mood in Washington, future spending could be down even further. This would mean reduced visitor services, fewer rangers, less trail maintenance and cuts to programs that maintain the parks' ecosystems.

Hot Topics

System-wide challenges are not the only matters garnering national attention. From the ongoing debate about snowmobiles in Yellowstone to the concern about melting glaciers in Glacier National Park, there are plenty of park-specific issues fueling debate beyond the doors of local diners.

Congestion and crowds remain a constant source of concern, and several parks have introduced free shuttles to combat traffic. Most recently, Glacier National Park began a free shuttle in 2007 to ease traffic on Going-to-the-Sun Rd. By 2010, nearly 8% of Glacier's annual summer drivers parked their cars and rode the bus instead.

The successful reintroduction of wolves into Yellowstone has been wildly popular among park visitors and restored an ecological balance to the park. Yet opponents remain among ranchers and hunters who believe wolves threaten local elk populations. In 2011, the wolf lost its federally protected status, to howls and cheers from respective sides.

The Grand Canyon Skywalk, constructed on the Hualapai Reservation near Grand Canyon National Park, generated controversy both for its location, considered sacred, and because many feared it would fuel overdevelopment. The views from the space-age viewing platform are certainly incredible. But is the attraction appropriate? May you find yourself debating this and other topics beside a crackling campfire in a national park very soon.

417

History

JOHN ELK III / LONELY PLANET I

Few things are as quintessentially American as national parks. As writer Wallace Stegner famously put it, they are 'the best idea we ever had. Absolutely American, absolutely democratic.' That a handful of people had the foresight to pull in the reins on rampant hunting, logging and mining in the 19th century, so that we might save at least some of our most magnificent treasures for future generations, is one of the greatest chapters in US history.

A Magnificent Park

American portrait artist George Catlin (1796–1872) is credited with being the first person to conceptualize a 'nation's park.' He envisioned a 'magnificent park' to protect the country's remaining indigenous people, buffalo and wilderness from the onslaught of western expansion. But over three decades would pass before anything remotely resembling that vision existed.

1864
President Lincoln designates Yosemite Valley and the Mariposa Grove a protected state park.

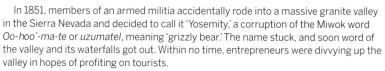

In 1851, members of an armed militia accidentally rode into a massive granite valley in the Sierra Nevada and decided to call it 'Yosemity,' a corruption of the Miwok word *Oo-hoo'-ma-te* or *uzumatel*, meaning 'grizzly bear.' The name stuck, and soon word of the valley and its waterfalls got out. Within no time, entrepreneurs were divvying up the valley in hopes of profiting on tourists.

Thanks to a handful of outspoken writers, artists, naturalists and – most importantly – the efforts of the great landscape architect Frederick Law Olmstead, Yosemite Valley was spared the plight of privatization. In 1864, President Lincoln signed a bill into law that put Yosemite Valley, and the nearby Mariposa Grove of giant sequoias, under the control of California. Although it wasn't a national park, it was the first time the US government – *any* government – had mandated the protection of a natural area for public use.

Birth of a National Park

Four years later, a group of men, bankrolled by Northern Pacific Railroad, headed into the Wyoming wilderness to investigate reports of thermal pools and geysers. Among their discoveries were the Great Fountain Geyser and another geyser they would name Old Faithful. Soon, lobbyists at Northern Pacific, with their eyes on tourist dollars, rallied alongside conservationists for a public park like Yosemite. Finally, in 1872, Ulysses S Grant signed the landmark Yellowstone National Park Act, creating the country's first national park.

Meanwhile, in Yosemite, the famed naturalist John Muir lamented the destruction that logging companies, miners and sheep – which he famously deemed 'hoofed locusts' – were wreaking upon the park. Muir took President Theodore Roosevelt on a camping trip in Yosemite and ultimately convinced him Yosemite needed federal protection. In 1890, Yosemite became the country's second national park. Over the next 25 years, presidents signed off on six more national parks, including Mt Rainier (1899), Crater Lake (1902), Mesa Verde (1906) and Glacier (1910).

Mather & the National Park Service

Still, there existed no effective protection or management of the new parks until the creation of the National Park Service (NPS) in 1916. The NPS was the brainchild of an industrialist and conservationist named Stephen Mather, who convinced the Department of Interior that a single governing body was precisely what the parks needed. When President Woodrow Wilson signed the National Park Service Act into law, Mather became the first director.

Mather believed that the best way to promote and improve the parks was to get people into them. A public relations guru, Mather encouraged park superintendents to

1872
President Ulysses S Grant designates Yellowstone the world's first national park.

1916
Stephen Mather convinces Department of Interior to create the National Park Service.

1933
FDR creates Civilian Conservation Corps, and CCC workers improve infrastructure in national parks.

The Father of Our National Parks

A self-described 'poetico-trampo-geologist-botanist', Scottish-born John Muir (1838–1914) was an eloquent writer, naturalist and arguably the greatest defender of our early national parks. His writings were pivotal in the creation not just of Yosemite, but of Sequoia, Mt Rainier, Petrified Forest, and Grand Canyon National Parks. Famously – but unsuccessfully – Muir fought to save Yosemite's Hetch Hetchy Valley, which he believed rivaled Yosemite Valley in beauty and grandeur. Although he couldn't stop the dam, his writings on the issue cemented the now widely held belief that our national parks should remain as close as possible to their natural state.

run publicity campaigns, created the park ranger system, initiated campfire talks and opened the first park museums. His efforts – always coupled with media outreach – were so successful that by 1928 he had tripled the number of park visitors to three million.

While Mather was extremely successful in developing the parks, some felt he'd gone too far. Conservation groups such as the National Parks Association and the Sierra Club felt that Mather's emphasis on development came at the expense of the parks themselves. Mather's successor and protégé, Horace Albright, partially addressed these concerns by creating a national wildlife division within the NPS.

FDR & the CCC

With the Great Depression, the parks went through significant changes. President Franklin Delano Roosevelt created the Civilian Conservation Corps (CCC) and put thousands of young men to work improving national park roads, visitors shelters, campsites and trails. During his presidency, FDR also created Joshua Tree, Capitol Reef and Channel Islands National Monuments (all of which would become national parks) and Olympic and Kings Canyon National Parks.

With the beginning of WWII, the country's greatest public relief program came to an end, CCC workers went off to war, and the national park budget was slashed. Simultaneously, postwar prosperity allowed more Americans to travel – and hordes of them headed to the parks. By 1950 some 32 million people visited America's national parks. Within five years the number topped 60 million.

1941–49

Ansel Adams photographs every national park in the US, bar the Everglades, for the NPS.

1956–66

Mission 66 improves park facilities and creates first national park visitor centers.

Mission 66

The number of travelers descending on the parks put tremendous pressure on them. Finally, in 1956, NPS Director Conrad Wirth created Mission 66, a 10-year plan to improve park infrastructure and dramatically increase visitors' services. The plan established the first park visitor centers, more staff and improved facilities. Over the course of Mission 66, Congress also added more than 50 new protected areas to the national park system.

In 1964 George Hartzog succeeded Wirth as director of the NPS and continued to add new acquisitions. During his tenure, nearly 70 new parks would become jurisdiction of the NPS. In 1972, President Nixon replaced Hartzog with his own appointee, and expansions to the park service were halted.

Doubling Down

Little was added to the national parks until 1980, when President Carter signed the Alaska National Interest Lands Conservation Act into law. The landmark legislation instantly protected over 80 million acres and doubled the amount of land under control of the national parks. Ten new national parks and monuments were created in the process. Although controversial in Alaska, the move has been widely heralded as one of the greatest conservation measures in US history.

Since 1980, 10 sites have been designated or reclassified as national parks, including, with the passing of the California Desert Protection Act of 1994, Joshua Tree and Death Valley. Today 395 locations are managed by the NPS. Of them, 58 are distinguished as national parks.

The Best...
History Lessons

1 Cable Mill Historic Area (p146)

2 Yellowstone Heritage & Research Center (p283)

3 Bodie State Historic Park (p311)

4 Human History Museum (p361)

5 Enos Mills Cabin Museum & Gallery (p226)

IN FOCUS   HISTORY

1972
Yellowstone celebrates 100 years as a national park.

1980
Alaska National Interest Lands Conservation Act doubles amount of land under control of the NPS.

1994
California Desert Protection Act designates Death Valley and Joshua Tree as national parks.

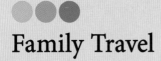

Family Travel

Hiking (p401), Arches

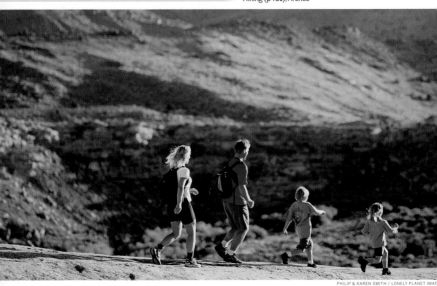

PHILIP & KAREN SMITH / LONELY PLANET IMAG

There's something inherently gratifying about bringing kids to a national park. Seeing your child spot a moose or a roaring waterfall can be as thrilling as the experience itself. Along with the natural wonders that will dazzle even the most Xbox-addicted child, national parks have educational programs and activities designed to engage children in the environments around them. Planning, however, is always key to a successful trip with kids.

Kids Activities

To keep kids happy in a national park, keep them busy. Rock-climbing classes and rafting trips can be great ways to instill confidence in kids and keep them excited. Horseback rides are almost always a hit. And don't forget the campfire chats and ranger-led walks. The parks abound with child-friendly hikes, ranging from easy, flat, paved paths you can push a stroller down to more strenuous trails that will challenge and entertain an active 10-year-old. 'Starry night' walks with volunteer astronomers are particularly memorable for children. In this book, the easiest hikes, which are listed first in Hiking sections, are all great for families.

Junior Ranger Programs

Every national park has a junior ranger program, an activity-based educational program geared toward children five to 12 years old.

Through a myriad of hands-on activities, children earn junior ranger badges and learn about the parks they're visiting. Before hitting the road, visit **Web Rangers** (www.webrangers.us) and the **NPS website** (www.nps.gov). Programs are free, but there's usually a small charge (under $5) for associated activity packets.

Sleeping & Eating

The vast majority of accommodations and restaurants listed in this book are kid-friendly. For places that are particularly family-friendly, we use a 🖶 icon, but you can rest assured that all but the quietest B&Bs or upscale restaurants are fine for children. Campgrounds, of course, are the closest thing to an earthly paradise for kids.

What to Pack

Never underestimate the misery (and power) of a thirsty, sunburned, mosquito-bitten, exhausted child on a hike. Remember the basics: hat, sunscreen, water and bug repellent. (DEET-based products are the most effective, but citronella- or eucalyptus-based products are less toxic.)

A great way to ensure a successful trip with younger children is by encouraging them to pack their own fun kit: kids' binoculars, a cheap digital camera, star charts, animal and plant identification books, dirt-friendly toys for the campsite, a small flashlight, a compass, a pen knife, and books or games for the car ride can all be saviors for parents.

Safety

While national parks are generally a very safe destination for children, precautions should still be taken. Overlooks (Yosemite, Grand Canyon, Bryce Canyon and Zion) are highlights of any trip, but guardrails aren't always present; be mindful of where your children are. The same is true with rivers – every year, children get swept away in currents. Educate them and only swim where you know it's safe. *Never* let your children feed animals.

Need to Know

○ **Changing Facilities** Available in some park restrooms.

○ **Cribs** Often available at larger hotels for no extra charge.

○ **Diapers** Available but pricey in general stores near parks.

○ **Highchairs** Available in most restaurants.

○ **Strollers** Bring your own; these are rarely available for rental. Most parks have one or two paved trails.

○ **Kids' menus** Common in midrange restaurants.

The Best...
Kids' Adventures

1 Wildlife watching, Lamar Valley, Yellowstone (p253)

2 Rock climbing, Yosemite Mountaineering School, Yosemite (p337)

3 Grand Canyon Cookout Experience, Grand Canyon (p138)

4 Sol Duc Hot Springs, Olympic National Park (p201)

5 Cable Mill Historic Area, Cades Cove, Great Smoky Mountains (p146)

IN FOCUS FAMILY TRAVEL

Outdoor
Activities

Rafting, Glacier (p65)

JOHN ELK III / LONELY PLANET IMAG

*We've yet to meet someone visiting
a national park so they can hang
around inside. The outdoors is what
the parks are all about, and getting
out usually means getting active.
With environments ranging from
the subtropics of the Everglades to
the Rocky Mountain tundra, the
possibilities are boundless.*

Hiking

Nothing encapsulates the spirit of the
national parks like hiking. Thousands of
miles of trails crisscross the parks, offering access to their most scenic mountain passes, highest waterfalls, deepest
canyons and quietest corners. Trails run
the gamut of accessibility, from the flat,
paved paths of Yosemite's Loop Trails to
the infamous, thigh-busting grunt up to
Zion's Angels Landing.

Each park chapter in this book has
its own Hiking or Activities section with
descriptions of the parks' top hikes. We've
done our best to cover not just our favorite
trails, but a variety of trails. Our goal with
descriptions is less about navigation than
it is about helping you choose which hikes
to squeeze into your trip. Detailed trail
descriptions and maps are readily available

at visitor centers in every park, and they will complement this book well.

Most visitor centers and outdoor stores stock USGS topographical maps, but our favorite maps are those in the *Trails Illustrated* series by **National Geographic** (www.nationalgeographic.com).

Day Hikes

Most of the hikes covered in this book are day hikes. At higher elevations, in parks like Yellowstone, Glacier and Mt Rainier, snow can keep some trails closed until late July. At lower elevations and in desert parks, always inquire about ticks, poison oak, poison ivy and rattlesnakes before heading out. Most day hikes are on well-maintained trails, but it's good to know what's out there.

Always carry more water than you think you'll need, and prepare for unpredictable weather, especially in the Rockies and the Sierras. Afternoon thunderstorms can turn a hot day cold and wet *very* quickly. When hiking at altitude, acclimate before tackling a long hike to avoid altitude sickness. Always lather on the sunblock, especially at higher elevations. Planning is the most important safety precaution. Know your limitations, know the route you plan to take and pace yourself. With proper preparation, hiking is safe and incredibly rewarding.

The Best...
Day Hikes

1 Bright Angel Trail (p107)

2 Hoh River Trail (p203)

3 Vernal & Nevada Falls (p332)

4 The Narrows (p370)

5 Kuloa Point Trail (p409)

IN FOCUS OUTDOOR ACTIVITIES

Backpacking

If you really want to ditch the crowds, hit the backcountry. Even if you have no backpacking experience, don't consider it out of reach. Most national parks have at least a few backcountry campsites within a couple hours' walk of a trailhead, making them excellent options for first-time backpackers.

Whatever you do, know the park rules and be familiar with backcountry ethics before heading out. Most park visitor centers have a backcountry desk, where you can apply for permits, get trail information, learn about bears (very important), check conditions and, usually, purchase maps. Before hitting the trail, familiarize yourself with low-impact camping principles at **Leave No Trace** (www.lnt.org).

Cycling

Many of the national parks have bicycle rentals inside or just outside the park. In Yosemite the 12 miles of paved pathways along the **Loop Trails** make for incredibly scenic and leisurely pedaling. In Zion, you can rent a bike and ride the 6.2-mile **Zion Canyon Scenic Dr** (closed to cars April through October) or the paved **Pa'rus Trail**. In Bryce, the 34-mile **Bryce Canyon Scenic Dr** makes for an excellent longer ride.

On the down side, cycling within national parks can sometimes be challenging due to traffic and steep grades. Anyone who's been grazed by an RV mirror can attest to that.

Mountain biking on trails is largely prohibited in the national parks, but some parks have dirt roads that make for great mountain biking. **Canyonlands National Park** is particularly full of them, and there are several gravel roads in Great Smoky.

Rafting, Canoeing & Kayaking

Canoes, kayaks and rafts are a wonderful way to get to parts of the parks that landlubbers can't reach. In Glacier National Park, the lake paddling is excellent and accessible, thanks to boat ramps and rentals on several lakes. In Grand Teton, **String** and **Leigh Lakes** are great for family and novice paddlers, and you can rent boats at Teton's **Colter Bay**. In Yosemite, **Tenaya Lake** makes for spectacular paddling. Yellowstone's **Shoshone Lake** is the largest backcountry lake in the Lower 48 and offers boat-in access to some of the remotest areas of the park.

River-running opportunities abound in the parks, but none stand out as famously as the Grand Canyon stretch of the **Colorado River**. You'll escape the crowds and see parts of the canyon that most people only see in photos. The **Snake River** in Grand Teton National Park has water for all skill levels. Superb rafting can also be found in and around Great Smoky Mountain and on the **Rio Grande** in Big Bend.

For white-water rafting, you usually have to head to outfitters in satellite towns outside the parks. Full-day guided trips on most rivers cost $50 to $100.

Rock Climbing & Mountaineering

If there's one park that's synonymous with rock climbing, it's **Yosemite**, the world's holy grail of rock. Best advice for novices? Head straight to the Yosemite Mountaineering School for lessons and information.

Next up, **Joshua Tree**. From boulders to cracks to multipitch faces, there are more than 8000 established routes in this desert park. The huge granite faces of the **Grand Tetons** are also among America's premier climbing destinations. **Rocky Mountain National Park** has a long tradition of climbing, with loads of granite, exceptional peaks and climbs that range from bouldering to multiday, big-wall climbs.

Kayaking (p58), Everglades

PHOTOGRAPHER: MARK NEWMAN / LONELY PLANET IMAGES ©

Winter Sports

Downhill Skiing & Snowboarding

Most of the best downhill skiing takes place outside the parks. Two parks, however, do have downhill ski resorts: Badger Pass in Yosemite National Park is an affordable, family-friendly resort and, just inside the border of Olympic National Park, Hurricane Ridge has only three lifts and is the westernmost ski resort in the Lower 48. The most notable skiing adjacent to parks covered in this book is Jackson Hole, Wyoming, which has long runs, deep powder and a screeching 4139ft vertical drop.

Cross-Country Skiing & Snowshoeing

Come winter, trails and roads in many parks get blanketed with snow, and the crowds disappear. It's a magical time to visit, and those willing to step into skis or snowshoes and brave the elements will be rewarded. The best parks for both activities are Glacier, Yellowstone, Grand Teton, Yosemite, Olympic, Mt Rainier, Zion, Bryce Canyon, and Sequoia and Kings Canyon. Surprisingly, there's even cross-country skiing at the Grand Canyon.

In most of these parks, rangers lead snowshoe hikes, which can be an excellent entry to the sport and a great way to learn about the winter environment. Visitor centers are the best place to check for information.

Swimming

With the exception of the higher-elevation parks (like Glacier and Rocky Mountain) and northern parks like Denali, summer means heat, and heat means swimming. Alpine lakes make for wonderful but often frigid swimming, and many of the larger lakes have beaches and designated swimming areas.

As river rats the world over will attest, nothing beats dipping into a swimming hole and drip-drying on a rock in the sun. But be careful; every year, swimmers drown in national park rivers. Always check with visitor centers about trouble spots and the safest places to swim. Unless you're certain about the currents, swim only where others are swimming.

Wildlife Watching

North America is home to some of the largest land mammals in the world, and the USA's national parks are by far the best places to see them. If wildlife watching – and we're talking the big mammal, 'megafauna' type – is a priority for you, head directly to **Yellowstone**, **Glacier** or **Grand Teton** National Parks. These are the places where you'll see the biggest of the beasts, including bison, moose, elk, mule deer, black bears and, if you're lucky, grizzly bears and wolves (from a distance, of course). Although too far afield for most people, Alaska's **Denali National Park** is big-mammal wonderland.

Black bears are prevalent in **Yosemite** (where you sometimes have to chase them out of your campsite banging pots and pans) and in **Great Smoky** and **Olympic**. For bird-watching, think **Everglades**.

As always, the best times for wildlife watching are at dawn and dusk, away from major roads. That said, even from the main roads in places like Grand Teton and Yellowstone, sightings are commonplace. If you're serious about wildlife watching, invest in a good pair of binoculars and head out early.

So Much to Do...

For those that want to try it all, here's some more fodder for fun:

- **Stargazing** It's outstanding in Bryce. Also check park newspapers for nightly astronomy walks.
- **Soaking** Submerge your sore muscles in thermal hot springs at Yellowstone and Olympic.
- **Ice Skating** The outdoor rink in Yosemite Valley is the perfect place to pirouette.
- **Tide pooling** Olympic and Acadia National Parks are tide-pool heaven.
- **Canyoneering** Rope up and descend into Zion's slot canyons; with a guide, no experience is necessary.
- **Napping** Outstanding in all parks, preferably on a hot day in the shade of a tree near water.

Our favorite places to get wet are Zion's Virgin River, the Merced River in Yosemite Valley, Sedge Bay in Yellowstone, Leigh Lake in Grand Teton, Midnight Hole in Great Smoky and Sol Duc Hot Springs in Olympic.

Fishing

For many, the idea of heading to the national parks without a fishing rod is ludicrous. Yellowstone offers some of the best fly-fishing in the country. Olympic's Hoh and Sol Duc Rivers are famous for their runs of salmon and winter steelhead. Waters in Yosemite's high country, particularly the Tuolumne River, can be great for small, feisty trout. Glacier, Grand Teton and, of course, Denali all offer outstanding fishing. Great Smoky has exceptional fishing for trout and bass.

Wherever you fish, read up on local regulations. Fishing permits are always required, and those caught fishing without one will be fined. (Children under 15 are generally not required to have a license.) Some waters, including many streams and rivers, are catch-and-release only, and sometimes bait-fishing is prohibited. Certain native fish, such as bull trout, kokanee salmon and wild steelhead, are often protected, and anglers in possession of one can be heavily fined. The best place to check regulations is online. For details on regulations, check the park's NPS website (www.nps.gov) and refer to the respective state's department of fish and game website. Find the latter by searching for the state plus 'fish and game.'

Horseback & Mule Riding

Our most time-tested form of transport still makes for a wonderful way to experience the great outdoors. Horseback riding is possible in many of the parks, and outfitters within or immediately outside the parks offer everything from two-hour rides to full- and multiday pack trips. Rides run around $25 to $35 per hour, $60 to $70 per half-day and up to $150 for a full day. In the Grand Canyon, an overnight mule trip costs around $480 per person.

In Great Smoky, over 550 miles of trails are open to horses, and outfitters abound. Popular horseback excursions such as the descent into the Grand Canyon or the High Sierra Camps in Yosemite require reservations far in advance.

Geology

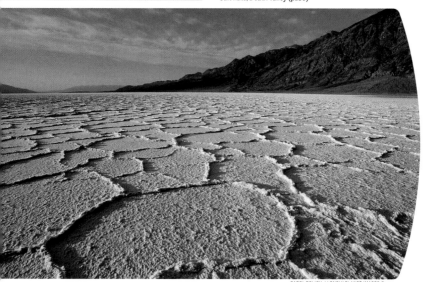

Salt flats, Death Valley (p185)

CAROL POLICH / LONELY PLANET IMAGES ©

Tectonic collisions, glaciation, volcanic eruptions, erosion – the forces of nature and time have worked wonders on the continent, and nowhere is that geologic history more beautifully evident than in the national parks. From east coast to west coast, each park tells its own ancient story through landscapes that are as unique as they are complex.

The Atlantic Ocean

Acadia National Park is the easternmost national park in the United States. It occupies about two-thirds of Mt Desert Island, the largest island off the coast of Maine. The island was created some 20,000 years ago, when glacial ice sheets sheared it from the mainland and sea levels rose with the close of the ice age. At 1530ft, Cadillac Mountain is the island's highest point.

Also on the Atlantic, **Everglades National Park** sits at the tip of the Florida Peninsula, which was covered by a shallow sea as recently as 5000 to 10,000 years ago. Today, the park protects the largest subtropical wilderness in North America. With an average elevation of only 6ft, the park is an expansive wetland atop an ancient seabed, with a tremendous variety of coastal and marine ecosystems.

The Appalachians

Great Smoky Mountains and **Shenandoah National Parks** reside in the Appalachian Mountains, one of the oldest mountain ranges in the world. Paralleling the Atlantic Ocean and stretching from Canada to Alabama, the Appalachians are a complex of scattered peaks and ridges that form an elevated axis across eastern North America. The range's easternmost ridge, known as the Blue Ridge, connects the two parks. Peaks in the central Appalachian region (home to Shenandoah) top out around 4000ft, while those in the southern part of the range (including Great Smoky) extend over 6000ft. Steep elevation gradients, deep V-shaped valleys, ridges, abundant rainfall and high summertime humidity make the Appalachians one of the most diverse ecosystems in all of North America.

The Rockies

Nearly 1000 miles west of the Appalachians, the Rocky Mountains begin their ascent from the western reaches of the Great Plains and climb to over 14,000ft. Much newer geologically than the Appalachians, the Rockies were created by tectonic uplift between 70 million and two million years ago. The mountains were carved and eroded by water and wind and finally, during the Pleistocene Ice Age of two million years ago, hewn by glaciers into the landscapes we see today.

Yellowstone was shaped by the same ice age, but what really differentiates it from other parks in the range is its volcanic activity. Yellowstone sits on a geological 'hot spot,' a thin piece of the earth's crust that is essentially floating atop a massive, 125-mile-deep plume of molten rock. Fueled by this underground furnace, Yellowstone bubbles like a pot on a hot stove to produce over 10,000 geothermal features – more than all other geothermal areas on the planet combined.

Yellowstone, **Grand Teton**, **Glacier** and **Rocky Mountain National Parks** together protect almost 6000 sq miles of the Rockies. Rocky Mountain National Park sits near the top of the range, its massive Longs Peak punching 14,259ft into the sky.

The Colorado Plateau

At the southwest end of the Rockies, the mountains descend to the Colorado Plateau, a 130,000-sq-mile region centered on the Four Corners area of the United States. Home to **Grand Canyon**, **Zion** and **Bryce Canyon National Parks**, the Colorado Plateau is one of the world's densest concentrations of exposed rock.

National Park Extremes

- **Highest peak** Mt Whitney, Sequoia & Kings Canyon; elevation: 14,505ft
- **Lowest point** Badwater Basin, Death Valley; elevation: -282ft
- **Wettest region** Hoh Rainforest, Olympic; annual rainfall: 11.25ft
- **Mountain with the most glaciers** Mt Rainier; number: 25
- **Greatest geothermal activity** Yellowstone; number of geysers: 300+
- **Largest granite monolith** El Capitan, Yosemite; base-to-summit: 3593ft
- **Deepest Canyon** Grand Canyon; greatest depth: 6000ft
- **Largest park** Death Valley; total area: 5270 sq miles

(All comparisons within contiguous United States.)

Unlike the Rocky Mountains to the east and the Sierras to the west, the plateau has remained stable for millions of years, during which the deep cracks that formed through uplift some 60 million years ago slowly eroded into the smaller plateaus seen today. From an aerial perspective, these plateaus and cliffs form a remarkable staircase that steps downward from the pink cliffs of Bryce Canyon, to the gray cliffs of Zion and finally to the chocolate cliffs abutting the Grand Canyon. This so-called 'Grand Staircase' exposes millions of years of layered rock that make the region so visually spectacular.

Mojave & Colorado Deserts

South of Zion, the Colorado Plateau meets the Mojave Desert, which is home to the hottest, driest places in North America. The Mojave is also home to **Death Valley National Park**, which protects over 5000 sq miles of what is no less than a crazy quilted geological playground. Encompassing far more than Death Valley itself, the park contains giant sand dunes, marbled canyons, extinct volcanic craters and palm-shaded oases.

At the southernmost edge of the Mojave lies **Joshua Tree National Park**, which straddles both the Mojave and the Colorado Deserts. The Mojave section of the park is home to a member of the yucca family, the Joshua Tree.

The Sierra Nevada

Northwest of the California deserts, the Sierra Nevada is a 400-mile-long mountain range with tremendous biological and geological diversity. The Sierras are an uplifted, westward-tilting slab of granite that broke off from the Earth's crust and thrust upward beginning roughly 10 million years ago.

Between two million and 10,000 years ago, glaciers 'flowed' from high-elevation ice fields, scouring out canyons and valleys and sculpting the range into a granite masterpiece. In **Yosemite**, evidence of glaciation is everywhere and is what makes the park so spectacular.

The Sierras' highest peaks stand within the areas protected by Yosemite, and Sequoia and Kings Canyon National Parks, with Mt Whitney (in Sequoia), standing taller than any other peak in the Lower 48.

The Pacific Northwest

North of the Sierra Nevada stands the Cascade Range, a volcanic mountain range stretching from northern California into British Columbia. The range's highest peak is 14,411ft Mt Rainier, a massive stratovolcano protected by **Mt Rainier National Park**. The volcano is 'episodically active' and is considered the most hazardous volcano in the Cascades. The mountain is covered in snow for much of the year and contains expansive ice fields and 25 glaciers. It last erupted in 1854.

West of the Cascades, on Washington's Olympic Peninsula, the Olympic Mountains plunge dramatically into the Pacific Ocean. They are a separate range entirely and, unlike the volcanic Cascades, were formed five to 15 million years ago during convergence of the Juan de Fuca and North American plates. Between the Olympic's highest peaks, which top out at 7965ft, and the ocean below, **Olympic National Park** protects a landscape drenched in rain, hammered by wind and pounded by waves.

The Best...
Rockstar Vistas

1 Olmsted Point, Yosemite National Park (p324)

2 Wall Street, The Narrows, Zion (p370)

3 Bryce Canyon Amphitheater, Bryce Canyon (p386)

4 Bright Angel Point, Grand Canyon (p132)

5 Hidden Valley, Joshua Tree (p181)

Wildlife

HOLGER LEUE / ;LONELY PLANET IMAGES

With habitats ranging from subtropical marshlands to alpine tundra, from the lowest point in the United States to the highest, the parks protect thousands of species of plants and animals. Moose, bears, eagles, elk, giant sequoias and Joshua trees – the list seems endless, and even the tiniest flower can be a marvel to see.

Bears

If you see a bear on your trip to a national park, odds are it will be a **black bear**. These mostly vegetarian foragers are much more common than their larger, more elusive cousins, grizzly bears. Black bears are very adaptable and in some places, such as Yosemite, have become so accustomed to humans that they regularly roam campsites and break into cars at night for food.

Black bears, which are sometimes brown or cinnamon colored, roam montane and subalpine forests throughout the Rockies and the Sierras and parts of the Southern Appalachians. Yellowstone, Grand Teton, Yosemite, Mt Rainier, Great Smoky Mountain, Shenandoah and parts of Grand Canyon National Park all have black bears.

The endangered **grizzly bear** once ranged across the western US, but today its population in the Lower 48 is less than

1200. In the continental US, they're only found in the mountainous regions of Montana, Idaho, Wyoming and Washington. In other words, unless you head to Denali in Alaska, Yellowstone, Glacier and Grand Teton are the only parks covered in this book where you'll see one. Of the three parks, Yellowstone has the most, with a population between 200 and 600 bears. Grizzlies can reach up to 800lb and can be distinguished from black bears by their concaved snout, rounded ears and prominent shoulder hump.

Grizzly attacks are rare, but they do happen. Most occur because people surprise them or inadvertently come between a sow and her cub. The **National Park Service** (www.nps.gov) has excellent information on bears and how to handle encounters.

Ungulates

The continent's largest land mammal is the **American bison** (or buffalo). Some 60 million bison once roamed North America, but Euro-American settlers, in one of the saddest chapters of American history, reduced their numbers to about 300 in order to deprive the Plains Indians of their primary food source. In Yellowstone, they were bred back from the brink of extinction, and today an estimated 3000 roam the park. Sightings are commonplace.

Moose, the largest of the world's deer species, stand 5ft to 7ft at the shoulder and can weigh up to 1000lb. They're common in Yellowstone, Glacier, Rocky Mountain, Grand Teton and Denali. The same parks are home to **elk**, which grow antlers up to 5ft long and weigh up to 700lb. These majestic herbivores graze along forest edges and are commonly sighted. They were reintroduced to Great Smoky in 2001.

Bighorn sheep are synonymous with the Rocky Mountains, and have made a slow but steady comeback after nearing extinction in the 1800s. Today they are sighted throughout the Rockies, and in Joshua Tree, Zion and Bryce Canyon. During late-fall and early-winter breeding seasons, males charge each other at 20mph and clash their horns so powerfully that the sound can be heard for miles.

Wolves & Coyotes

The **gray wolf** was once the Rocky Mountains' main predator, but relentless persecution reduced its territory to a narrow belt stretching from Canada to the Northern Rockies. Wolves were successfully reintroduced to Yellowstone beginning in 1995 and the last official count, in 2009, showed 98 wolves (down from 124 in 2008). They're very hard to see, but you can take a wolf course through the **Yellowstone Association** (www.yellowstoneassociation.com) and get your fix that way. Gray wolves are also found in Glacier, Grand Teton and Denali National Parks.

Coyotes and **foxes** are common in many of the parks. When it comes to coyotes, you're far more likely to hear them than see them. Listening to them yowl at night as you doze off to sleep is an eerie and wonderful experience.

The Best...
Wildlife Experiences

1 Bison, Yellowstone National Park (p246)

2 Giant Sequoias, Yosemite National Park (p321)

3 Moose, Grand Teton National Park (p286)

4 Mangroves, Everglades National Park (p52)

5 Temperate Rainforests, Olympic National Park (p198)

Cats

North America's largest cat is the **mountain lion** (aka, cougar), an elusive predator about the size of a rottweiler. Mountain lions prefer remote, forested areas and are extremely difficult to spot. They're present in many of the parks, including Yellowstone, Grand Teton, Glacier, Yosemite, Joshua Tree and Grand Canyon. Although they are seldom seen, they have been known to attack humans on rare occasions. Visitor center staff can tell you if any trouble spots exist in the parks. **Bobcats** and **lynx** are also present in most of these parks and are equally hard to spot.

Small Mammals

Small mammals often get short shrift on people's watch lists, but animals like beavers, pikas, marmots and river otters are a delight to see. **Beavers** (and their dams) are found in Rocky Mountain, Yellowstone, Grand Teton and Glacier National Parks and are particularly fun to watch. **Marmots**, despite being little more than a glorified ground squirrel, are enjoyable to watch hopping around on rocks in the high country. They are found in the subalpine regions of both the Rockies and the Sierras. Other critters you might come across include bats, squirrels, voles, mice, chipmunks, raccoons, badgers, skunks, shrews and martens.

Birds

Birds of prey, including eagles, falcons, hawks, owls and harriers, are common in the parks, especially the western ones. **Osprey**, which nest and hunt around rivers and lakes, are a commonly spotted raptor. Keep your eyes peeled for **bald eagles**, which can be seen throughout the Rockies, as well as in Mt Rainier and Olympic National Parks. Extremely rare, **California condors** are sometimes spotted in Grand Canyon

Gray wolf, Grizzly & Wolf Discovery Center (p279), Yellowstone
PHOTOGRAPHER: MARK NEWMAN / LONELY PLANET IMAGES ©

and Zion National Parks, and very occasionally in Bryce Canyon. Of the 195 known wild California condors, 68 are in Utah and Arizona.

Everglades National Park is famous for its birds. Over 350 species have been spotted there, including 16 different wading birds and dozens of terns, gulls and other shorebirds. Acadia National Park is close behind with 338 species on record. Needless to say, bird-watching in both parks is outstanding. But don't rule out the inland parks. In Yellowstone, 316 bird species have been sighted. Most of the **NPS park websites (www.nps.gov)** have complete bird lists.

Amphibians & Reptiles

Frogs, toads and salamanders thrive in and around streams, rivers and lakes in several of the parks. With 24 species of salamanders, Great Smoky Mountains is often deemed the Salamander capital of the world. The creepy-looking **Pacific giant salamander**, which can reach up to 12in in length, is found in Olympic and Mt Rainier National Parks.

When it comes to reptiles, Everglades National Park reigns supreme. Not only does it have **crocodiles**, **alligators** and **caiman**, but the park is home to over 20 species of snakes, including the eastern coral snake, diamondback rattlers and boa constrictors. Everglades is also home to 16 **turtle** and **tortoise** species.

Love 'em or hate 'em, **snakes** are here to stay in most of the parks – but snakebites are rare (in Yellowstone, the NPS reports two in the history of the park). Western and prairie rattlesnakes are common, but they are generally docile and would rather rattle and scram than bite. Gopher and garter snakes are the most common snakes of all.

Trees & Plants

If you were to travel to every national park in this book, you'd experience a vast array of plant life, from the salty mangroves of the Everglades, to bizarre Joshua trees of the Mojave Desert, to stunted, twisted conifers high in the Rockies.

Trees

The national parks protect some of the greatest forests on Earth. Yosemite's Mariposa Grove of giant sequoias is home to some of the planet's largest trees, while the park's high country holds subalpine forests that are nothing short of high-altitude fairylands. North of the Sierra Nevada, in the Cascade Range, Mt Rainier National Park protects thick forests of western hemlock, Douglas fir, cedar, true firs, and western white pine.

In the Realm of Giants

Yosemite, and Sequoia and Kings Canyon are home to the world's largest living things: giant sequoias. Although they aren't the tallest trees, nor the girthiest, they are the biggest in terms of sheer mass. Living up to 3000 years, giant sequoias also are one of the oldest living things. The General Sherman tree, in Sequoia, stands 275ft tall and measures 100ft around, making it the largest living single-specimen organism on earth. Think of it this way: according to the National Park Service, its trunk alone is equivalent to 15 blue whales or 25 military battle tanks. Now that's a big tree.

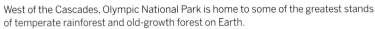

West of the Cascades, Olympic National Park is home to some of the greatest stands of temperate rainforest and old-growth forest on Earth.

In the Rockies (Yellowstone, Glacier, Grand Teton and Rocky Mountain National Parks), sparse piñon-juniper forests cover the lower slopes, while ponderosa pines dominate the montane zone. Deciduous alders, luscious white-barked aspens, willows and the distinctive blue spruce flourish in damper areas, while Engelmann spruce dominate the high subalpine zone. One of the Rockies' most striking trees is the quaking aspen, whose leaves flutter and shimmer in the mountain breeze and turn fiery-orange in fall.

In the dryer, hotter climates of Zion, Bryce Canyon and Grand Canyon, trees are fewer, but common still. Many Zion visitors are surprised to find a lush riparian zone along the Virgin River that supports beautiful stands of cottonwoods. In the Mojave Desert, Joshua Tree National Park protects one of the strangest looking trees of all, the Joshua tree.

To the east, Great Smoky Mountains National Park is home to more native tree species than any other park in the United States. Drive 900 miles south from Great Smoky and you end up in Everglades National Park, home to vast mangroves forests and tropical hardwoods.

Smaller Plants

When it comes to the smaller plants of the national parks, none seem to make an impression like wildflowers do. If you're traveling in spring or summer, it's always worth doing a little research on your park of choice to find out what's blooming when. For example, wildflowers put on a spectacular show in Death Valley every spring, usually in late February and March, and on good years it's worth planning a trip around them. Throughout the Rockies, July and August are prime wildflower months. In the Sierras, wildflowers bloom in spring at lower elevations, in early summer up around Tuolumne Meadows, and as late as mid-July at the highest elevations.

On the Colorado Plateau (Zion, Bryce, Grand Canyon), wildflowers such as desert marigolds and slickrock paintbrush bloom for a short period in early spring. The plateau's most interesting plants are arguably the cacti and desert succulents that make this mostly desert region so unique. Although many plants are specific to the plateau, others are drawn from adjacent biological zones such as the Great Basin, Mojave Desert and Rocky Mountains.

In the Southern Appalachians, Great Smoky Mountains boasts tremendous biodiversity. In fact, the park has so many plant species – more than 3500 – it was declared an International Biosphere Reserve by Unesco in 1976. Three years later, Unesco honored Everglades National Park with a World Heritage designation because the park protects the largest mangrove ecosystem *and* the largest continuous sawgrass prairie in the western hemisphere.

Conservation

Protecting the national parks has been a challenge since the day Yellowstone was created in 1872. Thanks to the efforts of passionate individuals, the parks now safeguard some of the greatest natural treasures on the planet. But they face new, often concurrent threats. Climate change, invasive species, overuse and irresponsible land use on park peripheries all jeopardize the national parks today.

Climate Change

According to National Park Service Director Jon Jarvis, climate change is 'the greatest threat to the integrity of our national parks that we have ever experienced.' Although park biologists are only just beginning to understand its impact, nearly all agree that it's taking a toll.

For example, scientists worry that, due to rising temperatures in the Mojave Desert, Joshua trees may disappear almost entirely from Joshua Tree National Park within the next 60 to 90 years. Glacier National Park may be devoid of glaciers by 2030 if melting continues at current rates (in 1850 the park contained 150 glaciers; today there are 25). And in Sequoia and Kings Canyon National Parks, there is concern that changing temperatures and rainfall patterns may threaten the park's giant sequoias.

Invasive Species

Invasive species pose a severe threat to the national parks. In the Southern Appalachians, a non-native insect called the hemlock woolly adelgid is decimating eastern
hemlock forests. In Great Smoky Mountains National Park, where the insect was discovered in 2003, trees are already beginning to die. In Shenandoah, where the insect
has been present since 1980, nearly 80% of the hemlocks have perished.

In Glacier National Park, botanists have identified over 125 non-native plants that
are reducing food sources for local wildlife. In Sequoia and Kings Canyon National
Parks, non-native trout have practically wiped out the mountain yellow-legged frog
population, landing the frog on the candidate list for endangered species. In Hawaii
Volcanoes National Park, invasive species, including feral animals, mongooses and
numerous plant species, pose tremendous threats to native flora and fauna.

Of course, we can hardly remove ourselves from the list of invasive species. Each
year, nearly 230 million visitors clock up more than a *billion* cumulative hours in
the parks. Traffic, auto emissions, roads and the simple fact of human presence in
sensitive wildlife areas all take their toll on the park ecosystems.

Park Peripheries

Aside from the impact visitors make on the parks, humans are putting immense pres-
sure on many locations by operating high-impact businesses outside park boundaries.
For example, conservationists have battled more than two decades to prevent Kaiser
Ventures, LLC from creating the nation's largest landfill on the edge of Joshua Tree
National Park. In Alaska, mining companies hope to create the continent's largest
open-pit gold and copper mine only miles from Clark Lake National Park. Great Smoky
Mountains, Grand Canyon and Big Bend National Parks are all affected by emissions
from coal-fired power plants, which drift over the parks and contaminate the air. Sensitive riparian areas along the Grand Canyon's Colorado River have long been impacted
by upriver damming and water holding. And on Washington's Olympic Peninsula,
logging companies have clear-cut forests right up to the borders of the park, which has
displaced the northern spotted owl from the region.

Sustainable Visitation

According to Jim Nations, senior media relations manager at the National Parks Conservation Association, 'less than one fourteenth of 1% of the national budget goes to
the national parks.' Despite this, park visitors can make a positive impact by traveling
sustainably and getting involved with park associations. Whenever you can, ride park
shuttles instead of driving your car. Skip high-impact park activities such as snowmo-
biling in Yellowstone and flight-seeing trips over the Grand Canyon. Trite as it sounds,
conserve water in the desert parks and prevent erosion by always staying on trails. If
you're backpacking, use biodegradable soaps (or skip them altogether) and follow the
principles of **Leave No Trace** (www.lnt.org).

Nearly every national park has an associated foundation or other nonprofit that
supports its parent park. These organizations, which include **Yellowstone Park
Foundation** (www.ypf.org), **The Yosemite Fund** (www.yosemitefund.org) and **Friends of the
Smokies** (www.friendsofthesmokies.org), conduct everything from trail maintenance to
habitat restoration. Members can volunteer or donate to programs that are critical to
the parks' well-being.

The **National Parks Conservation Association** (www.npca.org) covers all of the parks.
Since 1919, this nonprofit organization has been protecting and preserving America's
national parks through research, advocacy and education.

Survival
Guide

Mesquite Flat Sand Dunes (p187), Death Valley
PHOTOGRAPHER: CAROL POLICH / LONELY PLANET IMAGES ©

Directory

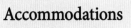

Accommodations

National park accommodations run the gamut from basic (campgrounds, cabins and tent cabins) to luxurious (some national park lodges). For the sake of convenience, not to mention the experience, sleeping inside the parks is usually the ideal, but satellite towns often have better deals on hotels and posher accommodations. RV-ers in particular will find better facilities outside the parks.

CAMPGROUNDS

National park campgrounds are usually expansive, busy places, but beautiful nonetheless. Most are designed for car and RV camping, though many parks have additional smaller campgrounds designed for car/tent camping only, or the smallest RVs. Occasionally, you'll find walk-in sites, which offer tent campers the most solitude.

Some campgrounds have hot showers, and most have flush toilets. Showers, full hookups and swimming pools are more common in outlying private campgrounds and RV parks.

If park campgrounds are full and you don't mind rugged camping, you can often camp for free in national forest or Bureau of Land Management (BLM) land on the outskirts of the park. For information and maps, visit the **US Forest Service** (www.fs.fed.us) and **BLM** (www.blm.gov) websites.

If you do turn up at a national park without a reservation, don't give up. Many parks have a campground reservation office, and, if there are cancellations (which there often are), you can 'make a reservation' on the spot. Those who arrive before noon usually have the best luck with this back-door approach.

RVS

All the national parks listed in this book can accommodate RVs and trailers, but most lack dump stations and full hookups. If you want conveniences such as electricity, wi-fi, swimming pools and cable, you're best off staying in one of the many private RV parks located outside the national parks. The **National Park Service (NPS) websites** (www.nps.gov) all have camping sections with details on RV services and maximum lengths.

LODGING

National park lodgings include basic tent cabins, rustic wood cabins, hotels and historic park lodges. They are run by concessionaires, rather than the NPS, and can be booked online or by phone. Tent cabins and cabins are usually very basic, and it's often good to have your own sleeping

bag. Most park accommodations lack TVs and radios.

Price-wise, most park lodges and hotels fall into the upper midrange category (rarely exceeding $200 for a double), though some lodges, such as Yosemite's Ahwahnee Hotel, have doubles that far exceed $200. Children under 12 usually stay free, and cots or roll-aways are provided. B&Bs, which are outside the parks, usually cost $100 to $175, and the occasional luxury inn will cost over $200.

SEASONS

For most of the parks, high season runs from Memorial Day (last Monday in May) to Labor Day (first Monday in September). During the winter season (generally October through March, April or May, depending on the location) many campgrounds, lodges and some B&Bs close. If a place is open only part of the year, we've included its opening hours following the ⏰ symbol.

Joshua Tree and Death Valley, because they are in warmer regions, have a slightly different season. Compared to the other parks, they get fewer people in summer and are busier in winter.

RESERVATIONS

June through early September, reservations are essential if you wish to stay inside or near the parks. The exceptions are first-come, first-served campgrounds, available in most of the parks. To nab one of these sites during peak season, however, you usually have to arrive by Friday midmorning at the latest. Outside high season, reservations are recommended but not essential.

In the most popular parks, reservations should be made up to a year in advance. As soon as you have your dates, book. National park campgrounds are reserved through **Recreation.gov** (☏ 877-444-6777; www. recreation.gov), unless the campgrounds are operated by a concessionaire.

PRICE ICONS

Room rates quoted in this book are for single (s) and double (d) occupancy per night; if there's no rate difference for one or two people, the general room (r) or suite (ste) rate is listed. Unless otherwise noted, breakfast is not included and bathrooms are private. Throughout this book, we provide the following quick-glance price categories at the top of each review:

CATEGORY	ICON	COST
Budget	$	< $100
Midrange	$$	$100-200
Top End	$$$	> $200

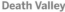

Business Hours

The **national park newspapers**, available at all entry kiosks and visitor centers, are the best sources for up-to-date operating hours for all park sights and services. Visitor centers are open roughly 8am to 7pm during peak season (June to September), and have reduced hours the rest of the year. More remote visitor centers close during winter. Restaurants and out-

fitters in satellite towns also maintain reduced hours, or close altogether, during winter. Reviews for restaurants, visitor centers, museums and sights in this book include operating hours.

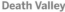

Discount Cards

The following America the Beautiful passes can be purchased at any park entry kiosk, online or by phone through the **National Park Service** (☏ 888-275-8747, ext 1; www.nps.gov). Only the Access Pass must be purchased in person.

Annual Pass ($80) Valid for admission to all national parks and federal recreation lands for 12 months from date of purchase. Each pass admits four adults and all accompanying children under 16.

Senior Pass ($10) US citizens and permanent residents 62 or older receive free admission to all national parks and federal recreation lands, plus 50% off select activity fees (including park campgrounds).

Access Pass (free) Gives US citizens or permanent residents with disabilities free

Climate

Acadia

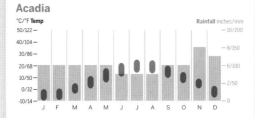

Death Valley

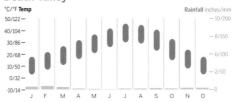

Yellowstone

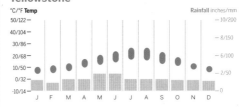

access to national parks and federal recreation lands. Members of the **American Automobile Association** (AAA; ☎ 800-564-6222; www.aaa.com; annual membership from $67) receive discounts up to 15% at many hotels outside the parks.

●●●
Electricity

120V/60Hz

120V/60Hz

●●●
Food

Although meals in the national park lodges are often good, the experience is usually about the setting as much as the food. Price-wise, they're the costliest places to eat in the parks. Most parks also have cafeterias and cafes. Depending on what part of the country you're in, restaurants outside the parks vary from mom-and-pop joints with stick-to-your-rib dinners to upscale eateries.

Throughout this book, we provide the following quick-glance price categories at the top of each review:

CATEGORY	ICON	COST
Budget	$	< $10
Midrange	$$	$10-20
Top End	$$$	> $20

●●●
Health

Every year the National Park Service conducts thousands of search-and-rescue missions in the parks. Hundreds of people are injured or go missing, and thousands more put themselves unnecessarily at risk. The wilderness can be an unforgiving place, and the best way to prevent injury is to know what you're getting into, prepare, and play within your own limits.

ANIMALS

BEARS

Travelers to parks like Yellowstone, Glacier, Rocky Mountain, Grand Teton or Yosemite need to be bear aware, whether camping in a developed site or hiking in the backcountry. Although bear attacks are rare, grizzlies can be extremely dangerous, and black bears can be destructive in their relentless quest for food.

In the Rockies, where both black and grizzly bears are present, it's helpful to learn the difference between the two. The easiest way to recognize grizzlies is by their large shoulder hump, rounded ears and concave snout.

Most grizzly attacks on humans occur when a person inadvertently comes between a sow and her cub. The presence of food and surprise encounters can also provoke aggressive behavior.

Bears will typically avoid contact if given sufficient warning. For this reason, many hikers in the Rockies wear 'bear bells' on their packs or yell 'Hey, bear!' when they can't see far ahead.

If you encounter a bear, do not run; it can trigger a bear's chase instinct. Instead, stand your ground, talk, and back slowly away.

OTHER MAMMALS

Avoid petting, handling, feeding or approaching any wild animal, no matter how harmless it looks. Not only is approaching larger mammals illegal in most parks, but it's dangerous. Smaller animals can be dangerous as well. In some parks, squirrels have gotten notoriously aggressive because so many people have (illegally) fed them. If you are bitten, thoroughly clean and sterilize the wound and contact local health authorities immediately for possible rabies treatment.

SNAKES

Rattlesnakes and other venomous snakes are present in many parks, particularly at lower elevations and in desert climates. Snakebites are uncommon, however, and fatalities are extremely rare. That said, getting bit by a rattler is not a good idea.

If you encounter a snake or hear a rattle, identify its location and back slowly away. If someone is bitten, stay calm. Remove any constricting jewelry or clothing from the bite area, and apply a light constricting bandage over the bite. Keep the bitten limb elevated above the level of the heart. Get the victim to a medical center for antivenom treatment immediately. Do not apply a tourniquet, slice the wound or attempt to suck out the venom.

ENVIRONMENTAL HAZARDS

Heat stroke, altitude sickness, hypothermia and dehydration are all serious dangers for hikers, climbers, cyclists and anyone else spending time in the wilderness. Fortunately, all are preventable. Read up on the symptoms of all these conditions – recognizing them in their early stages is the single most important method of avoiding injury. When hiking, always carry more water than you think you'll need, particularly in the desert parks.

GIARDIASIS (GIARDIA)

This parasitic infection of the small intestine occurs throughout North America.

Symptoms may include nausea, bloating, cramps and diarrhea, and may last for weeks. Giardia is easily diagnosed by a stool test and readily treated with antibiotics.

To protect yourself from giardia, avoid drinking (or treat all water) from lakes, ponds, streams and rivers, which may be contaminated. Giardia can also be transmitted from person to person if proper hand washing is not performed.

LIGHTNING

In the Rockies and the High Sierra, getting struck by lighting during a summer afternoon storm is a real possibility. Your best bet is to hike early, especially if you're going up high. If you do get caught in a lightning storm, steer clear of exposed ridges, open areas, lone trees, cliff bases and shallow caves or depressions. Move away from bodies of water. If camping, move metal tent poles and pack frames away from you and sit on a foam mattress in a crouched position, your arms around your knees. Seek the lowest ground and pay attention to your hair – if it stands on end, move immediately.

MOSQUITOES

Mosquitoes can be rampant in many of the parks, particularly early to midsummer at the higher elevations. If you have a flexible schedule and you plan to be at altitude in the Rockies or Sierras, it's worth calling the visitor center and asking what the mosquitoes are like in the high country. The season varies year to year, depending on snowmelt.

The best ways to prevent mosquito bites are to cover up and wear repellent. The most effective repellents have DEET – the higher the DEET content, the better. However, DEET is toxic stuff and can even decompose plastics (like watch-faces) and should not be used on young children. Eucalyptus and citronella-based repellents are gentler alternatives.

TICKS

Ticks are common in grassy, bushy and thickly forested areas, particularly at lower elevations. Tick bites can cause skin infections or more serious problems, including Lyme disease. If hiking where ticks might be present, be sure to conduct periodic tick checks, particularly in hidden areas beneath your clothes.

If a tick is found attached, press down around the tick's head with tweezers, grab the head and gently pull upwards. Avoid twisting the tick or squeezing its body. Do not douse an attached tick with oil, alcohol or petroleum jelly.

SAFE HIKING

From deserts to high altitude, the national parks present all manner of extreme conditions that can present dangers on even the shortest hikes. Planning and preparedness are the best ways to prevent problems on the trail.

○ Wear sunblock and a wide-brimmed hat.

○ Carry more water than you think you'll need, and know where water is available along the trail.

○ Pack a water filter or purification tablets.

443

- Get a local weather forecast (available at all visitor centers) before hitting the trail.

- When fording streams, unclip your pack and use a stick or pole (planted upstream) for support.

- Carry a whistle, mirror, compass, topo map and multi-use knife.

- Pack a rain shell and extra layer, regardless of how the weather looks when you set out.

- Know your own limits and hike within them.

RESCUE & EVACUATION

In case of an accident, self-rescue should always be your first consideration, as search-and-rescue operations into the backcountry are very expensive and require emergency personnel to put their own safety at risk.

If a person in your group is injured and a rescue is necessary, leave someone with the injured person while others seek help. If there are only two of you, leave the injured person with as much warm clothing, food and water as is sensible to spare, plus a whistle and flashlight. Mark their position with something conspicuous.

WATER PURIFICATION

Water from even the wildest mountain lakes and streams may contain harmful pathogens (especially those causing giardia and amoebic cysts) and should always be properly treated. Mountain spring water – ie water gushing straight out of the ground – is usually free of pathogens if taken directly from the source. Water from desert seeps, however, is generally considered unsafe until treated. All other water should be treated with a filter, Steri-PEN or iodine tablets or – most effectively – by boiling it for at least one minute, regardless of altitude.

MEDICAL KIT CHECKLIST

Recommended items for a first aid kit:

- Acetaminophen (Tylenol) or aspirin

- Adhesive or paper tape

- Antibacterial ointment (eg Bactroban) for cuts and abrasions

- Anti-diarrhea drugs

- Antihistamines (for hay fever and allergic reactions)

- Anti-inflammatory drugs (eg ibuprofen)

- Bandages, gauze, gauze rolls, butterfly bandages

- Emergency (Space) blanket

- Insect repellent containing DEET

- Iodine tablets or water filter

- Moleskin (for blisters)

- Oral rehydration salts

- Paper and pencil

- Permethrin-containing insect spray for clothing, tents and bed nets

- Pocket knife

- Scissors, safety pins, tweezers

- Sterile alcohol wipes

- Sunscreen and lip balm

- Thermometer

Insurance

No matter how long or short your trip, make sure you have adequate travel insurance and health insurance purchased before departure. You should also consider getting coverage for luggage loss and trip cancellation. If you already have a home-owner's or renter's policy, see what it will cover and consider getting supplemental insurance to cover the rest. If you have prepaid a large portion of your trip, cancellation insurance is a worthwhile expense.

For information on auto insurance, see p450.

Internet Access

Cybercafes are rare, but wireless access is commonplace in satellite towns. Nearly every hotel has wireless, including many of the national park lodges. Chain hotels often charge a fee (usually around $10 per day) for wireless access, but most smaller hotels include it in the cost of the room. Cafes often have wi-fi.

This guide uses an internet icon (@) when a place has a net-connected computer for public use and the wi-fi icon (🛜) when it offers wireless internet access, whether free or fee-based.

Maps

Every national park publishes a park newspaper which includes detailed maps to help you find visitor sites, trailheads and transportation routes. The maps in this

International Visitors

ENTERING THE USA

Every foreign visitor entering the USA needs a passport (valid for at least six months longer than the intended stay). Apart from most Canadian citizens and those under the Visa Waiver Program, all visitors need to obtain a visa from abroad. For more information, visit www.travel.state.gov/visa. For a complete list of US customs regulations, including information on passport and requirements, visit the official portal for **US Customs & Border Protection** (www.cbp.gov).

HEALTH INSURANCE

If your health insurance does not cover you for medical expenses while visiting the United States, consider supplemental insurance. Medical treatment in the USA is of the highest caliber, but the expense could kill you. At a minimum, you need coverage for emergencies, including hospital stays and a flight home if necessary. Check the Travel Services section of the **Lonely Planet website** (www.lonelyplanet.com) for more information. Some insurance providers require that you pay all costs before they will reimburse you; others will pay the medical provider directly.

EMBASSIES & CONSULATES

International travelers who want to contact their home country's embassy while in the US should visit **Embassy.org** (www.embassy.org), which lists contact information for all foreign embassies in Washington, DC. Some countries have consulates in other large cities; look under 'Consulates' in the Yellow Pages, or call **directory assistance** (☏ 411).

MONEY

ATMs are widely available in stores and businesses. Most businesses accept credit cards. Ask your bank or credit-card company for exact information about using its cards in US ATMs. The exchange rate on ATM transactions is usually as good as you'll get anywhere. Before traveling, notify your bank and credit-card providers in order to avoid triggering fraud alerts, which can result in a temporarily frozen account.

POST

The **US Postal Service** (USPS; www.usps.com) provides great service for the price. Private shippers such as **United Parcel Service** (UPS; ☏ 800-742-5877; www.ups.com) and **FedEx** (☏ 800-463-3339; www.fedex.com) are useful for sending more important or larger items.

TELEPHONE

If you plan to use a foreign cell phone in the USA, you'll need a multiband GSM model in order to make calls. A prepaid SIM card is usually cheaper than using your home network. For important telephone numbers, see p447.

VACCINATIONS

No special vaccines are required or recommended for travel to or within the USA (although evidence of cholera and yellow fever vaccinations may be required if arriving from an infected area). All travelers should be up-to-date on routine immunizations, particularly tetanus.

book are excellent for general orientation but are not intended for trail or wilderness navigation. For this, you'll need topographic maps.

Published by **National Geographic** (www.natgeomaps.com), *Trails Illustrated* maps are the best general-purpose topographical hiking maps and are available for most of the parks. They are water-resistant, color-coded for easy reading, and clearly mark trails, trailheads and important landmarks.

The **United States Geological Survey** (USGS; ☎ 888-275-8747; www.store.usgs.gov) publishes detailed 1:24,000 topographic maps ('quads'), covering the entire country. While their scale provides great detail, they are sometimes outdated, and you usually need multiple maps to cover longer hikes.

Outside the parks, **Bureau of Land Management** (BLM; www.blm.gov) and **United States Forest Service** (USFS; www.fs.fed.us) offices sell or give away maps that cover lands under their jurisdiction.

Money

Most national parks have at least one ATM machine, and ATMs are widely available in towns around the parks. Front desks at some of the park lodges will exchange foreign currency.

If you plan to camp in USFS or BLM campgrounds outside the parks, you usually must pay with cash using a drop box. USFS and BLM officials rarely carry change.

Nearly all businesses accept major credit cards.

Sales tax, which varies by state and county, ranges from 0% to 8%. Hotel taxes, which can be as high as 14%, vary by city.

Prices quoted in this book are in US dollars and exclude taxes, unless otherwise noted.

Public Holidays

On the following national public holidays, banks, schools and government offices (including post offices) close, and transportation, museums and other services operate on a Sunday schedule. Holidays falling on a weekend are usually observed the following Monday.

○ **New Year's Day** January 1

○ **Martin Luther King Jr Day** Third Monday in January

○ **Presidents' Day** Third Monday in February

○ **Memorial Day** Last Monday in May

○ **Independence Day** July 4

○ **Labor Day** First Monday in September

○ **Columbus Day** Second Monday in October

○ **Veterans' Day** November 11

○ **Thanksgiving** Fourth Thursday in November

○ **Christmas Day** December 25

Entry to the national parks is free on the weekends of Martin Luther King Jr Day, Veterans' Day, the first day of summer (June 21), and National Public Lands Day (Saturday, late September). During the annual **National Parks Week** (sometime in April), access to the parks is free for at least seven days. Check the **National Park Service** (www.nps.gov) for the year's free days.

Safe Travel

Despite its seemingly Babylonian list of dangers – guns, violent crime, riots, earthquakes, tornadoes – the USA is actually a pretty safe country to visit. The greatest danger for travelers is posed by car accidents. In the national parks, auto accidents are most often caused by drivers speeding or gawking at animals or natural features.

Most areas with predictable natural disturbances – tornadoes in the Midwest, tsunamis in Hawaii, hurricanes in the south, earthquakes in California – have an emergency siren system to alert communities to imminent danger. If you hear one and suspect trouble, turn on a local TV or radio station, which will be broadcasting safety warnings and advice.

The **US Department of Health & Human Services** (www.phe.gov) has preparedness advice, news and information.

Telephone

Nearly every national park covered in this book has pay phones in developed locations. Cell-phone coverage in the parks is spotty at best and available only in the most developed locations. Most – but certainly not all – satellite towns around the parks get cell phone service.

IMPORTANT NUMBERS

- ☎ 911 Emergency
- ☎ 1 USA country code
- ☎ 411 Directory assistance
- ☎ 00 International directory assistance
- ☎ 011 International access code from the USA
- ☎ 511 Road conditions (participating states only)

Time

The USA uses Daylight Saving Time (DST). On the second Sunday in March, clocks are set one hour ahead. Then, on the first Sunday of November, clocks are turned back one hour. Just to keep you on your toes, Arizona, Hawaii and much of Indiana don't follow DST.

The US date system is written as month/day/year. Thus, June 8 2012 becomes 6/8/12.

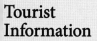

Tourist Information

The **National Park Service** websites are hands-down the best sources of information on the parks.

Acadia National Park www. nps.gov/acad

Bryce Canyon National Park www.nps.gov/brca

Death Valley National Park www.nps.gov/deva

Everglades National Park www.nps.gov/ever

Glacier National Park www. nps.gov/glac

Grand Canyon National Park www.nps.gov/grca

Grand Teton National Park www.nps.gov/grte

Great Smoky National Park www.nps.gov/grsm

Joshua Tree National Park www.nps.gov/jotr

Mt Rainier National Park www.nps.gov/mora

Olympic National Park www. nps.gov/olym

Rocky Mountain National Park www.nps.gov/romo

Shenandoah National Park www.nps.gov/shen

Yellowstone National Park www.nps.gov/yell

Yosemite National Park www.nps.gov/yose

Zion National Park www.nps. gov/zion

Websites for official state travel associations are also good sources of information. They can almost always be found online by searching for the state name, followed by 'tourist office.'

Travelers with Disabilities

Nearly every national park has at least one paved wheelchair-accessible trail, and most visitors sites are wheelchair accessible. National park lodges offer wheelchair accessible rooms, and some parks have specific wheelchair-accessible campsites. Many national parks have features and services for people with hearing or vision impairments. The best source of information on accessibility is the National Park Service's comprehensive listing at www.nps.gov/pub_aff/access.

All national parks publish an accessibility brochure, available at entry kiosks and visitor centers. These are also available online at each national park's **NPS website (www.nps.gov)**.

Volunteering

With national parks facing federal budget cuts or freezes, the need for volunteers is greater than ever. Every park has an associated foundation or nonprofit that relies on volunteers to help with everything from trail maintenance to habitat restoration. Other excellent resources for volunteering include the following:

National Park Service (NPS; www.nps.gov/volunteer) Apply for the Volunteer in Parks (VIP) program and search for opportunities by park name online.

Sierra Club (www.sierraclub.org) Hosts fee-based volunteer trips lasting one to 10 days; many are in national parks.

Student Conservation Association (SCA; www.thesca.org) Nonprofit organization offers conservation internships that earn academic credit, as well as summer trail-crew work.

Volunteer.gov (www.volunteer.gov) Online searchable database of volunteer opportunities for all public lands agencies.

Transport

●●●

Getting There & Away

Flights, tours and rail tickets can be booked online at lonely planet.com/bookings.

ENTERING THE USA

Entering the USA is straightforward, though all the red tape can make it a bit nerve-wracking. Upon arrival, international visitors must register with the **US-VISIT program** (www.dhs.gov/us-visit), which entails having your fingerprints scanned and a digital photo taken. For more information on visa requirements, see p445.

Be sure to read up on all official passport and visa requirements on the official website for **US Customs & Border Protection** (www.cbp.gov).

 AIR

For information on the regional airports see the Getting There & Around sections within the individual park chapters.

LAND BORDER CROSSINGS

The USA has more than 20 official border crossings with Canada in the north and almost 40 with Mexico in the south. It is relatively easy crossing from the USA into either country; it's crossing *into* the USA that can pose problems if you haven't brought all your documents. US Customs & Border Protection tracks current wait times (see http://apps.cbp.gov/bwt) at every border crossing. Some borders are open 24 hours, but most are not.

BUS

Greyhound has direct connections between main US cities and cities in Canada and Mexico. You may have to transfer to a different bus at the border.

Greyhound Canada (📞 in Canada 800-661-8747; www.greyhound.ca) For bus rides from Canada.

Greyhound México (📞 in Mexico 800-710-8819; www.greyhound.com.mx) Operates direct bus routes between main towns in Mexico and the USA.

Greyhound USA (📞 800-231-2222, international customer service 214-849-8100; www.greyhound.com) For all trips originating in the USA.

CAR & MOTORCYCLE

If you're driving into the USA from Canada or Mexico, bring the vehicle's registration papers, proof of liability insurance and your home driver's license. Canadian auto insurance is typically valid in the USA, and vice-versa. Mexican auto insurance is not. Canadian and Mexican driver's licenses are also valid, but an International Driving Permit (IDP) is a good supplement.

If your papers are in order, taking your own car across the US-Canadian border is usually fast and easy, but occasionally the authorities of either country decide to search a car *thoroughly*. On weekends and holidays, especially in summer, traffic at the main border crossings can be heavy.

TRAIN

Amtrak (📞 800-872-7245; www.amtrak.com) and **VIA Rail Canada** (📞 888-842-7245; www.viarail.ca) run daily services between Montreal and New York; Toronto and New York via Niagara Falls; Toronto and Chicago via Detroit; and Vancouver and Seattle. Customs inspections happen at the border.

Flying Visits

The following table shows the major international airports closest to each park. Some require long drives (up to eight hours), something to consider when making plans.

PARK	NEAREST AIRPORT	LOCATION	AIRPORT CODE
Acadia	Logan International	Boston, MA	BOS
Bryce Canyon	McCarran International	Las Vegas, NV	LAS
Death Valley	Los Angeles International	Los Angeles, CA	LAX
Everglades	Miami International	Miami, FL	MIA
Glacier	Glacier Park International Airport	Kalispell, MT	FCA
Grand Canyon (North Rim)	McCarran International	Las Vegas, NV	LAS
Grand Canyon (South Rim)	Sky Harbor International	Phoenix, AZ	PHX
Grand Teton	Salt Lake City International	Salt Lake City, UT	SLC
Great Smoky Mountains	Hartsfield-Jackson	Atlanta, GA	ATL
Joshua Tree	Los Angeles International	Los Angeles, CA	LAX
Mt Rainier	Seattle-Tacoma International	Seattle, WA	SEA
Olympic	Seattle-Tacoma International	Seattle, WA	SEA
Rocky Mountain	Denver International	Denver, CO	DEN
Shenandoah	Dulles International	Washington DC	IAD
Yellowstone	Salt Lake City International	Salt Lake City, UT	SLC
Yosemite	San Francisco International	San Francisco, CA	SFO
Zion	McCarran International	Las Vegas, NV	LAS

Getting Around

✈ AIR

The US domestic air system is extensive and reliable. Flying is usually more expensive than traveling by bus, train or car, but it's the way to go when you're in a hurry.

Most parks have at least one regional airport within 100 miles of the park, but flights are usually limited to the nearest major 'hub' airport. Consult the Getting There & Around sections within this book's individual park chapters for information on the nearest airports (where applicable).

AIR PASSES

Passes are normally available only to non–North American citizens, and they must be purchased in conjunction with an international ticket. Conditions and cost structures can be complicated, but all passes include a certain number of domestic flights (from two to 10) that typically must be used within a 60-day period. Two of the biggest airline networks offering air passes are **Star Alliance** (www.staralliance.com) and **One World** (www.oneworld.com).

BICYCLE

Bicycle touring can be outstanding within the USA and a great way to travel between the parks. Most national parks hold campsites for cyclists who turn up without reservations, and they can be some of the best sites in the park.

Some states have mandatory helmet laws. Bicycles are not permitted on freeways, so touring is limited to back roads (generally a good thing). Cyclists must follow the same rules of the road as automobiles, but drivers don't always allow cyclists right of way.

Better World Club (www.betterworldclub.com) Offers bicycle roadside assistance for $40 per year, plus a $12 sign-up fee.

League of American Bicyclists website (www.bikeleague.org) Publishes advice and lists of local bike clubs and repair shops. Has information on local helmet laws.

International Bicycle Fund website (www.ibike.org) Lists bike regulations by airline and contains loads of cycling advice.

 BUS

Greyhound serves many of the larger towns on the outskirts of the parks and offers a cost-effective, but definitely slow-going, way to reach the parks. As a rule, buses in the USA are reliable and clean, with air-conditioning, moderately comfortable seats, onboard lavatories and strict no-smoking policies. To reach most national parks, you need to transfer to local or county bus systems.

Greyhound (📞 800-231-2222; www.greyhound.com) The USA's major long-distance bus company.

Discovery Pass (www.discoverypass.com) Available to domestic and international travelers, Greyhound's Discovery Pass allows unlimited, unrestricted travel for periods of seven ($246), 15 ($356), 30 ($456) or 60 ($556) consecutive days in both the USA and Canada.

Trailways (📞 703-691-3052; www.trailways.com) Offers vacation-oriented bus transportation.

Megabus (📞 877-462-6342; www.megabus.com) Bus company serving the Northeast and Midwest.

 CAR & MOTORCYCLE

For maximum flexibility and convenience, a car is essential. In many states you can get road conditions by dialing 📞 511.

AUTOMOBILE ASSOCIATIONS

American Automobile Association (AAA; 📞 800-874-7532; www.aaa.com) The USA's main motoring club offers travel and car insurance, road maps, tour books, regional information offices, roadside assistance and towing for all members. It has reciprocal membership agreements with many international auto clubs. AAA card-carriers receive 5% to 15% discounts at many hotels.

Better World Club (📞 866-238-1137; www.betterworldclub.com) Ecofriendly alternative to AAA with similar services.

DRIVER'S LICENSE

An International Driving Permit, obtained before you leave home, is not required but advisable if your country of origin is non-English-speaking or your license lacks a photo.

INSURANCE

Drivers are required by law to have (at minimum) liability insurance and must carry proof of insurance in the vehicle at all times. Rental-car companies will provide liability, collision and other insurance for an extra charge. Paying extra for some or all of this insurance increases the cost of a rental car by as much as $30 a day. If you are paying by credit card, these may all be covered by the card company. Check your credit-card policy.

RENTAL

Car rental is a competitive business in the USA. Most rental companies require that you have a major credit card, be at least 25 years old and have a valid driver's license. Some major national companies may rent to drivers between the ages of 21 and 24 for an additional charge of around $25 per day.

Daily rates for small cars start around $30 per day, or $200 per week. One-way rentals are usually far more expensive. Airport-based rental offices charge extortionate fees, unless you reserve your car online.

Major national car-rental companies:

Alamo (📞 877-222-9075; www.alamo.com)

Avis (📞 800-230-4898; www.avis.com)

Budget (📞 800-527-0700; www.budget.com)

Dollar (📞 800-800-3665; www.dollar.com)

Enterprise (📞 800-261-7331; www.enterprise.com)

Hertz (📞 800-654-3131; www.hertz.com)

National (📞 877-222-9058; www.nationalcar.com)

Rent-a-Wreck (📞 877-877-0700; www.rentawreck.com)

Simply Hybrid (www.simplyhybrid.com) Southern California company that only rents hybrid vehicles.

Thrifty (📞 800-847-4389; www.thrifty.com)

For motorcycle or recreational vehicle (RV) rental, try the following:

Adventures on Wheels (📞 866-787-3682; www.wheels9.com) RV rentals.

Cruise America (📞 800-671-8042; www.cruiseamerica.com) RV rentals.

EagleRider (📞 888-900-9901; www.eaglerider.com) Motorcycle rentals and tours.

Happy Travel Camper Rental & Sales (📞 800-370-1262; www.camperusa.com) RV rentals.

 TRAIN

Compared with other modes of travel, trains are rarely the quickest, cheapest, timeliest or most convenient option, but they turn the journey into a relaxing, social and scenic experience.

Amtrak (📞 800-872-7245, 215-856-7953; www.amtrak.com) The USA's only national train service. Amtrak's Thruway buses provide connections to and from the rail network to some smaller centers and national parks.

Amtrak Vacations (📞 800-268-7252; www.amtrakvacations.com) Offers train-travel vacation packages that include rental cars, hotels, tours and attractions.

USA Rail Pass Amtrak's rail pass offers coach-class travel for 15 ($389), 30 ($579) or 45 ($749) days, with travel limited to eight, 12 or 18 one-way 'segments,' respectively.

LOCAL TRANSPORTATION

BICYCLE

Bicycle can be a fun way to get around inside the main visitor areas of the national parks (ie between the campground and the cafeteria), but outside these areas, roads can be steep and narrow, and traffic can be dangerous. Experienced cyclists usually enjoy the adventure, but casual bikers likely will not. Each park is different, however, so consult the Activities section in the park chapters of this book.

Bicycle rentals are available in some of the parks. Mountain bikes are prohibited from nearly all trails throughout the national park system.

PARK SHUTTLES

Park shuttles are a great, free and sometimes required way to get around inside the parks. They offer access to the most popular trailheads and visitor sites and save you the headache of having to find parking, which is often limited, especially at trailheads. During peak season (generally late May to early September), shuttle services are frequent.

Shuttles are often available between satellite towns and the national parks. If you're staying outside the park, these are highly recommended as they eliminate your need to find parking, which can be hellish in parks like Yosemite and Zion.

Behind the Scenes

Author Thanks

DANNY PALMERLEE

Thanks to the authors who researched and wrote the original national park books from which these chapters came. A big hug to Julia Happ-Shine for helping with Nadine. Thank you, Sam Hendricks, for making this possible. To Nadine: let's go camping!

NED FRIARY & GLENDA BENDURE

Thanks to Paul and Sasha, who joined us on the climb up Acadia Mountain; Steve Howance, for his insights; Carol, in the breakfast room; and the rangers, park volunteers and fellow travelers who shared tips with us.

ADAM KARLIN

Thanks to Anna Whitlow, Paula Nino, Jordan Melnick, Megan Harmon, the Paquet family and my Keys crew. Thanks to my grandmother, Rhoda Brickman, for getting me down to Florida in the first place, to my parents who always give me a place to write, and to Rachel for being Rachel.

EMILY MATCHAR

Thanks to the park rangers of Shenandoah for letting me into the campground way after dark, and to my helpful Twitter tipsters. And thanks to Jamin Asay, my partner in travel and in life, for his tireless map-reading and, well, everything else.

BRENDAN SAINSBURY

Thanks to all the bus drivers, tourist info volunteers and park rangers; and to Danny Palmerlee for being a supportive coordinating author. Special thanks to Andy McKee. Thanks also to my wife Liz and son Kieran for their company on the road.

This Book

This 1st edition of Lonely Planet's *Discover USA's Best National Parks* guide was researched and written by Danny Palmerlee, Glenda Bendure, Ned Friary, Adam Karlin, Emily Matchar and Brendan Sainsbury. Additional chapters were based on material from various national park and state guides by the following authors: Sara Benson, Nate Cavalieri, Jennifer Denniston, Lisa Dunford, Beth Kohn, Bradley Mayhew, Carolyn McCarth Brendan Sainsbury, Andrea Schulte-Peevers and Wendy Yanagihara. This guidebook was commissioned in Lonely Planet's Oakland office, and produced by the following:

Commissioning Editor Kathleen Munnelly
Coordinating Editor Dianne Schallmeiner
Coordinating Cartographers Hunor Csutoros, Corey Hutchison, Joelene Kowalski, Peter Shields
Coordinating Layout Designer Nicholas Colicchia
Managing Editors Brigitte Ellemor, Annelies Mertens, Anna Metcalfe
Managing Cartographers David Connolly, Alison Lyall
Managing Layout Designer Chris Girdler
Assisting Editors Andrew Bain, Elizabeth Harvey, Briohn Hooper, Pat Kinsella, Charlotte Orr, Martine Power
Assisting Cartographers Jolyon Philcox, Andy Rojas
Cover Research Naomi Parker
Internal Image Research Sabrina Dalbesio
Thanks to Shahara Ahmed, Sasha Baskett, Helen Christinis, Ruth Cosgrove, Ryan Evans, Gerard Walker

Climate map data adapted from Peel MC, Finlayson BL McMahon TA (2007) 'Updated World Map of the Köppen Geiger Climate Classification', Hydrology and Earth System Sciences, 11, 1633¬44.

Cover photographs:
Front: Grand Canyon, George HH Huey/Corbis
Back: Half Dome, Yosemite, Richard I'Anson/Lonely Planet Images

Many of the images in this guide are available for licensin from Lonely Planet Images: www.lonelyplanetimages.com

SEND US YOUR FEEDBACK

We love to hear from travelers – your comments keep us on our toes and help make our books better. Our well-traveled team reads every word on what you loved or loathed about this book. Although we canno reply individually to postal submissions, we always guarantee that your feedback goes straight to the ap propriate authors, in time for the next edition. Each person who sends us information is thanked in the next edition, and the most useful submissions are rewarded with a free book.

Visit **lonelyplanet.com/contact** to submit your updates and suggestions or to ask for help. Our award-winning website also features inspirational travel stories, news and discussions.

Note: We may edit, reproduce and incorporate your comments in Lonely Planet products such as guidebooks, websites and digital products, so let u know if you don't want your comments reproduce or your name acknowledged. For a copy of our privacy policy visit lonelyplanet.com/privacy.

NOTES

455

NOTES

Index

000 Map pages

000 Map pages

S

000 Map pages

3 1170 00893 2414

How to Use This Book

These symbols will help you find the listings you want:

- ⊙ Sights
- 🏖 Beaches
- ➕ Activities
- ☕ Courses
- 📷 Tours
- 🎉 Festivals & Events
- 🛏 Sleeping
- 🍴 Eating
- 🍷 Drinking
- ⭐ Entertainment
- 🛍 Shopping
- ℹ Information/Transport

Look out for these icons:

FREE No payment required

🌿 A green or sustainable option

Our authors have nominated these places as demonstrating a strong commitment to sustainability – for example by supporting local communities and producers, operating in an environmentally friendly way, or supporting conservation projects.

These symbols give you the vital information for each listing:

- 🎵 Telephone Numbers
- ⊙ Opening Hours
- P Parking
- ⊖ Nonsmoking
- ❄ Air-Conditioning
- @ Internet Access
- 🛜 Wi-Fi Access
- 🏊 Swimming Pool
- 🥗 Vegetarian Selection
- 🖹 English-Language Menu
- 👪 Family-Friendly
- 🐾 Pet-Friendly
- 🚌 Bus
- 🚢 Ferry
- Ⓜ Metro
- Ⓢ Subway
- ⊖ London Tube
- 🚋 Tram
- Ⓡ Train

Reviews are organised by author preference.

Map Legend

Sights
- 🏖 Beach
- ☸ Buddhist
- ✪ Castle
- ✝ Christian
- 🕉 Hindu
- ☪ Islamic
- ✡ Jewish
- 🏛 Monument
- 🏛 Museum/Gallery
- ✹ Ruin
- 🍇 Winery/Vineyard
- 🐘 Zoo
- ⊙ Other Sight

Activities, Courses & Tours
- 🤿 Diving/Snorkelling
- 🛶 Canoeing/Kayaking
- ⛷ Skiing
- 🏄 Surfing
- 🏊 Swimming/Pool
- 🥾 Walking
- 🏄 Windsurfing
- ➕ Other Activity/Course/Tour

Sleeping
- 🛏 Sleeping
- 🏕 Camping

Eating
- 🍴 Eating

Drinking
- ☕ Drinking
- ☕ Cafe

Entertainment
- 🎭 Entertainment

Shopping
- 🛍 Shopping

Information
- 💲 Bank
- 🏛 Embassy/Consulate
- ✚ Hospital/Medical
- @ Internet
- 👮 Police
- 📮 Post Office
- ☎ Telephone
- 🚻 Toilet
- ⓘ Tourist Information
- ● Other Information

Transport
- ✈ Airport
- ⊗ Border Crossing
- 🚌 Bus
- ⊕ Cable Car/Funicular
- ⊙ Cycling
- ⊖ Ferry
- Ⓜ Metro
- ⊕ Monorail
- P Parking
- ⛽ Petrol Station
- 🚕 Taxi
- ⊕ Train/Railway
- ⊕ Tram
- ● Other Transport

Routes
- Tollway
- Freeway
- Primary
- Secondary
- Tertiary
- Lane
- Unsealed Road
- Plaza/Mall
- Steps
-)=(Tunnel
- Pedestrian Overpass
- Walking Tour
- Walking Tour Detour
- Path

Geographic
- 🏠 Hut/Shelter
- 💡 Lighthouse
- 👁 Lookout
- ▲ Mountain/Volcano
- 🌴 Oasis
- 🌳 Park
-)(Pass
- 🏞 Picnic Area
- 💧 Waterfall

Population
- ✪ Capital (National)
- ◉ Capital (State/Province)
- ● City/Large Town
- ○ Town/Village

Boundaries
- — — — International
- – – – – State/Province
- — — Disputed
- Regional/Suburb
- Marine Park
- ⌐ Cliff
- ▬▬▬ Wall

Hydrography
- River/Creek
- Intermittent River
- Swamp/Mangrove
- Reef
- Canal
- Water
- Dry/Salt/Intermittent Lake
- Glacier

Areas
- Beach/Desert
- Cemetery (Christian)
- Cemetery (Other)
- Park/Forest
- Sportsground
- Sight (Building)
- Top Sight (Building)

Our Story

A beat-up old car, a few dollars in the pocket and a sense of adventure. In 1972 that's all Tony and Maureen Wheeler needed for the trip of a lifetime – across Europe and Asia overland to Australia. It took several months, and at the end – broke but inspired – they sat at their kitchen table writing and stapling together their first travel guide, *Across Asia on the Cheap*. Within a week they'd sold 1500 copies. Lonely Planet was born.

Today, Lonely Planet has offices in Melbourne, London and Oakland, with more than 600 staff and writers. We share Tony's belief that 'a great guidebook should do three things: inform, educate and amuse'.

Our Writers

DANNY PALMERLEE

Coordinating author, Plan Your Trip, Glacier National Park, Grand Canyon National Park, Joshua Tree & Death Valley National Parks, Rocky Mountains National Park, Yellowstone & Grand Teton National Parks, Yosemite National Park, Zion & Bryce National Parks, Best of the Rest, In Focus and Survival Guide Danny is a freelance writer and photographer based in Portland, Oregon. He has co-authored numerous Lonely Planet guidebooks, including *Yosemite, Sequoia & Kings Canyon National Parks*, *USA's Best Trips* and several Latin American titles. His favorite national park is Yosemite, followed closely by Glacier. To view his work, visit www.travelburro.com.

NED FRIARY & GLENDA BENDURE

Acadia National Park Ned and Glenda make their home on Cape Cod. Their first trip to Acadia National Park was in the 1980s and they've returned many times since to hike the park's trails, cycle the carriage roads and just unwind. They love the untamed surf, quiet lakes and dramatic views of New England's only national park. They've written extensively on the region and are co-authors of Lonely Planet's *New England* and *USA* guides.

ADAM KARLIN

The Everglades Growing up, Adam had grandparents in Florida, and fondly remembers many a December snowbirding in West Palm Beach. Later in life he worked as a reporter for the *Key West Citizen* before being hired by Lonely Planet to cover South Florida. Since then he's written or contributed to over two dozen guidebooks for the company, almost always in tropical places: the Southern USA, Caribbean, Africa and Southeast Asia. Follow Adam at www.walkonfine.com.

EMILY MATCHAR

Great Smoky Mountains & Shenandoah National Parks A native Tarheel, Emily lives and works in Chapel Hill, North Carolina (when she's not bopping around the globe, that is). Though she doesn't have a Southern accent, she does know how to smoke a hog, hotwire a pickup truck and bake a mean coconut cake. She writes about culture, food and travel for a variety of national magazines and newspapers, and has contributed to a dozen Lonely Planet guides.

BRENDAN SAINSBURY

Olympic & Mt Rainier National Parks UK-born Brendan once ran 100 miles across the Cascade Mountains in an ultra-distance marathon race, so researching the hikes for this book seemed like a dream job. He currently lives near Vancouver in Canada with his wife and young son. As well as contributing to this book, he is co-author of Lonely Planet's *Banff, Jasper & Glacier National Parks*. When not writing he likes playing guitar and visiting his favorite cities – London, Havana and Granada.

Published by Lonely Planet Publications Pty Ltd
ABN 36 005 607 983
1st edition – Mar 2012
ISBN 978 1 74220 491 8
© Lonely Planet 2012   Photographs © as indicated 2012
10 9 8 7 6 5 4 3 2 1
Printed in China